YBM
실전토익
RC1000
3

YBM
실전토익
RC 1000 3

발행인	권오찬
발행처	YBM

문항 개발	Marilyn Hook
편집	허유정
디자인	이현숙
마케팅	전경진, 정연철, 박천산, 고영노, 박찬경, 김동진, 김윤하

초판 발행	2021년 1월 4일
3쇄 발행	2022년 1월 3일

신고일자	1964년 3월 28일
신고번호	제 300-1964-3호
주소	서울시 종로구 종로 104
전화	(02) 2000-0515 [구입문의] / (02) 2000-0429 [내용문의]
팩스	(02) 2285-1523
홈페이지	www.ybmbooks.com

ISBN 978-89-17-23817-4

토익 주관사가 제시하는 진짜 토익
YBM 실전토익 RC 1000 3을 발행하며

지난 30여 년간 우리나라에서 토익 시험을 주관하면서 토익 시장을 이끌고, 꾸준히 베스트셀러를 출간해 온 YBM에서 〈YBM 실전토익 RC 1000 3〉을 출간하게 되었습니다.

YBM 토익은 이렇게 다릅니다!

YBM의 명성에 자부심을 가지고 개발했습니다!

YBM은 지난 1982년부터 우리나라의 토익 시험을 주관해온 토익 주관사로서, 지난 30여 년간 400여 권의 토익 베스트셀러를 출판해왔습니다. 그 오랜 시간 토익 문제를 분석하고 교재를 출판하면서 쌓아온 전문성과 실력으로 이번에 〈YBM 실전토익 RC 1000 3〉을 선보이게 되었습니다.

토익 주관사로서의 사명감을 가지고 개발했습니다!

토익 주관사로서 사명감을 갖고 최신 경향을 철저히 분석하여 〈YBM 실전토익 RC 1000 3〉을 개발하였습니다. 실제 시험과 가장 유사한 고난도 문제를 다수 수록하였고, 핵심 출제 포인트를 해설집에 상세히 담았습니다.

ETS 교재를 출간한 노하우를 가지고 개발했습니다!

출제기관 ETS의 토익 교재를 독점 출간하는 YBM은 그동안 쌓아온 노하우를 바탕으로 〈YBM 실전토익 RC 1000 3〉을 개발하였습니다. 본 책에 실린 1000개의 문항은 출제자의 의도를 정확히 반영하였기 때문에 타사의 어떤 토익 교재와도 비교할 수 없는 퀄리티를 자랑합니다.

YBM의 모든 노하우가 집대성된 〈YBM 실전토익 RC 1000 3〉은 최단 시간에 최고의 점수를 수험자 여러분께 약속 드립니다.

YBM 토익연구소

토익의 구성과 수험 정보

TOEIC은
어떤 시험인가요?

Test of English for International Communication(국제적 의사소통을 위한 영어 시험)의 약자로서, 영어가 모국어가 아닌 사람들이 일상생활 또는 비즈니스 현장에서 꼭 필요한 실용적 영어 구사 능력을 갖추었는가를 평가하는 시험이다.

시험 구성

구성	Part	내용		문항수	시간	배점
듣기 (L/C)	1	사진 묘사		6	45분	495점
	2	질의 & 응답		25		
	3	짧은 대화		39		
	4	짧은 담화		30		
읽기 (R/C)	5	단문 빈칸 채우기(문법/어휘)		30	75분	495점
	6	장문 빈칸 채우기		16		
	7	독해	단일 지문	29		
			이중 지문	10		
			삼중 지문	15		
Total		**7 Parts**		**200문항**	**120분**	**990점**

TOEIC 접수는
어떻게 하나요?

TOEIC 접수는 한국 토익 위원회 사이트(www.toeic.co.kr)에서 온라인 상으로만 접수가 가능하다. 사이트에서 매월 자세한 접수 일정과 시험 일정 등의 구체적 정보 확인이 가능하니, 미리 일정을 확인하여 접수하도록 한다.

시험장에 반드시 가져가야 할 준비물은요?

신분증 규정 신분증만 가능

(주민등록증, 운전면허증, 기간 만료 전의 여권, 공무원증 등)

필기구 연필, 지우개 (볼펜이나 사인펜은 사용 금지)

시험은 어떻게 진행되나요?

09:20	입실 (09:50 이후는 입실 불가)
09:30 – 09:45	답안지 작성에 관한 오리엔테이션
09:45 – 09:50	휴식
09:50 – 10:05	신분증 확인
10:05 – 10:10	문제지 배부 및 파본 확인
10:10 – 10:55	듣기 평가 (Listening Test)
10:55 – 12:10	독해 평가 (Reading Test)

TOEIC 성적 확인은 어떻게 하죠?

시험일로부터 12일 후 인터넷과 ARS(060-800-0515)로 성적을 확인할 수 있다. TOEIC 성적표는 우편이나 온라인으로 발급 받을 수 있다(시험 접수시, 양자 택일). 우편으로 발급 받을 경우는 성적 발표 후 대략 일주일이 소요되며, 온라인 발급을 선택하면 유효기간 내에 홈페이지에서 본인이 직접 1회에 한해 무료 출력할 수 있다. TOEIC 성적은 시험일로부터 2년간 유효하다.

TOEIC은 몇 점 만점인가요?

TOEIC 점수는 듣기 영역(LC) 점수, 읽기 영역(RC) 점수, 그리고 이 두 영역을 합계한 전체 점수 세 부분으로 구성된다. 각 부분의 점수는 5점 단위이며, 5점에서 495점에 걸쳐 주어지고, 전체 점수는 10점에서 990점까지이며, 만점은 990점이다. TOEIC 성적은 각 문제 유형의 난이도에 따른 점수 환산표에 의해 결정된다.

토익 경향 분석

PART 1 사진 묘사 Photographs

1인 등장 사진
주어는 He/She, A man/woman 등이며 주로
앞부분에 나온다.

2인 이상 등장 사진
주어는 They, Some men/women/people,
One of the men/women 등이며 주로
중간 부분에 나온다.

사물/배경 사진
주어는 A car, some chairs 등이며 주로 뒷부분에
나온다.

사람 또는 사물 중심 사진
주어가 일부는 사람, 일부는 사물이며 주로 뒷부분에
나온다.

현재 진행 능동태
〈is/are + 현재분사〉 형태이며 주로 사람이 주어이다.

단순 현재 수동태
〈is/are + 과거분사〉 형태이며 주로 사물이 주어이다.

기타
〈is/are + being + 과거분사〉 형태의 현재 진행 수동
태, 〈has/have + been + 과거 분사〉 형태의 현재 완
료 수동태, '타동사 + 목적어' 형태의 단순 현재 능동태,
There is/are와 같은 단순 현재도 나온다.

PART 2 질의 & 응답 Question-Response

총 25문제

평서문
질문이 아니라 객관적인 사실이나 화자의 의견 등을 나타내는 문장이다.

명령문
동사원형이나 Please 등으로 시작한다.

의문사 의문문
각 의문사마다 1~2개씩 나온다. 의문사가 단독으로 나오기도 하지만 What time ~?, How long ~?, Which room ~? 등에서처럼 다른 명사나 형용사와 같이 나오기도 한다.

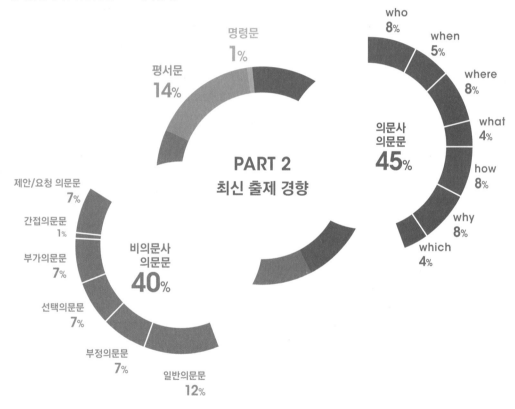

비의문사 의문문
일반(Yes/No) 의문문 적게 나올 때는 한두 개, 많이 나올 때는 서너 개씩 나오는 편이다.
부정의문문 Don't you ~?, Isn't he ~? 등으로 시작하는 문장이며 일반 긍정 의문문보다는 약간 더 적게 나온다.
선택의문문 A or B 형태로 나오며 A와 B의 형태가 단어, 구, 절일 수 있다. 구나 절일 경우 문장이 길어져서 어려워진다.
부가의문문 ~ don't you?, ~ isn't he? 등으로 끝나는 문장이며, 일반 부정 의문문과 비슷하다고 볼 수 있다.
간접의문문 의문사가 문장 처음 부분이 아니라 문장 중간에 들어 있다.
제안/요청 의문문 정보를 얻기보다는 상대방의 도움이나 동의 등을 얻기 위한 목적이 일반적이다.

PART 3 짧은 대화 Short Conversations

총 13대화문 39문제 (지문당 3문제)

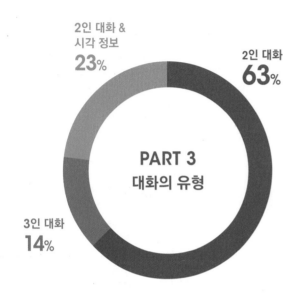

- 3인 대화의 경우 남자 화자 두 명과 여자 화자 한 명 또는 남자 화자 한 명과 여자 화자 두 명이 나온다. 따라서 문제에서는 2인 대화에서와 달리 the man이나 the woman이 아니라 the men이나 the women 또는 특정한 이름이 언급될 수 있다.

- 대화 & 시각 정보는 항상 파트의 뒷부분에 나온다.

- 시각 정보의 유형으로 chart, map, floor plan, schedule, table, weather forecast, directory, list, invoice, receipt, sign, packing slip 등 다양한 자료가 골고루 나온다.

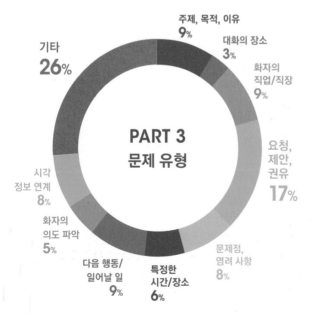

- 주제, 목적, 이유, 대화의 장소, 화자의 직업/직장 등과 관련된 문제는 주로 대화의 첫 번째 문제로 나오며 다음 행동/일어날 일 등과 관련된 문제는 주로 대화의 세 번째 문제로 나온다.

- 화자의 의도 파악 문제는 주로 2인 대화에 나오지만, 가끔 3인 대화에 나오기도 한다. 시각 정보 연계 대화에는 나오지 않고 있다.

- Part 3 안에서 화자의 의도 파악 문제는 2개 나오고 시각 정보 연계 문제는 3개 나온다.

PART 4 짧은 담화 Short Talks

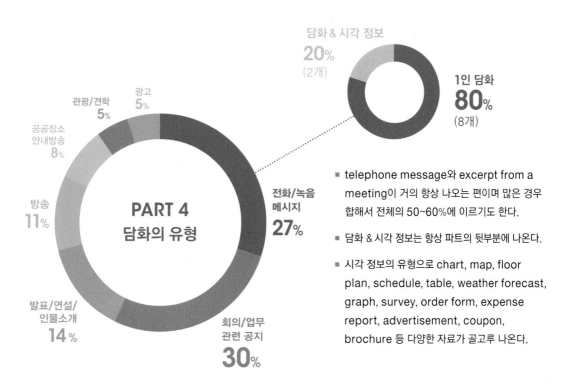

담화 & 시각 정보
20%
(2개)

1인 담화
80%
(8개)

관광/견학 **5%**
광고 **5%**
공공장소 안내방송 **8%**
방송 **11%**

PART 4
담화의 유형

전화/녹음 메시지 **27%**

발표/연설/인물소개 **14%**

회의/업무 관련 공지 **30%**

- telephone message와 excerpt from a meeting이 거의 항상 나오는 편이며 많은 경우 합해서 전체의 50~60%에 이르기도 한다.

- 담화 & 시각 정보는 항상 파트의 뒷부분에 나온다.

- 시각 정보의 유형으로 chart, map, floor plan, schedule, table, weather forecast, graph, survey, order form, expense report, advertisement, coupon, brochure 등 다양한 자료가 골고루 나온다.

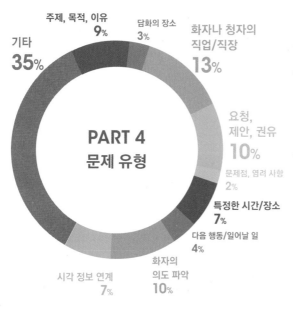

주제, 목적, 이유 **9%**
담화의 장소 **3%**
화자나 청자의 직업/직장 **13%**

기타 **35%**

PART 4
문제 유형

요청, 제안, 권유 **10%**
문제점, 염려 사항 **2%**
특정한 시간/장소 **7%**
다음 행동/일어날 일 **4%**

시각 정보 연계 **7%**
화자의 의도 파악 **10%**

- 문제 유형은 기본적으로 Part 3과 거의 비슷하다.

- 주제, 목적, 이유, 담화의 장소, 화자나 청자의 직업/직장 등과 관련된 문제는 주로 담화의 첫 번째 문제로 나오며 다음 행동/일어날 일 등과 관련된 문제는 주로 담화의 세 번째 문제로 나온다.

- Part 4 안에서 화자의 의도 파악 문제는 3개 나오고 시각 정보 연계 문제는 2개 나온다.

토익 경향 분석

PART 5 단문 빈칸 채우기 Incomplete Sentences 총 30문제

문법 문제
시제와 대명사와 관련된 문법 문제가 2개씩, 한정사와 분사와 관련된 문법 문제가 1개씩 나온다. 시제 문제의 경우 능동태/수동태나 수의 일치와 연계되기도 한다. 그 밖에 한정사, 능동태/수동태, 부정사, 동명사 등과 관련된 문법 문제가 나온다.

어휘 문제
동사, 명사, 형용사, 부사와 관련된 어휘 문제가 각각 2~3개씩 골고루 나온다. 전치사 어휘 문제는 3개씩 꾸준히 나오지만, 접속사나 어구와 관련된 어휘 문제는 나오지 않을 때도 있고 3개가 나올 때도 있다.

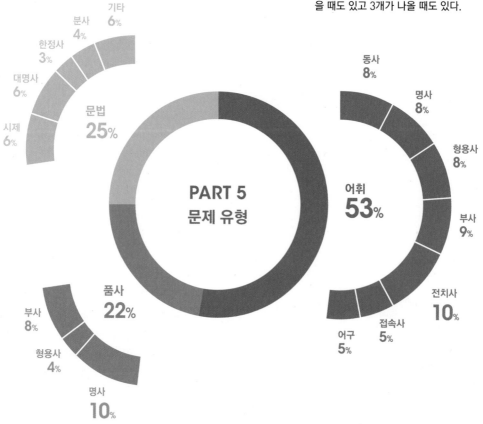

품사 문제
명사와 부사와 관련된 품사 문제가 2~3개씩 나오며, 형용사와 관련된 품사 문제가 상대적으로 적은 편이다.

PART 6 장문 빈칸 채우기 Text Completion

한 지문에 4문제가 나오며 평균적으로 어휘 문제가 2개, 품사나 문법 문제가 1개, 문맥에 맞는 문장 고르기 문제가 1개 들어간다. 문맥에 맞는 문장 고르기 문제를 제외하면 문제 유형은 기본적으로 파트 5와 거의 비슷하다.

어휘 문제
동사, 명사, 부사, 어구와 관련된 어휘 문제는 매번 1~2개씩 나온다. 부사 어휘 문제의 경우 therefore(그러므로)나 however(하지만)처럼 문맥의 흐름을 자연스럽게 연결해 주는 부사가 자주 나온다.

문맥에 맞는 문장 고르기
문맥에 맞는 문장 고르기 문제는 지문당 한 문제씩 나오는데, 나오는 위치의 확률은 4문제 중 두 번째 문제, 세 번째 문제, 네 번째 문제, 첫 번째 문제 순으로 높다.

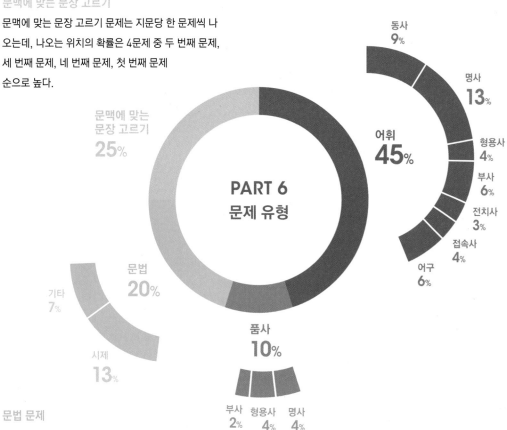

PART 6
문제 유형

- 문맥에 맞는 문장 고르기 25%
- 기타 7%
- 시제 13%
- 문법 20%
- 품사 10%
  - 부사 2%
  - 형용사 4%
  - 명사 4%
- 어휘 45%
  - 동사 9%
  - 명사 13%
  - 형용사 4%
  - 부사 6%
  - 전치사 3%
  - 접속사 4%
  - 어구 6%

문법 문제
문맥의 흐름과 밀접하게 관련이 있는 시제 문제가 2개 정도 나오며, 능동태/수동태나 수의 일치와 연계되기도 한다. 그 밖에 대명사, 능동태/수동태, 부정사, 접속사/전치사 등과 관련된 문법 문제가 나온다.

품사 문제
명사나 형용사 문제가 부사 문제보다 좀 더 자주 나온다.

토익 경향 분석

PART 7 독해 Reading Comprehension

총 15지문 54문제 (지문당 2~5문제)

지문 유형	지문당 문제 수	지문 개수	비중 %
단일 지문	2문항	4개	약 15%
	3문항	3개	약 16%
	4문항	3개	약 22%
이중 지문	5문항	2개	약 19%
삼중 지문	5문항	3개	약 28%

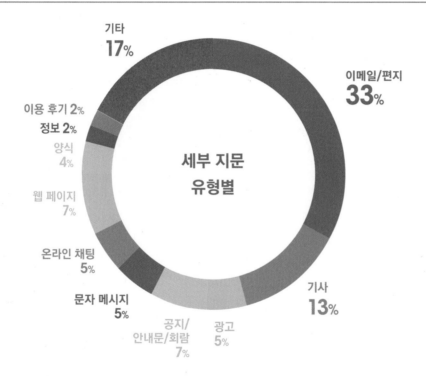

세부 지문 유형별

- 기타 17%
- 이메일/편지 33%
- 이용 후기 2%
- 정보 2%
- 양식 4%
- 웹 페이지 7%
- 온라인 채팅 5%
- 문자 메시지 5%
- 공지/안내문/회람 7%
- 광고 5%
- 기사 13%

- 이메일/편지, 기사 유형 지문은 거의 항상 나오는 편이며 많은 경우 합해서 전체의 50~60%에 이르기도 한다.

- 기타 지문 유형으로 agenda, brochure, comment card, coupon, flyer, instructions, invitation, invoice, list, menu, page from a catalog, policy statement, report, schedule, survey, voucher 등 다양한 자료가 골고루 나온다.

(이중 지문과 삼중 지문 속의 지문들을 모두 낱개로 계산함 – 총 23지문)

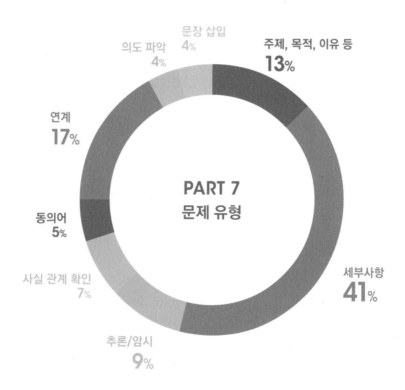

문장 삽입
4%

의도 파악
4%

주제, 목적, 이유 등
13%

연계
17%

세부사항
41%

동의어
5%

사실 관계 확인
7%

추론/암시
9%

PART 7
문제 유형

- 동의어 문제는 주로 이중 지문이나 삼중 지문에 나온다.
- 연계 문제는 일반적으로 이중 지문에서 한 문제, 삼중 지문에서 두 문제가 나온다.
- 의도 파악 문제는 문자 메시지(text-message chain)나 온라인 채팅(online chat discussion) 지문에서 출제되며 두 문제가 나온다.
- 문장 삽입 문제는 주로 기사, 이메일, 편지, 회람 지문에서 출제되며 두 문제가 나온다.

점수 환산표

LISTENING Raw Score (맞은 개수)	LISTENING Scaled Score (환산 점수)	READING Raw Score (맞은 개수)	READING Scaled Score (환산 점수)
96-100	480-495	96-100	460-495
91-95	435-490	91-95	410-475
86-90	395-450	86-90	380-430
81-85	355-415	81-85	355-400
76-80	325-375	76-80	325-375
71-75	295-340	71-75	295-345
66-70	265-315	66-70	265-315
61-65	240-285	61-65	235-285
56-60	215-260	56-60	205-255
51-55	190-235	51-55	175-225
46-50	160-210	46-50	150-195
41-45	135-180	41-45	120-170
36-40	110-155	36-40	100-140
31-35	85-130	31-35	75-120
26-30	70-105	26-30	55-100
21-25	50-90	21-25	40-80
16-20	35-70	16-20	30-65
11-15	20-55	11-15	20-50
6-10	15-40	6-10	15-35
1-5	5-20	1-5	5-20
0	5	0	5

* 이 환산표는 본 교재에 수록된 Test용으로 개발된 것이다. 이 표를 사용하여 자신의 실제 점수를 환산 점수로 전환하도록 한다. 즉, 예를 들어 Listening Test의 실제 정답 수가 61~65개이면 환산 점수는 240점에서 285점 사이가 된다. 여기서 실제 정답 수가 61개이면 환산 점수가 240점이고, 65개이면 환산 점수가 285점임을 의미하는 것은 아니다. 본 책의 Test를 위해 작성된 이 점수 환산표가 자신의 영어 실력이 어느 정도인지 대략적으로 파악하는 데 도움이 되긴 하지만, 이 표가 실제 TOEIC 성적 산출에 그대로 사용된 적은 없다는 사실을 밝혀 둔다.

CONTENTS

TEST 01   4

TEST 02   34

TEST 03   64

TEST 04   94

TEST 05   124

TEST 06   154

TEST 07   184

TEST 08   214

TEST 09   244

TEST 10   276

해설집

RC

TEST 1

In the Reading test, you will read a variety of texts and answer several different types of reading comprehension questions. The entire Reading test will last 75 minutes. There are three parts, and directions are given for each part. You are encouraged to answer as many questions as possible within the time allowed.

You must mark your answers on the separate answer sheet. Do not write your answers in your test book.

PART 5

Directions: A word or phrase is missing in each of the sentences below. Four answer choices are given below each sentence. Select the best answer to complete the sentence. Then mark the letter (A), (B), (C), or (D) on your answer sheet.

101. Mr. Ardary expressed concern that the proposed candidate ------- the required organizational skills.

(A) fails
(B) struggles
(C) lacks
(D) limits

102. Rayville's Public Works Department hired local ------- to clean up the lakeside.

(A) contract
(B) contracted
(C) contractor
(D) contractors

103. Submissions of translated writings must include the original text ------- your translation.

(A) along
(B) as well as
(C) altogether
(D) also

104. ------- a temporary problem with the speaker system, the product launch event went as planned.

(A) Apart from
(B) After all
(C) Instead of
(D) Not only

105. Please return the books to the library by the indicated date so that other patrons can borrow ------- freely.

(A) it
(B) its own
(C) them
(D) themselves

106. ------- this drug to strong light or heat will reduce its effectiveness.

(A) Consuming
(B) Handling
(C) Allowing
(D) Exposing

107. When the machine is out of paper or ------- unable to function, a notification will appear on the display screen.

(A) otherwise
(B) however
(C) in case
(D) anymore

108. The ------- of a MimEx smartphone may be extended by filling out an online form.

(A) warranty
(B) lifespan
(C) design
(D) vendor

109. In order to boost participation, ------- who enters the photo contest will receive a small gift.

(A) those
(B) everyone
(C) they
(D) many

110. The bulk of Eltis Automotive's financial resources is being directed ------- developing new vehicles.

(A) by
(B) besides
(C) towards
(D) onto

111. The radio towers will provide park rangers with a ------- means of communication despite the mountainous terrain.

(A) reliable
(B) reliably
(C) reliability
(D) reliant

112. Arrange the plants as ------- as possible on the aquarium's floor to create the ideal environment for your fish.

(A) densest
(B) densely
(C) density
(D) denser

113. Ms. Muir argues that technological advancements in manufacturing have led to ------- prices for consumers.

(A) comparable
(B) full
(C) market
(D) better

114. Grelf, Inc. held a press conference yesterday to announce plans to expand, ------- its rivals in the mining industry.

(A) surprised
(B) surprising
(C) surprises
(D) surprise

115. As Brenford Grill's most popular dish, Corinne's Chili Cheeseburger is ------- featured in advertisements for the restaurant.

(A) prominently
(B) inadvertently
(C) rapidly
(D) respectively

116. Hyall Health, Inc.'s claims about the benefits of its aromatherapy oils do not have scientific -------.

(A) result
(B) verification
(C) experiment
(D) excuse

117. Television advertising is appropriate for products with broad target markets, ------- mobile advertising is more suited to niche products.

(A) in spite of
(B) contrary to
(C) whereas
(D) only if

118. This memo details our proposal ------- the secondary storage closet into a small meeting space.

(A) will convert
(B) conversion
(C) was converted
(D) to convert

119. Assembly line workers may have facial hair as long as it does not ------- with their work.

(A) affect
(B) disrupt
(C) interfere
(D) compromise

120. The survey data show that interns found the written training materials more ------- than the video.

(A) informing
(B) information
(C) informatively
(D) informative

GO ON TO THE NEXT PAGE

121. New employees will be asked to wear temporary badges ------- their official identification cards are issued.

(A) whether
(B) rather than
(C) as though
(D) until

122. Thanks to Ms. Perry's tireless campaigning, education ------- as the central issue of the city council election.

(A) emerging
(B) will be emerged
(C) is emerging
(D) has been emerged

123. The commission system gives sales associates a strong ------- to work hard.

(A) incentive
(B) satisfaction
(C) supervision
(D) approach

124. As its name suggests, "Painting for Beginners" caters ------- to those who have never studied the craft before.

(A) specify
(B) specific
(C) specified
(D) specifically

125. The technical support department's budget is no longer ------- to cover its staffing expenses.

(A) vital
(B) plentiful
(C) accustomed
(D) sufficient

126. Taskko software helps managers ensure that tasks are being distributed ------- among the members of their team.

(A) briefly
(B) loosely
(C) evenly
(D) newly

127. Our services include the ------- of any required import and export documents.

(A) supplies
(B) supplier
(C) supplying
(D) supplied

128. Hogan & Partners' internship program gives law students the chance to learn ------- the guidance of seasoned attorneys.

(A) within
(B) under
(C) behind
(D) among

129. If his flight from Madrid had arrived on time, Mr. Martín ------- the conference's welcome reception.

(A) was attending
(B) could have attended
(C) can attend
(D) had attended

130. The success of its new line of beverages has reduced Genvia's ------- on its flagship snack bars for revenue.

(A) expertise
(B) dependence
(C) perspective
(D) shortage

PART 6

Directions: Read the texts that follow. A word, phrase, or sentence is missing in parts of each text. Four answer choices for each question are given below the text. Select the best answer to complete the text. Then mark the letter (A), (B), (C), or (D) on your answer sheet.

Questions 131-134 refer to the following Web page.

---

www.vegashift.com

VegaShift

VegaShift is a mobile app that gives restaurants, stores, and other shift-based businesses a fast, simple way to facilitate shift trades. Workers offer unwanted shifts ------- to their coworkers, **131.** who can choose whether or not to take them. This enables employees to increase the flexibility of their working hours without inconveniencing their supervisors. -------, VegaShift allows **132.** management to retain control of the schedule. Supervisors can require all trades to be approved so that no workers are scheduled to work more than their ------- hours. The app can **133.** also alert management to added costs that may arise due to differences in employees' hourly pay.

We are so confident in VegaShift's quality that we give businesses the chance to use it for a whole month at no cost. -------. **134.**

---

131. (A) directs
(B) directly
(C) directing
(D) direction

132. (A) As a result
(B) In other words
(C) On the contrary
(D) At the same time

133. (A) permitted
(B) shortened
(C) preferred
(D) extra

134. (A) Learn why *Tech Z* named us one of the industry's top employers.
(B) Enter your information below to start your free trial today.
(C) For a full list of products, click on "Offerings".
(D) Additional technical support is available at 1-800-555-0184.

Reyno to Host National Science Festival

REYNO (December 11)—The National Department of Science and Technology (NDST) has announced that the city of Reyno will host the second annual National Science Festival in June.

NDST spokesperson Isaac Hodges said that ------- for the honor was fierce, but Reyno was
135.
chosen because of its "fast-growing agricultural science and biotechnology industry." He also mentioned the city's recent establishment of the Reyno 300 complex for technology start-ups.

-------.
136.

The National Science Festival is a weeklong event showcasing the country's scientific achievements and projects. It features lectures that introduce cutting-edge concepts to the general public, exhibitions for all ages, and ------- demonstrations. The first one ------- in
137.   138.
Oglesby.

135. (A) selection
(B) opportunity
(C) competition
(D) recommendation

136. (A) Visitors hoping to stay there should make their reservations soon.
(B) He has initiated several such projects during his time in city government.
(C) Companies accepted as tenants there receive special funding and advice.
(D) There is concern that its construction will cause traffic problems during the festival.

137. (A) fascinating
(B) fascinatingly
(C) fascinated
(D) fascinates

138. (A) was being held
(B) was held
(C) is held
(D) will be held

Questions 139-142 refer to the following e-mail.

From: Patrick Holbrook
To: Library Services Staff
Subject: Peer Evaluations
Date: November 15
Attachment: Evaluation Forms

Hi all,

Your yearly employee performance evaluations will take place over the next month. As before, evaluations will be conducted by me but will include input ------- your peers in the Library
139.
Services Department. To gather this feedback, I need each of you to fill out and send back the evaluation forms in the attached file. Please ------- one for every member of the department.
140.
-------. Like last time, you will be asked to first rate your coworker's performance in a range of
141.
areas and then write a paragraph explaining and expanding on your answers. However, I urge you to take special care with the latter part this year. Remember, thoughtful feedback can benefit your peers -------.
142.

Patrick Holbrook
Vice Director of Library Services

139. (A) from
(B) on
(C) like
(D) over

140. (A) grant
(B) compile
(C) complete
(D) attend

141. (A) Surveys were distributed to library patrons, as well.
(B) The format of the questionnaires has not been altered.
(C) Head Director Htun will be present at each review.
(D) You appear to have left some boxes blank.

142. (A) consider
(B) considers
(C) considerable
(D) considerably

GO ON TO THE NEXT PAGE

Questions 143-146 refer to the following notice.

NOTICE TO CUSTOMERS

Due to increases in the cost of raw materials such as paper and ink, Wheeler Printing Shop has

decided to raise the prices of our printing services as of February 1. ------.
143.

This is our first such ------ in over five years. We have delayed it out of respect for our
144.

customers, but it has now become unavoidable because of the abovementioned economic

factors. ------ our prices is necessary to enable us to continue providing top-notch service well
145.

into the future.

Our price list boards will be updated on February 1 to reflect the changes, and employees will

be encouraged to state the cost of all printing services upfront to avoid misunderstandings.

Questions about this matter ------ to Lucia Zaiser, our manager. Thank you for your
146.

understanding.

---

143. (A) We are not able to accept any other
       digital file formats.
    (B) Our regular business hours will resume
        on February 8.
    (C) To print packaging materials, please
        visit our Holloway location.
    (D) The prices of our graphic design
        services will remain the same.

144. (A) adjustment
    (B) expenditure
    (C) departure
    (D) error

145. (A) Having raised
    (B) Raised
    (C) To be raised
    (D) Raising

146. (A) have been addressed
    (B) can be addressed
    (C) are addressing
    (D) will be addressing

10

PART 7

Directions: In this part you will read a selection of texts, such as magazine and newspaper articles, e-mails, and instant messages. Each text or set of texts is followed by several questions. Select the best answer for each question and mark the letter (A), (B), (C), or (D) on your answer sheet.

Questions 147-148 refer to the following information.

Howell Airlines

Howell Sky Lounge Guest Policy

Sky Lounge members are allowed to bring holders of tickets for same-day Howell Airlines flights into the lounge as guests. Platinum Membership holders may bring two guests or a spouse and any children under 21 years of age into the Sky Lounge at no cost; Gold Membership holders may do the same for a fee of $25 per person. Guests must be accompanied by the admitting member for the duration of their visit. They are also subject to Sky Lounge rules regarding attire, behavior, and use of lounge amenities.

147. According to the information, what is different between membership types?

(A) The amount of time guests can stay
(B) The number of guests allowed
(C) The cost of bringing a guest
(D) The qualifications required of guests

148. What must guests do after entering the Sky Lounge?

(A) Remain with an escort
(B) Wear a form of identification
(C) Leave baggage in a designated area
(D) Pay a fee for amenities

Questions 149-150 refer to the following e-mail.

≡ E-Mail message ≡

From:	Natasha Akers
To:	Satchelton Running Club
Subject:	March events
Date:	February 28

Hi runners! Isn't it great that the weather is starting to get warmer? Soon we'll have a lot of greenery to admire during our outings.

Here's what will be going on in the club in March:

- Nearby event alert: the Spratt City Marathon. Details are below. If you're interested in carpooling to the city the night before, contact me by the race registration deadline.
  - Date: March 30
  - Location: Spratt
  - Course length: 26.2 miles
  - Registration deadline: March 16
  - Web site: www.sprattcitymarathon.com

- We'll continue going on group runs every Sunday at 10 A.M. (seven-mile course) and Wednesday at 7 P.M. (five-mile course) at Cosmon Park. Remember to sign up in advance on the club Web site so I know to send you text message notifications about cancellations or other changes.

I hope to see you on the course!

-Natasha

---

149. By what date should Ms. Akers be contacted about sharing transportation to Spratt?

(A) February 28
(B) March 16
(C) March 29
(D) March 30

150. What does Ms. Akers remind recipients to do?

(A) Send her a text message on Sundays
(B) Warm up before going on a group run
(C) Register to receive updates about events
(D) Study course routes in advance

Questions 151-153 refer to the following e-mail.

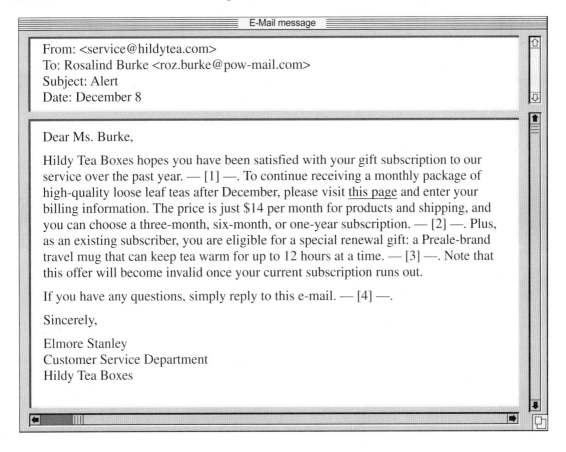

E-Mail message

From: <service@hildytea.com>
To: Rosalind Burke <roz.burke@pow-mail.com>
Subject: Alert
Date: December 8

Dear Ms. Burke,

Hildy Tea Boxes hopes you have been satisfied with your gift subscription to our service over the past year. — [1] —. To continue receiving a monthly package of high-quality loose leaf teas after December, please visit this page and enter your billing information. The price is just $14 per month for products and shipping, and you can choose a three-month, six-month, or one-year subscription. — [2] —. Plus, as an existing subscriber, you are eligible for a special renewal gift: a Preale-brand travel mug that can keep tea warm for up to 12 hours at a time. — [3] —. Note that this offer will become invalid once your current subscription runs out.

If you have any questions, simply reply to this e-mail. — [4] —.

Sincerely,

Elmore Stanley
Customer Service Department
Hildy Tea Boxes

---

151. Why was the e-mail sent to Ms. Burke?

(A) She complained about Hildy Tea Boxes.
(B) She referred a friend to Hildy Tea Boxes.
(C) A new product has become available.
(D) Her subscription period will end soon.

152. What does Mr. Stanley offer to Ms. Burke?

(A) A drinking container
(B) Some cold-weather apparel
(C) Free shipping for one year
(D) Advance notice of a sales promotion

153. In which of the positions marked [1], [2], [3], and [4] does the following sentence best belong?

"I or another representative will respond within 24 hours."

(A) [1]
(B) [2]
(C) [3]
(D) [4]

GO ON TO THE NEXT PAGE

Questions 154-155 refer to the following online chat discussion.

Alex Collins [9:02 A.M.]

Mercedes, I have a quick question. What's going on with my purchase request for a new laptop? I thought it would be processed by now.

Mercedes Burch [9:03 A.M.]

Hi, Alex. Didn't you get my e-mail? The IT department is recommending a different model. Once you approve the change, we can finish processing the request.

Alex Collins [9:07 A.M.]

Oh, I see. Well, it looks like the model they're recommending is heavier than what I requested. But I often have to carry my laptop around construction sites, so having a lightweight model is important.

Mercedes Burch [9:08 A.M.]

In that case, you can oppose the change. Just write a short paragraph explaining the situation, and I'll append it to the request.

Alex Collins [9:08 A.M.]

I'm glad to hear that that's an option. I'll do that. Thanks.

---

154. At 9:03 A.M., what does Ms. Burch imply when she writes, "Didn't you get my e-mail"?

(A) Her e-mail provides an explanation for a delay.
(B) Her e-mail gives notification of the conclusion of a process.
(C) Her e-mail describes a change to a policy.
(D) Her e-mail announces a staff transfer.

155. What does Mr. Collins state that his job frequently requires?

(A) Carrying out training
(B) Visiting work sites
(C) Doing persuasive writing
(D) Researching personal electronics

Questions 156-157 refer to the following notice.

NOTICE FOR RESIDENTS
OF SANDLING APARTMENTS

Over the past few months, the volume of tenants' packages being delivered to the apartment management office has grown beyond our capacity to handle them. The result has been an excessive amount of work for our employees, reduced space in our facility, and several incidents of packages being lost. Therefore, the office will no longer accept delivery of packages for tenants from <u>Monday, October 1</u>. Please take advantage of this ample advance notice to make other arrangements for any packages that will likely arrive on or after that date. These could be taking delivery at the door of your building or a third location like a post office box or your workplace.

- Sandling Apartments Management

156. What are apartment residents mainly being notified of?

(A) The holding of a tenant meeting
(B) The elimination of a receiving service
(C) The installation of a convenience facility
(D) The misplacement of some goods

157. What is suggested about Sandling Apartments?

(A) Its office is closed on weekends.
(B) It will soon be under new management.
(C) It recently reduced its number of employees.
(D) It occupies multiple buildings.

GO ON TO THE NEXT PAGE

From: Shane Maxwell
To: All employees
Re: Announcement
Date: May 8

It's the time of year when Goldwin Publishing gives all of its employees a chance to show their creativity. We are again seeking proposals for innovative additions to our range of Spanish language education solutions. Any type of product that is among those we already offer—books, flash cards, board games, etc.—or reasonably similar to them is welcome.

We believe that valuable contributions can come from unconventional sources, so employees in every area are encouraged to participate. Last year, Lois Edwards in the accounting department suggested a book that not only was published but ended up selling very well. If you have a fresh idea, we urge you to temporarily put aside your regular workload and write a proposal for it.

Each employee can submit up to two proposals. There is no specific format for proposals, but they should include a detailed description of the product and its target market. To keep submissions manageable, however, we ask that they be no more than one page in length. Please send them to my assistant, Ivan Briggs, at ivan@goldwinpublishing.com by Friday, May 19.

158. What does Mr. Maxwell ask recipients of the memo to submit?

(A) Reviews of existing products
(B) Ideas for potential new products
(C) Applications for joining a product development team
(D) Proposals for improving the product development process

159. Who most likely was Ms. Edwards's book intended for?

(A) Board game fans
(B) Amateur cooks
(C) Language learners
(D) Accounting students

160. What is indicated about submissions?

(A) They should be sent to two people.
(B) They are accepted twice a year.
(C) They can be up to two pages long.
(D) They must include two pieces of information.

Questions 161-164 refer to the following Web page.

---

www.shopslam.com/hiring/faq

Frequently Asked Questions about Hiring at Shopslam

Due to our exciting work environment and excellent employee benefits, thousands of people each year express interest in becoming part of the Shopslam team. Our recruiters cannot respond to all of the inquiries that we receive, so we have collected some common questions and their answers on this page.

1. Can I apply for more than one job?

This is permitted. However, we strongly recommend that you focus on the position for which you are best qualified.

2. Do you provide disability accommodations during the hiring process?

We are happy to offer accommodations such as sign language interpreters, wheelchair-accessible hotels for interviewees coming from out of town, etc. Simply fill out the optional "Accessibility Request Form" and include it with your other application materials.

3. Will you notify me if my application is rejected?

The high volume of applications means that we are only able to send updates about the hiring process to successful candidates.

4. After being rejected, can I reapply for the same job?

Yes, but if it is a technical position, we ask that you gain substantial additional experience before doing so.

---

161. What is most likely true about Shopslam?

(A) It hires thousands of people annually.
(B) It sends recruiters to university campuses.
(C) It has lower requirements for some technical jobs.
(D) It has a reputation for being a good employer.

162. What is mentioned as an example of a disability accommodation?

(A) Help with in-person communication
(B) Forms with large lettering
(C) An easily accessible interview site
(D) Additional time to fill out paperwork

163. According to the Web page, what should job applicants do?

(A) Check a Web page for hiring updates
(B) Concentrate their efforts on a single opening
(C) Include work samples with their application materials
(D) Review a list of commonly asked interview questions

164. Which question does NOT receive an affirmative reply?

(A) 1
(B) 2
(C) 3
(D) 4

GO ON TO THE NEXT PAGE

Questions 165-168 refer to the following text-message chain.

Lynne Fleming   [1:45 P.M.]

Johnny, are you still at the supermarket?

John Rivera   [1:47 P.M.]

No, I'm on my way back. I pulled over to the side of the road to answer your text. Why do you ask?

Lynne Fleming   [1:48 P.M.]

I was just cleaning up the Rose Room for the guests who are coming at five, and I ran out of some of our cleaning supplies. Would you mind going back and picking some up? I know it's inconvenient.

John Rivera   [1:49 P.M.]

Well, I am right by Nash Mart.

Lynne Fleming   [1:50 P.M.]

Oh, that would work! We need paper towels and window cleaner.

John Rivera   [1:51 P.M.]

Really? We're out of paper towels? I bought a 12-pack just last week.

Lynne Fleming   [1:52 P.M.]

Yes, the family with young kids that stayed in the Lilac Suite last weekend used a lot of them to clean up spills. Why don't you get a 24-pack this time? That should last us for a while.

John Rivera   [1:53 P.M.]

OK, will do. I should be back in half an hour.

Lynne Fleming   [1:53 P.M.]

Great. Don't forget to get a receipt for this purchase too.

---

165. Where do the writers most likely work?

(A) At a small hotel
(B) At a landscaping firm
(C) At a cleaning company
(D) At an educational institution

166. At 1:49 P.M., what does Mr. Rivera mean when he writes, "I am right by Nash Mart"?

(A) His journey is progressing quickly.
(B) He might be able to shop at Nash Mart.
(C) He would like Ms. Fleming to pick him up.
(D) Ms. Fleming should be able to see him from her location.

167. What most likely surprises Mr. Rivera?

(A) That he has been chosen to do a task
(B) That Ms. Fleming is aware of a problem
(C) That it has been a full week since an event occurred
(D) That some supplies have been used up

168. What does Ms. Fleming remind Mr. Rivera to do?

(A) Put fuel in a vehicle
(B) Avoid spilling a liquid
(C) Receive proof of a payment
(D) Send a notification to a coworker

Questions 169-171 refer to the following e-mail.

From:	Wally Barnes <w.barnes@mclerdon.com>
To:	Araceli Diaz <araceli@hevneymanufacturing.com>
Subject:	Request
Date:	April 28

Dear Ms. Diaz,

My name is Wally Barnes, and I am a marketing specialist at McLerdon, Inc. My department was established earlier this year thanks to growth fueled by the loyal patronage of clients like Hevney Manufacturing. Your account manager, Mr. Quinn, has told me that McLerdon staff have had the honor of guarding Hevney's factory premises for nearly five years now.

In addition to introducing myself, I am writing to make a request. I am currently adding client logos to McLerdon's Web site and would like to include your company's. This would normally be authorized by the service agreement between your company and ours, but our low level of marketing expertise at the time the contract was written meant that no such provision was included. If you agree to this request, all we need is a clear image of your current logo at a size of 150 pixels by 150 pixels. However, if you prefer that we do not display your logo, please do not hesitate to let me know.

McLerdon thanks you again for your business. We hope to hear from you soon.

Best regards,

Wally Barnes
McLerdon, Inc.

169. What is suggested about Mr. Barnes?

(A) Mr. Quinn is his manager.
(B) He helped draft an agreement.
(C) He holds a newly-created position.
(D) He has visited Hevney Manufacturing's Web site.

170. What most likely does McLerdon, Inc. do for its clients?

(A) Conduct marketing campaigns
(B) Provide security personnel
(C) Repair factory equipment
(D) Give legal advice

171. What does Mr. Barnes ask Ms. Diaz for?

(A) A client testimonial
(B) A signed copy of a contract
(C) Confirmation of a machine's dimensions
(D) Permission to use an image

GO ON TO THE NEXT PAGE

Doretta Creates Stir in Podcast Industry

By Filip Knutsen

Fans of *Doretta*, the eight-episode audio podcast chronicling the life of novelist Doretta Worth, will soon have many similar offerings to listen to. *Doretta*'s success has inspired its production company, Elgior Media, and several other podcast giants to develop scripted podcasts depicting interesting events and people in history. — [1] —.

According to podcast industry analytics firm Casteye, the majority of the top ten most popular podcasts are usually current events or interview shows. That is why *Doretta*'s achievement of mainstream popularity has made such an impression. As a historical fiction podcast, the show featured scripted dialogue performed by professional actors, sound effects, and a musical score. — [2] —. And yet, in the second month of its run, it reached number four on Casteye's ranking list. The show still has an active discussion board on Elgior's Web site, and the cast gave five sold-out live performances of an abridged version of its story shortly after it ended.

Some have speculated that *Doretta*'s distinctness was the cause of its popularity instead of a barrier to it. — [3] —. However, Casteye analyst Cynthia Myers disagrees. "After all, *Doretta* was not the first historical fiction podcast," she said. "Our research indicates that it was the excellence of the show's writing and performances that appealed to listeners."

Still, the industry believes that there is now an audience for similar projects. Elgior offered Kent Mulligan, *Doretta*'s creator, a lucrative deal to develop another historical fiction podcast next year. —[4]—. Meanwhile, Lenston Studios will release *1955*, a podcast detailing a championship season for the Marchand Panthers, next month, and Carryover Radio says it is currently in production on a show depicting the Murrell v. Talbert court case.

172. What is indicated about *Doretta*?

(A) It was based on a bestselling book.
(B) It was expected to run for more episodes.
(C) It was in a different genre from other popular podcasts.
(D) It was the first show made by its production company.

173. What can *Doretta* fans most likely do on Elgior Media's Web site?

(A) Purchase themed merchandise
(B) Post messages to each other
(C) Read some biographical facts
(D) View photographs of a performance

174. What does Ms. Myers provide an expert opinion on?

(A) The cause of *Doretta*'s success
(B) The historical accuracy of *Doretta*
(C) The reliability of Casteye's rankings
(D) The future prospects of Elgior Media

175. In which of the positions marked [1], [2], [3], and [4] does the following sentence best belong?

"A spokesperson for the company said it would deal with the building of Corbitt Bridge."

(A) [1]
(B) [2]
(C) [3]
(D) [4]

GO ON TO THE NEXT PAGE

Questions 176-180 refer to the following e-mail and Web page.

From:	Yeon-Hee Nam
To:	Research Team
Subject:	Workshop
Date:	January 30

Hi all,

I'm sure most of you have heard of Slinview, the new data visualization software. Well, Vazent Tech, its maker, is going to hold an educational workshop here next month. At just $40 per person for eight hours of instruction, this would be a great chance for us to become familiar with Slinview before investing a large sum of money to purchase it. I'd like to send two members of the team to attend the workshop and determine if it would benefit Fannon Agricultural Consulting to adopt Slinview.

You can find information about the workshop on <u>this page</u>. Note that we'll pay for your lunch at a nearby restaurant, but you'll need to coordinate your own transportation to the Grenory Hotel and get there by 8 A.M.

If you're interested, respond to this e-mail by the end of the day with a brief outline of the arguments for sending you. I'll notify those chosen tomorrow and have my assistant call to sign them up.

–Yeon-Hee

http://www.vazenttech.com

About   **Products**   **News**   **Contact**

One-day Slinview Workshops in Ontario

Vazent Tech invites Ontario-based businesses and individuals interested in learning the basics of Slinview to join one of four introductory workshops that will be held around the province in February. Our expert instructors will demonstrate Slinview's many features and then give participants the chance to try out the software through hands-on exercises. Please note that the number of participants is capped at 20 to match the number of computers available for this activity.

Workshops will run from 8 A.M. to 5 P.M., with a one-hour lunch break. The cost is $55 per person, or $40 for those with corporate or individual memberships in the Ontario Business Association. Snacks and water will be provided but participants must bring their own lunch or buy it in the area.

Locations and dates:

West Toronto (Sindley Convention Center)	February 17
East Toronto (Hernot Plaza)	February 19
Ottawa (Grenory Hotel)	February 21
Hamilton (Blaines University)	February 24

Click <u>here</u> to register.

176. Who most likely is Ms. Nam?

(A) A team manager
(B) A software developer
(C) An executive assistant
(D) A freelance event coordinator

177. In the e-mail, the word "arguments" in paragraph 3, line 2, is closest in meaning to

(A) procedures
(B) attitudes
(C) disputes
(D) reasons

178. What is implied about Fannon Agricultural Consulting?

(A) It is located on the west side of Toronto.
(B) It regularly pays for its staff to undergo skills training.
(C) It belongs to the Ontario Business Association.
(D) It recently adopted a new technique for data collection.

179. Which detail given by Ms. Nam about the workshops differs from the information in the Web page?

(A) The time she recommends arriving
(B) The method she describes for registering
(C) The place where she expects participants to eat
(D) The duration she attributes to the instructional portion

180. According to the Web page, why is the number of workshop participants limited?

(A) To ensure that participants can practice using the software
(B) To prevent venues from becoming difficult to access
(C) To allow participants to speak with the instructor
(D) To generate interest in an exclusive experience

GO ON TO THE NEXT PAGE

Questions 181-185 refer to the following article and e-mail.

Shrader Extension to Offer Certificate in Remote Work

SHRADER CITY (December 1)—The University of Shrader Extension has announced that it will begin offering a "Remote Work Proficiency Certificate".

Operated by the university, the extension is a Shrader-wide network of offices that is charged with sharing knowledge through continuing education classes and other programs. The extension's dean, Dr. Irwin Hirano, said that the goal of this program is to give opportunities to underemployed people in rural areas: "We want them to be able to make a living while remaining a part of their community, instead of feeling forced to move to a city."

For students' convenience, the program will be administered entirely online. Dr. Hirano explained, "All that people will need is a computer, moderate computer literacy, and a good Internet connection." He did point out that a background in fields like marketing or graphic design is helpful, but said that "there are remote work jobs, like customer service representative, that require little previous work experience."

The five-week program, which will cost nothing for residents of certain rural areas, centers around a course teaching the technological tools and job skills needed for remote work. Once the course ends, certificate-holders will have access to a career coach as they launch their job search.

Potential students must register by December 26 for the inaugural session, which will begin classes on January 2, and by February 24 for the session beginning March 3. More information about the program can be found at www.extension.shrader.edu/rwpc.

E-mail

From:	Tracy Byrne <tracy.byrne@obr-mail.com>
To:	<editor@shraderherald.com>
Subject:	Shrader's Remote Work Proficiency Certificate
Date:	November 7

Dear Editor,

Nearly a year ago, your paper reported on the University of Shrader Extension's program to train people to do remote work. I signed up to be a student in its first session, and within two weeks of earning my certificate, I got a remote work job that I still hold today. Most of the other people in my session had a similar experience.

That is why I was very surprised to find out recently that the program appears to no longer be available. Its Web page has been taken down. Dr. Hirano has left the university, and when I sent an e-mail to his successor about the program, I did not receive an answer. Could one of your reporters look into this issue? I think the people of our region deserve to know why such a successful initiative has been discontinued.

Thank you for your attention to this matter.

Sincerely,

Tracy Byrne

181. What kind of people is the program intended for?

(A) People who live in areas with low population density

(B) People who have family care responsibilities

(C) People who do not have university degrees

(D) People who previously worked in certain industries

182. What does the article state about the program's course?

(A) Its contents include a final exam.

(B) Some of its students are charged a reduced fee.

(C) Some of its classes are held at university extension offices.

(D) Its graduates can get job seeking assistance.

183. What is the purpose of the e-mail?

(A) To ask for an investigation into the program's status

(B) To complain about changes to the program's design

(C) To recommend the program to other potential students

(D) To thank a publication for promoting the program

184. What did Ms. Byrne most likely do on January 2 ?

(A) Notice an article

(B) Complete enrollment

(C) Start her course

(D) Receive her certificate

185. What is suggested about the University of Shrader Extension?

(A) It is Ms. Byrne's current employer.

(B) It did not fulfill a promise it made to Ms. Byrne.

(C) It no longer has an online presence.

(D) It has a new dean.

GO ON TO THE NEXT PAGE

Questions 186-190 refer to the following Web pages and e-mail.

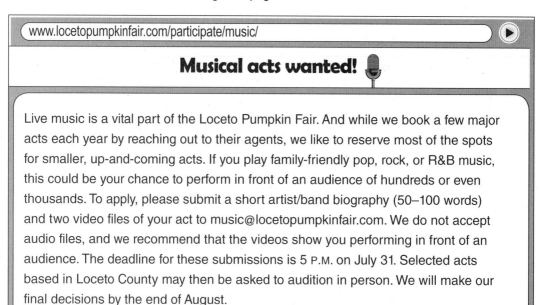

www.locetopumpkinfair.com/participate/music/

Musical acts wanted!

Live music is a vital part of the Loceto Pumpkin Fair. And while we book a few major acts each year by reaching out to their agents, we like to reserve most of the spots for smaller, up-and-coming acts. If you play family-friendly pop, rock, or R&B music, this could be your chance to perform in front of an audience of hundreds or even thousands. To apply, please submit a short artist/band biography (50–100 words) and two video files of your act to music@locetopumpkinfair.com. We do not accept audio files, and we recommend that the videos show you performing in front of an audience. The deadline for these submissions is 5 P.M. on July 31. Selected acts based in Loceto County may then be asked to audition in person. We will make our final decisions by the end of August.

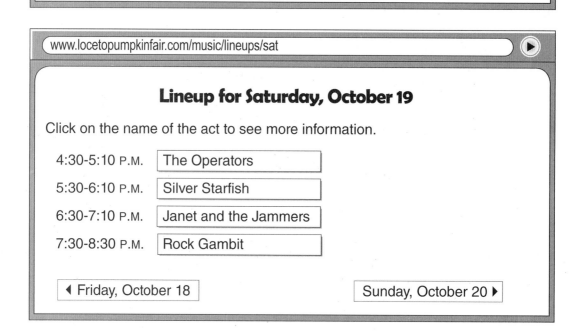

www.locetopumpkinfair.com/music/lineups/sat

Lineup for Saturday, October 19

Click on the name of the act to see more information.

4:30-5:10 P.M.   The Operators

5:30-6:10 P.M.   Silver Starfish

6:30-7:10 P.M.   Janet and the Jammers

7:30-8:30 P.M.   Rock Gambit

◀ Friday, October 18   Sunday, October 20 ▶

From:	\<music@locetopumpkinfair.com\>
To:	Lora Gordon \<lora.g@pmt-mail.com\>
Subject:	Loceto Pumpkin Fair
Date:	September 23

Dear Ms. Gordon,

One of the bands scheduled to perform at the Loceto Pumpkin Fair on October 19 has dropped out unexpectedly, and we would like to offer your band the chance to take its place. As I mentioned in my earlier e-mail, the other members of the music committee and I were very impressed by the Hairpins' audition and were sorry that we were initially unable to offer you a spot. You're the first act we're contacting about this opening.

You would play a 40-minute set starting at 4:30 P.M., and the pay is $300. We understand that the Hairpins may have found another engagement that day, so please discuss our offer with your bandmates and let us know what you decide. We need to hear from you by the end of the day tomorrow.

Thanks,

Wendell Fox
Loceto Pumpkin Fair Music Committee

---

186. What does the first Web page indicate about the application process?

(A) It is simpler than it was the previous year.
(B) There is a video guide explaining it.
(C) Some bands do not go through it.
(D) It requires applicants to submit a payment.

187. In the first Web page, the word "reserve" in paragraph 1, line 2, is closest in meaning to

(A) possess
(B) set aside
(C) take over
(D) exert

188. What is the purpose of the e-mail?

(A) To alert Ms. Gordon to an opportunity
(B) To revise the terms of an offer
(C) To give some preparation instructions
(D) To warn Ms. Gordon about a problem

189. What is most likely true about the Hairpins?

(A) It plays R&B music.
(B) It gave a performance on July 31.
(C) It is represented by a professional agent.
(D) Its members live in Loceto County.

190. Which band will NOT perform on October 19 ?

(A) The Operators
(B) Silver Starfish
(C) Janet and the Jammers
(D) Rock Gambit

GO ON TO THE NEXT PAGE

High Efficiency Fume Hoods from Belker Science

Almost every type of laboratory needs fume hoods so that its scientists can safely work with chemicals that give off hazardous gases. Unfortunately, fume hoods are also among the most energy-hungry pieces of lab equipment. That is why Belker Science created its range of high efficiency fume hoods. Each has a sophisticated controller and three-speed blower that together can reduce the hood's airflow usage and thus its energy requirements. In addition, the special motor uses less energy than a traditional motor. Available in 2-foot, 4-foot, 6-foot, and 8-foot models, the hoods also feature a vertical safety glass sash for maximum safety and usability.

Visit www.belkerscience.com today to learn more about these and other innovative products.

From:	Linda Murphy <l.murphy@simonroylabs.com>
To:	Jabril Nasser <j.nasser@simonroylabs.com>
Date:	February 2
Subject:	Replacing fume hoods

Hi Jabril,

As you requested, I spent last week's trade fair looking for ways for the lab to save money, and I was most impressed by what I saw at Belker Science's booth. Their high efficiency fume hoods seem to be just what we're looking for. Our fume hoods are all over 10 years old, so I'm sure that replacing them would result in noticeably lower energy bills. Plus, the salesperson mentioned that Wisenway, our energy provider, is offering an "EE" (energy efficiency) rebate through May, so if we hurry, we can get a rebate of up to $500 for upgrading.

You can see the collection of models at www.belkerscience.com/fumehoods/he. I think we should take advantage of the change to move up a size from our current 4-foot hoods, but I know that depends on our budget.

I hope this recommendation is helpful!

-Linda

```
┌─────────────────────────────────────────────────────────────┐
│                    ┌──────────────────────┐                   │
│                    │   Wisenway Energy    │                   │
│                    └──────────────────────┘                   │
│  Simonroy Laboratories              Account #: 4018532        │
│  540 Cole Lane                      Amount due: $648.86       │
│  Crawfend, CO 80022                 Due date: July 22         │
│                                                               │
│                         Energy Bill                           │
│  Billing period: June 1–June 30                               │
│  Energy usage: 7,348 kWh       Historical usage:              │
│  Meter #: 8231004248           - Previous billing period: 8,011 kWh │
│  Read date: June 30            - This billing period last year: 8,104 kWh │
│  Rate type: Commercial                                        │
└─────────────────────────────────────────────────────────────┘
```

Charge type	Rate	Total charge
Energy	$0.120 per kWh	$ 881.76
Distribution	$0.032 per kWh	$ 235.14
System Access	$7.00 per month	$ 7.00
EE Rebate	-$500.00 (one-time)	-$ 500.00
	Subtotal	$ 623.90
	Taxes (4.0%)	$ 24.96
	Total	$ 648.86

See reverse for payment options. →

191. Which part of the fume hoods is NOT described as increasing energy efficiency?

(A) The controller
(B) The blower
(C) The sash
(D) The motor

192. In the e-mail, the word "spent" in paragraph 1, line 1, is closest in meaning to

(A) contributed
(B) passed
(C) paid
(D) clarified

193. What size of fume hood does Ms. Murphy suggest buying?

(A) 2-foot
(B) 4-foot
(C) 6-foot
(D) 8-foot

194. What is implied about a rebate program?

(A) It has been extended.
(B) Its maximum amount was raised.
(C) It is now offered by two organizations.
(D) Its name has been changed.

195. What does the bill indicate about Simonroy Laboratories?

(A) Its current bill is due at the end of the next billing period.
(B) It has been a Wisenway Energy customer for at least a year.
(C) Its energy expenses are automatically withdrawn from its bank account.
(D) All of its regular energy charges vary based on its energy usage.

GO ON TO THE NEXT PAGE

Flickinger Corporate Dining Services

www.delicious-fcds.com

Flickinger Corporate Dining Services (FCDS) has become the number-one operator of corporate cafeterias in the Birmingham area because of our dedication to excellence and range of flexible services. We can plan the creation of a new cafeteria or take over operation of an existing facility from an in-house provider to increase efficiency. If desired, we can serve meals from 6 A.M. to 10 P.M. For businesses with environmental concerns, we offer menu plans with dishes made only with foods from regional suppliers. Above all, we guarantee delicious, nutritious meals and snacks. Visit our Web site for more information and resources, including footage of our chefs at work.

E-Mail	
From:	Ronald Scherba <r.scherba@wibbenslogistics.com>
To:	<inquiries@delicious-fcds.com>
Subject:	Inquiry
Date:	14 January

Hello,

My name is Ronald Scherba, and I'm the head of the administrative services department at Wibbens Logistics. We're a small firm of about 60 people located in the city centre. I'm writing because we're looking for a new service provider to operate our employee cafeteria, and I was impressed by a recent advertisement of yours. Our current provider doesn't offer environmentally-friendly menu plans or late-night service, and we especially need the latter because our employees keep unusual hours in order to communicate with overseas contacts.

Still, our main concerns are basic issues like meal quality and customer service. To that end, I would like to tour one of the cafeterias you currently manage. This would help me determine whether your services will be a good fit for our business before we begin negotiating a contract. Would it be possible to set up something like that? Please let me know by replying to this e-mail.

Sincerely,

Ronald Scherba
Director of Administrative Services
Wibbens Logistics

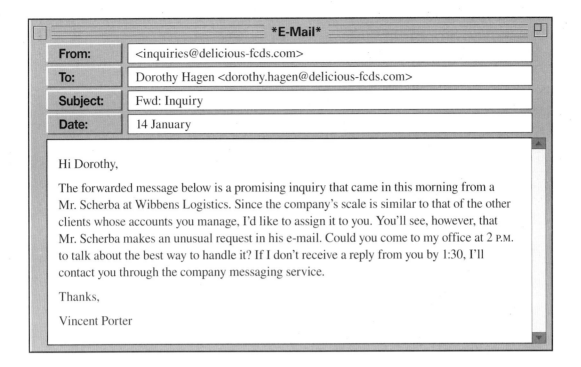

```
*E-Mail*

From:      <inquiries@delicious-fcds.com>

To:        Dorothy Hagen <dorothy.hagen@delicious-fcds.com>

Subject:   Fwd: Inquiry

Date:      14 January
```

Hi Dorothy,

The forwarded message below is a promising inquiry that came in this morning from a Mr. Scherba at Wibbens Logistics. Since the company's scale is similar to that of the other clients whose accounts you manage, I'd like to assign it to you. You'll see, however, that Mr. Scherba makes an unusual request in his e-mail. Could you come to my office at 2 P.M. to talk about the best way to handle it? If I don't receive a reply from you by 1:30, I'll contact you through the company messaging service.

Thanks,

Vincent Porter

196. According to the advertisement, what can visitors to FCDS's Web site do?

(A) Read comments made by current customers
(B) Access a variety of sample menu plans
(C) See a list of the company's suppliers
(D) Watch videos of meals being prepared

197. What is a service mentioned in the advertisement Mr. Scherba does NOT inquire about?

(A) Special occasion catering
(B) Cafeteria construction planning
(C) A locally-sourced food program
(D) Extended serving hours

198. What does Mr. Scherba hope to arrange?

(A) A visit to a food service facility
(B) A conference call with FCDS staff
(C) A delivery of informational materials
(D) A collaboration between two food service providers

199. What is most likely true about Ms. Hagen?

(A) She manages all clients within a certain city district.
(B) She met Mr. Scherba at a networking event.
(C) She has experience with small firms.
(D) She specializes in overseas accounts.

200. Why is Ms. Hagen asked to go to Mr. Porter's office?

(A) To present the results of some research
(B) To assist with assigning tasks to other employees
(C) To discuss strategies for responding to a request
(D) To resolve an issue with some software

Stop! This is the end of the test. If you finish before time is called, you may go back to Parts 5, 6, and 7 and check your work.

RC

TEST 2

READING TEST

In the Reading test, you will read a variety of texts and answer several different types of reading comprehension questions. The entire Reading test will last 75 minutes. There are three parts, and directions are given for each part. You are encouraged to answer as many questions as possible within the time allowed.

You must mark your answers on the separate answer sheet. Do not write your answers in your test book.

PART 5

Directions: A word or phrase is missing in each of the sentences below. Four answer choices are given below each sentence. Select the best answer to complete the sentence. Then mark the letter (A), (B), (C), or (D) on your answer sheet.

---

101. Authorities ------- a warning to drivers about poor road conditions caused by the recent storm.

(A) is issuing
(B) was issued
(C) will be issued
(D) have issued

102. Ben Johnson was ------- one of the most influential photographers of the year.

(A) easy
(B) ease
(C) easily
(D) easiest

103. The city is considering turning the vacant land ------- a small playground or some plots for community gardening.

(A) into
(B) apart
(C) across
(D) only

104. Since Ms. Huff's lecture dealt with the most controversial topic, the audience directed the majority of its questions to -------.

(A) herself
(B) hers
(C) her
(D) she

105. Collis Group regularly appears ------- lists of banks with the highest level of customer satisfaction.

(A) at
(B) on
(C) of
(D) to

106. Please confirm that you have closed the paper drawers ------- before attempting to operate the printer.

(A) securely
(B) widely
(C) hardly
(D) strictly

107. The release of the SwiftPlay game console was ------- timed to occur at the start of the holiday shopping season.

(A) strategy
(B) strategized
(C) strategic
(D) strategically

108. Flexible working arrangements are increasingly favored by full-time and part-time workers -------.

(A) neither
(B) alike
(C) both
(D) same

109. After careful consideration, Mr. Marsh's reasons for requesting a deadline ------- were determined to be insufficient.

(A) extension
(B) extended
(C) extendable
(D) extensions

110. Candidates may be asked to provide ------- of their qualifications in the form of diplomas, certificates, etc.

(A) access
(B) renewal
(C) evidence
(D) compensation

111. Alonta Associates requires its employees to ------- the company of a change in their home address.

(A) note
(B) reveal
(C) educate
(D) inform

112. ------- draws readers to the *Willard Daily News* is our commitment to fair and honest reporting.

(A) Something
(B) What
(C) Whom
(D) Whoever

113. Bailey Studios' new comedy has performed ------- better at the box office than movie industry analysts predicted it would.

(A) far
(B) so
(C) very
(D) beyond

114. ------- the construction permit application took longer than the contractor had anticipated.

(A) Prepare
(B) Preparing
(C) Preparation
(D) Prepared

115. At the orientation, trainees should listen attentively while the representative from headquarters ------- our corporate values.

(A) described
(B) has described
(C) describe
(D) is describing

116. Bauft Software's booth was crowded with visitors ------- its inconvenient placement in a back corner of the exhibition hall.

(A) despite
(B) between
(C) except
(D) unlike

117. ------- upgraded with the latest hardware, our data centers offer safe, reliable data storage.

(A) Frequent
(B) Frequenting
(C) Frequency
(D) Frequently

118. The year-end report your department will produce must include summaries of both concluded and ------- projects.

(A) multiple
(B) ambitious
(C) tailored
(D) ongoing

119. Due to the mild weather, this seems likely to be Jennings Winter Recreation Area's ------- season of the past fifteen years.

(A) shorten
(B) shortest
(C) shorter
(D) shortly

120. The office's energy ------- has been successfully reduced by the campaign to power down idle electronics at night.

(A) transition
(B) efficiency
(C) consumption
(D) awareness

GO ON TO THE NEXT PAGE

121. An e-mail notification about an upcoming series of training sessions was sent to -------.
(A) recruiter
(B) recruits
(C) recruit
(D) recruiting

122. The recipe calls for one pound of ground beef, but this can be replaced with an ------- amount of a vegetarian substitute such as cooked lentils.
(A) existing
(B) accountable
(C) equivalent
(D) overall

123. The business world and the academic community must be encouraged to collaborate with ------- to engage in practical research.
(A) other
(B) which
(C) itself
(D) one another

124. Moxis Motors ------- to supply transportation providers with economical, fuel-efficient commercial vehicles.
(A) strives
(B) conforms
(C) discontinues
(D) specializes

125. The final step of the licensing process is a practical exam that verifies applicants' ------- in the art of styling hair.
(A) insight
(B) privilege
(C) proficiency
(D) compliance

126. ------- joining Keller Fox Ltd., Ms. Jang was the vice president of sales at Cortiss Hotels.
(A) Prior to
(B) Compared to
(C) Ever since
(D) According to

127. The IT director has assured us that the technicians ------- the system repairs by this time tomorrow.
(A) will have finished
(B) have finished
(C) are finishing
(D) were finishing

128. Mr. Easton released a statement ------- his spokesperson instead of speaking directly to the press.
(A) even
(B) officially
(C) announced
(D) through

129. The committee proposed ------- the Sparks and Corgan courts in a new building to be located in western Corgan.
(A) expediting
(B) consolidating
(C) delegating
(D) waiving

130. Wunch Consulting's strategic planning services will assist you in determining your business objectives ------- evaluating your progress in achieving them.
(A) yet
(B) beside
(C) and
(D) in regard to

PART 6

Directions: Read the texts that follow. A word, phrase, or sentence is missing in parts of each text. Four answer choices for each question are given below the text. Select the best answer to complete the text. Then mark the letter (A), (B), (C), or (D) on your answer sheet.

Questions 131-134 refer to the following letter.

February 25

Diana Townsend
407 Robin Rd.
Burkett, ME 04007

Ms. Townsend,

You are hereby invited to a community meeting on the proposal to construct an express train line paralleling part of the Gold Line. The meeting will be held in the auditorium of the Powlar Community Center from 6 to 8 P.M. on Thursday, March 18. -------.
                                                                                            131.

------- described in detail in the enclosure, the express line would run from Burkett to Grenham
132.
Central Station with just two stops in between. Therefore, it would enable ------- journeys to and
                                                                            133.
from the city center.

The meeting will be a chance for Burkett residents to provide input on the proposal. The agenda includes a presentation ------- by transit officials and a question-and-answer session.
                                 134.
We hope you will attend.

Sincerely,

Gary Murphy
Director, Grenham Regional Transit Authority

Encl.

131. (A) Unfortunately, this date does not suit my schedule.
     (B) The center is located at 150 Second Street, Burkett.
     (C) We expect construction to be nearly done by then.
     (D) Please come prepared with a revised draft of the proposal.

132. (A) Upon
     (B) For
     (C) Until
     (D) As

133. (A) swifter
     (B) cozier
     (C) more scenic
     (D) cheaper

134. (A) will conduct
     (B) was conducted
     (C) to conduct
     (D) conducted

GO ON TO THE NEXT PAGE

Questions 135-138 refer to the following e-mail.

From: Gwendolyn Ramsey

To: All volunteers

Subject: Policy

Date: 16 December

Dear Lyndie Fashion Museum volunteers,

I recently overheard a volunteer guide giving incorrect information ------- a tour of our exhibits.
                                                                          135.
Please do not do this. I understand that it may be embarrassing to be asked a question that you

can't answer. -------, the correct response in that situation is to direct the visitor to our
              136.
educational staff. -------. It's also wise to learn the answer yourself to prevent the problem from
                   137.
recurring.

I wanted to spell this policy out to all of you, as it's not clear ------- the incident I witnessed was a
                                                                    138.
one-time mistake or part of a widespread problem. Please reply briefly to confirm that you've

read and understood this e-mail.

Thanks,

Gwendolyn Ramsey

Volunteer Coordinator

Lyndie Fashion Museum

135. (A) like
(B) during
(C) though
(D) while

136. (A) Likewise
(B) On the contrary
(C) More importantly
(D) Nevertheless

137. (A) They will be able to give an overview of
our event calendar.
(B) The museum is open from 10 A.M. to
6 P.M., Tuesday through Sunday.
(C) If they are unavailable, the visitor may
e-mail them later at info@lfm.org.nz.
(D) We are always seeking additional
volunteers to lead tours.

138. (A) whether
(B) based on
(C) after all
(D) when

Thank you for ordering from Sarinta Studio!

The enclosed candle was handmade with high-quality ingredients. ------- its wick trimmed to a
139.
1/8-inch length for best results. We also advise burning it until the top layer of wax melts
completely each time to keep the top from becoming uneven.

If you are displeased with your purchase for any reason, please don't hesitate to contact us.

-------. Our decades of fragrance expertise are at your disposal. We are happy to recommend
140.
another ------- for you or even create a customized one. We can be reached by e-mail at
141.
sarinta@pexo-market.com or by phone during regular business hours at (864) 555-0192.

On the other hand, if you are satisfied with your Sarinta candle, please let ------- know! You can
142.
leave a positive review of our studio at www.pexo-market.com/sarinta. We would deeply
appreciate the support.

---

139. (A) To keep
    (B) Having kept
    (C) Keeping
    (D) Keep

140. (A) At present, Sarinta Studio does not
       operate any offline stores.
    (B) Our social media accounts are often
       updated with photos of new products.
    (C) Take 15% off of your next order with the
       coupon code "MYSARINTA".
    (D) Along with returns and exchanges, we
       can offer helpful advice.

141. (A) scent
    (B) shape
    (C) texture
    (D) pattern

142. (A) her
    (B) some
    (C) others
    (D) them

Questions 143-146 refer to the following memo.

To: All Pengler employees
Re: Rouse Commercial Services

I'm writing to share with you all a recent success story for our company.

Rouse Commercial Services, a maintenance and repair provider, used to have a paperwork problem. Its service visit report forms were long and easy to misplace. Customers complained about paying for the time technicians spent ------- them by hand after every visit, while lost forms
143.
often made it difficult for the company to bill correctly for the services it had provided.

Fortunately, Rouse chose to buy tablet computers and begin using Pengler Business. Its technicians ------- fill out electronic forms that are automatically saved to a shared, well-
144.
organized folder.

Rouse's service business supervisor told us, "You've made it possible for our technicians to be much more productive. -------." Thanks to these benefits, the company ------- its investment in
145.   146.
just one year.

We should all be proud of the assistance that Pengler provided for Rouse Commercial Services. Let's keep up the good work.

Gun-Woo Han
Chief Executive Officer

143. (A) on completion
(B) that complete
(C) completing
(D) completed

144. (A) now
(B) then
(C) rarely
(D) still

145. (A) We employ specialists in plumbing, electricity, and building repair.
(B) And just as importantly, we no longer lose money to underbilling.
(C) We want customers to know that we are keeping their data safe.
(D) As a matter of fact, we are exploring that possibility right now.

146. (A) reserved
(B) recovered
(C) maintained
(D) encouraged

PART 7

Directions: In this part you will read a selection of texts, such as magazine and newspaper articles, e-mails, and instant messages. Each text or set of texts is followed by several questions. Select the best answer for each question and mark the letter (A), (B), (C), or (D) on your answer sheet.

Questions 147-148 refer to the following e-mail.

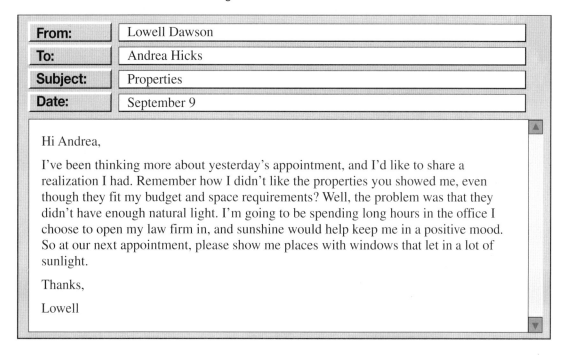

From:	Lowell Dawson
To:	Andrea Hicks
Subject:	Properties
Date:	September 9

Hi Andrea,

I've been thinking more about yesterday's appointment, and I'd like to share a realization I had. Remember how I didn't like the properties you showed me, even though they fit my budget and space requirements? Well, the problem was that they didn't have enough natural light. I'm going to be spending long hours in the office I choose to open my law firm in, and sunshine would help keep me in a positive mood. So at our next appointment, please show me places with windows that let in a lot of sunlight.

Thanks,

Lowell

147. Why did Mr. Dawson send the e-mail?

(A) To confirm a choice
(B) To inquire about a budget
(C) To provide a specification
(D) To make an appointment

148. What is suggested about Mr. Dawson?

(A) He will be spending a lot of time outdoors soon.
(B) He wants to upgrade some lighting fixtures.
(C) He is concerned about a property law.
(D) He plans to start his own business.

GO ON TO THE NEXT PAGE

Foxhead Rock

Foxhead Rock is the large rock formation visible on the rise opposite this point. Named for its resemblance to the head of a fox, it is one of the most famous geological features in the park. The 27-foot structure is made of sandstone shaped over millions of years by natural processes like erosion.

Though Foxhead Rock is visible from other points on the trail, this spot offers hikers the best photo opportunity. Please do not leave the trail and attempt to approach the rock, because the ground surrounding it is steep and rocky. Thank you.

Lundes National Park

149. Where would the information most likely appear?

(A) In a museum display
(B) In a park brochure
(C) On a product label
(D) On an outdoor sign

150. What does the information suggest that readers can do?

(A) Take photographs
(B) Touch an exhibit
(C) Buy souvenirs
(D) Sign up for a tour

Questions 151-152 refer to the following text-message chain.

Herman Ahderom [3:02 P.M.]
Ms. Ryan, the candidate you brought to us isn't responding to my attempts to video chat with him.

Eleanor Ryan [3:03 P.M.]
Matthew Kasper? The applicant for the data-entry position?

Herman Ahderom [3:03 P.M.]
That's right.

Eleanor Ryan [3:04 P.M.]
I'm sorry about that. Let me check in with him.

Eleanor Ryan [3:05 P.M.]
I think there must be a misunderstanding. He says he's online.

Herman Ahderom [3:06 P.M.]
Let's confirm our information. I'm calling him using the program "Chatrich", and his user name is "matthew_kasper", right?

Eleanor Ryan [3:07 P.M.]
Actually, it's "matthew.kasper", according to my materials. Try that.

Herman Ahderom [3:09 P.M.]
OK, now the call is going through. Thank you. I'll call you afterwards to let you know how the interview went.

151. Who most likely is Ms. Ryan?

(A) A computer technician
(B) A political reporter
(C) An event planner
(D) A job recruiter

152. At 3:07 P.M., what does Ms. Ryan recommend doing when she writes, "Try that"?

(A) Using different contact information
(B) Restarting a software program
(C) Reading some instructional materials
(D) Changing a computer's display setting

GO ON TO THE NEXT PAGE

Questions 153-154 refer to the following Web page.

◻ ◻ ☒

http://www.scheelerexpress.com/rail

Scheeler Express Rail Services

Rail can be an excellent way to move large amounts of freight. When compared with trucking, the other major over-the-land shipping method, rail can be slower and less convenient but offers increased safety and causes less harm to the environment. It is best suited to businesses that need to transport large amounts of freight over a long distance on a regular basis.

Scheeler Express's transportation experts can advise you on whether railway transport is right for your company. If you decide it is, we can assist you with navigating the complex systems of different railway companies on your route. We maintain relationships with all major operators, which enables us to stay up-to-date on their constantly changing technology.

Contact us today to get started.

153. Who is the Web page intended for?
(A) Employees commuting to work
(B) Companies shipping cargo
(C) Tourists visiting a certain region
(D) Train operators seeking repair services

154. According to the Web page, what is one advantage of Scheeler Express?
(A) It offers long hours of operation.
(B) It employs advanced technology.
(C) It has connections with other companies.
(D) It has exclusive use of a rail route.

Questions 155-157 refer to the following e-mail.

```
══════════════════ E-Mail message ══════════════════

  From:      Zaters Hardware

  To:        Wallace Glover

  Subject:   Announcement

  Date:      November 1
```

Dear Valued Customer,

Zaters Hardware is sorry to announce the discontinuation of our Zaters Points
program. For the last eight years, Zaters Points have been a great way for our
customers to earn discounts on our products. Unfortunately, the cost of running the
program has grown to the point where it no longer makes sense to continue offering it.
Starting today, no new applications for the program will be accepted. However, we
will allow existing participants to continue accruing Zaters Points until November 30
and spending them until January 31. Please keep the latter deadline in mind as you
determine how to use your remaining points. We will send out periodic reminder
e-mails about the situation as well.

As always, thank you for being a loyal Zaters Hardware customer.

Sincerely,

Darryl Harmon, CEO
Zaters Hardware

155. What does the e-mail notify recipients of?

(A) The closing of a retail store
(B) The end of a loyalty program
(C) The replacement of an executive
(D) The recall of a hardware product

156. According to the e-mail, what was the reason for the decision?

(A) A security issue
(B) A legal dispute
(C) Financial considerations
(D) Business restructuring

157. What are recipients asked to do?

(A) Fill out a form
(B) Wait for a future e-mail
(C) Choose between two options
(D) Remember a date

GO ON TO THE NEXT PAGE

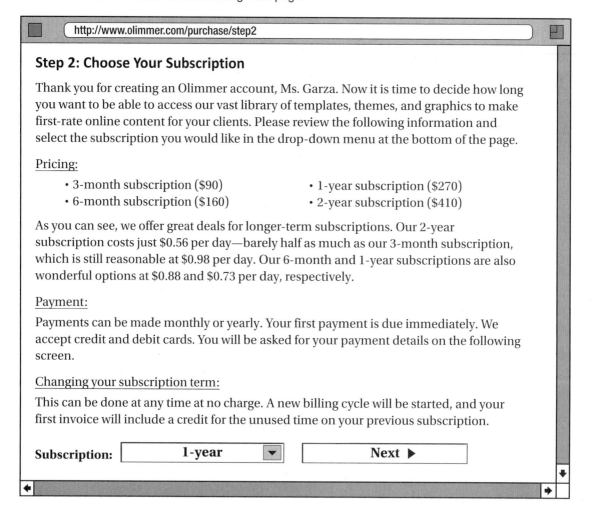

http://www.olimmer.com/purchase/step2

Step 2: Choose Your Subscription

Thank you for creating an Olimmer account, Ms. Garza. Now it is time to decide how long you want to be able to access our vast library of templates, themes, and graphics to make first-rate online content for your clients. Please review the following information and select the subscription you would like in the drop-down menu at the bottom of the page.

Pricing:

- 3-month subscription ($90)
- 6-month subscription ($160)
- 1-year subscription ($270)
- 2-year subscription ($410)

As you can see, we offer great deals for longer-term subscriptions. Our 2-year subscription costs just $0.56 per day—barely half as much as our 3-month subscription, which is still reasonable at $0.98 per day. Our 6-month and 1-year subscriptions are also wonderful options at $0.88 and $0.73 per day, respectively.

Payment:

Payments can be made monthly or yearly. Your first payment is due immediately. We accept credit and debit cards. You will be asked for your payment details on the following screen.

Changing your subscription term:

This can be done at any time at no charge. A new billing cycle will be started, and your first invoice will include a credit for the unused time on your previous subscription.

Subscription: 1-year ▼   Next ▶

158. Who most likely is Olimmer intended for?

(A) Freelance accountants
(B) Web designers
(C) Librarians
(D) Journalists

159. How much will Ms. Garza pay per day for her subscription?

(A) $0.56
(B) $0.73
(C) $0.88
(D) $0.98

160. What is stated about Olimmer subscriptions?

(A) They can be cancelled at any time.
(B) Their prices reflect the services they allow access to.
(C) There is no fee for switching from one to another.
(D) They must be paid for on a monthly basis.

Questions 161-163 refer to the following memo.

To: All employees
From: Diane Erickson
Re: Flexible hours

It has recently come to my attention that there is some confusion among employees about Prask's policy with regard to flexible working hours. — [1] —. I have rewritten the employee handbook as follows to clarify the issue:

"Prask requires all full-time employees to work in the office for 40 hours each week. — [2] —. However, employees approved to work flextime may fulfill this requirement by working any combination of hours between 7 A.M. and 8 P.M., Monday through Friday. Flextime is only available to employees whose job duties do not require them to be in the office at specific times. Employees must receive managerial approval in order to work flexible hours. The privilege of working flextime may be revoked at any time due to business needs or employee performance issues. — [3] —."

If you believe that you are eligible to work flextime and would like to do so, you should begin by creating a proposed schedule, and then meet with your manager to discuss it. Please do not bring flextime requests directly to the HR department. However, general inquiries about the policy can be made to our department by contacting John Burrows (ext. 72, john.burrows@prask.com). — [4] —.

Diane Erickson
Director of Human Resources

161. What is indicated about Prask's flextime policy?

(A) It allows weekend work.
(B) It was recently implemented.
(C) It excludes some employees.
(D) It is popular with staff.

162. According to the memo, what should an employee interested in working flextime do first?

(A) Determine their desired working hours
(B) Ask a manager for permission
(C) Submit a request to Human Resources
(D) Earn a positive performance evaluation

163. In which of the positions marked [1], [2], [3], and [4] does the following sentence best belong?

"In either case, the employee's manager should clearly explain the situation and give the employee advance notice of the change."

(A) [1]
(B) [2]
(C) [3]
(D) [4]

GO ON TO THE NEXT PAGE

Questions 164-167 refer to the following text-message chain.

Lana Norton	**[11:54 A.M.]**

Hi, everyone. I'm at a doctor's appointment that's running long, so I'm not going to be able to teach my 1 P.M. aerobics class today. Kyeong-Mo told me to text all of you to see if one of you could do it for me.

Henry Russell	**[11:54 A.M.]**

I would, but I'll be in the middle of a pilates class at that time.

Kenya Hunt	**[11:55 A.M.]**

I'm finished with my scheduled classes for the day. Could you give me some more details?

Lana Norton	**[11:55 A.M.]**

It's a low-intensity, dance-centered class that runs from 1 to 1:50 in Studio 3. It doesn't require any equipment, and the students are usually older women.

Kenya Hunt	**[11:56 A.M.]**

OK, that sounds doable. I'll take it. What kind of music do you usually play?

Kyeong-Mo Jeon	**[11:57 A.M.]**

Thank you, Kenya. I'll send out a text to let the regular attendees know that the class will go forward with a different instructor.

Lana Norton	**[11:58 A.M.]**

I actually have a video of the class that I recorded a few weeks ago. It should give you an idea of the music to play and the kind of moves that we usually do. What's your e-mail address?

Kenya Hunt	**[11:58 A.M.]**

It's kenya.hunt@pnb-mail.com. Thanks! That'll be really helpful.

Lana Norton	**[11:59 A.M.]**

No, thank you for volunteering to substitute! Let me know if you have any more questions. I should be able to check my phone periodically during the rest of my appointment.

164. Why does Ms. Norton message the other participants?

(A) To ask for a favor
(B) To promote an event
(C) To apologize for a situation
(D) To announce a schedule

165. At 11:56 A.M., what does Ms. Hunt most likely mean when she writes, "I'll take it"?

(A) She is accepting a teaching opportunity.
(B) She is volunteering to move an item.
(C) She would like to keep some equipment.
(D) She is interested in acquiring a new skill.

166. What is NOT indicated about the 1 P.M. class?

(A) It lasts for less than an hour.
(B) It requires registration in advance.
(C) It involves relatively easy exercise.
(D) It is attended routinely by some people.

167. What most likely will Ms. Norton e-mail to Ms. Hunt?

(A) A video clip
(B) A list of songs
(C) A sign-up sheet
(D) A neighborhood map

Questions 168-171 refer to the following letter.

Claire Fields
390 Holt Drive
4C24+8G Bridgetown

18 March

Ruthie's
2090 Philip Road
3CV4+9Q Bridgetown

To Whom It May Concern:

My name is Claire Fields, and I am a frequent customer at your shop. I love your iced mochas, and I think your service is excellent. However, as a wheelchair user, there is an accessibility issue that I would like to bring to your attention. Your service counter is quite high. It seems like it is about 150 centimeters off the floor. I cannot see things that are set on it, I struggle to reach over it, and it even obstructs my view of your menu.

It would probably be quite expensive to replace your counter, so I am not asking you to do that. Instead, I am writing because I heard that you are opening new locations in other areas of Bridgetown. Please consider equipping them with more wheelchair-friendly facilities. Also, I suggest contacting the Barbados Disability Authority (BDA) for more tips on accessible design. Its Web site is www.bda.bb.

Thank you for taking the time to read my letter, and good luck! It is always exciting to see locally-owned businesses thrive.

Sincerely,

Claire Fields

168. What kind of business is Ruthie's?

(A) A café
(B) A hair salon
(C) A flower shop
(D) A clothing store

169. What problem does Ms. Fields describe?

(A) A doorway is too narrow.
(B) The text on a sign is too small.
(C) Some flooring is too uneven.
(D) A piece of furniture is too tall.

170. What is indicated about Ruthie's?

(A) It is currently expanding.
(B) It offers an unusual service.
(C) It employs people with disabilities.
(D) It is an international chain.

171. Why does Ms. Fields recommend contacting the BDA?

(A) To schedule an inspection
(B) To receive further information
(C) To apply for financial support
(D) To report a difficulty

Test 2

Evarson Farmers' Petition Introduced in State Parliament

SCAVELL (8 September)—Today, member of State Parliament Naomi Black submitted a petition created by farmers in the Evarson area protesting a government plan to reduce their water licences.

Water licences authorize their holders to use specific, large amounts of groundwater. —[1]—. The government's reduction plan would slowly shrink the amount of water that licence-holders in the agricultural industry are entitled to by 10% over the next five years. It was developed by the Evarson Water and Agriculture Taskforce (EWAT) as a way to combat the regions increasing dryness.

"Everyone has to adjust," said Alvin Brooks, EWAT's chair. "The state government has already cut its own water use through actions like replacing grass in public parks with stone gravel. The licence plan will encourage farmers to use water more efficiently."

However, the farmers complain that the reductions will unfairly devalue their land and damage the local economy. —[2]—. Courtney Grant, head of the Evarson Farmers Association (EFA) and one of the creators of the petition, said, "We already use water efficiently. All that the reductions will do is lower our output."

EWAT representatives and EFA members discussed the plan at a public meeting soon after its announcement last month, but were unable to find a mutually acceptable compromise. —[3]—. The association then wrote and circulated the "Petition for Responsible Water Resources Management".

The petition proposes that the state government invest in finding or developing additional water sources instead. —[4]—. Now that it has been officially introduced into State Parliament, it will be referred to the appropriate parliamentary committee for review.

172. What does EWAT propose doing?

(A) Subsidizing water-efficient technology
(B) Allocating less water to farming efforts
(C) Raising the qualifications for water licences
(D) Using water-conserving landscaping on public property

173. What is suggested about EWAT's plan?

(A) It was developed without input from EFA.
(B) It will be implemented after a delay of several years.
(C) It is similar to proposals made in other states.
(D) It will require a large investment of government funds.

174. Who most likely is Ms. Black?

(A) A university professor
(B) A produce grower
(C) A regional politician
(D) An environmental activist

175. In which of the positions marked [1], [2], [3], and [4] does the following sentence best belong?

"It garnered more than 1,000 signatures in two weeks."

(A) [1]
(B) [2]
(C) [3]
(D) [4]

GO ON TO THE NEXT PAGE

Event Preparation and Wrap-up Plan

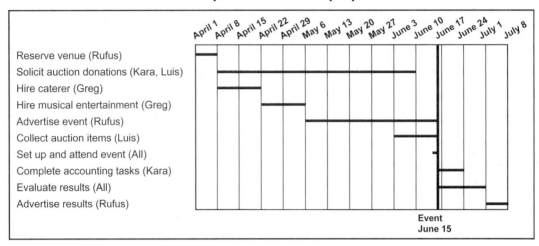

Event
June 15

From:	Kara Griffin
To:	Luis Rodriguez
Subject:	Good news
Date:	April 24

Hi Luis,

I have some good news from my meeting with Mr. Bobrova at Falcon Gallery this morning—he agreed to donate a Gabrielle Searcy painting! It's valued at nearly $500, so it could bring in a pretty high bid. It turns out that Mr. Bobrova loves Felix Forest, so he was very happy to help with our conservation efforts.

You should talk to him in advance about how to collect and transport the piece, though, because I suspect that that might be difficult. If you do need to use a packing or transportation service, make sure you keep the receipts and any other paperwork. We'll need them for accounting purposes after the event.

How are your efforts going? Have you heard back from the amusement park yet? Their admission tickets would be such an attractive item for families.

Also, I noticed that Greg hasn't met his first deadline. Do you know why? I thought that you might have heard something since your desk is next to his.

- Kara

176. According to the chart, what is Rufus NOT responsible for?

(A) Reserving a site
(B) Hiring a food provider
(C) Publicizing the event
(D) Setting up a venue

177. What has Ms. Griffin obtained a donation of?

(A) An artwork
(B) A gallery tour
(C) A set of painting lessons
(D) A meal with an artist

178. Who most likely would need the paperwork mentioned in the e-mail?

(A) Rufus
(B) Ms. Griffin
(C) Greg
(D) Ms. Searcy

179. What deadline did Greg fail to meet?

(A) April 8
(B) April 15
(C) April 22
(D) May 6

180. In the e-mail, what is suggested about the event that is being planned?

(A) It had to be rescheduled.
(B) It will require special transportation for attendees.
(C) It is being sponsored by an entertainment business.
(D) It will benefit an environmental cause.

GO ON TO THE NEXT PAGE

INVOICE

Brendan Echevarria Services
P.O. Box 10392
Toronto ON M4N 3P6
647-555-0129
www.brendanechevarria.com

Invoice #: 62
Work period: January 1–January 31
Date issued: February 1
Date due: March 2

Client: Baldora Online
Attn: Amanda Aoki
780 Richmond St.
Toronto ON M6J 1B9
416-555-0105

Service	Rate	Total
300-word news article on Werra, Inc. expansion	$0.30/word	$90.00
450-word informative article on management skills	$0.50/word	$225.00
30-minute phone call with client	$5/15 minutes	$10.00
Revision of 450-word article	$0.10/word	$45.00
	Total:	**$370.00**

Payment can be made by check to the above physical address or by WeisPay to payment@brendanechevarria.com.

Thank you for your business!

From:	Brendan Echevarria <contact@brendanechevarria.com>
To:	Amanda Aoki <amanda.aoki@baldora.com>
Subject:	Re: Questions
Date:	February 5

Dear Amanda,

I'm happy to address your question about my invoice for this month. First, you are correct that my rewriting rate increased this year. I'm sorry if it took you by surprise, but the new rate was stated in the rate sheet that I sent to your predecessor in December, and he agreed to it. I'll forward you the e-mail exchange separately so that you can confirm this. My guess is that he forgot to update my information in your company files.

As for your request to recommend other potential contributors, I do know someone that you may be interested in. Her name is Melody Thorpe, and she's a former colleague of mine from the *Yorkville Herald* who recently became a freelance science writer. She has a simple, engaging style that you can see in her old articles on the *Herald's* Web site. If you decide you'd like to contact her, her e-mail address is m.thorpe@vct-mail.com.

Let me know if you have any further questions or concerns. Unless you tell me otherwise, I'll continue working on my current 250-word news article.

Sincerely,

Brendan

181. What did Mr. Echevarria write about for Baldora Online in January?

(A) Sports
(B) Politics
(C) Business
(D) Entertainment

182. What is the purpose of the e-mail?

(A) To answer some client inquiries
(B) To report a problem with a payment
(C) To discuss changes to a project
(D) To apologize for a billing mistake

183. Which rate does Mr. Echevarria indicate recently changed?

(A) $0.30 per word
(B) $0.50 per word
(C) $5.00 for 15 minutes
(D) $0.10 per word

184. In the e-mail, the word "exchange" in paragraph 1, line 4, is closest in meaning to

(A) trade
(B) market
(C) conversion
(D) correspondence

185. What does the e-mail indicate about Ms. Thorpe?

(A) She is one of Mr. Echevarria's clients.
(B) She has a degree in a science field.
(C) She no longer has a full-time employer.
(D) She responded to an advertisement on a Web site.

GO ON TO THE NEXT PAGE

From:	Ed Padgett
To:	Rose Tate
Subject:	Office decoration
Date:	September 30
Attachment:	🖉 Office_decoration_request

Dear Ms. Tate,

Welcome to Lunsford & Associates! My name is Ed Padgett, and I'm the office administrator for your floor. Since you'll be very busy after you begin work, you might want to start shopping for your new office now. Our office decoration policies are as follows:

- Employees who have private offices (hereafter, "officeholders") should decorate them within one month in order to make a good impression on clients.
- Upon hiring or promotion, new officeholders may spend up to $1000 on office decoration.
- Purchases can be requested by submitting an electronic Office Decoration Request form to an office administrator.
- Requests to spend any additional funds at this or a later time must be approved by the officeholder's manager.
- Decorations must be tasteful and professional.
- Nearby officeholders should be notified of decorating activities in advance in case it may disturb their work.

For reference, your office is roughly 10 feet long by 10 feet wide. Also, you may remember from your visit that it has grey marble floors and already contains a desk, a small sofa, and a bookcase—but of course you can replace any of those items if you'd like.

I've attached the necessary form to this e-mail. Please let me know if you have any questions about this information.

Sincerely,

Ed

Office Decoration Request

Name: Rose Tate
Job Title: Senior Accountant

Effective Date of Hiring/Promotion: October 4
Office No.: 305

Item description	Seller	Web page link	Quantity	Approx. Total Price*
Desk chair	Mallorin	www.mallorin.com/4024	1	$235.00
Art print	Nicole Phan	Not available	1	$175.00
Armchair	Bohn Homes	www.bohnhomes.com/3421	2	$210.00
End table	Bohn Homes	www.bohnhomes.com/0257	1	$65.00
Coat rack	Bohn Homes	www.bohnhomes.com/6369	1	$40.00
			Estimated Total:	$725.00

Date of Submission: October 6   Submitted to: Ed Padgett

*Price estimates must include potential shipping/delivery/installation charges.

Hi Audrey,

I just wanted to let you know that I need to do some decorating in my office this morning. Please tell me if there are any times that would be especially inconvenient for you, because I have some flexibility on that.

Thanks,

Rose

186. What information does Mr. Padgett NOT provide about Ms. Tate's office?

(A) Its dimensions
(B) Its existing contents
(C) Its flooring material
(D) Its location

187. In the e-mail, the word "professional" in paragraph 6, line 1, is closest in meaning to

(A) receiving money
(B) durable
(C) appropriate for business
(D) polite

188. What is suggested about Ms. Tate's request?

(A) It will not require managerial approval.
(B) It includes replacements for some used furniture.
(C) It was submitted later than recommended.
(D) It has already been revised once.

189. What is indicated about the products listed on the form?

(A) One of them will be customized.
(B) Not all of them are sold online.
(C) Some of them are used items.
(D) They are all made by the same manufacturer.

190. What is implied about Audrey?

(A) She does not work in the mornings.
(B) Her office is near Ms. Tate's.
(C) She is a maintenance supervisor.
(D) Her job title is the same as Mr. Padgett's.

GO ON TO THE NEXT PAGE

Questions 191-195 refer to the following article and Web pages.

Hammell Wins Best Actor Prize at Vellon Springs

VELLON SPRINGS (May 17)—At its awards ceremony on Sunday night, the jury of the Vellon Springs Film Festival awarded Best Actor to veteran actor Christopher Hammell. Other big winners among the 22 independent films and countless performers competing in the festival included *Shouting in the Wind* (Best Picture) and Sylvia Mathis (Best Actress for her role in *The Advance*).

Mr. Hammell won for his superb performance in *Our Fence*. Directed by Vitomir Holmwood and costarring Felicia Carlson, *Our Fence* tells the story of a retired Seattle truck driver (Mr. Hammell) who finds his quiet life interrupted when an artist (Ms. Carlson) and her young daughter move in to the house next door. The moving film was an audience favorite and has been picked up for late summer distribution across the United States by RTY Films.

The award may represent a career comeback for Mr. Hammell, who stopped appearing in major studio-produced films about a decade ago after a string of disappointing box-office results. He has worked steadily in theater productions and smaller films since that time, but *Our Fence* is the first to gain widespread recognition.

During his acceptance speech onstage at the Vellon Theater, Mr. Hammell thanked Mr. Holmwood, Ms. Carlson, and the festival jury, and finished by saying, "It feels like I've been given a second chance. I can't believe it."

http://www.all-about-movies.com/053809

| Home | Recent Releases | Editors' Recommendations | Contact |

All About Movies

Our Fence

Genre: Drama, Comedy, Family
Release date: August 31 (wide)
Running time: 125 minutes
Directed by: Vitomir Holmwood
Written by: Ebony Francis
Music by: Cory Gibson

Summary: An elderly man gets unexpected life lessons from his new neighbors.

Trivia: Filmed in Toronto. See more

Main cast:
Christopher Hammell......Terrence Jones
Felicia Carlson.....................Vanessa Webb
Yvonne Park.............Eva Webb
Raul Alvizo.................Marco

(See full cast and crew)

http://www.all-about-movies.com/053809/reviews

| Home | Recent Releases | Editors' Recommendations | Contact |

All About Movies

Reviews of: *__Our Fence__*

"More drama than comedy" ★★★☆☆

I went to see this movie because the TV commercials for it made it look really fun, but it turned out to be quite sad in some parts. I'd still give it a positive review, though. The cast was great.

Silvia Flores, Sept. 3

"Great job all around!" ★★★★☆

Christopher Hammell definitely earns his festival award, but I think Ebony Francis is the real talent involved in this film. I'll certainly be seeking out more of her work.

Kurt Stewart, Sept. 1

---

191. What information does the article provide about the film festival?

(A) The president of its jury
(B) The length of time it lasts
(C) The number of times it has been held
(D) The venue of its awards ceremony

192. What does the article suggest that Mr. Hammell has done in recent years?

(A) Acted in independent films
(B) Worked as a film producer
(C) Taught students in a theater program
(D) Participated in a fund-raising campaign

193. What is most likely true about *Our Fence*?

(A) Its wide release was delayed.
(B) It was shortened after the film festival.
(C) It was not filmed where its story takes place.
(D) Its poster was not approved by RTY Films.

194. Why did Ms. Flores decide to see *Our Fence*?

(A) She read positive audience reviews of it.
(B) She is a fan of one of its cast members.
(C) She wanted to know more about its subject matter.
(D) She liked its promotional materials.

195. What did Mr. Stewart most appreciate about *Our Fence*?

(A) Its performances
(B) Its direction
(C) Its writing
(D) Its music

GO ON TO THE NEXT PAGE

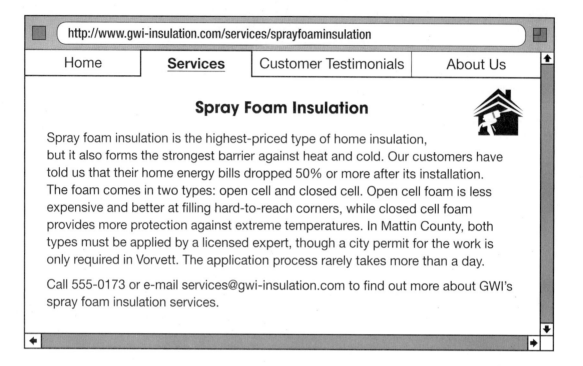

http://www.gwi-insulation.com/services/sprayfoaminsulation

| Home | **Services** | Customer Testimonials | About Us |

Spray Foam Insulation

Spray foam insulation is the highest-priced type of home insulation, but it also forms the strongest barrier against heat and cold. Our customers have told us that their home energy bills dropped 50% or more after its installation. The foam comes in two types: open cell and closed cell. Open cell foam is less expensive and better at filling hard-to-reach corners, while closed cell foam provides more protection against extreme temperatures. In Mattin County, both types must be applied by a licensed expert, though a city permit for the work is only required in Vorvett. The application process rarely takes more than a day.

Call 555-0173 or e-mail services@gwi-insulation.com to find out more about GWI's spray foam insulation services.

GWI Insulation

Warranty

Work Information

GWI Insulation installed <u>open-cell insulation foam</u> in the <u>attic of the house</u> located at <u>450 Brewer Street, Vorvett</u>, at the request of its owner, <u>Albert Mackie</u>.

Coverage

GWI Insulation will provide labor and goods at no charge to repair any problems with the insulation that arise from defective products or work performed incorrectly at the time of installation.

This warranty is valid throughout the life of the structure and can be transferred along with the ownership of the structure.

Exclusions

GWI Insulation will not be held responsible for problems with insulation in the following cases:
1. It or the surrounding area has been altered or replaced by the homeowner or another company.
2. It has been damaged by extreme wind, rain, or other natural occurrences.
3. The surface to which it has been attached is damaged by the collapse or shifting of the structure's foundation or walls.
4. The surface to which it has been attached is suffering from mildew, mold, or natural aging.

Lillian Thiel
Lillian Thiel
President, GWI Insulation

```
┌─────────────────────────────────────────────────────────────────────────┐
│                            *E-Mail*                                    ▣  │
├────────────────┬──────────────────────────────────────────────────────────┤
│    To:         │  Albert Mackie                                           │
├────────────────┼──────────────────────────────────────────────────────────┤
│    From:       │  Derek Sullivan                                          │
├────────────────┼──────────────────────────────────────────────────────────┤
│    Subject:    │  Re: Warranty claim                                      │
├────────────────┼──────────────────────────────────────────────────────────┤
│    Date:       │  February 24                                             │
├────────────────┼──────────────────────────────────────────────────────────┤
│    Attachment: │  🖉Warranty_Mackie                                        │
└────────────────┴──────────────────────────────────────────────────────────┘
```

Dear Mr. Mackie,

We at GWI Insulation were sorry to learn that you will need to replace some of the beams and boards in your attic because of mold issues. Unfortunately, this situation is one of those explicitly excluded from your warranty, so we would need to charge you for any work that we do on your attic insulation. I have attached a scan of our copy of the warranty for your reference.

Please let us know if you would like to hire us to repair or replace your installation. While the work would not be free, we could still offer you a good price.

Sincerely,

Derek Sullivan
GWI Insulation

196. According to the Web page, what have GWI Insulation's customers reported?

(A) Lower energy costs
(B) Better indoor air quality
(C) Reduced noise pollution
(D) Increased structural strength

197. What is suggested about the work done on Mr. Mackie's house?

(A) It was carried out in an underground space.
(B) It took place with a city government's permission.
(C) It involved the more expensive type of spray foam.
(D) It required more than one day to complete.

198. What is stated about the warranty?

(A) It has an expiration date.
(B) Mr. Mackie paid extra to obtain it.
(C) It will still be valid even if Mr. Mackie sells the house.
(D) It does not cover the cost of products needed for repairs.

199. Which exclusion in the warranty does Mr. Sullivan refer to?

(A) Exclusion 1
(B) Exclusion 2
(C) Exclusion 3
(D) Exclusion 4

200. In the e-mail, the word "learn" in paragraph 1, line 1, is closest in meaning to

(A) master
(B) discover
(C) memorize
(D) experience

Stop! This is the end of the test. If you finish before time is called, you may go back to Parts 5, 6, and 7 and check your work.

RC

TEST 3

READING TEST

In the Reading test, you will read a variety of texts and answer several different types of reading comprehension questions. The entire Reading test will last 75 minutes. There are three parts, and directions are given for each part. You are encouraged to answer as many questions as possible within the time allowed.

You must mark your answers on the separate answer sheet. Do not write your answers in your test book.

PART 5

Directions: A word or phrase is missing in each of the sentences below. Four answer choices are given below each sentence. Select the best answer to complete the sentence. Then mark the letter (A), (B), (C), or (D) on your answer sheet.

101. Edith Stanley says she has ------- regretted switching her university major from finance to engineering.
    (A) never
    (B) enough
    (C) very
    (D) less

102. Users should avoid closing the copy machine's lid more ------- than necessary.
    (A) forceful
    (B) forcefully
    (C) forcing
    (D) force

103. Mr. Hawkins hoped that hiring the career coach would enable ------- to pursue certain goals.
    (A) himself
    (B) him
    (C) his
    (D) he

104. Quezada Grill offers free delivery to locations ------- five miles of its store but charges relatively high fees for longer trips.
    (A) about
    (B) on
    (C) within
    (D) up to

105. Seasonal sporting equipment and other infrequently used items ------- in the apartment complex's basement.
    (A) can be stored
    (B) should store
    (C) are storing
    (D) stored

106. Just a few weeks after ------- responsibility for factory operations, Ms. Jennings began making changes to increase efficiency.
    (A) assumes
    (B) assuming
    (C) assumed
    (D) assume

107. With the exception of morning rush hour, the study found that city buses are ------- on time throughout the day.
    (A) general
    (B) generalized
    (C) generally
    (D) generalizing

108. Though this cannot be proven conclusively, archaeologists believe it is ------- that the object was used in preparing food.
    (A) actual
    (B) functional
    (C) usual
    (D) probable

109. Modern fans of Mr. Montano's books may be surprised to learn that few of ------- were popular with critics upon release.

(A) theirs
(B) their
(C) them
(D) themselves

110. In spite of the recent failure of her juice bar franchise, Ms. Diaz remains ------- among investors for her early success with Diaz Café.

(A) respectful
(B) respecting
(C) respectably
(D) respected

111. The Rostan Building has never been ------- popular before, though it has been considered a Hentville landmark for years.

(A) this
(B) high
(C) how
(D) much

112. The crew tasked with resurfacing Maple Street will begin at its intersection with Higgs Road and proceed in the ------- of Leskett Avenue.

(A) director
(B) most direct
(C) directing
(D) direction

113. ------- the Boyce Eagles have reached the final round of the Wicks Cup several times, they have not yet managed to win it.

(A) While
(B) Even
(C) Whenever
(D) Despite

114. Dr. Bak's article in *Organizational Psychology* explains how people ------- to strong leadership have difficulty in horizontally-structured workplaces.

(A) respond
(B) responsive
(C) responsively
(D) responded

115. Your signature will indicate your agreement ------- abide by the terms of this contract.

(A) with
(B) through
(C) regarding
(D) to

116. As of today, special bins for the disposal of used batteries ------- in front of all of the city's public libraries.

(A) have been placed
(B) placed
(C) will place
(D) is being placed

117. ------- the latest market report, the cosmetics industry will continue to expand thanks to growth in income levels.

(A) Except for
(B) Through
(C) In addition to
(D) According to

118. Our negotiator ------- Silmond Software to discount its services in exchange for a positive customer testimonial.

(A) argued
(B) persuaded
(C) assured
(D) settled

119. Jeralt, Inc., employees appreciate that telecommuting is ------- and very easy to arrange via an online scheduling system.

(A) permit
(B) permitting
(C) permission
(D) permitted

120. There is some evidence that regular tea drinkers have a reduced ------- of heart disease.

(A) treatment
(B) progress
(C) risk
(D) diagnosis

GO ON TO THE NEXT PAGE

121. When our employee complained about the issue, the hotel manager ------- offered to upgrade her to a better room.

(A) greatly
(B) collectively
(C) randomly
(D) readily

122. Air Primera will begin offering increased leg room on flights to ensure passenger -------.

(A) comforting
(B) comfortable
(C) comfort
(D) comfortably

123. The law requiring hospital fees to be published online is intended to make the medical industry's pricing more ------- to patients.

(A) transparent
(B) equivalent
(C) adequate
(D) knowledgeable

124. During the banquet, the recipient of the Reilter Prize will be introduced and given the opportunity to make remarks in ------- of the honor.

(A) reaction
(B) acceptance
(C) gratitude
(D) analysis

125. Our training courses are constantly updated to ensure that they ------- with the requirements of the workforce.

(A) collaborate
(B) implement
(C) equip
(D) align

126. Prost Agriculture's booth features a video screen ------- displays pictures taken by the trade show's attendees.

(A) whose
(B) just
(C) that
(D) of

127. Human resources staff must demonstrate ------- in handling the private information of their coworkers.

(A) prosperity
(B) discretion
(C) consensus
(D) aspiration

128. In preparation for their stay in Japan, the JFLT program provides its participants with 50 hours of Japanese language -------.

(A) instruction
(B) instructed
(C) instructive
(D) instructors

129. Goines Corporation will ------- construction of the building when all necessary approvals have been obtained.

(A) redeem
(B) exercise
(C) commence
(D) maneuver

130. The decrease in Sparont's revenues is the ------- effect of a drop in demand for digital cameras, its chief product.

(A) scarce
(B) inevitable
(C) competent
(D) cooperative

PART 6

Directions: Read the texts that follow. A word, phrase, or sentence is missing in parts of each text. Four answer choices for each question are given below the text. Select the best answer to complete the text. Then mark the letter (A), (B), (C), or (D) on your answer sheet.

Questions 131-134 refer to the following article.

Groundswork to Hold 1,000th Weekly Garden Clean-up

Nonprofit organization Groundswork will hold its 1,000th Weekly Garden Clean-up this Saturday, September 8, at Schuler Park.

Since its ------- by a group of local conservationists, Groundswork has strived to promote a love
      131.
of nature among Mellin County residents. The enthusiastic volunteers ------- to Schuler Park
                                                                         132.
nearly every weekend are a major part of these efforts. Overseen by park staff, they have been picking up trash and helping with plant care tasks for over 19 years. The organization also holds regular hikes and classes on nature-related topics for all ages.

Groundswork plans to celebrate the ------- with a party after Saturday's clean-up. -------. Those
                                    133.   134.
interested in attending should visit its Web site, www.groundswork.org, for more information.

---

131. (A) granting
　　　(B) achieving
　　　(C) founding
　　　(D) joining

132. (A) have been sent
　　　(B) it sends
　　　(C) that send
　　　(D) are sending

133. (A) milestone
　　　(B) acquisition
　　　(C) improvement
　　　(D) decision

134. (A) Applications for membership are welcomed year-round.
　　　(B) In fact, a clean-up plan must be submitted for all park events.
　　　(C) It will feature music, family-friendly games, and refreshments.
　　　(D) Mayor Chan even posted a congratulatory message on social media.

GO ON TO THE NEXT PAGE

From: Imani Jackson

To: Toby Ortega

Subject: Receptionist job candidates

Date: April 2

Attachments: Candidate spreadsheet

Hi Toby,

As you may remember, the application period for the receptionist position ended last Friday. I'm happy to report that we received résumés from more than 50 people! ------.
135.

Anyway, I've narrowed down the candidate pool in accordance with the requirements that you specified, and the top ten prospects ------ in the attached spreadsheet. Please ------ the file
136. **137.**
when you have time and choose the people you would like to interview. ------, we should follow
138.
the timetable stated in the ad and begin calling them this week.

Let me know if there's anything else you need.

Sincerely,

Imani

---

135. (A) Posting the ad on that job seeking
    Web site certainly made a difference.
 (B) However, that is why we were unable to
    respond promptly to your application.
 (C) It may not be so difficult to fill all ten
    openings by the end of April after all.
 (D) It is lucky that Mark will have time next
    week to help me review each one.

136. (A) have described
 (B) having described
 (C) being described
 (D) are described

137. (A) pass up
 (B) call for
 (C) look over
 (D) turn around

138. (A) If possible
 (B) Instead
 (C) Therefore
 (D) In particular

Questions 139-142 refer to the following letter.

Lauryl County Toll Road Authority

430 Main Street, Carlson, VA 22432

April 10

Melba Graves

108 Franklin Lane

Carlson, VA 22433

Dear Ms. Graves,

You are receiving this letter because a vehicle registered to you used Knapp Toll Road on April 2. As the vehicle is not enrolled in Lauryl County's Electronic Toll Collection System (ETCS), this action was a violation of county law. Please see the enclosed ------. The amount
139.
requested on it must be paid by May 2. Note that if your payment has not been received by ------, you will be charged an additional fee.
140.

Also, if you are likely to use a toll road again in the future, we strongly suggest that you enroll in the ETCS. ------. Enrollment is free and will prevent ------ issues of this sort.
141. **142.**

If you believe you have received this notice in error, follow the instructions on the back of this page to dispute it.

Encl.

---

139. (A) invoice
(B) photograph
(C) manual
(D) license

140. (A) many
(B) then
(C) yourself
(D) tomorrow

141. (A) The money collected from tolls is used for road upkeep projects.
(B) It has eased traffic congestion in other neighborhoods as well.
(C) This can be done by visiting our office at the address above.
(D) A device in your vehicle transmits an electronic signal each time.

142. (A) total
(B) identical
(C) valuable
(D) further

GO ON TO THE NEXT PAGE

Verification of Information

As an open-source online encyclopedia whose contributors may not be experts, Calhoun Science Encyclopedia takes the verification of information ------. Contributors must specify the source of ------ content they add to the encyclopedia's articles. To do this, append a footnote link to the relevant part of the text and give all necessary information in the connected footnote. (See this page for information on footnote formatting.) Sources must be reliable and professionally published. ------. Content that is not accompanied by a footnote citing such a source should be ------. The reason for the removal should be explained in the article's discussion page so that others can review it. Finally, in the case that trustworthy sources disagree, contributors should provide a neutral account of the positions of all sides.

143. (A) serious
     (B) seriously
     (C) seriousness
     (D) more serious

144. (A) any
     (B) either
     (C) which
     (D) another

145. (A) The latter kind of claim requires additional verification.
     (B) Ideal examples are academic journal articles and textbooks.
     (C) Otherwise, the quotation might violate publishing copyrights.
     (D) This includes the title, author, publisher, and date of the work.

146. (A) highlighted
     (B) reorganized
     (C) condensed
     (D) deleted

PART 7

Directions: In this part you will read a selection of texts, such as magazine and newspaper articles, e-mails, and instant messages. Each text or set of texts is followed by several questions. Select the best answer for each question and mark the letter (A), (B), (C), or (D) on your answer sheet.

Questions 147-148 refer to the following notice.

NOTICE OF STREET TREE TRIMMING

The trees on your street will be trimmed between the hours of 8 A.M. and 5 P.M. on June 28–29. Branches hanging less than thirteen feet above the street or eight feet above the sidewalk will be trimmed or removed.

The Dawston Parks Department regularly performs this work in city parks and adjacent streets in order to improve the trees' structural stability and protect them from damage caused by possible breakages. A certified tree care professional supervises our crew to make certain that the work is done properly.

Please keep the street clear on these days by parking automobiles in driveways or on other streets. Also, we ask for your understanding regarding the loud noise made by the trimming machinery.

147. Why are the trees being trimmed?

(A) To protect residents' automobiles
(B) To prevent damage to power lines
(C) To improve their appearance
(D) To maintain their well-being

148. According to the notice, how will the city ensure the work is done well?

(A) By having an expert monitor it
(B) By incorporating feedback from citizens
(C) By sending multiple work crews
(D) By using special machinery

GO ON TO THE NEXT PAGE

```
~~~~~~~~~~~~~~~~~~~~~~~~~~~~~~~~~~~~~~~~~~~~~~

                    Barry's Books #4
                       47 Fir Street
                   Central City, IL 61087
                        555-0161

   Store number: 4     Register number: 3    Cashier: Kate G.
   Card: Barry's Loyalty Club Member         Expires: May 11

   Book: Heritage in Mumbai                      $26.00
           10% member card discount(-2.60)    →$23.40
   Magazine: Movie Monthly                        $7.00
           10% member card discount(-0.70)     →$6.30
                              Sale subtotal    $29.70

   Customer special order #1127      *In-store pickup
                                     *Notification method: text message

   Book: Bold Architecture                        $34.00
             Promotion 2848 – 50% off (-17.00)    $17.00
             10% member card discount (-1.70)     $15.30

        Special order subtotal                    $15.30

        TOTAL                                      $45.00
        CASH PAID                                  $50.00
        CHANGE                                     $ 5.00

   Visit our in-store café – open during regular store hours

   Date/time of purchase: March 7  04:09 P.M.

~~~~~~~~~~~~~~~~~~~~~~~~~~~~~~~~~~~~~~~~~~~~~~
```

149. What is NOT indicated on the receipt about Barry's Books?

(A) It only accepts returns for a limited period.
(B) It has a customer loyalty program.
(C) It has more than one store.
(D) It also operates a café.

150. According to the receipt, what is true about *Bold Architecture*?

(A) It can only be purchased online.
(B) It was part of a sales promotion.
(C) It was ordered by telephone.
(D) It was a staff recommendation.

Questions 151-152 refer to the following text-message chain.

Jody Rodriguez (1:43 P.M.)
Grady, are you on the construction site right now?

Grady Webb (1:44 P.M.)
Yes, I'm over on the north side talking to the electrical team. What's up?

Jody Rodriguez (1:44 P.M.)
I wanted to check with you that it's all right to send up the RBX80.

Grady Webb (1:45 P.M.)
The RBX80? I'm sorry, but I don't know what that is.

Jody Rodriguez (1:46 P.M.)
Oh, it's a new technology. It's a drone aircraft equipped with cameras. We're going to fly it around the outsides of the building to make sure there are no problems in the walls that have been put up so far.

Grady Webb (1:47 P.M.)
Ah, I see. That should be fine, but please give advance notice to the teams that are working on any of the floors you'll be looking at—especially the high ones. It could be dangerous to surprise them.

Jody Rodriguez (1:48 P.M.)
I'll send out a group text to the team leaders now.

151. At 1:46 P.M., what does Ms. Rodriguez mean when she writes, "it's a new technology"?

(A) She cannot guarantee that the RBX80 will work well.
(B) Mr. Webb's unfamiliarity with the RBX80 is understandable.
(C) A problem that occurred in the past will be avoided today.
(D) Her team will need time to prepare for a procedure.

152. What is suggested about the building being constructed?

(A) It has a round shape.
(B) It has brick walls.
(C) It is in an airport.
(D) It will be tall.

GO ON TO THE NEXT PAGE

Questions 153-154 refer to the following advertisement.

The Forance Company
Announcing: the Blue Sky Line of Greeting Cards

When Rufus Forance started The Forance Company more than 70 years ago to publish a lifestyle magazine, he did not imagine what it would become. Rufus only began making greeting cards to earn extra profit via his printing presses. However, the cards, designed by the magazine's staff artists, were an instant success, and Rufus soon decided to focus exclusively on them. Since then, The Forance Company has become one of the nation's most trusted sources of beautiful, thoughtful greeting cards.

Now, The Forance Company is proud to add a new line of cards to our catalog: the Blue Sky line. Blue Sky cards are for sending heartfelt messages of love, support, and friendship in everyday life. Their simple, charming style is designed to put the focus on the sender's words. Instead of waiting for a birthday or holiday, let people know you care about them right now. Visit any major stationery store to browse the Blue Sky line today.

153. What is mentioned about The Forance Company?

(A) It is still owned by the Forance family.
(B) It began with 70 employees.
(C) It achieved success through print advertising.
(D) It used to make a different type of product.

154. What is the Blue Sky line intended to enable customers to do?

(A) Customize the design of a greeting card
(B) Express goodwill outside of special occasions
(C) Send positive messages electronically
(D) Support local artists through their purchase

```
========================= E-Mail message =========================

From:      Simon Burgess

To:        Viola McDonald

Subject:   Re: Inquiry

Date:      July 30
```

Dear Ms. McDonald,

Thank you for your inquiry regarding Rolent smart glass. From what you wrote, I believe that our RC-2 Glass would be an excellent fit for your project. In its transparent setting, it will eliminate the dark, cramped feeling you describe your building as having, and in its opaque "frosted" setting, it will provide your conference rooms, copy rooms, etc. with the same privacy you currently enjoy.

I can also address your concern about cost. Though smart glass does require electric power to switch settings, it does not need electricity to maintain either setting. None of our many satisfied clients have found it to have a significant impact on their utility bills.

I would be happy to visit your site to provide more information on RC-2 Glass and suggestions on its best use in your project. If you are interested, please reply to this e-mail or call me at 555-0196.

Sincerely,

Simon Burgess
Sales Associate, Rolent Ltd.

155. What most likely is Ms. McDonald planning to do?

(A) Construct a building
(B) Improve a vehicle's design
(C) Renovate an office
(D) Create an outdoor display

156. What does Mr. Burgess write to reassure Ms. McDonald about smart glass?

(A) It does not use much energy.
(B) It is not expensive to install.
(C) It is not difficult to keep clean.
(D) It does not break easily.

157. What does Mr. Burgess offer Ms. McDonald?

(A) A reference
(B) A consultation
(C) A demonstration
(D) A discount

Questions 158-160 refer to the following notice.

Thornton Burger, Lakeside Branch

Notice

Our staff workshop is due to take place next Tuesday from 9 A.M. to 12 P.M. It is mandatory for all staff regardless of seniority level, so the restaurant will be closed during those hours. If you have a prior commitment, please contact your line manager to make appropriate arrangements. — [1] —.

The workshop's leader will be Karen Downing. She will be talking about maintaining hygiene standards at our restaurant. — [2] —. Ms. Downing has already delivered this workshop at branches all over the country and is up to date with the latest regulations and research. — [3] —. I am sure you will find it to be an informative day.

You have all been pre-registered for this event automatically. Uniforms are not required for this day. — [4] —. See the relevant section of the employee handbook.

---

158. What is the notice announcing?

(A) A training event
(B) A job opening
(C) A facility inspection
(D) A new dress code

159. What is indicated about Ms. Downing?

(A) She was recently promoted to management.
(B) She will observe the restaurant's operations.
(C) She proposed some company regulations.
(D) She is an expert in food hygiene.

160. In which of the positions marked [1], [2], [3], and [4] does the following sentence best belong?

"However, we expect you to wear company-recognized business casual clothing."

(A) [1]
(B) [2]
(C) [3]
(D) [4]

Leopard Automotive

I may, during my period of employment, be exposed to information confidential to Leopard Automotive. This includes but is not limited to technical specifications of automobiles and manufacturing equipment, business practices, company plans, data from market research, sales and revenue information, and details about security procedures. I understand that this category also includes information and materials that I myself develop while employed at Leopard Automotive.

I will not disclose such information to third parties, including competitors, journalists and members of the public, during or following my employment at Leopard Automotive.

At the end of my employment period, I will immediately return to the company all physical security credentials and company-issued devices, and supply all passwords to company systems.

I have been provided with a copy of this document for my own records.

Signed: *Jeremy Fulton*

Title: *Manufacturing Manager*

Date: *November 19*

---

161. What is suggested about the agreement?

(A) It must also be signed by a company representative.
(B) It extends past Mr. Fulton's period of employment.
(C) It cannot be removed from the business's premises.
(D) It has been modified at Mr. Fulton's request.

162. What is NOT mentioned as confidential information?

(A) Results of consumer studies
(B) Company earnings
(C) Names of suppliers
(D) Vehicle specifications

163. What does the agreement specify?

(A) What Mr. Fulton should do upon leaving his job
(B) What penalties Mr. Fulton may face for violating it
(C) Whom Mr. Fulton may share some information with
(D) How Mr. Fulton may use company-issued devices

GO ON TO THE NEXT PAGE

Questions 164-167 refer to the following e-mail.

To:	Louise Anderson
From:	Jesse Reed
Subject:	Panel discussion invitation
Date:	18 June

Dear Ms. Anderson,

Hello. My name is Jesse Reed, and I am one of the organizers of IT Healthlink. IT Healthlink has become one of the UK's most exciting conferences on information technology in healthcare, bringing together hundreds of medical care providers, entrepreneurs, investors, government representatives, and others annually. — [1] —. We are currently seeking speakers and panelists for this year's conference, which will be held in London's Fiore Hall on 5–7 October.

The particular session I am contacting you about is an hour-long panel discussion titled "The Next Generation of Health Tech". — [2] —. We have already engaged Clive Minamore, Kwame Obeng, Logan Norwick, and Andrew Earle, four of the industry's most innovative young minds, to participate. However, as you might have realized immediately, there is something missing from that group—a female perspective. So I asked around my network for recommendations, and Harold Kirby said he was very impressed with your speech at Health Liverpool last year. — [3] —. After watching the video of it that is available online, I am too. It would be an honor if you would join our panel to share your inventive ideas with our attendees.

If you are interested, all you need to do at this stage is respond to this e-mail with your affirmative answer and, for our Web site, a professional headshot and your official job title. I would send you the speaking agreement with all of the details of the event by the end of this month. — [4] —. Alternatively, if you have any questions or concerns, you can reply to this e-mail or call me at 020 7043 5214 during business hours.

I hope to hear from you soon.

Sincerely,

Jesse Reed

---

164. What is stated about the panel discussion?

(A) It will take place on October 7.
(B) It will be moderated by Mr. Kirby.
(C) It is not currently scheduled to include any women.
(D) It has been part of previous conferences.

165. How did Mr. Reed find out about Ms. Anderson?

(A) By attending a talk
(B) By reading a newspaper
(C) By searching the Internet
(D) By receiving a referral

166. What should Ms. Anderson provide first if she wants to participate?

(A) A photograph of herself
(B) A signed contract
(C) A fee quote
(D) A suggested topic

167. In which of the positions marked [1], [2], [3], and [4] does the following sentence best belong?

"Over the three-day event, participants form connections, share practical tips, and discuss big ideas."

(A) [1]
(B) [2]
(C) [3]
(D) [4]

Auckland Business News

(19 February)—Christine Redman recently found herself unable to pay for the iced latte she had ordered at her favorite coffee shop—even though she had plenty of cash. "They'd made the switch to electronic payments a few weeks before," Ms. Redman explained. "But that day, I forgot to bring my debit card. It was embarrassing."

The coffee shop, Seeley's Beans, is one of several New Zealand retailers that have stopped accepting cash at their stores. Supporters of the trend say that electronic payments have benefits like faster transactions, error-free record-keeping, and less handling of potentially-unsanitary bills and coins. Seeley's Beans spokesperson Sharon Wright said, "It was an easy choice, frankly."

Consumers, however, are not convinced. Although there has been a steady move toward using cards and apps instead of paper money, many still prefer to use cash or at least to have the option of doing so. "For me, it's about privacy. I wouldn't go to a cashless store, because I don't like the credit card company knowing everything I buy," said Auckland citizen Chad Williams.

Similar consumer resistance has led some city governments in the United States to prohibit businesses from going cashless. Retail analyst Sang-Wook Jung believes that could happen here as well, but not right away. "At this point, there are only a few cashless places, so it's not a big inconvenience. But if a lot of stores start to switch over, we may see a backlash too."

Have you visited a cashless store? Tell us about it in the comments! (Note that commenters must create an Auckland Tribune account.)

168. What is the article about?

(A) A trend in retail payment methods
(B) The expansion of a coffee shop chain
(C) A proposal for a city ordinance
(D) A dispute between a customer and a store

169. What is implied about Mr. Williams?

(A) He works in the finance field.
(B) He will not patronize cafés like Seeley's Beans.
(C) He spoke with Ms. Redman earlier in February.
(D) He hopes to become a local politician.

170. Why does the article mention another country?

(A) To explain a management practice's origin
(B) To highlight a company's structure
(C) To introduce a situation's potential outcome
(D) To express pride about a region's achievements

171. What are readers of the article encouraged to do?

(A) Sign up to receive updates on a story
(B) Discuss any relevant experiences
(C) Look at a list of similar writings
(D) Report any factual errors

GO ON TO THE NEXT PAGE

Monica Dietrich [2:11 P.M.]	Great news! A representative from Ramona Enterprises has finally agreed to do an interview with me!
Tao Hou [2:12 P.M.]	That's wonderful! Our readers will be thrilled to get some insights into one of the fastest-growing software companies in the industry. When will you go there?
Monica Dietrich [2:14 P.M.]	Next Monday at 2 P.M. That doesn't give me much time to prepare, and I've only been given a one-hour time slot, but I'll take what I can get.
Roxanne Toro [2:16 P.M.]	Jacques, are you free to go with Monica and take pictures?
Monica Dietrich [2:17 P.M.]	Actually, I'm the only one who will be allowed in the offices. The company said it prefers to supply its own pictures.
Jacques Favreau [2:18 P.M.]	That's a shame. I would love to see their offices. I heard that employees are allowed to personalize their workspaces, so you see everything from standing desks with treadmills to recliner chairs.
Monica Dietrich [2:19 P.M.]	I'll be sure to let you know if that's true!
Roxanne Toro [2:22 P.M.]	Will you have the article ready in time for this month's issue? The deadline is March 18, just two days after you visit Ramona Enterprises.
Monica Dietrich [2:23 P.M.]	I don't think that's a good idea.
Tao Hou [2:24 P.M.]	I agree. Quality has to be the top priority.

172. What is suggested about Ms. Dietrich?

(A) She used to be employed by Ramona Enterprises.
(B) She made multiple requests to Ramona Enterprises.
(C) She checks Ramona Enterprises' Web site regularly.
(D) She has confirmed a sale to Ramona Enterprises.

173. Where most likely do the writers work?

(A) At a technology company
(B) At a news station
(C) At a recruiting agency
(D) At a magazine publisher

174. Why is Mr. Favreau unable to accompany Ms. Dietrich?

(A) He is too far away to arrive in time.
(B) He has not been granted access.
(C) He is busy with other work.
(D) He is not qualified for an assignment.

175. At 2:23 P.M., what does Ms. Dietrich mean when she writes, "I don't think that's a good idea"?

(A) She plans to supervise a process.
(B) She prefers to meet in-person.
(C) She wants more time for a task.
(D) She thinks a workspace policy is unwise.

Test 3

GO ON TO THE NEXT PAGE

```
                               E-Mail message
┌──────────────┬─────────────────────────────────────────────────────┐
│ From:        │ Megan Danner                                          │
├──────────────┼─────────────────────────────────────────────────────┤
│ To:          │ Liling Yang                                           │
├──────────────┼─────────────────────────────────────────────────────┤
│ Subject:     │ Request                                               │
├──────────────┼─────────────────────────────────────────────────────┤
│ Date:        │ 3 September                                           │
├──────────────┼─────────────────────────────────────────────────────┤
│ Attachment:  │ 🖉 7 files                                            │
└──────────────┴─────────────────────────────────────────────────────┘
```

Dear Professor Yang,

Hello! I hope this e-mail finds you well. I'm writing to take you up on the offer you made when I graduated last summer. In particular, I've decided to enter the Queensland Young Designers Contest, and I'm hoping that you'll review my submission before I turn it in.

I suspect you're already familiar with the contest, but let me give you an overview just in case. It's organised by the Queensland Fashion Council in order to support talented young designers. The first prize winner is featured in the council yearbook, but I'm just hoping for one of the top five spots, as all of them come with an invitation to the council's yearly fashion show. As for the entries, contestants have to submit three collections. Each collection consists of sketches of three clothing designs connected by a creative concept chosen by the applicant.

So, I'm sending you my sketches and the accompanying explanations of the creative concepts I chose. I've also included a document listing the judging criteria, for reference. I know you are busy, but I would be very grateful if you could take a look at these materials sometime before 10 September and share any comments that come to mind. Thank you in advance for any help you can give.

Sincerely,

Megan

Queensland Young Designers Contest Award Winner Announced

BRISBANE (12 December)—The Queensland Fashion Council (QFC) revealed the winner of its fourth annual contest for young fashion designers yesterday. Jacquelyn Abbot, an assistant buyer at Sandpace Apparel and a recent graduate of Wilburt University, took first place among nearly 500 entrants.

The QFC has over 3,000 members, including designers, other industry employees, and investors, and the judges committee for the Queensland Young Designers Contest consists of some of the top names in eastern Australian fashion.

Ms. Abbot's design entry, which embodied the concepts "Fresh", "Reflections", and "Flight", impressed the judges with its original interpretations of classic styles. Gary Odell, the chair of the committee and a member of the QFC board, said, "Ms. Abbot's clothes and accessories are fascinating, becoming more complex the longer you look at them. We think she has a bright future in this industry."

Ms. Abbot, as well as top runners-up Jedda Ryan, Hayden Noe, Megan Danner, and Kevin Naylor, will receive a range of support services from the council.

176. Why was the e-mail sent?

(A) To request clarification about a requirement

(B) To respond to a suggestion to enter a contest

(C) To ask for feedback on some entry materials

(D) To provide a reminder about a deadline

177. What is NOT attached to the e-mail?

(A) A sample template for a document

(B) A list of some evaluation standards

(C) Descriptions of design concepts

(D) Drawings of fashion items

178. What is suggested about Ms. Danner?

(A) She completed an internship at the QFC.

(B) She will be promoted in an annual publication.

(C) She wrote an e-mail to a Wilburt University professor.

(D) She will receive a pass to a fashion event.

179. According to the article, what is true about the QFC?

(A) It has around 500 members.

(B) Its board of directors is headed by Mr. Odell.

(C) It has held the competition three times before.

(D) It is affiliated with Sandpace Apparel.

180. In the article, the word "bright" in paragraph 3, line 9, is closest in meaning to

(A) sunny

(B) cheerful

(C) promising

(D) clever

GO ON TO THE NEXT PAGE

Thornwood Monthly City Council Meeting
Room 105, Thornwood Community Center
Tuesday, February 10, 7 P.M.

Attendance: 10 out of 12 council members　　**Absent:** Patrick Chu, Tamara Walton
Minutes from January's meeting were read and approved.

Department Reports:
Finance: Request for March's operating expenses approved Parks and Recreation: Explanation of park improvement grant
Public Presentations:
Suggestions for the usage of the grant funds at Randall Park -Richard Dejean, former council member: building a covered picnic shelter with several picnic tables -Lorena Palermo, Thornwood resident: adding an asphalt path that joggers can use to exercise in the park -Veer Kamath, Thornwood resident: installing a fenced-in basketball court near the soccer fields -Heather Bolin, president of the Nature Now charity: planting a flower garden to enhance the park's appearance
Deliberation:
Council members debated the merits of the various proposals.
Next Meeting (March 13):
The council will vote on the park improvement grant. The meeting will be held in the main auditorium because unusually large attendance is predicted.

To:	Lewis Knutson <lknutson@thornwood.gov>
From:	Victoria Pickard <vpickard@thornwood.gov>
Date:	March 15
Subject:	Randall Park Project

Hi Lewis,

Now that we have selected the project for Randall Park, we need to get started on the planning. I would like to sit down with the director and assistant director of the parks and recreation department sometime this week—could you arrange that? We need to get an accurate map of where the jogging path will be installed.

Once a tentative plan is in place, we can begin advertising the project and collecting bids from construction companies. I believe this project will be an excellent use of the grant funds we received. However, I'm worried that the process will be much lengthier than citizens expect. We'll have to hurry if we want it to be ready by the end of the summer.

Please keep me posted on your progress.

Thanks!

Victoria

181. What is NOT indicated about the February meeting?

(A) A monthly budget was approved.
(B) A charity representative gave a presentation.
(C) The majority of council members were present.
(D) There was a debate over the venue of the next meeting.

182. What does the meeting agenda suggest about the vote on the park improvement grant?

(A) Some council members would not participate in it.
(B) It was supposed to take place in February.
(C) It would be broadcast to local audiences.
(D) It was expected to attract a lot of public interest.

183. Whose proposal was successful?

(A) Mr. Dejean's
(B) Ms. Palermo's
(C) Mr. Kamath's
(D) Ms. Bolin's

184. What is Mr. Knutson asked to do this week?

(A) Train some volunteers
(B) Set up a meeting
(C) Contact construction companies
(D) Post an advertisement

185. What does Ms. Pickard mention about the park improvement project?

(A) A grant organization may not approve plans for it.
(B) It will not use all of the available funds.
(C) She is concerned about its duration.
(D) It may disrupt a seasonal festival.

GO ON TO THE NEXT PAGE

www.bernlakeoutfitters.com

| **Home** | Staff | Watercraft | Testimonials | Contact |

Bern Lake Outfitters

Welcome to the online home of Bern Lake Outfitters! Paolo Gaspar opened Bern Lake Outfitters ten years ago when he began renting his personal kayak, Little Rush, to friends for the weekend. Now, with the purchase of a 50-meter yacht we call "The Spirit of the Lake" earlier this year, we have the most watercraft of any company in the area. We can satisfy the needs of all customers, whether they want to participate in fast-paced aquatic sports with one of our Golden Blaze speedboats, or spend an afternoon fishing with a few friends in a Quiet Ripple rowboat.

***If you're staying in the area, let us help you with your lodgings. We can get you a discounted rate at our longtime partner hotel, the Laguna Lodge.

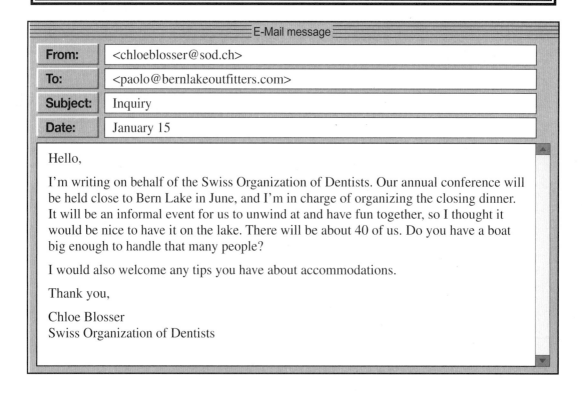

E-Mail message

From:	<chloeblosser@sod.ch>
To:	<paolo@bernlakeoutfitters.com>
Subject:	Inquiry
Date:	January 15

Hello,

I'm writing on behalf of the Swiss Organization of Dentists. Our annual conference will be held close to Bern Lake in June, and I'm in charge of organizing the closing dinner. It will be an informal event for us to unwind at and have fun together, so I thought it would be nice to have it on the lake. There will be about 40 of us. Do you have a boat big enough to handle that many people?

I would also welcome any tips you have about accommodations.

Thank you,

Chloe Blosser
Swiss Organization of Dentists

```
┌─────────────────────────────────────────────────────────┐
│                   E-Mail message                         │
├──────────┬──────────────────────────────────────────────┤
│ From:    │ <paolo@bernlakeoutfitters.com>               │
├──────────┼──────────────────────────────────────────────┤
│ To:      │ <chloeblosser@sod.ch>                        │
├──────────┼──────────────────────────────────────────────┤
│ Subject: │ RE: Inquiry                                  │
├──────────┼──────────────────────────────────────────────┤
│ Date:    │ January 15                                   │
└──────────┴──────────────────────────────────────────────┘
```

Dear Ms. Blosser,

Thanks for getting in touch!

Our operation certainly has a boat that can suit your needs. Could you let me know the exact date in June you'll need it?

As far as your inquiry about accommodations goes—I know that the Laguna Lodge has some openings for that time frame, while the Brand New Sunset Hotel may be a less pricey option, if it's not fully booked already. Let me know what you decide, because depending on which one you choose, we may be able to make bookings for you at a discounted rate.

Sincerely,

Paolo Gaspar

Test 3

186. What is mentioned as a special characteristic of Bern Lake Outfitters?

(A) The length of its history
(B) The rental price of its boats
(C) The convenience of its locations
(D) The number of boats it owns

187. Why is Ms. Blosser visiting the Bern Lake area?

(A) To attend a professional gathering
(B) To take an overseas vacation
(C) To watch a series of sporting events
(D) To conduct scientific research

188. Which boat will most likely be recommended to Ms. Blosser?

(A) The Little Rush
(B) The Spirit of the Lake
(C) The Golden Blaze
(D) The Quiet Ripple

189. In the second e-mail, the word "goes" in paragraph 3, line 1, is closest in meaning to

(A) is available
(B) is concerned
(C) functions
(D) departs

190. What does Mr. Gaspar indicate about Bern Lake Outfitters' partner hotel?

(A) It is relatively inexpensive.
(B) It recently reopened.
(C) It currently has vacancies for June.
(D) There is a dining establishment in it.

GO ON TO THE NEXT PAGE

Making the World a Better Place

(August 4)—Though corporate social responsibility is becoming more important to consumers around the world, some companies are finding that giving back can be tricky.

Pinflash was embarrassed last year when a Charity Monitor report gave its main charitable partner a "D" rating because of its lack of impact. Similarly, Dunne Galloway recently ended its relationship with an arts nonprofit because of a disagreement over accounting processes.

This is why Peter Gandy started Giveler, a for-profit company that tries to make corporate giving as easy and efficient as possible.

"We do it all," says Mr. Gandy. "We help businesses choose a cause to support, connect them with a reputable charity or nonprofit organization, handle the donation logistics, and supply publicity tools."

In the two years it has been in business, Giveler has served over one hundred corporations and estimates that its clients have donated roughly three million dollars to various causes.

Among these successes, Mr. Gandy says he is most proud of Rickard Paper Co.: "We set up a program in which a tree is planted for almost every stationery product they sell. Not only have 56,000 trees been planted so far, but the publicity from the program has led to a 10% bump in Rickard's sales. That's the kind of mutually beneficial relationship we want for all of our clients and their partner organizations."

From:	Samuel Akagi <samuel.akagi@giveler.com>
To:	Janelle Hawn <janelle.hawn@weatherfordpro.com>
Subject:	Potential partners
Date:	August 24
Attachment:	📎 Nonprofit Review

Dear Janelle,

It was a pleasure to meet you yesterday. As I promised then, I'm now sending you an overview of our process for connecting corporations with partner charities and nonprofits. I believe it will relieve the concerns you mentioned about experiencing the same setback as Dunne Galloway.

In addition, here are some organizations that we think might be a good fit for Weatherford Pro:

- Kirchner Foundation - Operates free rural summer camp for kids
- Green Now! - Lobbies government to expand national parks
- Withrow Society - Protects endangered animals in a variety of habitats
- Mission Clean - Removes garbage from beaches and oceans

The Web site of each one is linked in its name so that you can learn a little more about them. If some questions come up or you feel ready to make a selection, just e-mail or give me a call at 555-0186.

Sincerely,

Samuel Akagi
Client Account Manager

```
http://www.weatherfordpro.com                                    ▶
```

HOME	PRODUCTS	PROMOTIONS	ABOUT

Weatherford Pro

Shipping Information: Victoria Cole
340 Griffin St.
Pueblo, CO 81008

Billing Address: Same as shipping ☑
Payment Method: PayRight
Account: vicky100@efr-mail.com

Product No.	Description	Quantity	Price
H2420	Trail Master Backpack – Navy	1	$59.99
R4371	Onivin Trekking Shoes – Size 10	1	$89.99
		Subtotal	$149.98
		Taxes	$10.50
		Total	$160.48

Did you know? Weatherford Pro passes on 5% of each pre-tax sale to the Withrow Society! Click "Complete My Order" to help us donate $7.50 right now.

Complete My Order

---

191. What is the purpose of the article?

(A) To examine some corporations' mistakes
(B) To profile a local entrepreneur
(C) To promote a company's services
(D) To urge consumers to make certain choices

192. In the article, the word "bump" in paragraph 6, line 7, is closest in meaning to

(A) difficulty
(B) collision
(C) opportunity
(D) increase

193. What is implied about Ms. Hawn?

(A) She thinks that publicity methods should be simple.
(B) She hopes to avoid becoming engaged in a financial dispute.
(C) She is worried about the effectiveness of potential partner organizations.
(D) She is concerned about accidentally breaking a law.

194. What is Ms. Cole ordering from Weatherford Pro?

(A) Bicycling gear
(B) Camping supplies
(C) Fishing equipment
(D) Hiking accessories

195. What cause did Weatherford Pro choose to support?

(A) Saving rare animals from extinction
(B) Enabling children to spend time outdoors
(C) Affecting government policy on nature areas
(D) Clearing waste from coastal habitats

GO ON TO THE NEXT PAGE ➤

http://www.kurgess.com/packages

| HOME | ABOUT | PACKAGES | CONTACT |

Kurgess Property Management offers a range of packages representing different levels of involvement in the management of your house, apartment, or condominium. Whichever you choose, you can be certain that all services will be performed by dedicated specialists committed to taking care of your property.

- Bronze – Services include property showings, rental application processing, credit and background checks, tenancy agreement signing, and deposit collection.
  Cost: 100% of the monthly rental fee (one time).

- Silver – All services in the bronze package plus collection of monthly rent.
  Cost: 4% of the monthly rental fee (monthly).

- Gold – All services in the silver package plus maintenance and repair services.
  Cost: 6% of the monthly rental fee (monthly).

- Gold Plus – All services in the gold package but offered at a discount for those who hire Kurgess to manage three or more properties.
  Cost: For each property, 5% of the monthly rental fee (monthly).

E-Mail message

From: Rex Campbell <rex@kurgess.com>
To: Dora McLaughlin <d.mclaughlin@rui-mail.com>
Subject: Good news
Date: March 21
Attachment: 🖉 Application, Background Check, Credit Check, Contract

Dear Ms. McLaughlin,

I am pleased to notify you that we have found a suitable tenant for your property located at 682 Perry Road in Hennisberg. We have carried out his credit and background checks with a high degree of thoroughness; the results are attached for your perusal. As you can see, Isaiah Pritchard has a steady job as a high school teacher and a history of financial responsibility. Also, of course, he is willing to agree to all of the property usage terms you specified.

Mr. Pritchard would like to begin his one-year lease on Saturday, April 14. If you are satisfied with the information we have provided, please print out the contract, sign it, and send it to my office by certified mail as soon as possible. Thank you.

Regards,

Rex Campbell
Account Manager
Kurgess Property Management
Hennisberg Branch

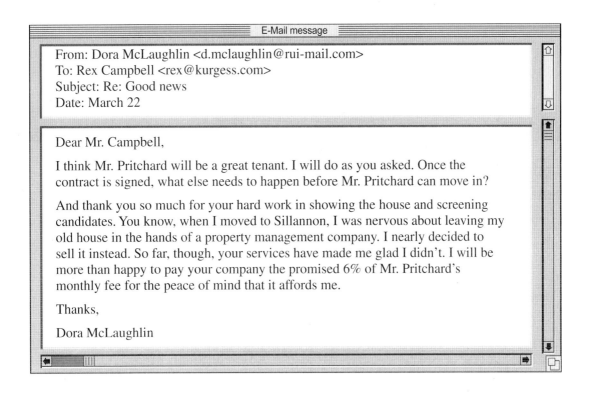

From: Dora McLaughlin <d.mclaughlin@rui-mail.com>
To: Rex Campbell <rex@kurgess.com>
Subject: Re: Good news
Date: March 22

Dear Mr. Campbell,

I think Mr. Pritchard will be a great tenant. I will do as you asked. Once the contract is signed, what else needs to happen before Mr. Pritchard can move in?

And thank you so much for your hard work in showing the house and screening candidates. You know, when I moved to Sillannon, I was nervous about leaving my old house in the hands of a property management company. I nearly decided to sell it instead. So far, though, your services have made me glad I didn't. I will be more than happy to pay your company the promised 6% of Mr. Pritchard's monthly fee for the peace of mind that it affords me.

Thanks,

Dora McLaughlin

196. What is suggested about Kurgess Property Management?

(A) It outsources some of its maintenance services.
(B) It handles only residential properties.
(C) It requires an advance deposit.
(D) It offers a discount to clients after three years.

197. What is mentioned as a positive characteristic of Mr. Pritchard?

(A) A history of home ownership
(B) A flexible move-in date
(C) A stable career
(D) A lack of pet animals

198. What service package did Ms. McLaughlin most likely choose?

(A) Bronze
(B) Silver
(C) Gold
(D) Gold Plus

199. What does Ms. McLaughlin ask about?

(A) Some steps in a process
(B) Some changes to an agreement
(C) The reason for a recommendation
(D) The person responsible for a task

200. What is implied about Ms. McLaughlin?

(A) She will visit Kurgess Property Management's offices.
(B) She will move out of her current house by April 14.
(C) She will call Mr. Campbell's work phone.
(D) She will send some paperwork to Hennisberg.

Stop! This is the end of the test. If you finish before time is called, you may go back to Parts 5, 6, and 7 and check your work.

Test 3

RC

TEST 4

READING TEST

In the Reading test, you will read a variety of texts and answer several different types of reading comprehension questions. The entire Reading test will last 75 minutes. There are three parts, and directions are given for each part. You are encouraged to answer as many questions as possible within the time allowed.

You must mark your answers on the separate answer sheet. Do not write your answers in your test book.

PART 5

Directions: A word or phrase is missing in each of the sentences below. Four answer choices are given below each sentence. Select the best answer to complete the sentence. Then mark the letter (A), (B), (C), or (D) on your answer sheet.

101. In her e-mail, the CEO assured shareholders that she was ------- in control of the situation.

(A) filling
(B) filled
(C) fuller
(D) fully

102. Mr. Moss and I attended the conference and shared what ------- had learned there with the rest of the team upon returning.

(A) we
(B) us
(C) our
(D) ourselves

103. Train conductors are ------- to reduce the machines' speed during heavy rainfall.

(A) examined
(B) instructed
(C) referred
(D) fixed

104. Mr. Maeda urges readers not to overlook ------- effects of social media use.

(A) benefited
(B) benefit
(C) beneficial
(D) beneficially

105. The registration ------- for our classes will last ten business days in total.

(A) requirement
(B) administrator
(C) period
(D) form

106. The recent improvements to the Walton Ballroom ------- its popularity as a venue for formal events.

(A) enhances
(B) have enhanced
(C) are enhanced
(D) enhancing

107. Customers wishing to use the free parking lot should drive ------- the Botanic Garden Café and take a left on Elm Street.

(A) between
(B) upon
(C) past
(D) through

108. Ms. Yates agreed to photograph Emburg's daylong dance ------- for a national newspaper.

(A) competed
(B) competitor
(C) competitors
(D) competition

109. As its manager, Mr. Staley is ------- for the outcome of the building project.
    (A) confident
    (B) accountable
    (C) sensible
    (D) obliged

110. Although Warron's spreadsheet software is widely used, ------- are aware of its specialty functions.
    (A) few
    (B) that
    (C) each
    (D) many

111. Cobb Buffet is booked solid in December, ------- you will need to find a different site for the year-end banquet.
    (A) until
    (B) then
    (C) but
    (D) so

112. Angul Timepieces will make a series of animated advertisements in an attempt to be ------- in its marketing.
    (A) creatively
    (B) creative
    (C) creators
    (D) creations

113. It is necessary for receptionists to answer the telephone promptly, ------- busy they may be.
    (A) very
    (B) even
    (C) likewise
    (D) however

114. Mr. Woods will require assistance in order to finish the budget report ------- before its deadline.
    (A) successfully
    (B) succeeded
    (C) successful
    (D) success

115. The Franklin warehouse was built to enable faster ------- of our products in the region.
    (A) proximity
    (B) destination
    (C) distribution
    (D) fulfillment

116. Jocabia Market will reopen now that its organizers have ------- a dispute with the city over the market's operating license.
    (A) settled
    (B) resigned
    (C) conveyed
    (D) elected

117. Luigi Mancini, ------- achievements as a player included winning a "Most Valuable Player" award, has been hired to coach the Ardshire Ravens.
    (A) whichever
    (B) whose
    (C) who
    (D) his

118. Some offices prefer Horizon air purifiers due to their ------- size and portability.
    (A) brief
    (B) compact
    (C) demanding
    (D) authentic

119. The services Sephat Hotel offers ------- the needs of travelers on the go include digital check-in.
    (A) accommodate
    (B) accommodated
    (C) are accommodating
    (D) to accommodate

120. The Zambardi-Z backpack has side pockets to allow easy ------- to essential items such as water bottles and snacks.
    (A) accesses
    (B) accessing
    (C) access
    (D) accessed

GO ON TO THE NEXT PAGE

121. While the staff handbook prohibits smartphone use on the job, it does not specify the ------- of breaking this rule.

(A) offenders
(B) consequences
(C) alternatives
(D) objectives

122. Woolio uses information gathered through its mobile app to improve its own services, but it does not share customer data -------.

(A) externally
(B) inaccurately
(C) meticulously
(D) originally

123. The mayor's attendance at the gathering marked his first public appearance ------- nearly a month.

(A) in
(B) over
(C) since
(D) around

124. Storgan Education's language programs produce self-motivated learners capable of ------- to new circumstances.

(A) cooperating
(B) converting
(C) addressing
(D) adapting

125. One of the duties of the stock clerk is to ensure that all of the merchandise ------- in the store is placed on the right shelves.

(A) are selling
(B) will sell
(C) being sold
(D) have sold

126. Our monthly utility bills have been ------- lower since the new temperature control system was installed.

(A) deeply
(B) forcefully
(C) substantially
(D) extremely

127. Ms. Ok has been tasked with investigating ------- standard procedures are being properly followed.

(A) into
(B) whether
(C) before
(D) any

128. The establishment of the call center complex will make Blundell's economy less ------- on manufacturing.

(A) reliance
(B) relying
(C) reliant
(D) reliable

129. Despite their careful preparations, the party's caterers were forced to ------- when the refrigeration unit suddenly broke down.

(A) improvise
(B) designate
(C) condense
(D) attain

130. The most popular of Mortel Consulting's leadership seminars teaches managers how to foster teamwork while respecting employee -------.

(A) individual
(B) individually
(C) individualized
(D) individuality

PART 6

Directions: Read the texts that follow. A word, phrase, or sentence is missing in parts of each text. Four answer choices for each question are given below the text. Select the best answer to complete the text. Then mark the letter (A), (B), (C), or (D) on your answer sheet.

Questions 131-134 refer to the following article.

City News Times   *Week of March 3*

The highly anticipated grand opening of Fusion Foods, ------- chef David Huu's new restaurant,
                                                                                 131.
is scheduled for Thursday, March 13 at 5 P.M. The event ------- a ribbon-cutting ceremony and
                                                                                    132.
reception with complimentary delicacies.

During his 24-year career, Mr. Huu has become one of the region's most prominent and popular

chefs. -------. His first eatery, Café West 24, opened early last year to strong reviews and
         133.
continues to be a popular option for city diners. ------- running his own restaurants, Mr. Huu
                                                                          134.
worked for a decade as head chef at Gianmati's Bistro on Third Street.

Fusion Foods is located at 3402 Jordan Street. From March 14, it will be open for lunch and

dinner, Tuesday through Sunday. Its menu is already available online at www.fusion-food.com.

131. (A) aspiring
    (B) visiting
    (C) retired
    (D) noted

132. (A) featured
    (B) would have featured
    (C) is to feature
    (D) will have featured

133. (A) He currently teaches culinary arts classes
       there.
    (B) Fusion Foods is his second restaurant.
    (C) Fusion Foods may change ownership
       soon.
    (D) He also plans to extend its business hours.

134. (A) As soon as
    (B) Prior to
    (C) Afterward
    (D) In addition

GO ON TO THE NEXT PAGE

Questions 135-138 refer to the following e-mail.

To: <customerservice@romerouniforms.com>
From: <natasha.maxwell@odn-mail.com>
Subject: Uniform logo
Date: November 25
Attachment: lion_image

Hello,

I'm trying to use your Web site to order customized uniforms for the youth basketball team I coach, but it doesn't seem to be working ------. We are the Lions, and one of our team
                                                    135.
member's parents designed an image of a lion that we plan to use as our logo. ------, when we
                                                                              136.
upload it to your site, it looks distorted in the uniform preview image. We've tried different image sizes and all of the possible file types, but the issue ------. So, I'm sending you the image as an
                                                                    137.
attachment to this e-mail. ------. I'm not sure if this matters, but we've chosen the "Winner
                           138.
Diamond Dunk" uniform style with an emerald green background and white diamonds.

Thanks,

Natasha Maxwell

---

135. (A) corrected
(B) correct
(C) correctly
(D) corrections

136. (A) Instead
(B) Namely
(C) Similarly
(D) Unfortunately

137. (A) persists
(B) resides
(C) determines
(D) asserts

138. (A) Please give us your honest opinion of its appeal.
(B) You will not have to come by my office in person after all.
(C) We would like you to use it as the basis for your logo design.
(D) I hope you can figure out what the problem is.

http://www.russontmining.com/careers/tp

Trainee Program

The Trainee Program is ------- an exciting career opportunity for recent university graduates and
                               139.
an important way for Russont Mining Co. to cultivate our future leaders. We choose promising
young people from a variety of fields and give them the tools and knowledge they need to
become valuable members of the Russont team. Over the twelve-month program, trainees
travel to Russont sites across Canada and speak with employees and executives at all levels.
-------. Room, board, and a generous living stipend are provided. Successful completion of the
  140.
program entitles trainees to a full-time position at Russont in the area to which their
qualifications and interests are best -------.
                                       141.

Would you like to find out how to become a trainee? Click here to learn about the ------- process.
                                                                                      142.

139. (A) both
(B) what
(C) either
(D) intended

140. (A) In particular, they should have excellent
communication skills.
(B) They are even given opportunities to
work on major projects.
(C) For example, our current vice president
of operations is a graduate.
(D) We will review submissions on a rolling
basis throughout this time.

141. (A) to suit
(B) suits
(C) suited
(D) suitable

142. (A) development
(B) appraisal
(C) application
(D) procurement

Test 4

Notice to Online Banking Customers:

Starting from January 1, Meypt Bank will provide account statements electronically by default. After that date, you will no longer receive paper statements in the mail ------- you specifically
143.
inform us that you wish to. You can do this by logging in to your online banking account, opening the "Settings" tab, and selecting "Continue to receive paper statements".

Electronic statements are available under the "Statements" tab on your account page. We will send you an e-mail ------- upon the release of your statement each month. -------. It will only
144.   145.
mention your name and the last four digits of your account number. Please keep the e-mail address associated with your account updated at all times. This will ensure the ------- of these
146.
and other important messages from Meypt Bank.

143. (A) wherever
(B) unless
(C) besides
(D) once

144. (A) notification
(B) notifying
(C) notified
(D) notifiable

145. (A) This message is designed to protect customer privacy.
(B) The process is the same for joint account holders.
(C) The statement lists all of your recent transactions.
(D) At present, this date cannot be changed online.

146. (A) clarity
(B) deletion
(C) relevance
(D) delivery

PART 7

Directions: In this part you will read a selection of texts, such as magazine and newspaper articles, e-mails, and instant messages. Each text or set of texts is followed by several questions. Select the best answer for each question and mark the letter (A), (B), (C), or (D) on your answer sheet.

Questions 147-148 refer to the following coupon.

Hones Hill Nursery
Spring sale

Bring this coupon to Hones Hill Nursery between April 14 and April 23 to get 25% off all plants and 15% off all pottery. Celebrate the first warm weather of the new year by buying beautiful flowers, bushes, and even trees for your home or business at amazing prices. Delivery and planting assistance for our everyday low fees will be available for all purchases.

147. What is indicated about the promotion?
(A) It involves giving out free plants.
(B) It applies to multiple types of items.
(C) It rewards the nursery's long-time customers.
(D) It requires shoppers to spend a certain amount of money.

148. What is suggested about Hones Hill Nursery?
(A) It also stocks outdoor furniture.
(B) It is closed one day per week.
(C) It offers some off-site services.
(D) It mainly serves other businesses.

GO ON TO THE NEXT PAGE

Jamar Richardson [6:14 P.M.]
Hi, Amina. I just got approved to attend the University Financial Aid Professionals conference this year, and I saw that you're presenting. Why don't we meet up while we're there?

Amina Ndiaye [6:28 P.M.]
Hi, Jamar. Sure, I'd love to catch up. It's been two years since you left, right? I can't believe it. It seems like only yesterday that you were our newest student counselor.

Jamar Richardson [6:31 P.M.]
I know! So, my plane will arrive on Thursday at around 7. Could we get together for a late dinner?

Amina Ndiaye [6:33 P.M.]
Hmm. How about lunch on Saturday? I'd like to use Thursday evening to prepare for my presentation.

Jamar Richardson [6:34 P.M.]
That should work.

Amina Ndiaye [6:35 P.M.]
Great. If we don't run into each other before then, let's text again on Friday to figure out the details.

149. Who most likely is Mr. Richardson?

(A) Ms. Ndiaye's former coworker
(B) Ms. Ndiaye's co-presenter
(C) A university student
(D) A conference organizer

150. At 6:34 P.M., what does Mr. Richardson mean when he writes, "That should work"?

(A) He thinks some preparations will be useful.
(B) He believes some equipment is reliable.
(C) He does not mind providing some assistance.
(D) He can probably meet at a suggested time.

E-Mail message	
From:	<lester.knight@eorp.com>
To:	<benita.garza@niy-mail.com>
Subject:	Upcoming appointment
Date:	January 2
Attachment:	📎 Information

Dear Ms. Garza,

Thank you for making an appointment to meet with me on **January 17 at 2 P.M.** I am excited to have the chance to help you achieve your goals—whether they are buying a house, sending children to university, or something else—through careful money management and smart investing.

In order to make our first meeting as productive as possible, there is some information about your income, assets, debts, and so on that you will need to have at hand. Please review the attachment to this e-mail to see the full range of paperwork that will be necessary. It is also a good idea to think of and write down any questions that you may have for me before coming to my office.

I look forward to meeting you.

Sincerely,

Lester Knight

151. What most likely is Mr. Knight's job?

(A) Real estate agent
(B) Private tutor
(C) Financial advisor
(D) Job recruiter

152. According to Mr. Knight, what is the purpose of the attachment?

(A) To describe the location of an office
(B) To justify a request for payment
(C) To summarize the details of an offer
(D) To provide a list of required documents

GO ON TO THE NEXT PAGE

Questions 153-155 refer to the following notice.

PUBLIC NOTICE

March 6: The City of Donnerly proposes the upgrading of a portion of its water distribution system starting in April.
— [1] —. Steel pipes of insufficient size for the city's current needs will be replaced with high-density plastic pipes.
— [2] —. A city assessment has determined that this project may have an impact on local wetlands. Therefore, this notice is being given in order to provide residents with an opportunity to express their environmental and safety concerns. — [3] —.
The project file, which includes the results of the assessment, is available for public viewing at the Water Services Department in City Hall. Comments on the project may be submitted at the same place until March 27. — [4] —.

---

153. Why was the notice written?

(A) To announce a business opportunity
(B) To seek feedback on a proposal
(C) To caution residents about service interruptions
(D) To correct a misunderstanding about a project

154. What is suggested about Donnerly?

(A) Its water usage has increased.
(B) It is located in a relatively dry region.
(C) Its officials will hold a public meeting.
(D) It evaluated the quality of its drinking water.

155. In which of the positions marked [1], [2], [3], and [4] does the following sentence best belong?

"Valves will also be added to the remaining pipes to limit water loss from line breaks."

(A) [1]
(B) [2]
(C) [3]
(D) [4]

Questions 156-157 refer to the following sign.

Nabors Associates

Please read before using the microwave!

1. Do not use the microwave to heat any foods that are likely to give off a strong smell (e.g., fish).

2. Cover your dish with a lid or paper towel to prevent food from splattering inside the microwave.

3. If your food does splatter or drip in the microwave, clean it up immediately. Cleaning products can be found under the sink.

4. Any problems with the microwave should now be reported to Tony Mitchell in Maintenance (ext. 32), not an office administrator.

---

156. What is the purpose of the sign?

(A) To publicize the features of an amenity
(B) To warn about some dangers
(C) To explain a process
(D) To issue a set of rules

157. What is most likely true about Mr. Mitchell's job duties?

(A) They are specified in a handbook.
(B) They have recently grown.
(C) They mainly consist of cleaning tasks.
(D) They include communicating with office administrators.

Questions 158-160 refer to the following e-mail.

From:	Scott Pham
To:	Volunteer List
Subject:	Munseck Book Fair
Date:	August 7

Hello, Volunteers!

On behalf of the Munseck Book Fair Organizing Committee, I'd like to welcome you all to the team responsible for putting on this wonderful event.

You'll receive an e-mail later this month from the supervisor of your particular area (e.g., exhibitor assistance, transportation, etc.) that specifies details such as where to report for your shift, but I have some general tips and information to share first.

We recommend that all volunteers wear comfortable shoes, as well as bring sunscreen just in case it is needed. Also, because the Hondina Convention Center is a large venue, you should plan to arrive 15 minutes early to ensure that you make it to your shift on time.

No matter what you do at the fair, your priority once you put on your "Volunteer" badge will be to assist the guests. Please take a look at the "Fairgoers Guide" booklet that you will be given at the entrance so that you can help them find convenience facilities. If you're asked a question that you can't answer, direct the asker to the nearest information booth.

See you at the fair!

Regards,

Scott Pham
Head Volunteer Coordinator

---

158. What information does Mr. Pham mention will be provided in a future e-mail?

(A) Some training session dates
(B) Some uniform requirements
(C) Some transportation costs
(D) Some work sites

159. What is suggested about the volunteers?

(A) Some of them will be stationed outside.
(B) There will be 15 of them in each activity area.
(C) They will receive a badge at the entrance to the fair.
(D) They will be entitled to free lodging.

160. How are volunteers encouraged to learn about the fair?

(A) By asking their supervisors
(B) By exploring it on foot
(C) By reading a publication
(D) By visiting an information booth

Excitement, Controversy Surround Tourism Board Contest

The Haspanton Tourism Board has caused a stir with its latest event, the "#MyHaspanton Contest." The contest offers $1,000 to the person who creates a short video that best embodies Haspanton. Videos must be posted to the social media platform Shoutster and tagged with "#MyHaspanton." The winner will be determined by a combination of the number of "Likes" that each video receives and votes to be submitted by members of the tourism board.

The contest was dreamed up by Ella Forte, the board's newest member as well as its only one under 35. In a phone call yesterday, Ms. Forte said the contest "makes use of both technology and Haspanton's greatest resource — its people." It has certainly been met with enthusiasm from Shoutster users. Nearly 80 videos have been posted so far, and they have garnered more than 10,000 "Likes" in total.

However, not everyone is pleased with the contest. At last week's city council meeting, local restaurant owner Ernest Mathews complained that the board was essentially ignoring the ideas of anyone who does not use Shoutster. "Most of my customers are seniors, and none of them are on Shoutster," he said. "The side of Haspanton that is represented in this contest is too narrow." In response, Council Member Juanita Padilla said she would urge the board to consider multiple participation methods for future promotions.

161. What phase is the contest currently in?

(A) It has not yet begun.
(B) Entries are being submitted.
(C) The tourism board is voting.
(D) The winner has been chosen.

162. What is stated about Ms. Forte?

(A) She was present at a city council meeting.
(B) She has a personal Shoutster account.
(C) She appeared in a short promotional video.
(D) She is the youngest member of an organization.

163. What does Mr. Mathews dislike about the contest?

(A) That the tourism board can influence its results
(B) That it excludes some residents' perspectives
(C) That it has been unsuccessful in the past
(D) That it is expensive for the city

GO ON TO THE NEXT PAGE

Questions 164-167 refer to the following online chat discussion.

Selena Horvath — 3:49 P.M.

The consultant from Welk Material Handling came in this morning to present her ideas for redesigning the Pookville warehouse, right? What did you think?

Amy Carroll — 3:50 P.M.

Most of her suggestions were great. For example, she recommended setting up an area near the entrance that would have small quantities of the materials that customers order most frequently. That would cut down our retrieval times.

Selena Horvath — 3:50 P.M.

That does sound like a good idea. Did she think we'll need to invest in pallet racks, like we suspected?

Amy Carroll — 3:51 P.M.

Yes, but only for that special front area. We could keep stacking the rest of the stock on the floor.

Ronald Eguchi — 3:51 P.M.

But she also said we should implement a location-finding system with scannable labels.

Selena Horvath — 3:52 P.M.

Hmm, that sounds expensive. But I'm sure it has a huge potential to improve our efficiency.

Amy Carroll — 3:53 P.M.

Our thoughts exactly. We asked her how long it would take to recover the cost of the system through the increase in productivity, and she said it depends on which provider we choose.

Ronald Eguchi — 3:54 P.M.

We're looking for a provider that might be willing to offer us a discount for adopting the system in several warehouses instead of just one.

Selena Horvath — 3:55 P.M.

Well, we may decide to try out the system in one location before implementing it in the others. But that's an interesting idea. Let me know what you find out.

164. Why did Ms. Horvath begin the online chat discussion?

(A) To learn about the outcome of a meeting
(B) To clarify the contents of a document
(C) To discuss arrangements for an inspection
(D) To share her opinions on a presentation

165. What is NOT a recommendation that a consultant made?

(A) Installing racks in one part of a facility
(B) Painting lines on a floor to mark aisle sizes
(C) Using stickers that can be read electronically
(D) Making popular types of stock more accessible

166. At 3:53 P.M., what does Ms. Carroll most likely mean when she writes, "Our thoughts exactly"?

(A) She and Mr. Eguchi have mixed feelings about an idea.
(B) She and Mr. Eguchi are confused by some findings.
(C) A warehouse's output is disappointingly low.
(D) The budget for a project should not be increased.

167. According to Ms. Horvath, what might the chat participants' company choose to do?

(A) Open a new location in Pookville
(B) Customize some features of a system
(C) Conduct a small-scale test of a scheme
(D) Discount some older merchandise

Questions 168-171 refer to the following Web page.

http://www.allstons.com/corporate ▾

Allston's >> Corporate Inquiries

For over 40 years, Allston's has been committed to giving our customers the best selection of quality apparel and footwear for every athletic activity. — [1] —. Today, we maintain business relationships with hundreds of vendors who represent some of the country's most popular and exciting products. Still, we are always seeking new brands and styles to sell under the "Allston's" banner. We boast a large, loyal customer base and fast, dependable payment schedules. In return, we merely ask vendors to follow our reasonable standards for merchandise packing and truck deliveries. — [2] —. To inquire about establishing a vendor relationship with us, please call us at (809) 555-0162 or e-mail us at vendors@allstons.com. — [3] —. We will be happy to provide testimonials from select existing vendors.

In addition, Allston's is constantly reviewing potential locations for opening new stores throughout the Midwestern region of the U.S. — [4] —. If you own a suitable commercial property and would like to discuss leasing it to us, please call our Chicago head office at (809) 555-0160.

168. What kind of business mostly likely is Allston's?

(A) A health food supplier
(B) A sports clothing store
(C) A chain of fitness centers
(D) An event planning firm

169. What is suggested about Allston's?

(A) It recently moved its headquarters.
(B) It will soon change its name.
(C) It is attempting to expand.
(D) It attends regional trade shows.

170. According to the Web page, what are all existing vendors required to do?

(A) Pack items according to company policies
(B) Give a testimonial upon request
(C) Display the Allston's logo on their trucks
(D) Prove that their operations are environmentally-friendly

171. In which of the positions marked [1], [2], [3], and [4] does the following sentence best belong?

"Our minimum requirement for floor space is generally 15,000 square feet."

(A) [1]
(B) [2]
(C) [3]
(D) [4]

GO ON TO THE NEXT PAGE

TEST 4 **109**

To: Managers
From: Joon-Tae Shin
Re: Employee treatment
Date: July 20

As you all know, Ms. Noolan hired me earlier this year to be Noolan Software's first full-time human resources employee. One of my duties is looking at our overall situation from a personnel perspective, and now that I have been here for a few months, I have developed some suggestions for improvements. As a small business that hopes to grow into a larger one, it is important that we provide working conditions that attract and keep talented employees.

One important consideration is workload. We should be checking in with employees regularly to ensure that their tasks can be completed in a standard workweek. If your department's workload becomes too heavy, please set up a meeting with Ms. Noolan and me to discuss adding more personnel.

Similarly, employees should feel comfortable taking sick time when needed and using their full allotment of vacation days. This is an important way of protecting their health and morale.

Finally, please allow employees some flexibility in their hours as long as they meet their performance targets. While we are not yet able to support remote work, we can at least empower our employees to manage their own schedules within reason.

All of you, Ms. Noolan, and I will meet on Thursday at 10 A.M. to talk about the contents of this memo. Please note that Ms. Noolan has already given her approval to my recommendations, so the meeting will not be an opportunity to debate them. Instead, we will focus on how best to achieve them. Thank you.

172. What is indicated about Noolan Software?

   (A) It recently opened a new office.
   (B) It was founded less than a year ago.
   (C) It does not have many employees.
   (D) It must satisfy its shareholders.

173. What is NOT mentioned as a way to improve treatment of employees?

   (A) Adjustable working hours
   (B) A reasonable workload
   (C) Easy usage of leave time
   (D) An on-site health program

174. According to the memo, why should recipients schedule a meeting with Mr. Shin?

   (A) To express opposition to his ideas
   (B) To propose hiring more workers
   (C) To recommend a performance-based bonus
   (D) To secure permission for a staff member to work remotely

175. What does Mr. Shin suggest about the recommendations in the memo?

   (A) They will also be announced to the entire staff.
   (B) They are supported by scientific research.
   (C) They are endorsed by the business's owner.
   (D) They have been adopted by a competitor.

GO ON TO THE NEXT PAGE

Questions 176-180 refer to the following Web page and e-mail.

www.orosco-pac.org/fscs

Orosco Performing Arts Center

Free Autumn Concert Series

Every Thursday evening from September through November, the center offers a free concert in the Ervin Amphitheater, its most intimate performance space. The series, which is carefully planned to represent a variety of genres, is an excellent chance to see established musicians and discover exciting new ones.

Performances begin at 7 P.M. Reservations are only allowed for bookings of more than 10 people. All other attendees are encouraged to line up at the box office well before the concert in order to secure their tickets.

Upcoming Concerts (Full Schedule)

October 19	**Emilia Bernauer:** Ms. Bernauer, called "the next big star in classical piano" by renowned concert pianist Roman Huff, will give a recital of works by French composers.
October 26	**The Green Cliff Trio:** Enjoy the smooth blending of piano, double bass, and drums that earned the group its prestigious "Album of the Year" honor from the Academy of Jazz Music.
November 2	**Johnny and The Farmers:** The legendary folk band makes its first visit to Helmsped in over a decade! Come and listen to "Broken Banjo" and other hits from its bestselling records.
November 9	**Orosco Opera Company:** Talented singers from right here in Helmsped will perform famous arias and duets from various operas in Italian and English.

Call 555-0180 for more information, or follow us on social media to see photos of past concerts and receive reminders of upcoming ones.

From:	Eloise Flynn
To:	Trina McGee
Subject:	Re: Free Autumn Concert
Date:	October 10

Dear Trina,

Sure, I would love to go to the concert with you. I can't believe we'll be able to see opera singing in the Orosco Performing Arts Center for free! I've never been there before, and I've heard that it's really nice. You always seem to know about the most interesting events around the city—someday you'll have to tell me how you do that! And no, I wouldn't mind handling the tickets, since you work on Thursdays. It will just be the two of us, right?

–Eloise

176. What is indicated about the Orosco
     Performing Arts Center?

     (A) It has more than one stage.
     (B) It displays various architectural styles.
     (C) It posts interviews on its social media
         accounts.
     (D) It allows children under age 10 to
         attend some events.

177. On the Web page, what is NOT
     mentioned as an accomplishment of the
     listed performers?

     (A) Selling many albums
     (B) Winning a major award
     (C) Performing around the world
     (D) Receiving acclaim from a famous
         musician

178. Why was the e-mail written?

     (A) To request a change to some plans
     (B) To answer a question about a
         completed booking
     (C) To confirm that a reservation has been
         made
     (D) To accept a friendly invitation

179. On which date does Ms. Flynn probably
     want to see a concert?

     (A) October 19
     (B) October 26
     (C) November 2
     (D) November 9

180. What will Ms. Flynn most likely do?

     (A) Arrive early on the day of the
         performance
     (B) Call the performing arts center's box
         office
     (C) Go through an online process on a
         certain date
     (D) Download a tourism-related mobile
         app

GO ON TO THE NEXT PAGE

(February 7)—A Waymarr convenience store is coming to Denold City.

The city's Economic Development Committee (EDC) unanimously approved Waymarr's plans to construct a 4,600-square-foot convenience store, which will feature a tiled canopy above its 12 gas pumps. It will be built on a plot of vacant land on Milden Drive, near Route 7, and remain open 24 hours a day, 7 days a week.

To operate the store, the company will have to comply with the city's noise and traffic reduction regulations. Among other things, it will not be allowed to accept deliveries via heavy trucks between 1:00 A.M. and 5:00 A.M., with the exception of gasoline. Trucks will also be unable to access the store from Milden Drive, so Waymarr will build a private road leading to the store's receiving area.

Approval came after a public meeting that included presentations by the company's own traffic engineers. The residents in attendance voiced a mixture of support and opposition. Betty Timpano, who lives on the 400 block of Milden Drive, said she liked the idea of a convenience store in the neighborhood but had concerns about increased traffic along nearby Ramona Way. As evidence, she showed a digital video she had shot from her car window during rush hour. It showed heavy vehicle congestion on Ramona Way near Brook Street.

On the other hand, resident Steve Grossick said he would welcome the store because it would provide a "quick, warm bite to eat" after work. Currently, the nearest convenience store is a Weisbold Plus shop on Laurel Street, about three kilometers away.

Dear Editor,

As a lifelong resident of Denold City, I was grateful for your February 7 report on the planned Waymarr convenience store. However, the article contained some incorrect information. The digital video I presented at the public meeting was a recording of congested traffic on my street of residence.

Also, I would like to remind you that two citizens voiced concerns about the modern design of the store. I agree with them that we must try to retain our city's distinctive architectural character. New buildings should, if possible, blend in with our historical structures.

Again, thank you for your reporting.

Sincerely,

Betty Timpano

181. What is NOT true about the planned convenience store?

(A) It will have a covered fueling area.
(B) It will not sell gas in the early mornings.
(C) It will offer cooked food selections.
(D) It will be constructed on empty land.

182. What is mentioned about Denold City?

(A) It is known for its large warehouse district.
(B) It is the site of an annual engineering conference.
(C) It has three other convenience stores.
(D) It has implemented policies to decrease traffic.

183. Where did Ms. Timpano most likely film a video for a public meeting?

(A) On Milden Drive
(B) On Ramona Way
(C) On Brook Street
(D) On Laurel Street

184. What does the letter to the editor indicate about Ms. Timpano?

(A) She is a local historian.
(B) She prefers modern architecture.
(C) She has never lived outside of Denold City.
(D) She has been to a Waymarr convenience store.

185. In the letter to the editor, the word "retain" in paragraph 2, line 2, is closest in meaning to

(A) appoint
(B) conceal
(C) preserve
(D) confine

GO ON TO THE NEXT PAGE

MINTANA SPA

Proposal for a Sales Promotion

Submitted by Joseph Barham, Sales Assistant
September 2

Form of Promotion: A 15% discount on any service

Target Customer: Nurses

Dates/Duration: Ongoing, starting as soon as possible

Advantages:

- New group of customers. As holders of a job that is high stress but not always well paid, nurses could benefit greatly from our services but may feel that they are not affordable at full price.
- Improvement of our corporate image among the general public.

Challenges:

- Logistical issues. Our staff would have to carefully check the credentials of participants and remember that only services are included in the discount.

Mintana Spa Supports Medical Personnel!

Mintana Spa knows that saving lives and providing day-to-day medical care is difficult work. That is why, starting November 1, we will offer a 15% discount on all of our services to nurses, paramedics, and emergency medical technicians.* These include relaxing massages, refreshing facial and body treatments, and cleansing sauna time—even in our new infrared sauna pods, which use infrared light to induce detoxifying sweat and improve circulation! This is our small way of thanking the heroes who keep our community healthy.

Mintana Spa is located at 1200 Whitcomb Road in Bruner. Walk-ins are accepted, but we recommend making an appointment, as our schedule does frequently fill up. Call 555-0122 for more information.

Proof of eligible employment is required. Note that the discount cannot be used toward spa gift certificates or merchandise.

http://www.brunerbusinessreviews.com/mintanaspa

Bruner Business Reviews

Latest reviews for Mintana Spa:

"I had a day off yesterday, so I visited in the early afternoon to take advantage of their new discount for nurses. They were quite busy for a weekday, and I was lucky that I didn't get turned away for not having an appointment. Still, I never felt hurried by the staff. Everyone was very attentive and treated me like I was the only customer that day. That's what I appreciated the most. In contrast, the benefits of the blueberry extract facial faded by this morning, and the sauna pod, while relaxing, wasn't much better than a hot bath. I will probably go to this spa again but try some different services next time."

By Teisha Coyne, November 12

Test 4

186. What does the proposal mention as a potential difficulty of a promotion?

(A) Making potential participants aware of it
(B) Serving large numbers of new patrons
(C) Maintaining sufficient profit margins
(D) Evaluating participants' qualifications

187. What is different about the promotion in the proposal and the advertisement?

(A) The size of its discount
(B) The duration it is available
(C) The people eligible for it
(D) The purchases to which it can be applied

188. In the customer review, the phrase "turned away" in paragraph 1, line 3, is closest in meaning to

(A) dismissed
(B) rejected
(C) avoided
(D) abandoned

189. What is implied about Ms. Coyne?

(A) She visited on the first day of the promotion.
(B) She received a light-based treatment.
(C) She tried Mintana Spa's most popular offering.
(D) She called the phone number listed in the advertisement.

190. What did Ms. Coyne especially like about Mintana Spa?

(A) Its considerate customer service
(B) Its luxurious interior decoration
(C) The effectiveness of its procedures
(D) The privacy afforded by its layout

Arabic Language Exam To Be Administered in Cobshaw

By Sheila Ridenour

COBSHAW (May 13)—The National Foreign Language Association (NFLA), a non-profit organization committed to advancing Americans' competency in languages other than English, will begin offering its Arabic language proficiency test in Cobshaw. The Test of Competency in Arabic (TOCIA) will be administered twice a year starting this July.

Ken Reed, an NFLA official, says the decision was an easy one to reach. "We noticed that there have been a lot of test-takers coming from the Cobshaw region." He believes that this is thanks to the University of Cobshaw's Arabic language program. The program also, he says, supplies local people qualified to administer the test, as such work requires some knowledge of the language.

The TOCIA consists of a 50-minute listening section and a 70-minute reading section. The first exam will be held in the university's Duckett Auditorium, though Mr. Reed says other venues may be added if there are over 150 test-takers. Registration, which costs $40, must be completed online at www.nfla.org/tocia by 5 P.M. on June 4.

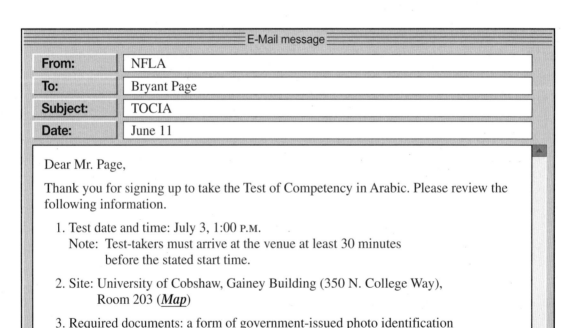

E-Mail message

From:	NFLA
To:	Bryant Page
Subject:	TOCIA
Date:	June 11

Dear Mr. Page,

Thank you for signing up to take the Test of Competency in Arabic. Please review the following information.

1. Test date and time: July 3, 1:00 P.M.
   Note: Test-takers must arrive at the venue at least 30 minutes before the stated start time.

2. Site: University of Cobshaw, Gainey Building (350 N. College Way), Room 203 (*Map*)

3. Required documents: a form of government-issued photo identification

For details about the test-taking process, please visit ***this page***.

Test of Competency in Arabic (TOCIA)
Report on the Observance of Testing Procedures

Test Site: University of Cobshaw, Duckett Auditorium
Test Date: July 3
Test Administrator: Savanna Keenan

Please check the box next to each item to indicate that the relevant procedure
was executed. If any box is left unmarked, a full explanation of the reason must be
appended to this report.

- No test-takers were admitted to the site fewer than 30 minutes
  before the start of the test. ☑
- The identity of each test-taker was verified. ☑
- All personal electronics brought by test-takers were stored away
  from the site. ☐
- Test-takers filled out all of the required pre-test forms. ☑

191. In the article, the word "reach" in paragraph
     2, line 2, is closest in meaning to

     (A) stretch
     (B) accomplish
     (C) contact
     (D) make

192. Why was the e-mail sent to Mr. Page?

     (A) To prepare him for the test
     (B) To ask him to finalize his registration
     (C) To advertise a study service
     (D) To respond to an inquiry

193. What is suggested about the TOCIA?

     (A) More than 150 people signed up to take
         it in Cobshaw.
     (B) There is a 30-minute break between its
         sections.
     (C) It is usually administered on a weekend
         day.
     (D) There are practice versions of it on the
         NFLA Web site.

194. What will most likely be explained in an
     attachment to the report?

     (A) When the last test-taker arrived
     (B) How test-takers proved their identities
     (C) What paperwork test-takers completed
         before the test
     (D) Where test-takers' belongings were
         kept during the test

195. What is most likely true about Ms. Keenan?

     (A) She participated in a training session in
         June.
     (B) She has some Arabic language skills.
     (C) She was interviewed by Ms. Ridenour.
     (D) She is a professor at the University of
         Cobshaw.

GO ON TO THE NEXT PAGE

To:	Nick Borrows <nickborrows1@renseed.com>
From:	Vanessa Castle <vanessacastle@renseed.com>
Date:	April 20
Subject:	San Diego
Attachment:	📎 Revised presentation

Hi Nick,

I just wanted to give you an update on the slides for our presentation in San Diego next week. I've left the graphs and balance sheet as they are, but I've made the pictures of our products a little bigger and sharper. I also have some notes about the text of the slides, but I didn't want to alter it without talking to you first. I'll send my ideas in a separate file.

Also, we need to book a flight. For the way there, there are four options available on our preferred carrier. I don't know about you, but I'd like to take the one that gets us there in the evening. It would allow us to prepare here in the office for most of the day but also arrive in time to relax a bit. If you agree, I'll book it before I leave today.

Let me know.

–Vanessa

◀ ▶ www.lightningair.com/departures/april28/query83789

Lightning Air - Operating Budget Flights Daily Across the US!

Departure Date: April 28
Departure Airport: San Francisco
Arrival Airport: San Diego

○ Flight No: L106	Departure: 4:30 A.M.	Arrival: 6:00 A.M.
○ Flight No: L982	Departure: 11:00 A.M.	Arrival: 12:30 P.M.
○ Flight No: L392	Departure: 1:00 P.M.	Arrival: 2:30 P.M.
○ Flight No: L720	Departure: 5:45 P.M.	Arrival: 7:15 P.M.

Important note: We have eliminated our complimentary meal service for economy class passengers on flights shorter than three hours. These passengers may purchase a meal for an additional cost. Business class passengers are still entitled to this meal free of charge. Club class passengers receive the meal and their choice of unlimited beverages. Premium class passengers get the same as club class, as well as entry to our exclusive Lightning Air lounge.

NEXT PAGE ▶

To:	Vanessa Castle <vanessacastle@renseed.com>
From:	Nick Borrows <nickborrows1@renseed.com>
Subject:	Re: San Diego
Date:	April 22

Hi Vanessa,

Thank you for your e-mail and your hard work on the presentation slides.

I've got the company credit card with me right now, so I went ahead and got tickets for the flight that you wanted, plus another one coming back on the thirtieth. The prices were quite reasonable, although I had to pay a little extra to get in-flight meals for us.

If you don't mind, I'll make reservations now at the hotel I usually use in the city center. We won't have to book transportation from the airport, because the hotel has a free shuttle bus. It also has a nice business center where we can print our presentation slides. Does that sound all right?

Nick

Test 4

196. What did Ms. Castle do to some images?

(A) She made them more visible.
(B) She put them in a different file.
(C) She added text to them.
(D) She removed flaws from them.

197. What does Ms. Castle promise to send to Mr. Borrows?

(A) Verification of a reservation
(B) Details about some travel options
(C) An audio recording of a presentation
(D) Suggestions for revising some writing

198. Which flight does Ms. Castle prefer?

(A) L982
(B) L106
(C) L720
(D) L392

199. What class of flight ticket did Mr. Borrows most likely purchase?

(A) Economy class
(B) Club class
(C) Business class
(D) Premium class

200. What does Mr. Borrows indicate he will do next?

(A) Apply for reimbursement for an expense
(B) Arrange ground transportation
(C) Book some accommodations
(D) Print some computer screenshots

Stop! This is the end of the test. If you finish before time is called, you may go back to Parts 5, 6, and 7 and check your work.

TEST 5

In the Reading test, you will read a variety of texts and answer several different types of reading comprehension questions. The entire Reading test will last 75 minutes. There are three parts, and directions are given for each part. You are encouraged to answer as many questions as possible within the time allowed.

You must mark your answers on the separate answer sheet. Do not write your answers in your test book.

PART 5

Directions: A word or phrase is missing in each of the sentences below. Four answer choices are given below each sentence. Select the best answer to complete the sentence. Then mark the letter (A), (B), (C), or (D) on your answer sheet.

101. The amount of each employee's ------- is based on his or her performance review.
(A) workstation
(B) bonus
(C) uniform
(D) promotion

102. Gillis Mining Group issued a firm ------- of rumors that it plans to replace its CEO.
(A) deny
(B) denies
(C) denied
(D) denial

103. ------- a minimal additional charge, our design professionals can produce eye-catching illustrations you can add to your promotional pieces.
(A) For
(B) As
(C) With
(D) To

104. Fellant Inn ------- a considerable amount of effort into maintaining its reputation for style and comfort.
(A) shows
(B) spends
(C) puts
(D) needs

105. One way to shorten the preparation time of this dish is by buying cabbage that has ------- been cut into strips.
(A) sometimes
(B) already
(C) finally
(D) since

106. The warehouse manager praised the members of the sprinkler installation team for ------- skilled and careful work.
(A) they
(B) them
(C) theirs
(D) their

107. The Galaxxania Plus navigation device for drivers ------- automatically as soon as the vehicle is started.
(A) activation
(B) activator
(C) activates
(D) activated

108. The responses to the recent student survey on the university's health services vary ------- .
(A) wide
(B) widened
(C) widening
(D) widely

109. Ms. Dudley's article calls on the authorities to increase ------- of some sectors of the telecommunications industry.

(A) supervision
(B) supervised
(C) supervisors
(D) supervises

110. Mr. Flores, the assistant manager, is in charge of the store ------- Ms. Weaver is gone.

(A) during
(B) if not
(C) so that
(D) when

111. Our consistently high customer satisfaction ratings ------- the excellent quality of our product line.

(A) transmit
(B) reflect
(C) deliver
(D) arrange

112. Handdahar Chemicals, Inc. has 12 research laboratories spread ------- the major regions of the world.

(A) between
(B) out
(C) upon
(D) across

113. Nishioka Industrial's leadership is ------- supportive of staff efforts to develop environmentally-friendly detergents.

(A) enthusiastically
(B) enthusiasm
(C) enthusiastic
(D) enthusiast

114. According to the janitor, ------- has been leaving unwashed dishes in the break room sink.

(A) who
(B) whoever
(C) someone
(D) one another

115. Mastery of a foreign language is not a fast process, and it is normal for skills to develop ------ over a long period of time.

(A) hurriedly
(B) affirmatively
(C) gradually
(D) reluctantly

116. In some small companies, the person ------- for ordering supplies may work in the accounting or finance department.

(A) responsibly
(B) responsible
(C) responsibility
(D) responsibilities

117. The casting director conducted an ------- search to find the perfect performer for the film's starring role.

(A) absolute
(B) eligible
(C) exhausted
(D) extensive

118. An extraordinary number of citizens participated ------- in the city's campaign to reduce water usage.

(A) voluntarily
(B) voluntary
(C) volunteers
(D) volunteering

119. ------- its materials' delicacy and high value, access to the rare books collection is limited to library staff only.

(A) Because of
(B) Along with
(C) In spite of
(D) Regardless of

120. This week's issue includes a review of jogging accessories that ------- in detail the differences in functionality, price, and durability.

(A) have analyzed
(B) analyzes
(C) analyze
(D) is analyzed

GO ON TO THE NEXT PAGE

121. Casey Street has become famous for having a high ------- of technology start-ups.
(A) position
(B) standard
(C) concentration
(D) attendance

122. Please reserve Conference Room 3 so that we can practice our sales ------- in advance of the client visit.
(A) presentation
(B) presentable
(C) presenter
(D) presented

123. Submitting this application does not ------- you to accept a loan from Masple Bank.
(A) ensure
(B) relieve
(C) obligate
(D) expedite

124. ------- construction of the condominiums is complete, they may be exhibited to prospective buyers.
(A) Now that
(B) Throughout
(C) Whatever
(D) In order that

125. All ------- to the logo design should be discussed in advance with a copyright expert and approved by Mr. Wang.
(A) proposals
(B) concepts
(C) modifications
(D) necessities

126. For the sake of its patients, Morrol Hospital urges medical personnel ------- sick leave as needed.
(A) have taken
(B) to take
(C) took
(D) taking

127. Boasting scenic views of the ocean, Raynor Highway was ------- the only route between the coastal cities of Autry and Lambort.
(A) what
(B) among
(C) far
(D) once

128. Several times in the past year, production at the Nettsald factory ------- by easily preventable machine breakdowns.
(A) was delaying
(B) has been delayed
(C) would have delayed
(D) can be delayed

129. Investors in Balters Incorporated are requesting that the company undergo an audit to prove that it is financially -------.
(A) sound
(B) equivalent
(C) feasible
(D) detailed

130. After the meal, Harkon Catering's servers will clear tables ------- to avoid distracting guests' attention from speeches or other events.
(A) accurately
(B) discreetly
(C) persistently
(D) luxuriously

PART 6

Directions: Read the texts that follow. A word, phrase, or sentence is missing in parts of each text. Four answer choices for each question are given below the text. Select the best answer to complete the text. Then mark the letter (A), (B), (C), or (D) on your answer sheet.

Questions 131-134 refer to the following notice.

Important Customer Notice

Deldunne's Bargain Store will be closed for inventory and computer updates on Monday, January 13. We apologize for any inconvenience this may cause, and we thank you in advance for your patience. On occasion, it is not possible for our staff to handle every task ------- to **131.** inventory processing during normal opening hours. -------. We chose to take care of these **132.** important business functions on this day because we have ------- few shoppers on Mondays. It **133.** is usually the ------- day of the week. Our store will open again promptly at 9 A.M. on Tuesday, **134.** January 14. Thank you.

---

131. (A) relates
(B) related
(C) relation
(D) relatively

132. (A) Therefore, closing for one day is our only option.
(B) The software program is a new addition.
(C) However, most of them are still available online.
(D) Please ask the customer service desk for assistance.

133. (A) solely
(B) considerably
(C) comparatively
(D) regularly

134. (A) shortest
(B) slowest
(C) earliest
(D) busiest

GO ON TO THE NEXT PAGE

Questions 135-138 refer to the following e-mail.

From: Douglas Bailey
To: <totycontest@inspiriteach.com>
Subject: Recommendation for Kerri Wilkinson
Date: November 26

To Whom It May Concern:

I would like to endorse Kerri Wilkinson's nomination for InspiriTeach's "Teacher of the Year" award. ------. Ms. Wilkinson has been my coworker at Winkfield Middle School for five years, **135.**
and I cannot imagine ------- more representative of these qualities. **136.**

Ms. Wilkinson demonstrates endless creativity in her lesson plans for her sixth grade class. For example, she recently made excellent use of the school's technological capabilities for a unit on ------. Her students planned, filmed, and edited a newscast about the school. **137.**

Ms. Wilkinson is also very compassionate. She shows nothing but understanding toward even our most difficult students. -------, she is able to handle disruptive behavior with patience and **138.**
kindness that are an inspiration to her coworkers.

In closing, I recommend you strongly consider Ms. Wilkinson for Teacher of the Year.

Sincerely,

Douglas Bailey

---

135. (A) She deserves recognition for her dedication to the campaign.
(B) I am a wholehearted supporter of InspiriTeach's activities.
(C) Please route my e-mail to the appropriate person or committee.
(D) Your Web site says you seek to reward innovation and caring.

136. (A) educating that
(B) an educator
(C) she educates
(D) whose education

137. (A) journalism
(B) geography
(C) economics
(D) government

138. (A) At first
(B) In fact
(C) Otherwise
(D) Nevertheless

Requirements for VieraGo Hotels

Being listed on VieraGo is a privilege that comes with a variety of responsibilities. ------- the key
139.
one is to provide guests with a pleasant stay, we also expect our member hotels to assist in

upholding VieraGo's good reputation through the following actions.

First, respond quickly to any inquiries made through VieraGo about your hotel—even those

from guests you are not able to accept. Next, after a booking has been made through VieraGo,

do not cancel it unless it is absolutely necessary. -------. Finally, please try to achieve a high
140.
rating on VieraGo by both taking good care of your property and ------- issues that are
141.
mentioned in guest reviews.

VieraGo tracks the performance of each member hotel in these areas (responsiveness,

cancelation rate, and guest ratings) and may impose penalties on hotels that drop below certain

levels. To avoid this, we recommend ------- this data yourself through your account page.
142.

---

139. (A) While
(B) Regarding
(C) Whether
(D) Besides

140. (A) You can also provide a physical copy at
your front desk.
(B) Some hotels may not benefit from
advertising on VieraGo.
(C) For most reservations, these would be
toiletries and towels.
(D) Remember, your guests' travel plans
depend on you.

141. (A) resolve
(B) resolved
(C) resolving
(D) resolution

142. (A) supplying
(B) revising
(C) monitoring
(D) saving

GO ON TO THE NEXT PAGE

FOR IMMEDIATE RELEASE

Contact: publicrelations@pearron.com

TORONTO (October 22)—Pharmaceutical firm Pearron, Inc. has announced the signing of a deal with Wompler Capital. Under the terms of the agreement, Wompler Capital has purchased a minority stake in Pearron for C$72 million, ------- providing funding to realize Pearron's growth
143.
strategy.

Pearron's shareholders support ------- landmark deal. They firmly believe that it ------- the
144. **145.**
company to expand significantly in the coming years.

Pearron develops and commercializes medications for a variety of skin, hair, and nail conditions. -------. In the future, it will focus on refining its rigorous development process that
146.
prioritizes the needs and safety of patients. It will also build up the dedicated sales force that markets its drugs to medical providers throughout Canada.

143. (A) yet
(B) instead
(C) thereby
(D) quite

144. (A) this
(B) every
(C) most
(D) our

145. (A) allows
(B) will allow
(C) has allowed
(D) allowing

146. (A) Many patients still prefer conventional medicine to alternative remedies.
(B) Its machines can be found in hospital rooms around the country.
(C) Its products include Travarin, a cream used to treat nail infections.
(D) The early results of an ongoing clinical trial have been promising.

Directions: In this part you will read a selection of texts, such as magazine and newspaper articles, e-mails, and instant messages. Each text or set of texts is followed by several questions. Select the best answer for each question and mark the letter (A), (B), (C), or (D) on your answer sheet.

Questions 147-148 refer to the following advertisement.

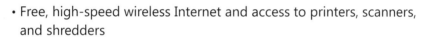

Swann Space

Swann Space provides a comfortable, high-tech working environment for individuals and small businesses. Our facility offers options ranging from flexible coworking lounges to private offices with dedicated conference space. Amenities available to all members include:

- Free, high-speed wireless Internet and access to printers, scanners, and shredders
- A kitchen and break lounge with free beverages and well-stocked vending machines
- Package receiving services and use of our building's impressive Highlands District address (3100 Barney Street) for business mailings

Want to know more? Join our next Swann Space Open Reception on May 3 to connect with us, our current members, and other leaders of the Linkley business community. Alternatively, you can visit us between 8 A.M. and 6 P.M. on weekdays for a personal tour or simply go to www.swannspace.com.

147. What is indicated about Swann Space?

(A) It caters mainly to workers in creative industries.
(B) It provides technical support to its members.
(C) It is located in a prestigious neighborhood.
(D) Its members have access to exercise machines.

148. What will Swann Space do on May 3 ?

(A) Raise a monthly rate
(B) Lead a tour of a facility
(C) Welcome a new executive
(D) Host a networking event

Questions 149-150 refer to the following e-mail.

```
═══════════════════════════════ E-Mail message ═══════════════════════════════

  From:        Eiji Furuta

  To:          Jill Bennett

  Subject:     Delivery packaging

  Date:        April 3
```

Hi Jill,

Customer Service has let me know that several of our grocery delivery customers have contacted us about our meat packaging. Apparently, they are concerned that the meat is only packed in our normal packaging (a foam tray covered with stretchable film). They would like another layer to be added to protect the other products from bacteria in case this packaging fails and the meat's juices leak.

Now, we haven't received any reports of the normal packaging actually failing, so I'm not convinced that it has to be upgraded. However, I think we should at least look into ways to accommodate these customers' wishes. Could you research additional packaging options and the cost and environmental impact involved in using them? I'd like a short report on your findings by the end of the month.

Thanks,

Eiji

149. What are customers concerned about?

(A) The use of non-recyclable packaging materials
(B) The temperature of meat rising to an unsafe level
(C) Staff not handling delivery containers gently
(D) Foods becoming cross-contaminated

150. What does Mr. Eiji suggest about a potential change to some packaging?

(A) It may not be necessary.
(B) It must be introduced slowly.
(C) It requires Ms. Bennett's approval.
(D) It will be unpopular with employees.

Hadnar City Community Newsletter

Hadnar City Garden Club (HCGC)

Come and join us as we begin our new season! Our first meeting of the year will be held on Monday, March 13 at 7:00 P.M. at our usual venue, the Hadnar Community Center. Patrick Lett and Gina Lu will give a lecture and demonstration about "How Honeybees Help Gardeners." As members of the Hadnar City Beekeepers Association, they are committed to educating the public on the environmental benefits of honeybees. Their lecture will include valuable advice on designing gardens that will attract bees. This program will be interactive, so please bring your questions.

We hope to see a lot of new faces next Monday. An individual membership to the HCGC costs $20 per year, and membership registration forms will be available at the meeting. A complete calendar of our upcoming field trips, plant sales, and volunteer activities can be found online at www.hcgc.org.

Test 5

151. What is one purpose of the information?

(A) To announce a change in venue
(B) To recruit new members for a club
(C) To seek feedback about a previous lecture
(D) To highlight a local environmental problem

152. According to the information, what is available on the HCGC Web site?

(A) A schedule of events
(B) A membership application
(C) A map of the city
(D) A discussion forum

Questions 153-154 refer to the following text-message chain.

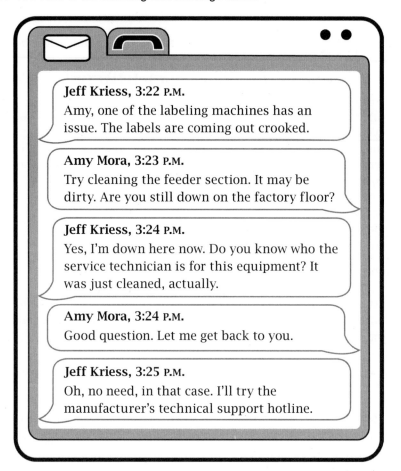

Jeff Kriess, 3:22 P.M.
Amy, one of the labeling machines has an issue. The labels are coming out crooked.

Amy Mora, 3:23 P.M.
Try cleaning the feeder section. It may be dirty. Are you still down on the factory floor?

Jeff Kriess, 3:24 P.M.
Yes, I'm down here now. Do you know who the service technician is for this equipment? It was just cleaned, actually.

Amy Mora, 3:24 P.M.
Good question. Let me get back to you.

Jeff Kriess, 3:25 P.M.
Oh, no need, in that case. I'll try the manufacturer's technical support hotline.

153. Where most likely is Mr. Kriess?

(A) In a production plant
(B) In a printing shop
(C) In a building's lobby
(D) In a computer store

154. At 3:24 P.M., what does Mr. Mora most likely mean when she writes, "Good question"?

(A) Mr. Kriess has pointed out an important problem.
(B) She is unsure of whom to contact about a repair.
(C) She does not know why a machine is malfunctioning.
(D) Mr. Kriess has reminded her about an urgent task.

8. Code of Conduct

As the exposition is primarily intended as a venue for the sharing of knowledge, the exhibitor and its representatives will not engage in selling, order-taking, etc., on the expo floor. Similarly, no prices may be displayed in the contracted exhibition space.

In order to encourage the free flow of visitors throughout the venue, exhibitors will not place any representatives or materials outside of the contracted exhibition space. Similarly, the placement of representatives and materials within the space must be arranged so that they draw attendees in instead of filling the aisles.

Like all attendees, exhibitor representatives must wear their official expo credentials and be appropriately dressed in business or business casual attire at all times.

Any demonstrations or other activities engaged in by the exhibitor will not generate a noise of greater than 85 decibels.

Exhibitors will not be allowed to dismantle their exhibits or begin packing before the official end of the expo.

Test 5

155. What is stated about the exposition?

(A) Its purpose is educational.
(B) It will occupy several buildings.
(C) It has been held before.
(D) It is free for members of the press.

156. The word "flow" in paragraph 2, line 1, is closest in meaning to

(A) sequence
(B) direction
(C) quantity
(D) circulation

157. What does the excerpt specify about exhibitors?

(A) The amount of electricity they can use
(B) The kind of handouts they can distribute
(C) The loudness of the sounds they can make
(D) The number of representatives they can send

GO ON TO THE NEXT PAGE

Questions 158-161 refer to the following article.

Local Business

(September 13)—With the opening of a Cainlen Superstore just two weeks away, the Bakert Merchants Association (BMA) has begun an initiative that encourages consumers to support local businesses. At least thirty stores have hung "Buy from Bakert" signs in their front windows.

Like other Cainlen locations across the nation, the new Bakert store stretches over 180,000 square feet of land and will sell groceries, clothing, and electronics and boast a garden supply center and a photo developing lab. The massiveness of its floor plan meant that its construction was subject to public review regarding potential harm to plants and wildlife near its site on Todd Road.

At that time, the BMA almost succeeded in blocking the development by pressing the city council to consider its effects in another area—that of local commerce. The BMA argued that Cainlen would put smaller retailers out of business and thus weaken the community in the long term.

However, the council was more persuaded by Cainlen representatives' claims that the store would ultimately benefit Bakert by creating new jobs for its citizens and allowing them to enjoy the chain's famously low prices.

BMA president and Bakert Sporting Goods owner Laura Comstock says the Buy from Bakert campaign "just asks people to think before they shop" and adds that it will continue "for as long as it feels necessary".

158. Why was the article written?

(A) To publicize a campaign led by local retailers
(B) To explain the history of a nationwide company
(C) To describe the opening celebration of a new store
(D) To invite citizens to a city council meeting

159. According to the article, what can visitors to a Cainlen Superstore do?

(A) Have a portrait photograph taken
(B) Fill a prescription for medication
(C) Buy landscaping goods
(D) Eat at a restaurant

160. The word "area" in paragraph 3, line 3, is closest in meaning to

(A) size
(B) field
(C) distance
(D) region

161. What is NOT mentioned as a possible effect of a new Cainlen Superstore?

(A) An increase in employment opportunities
(B) New types of products becoming available
(C) The closing of other businesses
(D) Damage to the environment

Molsher University

Department of Music

Ottawa, ON K1A 4H9

Dear Alumni and Friends:

Molsher University has had the use of new pianos for the past year thanks to the "Giving Music" program operated by the Tynor Arts Foundation (TAF). — [1] —. Now, as part of the program, we are offering a selection of the pianos to the public for purchase.

The instruments available will include grand pianos, upright pianos, and digital pianos from leading manufacturers. Most of them are still under warranty, and delivery arrangements can be made on site upon purchase. — [2] —.

To view and purchase an instrument, please visit the Center for the Arts on Saturday, February 10 between 2:00 P.M. and 6:00 P.M. No appointment is needed. — [3] —. The center is located on Canby Road, between First and Second Street. A $2-per-hour rate applies to all street parking in the vicinity. Alternatively, paid parking is available in the center's garage. For directions, please visit www.arts-center.org. — [4] —.

A portion of the proceeds from each instrument is returned to the TAF to maintain Giving Music, which plays an important part in our department's ability to give quality music instruction.

Regards,

Paul Lembke
Interim Chair, Department of Music
Molsher University

162. What is the main purpose of the letter?

(A) To welcome new staff to a department
(B) To give details about a fund-raising sale
(C) To thank donors for their contributions
(D) To announce a program's expansion

163. What is suggested about the Center for the Arts?

(A) It is usually closed on weekends.
(B) It has more than one entrance.
(C) It does not have free parking nearby.
(D) It is operated by volunteers from the TAF.

164. In which of the positions marked [1], [2], [3], and [4] does the following sentence best belong?

"It generously supplies our department with high-quality instruments at no cost every year."

(A) [1]
(B) [2]
(C) [3]
(D) [4]

GO ON TO THE NEXT PAGE

Padgino Employee Satisfaction Survey Report

Executive Summary

Tayona Consulting Services conducted a survey to measure the job satisfaction of employees of Padgino. Data was primarily collected with the use of the survey platform ZestSurvey. Employees were asked to numerically rate their satisfaction with factors such as company management, job duties, and employee benefits. The list of questions and a detailed analysis of the collected data are included in this report's appendices. Four supplementary interviews were conducted with employees who indicated willingness to further discuss their answers. To protect these employees' privacy, these interviews are not described in detail in this report.

The findings indicate that employees are satisfied with most aspects of their jobs and particularly their pay. The only part of the survey with a significant number of negative ratings is that of employee support. It appears that when employees encounter a problem during a call, they are often directed to connect the customer to a manager. In such cases, the employee does not learn how the problem can be resolved in the future. Employees expressed frustration with this situation. Therefore, this report proposes that regular training sessions be held to teach employees how to successfully deal with recurring problems.

---

165. Who most likely were the survey participants?

(A) Retail store clerks
(B) Bank tellers
(C) Flight attendants
(D) Call center representatives

166. How was the survey data mainly obtained?

(A) Through specialized software
(B) Through individual interviews
(C) Through paper questionnaires
(D) Through focus group discussions

167. What does the report recommend doing?

(A) Discontinuing service to difficult customers
(B) Increasing employee compensation
(C) Providing ongoing instruction to staff
(D) Directing supervisors to manage less strictly

Questions 168-171 refer to the following online chat discussion.

        — ☐ X

Danica Fay [11:02 A.M.]
In-Tak, a law firm just ordered six Ivy desks through our Web site. I know our stock of the walnut wood is low, so I wanted to check with you before I gave them an estimated ship date.

In-Tak Lee [11:03 A.M.]
We don't have enough walnut left for that. Three of the desks would be delayed by an extra month.

Danica Fay [11:04 A.M.]
Well, I'd hate to lose this client. What if we offered them Ivy desks in another type of wood?

In-Tak Lee [11:04 A.M.]
Hmm. Let me bring Bente in. Her team builds them.

In-Tak Lee [11:05 A.M.]
Bente, are there any alternative woods that you could use to make the Ivy desk? We're almost out of walnut.

Bente Dahl [11:07 A.M.]
Oak would work. It's also a hard wood, and it's got a similar color.

Danica Fay [11:08 A.M.]
If we use that, could the order be shipped within the usual four weeks?

In-Tak Lee [11:08 A.M.]
Yes. We have plenty of oak.

Danica Fay [11:09 A.M.]
That's much better. I'll ask whether the law firm is interested.

In-Tak Lee [11:10 A.M.]
OK, but you should probably add "backordered" banners to the pages of our larger walnut products. We can't do custom orders for every client.

168. What does the chat participants' company manufacture?

(A) Packaging
(B) Car parts
(C) Clothing
(D) Furniture

169. What does Ms. Dahl confirm?

(A) A color scheme has been decided.
(B) A product could be made with another material.
(C) Her team understands a manufacturing process.
(D) Her schedule for the next month is not yet full.

170. At 11:09 A.M., what does Ms. Fay most likely mean when she writes, "That's much better"?

(A) A new sample item is more attractive.
(B) A shorter production time is preferable.
(C) A client will appreciate a price reduction.
(D) An order should be shipped over land.

171. What does Mr. Lee recommend that Ms. Fay do?

(A) Update a company Web site
(B) Withdraw from a negotiation
(C) Display an advertisement in a store
(D) Add a feature to the design of some goods

GO ON TO THE NEXT PAGE

Test 5

Questions 172-175 refer to the following article.

Galtwood Native to Open Restored Antrell Theater

GALTWOOD (June 22)—After much painstaking restoration work, Galtwood native Jude Raglan says that the Antrell Theater will reopen in the fall with a performance of *A Faraway Year*.

During an interview at a Lockett Street café, Mr. Raglan says that the idea of restoring the theater drew him back to Galtwood after twenty years away. — [1] —. He was working as an administrator at a Latimev theater when he learned during a family visit two years ago that Antrell Theater was about to close.

"I was shocked," he says. The old theater, which sits at the corner of Fourth Street and Nichols Boulevard, had been a beloved part of his youth. He recalls, "We used to walk over from our house on Carden Lane. Seeing *The Glass Flag* there even inspired me to work in theater."

Antrell Theater's owners, however, said that it was no longer profitable. — [2] —. So Mr. Raglan bought it for the low price they were asking, quit his job, and set about restoring it with the help of a grant from the Galtwood city council.

The work, he explains, has focused on revealing and replicating the beauty of its original design. — [3] —. At the same time, some modernizing improvements, such as better accessibility for wheelchairs, have also been made.

Mr. Raglan says he chose *A Faraway Year*, the story of a group of friends' journey through a fantastical land of witches and giants, for the theater's first show because "it's a production that people of all ages can enjoy". — [4] —. He encourages those interested in being part of its cast or crew to visit www.antrelltheater.com for more information.

172. What does the article mention about Mr. Raglan?

(A) He is a friend of the theater's previous owners.
(B) He was a professional actor for two decades.
(C) He received funding from the city of Galtwood.
(D) The first play he attended was *The Glass Flag*.

173. Where did Mr. Raglan live when he was young?

(A) On Lockett Street
(B) On Fourth Street
(C) On Nichols Boulevard
(D) On Carden Lane

174. What is stated about *A Faraway Year*?

(A) Its plot includes magical elements.
(B) It is based on a popular film.
(C) Some of its characters are children.
(D) Mr. Raglan will modernize its setting.

175. In which of the positions marked [1], [2], [3], and [4] does the following sentence best belong?

"Work crews used old photographs of the theater for reference."

(A) [1]
(B) [2]
(C) [3]
(D) [4]

GO ON TO THE NEXT PAGE

Test 5

From	Rodolfo Escorza <r.escorza@oqui-mail.com>
To	Marcella Perry <anb-recruiting.com>
Subject	Re: Opportunity at Osborne Rental Cars
Date	August 7
Attachment	Résumé

Dear Ms. Perry,

Thank you for contacting me. I am familiar with Osborne Rental Cars and interested in this opening. Please see my attached résumé. It will give you a fuller understanding of my career than what you saw on my profile page on Exec-Link.

However, I should tell you up front that I am content at Panella and wouldn't consider leaving for anything less than a very good opportunity. This means a situation where I have both the support of global management and the autonomy to make the best decisions for the U.S. market. If Osborne is willing to meet these conditions, I would be happy to discuss this position further.

If you do decide to move forward with my candidacy, please let me know what the next steps will be. I will be away from Atlanta on a business trip for the next few days, but I will make sure to keep up with my correspondence.

Sincerely,

Rodolfo Escorza

Senior Vice President of Operations
Panella Airlines

Osborne Rental Cars Appoints New U.S. Executive

(October 22)—Osborne Rental Cars has hired Rodolfo Escorza as the director of its operations in the United States. Mr. Escorza will replace Jeanette Huff, who is retiring.

Mr. Escorza has worked in many sectors of the travel and airline industries over his 23-year career. As a senior product officer for Globastic, an online seller of consumer travel products, he oversaw the creation of its popular rental car booking service. Most recently, he served as the senior vice president of operations for Panella Airlines. In that position, he built up the airline's safety ratings without increasing its operational costs.

Osborne Rental Cars is a British company that entered the U.S. market just four years ago. It now has 18 locations and over 500 vehicles in the states of Florida and Georgia. From its national headquarters in Atlanta, Mr. Escorza is expected to lead its continued growth throughout the southeastern United States and beyond.

176. How does Mr. Escorza suggest that Ms. Perry became aware of him?

(A) Through a Web site
(B) Through a magazine article
(C) Through a mutual acquaintance
(D) Through a conference

177. In the e-mail, the word "meet" in paragraph 2, line 4, is closest in meaning to

(A) gather
(B) perform
(C) border
(D) fulfill

178. What is implied about Mr. Escorza?

(A) Osborne Rental Cars agreed to raise his salary.
(B) His hiring process took less than two months.
(C) He spoke to Ms. Perry on the phone.
(D) He will not have to relocate.

179. According to the press release, what did Mr. Escorza accomplish at Panella Airlines?

(A) A reduction in spending
(B) Improvements in safety
(C) The implementation of a new offering
(D) Higher passenger satisfaction ratings

180. What is mentioned about Osborne Rental Cars?

(A) It has branches in many countries.
(B) It is attempting to expand.
(C) Its founder is leaving the workforce.
(D) It was acquired by another company.

GO ON TO THE NEXT PAGE

```
www.nationalbaseballfederation.com/llions/tickets/groups
```

Group and Corporate Options for Single Games

Attending a Lanchner Lions game is a fun way to celebrate events with family or friends, entertain clients, or show appreciation for employees. Lanchner Field boasts an array of amenities to suit the needs of groups and corporations, and all options include discounts on stadium parking.

The Dugout Section	Lions Patios
- Regular outdoor seating - $15 in "Lions Bucks", which can be used at Lanchner Field shops - Pay per ticket; available for groups of 10 to 200	- Outdoor seating at tables with excellent sight lines - Unlimited ballpark fare (hot dogs, popcorn, etc.) from admission through the 7th inning - Pay per ticket; best for groups of 2 to 6
The Fastball Deck	**Diamond Lounges**
- Indoor, non-private seating - Unlimited ballpark fare from admission through the last inning - Pay per ticket; best for groups of 2 to 10	- Indoor, private seating - "Classic" catering package - 25 tickets
Home Run Suites	
- Indoor, private seating in one of two premium locations behind home plate - "Premium" catering package - 50 tickets	

For more information, call the hospitality department at (708) 555-0186 or click here to access its live chat service.

From:	Andre Delgado
To:	Keith Holt
Subject:	Request
Date:	July 15

Keith,

I'd like you to look into purchasing tickets for the Lions baseball game on the evening of August 4. I was just speaking with Ms. Walsh, the head of the group visiting us from Rioso Electronics that week, and she mentioned that she loves the sport. I feel confident about the proposal we're putting together for marketing their tablet computers, but we should also make sure the delegation enjoys their time in Lanchner.

As for the type of seats, please choose a climate-controlled option so that we can avoid the summer heat. And of course, it will need to accommodate between 15 and 20 people, since the group will also include members of our staff.

Please research the options and send me your recommendation.

Thanks,

Andre

181. What is indicated about the Lanchner Lions hospitality department?

(A) Its office overlooks Lanchner Field.
(B) It operates an online messaging platform.
(C) It offers service in multiple languages.
(D) It is seeking new employees.

182. What is NOT a benefit of Lions Patios?

(A) Complimentary food
(B) A lower parking fee
(C) Early admission to the stadium
(D) A clear view of the game

183. Where does Mr. Delgado most likely work?

(A) At a sports television network
(B) At an industrial supply company
(C) At an electronics manufacturer
(D) At an advertising agency

184. What is indicated about Ms. Walsh?

(A) She is a baseball fan.
(B) She will lead a presentation.
(C) She used to live in Lanchner.
(D) Her birthday is August 4.

185. Which option will Mr. Holt most likely recommend?

(A) The Dugout Section
(B) The Fastball Deck
(C) A Diamond Lounge
(D) A Home Run Suite

GO ON TO THE NEXT PAGE

Questions 186-190 refer to the following Web page, work schedule, and client reviews.

http://www.jackfogelphotography.com

Jack Fogel Photography

☛ Jack Fogel Photography is the county's top real estate photography company. Whether you are a real estate agent or a private homeowner seeking to sell a property quickly, we will provide the highest quality photos possible. Unlike other local real estate photography companies, we offer the following:

- Guaranteed next-day turnaround – you will get your images by the next day, or you pay nothing* (*two-day turnaround for Saturday visits)
- Easy payment options – pay by credit card or company check on the day of the photo shoot
- Fixed pricing, regardless of the property's size – visit our rates page for details

Our founder, Jack Fogel, still conducts many photo shoots himself, and every photographer in our network has at least 10 years of experience. They will choose the best angles and lighting to help you sell your property faster. To read reviews about our services, visit our testimonials page.

Today's Photo Sessions

Date: *August 23*

Photographer	Time	Address	# of photos	Payment	Notes
Jack Fogel	11:00 A.M.	177 Dunn Street	25	Credit card	External flash needed
Jack Fogel	2:00 P.M.	865 Reyes Avenue	15	Credit card	
Brad Mull	3:00 P.M.	262 Fir Drive	10	Check	
Ellen Sato	1:00 P.M.	190 Moy Road	35	Credit card	Repeat client

http://www.jackfogelphotography.com/testimonials

Most recent client reviews

"As a real estate agent, I highly recommend this company. I booked a photo shoot with little notice a few weeks ago, and the photographer, Ms. Sato, arrived early and worked hard. I got the high-quality images back in only two days, and I was even allowed to pay with a company check."

— Lisa Tobias, Wednesday, August 26

"They are professional yet affordable. I originally booked the 10-photo package, but at the last minute I decided to have 15 pictures taken. I'm glad I did. Mr. Mull, the photographer, was excellent. I just received my photos today, two days after the shoot. They look great."

— Larry Hodges, Monday, August 25

186. What is NOT listed as a unique feature of Mr. Fogel's company?

(A) Its guaranteed delivery times
(B) The payment methods it accepts
(C) Its use of sophisticated equipment
(D) The price structure of its services

187. In the work schedule, what is implied about the 11:00 A.M. photo session?

(A) It is the largest session of the day.
(B) It will mainly take place indoors.
(C) It is for a regular client.
(D) It will last less than three hours.

188. In the client reviews, the word "notice" in paragraph 1, line 2, is closest in meaning to

(A) warning
(B) attention
(C) resignation announcement
(D) public posting

189. What do the clients who posted the recent reviews have in common?

(A) Their photos required special editing.
(B) Their shoots happened on a Saturday.
(C) They work for real estate agencies.
(D) They paid deposits in advance.

190. Which property did Mr. Hodges most likely have photographed?

(A) 177 Dunn Street
(B) 865 Reyes Avenue
(C) 262 Fir Drive
(D) 190 Moy Road

Telges Hotel

Morning Sun Four-Cup Coffee Maker Instructions for Use

1. Remove the pot from the hotplate.
2. Open the cover of the pot and use the pot's indicator lines to fill it with the desired amount of water. Close the pot.
3. Pour the water from the pot into the water reservoir in the top of the coffee maker.
4. Return the pot to the hotplate.
5. Insert a paper filter into the filter basket in the top of the coffee maker.
6. Put the desired amount of ground coffee into the filter. We recommend 1 to 1.5 tablespoons of ground coffee per cup.
7. Close the top of the coffee maker securely.
8. Push the "On" button to begin brewing. Do not remove the pot from the hotplate until the power light shuts off.

The machine must be cleaned between uses, but we ask that you do not attempt to do it yourself. The cleaning staff will do it during their daily visit to your room.

From:	Vicky Schmidt
To:	Travis Peters
Subject:	Coffee maker issue
Date:	January 11

Hi Travis,

We've received some minor guest complaints about the Lywen "Morning Sun" coffee makers that we bought through Bruggins Limited. Guests are saying that you can't actually put the filter into the filter basket without taking it out of the coffee maker first. But the instructions we've provided don't specify that, and the filter is a little hard to remove, so people aren't sure if it's the right thing to do or not.

I checked the instructions for the Jares Home coffee makers in our business suites and the Qualcedo in the breakfast room, and the results were mixed—the Qualcedo model mentions removing the basket and the Jares doesn't. But we've never had complaints about the Jares.

Could you look into the issue?

Thanks,

Vicky

From:	Travis Peters
To:	Vicky Schmidt
Subject:	Re: Coffee maker issue
Date:	January 12

Hi Vicky,

I called the manufacturer, and they confirmed that the instructions should have specified that extra step. They were very apologetic and said they're planning to revise the product manual. So, I will replace the current instructions in our guest rooms with a corrected version.

You know, this happened because I just copied the instructions in the manual without actually trying them out. That had been fine for our other machines. But now I see that it is risky. I'm sorry, and I won't make that mistake again.

Best,

Travis

191. In the instructions, what is suggested about the Morning Sun coffeemaker?

(A) It allows users to adjust a brewing duration.
(B) Telges Hotel supplies a special type of water for it.
(C) Its indicator light comes on to signal that it must be cleaned.
(D) Telges Hotel expects it to be needed only once per day.

192. Which step does Ms. Schmidt indicate users are unsure about?

(A) Step 2
(B) Step 3
(C) Step 5
(D) Step 6

193. According to the first e-mail, what does Telges Hotel have?

(A) A clothes-washing service
(B) A dedicated place for morning meals
(C) A computerized system for analyzing guest complaints
(D) A loyalty program for business travelers

194. Which company did Mr. Peters most likely contact?

(A) Lywen
(B) Bruggins Limited
(C) Jares Home
(D) Qualcedo

195. What does Mr. Peters apologize for?

(A) Not testing the instructions himself
(B) Copying a manual's contents incorrectly
(C) Not buying a different coffee machine instead
(D) Dismissing a coworker's concerns

GO ON TO THE NEXT PAGE

◄ ► http://www.cityofrowder.gov/business/signs

Sign Regulations

Rowder's Department of Planning and Development Services (DPDS) oversees the enforcement of city regulations relating to commercial uses of signs. Its staff is committed to providing a favorable atmosphere for businesses while also maintaining a pleasant living space for citizens.

The city's comprehensive sign ordinances are listed here, but for your convenience, information on the most common types of temporary commercial signs is provided below in a simplified form.

Grand opening signs: With the approval of the DPDS, a new business can display signs advertising its opening for up to 30 days. This is the only circumstance in which free-standing outdoor signs are permitted.

Holiday promotional signs: Businesses do not need the DPDS's approval to display promotional signs related to Christmas or New Years for up to 15 days, and signs related to six other specified holidays for up to 5 days.

Other large promotional banners: The DPDS's approval is required for all other promotional banners over 20 square feet in surface area. These banners may be displayed for up to 14 days at a time, three times per year.

Do you disagree with a DPDS decision? Click here to find out how to file an appeal with the city council.

City of Rowder
Department of Planning and Development Services

Commercial Sign Permit Application

Applicant: Gail Brock

Address: 922 Ellis Drive, Rowder, MI 48097

Phone: (810) 555-0124   **E-mail:** gail.brock@ubi-mail.com

Business: Radiant Gem Salon

Address: 640 Main Street, Rowder, MI 48097   **Site ID:** 0943-886

Project description:

I would like to hang a 24-square-foot banner to advertise the fifth anniversary of the salon's opening and a related sales event. The banner would display "Radiant Gem Salon Celebrates 5 Years in Business" in large text and "15% Off All Services June 6–8" in smaller text. It would have a pink background and black writing. Please see the attachment for a mock-up image of the design. I would hang it over the top half of one of the salon's windows for the maximum time allowed, ending on June 8.

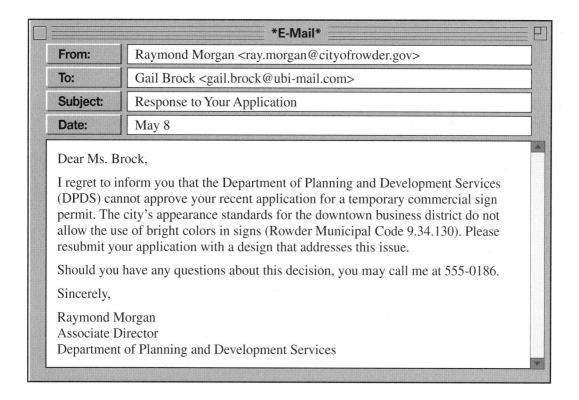

```
*E-Mail*

From:      Raymond Morgan <ray.morgan@cityofrowder.gov>
To:        Gail Brock <gail.brock@ubi-mail.com>
Subject:   Response to Your Application
Date:      May 8
```

Dear Ms. Brock,

I regret to inform you that the Department of Planning and Development Services (DPDS) cannot approve your recent application for a temporary commercial sign permit. The city's appearance standards for the downtown business district do not allow the use of bright colors in signs (Rowder Municipal Code 9.34.130). Please resubmit your application with a design that addresses this issue.

Should you have any questions about this decision, you may call me at 555-0186.

Sincerely,

Raymond Morgan
Associate Director
Department of Planning and Development Services

196. What does the Web page state about the DPDS?

(A) Its employees are highly qualified.
(B) It is the result of a departmental merger.
(C) It tries to serve the needs of two groups.
(D) It recently created new sign-related ordinances.

197. How long could Ms. Brock potentially display her sign?

(A) For up to 5 days
(B) For up to 14 days
(C) For up to 15 days
(D) For up to 30 days

198. What does Ms. Brock suggest about her business?

(A) It appears in a photograph attached to the form.
(B) It is located at an intersection.
(C) It used to have another owner.
(D) It will offer customers a temporary discount.

199. Why does Mr. Morgan reject Ms. Brock's application?

(A) A required piece of text is missing from a design.
(B) Her sign's color would not conform to a regulation.
(C) A city district does not allow certain advertising methods.
(D) The placement of her sign would not obey safety standards.

200. What is NOT mentioned as an action Ms. Brock could take?

(A) Contacting Mr. Morgan
(B) Altering the plan for the sign
(C) Asking the city council to review a decision
(D) Submitting an application for a different permit

Stop! This is the end of the test. If you finish before time is called, you may go back to Parts 5, 6, and 7 and check your work.

TEST 6

READING TEST

In the Reading test, you will read a variety of texts and answer several different types of reading comprehension questions. The entire Reading test will last 75 minutes. There are three parts, and directions are given for each part. You are encouraged to answer as many questions as possible within the time allowed.

You must mark your answers on the separate answer sheet. Do not write your answers in your test book.

PART 5

Directions: A word or phrase is missing in each of the sentences below. Four answer choices are given below each sentence. Select the best answer to complete the sentence. Then mark the letter (A), (B), (C), or (D) on your answer sheet.

101. Penelope Styles is proud of the artwork ------- created for the lobby of the Andrews Plaza Building.

(A) hers
(B) her
(C) she
(D) herself

102. Call Klinter Associates today to schedule an initial ------- with one of our experienced attorneys.

(A) consultant
(B) consultation
(C) consulted
(D) consults

103. Peltzer Real Estate's Web site provides an ------- of the monthly energy expenses for each of its listed properties.

(A) advice
(B) estimate
(C) evidence
(D) advantage

104. Thanks to the new television commercials, enrollment in carpentry classes is up 22% ------- last semester.

(A) than
(B) above
(C) throughout
(D) from

105. Lina Oakes will be ------- employee productivity this month at Deerford Cosmetics' main warehouse.

(A) assessing
(B) presenting
(C) disciplining
(D) resuming

106. Redesigning our Web site might help us attract a broader range of clients and ------- boost profits.

(A) closely
(B) rarely
(C) typically
(D) consequently

107. The emergency exit row seats are the only ------- equipped with a fold-out table that is stored in the armrest.

(A) some
(B) these
(C) whose
(D) ones

108. The employee handbook provides guidance on acceptable apparel and footwear, ------- not on hairstyles.

(A) but
(B) for
(C) or
(D) even

109. Situated at the foot of Emerald Mountain, Selway Valley ------- the cleanest natural spring water in the country.

(A) excels
(B) emphasizes
(C) distinguishes
(D) boasts

110. Now that the bank has switched to electronic billing, its stationery expenses are ------- lower.

(A) highly
(B) heavily
(C) considerately
(D) noticeably

111. Lost property is kept at the gym's reception desk for a maximum of two months, after which the item -------.

(A) is discarded
(B) has been discarded
(C) will be discarding
(D) discards

112. All employees ------- for any reason must submit an official letter to Human Resources for recordkeeping purposes.

(A) resign
(B) resigned
(C) resigning
(D) resignation

113. The hotel manager says there are ------- ten complaints about the noise from the poolside renovations.

(A) all
(B) already
(C) other than
(D) as many

114. The school board will debate a ------- educational proposal to change the way that the region's history is taught.

(A) controversy
(B) controversially
(C) controversial
(D) controversies

115. The new ward was named after Dr. Suzuki in ------- of his valuable contributions to the hospital.

(A) association
(B) obligation
(C) recognition
(D) occasion

116. Before he steps down as CFO of Hardin Furniture in July, Mr. Grady will play an active role in choosing his -------.

(A) successor
(B) succeeds
(C) succeeding
(D) success

117. In the summer, Colfax Public Library will be showing animated movies ------- for children as young as three.

(A) appropriate
(B) equivalent
(C) cautious
(D) tentative

118. To ensure a fun and effortless trip, book your summer vacation ------- Royes Travel Agency.

(A) to
(B) with
(C) around
(D) by

119. Caroba Manufacturing ------- strict safety policies to prevent accidents in its factories.

(A) entails
(B) produces
(C) presumes
(D) enforces

120. By the time the workers arrived to repair the store's roof, a large amount of merchandise -------.

(A) has damaged
(B) had been damaged
(C) will be damaged
(D) is damaged

GO ON TO THE NEXT PAGE

Test 6

121. The museum's south wing is temporarily off-limits to visitors ------- the new prehistoric fossil exhibits are being set up.

(A) touring
(B) as
(C) so that
(D) who

122. The first customer ------- the café's reward book with one hundred stickers will receive a year's supply of free coffee.

(A) fills
(B) is filling
(C) to fill
(D) filled

123. Mr. Sulaiman prefers training new hires in customer service etiquette ------- after they join his company.

(A) personally
(B) more personal
(C) personal
(D) personalizes

124. Individuals caught littering ------- 50 meters of a body of water are subject to a $250 fine.

(A) nearby
(B) during
(C) within
(D) anywhere

125. Mr. Menzel is doubtful that an expansion will truly make the CEO's annual sales target ------- by the end of the year.

(A) attain
(B) attainable
(C) attained
(D) attainment

126. Some government offices ------- avoid providing a contact phone number in an effort to cut down on the volume of public inquiries.

(A) adequately
(B) formerly
(C) proficiently
(D) intentionally

127. Many fast food outlets have significantly changed their menus in response to a ------- in demand for vegan-friendly products.

(A) pace
(B) flow
(C) surge
(D) phase

128. If we do not clearly determine our objectives ------- the commencement of negotiations, we will be unable to bargain effectively.

(A) before
(B) on behalf of
(C) according to
(D) against

129. The Owenberg Fresh Air Society uses sensors placed around the city to carry out pollution ------- in real-time.

(A) monitor
(B) monitors
(C) monitored
(D) monitoring

130. On the weekend of the music festival, the city council will ------- the charges for parking along Main Street.

(A) contend
(B) waive
(C) delegate
(D) redeem

Directions: Read the texts that follow. A word, phrase, or sentence is missing in parts of each text. Four answer choices for each question are given below the text. Select the best answer to complete the text. Then mark the letter (A), (B), (C), or (D) on your answer sheet.

Questions 131-134 refer to the following notice.

Attention Fairfax Public Library Members:

When using the library's hold system, please bear in mind that items are only held at the circulation desk for 24 hours. ------- you fail to collect an on-hold item within that timeframe, it will
131.
be put back into circulation.

-------. First, you can speak with an employee at the circulation desk. When the item you desire
132.
becomes available, it will be set aside for you. You may also request a hold on items using the database terminals ------- throughout the library, or through our Web site.
133.

Please keep the above time limit in mind when ------- items. It is one of the policies that support
134.
our goal of ensuring that our members have a wide selection of books, magazines, and multimedia materials to enjoy.

131. (A) Should
(B) Although
(C) Yet
(D) Until

132. (A) Applying for a membership could not be easier.
(B) Our collections can be browsed in person or online.
(C) There are several ways to put a hold on library items.
(D) Please follow these steps to file a complaint.

133. (A) to install
(B) install
(C) installing
(D) installed

134. (A) purchasing
(B) reserving
(C) returning
(D) reading

Questions 135-138 refer to the following e-mail.

From: Mina Wang
To: All staff members
Subject: Customer Service Workshops
Date: January 21

Dear employees,

I am writing to remind you all about our first Positive Customer Interaction (PCI) workshop on February 5. It ------- by Tim Ellison, a renowned motivational speaker and the author of *Key Factors for Customer Satisfaction*.
    135.

We have asked Mr. Ellison to discuss the attitudes and practices that are most ------- to
                                                                                136.
attracting, satisfying, and retaining customers. As the first in our series, this session will also be

------- by an introductory talk by our president, Howard Botting, who will discuss the overall aims
137.
of the workshops. There is space for no more than 100 participants at each workshop, and

registrations will be accepted on a first-come, first-served basis. -------.
                                                                    138.

Regards,
Mina Wang
Personnel Manager

---

135. (A) was led
(B) leads
(C) is leading
(D) will be led

136. (A) critics
(B) critical
(C) critically
(D) criticisms

137. (A) preceded
(B) officiated
(C) combined
(D) recorded

138. (A) Rest assured that these fees will be used to enhance your experience.
(B) A makeup session for the canceled seminars will be held at later dates.
(C) Requests for a full refund can be made by phone or e-mail.
(D) Please visit the personnel office if you are interested in attending.

Questions 139-142 refer to the following letter.

May 22

Gabriella Heron

4827 Dayton Avenue

Bakersfield, CA 93311

Dear Ms. Heron,

Please be advised that Hercules Fitness Center is scheduled to undergo renovations in order to expand. ------, we will be shut down from June 3 to June 9. We have acquired the adjacent
139.
commercial unit recently vacated by Rantillo Apparel and will be converting it into an additional space mainly containing fitness studios of various specifications. ------. The currently available
140.
areas of the center will reopen for business as usual at 7 A.M. on June 10, and the new space will be brought into ------ the next month.
141.

We apologize for this temporary ------ and appreciate your understanding. Also, we encourage
142.
you to check our July schedule, available at our front desk and online at www.herc-fitness.com/ schedule from June 15, to see the new offerings.

Best wishes,

Gary Salinger

Hercules Fitness Center

Test 6

139. (A) Occasionally
(B) After that time
(C) Accordingly
(D) Even so

140. (A) This will allow us to offer a wider range of exercise classes.
(B) An increasing number of people are shifting to a healthier lifestyle.
(C) There is no longer sufficient room in the existing parking lot.
(D) Our facilities have been highly praised by local publications.

141. (A) used
(B) use
(C) using
(D) users

142. (A) relocation
(B) negligence
(C) congestion
(D) closure

Questions 143-146 refer to the following article.

Midlands Biosciences Names New R&D Director

Midlands Biosciences ------- Clifford Maxwell of its R&D department to be the company's new
143.
research and development director. The biofuel maker announced Mr. Maxwell's ------- in a post
144.
on its Web site yesterday. Midlands CEO Ellen Stern is quoted as saying, "It is my pleasure to
welcome Mr. Maxwell to our executive team. His expertise will enable us to succeed ------- our
145.
research goals."

According to the Web post, Mr. Maxwell joined Midlands soon after earning a doctoral degree in
biotechnology. -------. He rose steadily through the company's ranks thanks to his diligence and
146.
innovative ideas. In his new role, which he will assume on December 10, Mr. Maxwell will
determine and implement Midlands' research and development objectives.

---

143. (A) to choose
(B) has chosen
(C) was chosen
(D) choose

144. (A) retirement
(B) candidacy
(C) initiative
(D) appointment

145. (A) that reaches
(B) reached by
(C) in reaching
(D) the reaching of

146. (A) The move reflects the company's goal of
becoming more streamlined.
(B) While he began as a junior researcher, he
did not hold that position for long.
(C) The board of directors is conducting an
extensive search to find his replacement.
(D) His latest research project received a lot of
attention within the industry.

PART 7

Directions: In this part you will read a selection of texts, such as magazine and newspaper articles, e-mails, and instant messages. Each text or set of texts is followed by several questions. Select the best answer for each question and mark the letter (A), (B), (C), or (D) on your answer sheet.

Questions 147-148 refer to the following invitation.

You are invited to enjoy an exclusive demonstration here at Salisbury Culinary Institute!

Visiting Guest Chef:

Gustav Perot

Owner of the five-star restaurant
The Partridge Bistro in New York City

Chef Perot will demonstrate how to expertly prepare a variety of Mediterranean dishes in Instruction Kitchen 3 on June 14 from 9:15 to 11:45 A.M.

This demonstration has been specifically arranged for those currently enrolled in the institute's advanced cooking courses. Space is limited to 250 people, and you must confirm your intention to attend by speaking with Ms. Ibrahim in the administration office before June 8.

---

147. For whom is the invitation most likely intended?

(A) Culinary instructors
(B) Food critics
(C) Aspiring cooks
(D) Restaurant diners

148. What is indicated about the event?

(A) It happens every year.
(B) Attendees will take part in the activity.
(C) It will finish in the afternoon.
(D) Admission is restricted.

Rialto Pet Mart would like to reward our loyal customers as part of
our tenth anniversary celebrations. From March 1 to March 14,
you may hand over this voucher to any checkout operator to receive
$15 off any purchase valued at $50 or more. This voucher may not be
exchanged for cash, cannot be used at our automated checkout
kiosks, and will expire at 9 P.M. on March 14. Please visit
www.rialtopetmart.ca/voucher for full terms and conditions.

149. What is mentioned about Rialto Pet Mart?

(A) It recently launched a new branch.
(B) It is currently hiring checkout operators.
(C) It runs a membership reward program.
(D) It has self-checkout machines.

150. What must shoppers do in order to use the voucher?

(A) Spend a minimum amount
(B) Visit the store twice
(C) Present it to a store manager
(D) Activate it on a Web page

Susie Levy	**2:04 P.M.**
Hideo, are you still down on the third floor?	
Hideo Fujita	**2:05 P.M.**
Yes, the meeting just finished. Do you need something?	
Susie Levy	**2:06 P.M.**
I'm trying to set up that new graphic design suite on my computer, but I'm having problems. I was hoping you could find the person who recommended it to me.	
Hideo Fujita	**2:07 P.M.**
Was it someone from here in our company?	
Susie Levy	**2:08 P.M.**
Yes, the tall guy on the Web design team.	
Hideo Fujita	**2:10 P.M.**
Our Web design team is rather large.	
Susie Levy	**2:11 P.M.**
Oh, sorry. He's the one who has short blonde hair. He might be new.	
Hideo Fujita	**2:13 P.M.**
I think I know who you're talking about. His name is Chris, right?	
Susie Levy	**2:14 P.M.**
Yes, that sounds right! Please ask him to stop by my office whenever he's free. Thanks, Hideo.	

151. What's Ms. Levy's problem?

(A) She is running late for a meeting.
(B) An electronic device will not turn on.
(C) She cannot install some software.
(D) Some graphics are confusing.

152. At 2:10 P.M., what does Mr. Fujita mean when he writes, "Our Web design team is rather large"?

(A) It is unnecessary to hire new workers.
(B) He needs a more detailed description.
(C) He is worried about the size of a space.
(D) Someone on the team probably has a certain skill.

GO ON TO THE NEXT PAGE

Test 6

Glow **Car Wash**

3476 Kingsman Street, Lansing 48213

Try our new Deluxe Wash & Premium Detailing services!

Deluxe Wash

$25 per car, approximately 15 minutes required
- Pre-wash, undercarriage wash, exterior wash
- Machine air dry plus manual soft towel dry

Premium Detailing

$35 per car, approximately 45 minutes required
- Full interior cleaning (X-Press Air technology to remove dust and dirt from all crevices and cracks)
- Conditioning of all upholstery and shampooing of carpeted areas
- Hand-applied "X-polymer" wax for supreme paint protection and shine

Deluxe Wash + Premium Detailing Package Deal available on request for only $50!

---

153. What is indicated about Glow Car Wash?

(A) Its Deluxe Wash takes over half an hour.
(B) It offers a discount for combined services.
(C) It specializes in a certain type of automobile.
(D) It sells some cleaning products.

154. What is the X-polymer product used for?

(A) Conditioning a vehicle's interior
(B) Repelling water from a vehicle's windows
(C) Protecting a vehicle's paint job
(D) Removing dirt from a vehicle's exterior

Dear Martino Health Foods Customers,

Our owner, Dino Martino, and the rest of the Martino Health Foods team have enjoyed serving you at our location on Harrison Street for the past five years, but it is now time for a change. Ever since we expanded our range of stock to include organic groceries, we have been struggling to keep up with demand. You may have noticed that checkout lines continue to get longer, and we can barely cope with the number of downtown orders we receive per day.

Therefore, we will move to a larger building in the downtown core on July 1 so that we can increase our stock volume and serve our customers more efficiently. The new and improved Martino Health Foods will be situated at 411 Thrush Drive.

Rest assured that all customer memberships and rewards will remain valid and unchanged. Further details regarding the move will be provided via our monthly newsletter. If you do not already receive the newsletter, please visit the customer service desk to subscribe.

Thank you!

Test 6

155. What is the main purpose of the notice?

(A) To publicize a new type of merchandise
(B) To announce the store's relocation
(C) To introduce a new business owner
(D) To provide details of upcoming renovations

156. What is most likely true about Martino Health Foods?

(A) It solicits feedback from employees.
(B) It is a family-operated business.
(C) It is experiencing financial difficulties.
(D) It is becoming increasingly popular.

157. What are some readers of the notice encouraged to do?

(A) Sign up for a regular mailing
(B) Recommend a friend for a membership
(C) Attend a grand opening event
(D) Make use of rewards points quickly

GO ON TO THE NEXT PAGE

PLAYSMART TOYS, INC.
OFFICIAL PRESS RELEASE

Playsmart has become aware of recent reports and rumors that one of our toy ranges is made using low-quality materials and workmanship. These stories have understandably led to many customers contacting us to ask whether the toys are truly of inferior quality, and in some cases, demanding a refund. — [1] —. The range in question is our recently-launched Galaxy Pirate toy line, which includes action figures and vehicles from the animated television show of the same name. Rumors have been circulating online that the toys are manufactured abroad and break very easily as a result of poor construction and cheap plastic. This has resulted in a noticeable drop in sales, and several Web sites have even removed our advertisements for the range. — [2] —.

While it is true that the toys are produced at a plant overseas, Playsmart works in close collaboration with the plant operators to ensure that high-grade materials are being used and proper manufacturing steps are being adhered to. — [3] —. We can unequivocally state that the toys are professionally assembled and highly durable. This morning, we have posted a video on our Web site that shows the entire manufacturing process for the Galaxy Pirate toys. — [4] —. We guarantee all customers that Playsmart remains fully committed to producing the best toys on the market.

---

158. What is the purpose of the press release?

(A) To launch a new line of toys
(B) To issue a product recall
(C) To describe how to obtain a refund
(D) To address customer concerns

159. What is NOT stated about the Galaxy Pirate toys?

(A) They are manufactured in a different country.
(B) They have been discontinued.
(C) They have been advertised online.
(D) They are based on some entertainment media.

160. In which of the positions marked [1], [2], [3], and [4] does the following sentence best belong?

"In fact, we carry out weekly quality assurance checks on the assembly line."

(A) [1]
(B) [2]
(C) [3]
(D) [4]

========================= E-Mail message =========================

From:	Chinenye Umeh
To:	All Employees
Subject:	Employee referral bonus
Date:	June 29

Hi everyone,

Now that we have to quickly expand our workforce as a condition of the funding we received from Ribdins Group, it seems like a good time to remind all of you about our employee referral bonus program. This entitles employees to a $500 bonus for a successful referral for an open position. If you are interested in participating, please regularly check the "Jobs" page on our Web site.

Note that it is very important that you only recommend candidates that have all of the qualifications required for the position. We instituted the new tiered payment system at the beginning of this year to cut down on the number of unhelpful recommendations. As you might remember, it entails issuing the bonus to the referrer in stages:

- First 20% when the referred person is chosen for an in-person interview
- Additional 30% when the candidate is hired
- Remaining 50% when the new hire is still an employee after 90 days

See page 28 of the employee handbook for more details on the program, including instructions on how to submit your referral. For any issues not covered in the handbook, you may call (ext. 233) or e-mail me.

Thanks,

Chinenye Umeh
Director of Human Resources
Patondo Technology

---

161. What is indicated about Patondo Technology?

(A) It recently attracted outside investment.
(B) A new page has been added to its Web site.
(C) Its employee handbook is distributed electronically.
(D) It implemented referral bonuses for the first time this year.

162. What does Ms. Umeh suggest has been a problem with the program in the past?

(A) Submission of referrals through incorrect channels
(B) Lack of diversity among referred people
(C) Endorsement of unsuitable candidates
(D) Late payment of bonuses

163. At what point will a referrer have received exactly half of the bonus?

(A) After an application has been completed
(B) After a face-to-face interview has been proposed
(C) After a job offer has been accepted
(D) After a probationary period has passed

GO ON TO THE NEXT PAGE

Questions 164-167 refer to the following online chat discussion.

 — □ X

Leah Young [1:04 P.M.]
Do you have a moment, Wade and Ursula? Management just told me about two new destinations they have chosen for us to cover in our next European Explorer travel books — one country and one city.

Wade Corbin [1:08 P.M.]
Great! What are they?

Leah Young [1:10 P.M.]
They want a full extensive guide for Luxembourg and a pocket-sized city guide for Venice.

Ursula Eriksson [1:11 P.M.]
Oh, I've spent a lot of time in Luxembourg, and it's an amazing place.

Leah Young [1:14 P.M.]
Definitely. So, we'll be sending two field researchers to Luxembourg from May 1 to June 29, and one to Venice from June 1 to June 30. We'll receive all of their notes in the first week of July, and then we'll have approximately one month to edit the information before the scheduled publication and launch dates.

Ursula Eriksson [1:16 P.M.]
That gives us plenty of time. And I can start designing the layout for each publication this week so that we're all prepared for the editing stage.

Wade Corbin [1:22 P.M.]
I'm not sure that's wise, Ursula. Remember the Bulgaria book?

Ursula Eriksson [1:23 P.M.]
Good point, Wade. I'll wait to see exactly what Management wants to be included this time.

Leah Young [1:25 P.M.]
That sounds good. All right, I'll give you more information after my meeting with Management tomorrow.

---

164. Why did Ms. Young send the first message to her colleagues?

(A) To ask for their opinions on competing proposals
(B) To recommend some changes to their publications
(C) To thank them for their work on a project
(D) To let them know about upcoming assignments

165. What is suggested about the Venice book?

(A) It will be published in July.
(B) It will be compact.
(C) It is a revised edition.
(D) It is Mr. Corbin's responsibility.

166. What information does Ms. Young provide?

(A) The qualifications for some researchers
(B) The maximum length of some writings
(C) The durations of some trips
(D) The reasons for some edits

167. At 1:22 P.M., what does Mr. Corbin most likely mean when he writes, "Remember the Bulgaria book"?

(A) Ms. Eriksson has another task that must be finished soon.
(B) Ms. Eriksson's expectations for a new book's success are too high.
(C) Ms. Eriksson could use an existing layout template for reference.
(D) Ms. Eriksson should not begin a process too early again.

Winners Announced for This Year's British Architecture Awards

LONDON (15 December)—Fifty extraordinary structures chosen from around 250 shortlisted candidates have won the prestigious British Architecture Awards this year for the most innovative architecture by British architects or foreign architects with offices in Britain. Now in their twenty-second year, the British Architecture Awards are jointly presented by the London Museum of Architecture & Design and the British Centre for Urban Planning & Art. They recognize the architects of exceptional contemporary structures that shape our lives in a wide variety of ways, including skyscrapers, corporate headquarters, bridges, park pavilions, hospitals, private residences, and academic institutions.

Among this year's biggest winners were Simon Thorpe for Maitland Street Car Park, a stunning 9-level, 768-space car park with various eco-friendly features in Central Manchester; Marcus Fryer for Horizon Bridge, a breathtaking 195-meter-long pedestrian bridge uniquely equipped with 4,500 blinking LED stars synchronized with music; and Isobel McDuff for The Spire, an elegant 28-floor apartment building with a heated rooftop swimming pool that is located near Edinburgh's busy shopping areas.

As in previous years, because of the sheer number of winners, the awards were given out over the course of three evenings and three ceremonies from Friday, 12 December to Sunday, 14 December. The opening night saw the awards presented in the Corporate and Commercial categories, Saturday's awards were for the Residential and Urban Planning categories, and the final night recognized those in the Institutional category. Maitland Street Car Park made history by being the first structure to win its architect two awards in the same year: one in the Urban Planning category and the top honour, Most Innovative Design of the Year.

Test 6

---

168. What is stated about the British Architecture Awards?

(A) Two organizations collaborate to issue them.
(B) They come with various amounts of prize money.
(C) Their list of categories recently increased.
(D) Only British citizens are eligible for them.

169. According to the article, what is special about Mr. Fryer's design?

(A) Its integration with a commercial area
(B) Its environmentally-friendly features
(C) Its combination of light and sound
(D) Its impressive height

170. When most likely did Ms. McDuff accept her award?

(A) On December 12
(B) On December 13
(C) On December 14
(D) On December 15

171. What is suggested about Mr. Thorpe?

(A) He has won awards in the past.
(B) He presented an award on Saturday.
(C) He was given a lifetime achievement award.
(D) He received two awards this year.

GO ON TO THE NEXT PAGE

To:	Len Goldman <lgoldman@whizzomail.net>
From:	Mi-Kyung Choi <mkchoi@summitsc.com>
Subject:	SparkLite Fire Pit
Date:	September 6

Dear Mr. Goldman,

I was very excited to receive the information pack for your latest patented invention. The SparkLite Fire Pit seems fantastic and is certainly a product that we would be highly interested in making available in Summit Sports & Camping Stores. We love its portability and solar charging option. — [1] —. However, I do have a few questions about its design. First, would you mind clarifying how the air jets pump oxygen into the wood fire? — [2] —. Also, the information pack outlines how the fire intensity can be controlled via smartphone app. Which operating systems is the app compatible with?

— [3] —. While I would very much like for you to answer those quick questions at your earliest convenience, I would also like you to visit our headquarters in person with one of the fire pits. As I am sure you know, our executives prefer to see new products in use firsthand before approving a contract to purchase and sell them. We would be grateful if you could attend a meeting at 2 P.M. on September 13 at which you would be allotted one hour to showcase the device's functions and capabilities.

Based on the product specifications and photographs you sent me, not to mention the popularity of your camping stove and multifunctional cooler, which are still among our top sellers, I am confident that we will choose to stock the SparkLite Fire Pit. — [4] —. I look forward to hearing from you.

Sincerely,

Mi-Kyung Choi
Head of Purchasing
Summit Sports & Camping

172. What is NOT true about the SparkLite Fire Pit?

(A) It can use renewable energy.
(B) It is easy to transport.
(C) It connects to mobile devices.
(D) It is awaiting a patent confirmation.

173. What does Ms. Choi ask Mr. Goldman to do?

(A) Give a live demonstration
(B) Send over a prototype
(C) Suggest contract terms
(D) Visit a manufacturing site

174. What can be inferred about Summit Sports & Camping?

(A) It is planning to expand its selection of sportswear.
(B) It is Mr. Goldman's former employer.
(C) It stocks other products created by Mr. Goldman.
(D) It has placed an initial order for SparkLite Fire Pits.

175. In which of the positions marked [1], [2], [3], and [4] does the following sentence best belong?

"We have some minor concerns regarding the safety of such a mechanism."

(A) [1]
(B) [2]
(C) [3]
(D) [4]

GO ON TO THE NEXT PAGE

Questions 176-180 refer to the following advertisement and registration form.

Growth Strategies for Newly Founded Companies

Do you want to grow and improve your new company, but you are unsure where to start? Fulbridge Growth Strategies is the place for you. We offer seminars on an array of subjects that are useful to novice business owners. Each one is taught with a combination of wisdom earned through decades of hands-on professional work and cutting-edge understanding of the latest management techniques and trends. Below is a sample of what we will be offering this fall:

Coming Together (Seminar Code #1809) - Price: $48

This seminar provides a variety of strategies for encouraging your employees to work together effectively.

→ Wednesday, September 3, 10:00 A.M. - 12:00 P.M.; Main Building, Room 204

Tomorrow's Market (Seminar Code #3487) - Price: $95

This seminar offers advice on how to attract a wider range of clients to your products or services.

→ Wednesday, September 24, 10:00 A.M. - 3:00 P.M.; Training Center, Room 3

Broaden Your Horizons (Seminar Code #2276) - Price: $149

This seminar gives business owners essential tips on what to consider when planning to open a new branch.

→ Wednesday, October 15, 10:00 A.M. - 4:00 P.M.; Main Building, Room 206

Keeping the Pace (Seminar Code #3785) - Price: $109

This seminar introduces popular employee perks, such as flexible working hours, and explains how to implement them.

→ Wednesday, November 5, 10:00 A.M. - 4:00 P.M.; Training Center, Room 4

Visit www.fulbridge-gs.com for more information.

Fulbridge Growth Strategies - Seminar Registration

Name:	Robin Booky
Address:	84 Ballack Avenue, Seattle, WA 98121
Phone:	555-0139
E-mail:	r.booky@globenet.com
Seminar Code:	#3487
Payment Method:	Bank Transfer
Comments:	I am really looking forward to attending my first Fulbridge seminar at your training center in September. As requested, I have sent the $59 registration fee to your corporate account. My only concern is that I might not make it to the center by 10 A.M., as I live very far away. I would appreciate it if someone could let me know via e-mail whether this would be a major problem. Thank you.

176. What is implied about Fulbridge Growth Strategies?

(A) It provides sample teaching materials on its Web site.
(B) Its instructors have practical business experience.
(C) Its offerings can be customized upon request.
(D) It holds the same set of seminars every season.

177. What topic is NOT covered by the listed seminars?

(A) Advising customers on purchasing decisions
(B) Fostering teamwork between employees
(C) Adding new work sites to a company
(D) Granting certain benefits to staff

178. In the advertisement, the word "flexible" in paragraph 5, line 2, is closest in meaning to

(A) gradual
(B) obedient
(C) bendable
(D) variable

179. What information has Mr. Booky most likely read incorrectly?

(A) The location of the seminar
(B) The fee for the seminar
(C) The month of the seminar
(D) The start time of the seminar

180. What does Mr. Booky ask Fulbridge Growth Strategies to do?

(A) Determine the seriousness of a risk
(B) Make an exception to a policy
(C) Compile some alternative options
(D) Give regular updates on a situation

GO ON TO THE NEXT PAGE

CASTELLENTE STORAGE COMPANY
RESIDENTIAL STORAGE UNITS

Castellente's residential storage units come in a variety of sizes and can be rented for as little as two weeks or as long as you like. Each one is on the ground floor for convenient packing and unpacking, and has its own security alarm and camera. You keep the key to your unit's lock so that you can access your belongings at any time, on any day of the week. What's more, our built-in heating and cooling systems ensure that it never becomes dangerously hot or cold in your unit.

Unit Type	Size	Weekly / Monthly Price*	Suitable for:
A	13.6m²	£52 / £208	The contents of a three-bedroom house
B	6.7m²	£32 / £128	The contents of a one-bedroom apartment
C	3.4m²	£18 / £72	Several items of furniture
D	1.6m²	£10 / £40	A few boxes

*A deposit of £50.00 is also required. Castellente Storage Company may keep all or part of this if the rental unit is found to be dirty or damaged at the end of the rental period.

---

http://www.birminghamsmartreviews.com/storage/0421

Castellente Storage Company Reviews

I rented a unit from Castellente to store my belongings in when I had to move to Germany for a six-month study program. My experience couldn't have been better. First, I wasn't sure how much space I needed, so their representative kindly explained the options without pressuring me. She also made sure I understood the terms of the rental contract before I signed it. And when I brought over my stuff— a bed, a dresser, some small appliances—the worker on duty offered to help me unload it and organise it all efficiently. Six months later, everything was right where I'd left it, safe and dry. Castellente is an excellent self-storage facility.

By Kiera Ritz, 2 December

181. What is NOT mentioned as a feature of each storage unit?

(A) Temperature control
(B) 24-hour accessibility
(C) A security system
(D) An electric power outlet

182. According to the information, for what is there an additional charge?

(A) Choosing a rental period of less than two weeks
(B) Renting a unit on the ground floor
(C) Leaving a unit in poor condition
(D) Replacing the key to a unit

183. Which type of storage unit did Ms. Ritz most likely rent?

(A) Type A
(B) Type B
(C) Type C
(D) Type D

184. Why did Ms. Ritz need to store some items?

(A) She went to live abroad temporarily.
(B) She relocated to a smaller home.
(C) She was remodeling her residence.
(D) She bought supplies for a new hobby.

185. What does Ms. Ritz indicate about Castellente Storage Company?

(A) Its facilities are spacious.
(B) Its staff are helpful.
(C) Its reputation is excellent.
(D) Its contracts are easy to understand.

GO ON TO THE NEXT PAGE

Questions 186-190 refer to the following Web pages and e-mail.

---

http://www.rosensteinconcerthall.com/events

| About Us | Event | Tickets | Location | Contact |

Rosenstein Concert Hall
Upcoming Events

Click on the title of the event to learn more and purchase tickets. Alternatively, explore our themed series such as The Rosenstein Family (shows for music lovers of all ages) and Great Performers (showcases for instrumentalists from around the world) by clicking here.

Sat., Nov. 15, 7:30-9:30 P.M. **A Celebration of Celia Moody** *The Burgess Orchestra performs selected works of the famous composer.*	Sat.-Sun., Nov. 22-23, 7:30-10:00 P.M. **Renditions in Jazz** ** *XO Jazz Quartet presents a jazz spin on modern pop hits.*
Sat., Nov. 29, 7:00-8:30 P.M. **A Night to Remember** *Tenor Antonio Bianchi sings some of his signature pieces.*	Sun., Dec. 7, 7:00-9:00 P.M. **Songs of *Green Valley* *** *The Burgess Orchestra plays the score of the classic motion picture.*

*Events with an asterisk (*) are only available to subscribers. Click here to see the full list of benefits of becoming a Rosenstein Concert Hall subscriber.

**Events with two asterisks are not included in subscriptions and must be paid for separately.

---

http://www.rosensteinconcerthall.com/tickets/payment/18780

| About Us | Event | Tickets | Location | Contact |

Rosenstein Concert Hall
Thank you for your purchase!

Your tickets will be mailed to the address below. However, we recommend that you print or take a screenshot of this page in case you need to exchange or cancel your tickets before they arrive.

Booking Confirmation Number: 59289289

Name:	Wayne Judge	E-mail:	wjudge@solomail.com
Address:	114 Redwood Park Burgess, TX 77014	Telephone:	555-0103

Date of Event:	November 15		
Number of Tickets:	2	Seating Area:	C
Price:	$100	Payment Method:	YowzaPay Online
Purchase Date:	October 20		

Please check the details of your booking carefully. If you discover an error, e-mail us at inquiries@rosenstein.com for assistance.

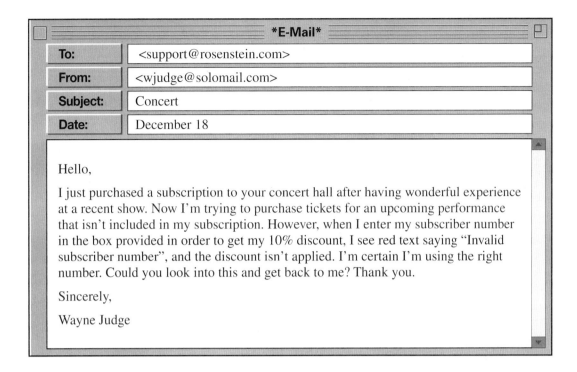

E-Mail

To:	<support@rosenstein.com>
From:	<wjudge@solomail.com>
Subject:	Concert
Date:	December 18

Hello,

I just purchased a subscription to your concert hall after having wonderful experience at a recent show. Now I'm trying to purchase tickets for an upcoming performance that isn't included in my subscription. However, when I enter my subscriber number in the box provided in order to get my 10% discount, I see red text saying "Invalid subscriber number", and the discount isn't applied. I'm certain I'm using the right number. Could you look into this and get back to me? Thank you.

Sincerely,

Wayne Judge

186. What do the events listed in the first Web page have in common?

(A) They take place on the weekend.
(B) They last the same amount of time.
(C) They involve groups of performers.
(D) They are each only offered on a single day.

187. What does the second Web page instruct Mr. Judge to do?

(A) Check his e-mail inbox
(B) Save his booking information
(C) Print his tickets at home
(D) Note a cancellation deadline

188. What did Mr. Judge hear at the concert he attended?

(A) A vocal performance
(B) Music created for a film
(C) Songs converted into a different genre
(D) Musical pieces written by one person

189. Why did Mr. Judge write the e-mail?

(A) To express appreciation for a service
(B) To report a technical problem
(C) To seek confirmation of a purchase
(D) To inquire about the terms of an agreement

190. What is most likely true about Mr. Judge?

(A) He is entitled to attend exclusive performances.
(B) He will begin receiving a regular publication.
(C) He has misunderstood a benefit of a special status.
(D) He is interested in child-friendly entertainment.

GO ON TO THE NEXT PAGE

Test 6

Charleston Central Museum

We will be hosting a reception on February 26 to mark the opening of the science exhibition "The Invisible World: Microorganisms" in March. As someone who has supported our institution with generous donations over the years, we hope you will join us to celebrate this exciting event.

Reception Details:

Saturday, February 26, 6 P.M.–9:30 P.M.

East Wing of Charleston Central Museum

Buffet provided by Silver Star Catering Co.

"The Invisible World: Microorganisms" will run from March 3 to May 31 and feature more than 250 exhibits depicting the wonders of the smallest forms of life.

The Midwestern Gazette

Charleston Central Museum Claims Prestigious Honor

by Jill Bradford

MERRITT (April 20)—Charleston Central Museum was awarded the Scientific Literature Award at the first-ever Midwestern Arts & Science Awards ceremony on April 18. Put on by the Midwestern Knowledge Foundation, the event took place at Washington Convention Hall in front of an audience of around 6,000 members of the arts and science communities.

Charleston Central Museum won the prize for the detailed and entertaining information pack that supplements its exhibition "The Invisible World: Microorganisms." Lead designer Yui Takahashi accepted the award and thanked graphic designer Raymond Schlupp, who provided many of the pack's illustrations. She also promised that the pack would be publically available on the new version of the museum's Web site, which is currently under construction.

"The Invisible World: Microorganisms" was conceptualized by scientist Thomas Ellson, who enlisted the knowledge and expertise of architect Fiona Watson to construct the exhibits. The exhibition has been a tremendous success for the museum, with ticket sales topping those of all previous exhibitions. After its run there comes to an end, it will be transported to neighboring Georgetown to be displayed at Georgetown Science Institute for approximately two months.

To:	<jillbradford@midwestern.com>
From:	<kevinshaw@gomail.net>
Date:	April 22
Subject:	Recent article

Dear Ms. Bradford,

I was initially happy to see your recent coverage of Charleston Central Museum's success at the Midwestern Art & Science Awards. However, as I read through the article, excitedly waiting to see my name in print, I found that my work had been mistakenly attributed to Fiona Watson, who merely served as an advisor to me during the process. This was very disappointing. I encourage you to carry out more thorough research for future articles.

Sincerely,

Kevin Shaw

191. Who is the notice intended for?

(A) Museum employees
(B) Potential exhibitors
(C) Financial donors
(D) University students

192. In the notice, the word "mark" in paragraph 1, line 1, is closest in meaning to

(A) characterize
(B) evaluate
(C) acknowledge
(D) brand

193. What is indicated about the Midwestern Art & Science Awards ceremony?

(A) It had not been held previously.
(B) It took place at Charleston Central Museum.
(C) It was hosted by Ms. Takahashi.
(D) It was broadcast to a live audience.

194. What most likely will happen on June 1 ?

(A) The nomination period for an honor will begin.
(B) Some educational materials will be released online.
(C) A talk will be sponsored by a funding organization.
(D) An exhibition will move to a different town.

195. What did Mr. Shaw probably do?

(A) Provided artwork for an information pack
(B) Accepted an award on behalf of an institution
(C) Developed the concept for an exhibition
(D) Constructed some museum displays

City of Sotorik

Temporary Food Facility Application

Please submit this application to receive permission to operate a temporary food and/or drink facility within Sotorik city limits during a special event.

Applicant: Lynne McKinley

Business: Lynne's Tacos

Address: 32 West Road, Sotorik, NY 47372

Phone: 555-0153

Event Name: Global Crafts Festival

Organizer: Sotorik Tourism Board

Date/s: May 8-10

Location: Sotorik Grand Park

Supplementary materials (required unless specified otherwise):

(a) Photographs of all facilities and equipment to be used on-site for food/drink preparation and service

(b) A list of all food/drink items to be sold and the ingredients of all of the non-prepackaged items

(c) A check payable to Sotorik City Hall for $50 OR, if the application is being submitted fewer than 10 days before the event, for $100

(d) A certificate of inspection from the Sotorik Department of Health (only required for vendors intending to use gas-powered appliances in their facility)

Signature of applicant: *Lynne McKinley*

Date: April 19

To	Angel Munoz and 3 others
From	Lynne McKinley
Date	May 3
Subject	Global Craft Festival booth
Attachment	⋃Schedule, Festival Map

Hi all,

Thanks for agreeing to represent Lynne's Tacos at the Global Crafts Festival this weekend. In addition to following the instructions on the attached schedule, please note that there will be a city-issued food safety checklist that the early shift workers must fill out, and that the late shift workers on Friday and Saturday must carefully store the food and lock up our booth. The actual food sale period will start a half hour later and end a half hour earlier than the shifts, so we should have plenty of time for these tasks.

If we start to run low on supplies before the dinner rush, if the gas grill stops working (which has happened before), or if another problem comes up, please contact me or Grady, who will be managing the restaurant all weekend.

Thanks,
Lynne

	Friday	Saturday	Sunday
Early shift (9:30 A.M.–2:00 P.M.)	Lynne Kwang-Sun	Lynne Ron	Dallas Kwang-Sun
Late shift (2:00 P.M.–6:00 P.M.)	Angel Dallas	Angel Ken	Dallas Lynne

Lynne's Tacos

Global Crafts Festival Schedule

- Use the vendors' parking area and entrance on Fourth Street.
- Bring a form of ID (your name will be checked against a vendor list).
- Arrive at least 15 minutes early so that you have time to get to the booth.

196. What was Ms. McKinley required to provide with the form?

(A) A list of staff members
(B) A blueprint of a temporary facility
(C) A photocopy of a business license
(D) A payment to a government office

197. In the e-mail, the word "following" in paragraph 1, line 2, is closest in meaning to

(A) complying with
(B) comprehending
(C) accompanying
(D) subsequent

198. What is implied about Ms. McKinley?

(A) Her application had to be expedited.
(B) Her equipment passed an inspection.
(C) She hired a professional food photographer.
(D) She chose to rent a cooking appliance.

199. What will Ron most likely do with a coworker?

(A) Complete some paperwork
(B) Carpool to the festival site
(C) Secure some company property
(D) Pick up some supplies

200. In the attachment, what is suggested about vendors at the Global Crafts Festival?

(A) They are grouped by merchandise type.
(B) They are given identification badges.
(C) They may enter before 9:30 A.M. each day.
(D) They can disassemble their booths on Monday.

Stop! This is the end of the test. If you finish before time is called, you may go back to Parts 5, 6, and 7 and check your work.

Test 6

RC

TEST 7

READING TEST

In the Reading test, you will read a variety of texts and answer several different types of reading comprehension questions. The entire Reading test will last 75 minutes. There are three parts, and directions are given for each part. You are encouraged to answer as many questions as possible within the time allowed.

You must mark your answers on the separate answer sheet. Do not write your answers in your test book.

PART 5

Directions: A word or phrase is missing in each of the sentences below. Four answer choices are given below each sentence. Select the best answer to complete the sentence. Then mark the letter (A), (B), (C), or (D) on your answer sheet.

101. As Ms. Roy's parking space is far from the entrance, Mr. Ezra has kindly agreed to let her park in ------- until her injury heals.

(A) he
(B) his
(C) him
(D) himself

102. The powerful ------- provided by the Yarov-A coat's fabric will make sure you stay warm in the world's coldest places.

(A) protected
(B) protects
(C) protectively
(D) protection

103. Designed to offer as much ------- as possible, the Lorene Convention Center is an ideal venue for a wide variety of events.

(A) flexibility
(B) enthusiasm
(C) financing
(D) accuracy

104. Pattison Bank has been providing entry-level career opportunities to recent university graduates ------- years.

(A) in
(B) following
(C) for
(D) during

105. Restaurant owners ------- face new challenges, especially in today's competitive business environment.

(A) heavily
(B) constantly
(C) diversely
(D) variably

106. When it runs updates, antivirus software may temporarily affect the ------- of your computer.

(A) innovation
(B) measurement
(C) performance
(D) representation

107. A market report indicated that social media marketing reaches young consumers ------- than television advertising.

(A) effective
(B) effectively
(C) more effectively
(D) effectiveness

108. At Klevaratix Supply, we aim to ------- the highest quality kitchen equipment for professional chefs.

(A) commit
(B) earn
(C) remain
(D) produce

184

109. ------- learning to play the guitar, practice with a durable model like the Franmawr-5.

(A) Whether
(B) Since
(C) From
(D) When

110. To prevent ------- of records, a notification appears if the same client number is entered in the database more than once.

(A) transportation
(B) duplication
(C) organization
(D) differentiation

111. Sales of signs and banners have continued to ------- decline as more businesses move online.

(A) steady
(B) steadied
(C) steadily
(D) steadying

112. The safety consultant recommended treating the flooring ------- non-slip finish in order to prevent workplace accidents.

(A) with
(B) of
(C) to
(D) until

113. At the next Town Hall meeting, officials will give a progress report on the construction of the ------- community center.

(A) planned
(B) nominated
(C) acquainted
(D) relieved

114. Smart-Tekk, Inc. makes educational toys that help young children gain ------- with scientific concepts.

(A) familiarly
(B) familiarity
(C) familiarized
(D) more familiar

115. Though some managers may think -------, using off-site storage for old paper documents is a very affordable solution.

(A) particularly
(B) otherwise
(C) moreover
(D) formerly

116. Many entrepreneurs, ------- experience, may make the mistake of expanding their businesses too quickly.

(A) regardless of
(B) instead of
(C) nevertheless
(D) as much as

117. Next time that we buy office furniture, I propose selecting chairs and desks that can ------- to a variety of heights.

(A) raising
(B) raise
(C) be raised
(D) being raised

118. Sunara Food Market ------- all of its produce from local organic farms.

(A) proceeds
(B) succeeds
(C) intends
(D) obtains

119. Keeping your customers fully ------- depends largely on the ability to resolve complaints in a professional manner.

(A) satisfies
(B) satisfied
(C) satisfying
(D) satisfaction

120. Researchers at Novarraic Tech, Inc. have been developing a robot that can teach ------- basic new tasks.

(A) themselves
(B) yourself
(C) itself
(D) ourselves

GO ON TO THE NEXT PAGE

121. Digital videos ------- larger amounts of data than most other applications, especially when they are viewed in high definition.
(A) requiring
(B) to require
(C) having required
(D) require

122. The road improvement project has faced several delays, and sources say that the work may extend ------- June.
(A) along
(B) above
(C) plus
(D) past

123. The recent drop in the value of the dollar has made importing goods from the United States more ------- for us.
(A) profitable
(B) profitability
(C) profiting
(D) profit

124. The new Web site is expected to be launched ------- the developers complete usability testing.
(A) once
(B) ever
(C) whereas
(D) upon

125. The museum's staff and a team of IT experts will work ------- to design a virtual reality exhibit.
(A) relatively
(B) unusually
(C) collaboratively
(D) absently

126. Although the merger discussions have progressed slowly, company negotiators are ------- that a deal will be reached.
(A) ongoing
(B) probable
(C) dedicated
(D) optimistic

127. The new policy allows selected staff to work from home, ------- regular deadlines are met.
(A) as for
(B) provided that
(C) concerning
(D) in case of

128. Rosemary is one of the most commonly used herbs in Italian cooking because the plant ------- in the region's warm, dry climate.
(A) thrives
(B) flatters
(C) characterizes
(D) absorbs

129. If ------- incorrectly, the software program will display an error message on the start-up menu.
(A) installation
(B) installer
(C) installed
(D) installs

130. Ms. Cho has made a detailed transcript of ------- was discussed in the last department meeting.
(A) that
(B) what
(C) everything
(D) it

Directions: Read the texts that follow. A word, phrase, or sentence is missing in parts of each text. Four answer choices for each question are given below the text. Select the best answer to complete the text. Then mark the letter (A), (B), (C), or (D) on your answer sheet.

Questions 131-134 refer to the following e-mail.

To: Don Chen <don-chen@mail.org>
From: Brundy Storage <brundy-storage@mail.com>
Date: January 30
Subject: Update on Space 1032

Dear Mr. Chen,

Please know that we at Brundy Storage appreciate your business and loyalty.

Recently, rental rates have increased due to greater ------- for storage space in this area. Based
                                                        131.
on these market conditions, the new monthly rent for Space 1032 ------- $208 starting on
                                                                  132.
Sunday, March 1.

This ------- represents less than a 2% increase in your rental rate. -------. Your new rate is still
     133.   **134.**
lower than the current rate for first-time customers renting a storage unit the same size as
yours.

Again, we are grateful for your business as a longtime customer of Brundy Storage.

Regards,
The Management at Brundy Storage

131. (A) range
     (B) sales
     (C) demand
     (D) renovation

132. (A) was to be
     (B) will be
     (C) has been
     (D) would have been

133. (A) adjusts
     (B) adjuster
     (C) adjustable
     (D) adjustment

134. (A) We would like to thank all of our
         customers for their input in this matter.
     (B) We wish to emphasize that, with fewer
         tenants, we are now downsizing.
     (C) Be aware that the terms and conditions
         of rental agreements can vary greatly.
     (D) Rest assured that, even at that price, you
         are still receiving a good value.

Petralla Publishing is a leading publisher of instructional books ------- to readers who enjoy

                                                                    135.

hands-on arts and crafts hobbies. Supporting fresh talent and ideas is a key part of our

business. -------, we actively seek book proposals from people who would to like to make a

            136.

useful addition to the body of writing in our field. -------. For many of our authors, writing a book

                                                     137.

was only a ------- dream, something they had hoped to do someday. With our encouragement

            138.

and guidance, they went on to create a beautiful new work for publication. Please click here to

see our submission guidelines.

---

135. (A) caters
(B) catering
(C) is to cater
(D) are catered

136. (A) For that reason
(B) By comparison
(C) Afterward
(D) Alternatively

137. (A) On certain days, educators may request copies of recent titles for review.
(B) We will set up a phone appointment to speak with you further about this.
(C) Our team of editors can make a promising concept for a book into a reality.
(D) Research shows that fairy tales still appeal more to younger readers.

138. (A) distant
(B) vacant
(C) subtle
(D) deep

Questions 139-142 refer to the following article.

DORTLUND (19 March)—The 25th annual Dortlund Folk Music Festival drew a record crowd of over 6,000 people last Saturday and Sunday. According to organizers, this impressive ------- can

139.

be credited to the new features of this year's event. -------. For the first time ever, the

140.

performance lineup included not only popular folk groups but also Cuban mambo bands, Polish dance ensembles, and ------- jazz soloists. There were also chances for attendees to take part

141.

in hands-on workshops ------- to show them techniques for playing various traditional

142.

instruments. Organizers say both of these popular changes will be carried over to next year's festival.

139. (A) prize
(B) funding
(C) turnout
(D) rating

140. (A) They noted that traditional culture may continue to change in the future.
(B) All volunteers received free meals and specially-made festival T-shirts.
(C) In fact, a background in music is not necessary for greater appreciation.
(D) For example, a more diverse array of musical styles was represented.

141. (A) yet
(B) very
(C) even
(D) much

142. (A) designer
(B) designed
(C) to design
(D) designs

GO ON TO THE NEXT PAGE

Questions 143-146 refer to the following information.

The HGA's annual Household Goods Trade Show in Dallas Texas – Why you should attend

For more than 60 years, the Household Goods Association (HGA) ------- the industry's largest
 143.

trade show featuring household goods from the world's leading manufacturers. Purchasing

managers for retail stores attend every year to meet with wholesale suppliers and seize

opportunities to form business partnerships. Are you looking for original merchandise to

distinguish your business from competitors and gain a market advantage? ------- walk the trade
 144.

floor and explore the displays. You are certain to ------- innovative new household products.
 145.

-------. By attending the HGA trade show, you are assured of staying up to date on the latest
 146.

trends in household goods.

---

143. (A) has hosted
(B) was hosted
(C) is being hosted
(D) would have hosted

144. (A) Simply
(B) Lately
(C) Closely
(D) Shortly

145. (A) utilize
(B) navigate
(C) demonstrate
(D) discover

146. (A) There are several other important ways to care for a home.
(B) In addition, there are talks and workshops on current industry issues.
(C) A few of the vintage items on display are over 50 years old.
(D) When your business is finished, enjoy our complimentary lunch buffet.

PART 7

Directions: In this part you will read a selection of texts, such as magazine and newspaper articles, e-mails, and instant messages. Each text or set of texts is followed by several questions. Select the best answer for each question and mark the letter (A), (B), (C), or (D) on your answer sheet.

Questions 147-148 refer to the following notice.

Meeting Room Policy

The Cleary City Public Library's meeting rooms are available at no charge to community groups under the following conditions. All community meetings held in the rooms must be free of charge and open to the public. Meeting rooms are available only during the library's normal opening hours. Requests to reserve a meeting room must be made via the library's online reservation system. Groups may reserve a room for the current month or the following month. Under no circumstances may any group reserve a room for more than one meeting within a 14-day period. Reservations are accepted on a first-come, first-served basis.

Please note that all rooms are equipped with chairs and conference tables. Library-owned audiovisual equipment may be requested on the meeting room application and must be checked out with a library card.

147. What is suggested about the library's meeting rooms?

(A) Their seating may be rearranged by patrons.

(B) They have different maximum capacities.

(C) They do not have audiovisual equipment.

(D) They may be used outside of the library's regular hours.

148. According to the notice, what is true about meeting room reservations?

(A) They will be taken in the order they are received.

(B) There is a penalty for canceling them after a certain point.

(C) They must be requested via an in-person visit.

(D) They must be made one month in advance.

GO ON TO THE NEXT PAGE

Wanted: Graphic Designer (Digital Media)

Company/Location: Strobbels, Inc. Headquarters, Hamilton, Ontario

----

Strobbels, Inc. is seeking a creative individual to design graphics for our digital marketing initiatives. These include the company Web site, online advertising, social media, and mobile phone apps. The successful candidate will also attend industry trade shows on the company's behalf and acquire in-house training to stay current on digital communication trends. Qualifications include a minimum of 2 years' experience as a graphic designer in an advertising agency and proficiency in digital design software.

Strobbels, Inc. is a family-owned chain of convenience stores that provide snacks and quick meals for customers on the go. We have earned recognition from the media as one of the province's five best companies for employees. We are also well known for our strong commitment to the communities in which we are located. Each year, the company sponsors fundraising activities for several charitable organizations.

149. What is mentioned as a requirement for the job?
(A) An educational background in computer programming
(B) Previous employment with an advertising agency
(C) Proven ability to design in-house training courses
(D) Experience with organizing trade show events

150. What is indicated about Strobbels, Inc.?
(A) It has various staff recognition programs.
(B) It recently relocated its headquarters.
(C) It runs a delivery service.
(D) It supports local charities.

Questions 151-152 refer to the following ticket.

City Railways   Ticket Coupon 01 of <u>01</u>   Retain During Trip

---

Name of passenger: Steven Rigby   **Reservation #:** 834253   19 March
Place of issue: Dover   **Issued:** In-person
Class of Seating: Business Class   **Train Number:** 192
From: Dover   **To:** Vernon Heights
Departs: 1:45 P.M.   **Arrives:** 3:44 P.M.

Photo ID required on board   Total charge: $53*
*Refund/exchange penalties apply   *Change fee applies

Join our Frequent Rider Program and get discounted upgrades from Coach to Premium Class seating. Visit www.city-railways.com for more details.

---

151. What is implied about Mr. Rigby?

(A) He will eat a meal while on board.
(B) He is a frequent rider on City Railways.
(C) He changed an itinerary at no charge.
(D) He must present identification during his trip.

152. What is suggested about City Railways?

(A) It accepts reservations by telephone.
(B) Its Web site was recently upgraded.
(C) Its trains have multiple classes of seating.
(D) It offers discounts for tickets booked online.

GO ON TO THE NEXT PAGE

Questions 153-154 refer to the following text-message chain.

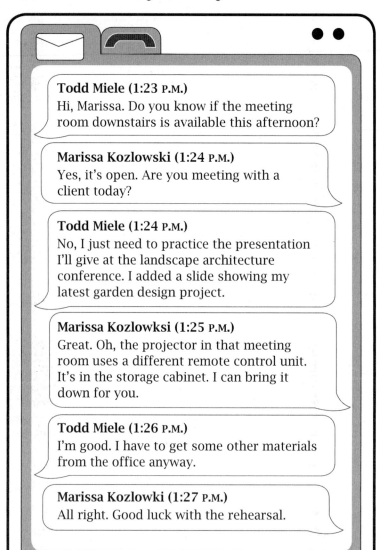

Todd Miele (1:23 P.M.)
Hi, Marissa. Do you know if the meeting room downstairs is available this afternoon?

Marissa Kozlowski (1:24 P.M.)
Yes, it's open. Are you meeting with a client today?

Todd Miele (1:24 P.M.)
No, I just need to practice the presentation I'll give at the landscape architecture conference. I added a slide showing my latest garden design project.

Marissa Kozlowksi (1:25 P.M.)
Great. Oh, the projector in that meeting room uses a different remote control unit. It's in the storage cabinet. I can bring it down for you.

Todd Miele (1:26 P.M.)
I'm good. I have to get some other materials from the office anyway.

Marissa Kozlowki (1:27 P.M.)
All right. Good luck with the rehearsal.

153. Who most likely is Mr. Miele?

(A) A building superintendent
(B) A conference organizer
(C) A landscape architect
(D) An information technology expert

154. At 1:26 P.M., what does Mr. Miele mean when he writes, "I'm good"?

(A) He is skilled at making presentations.
(B) He does not need further assistance.
(C) He has a suitable amount of storage space.
(D) He has a strong working relationship with a client.

Questions 155-157 refer to the following online article.

http://www.keys-to-success.com/articles/023421

Some common advice that experts share

Showing homes well requires preparation. Clients need to feel confident in your expertise in local neighborhoods and properties for sale. — [1] —. When you drive a prospective buyer to a home for viewing, be sure you have memorized the directions ahead of time. You may even want to practice driving to the home the day before the showing. — [2] —. Getting lost en route to a property will suggest a lack of knowledge about the community. When you are giving house tours to prospective buyers, it is a good idea to bring several copies of a buyers' packet with information about the home and the surrounding district. — [3] —. Even a paper map of the local area can be helpful. Also, confirm you have the correct key to access the home. — [4] —. Having the wrong key, or no key, will not make a good impression.

155. Who is the article most likely intended for?

(A) Real estate salespeople
(B) Residential renovation specialists
(C) Volunteer tour guides
(D) First-time home buyers

156. What does the writer of the article suggest doing?

(A) Having extra sets of door keys made
(B) Mastering travel routes in advance
(C) Stopping briefly at scenic viewpoints
(D) Researching community service opportunities

157. In which of the positions marked [1], [2], [3], and [4] does the following sentence best belong?

"Any recipients will appreciate it, and you will be able to refer to the material to answer questions if needed."

(A) [1]
(B) [2]
(C) [3]
(D) [4]

Test 7

GO ON TO THE NEXT PAGE

Yvonne Clark
803 Bates Street
Bowen City, IL 60419

Dear Ms. Clark,

As one of the coaches of Bowen City's Youth Soccer League, you should be aware of an upcoming special meeting of Bowen City's Parks and Recreation Committee. It will take place on Tuesday, February 4 at 6:30 P.M. in Room 5 of City Hall.

The topic will be Parks Department director Fiorello Sauro's proposal to allocate a portion of the Parks Department's budget to upgrade Hohman Park's recreational amenities. Specifically, photos taken of the Youth Soccer Stadium's equipment storage buildings show exposed nails, holes in the siding, and cracked windows that must be taken care of.

Director Sauro will also discuss installing modern electric lighting on the stadium's scoreboard. He has secured an estimate from Seiffert Electric, Inc. of the overall cost of these endeavors. At the meeting, the committee will seek the public's input on this plan.

The Youth Soccer League board urges you to attend to share your valuable opinion as one of the people who would be affected by the project.

Sincerely,

Calvin Waters
President of the Board, Bowen City Youth Soccer League

---

158. What most likely is the purpose of the upcoming meeting?

(A) To provide updates on a park's event schedule
(B) To discuss financing for park improvements
(C) To announce the results of a public contest
(D) To introduce a newly-appointed parks official

159. What is suggested about a stadium's storage buildings?

(A) They serve additional functions.
(B) They will be moved to a new location.
(C) They may be rented for a fee.
(D) They are in need of repair.

160. According to the letter, what has Mr. Sauro done recently?

(A) Received a cost estimate
(B) Photographed other city parks
(C) Attended a local sporting event
(D) Revised a park brochure

Book-bargains.com *"The most trusted Web-based seller of secondhand books"*

Customer review of: *Logo Design Inspirations* | soft-cover, 148 pages

Review number: 1 of 7 for items purchased from Book-bargains.com
click here to see other reviews

Date of review: May 26

Customer name: Jeff Starks [✓ Verified purchase]

Overall rating: Excellent

Comments:

This compact, easy-to-carry book presents 55 examples of famous, highly-effective logo designs. All of the logos are shown in full color against a white background, and the accompanying text outlines the history of their creation and analyzes their design elements. In addition to the main text, the publisher has thoughtfully provided about ten empty pages for taking notes—a nice feature. The logos have been selected from a wide range of companies, from software developers to package delivery services. The latter was covered in what was for me the most interesting chapter of the book: "Patterns Showing Movement." This section also features my favorite piece of design—the dynamic logo for Zlatariax, a maker of exercise machines that is known for its innovation. The book is a valuable resource for any commercial designer.

---

161. What most likely is true about Mr. Starks?

(A) He has purchased several used books online.
(B) He is a professional buyer for a bookstore.
(C) He recently joined a book discussion group.
(D) He has created logos for a variety of companies.

162. What is mentioned about *Logo Design Inspirations*?

(A) It includes a section of blank pages.
(B) It is also available in an electronic edition.
(C) A friend of Mr. Starks did research for it.
(D) It is currently out of print.

163. What kind of company is Zlatariax?

(A) A computer software developer
(B) A fitness equipment manufacturer
(C) A package delivery service
(D) A graphic design firm

GO ON TO THE NEXT PAGE

www.curiosom.com/news/0111

January 11 - Official announcement regarding Curiosom.com's change of payment processors – what it means for our subscribers

Since its inception nearly 15 years ago, Curiosom.com has grown to become the premier venue for photographers to share their pictures with the entire global community. When we started offering paid subscriptions for unlimited photo uploading privileges, our management chose the Brainard-Plus payment processing service to handle our billing for subscriptions. — [1] —. We based our decision primarily upon Brainard-Plus's ability to automatically renew our 1-year and 2-year subscription plans.

However, when we became a subsidiary of Panamat.com last June, we began the process of switching to their payment processing firm, Digitexx-D, in order to unify our billing systems. — [2] —. Unfortunately, we have been notified by Digitexx-D that they cannot renew any Curiosom.com subscriptions that originated on our prior payment processor. This affects all Curiosom.com members who began their subscription on or before June 30 of last year. To get around this problem, we are encouraging these members to take advantage of a 20% discount on early subscription renewals. — [3] —. If you do so, your subscription will continue uninterrupted until its end date and can be renewed automatically. If you take no action, you will have to update your subscriber profile and billing information at the end of your current subscription. — [4] —. We therefore urge all of our affected subscribers to renew early.

164. What type of business most likely is Curiosom.com?

(A) A digital magazine for visual artists
(B) An advertising analytics service
(C) An online accounting app
(D) A photo sharing platform

165. According to the announcement, what happened the previous year?

(A) An anniversary celebration
(B) A business acquisition
(C) A new product release
(D) An increase in subscription fees

166. Who is currently eligible for a discount?

(A) Subscribers who started their service within the past week
(B) Subscribers who select a renewal period of three or more years
(C) Subscribers who were initially billed by Brainard-Plus
(D) Subscribers who are also members of Panamat.com

167. In which of the following positions marked [1], [2], [3], and [4] does the following sentence best belong?

"The regular fee for your chosen subscription plan will then be charged."

(A) [1]
(B) [2]
(C) [3]
(D) [4]

Questions 168-171 refer to the following online chat discussion.

		— □ X

Aurelia Ramos [2:04 P.M.]	Hi, all. I'm just checking in. How is it going with the brainstorming for our customer forum page? Any article ideas?
Peter Xiu **[2:05 P.M.]**	Yes — I'd like to write a how-to guide for lighting a warehouse properly.
Aurelia Ramos [2:06 P.M.]	Good. We do have many commercial clients that purchase lighting supplies from us, so our forum's content should reflect their needs. Other ideas?
Linda Melo **[2:07 P.M.]**	For our consumer clients, I was thinking of writing tips on how to select the best lighting fixtures for recreation rooms. There are so many options.
Aurelia Ramos [2:07 P.M.]	For sure.
Linda Melo **[2:08 P.M.]**	I could also write a profile on Moishe Wietz, the artisan who makes wall lamps from recycled industrial pipes.
Aurelia Ramos [2:09 P.M.]	Great. You used to work with him, right?
Linda Melo **[2:10 P.M.]**	Yes, I was his apprentice.
Peter Xiu **[2:11 P.M.]**	That reminds me. I have another idea. We should create a post that clarifies some common technical terms, and make them easier to understand.
Aurelia Ramos [2:12 P.M.]	That would be very helpful. Could you do that?
Peter Xiu **[2:13 P.M.]**	Sure thing.
Aurelia Ramos [2:14 P.M.]	Great. Thank you, both, for your input. I'll check on your progress later this week.

168. What kind of company do the participants most likely work for?

(A) A maker of gardening tools
(B) A seller of lighting supplies
(C) A chain of storage facilities
(D) A trade publication for electricians

169. At 2:07 P.M., what does Ms. Melo most likely mean when she writes, "There are so many options"?

(A) A coworker may need more time for a decision.
(B) She is not sure how to begin a piece of writing.
(C) Customers may be overwhelmed by a selection.
(D) She is impressed by a list of suggestions.

170. What is indicated about Ms. Melo?

(A) She worked under Mr. Wietz's guidance.
(B) She organizes recycling initiatives.
(C) She is currently remodeling her home.
(D) She used to be a magazine journalist.

171. What does Mr. Xiu agree to do?

(A) Collect data to measure customer satisfaction
(B) Develop content that explains some expressions
(C) Post reminder notes on a shared calendar
(D) Supervise a new internship program

GO ON TO THE NEXT PAGE

Entrepreneur News-Times   *April 23*

What Café Owners Should Know...

By Kayla Leitch

➤ Those who run an independent café will soon find that their decision on how much to charge for their offerings will have a major effect on profits. Because there is much competition among cafés, it is important to determine the optimal prices for products and services.

➤ When I first opened Café Connective nearly 10 years ago, I aimed to charge the same prices as the major coffee shop chains while providing superior service. This strategy succeeded in attracting customers, but it did not result in decent earnings. After my first year in business, I commissioned a market research study and found that most customers already perceive independent coffee shops as offering higher levels of service and product quality. With this in mind, I began to serve higher-quality, more expensive gourmet coffee products.

➤ To further justify my higher prices, I have made efforts to carve out a niche for my café as a neighborhood meeting place. Every month, I hold fun special events, such as brewing workshops or coffee tasting sessions, for customers. These gatherings have had a positive impact on my establishment's image.

➤ It is, of course, possible to charge lower prices than the competition, but this may not bring in enough additional sales to ensure profitability. Independent café owners have, after all, invested a good amount of money in equipment and inventory, so they must maximize their returns.

About the writer: A native of Dee City, Ms. Leitch runs a successful café there, and just last week her online resource for café and tea shop owners worldwide, www.cafe-owners.com, went operational.

172. Why most likely was the article written?

(A) To explain why many cafés fail to make profits

(B) To give tips for managing a café's staff

(C) To offer pricing advice for café owners

(D) To outline recent trends in the café industry

173. What is indicated about Café Connective?

(A) It has been in business for over a decade.

(B) It hosts biweekly special events.

(C) It was profiled in a marketing book.

(D) It is located in Ms. Leitch's hometown.

174. What is one reason changes were implemented in Café Connective?

(A) To differentiate it from its competitors

(B) To shorten the wait time for customers

(C) To reduce its impact on the environment

(D) To make it a more enjoyable place to work

175. The word "good" in paragraph 4, line 3, is closest in meaning to

(A) satisfactory

(B) dependable

(C) substantial

(D) useful

GO ON TO THE NEXT PAGE

Questions 176-180 refer to the following article and notice on a Web page.

Colway City Theater Group to Present *Cagen Street*

COLWAY CITY (June 3)—The Colway City Theater Group (CCTG) will kick off its summer season with Donna Mason's delightfully comical play *Cagen Street*, running from Friday, June 10 through Sunday, June 26. Friday and Saturday performances will be at 7:00 P.M. and Sunday performances will be at 2:00 P.M.

The play centers around a day in the life of Brad and Mary, a young married couple who invite their new neighbors, Ken and Janice, over for a barbecue dinner. During the cookout, the two couples learn that they went on the same tour company's overland journey across Africa just a few weeks apart. As the characters share anecdotes about the funny, adventurous, and inspirational aspects of international travel, the play carries audiences toward a sense of wonder.

The cast includes Eric Griffey, of West Town; Amy Yoon, of Hillside City; Kevin Braddock, of East Valley; and Betsy Maliki, of West Town. After the performance on June 10, audience members can meet and take photos with the performers. The director, George Mulway, will be on hand to answer audience questions as well.

For more information about the CCTG, visit www.colway-theater.org. Tickets may be purchased via its Web site or at the box office.

---

http://www.colway-theater.org/home ▶

The Colway City Theater Group (CCTG)

Update for June 6: The management of the CCTG is happy to announce that we will offer extra performances, at 2:00 P.M. each Saturday, for *Cagen Street*, the first play of our summer season. Evening performances for Friday and Saturday are at 7:00 P.M., and the Sunday matinee is at 2:00 P.M.

The play, directed by Colway City native George Mulway, will feature the talented Kevin Braddock, making his stage debut with our group, in the role of Brad. He is joined by Amy Yoon, as Mary; Eric Griffey, as Ken; and Betsy Maliki, as Janice.

176. What is *Cagen Street* mainly about?

(A) Neighbors with a common experience
(B) A family's humorous cooking mistakes
(C) Immigrants adapting to a new culture
(D) The challenges of moving house frequently

177. In the article, the word "carries" in paragraph 2, line 11, is closest in meaning to

(A) propels
(B) maintains
(C) communicates
(D) captures

178. What will audiences at *Cagen Street*'s premiere receive?

(A) A preview of a future CCTG production
(B) The opportunity to interact with the cast
(C) Entry into a drawing for a theater tour
(D) A small gift related to the play's theme

179. What most likely is the main purpose of the notice?

(A) To encourage early ticket purchases
(B) To honor the director of a stage play
(C) To announce the retirement of an actor
(D) To publicize an expanded performance schedule

180. What is implied about Mr. Braddock?

(A) He appears in a video on the CCTG's Web site.
(B) He will perform at 7:00 P.M. on June 26.
(C) He will play the husband of Ms. Yoon's character.
(D) He is from the same city as Mr. Mulway.

GO ON TO THE NEXT PAGE

Goalmarkk Research	

Summary of market research study on four milkshake drinks

Name of client: Montroy's Spot

Description: Goalmarkk Research was hired by Montroy's Spot, a large chain of casual dining restaurants, to assess consumer reactions to four of its milkshake drinks. The study took place between mid-August and mid-September at the company's restaurant locations in Cleveland, Ohio and Pittsburgh, Pennsylvania. Participants were instructed to visit a restaurant in their local region, where they were randomly assigned one of the four flavors of milkshake drinks to sample. They then had to access a link via their mobile phone and take a survey consisting of multiple-choice and open-ended questions.

Overall findings:

Sample #1	*Banana and cherry flavor* Percent of respondents who indicated *"tasted great"* – 79% Most frequent comments: "too much banana flavor", "couldn't taste much cherry"
Sample #2	*Pineapple and mango flavor* Percent of respondents who indicated *"tasted great"* – 82% Most frequent comments: "refreshing flavor", "not enough pineapple taste"
Sample #3	*Salted caramel flavor* Percent of respondents who indicated *"tasted great"* – 84% Most frequent comments: "Strong flavor," "attractive color"
Sample #4	*Coconut and vanilla flavor* Percent of respondents who indicated *"tasted great"* – 87% Most frequent comments: "thick texture," "just sweet enough"

To:	Barbara Milligan <b.milligan@goalmarkkresearch.com>
From:	Carl Pella <c.pella@goalmarkkresearch.com>
Date:	October 2
Subject:	Results of Montroy's Spot research study
Attachment:	🔗 Graphs_and_tables

Hi, Barbara,

As per your request, I have attached the graphs and tables for the report for Montroy's Spot. The electronic questionnaire you designed was quite effective in eliciting feedback. I'm pleased the survey process went so smoothly, especially considering our firm had never used the online format before.

Based on our previous studies for this client, most of the results were consistent with what I had projected. One finding, however, did stand out. What I had thought would be the least popular flavor ended up being the second most popular. I really hadn't anticipated this.

Let me know if you need any more information to support our recommendations for the client.

Thanks,

Carl

181. What is NOT stated about the market
    research study?

    (A) It was conducted in two cities.
    (B) It required the use of a mobile device.
    (C) It had multiple-choice survey questions.
    (D) Each of its participants sampled four
        drinks.

182. What feedback did two of the drink
    samples receive in common?

    (A) The texture was too thick.
    (B) The taste was refreshing.
    (C) The flavor mix was uneven.
    (D) The color was appealing.

183. What most likely is true about Montroy's
    Spot?

    (A) It plans to expand into other regions.
    (B) It is based in Pittsburgh.
    (C) It offers a range of bottled beverages.
    (D) It has consulted Goalmarkk Research
        in the past.

184. Which sample received more positive
    feedback than Mr. Pella had expected?

    (A) Sample #1
    (B) Sample #2
    (C) Sample #3
    (D) Sample #4

185. What is indicated about Ms. Milligan?

    (A) She used to work for a food
        manufacturer.
    (B) She created a firm's first electronic
        survey.
    (C) She will meet with a client in October.
    (D) She revised graphs for a market report.

Questions 186-190 refer to the following newsletter article, flyer, and e-mail.

Altarr Properties Newsletter

Chicago—At Altarr Properties, residents' comfort and convenience are important to us. That is why we are pleased to announce that we have formed a partnership with Laundry Flash, an on-demand service that will pick up a tenant's laundry and deliver the cleaned garments back to a convenient storage locker.

The service will be available in both of our apartment buildings. Installation of the lockers will take place on August 20 in the tenant lounge of the Menworth Building and August 27 across from the fitness center in the Courtway Building. Each tenant will receive a key for an assigned locker from the building manager. The front desk attendant in each building's lobby will be entrusted with signing in the Laundry Flash personnel.

Laundry pick-ups are easy to schedule via the company's Web site, www.laundry-flash.com. Turnaround time is two days, with a same-day express option available. Cleaning fees are $3 per shirt, $5 per pair of pants, and $15 per suit or dress. A discount coupon is provided on the company's flyer, available in the lobby.

Laundry Flash
We pick up, clean, and deliver your laundry back in 2 days—guaranteed!

Attention Residents of Altarr Properties' Buildings
—we're all set to do business with you!

> ### *Special Coupon (mention code 166)*
> For residents of the Menworth Building and the Courtway Building, we are offering *10 percent off* any service totaling $20 or more.

- **How to Make a Service Request**
  Visit our Web site at www.laundry-flash.com and go to the online scheduling section. We are also available via phone at 555-0129.

- **Pickup Schedule**
  -NORTH ZONE (includes the Menworth Building at 5320 Avery Street)
  Monday, Wednesday, Friday.

  -SOUTH ZONE (includes the Courtway Building at 1811 Dixon Drive)
  Tuesday, Thursday, Saturday

- **Pricing** (standard 2-day service, includes pick-up and delivery)
  Shirt $3, Pair of Pants $5, Dress $8, Suit $15, Wash and Fold $1.60 per pound; same-day express service available for a $10 surcharge

- **Laundry Bags**
  Each customer will receive one complimentary laundry bag upon their first delivery—it is yours to keep for future service requests. Additional laundry bags can be purchased for $14 each.

LAUNDRY
WASH & FOLD

To:	Jacob Gritz <j-gritz@mail.com>
From:	<orders@laundry-flash.com>
Subject:	Laundry Flash Confirmation
Date:	September 1

Thank you for your service request—confirmation #22176158.

Customer name: Jacob Gritz **Locker number**: 12
Address: 5320 Avery Street **Laundry pick-up date**: Monday, September 2

Item	Price	Item total
Shirt (cleaning)	$3.00 × 4	$12.00
Pants (cleaning)	$5.00 × 4	$20.00
Laundry bag	$0.00	
	- $3.20 10% coupon code 166	
	Total	$28.80

Paid by: credit card ending in 1362

186. What is main purpose of the newsletter article?

(A) To solicit opinions from readers
(B) To thank tenants for their loyalty
(C) To give a progress report on renovations
(D) To give details about a new service

187. According to the newsletter article, what do the Menworth and the Courtway buildings have in common?

(A) They have exercise facilities for residents.
(B) They will have lockers installed on the same day.
(C) They have the same number of rental units.
(D) They have attended front desks.

188. In the flyer, the word "set" in paragraph 1, line 2, is closest in meaning to

(A) estimated
(B) restored
(C) ready
(D) fixed

189. What information in the article may NOT be accurate?

(A) An expedited turnaround option
(B) A garment cleaning fee
(C) A Web address
(D) A coupon's availability

190. What most likely is true about Mr. Gritz?

(A) He requested an additional laundry bag.
(B) He lives in the Menworth Building.
(C) His clothing will be returned on a Tuesday.
(D) He will receive a discount for using a credit card.

GO ON TO THE NEXT PAGE

www.jerroldssupply.com/about

Jerrold's Supply

About Us

We are the area's largest members-only warehouse store for food service operators.

Our membership is free for any qualified* business. Enjoy these great benefits:

- **One-stop shopping**—We stock food and beverages from all major brands, plus kitchen equipment and even chef's apparel. Get all of your supplies in just one trip.

- **No minimum purchase required**—We are different from Bascor Club and other open-to-the-public warehouse stores in the most important sense—you never have to buy items in bulk at Jerrold's Supply.

- **Advertised specials**—We keep our members informed with monthly e-mail updates about special sale events.

Note: We are a wholesale market and not open to the general public. Membership cards are issued only to those who own or manage a restaurant. On your first store visit, you must present a valid document showing you are licensed as a food service business. You will then be issued a card that is not transferable. You may, however, bring one guest shopper with you per month, as long as that person presents a photo ID upon entering.

═══════════════ E-Mail message ═══════════════

To:	Stella Adelson
From:	Tina Rawley
Date:	October 9
Subject:	Tomorrow's errand - of interest?

Hi Stella,

I have to run over to Jerrold's Supply tomorrow morning to stock up on napkins and carry-out containers for the restaurant. You had once expressed interest in seeing the warehouse store, so I was wondering if you'd like to come along. I can pick you up in front of your apartment at 9 A.M. sharp. Please text or e-mail me back and let me know if you can make it.

For the visit, be sure to bring ID and wear comfortable shoes. The warehouse store has a large floor area, so there is a lot of walking. Also, if you'd like to look around the freezer section, bring some kind of outerwear. It's quite cold.

Hope to see you tomorrow,

Tina

Reviewed by: Stella Adelson   **Reviewed on:** October 11

I visited Jerrold's Supply for the first time yesterday. Like Bascor Club, it is a warehouse store that sells goods at impressively low prices. But, unlike that store, it does not sell flat-screen TVs or computer equipment. Instead, it offers everything needed to keep a restaurant up and running. I saw paper napkins in huge packages of 6,000! Even more amazing was the vast selection of frozen seafood. I spent much longer in that area than I'd intended, and it made me wish I'd brought a sweater. The store is crowded and the checkout lines are long, but they move quickly. I am lucky that I know someone with a membership, so I was able to come as a guest while she was picking up supplies.

191. In the Web page, what is indicated about Jerrold's Supply?

(A) Its memberships may not be transferred.
(B) It is open every day of the week.
(C) It holds cooking classes for chefs.
(D) It has automated checkout stations.

192. What is required for a Jerrold's Supply membership card?

(A) An e-mailed invitation
(B) A minimum monthly purchase
(C) A valid business license
(D) Two forms of photo identification

193. What is NOT suggested about Bascor Club?

(A) It sells consumer electronics.
(B) The general public can shop there.
(C) Its goods are only available in large quantities.
(D) It shares a parent company with Jerrold's Supply.

194. In the e-mail, what is one thing Ms. Rawley mentions buying?

(A) Cookware
(B) Eating utensils
(C) Food packaging
(D) Raw ingredients

195. What is most likely true about Ms. Adelson?

(A) She did not follow some of Ms. Rawley's advice.
(B) Her trip to Jerrold's Supply was postponed.
(C) She did not end up traveling with Ms. Rawley.
(D) She visited Jerrold's Supply on an unusually busy day.

Test 7

GO ON TO THE NEXT PAGE

Questions 196-200 refer to the following presentation handout, agenda, and text message.

How To Improve Your Business's Web Site

Presented by: Greg Wu, Web site consultant
For: Brexby Cycle Co.   **Date:** May 2

Strengths of company's Web site:

• Attractive color schemes—comfortable to look at while browsing the site
• Appealing photos of all product lines—size and spacing are appropriate
• Section titled "Why Take Up Cycling?" persuasively outlines health benefits of cycling

---

Weaknesses of company's Web site:

• Too much text and information on each page—can be confusing
• Takes too much time to load—some customers may leave the site because of this
• Complicated checkout process for purchases—too many forms to fill out

---

Action plan – at company's approval, will improve Web site by:

• Removing a digital video that plays when the site is launched, which will greatly reduce the time needed for loading
• Streamlining the checkout process, while presenting the payment options (e.g., credit card, gift card, e-commerce accounts, etc.) with more prominent graphics
• Creating a separate section on the site for company's newest line of electric bikes, which would include a short explanation on how the bicycles are charged

---

Brexby Cycle Co.

Proposed Agenda for May 30 Strategy Meeting*

2:00 P.M.	**Overview of topic**—Ongoing efforts to upgrade company Web site
2:15 P.M.	**Item 1**—Walk-through of current site, with explanation of implemented (faster loading time, more visible payment options, added section for latest products) and rejected (shorter checkout process) suggestions from consultant
3:00 P.M.	**Item 2**—Presentation by Digital Marketing Director Troy Vaden of additional, smaller modifications to site suggested during consultant's visit
4:00 P.M.	**Item 3**—Discussion of pros and cons of offering online chat support; to be led by our in-house Web developer, Fred Calloway
4:30 P.M.	**Item 4**—Brainstorming of potential interactive features for site
5:00 P.M.	**Adjournment**

To be led by Sales Manager Allison Hull; attendees should bring laptop computers

From: Fred Calloway [10:17 A.M. on May 30]

Hi, Allison. I just researched a competitor's Web site and found something interesting. One section provides a digital image of a bicycle that can be 'customized' by manipulating a computer mouse or touch screen. I'll show this to everyone at the meeting, so I'd like to allot 15 more minutes to our discussion on potential interactive features. Thanks.

196. What is NOT mentioned as a strong point of Brexby Cycle Co.'s Web site?

(A) The images of merchandise
(B) The choice of colors
(C) The size of text
(D) The content on cycling and health

197. What will attendees at the May 30 meeting most likely do?

(A) Debate the merits of a proposal
(B) Use borrowed laptop computers
(C) Listen to a consultant's presentation
(D) Decide on some deadlines for a project

198. What change most likely was made recently to Brexby Cycle Co.'s Web site?

(A) An explanation page was shortened.
(B) A digital video was eliminated.
(C) A payment process was simplified.
(D) A product category was modified.

199. In the text message, the word "manipulating" in line 4 is closest in meaning to

(A) tricking
(B) operating
(C) altering
(D) installing

200. What item on the agenda does Mr. Calloway want to schedule more time for?

(A) Item 1
(B) Item 2
(C) Item 3
(D) Item 4

Stop! This is the end of the test. If you finish before time is called, you may go back to Parts 5, 6, and 7 and check your work.

Test 7

TEST 8

In the Reading test, you will read a variety of texts and answer several different types of reading comprehension questions. The entire Reading test will last 75 minutes. There are three parts, and directions are given for each part. You are encouraged to answer as many questions as possible within the time allowed.

You must mark your answers on the separate answer sheet. Do not write your answers in your test book.

PART 5

Directions: A word or phrase is missing in each of the sentences below. Four answer choices are given below each sentence. Select the best answer to complete the sentence. Then mark the letter (A), (B), (C), or (D) on your answer sheet.

101. At the end of each group tour, participants will receive a souvenir photo that is ------- to keep.

(A) they
(B) them
(C) theirs
(D) themselves

102. The key to success in running an ethnic food restaurant is -------.

(A) authenticity
(B) authentic
(C) authenticate
(D) authentically

103. The city's landscape architects are working to ------- how more trees can be included in the Spencer Canal project.

(A) reflect
(B) encourage
(C) strengthen
(D) determine

104. A printed catalog with descriptions and images of our products can be mailed to customers ------- request.

(A) after
(B) on
(C) for
(D) along

105. Schandrax Ltd.'s mining machinery is designed to perform ------- even under the harshest conditions.

(A) successively
(B) reliably
(C) spaciously
(D) thoughtfully

106. It is recommended that novice hikers walk at a relaxed ------- and avoid going too fast, especially on steep trails.

(A) level
(B) stretch
(C) approach
(D) pace

107. Your home's heating system should be checked every six months to ensure that it is operating as ------- as possible.

(A) efficiency
(B) efficient
(C) efficiently
(D) more efficient

108. There are plans to build a new R&D center in East Hills City, but its exact location is ------- to be decided.

(A) enough
(B) once
(C) yet
(D) later

109. The Xtelia X10 mobile phone is so durable that it will not ------- any damage even if it is dropped onto a hard surface.
(A) terminate
(B) sustain
(C) diminish
(D) commit

110. Lahxmitech Ltd. develops ------- personal and business Web sites at affordable prices.
(A) impressive
(B) impress
(C) impressively
(D) impression

111. Fairview City's new recycling containers are free to residents and available ------- supplies last.
(A) toward
(B) during
(C) while
(D) within

112. The company's vision and objectives are summarized briefly ------- its mission statement.
(A) of
(B) to
(C) in
(D) about

113. The VT-5 exercise bike is ------- for small apartments because it occupies very little space.
(A) ideal
(B) deliberate
(C) convincing
(D) capable

114. Renarc Co.'s model building kits feature ------- labeled pieces that can be assembled with minimum effort.
(A) extremely
(B) remotely
(C) promptly
(D) explicitly

115. The winner of the photo contest, Mark Murdo, says he finds ------- in empty desert scenery.
(A) inspired
(B) to inspire
(C) inspirational
(D) inspiration

116. Thanks to new educational applications, mobile phones can ------- as learning tools in the classroom.
(A) be used
(B) be using
(C) have used
(D) use

117. Greenveld Park does not allow any vehicle traffic on its scenic road ------- its own tour buses that run on bio-fuels.
(A) throughout
(B) except for
(C) regardless of
(D) out of

118. A highly ------- interior designer, Alfonso Grieco provides design solutions for a wide variety of clients.
(A) accomplishing
(B) accomplished
(C) accomplishes
(D) accomplishment

119. The Mangim Career Fair is open to ------- who is seeking a new job, without regard to current employment status.
(A) every
(B) all
(C) those
(D) anyone

120. Recent research has found that social media posts have a limited ------- on people's buying decisions.
(A) value
(B) function
(C) association
(D) impact

GO ON TO THE NEXT PAGE

121. Jenebec Catering Co. allows clients to ------- their meal options to suit their exact tastes.

(A) fasten
(B) monitor
(C) customize
(D) patronize

122. Candidates will be asked for the names of three people who can provide ------- professional references for them.

(A) positives
(B) positivity
(C) positively
(D) positive

123. Members of the marketing team are contributing articles to online news outlets to attract ------- for our brand.

(A) publicity
(B) publically
(C) publicizes
(D) public

124. Ms. Booth plans to transfer to an overseas office ------- her replacement is properly trained.

(A) beginning from
(B) as soon as
(C) no earlier
(D) up to

125. When salespeople exceed their quarterly sales goals, the company rewards them ------- in the form of bonuses.

(A) financial
(B) financially
(C) finances
(D) financed

126. If the package had been lost in transit, the shipping company ------- to compensate for the loss.

(A) would have been offered
(B) will have offered
(C) had been offered
(D) would have offered

127. ------- you are traveling for leisure or business, it is important to choose a hotel with a convenient location.

(A) Notwithstanding
(B) Either
(C) Whether
(D) No matter

128. Unfortunately, the ------- wording of the contract led to there being multiple interpretations of its meaning.

(A) ambiguous
(B) forceful
(C) widespread
(D) skeptical

129. FNR Metals has earned ample recognition, including ------- the first local manufacturer to receive an "eco-friendly factory" certification.

(A) that is
(B) to be
(C) being
(D) is to be

130. Alarax Graphics can print all types of signs, in ------- shape and size may be required.

(A) whatever
(B) particular
(C) contrast
(D) any

PART 6

Directions: Read the texts that follow. A word, phrase, or sentence is missing in parts of each text. Four answer choices for each question are given below the text. Select the best answer to complete the text. Then mark the letter (A), (B), (C), or (D) on your answer sheet.

Questions 131-134 refer to the following e-mail.

To: Current clients

From: Saffler Shipping Co.

Subject: Update

Date: November 30

UPDATE for e-commerce businesses – *a solution for making return shipping labels*

The ongoing rise in online sales transactions means that e-commerce businesses may also need to handle more requests from customers who wish to return ------- merchandise that they
131.
purchased recently. Including a return label with each outbound package makes the process of sending items back ------- for the customer. A return label is a sticker stating the address of the
132.
company ------- the goods were purchased. -------. Saffler Shipping's label solution software
133.   **134.**
makes elegant and functional return shipping labels. To try it out and create a sample label in just minutes, click here. You can then choose whether or not to purchase the software for your business.

---

131. (A) canceled
(B) unwanted
(C) unintended
(D) expired

132. (A) ease
(B) easily
(C) easier
(D) eased

133. (A) where
(B) whose
(C) that
(D) which

134. (A) It also has a barcode for tracking the package that is being returned.
(B) You may exchange merchandise that you are not completely satisfied with.
(C) For better results, we recommend that customers ship it at a later date.
(D) As an online business, you can sell goods from the comfort of your home.

GO ON TO THE NEXT PAGE

Longmont Real Estate, Inc. – virtual home tours

Thanks to today's digital technology, homebuyers can now take virtual tours of homes and look at properties ------- leaving their own residence. By providing such tours for most of our
135.
properties, Longmont Real Estate is at the forefront of this industry revolution.

-------. The tours ------- using a camera that provides three-dimensional images of all the spaces
136.   137.
in each home. These images allow the viewer to "move" around the home digitally in the same manner they would in person.

Once virtual tours have been uploaded to our site, our clients can use a computer or mobile device to review a virtual tour from ------- anywhere. The technology is guaranteed to save
138.
prospective homebuyers hours of travel time and tens of dollars in gas.

To view our current properties for sale that offer virtual tours, click here.

---

135. (A) until
(B) inside
(C) without
(D) behind

136. (A) Home prices are increasing in some regions but staying steady in others.
(B) Surveyed shoppers also indicated that they prefer to visit homes in person.
(C) All of our virtual tours include photos and interactive videos of each property.
(D) If you have questions about this residence, one of our experts can help you.

137. (A) were being created
(B) are created
(C) would have been created
(D) will be created

138. (A) even
(B) not
(C) hardly
(D) almost

Explore Florham City's nature trails—with upgraded amenities!

The Florham Parks and Recreation Department is proud to announce that its six-month trail improvement project has been completed in time for summer. ------- . **139.** We thank you for your patience during the construction process.

The upgrades include a new boardwalk that extends across Florham Park's pond, ------- **140.** providing access to wetland areas. ------- , **141.** the well-traveled Blue Trail, a favorite for both local residents and out-of-town visitors, has been widened to accommodate more hikers. Many more small improvements have been made to other trails as well.

From challenging climbs up steep hillsides to leisurely walks along flat meadows, the improved nature trails offer hikes for people of all ------- . **142.** Interactive trail maps can be found by visiting www.florham-trails.org.

139. (A) The park department's staff works closely with volunteers.
(B) Organized hiking clubs are becoming more and more popular.
(C) Our entire network of trails is now once again open to visitors.
(D) The city's park system has a long and interesting history.

140. (A) safe
(B) safety
(C) safest
(D) safely

141. (A) Still
(B) Instead
(C) For example
(D) In addition

142. (A) abilities
(B) holidays
(C) landscapes
(D) benefits

Test 8

Questions 143-146 refer to the following information.

Locally Grown Food – A Quick Overview

There is no specific definition for locally grown food. However, it is generally understood to be food that is grown relatively close to its ------- of sale. Purchasing locally grown food can help
143.
regional economies ------- more money goes directly to the food growers. Local farmers almost
144.
never require the services of an outside distributor to get their products to market. -------. During
145.
much of the year, locally grown food ------- at farmers' markets and outdoor farm stands.
146.
Produce items are sold only when they are in season, so they are fresh and full of flavor. This means that buying locally grown food also has advantages for individual consumers.

---

143. (A) date
    (B) point
    (C) volume
    (D) manner

144. (A) in that
    (B) based on
    (C) owing to
    (D) in case

145. (A) Moreover, farmers may give gardening tips to visitors.
    (B) In fact, eating a lot of processed foods may be less healthy.
    (C) Therefore, the food transportation industry continues to grow.
    (D) Thus, their earnings are more likely to stay within the region.

146. (A) available
    (B) is available
    (C) had been available
    (D) to be available

Directions: In this part you will read a selection of texts, such as magazine and newspaper articles, e-mails, and instant messages. Each text or set of texts is followed by several questions. Select the best answer for each question and mark the letter (A), (B), (C), or (D) on your answer sheet.

Questions 147-148 refer to the following receipt.

Ayali Supermarket
North Weaver City Branch
12 Devon Road
Store telephone: 555-0163

May 03 02:28 P.M.

Blueberry muffins (5-pack)	$3.70
Bottled water (12-pack)	$4.90
Vegetable soup (small can)	$2.20
Dried fruit snack (large bag)	$5.80
***TOTAL	$16.60
CASH	$20.00
CHANGE	$ 3.40

Thank you for shopping at our
North Weaver City location!

Store manager: Dave Soto
Your cashier: SELF-CHECKOUT, Station #3

Sign up at the customer service desk for a preferred shopper card and start saving money!

****

How are we doing? Visit www.ayali-survey.com and give us your feedback for the chance to win $500.*
Use PIN number **334 05081** to log in and complete the survey.
*Inquire at the customer service counter for more details on the prize drawing

147. What is NOT suggested about Ayali Supermarket?

(A) Its baked goods are made on the premises.
(B) It issues loyalty cards to some shoppers.
(C) It has more than one store location.
(D) Its customers can process their own purchases.

148. How are customers instructed to participate in a survey?

(A) By obtaining a form at a service counter
(B) By supplying a current phone number
(C) By accessing a designated Web site
(D) By speaking directly to management

Questions 149-150 refer to the following Web page.

Customer reviews for: Dennward Co.

Latest posting: June 9

Posted by: Jeff Andersen, District Manager, Standard Paper Company

Dennward Co. offers outstanding service. Owing to our recent expansion, I had to order extra uniforms for our newly hired production and warehouse staff on short notice. Dennward Co. provided us with what we needed and their delivery driver, Stan, was punctual and courteous. The quality of their clothing is excellent, and they can easily add a company logo. They are always responsive to a client's needs.

➥ **Company response:** Thanks, Mr. Andersen! Customer satisfaction has always been of utmost importance to Dennward Co. We were the first company in our region to employ ACPS (Advanced Client Processing System), an order management program that has won awards from the Business Software Developers Association. This cutting-edge solution enables us to track and sort orders faster and more accurately, giving us an on-time delivery rate of 99.6%.

---

149. What kind of business most likely is Dennward Co.?

(A) A food delivery service
(B) A manufacturer of paper products
(C) A building maintenance company
(D) A supplier of work apparel

150. What is indicated about ACPS?

(A) It has achieved industry recognition.
(B) It was tailored to suit Mr. Andersen's needs.
(C) It has been released in several versions.
(D) It is considered to be easy to use.

Brad Iqbal   **[10:40 A.M.]**

Maria, I just came down here to the computer room to install the new software. Did you know that the cooling system is acting strange again? It's pretty warm in here.

Maria Dee   **[10:41 A.M.]**

Yes, we're aware of the problem. I just called the HVAC company to have a repair person come by.

Brad Iqbal   **[10:42 A.M.]**

Really? Then I'll wait to finish this assignment until after they've fixed it. This temperature is uncomfortable.

Maria Dee   **[10:43 A.M.]**

Are you sure? They're coming in tomorrow.

Brad Iqbal   **[10:44 A.M.]**

Oh, I see. I guess there's no choice but to work in the heat.

151. Who most likely is Mr. Iqbal?

(A) An air conditioning repair person
(B) An office furniture installer
(C) A computer technician
(D) A building superintendent

152. At 10:43 A.M., what most likely does Ms. Dee mean when she writes, "They're coming in tomorrow"?

(A) She does not yet have some information.
(B) She will not be available to provide assistance.
(C) Mr. Iqbal should hurry to complete a task.
(D) A delay might be longer than Mr. Iqbal expected.

To:	Constance Baylor <constance-baylor@mail.com>
From:	<greenbrandtbooks@green-brandt.com>
Subject:	Your purchase
Date:	August 1

Dear Ms. Baylor,

Thank you for shopping with us. We would like to inform you that the book you ordered, *Carpentry for Novices*, was damaged during processing due to an unexpected malfunction with our mailing machine. However, we do have a used copy of this same book, with a slightly faded back cover and a small moisture stain on the bottom edge. Its pages are clean, with no folds or markings of any kind.

If you are interested in ordering this replacement book, we will credit $7.00 to your customer account to reflect its price difference with a new copy.

Please reply to this e-mail by Monday (August 4) to let us know how you would like to proceed. Otherwise, we will automatically cancel your order and return the full amount of the purchase price to you.

Thank you for your understanding,

All of us at Greenbrandt Books

153. Why most likely was the e-mail written?

(A) To give information about a new discount program

(B) To notify Ms. Baylor about a problem with her order

(C) To provide an explanation for a price increase

(D) To clarify guidelines for purchasing collectible books

154. What most likely will happen if Ms. Baylor does not respond to the e-mail by Monday?

(A) She will not earn a bonus credit.

(B) She will be given a substitute item.

(C) She will receive a full refund.

(D) She will lose an opportunity to upgrade her account.

Storeymoore Theater Company Debuts
Online Programming

For Immediate Release (June 22)—The Storeymoore Theater Company (STC) concluded its last season with a successful run of its highly-praised stage comedy *The Big Family Reunion*. The production, which brought in the biggest crowds in the company's history, included post-performance panel discussions on the play's topic—the joyful aspects of family gatherings. These lively conversations led the STC's public relations director, Gloria Chatham, to come up with the idea of developing an audio podcast in which the company's crew members talk about the creative processes in theater. — [1] —. The first episode, titled "Why Design Matters," was posted on June 19. It features an engaging conversation between Hal Brady, the costume designer for *The Big Family Reunion*, and Michelle Lindley, the play's stage designer. — [2] —. The second episode will go up on June 26 and will include a conversation with the play's director. — [3] —. Chatham plans to continue posting 30-minute episodes each week, or perhaps twice a week. — [4] —. The public can listen to the podcast for free by visiting www.stc-theater.org/podcast.

---

155. What is indicated about *The Big Family Reunion*?

(A) Its cast included Gloria Chatham.
(B) It had two different directors.
(C) It set an attendance record.
(D) It had high production costs.

156. What is stated about the STC's podcast?

(A) It was inspired by panel discussions.
(B) It will be funded by audience donations.
(C) It requires listeners to have a paid subscription.
(D) It was developed especially for journalists.

157. In which of the positions marked [1], [2], [3], and [4] does the following sentence best belong?

"She noted, however, that it can take a few days to produce just one half-hour program."

(A) [1]
(B) [2]
(C) [3]
(D) [4]

Questions 158-160 refer to the following online list.

Nigerian Sources—West Africa's most trusted business journal　　　*Online Edition*

A look at Nigeria's best ad agencies

Posted: 1 day ago　**by** Madalina Ikande 1242 views

In recent months, many of our subscribers have suggested that we publish a list of the top advertising agencies in Nigeria. The agencies listed below have been recommended enthusiastically by the business leaders I've interviewed in the past for this publication.

Marketing Reach—Founded 20 years ago, Marketing Reach is one of the largest ad agencies in Nigeria, with branches in the cities of Lagos and Abuja. To meet the needs of Dangoumie Food Manufacturing, a major client, the firm recently opened a field office in Senegal to conduct market research studies.

Fusiontekk—In its four years of operation, this domestic agency, with offices in Lagos and Abuja, has become highly respected for its digital marketing campaigns. Last year it added Sunmurru Brands, a maker of instant noodle products, to its client base. It was for this company that the agency created an award-winning series of online advertisements.

Olouwaa Solutions—This decade-old specialty agency has offices in Nigeria, Ghana, and Kenya. Unlike many other agencies, it focuses mainly on helping client companies develop and introduce new brands. Recently, it was tasked with ensuring a successful launch for BCC Industries' line of packaged snacks. The agency is also known for having partnered with Prospectar Tech to develop Infomatt-Plus, a software program that enables businesses to create online customer surveys in service of improving their brand image.

---

158. Who most likely is Ms. Ikande?

(A) The owner of an advertising agency
(B) The manager of a bookstore
(C) A software developer
(D) A business reporter

159. What do the listed advertising agencies have in common?

(A) They have offices in more than one country.
(B) They have been in business for over five years.
(C) They work with clients in the food industry.
(D) They are headquartered in the same city.

160. What is Infomatt-Plus most likely used to do?

(A) Track public mentions of brands
(B) Collect customer feedback
(C) Analyze market research data
(D) Manage social media accounts

Questions 161-163 refer to the following information.

Rohnart Properties

RENTING SOON > The Dunmawr Building, an amenity-rich rental complex at 2 Snyder Street

The Dunmawr Building stretches across nearly an entire city block and combines comfortable apartment living with an abundance of amenities, including a ground-floor fitness center with an indoor pool. The spacious lobby acts as a co-working space for tenants, and the building is just steps away from neighborhood shops and restaurants. Built originally as a garment production facility, the Dunmawr Building possesses a vintage look and beautifully preserved architectural details. Its 38 units consist of one-bedroom and two-bedroom apartments in a variety of layouts.

Available for occupancy starting July 1. Apply before June 5 and Rohnart Properties will waive its customary $50 fee to process new applications.

---

161. What is the information mainly about?

(A) An opening ceremony
(B) City neighborhoods
(C) Residential vacancies
(D) A business opportunity

162. What is indicated about the Dunmawr Building?

(A) It has entrances on two streets.
(B) It has outdoor recreation facilities.
(C) It was previously a factory.
(D) It is in a historic district.

163. What is suggested about Rohnart Properties?

(A) It usually charges a fee to rental applicants.
(B) It specializes in commercial properties.
(C) It offers short-term leases to renters.
(D) It plans to hire additional staff members.

Questions 164-167 refer to the following e-mail.

From:	Nutrition Newsletter <healthnutrition-newsletter@maynard.edu>
To:	Janet Lee <j.lee@mail.com>
Subject:	MU Nutrition Newsletter
Date:	March 1

Maynard University Nutrition Newsletter

Dear Ms. Lee,

These days, we have become overloaded with information about healthy eating. A vast number of sources, from TV shows to online cooking forums, dispense conflicting nutritional advice of questionable scientific authority. — [1] —. This leads me to bring up the primary reason you can trust everything you read in each monthly Maynard University Nutrition Newsletter.

Each article has been researched by the editorial staff and by leading nutrition experts at the Maynard University School of Nutritional Science, and gives science-based health advice that is easy to follow. — [2] —. What's more, the newsletter carries no advertising, giving us the freedom to discuss the nutritional quality of popular foods without any obligation to please corporate advertisers in the food industry.

Our current newsletter, for example, contains an impartial guide to the healthiest types of pasta. We invite you to sample the online version of this issue, in its entirety, by visiting www.mu-health.com and entering the code "A12." We are doing so in the hopes that you will want to subscribe to our extraordinary publication. — [3] —. With our introductory discount, you can subscribe to the print or digital edition for one year for $32—a savings of 35% from our regular rate.

We are reaching out to you because our records indicate you currently receive free "health update" e-mails from our university's alumni Web site. — [4] —. Our monthly newsletter provides even more detailed health guidance, so we urge you to take advantage of this special offer.

Sincerely,

David Ahmed
Editorial Director, Maynard University Nutrition Newsletter

164. What is the main purpose of the e-mail?

(A) To give an update on a newsletter's new editorial policies
(B) To compare health recommendations made by various experts
(C) To outline the benefits of a subscription-based publication
(D) To propose a collaboration on a series of articles

165. What most likely is true about the newsletter?

(A) It is no longer sold in a print edition.
(B) It does not have advertisements.
(C) It is aimed primarily at scientists.
(D) It is associated with a television show.

166. What is suggested about Ms. Lee?

(A) She graduated from Maynard University.
(B) She teaches an online cooking class.
(C) She used to work with Mr. Ahmed.
(D) She attempted to cancel a free service.

167. In which of the positions marked [1], [2], [3], and [4] does the following sentence best belong?

"The newsletter is always written in simple language, not full of complex medical terminology."

(A) [1]
(B) [2]
(C) [3]
(D) [4]

Questions 168-171 refer to the following online chat discussion.

Live chat		— ☐ X
Amir Nazari	[9:22 A.M.]	Hi, all. I'm here in the conference room practicing the presentation for our team. I just reviewed the slides with side-by-side comparisons of the original and new logos, with descriptions of the changes we made. They look good.
Nadia Ghosn	[9:23 A.M.]	Did you add my slides showing the reasons for our selection of graphics?
Amir Nazari	[9:24 A.M.]	Yes, they were very helpful.
Nadia Ghosn	[9:25 A.M.]	How does the video look on screen?
Amir Nazari	[9:26 A.M.]	That's our problem. It's not playing.
Linda Wade	[9:27 A.M.]	Try changing its format.
Amir Nazari	[9:28 A.M.]	OK. Just a minute.
Nadia Ghosn	[9:37 A.M.]	Any luck?
Amir Nazari	[9:38 A.M.]	Got it. It's working now.
Linda Wade	[9:39 A.M.]	Did the suggestion help?
Amir Nazari	[9:40 A.M.]	As always.
Dale Kang	[9:41 A.M.]	Remember too that you can pause the video with the remote control unit. You may want to try it out a few times. The buttons can be tricky.
Amir Nazari	[9:42 A.M.]	Good idea—thanks.

168. What most likely is the topic of the team's presentation?

(A) Revisions to the design of a logo
(B) Present and future sales forecasts
(C) An overview of competing brands
(D) How to describe a product's features

169. What is suggested about Mr. Nazari?

(A) He has not seen a promotional film yet.
(B) He gives workshops on presentation strategies.
(C) He hired all the graphic designers on the work team.
(D) He incorporated Ms. Ghosn's content into a presentation.

170. At 9:40 A.M., what does Mr. Nazari most likely mean when he writes, "As always"?

(A) The team regularly has to make changes on short notice.
(B) A colleague gives dependable troubleshooting advice.
(C) A problem occurs repeatedly on a computer.
(D) He often assists with converting the format of videos.

171. What does Mr. Kang suggest Mr. Nazari do?

(A) Memorize an introduction
(B) Brainstorm potential audience questions
(C) Schedule a break between sections
(D) Practice using an accessory

GO ON TO THE NEXT PAGE

Heritage museum showcases memorabilia from everyday life

HAZLETT VIEW—The Keeler Heritage Museum has been called "a hidden gem" by visitors who have explored its huge collection of vintage treasures. The museum is home to more than 30,000 items, displayed in four massive buildings on a repurposed farm complex. The exhibits represent the personal collection of Marvin Keeler, a lifelong resident of Hazlett View who has been gathering up local memorabilia since his childhood. Today, he is often seen relaxing in the museum's garden pavilion, where visitors can try their hand at operating the antique farm equipment on display. "It was Mr. Keeler's dream to start a museum," said facility manager Julia Halstead, who now leads tours for small groups.

The museum's exhibits and historical timelines cover a variety of aspects of daily life in the region. Part of the museum shows off memorabilia from local industries, including an intact seating booth and service counter from Centralia Diner, which Mr. Keeler owned and operated until his retirement. A wide range of other historical items are on exhibit, from antique printing presses to old school uniforms. Exploring the museum, many visitors connect the exhibits with their own memories of past times.

The museum is located at 1100 Ridge Road, just outside the small town of Hazlett View. It is open seven days a week, from 8 A.M. to 5 P.M. Admission is $8 for adults and $5 for students. Visitors should set aside three or more hours to view all of the museum's objects in a leisurely manner. The museum also offers a membership program that allows access to a range of special events. For more information on the museum, visit www.keeler-mus.org.

172. What is NOT mentioned about the museum's collection?

(A) It features interactive exhibits.
(B) It is housed in multiple buildings.
(C) It displays sections of Mr. Keeler's former business.
(D) It includes objects donated by past visitors.

173. The word "cover" in paragraph 2, line 2 is closest in meaning to

(A) fill in for
(B) relate to
(C) enclose
(D) guarantee

174. What is implied about Mr. Keeler?

(A) He also operates a local jewelry store.
(B) He purchased a farm from Ms. Halstead.
(C) He grew up near the site of his museum.
(D) He has taken up gardening as a hobby.

175. What does the writer of the article recommend doing?

(A) Allowing several hours to look around a facility
(B) Buying single tickets through a Web site
(C) Enrolling in a new membership program
(D) Participating in a special group tour

GO ON TO THE NEXT PAGE

Test 8

Questions 176-180 refer to the following online review and response.

Reviews Plus   -- The area's top online review site

Review of Alerro's Bistro   by: Matt Browski

Matt Browski's profile   → *Reviews Plus* member for: <u>5 years 7 months</u>
                              Total reviews posted: 32 Photos posted: 11

The quality of the food at Alerro's Bistro is good, but it could be better considering the prices that are charged. I ordered a tofu burger ($13.00), a bowl of mushroom soup ($7.00), cross-cut fries ($8.00), and a "farm special" salad plate ($9.00). Everything was reasonably tasty. There are several healthy salad options, but for some reason the taco salad was removed from the menu. I've had it here before and wish it would be brought back. In general, the food here would appeal to health-conscious diners who are not concerned with fancy artisanal food preparation. The most positive part of my visit was the responsiveness of the staff. Even though the small dining room was busy when I visited, I waited less than a minute for a server to arrive at my table.

➡ Response from: Lisa Trapani, General Manager, Alerro's Bistro

Hi Matt,

Thank you for your feedback. We pride ourselves on our hospitality and, above all, our high standards for sourcing food ingredients. In particular, all of our fries are made from organically grown potatoes. As supplies have been tight this season, we recently had to source some potatoes from a different grower. Accordingly, the charge for that dish was not applied to your bill. We hope that you noticed this gesture; if not, you can confirm it by checking your receipt.

We are certain we can offer you a better experience than the most recent one you had, so we would like to invite you back to our restaurant. Could you send me a message through this site and provide your e-mail address? Our customer service supervisor would like to know more about your visit.

Thank you again,

Lisa Trapani, www.alerro-bistro.com

176. What does Mr. Browski imply about the food at Alerro's Bistro?

(A) It is served in large portions.
(B) It is prepared in a simple way.
(C) Its prices are surprisingly low.
(D) It does not match the dining room's décor.

177. What most likely is true about Mr. Browski?

(A) He has eaten at Alerro's Bistro previously.
(B) He is an employee of a local health food store.
(C) He posts pictures with each of his online reviews.
(D) He went to Alerro's Bistro on a weekday.

178. In the response, the word "tight" in paragraph 1, line 3, is closest in meaning to

(A) strict
(B) lacking
(C) closely packed
(D) strongly fixed

179. Which amount was most likely removed from Mr. Browski's bill?

(A) $7.00
(B) $8.00
(C) $9.00
(D) $13.00

180. What does Ms. Trapani suggest that she will do if Mr. Browski responds?

(A) Refund the full cost of his meal
(B) Share his complaints with a business owner
(C) Send him an electronic coupon
(D) Pass on his contact details

GO ON TO THE NEXT PAGE

Welcome to Brightlane Publishing!

Brightlane Publishing is a publisher of cutting-edge guidebooks on marketing strategy. Since our founding nearly 15 years ago, we have put out hundreds of popular and useful titles. Here are our newest releases:

Write Better Product Descriptions In this illustrated volume, noted advertising copy-writer Jack Schoeffel gives practical advice on writing product descriptions that generate sales. This is Mr. Schoeffel's debut book, and we are confident it will become a classic in its field. *Paperback - $27 + $5 shipping, Electronic edition $13*

Start a Hotel Business This inspiring book focuses on entrepreneurship, making it different from any of our previous releases. The lively text, written by hospitality expert Hugh Tsangaras, lays down key principles for getting a hotel business off the ground, even in regions without a strong tourism base. *Paperback - $22 + $4 shipping*

Boost Your E-Commerce Sales This book's author, Lois Mazza, holds the view that marketing skills are even more important than technical expertise in building a profitable online business. She supplies tips for increasing your online sales, and lists contact information for top e-commerce consultants. *Paperback - $29 + $6 shipping, Electronic edition $14*

Selling via Social Media Written by *Online Age* magazine editor Amy Kang, this comprehensive volume provides detailed direction on effective selling via social media sites, and includes a bonus 24-page pocket book listing words that are proven to increase sales. *Hardcover - $37 + $7 shipping*

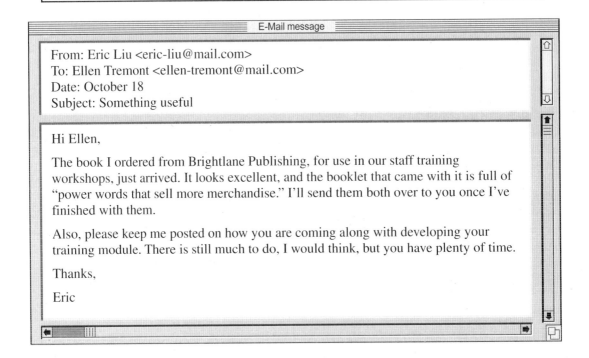

E-Mail message

From: Eric Liu <eric-liu@mail.com>
To: Ellen Tremont <ellen-tremont@mail.com>
Date: October 18
Subject: Something useful

Hi Ellen,

The book I ordered from Brightlane Publishing, for use in our staff training workshops, just arrived. It looks excellent, and the booklet that came with it is full of "power words that sell more merchandise." I'll send them both over to you once I've finished with them.

Also, please keep me posted on how you are coming along with developing your training module. There is still much to do, I would think, but you have plenty of time.

Thanks,

Eric

181. What most likely is NOT true about Brightlane Publishing?

(A) It published a work by a first-time author.
(B) It imposes a separate charge for delivery.
(C) It offers digital editions for some titles.
(D) It was founded by a magazine editor.

182. What is suggested about *Start a Hotel Business*?

(A) It cannot be shipped to some regions.
(B) It is the first book of its type for the publisher.
(C) It is recommended by experts in the tourism industry.
(D) It took longer to write than the other new titles.

183. In the Web page, the word "holds" in paragraph 4 line 1, is closest in meaning to

(A) contains
(B) secures
(C) adheres to
(D) suspends

184. Which book did Mr. Liu most likely purchase recently?

(A) *Write Better Product Descriptions*
(B) *Start a Hotel Business*
(C) *Boost Your E-commerce Sales*
(D) *Selling via Social Media*

185. What does Mr. Liu ask Ms. Tremont to do?

(A) Provide him with a progress report on a project
(B) Find a replacement leader for a training session
(C) Proofread the content of a staff presentation
(D) Reimburse him for a business expense

GO ON TO THE NEXT PAGE

Questions 186-190 refer to the following Web page, meeting summary, and online registration form.

http://www.cityofstenley.gov/services/recycling-waste

Stenley City >> *Recycling and Waste Removal Services for Residents*

➢ Stenley City contracts with Grunby Industries Co. (GIC) to collect waste from all parts of the city. Non-recyclable waste is first taken to the Stenley City Transfer Facility (SCTF) on the city's north side, and then transported to a landfill. All recyclable material is sent to the GIC-managed recycling facility for on-site processing. Recyclable waste must be placed by the curb before 6:00 A.M. on your designated recycling pick-up day each week. The city provides every home and business with one (1) of each type of bin for recyclables:

➢ Blue – for household recyclables, including cans and bottles

➢ Red – for compostable yard waste, such as weeds and leaves*

➢ Green – for all other yard waste, including branches and tree limbs

➢ Yellow – for electronic waste, including computers and peripherals, mobile phones, and electrical accessories

*Pick-up available from mid-March to mid-December

Summary of Stenley City regular weekly meeting for Tuesday, April 28

Attending: Mayor Ray Conley, Director of Waste Management Drew Morro, All Members of the Budget Committee, GIC representative Eunice Woo

New mobile application: Mr. Morro announced that the *Recycling Reminder* mobile phone app, created by GIC (Grunby Industries Co.) specifically for city residents, will go live on Friday, May 1. Ms. Woo, the lead developer of the app, gave a demonstration on navigating its features. Mr. Morro confirmed that the weekly recycling pick-up schedule will be divided into the following sectors: Zone 1 (residences with "North" addresses) – every Tuesday; Zone 2 (businesses with "North" addresses) – every Wednesday; Zone 3 (residences with "South" addresses) – every Thursday; Zone 4 (businesses with "South" addresses) – every Friday. The first pick-up dates for the month will be May 5, 6, 7, and 8 for Zones 1, 2, 3, and 4 respectively.

Recycling Reminder
Registration Screen

Complete the fields below and press "submit" to register for reminders.

Today's date | May 1

Name of resident | Debbie Guarini   **E-mail** | Debbie@mail.com

Address | 1736 Bradley Street North

Type of property: [V] residential [ ] commercial

(Optional) Ask the *Recycling Helper* your question.

How do I dispose of | Computer keyboards and speakers, power cables | **?**

[submit]

You will receive a reminder text message one day before your pick-up day each week. Recycling Helper is available to advise you on which container to use.

---

186. What is mentioned about the GIC?

(A) It is expanding its information technology department.
(B) It operates its own recycling facility.
(C) It manufactures recycling containers.
(D) It is located next to the SCTF.

187. What is most likely true about Stenley City?

(A) Many of its residential properties include outdoor land.
(B) Its non-recyclable waste is transported overseas.
(C) It does not pick up some recyclables in November.
(D) It asks citizens to dispose of glass separately from metal.

188. What is stated about Ms. Woo?

(A) She is a member of a financial committee.
(B) She is currently a resident of Stenley City.
(C) She illustrated how to use a mobile app on April 28.
(D) She used to work in Mr. Conley's office.

189. When most likely will Ms. Guarini receive a reminder message?

(A) On May 4
(B) On May 5
(C) On May 6
(D) On May 7

190. What container will Ms. Guarini need to use for the waste she inquired about?

(A) A blue bin
(B) A red bin
(C) A green bin
(D) A yellow bin

GO ON TO THE NEXT PAGE

Test 8

Enter *Barbados Life* magazine's photo contest!

Your winning photograph could be seen by our magazine's more than 70,000 readers living in Barbados and internationally. Our photo contest is open to all amateur photographers—that is, anyone who does not earn any income as a photographer. All entrants must be residents of Barbados. Each entrant may submit up to 10 images in any one category.

Please ensure that your entry form—available via www.magazine-contest.com—and your photos are submitted electronically no later than February 15.

The top three photos will appear in our June special issue, "Best of Barbados," and Honorable Mention entrants will be mentioned by name. Our editors will also review Honorable Mention photos for inclusion in future monthly issues. If we wish to run your photo in the magazine, we will contact you to arrange for its one-time use.

Prizes in each category:

First Place - $300 cash   Third Place – a two-year subscription to Barbados Life
Second Place - $150 cash   Honorable Mention – A *Barbados Life* T-shirt

Questions? E-mail us at editor@barbados-mag.com

Barbados Life Photo Contest
Entry Form

Category of photo(s): _____ Festivals (taken at an event)

_____V_____ Wildlife (animals, insects, or plants)

_____ Scenery (views and vistas)

Name: *Ida Serrano*   **E-mail address:** *serrano@mail.com*

Please attach a title and description to each photo, specifying where and when it was taken. In the space below, explain any unique circumstances surrounding the photo(s):

I captured these images while I was leading tours as a volunteer guide.

Signature: *Ida Serrano*

```
╔══════════════════ E-Mail message ══════════════════╗
║  From:     │ James Marlin <marlin@barbados-mag.com>   ║
║  To:       │ Ida Serrano <serrano@mail.com>            ║
║  Date:     │ April 17                                  ║
║  Subject:  │ Congratulations!                          ║
╚═════════════════════════════════════════════════════╝
```

Dear Ms. Serrano,

Congratulations—*Barbados Life* magazine has recognized one of your photographs
(Butterfly #2), taken at the Tropical Butterfly Garden on January 24, as an Honorable
Mention photo. We have confirmed that you have met all entry requirements. To
claim your prize, please e-mail me back within five days. In your e-mail, please
confirm that it is OK for us to include your name in our special issue.

Please e-mail me if you have any questions as well.

Regards,

James Marlin, Photo Editor

191. What does the announcement indicate
about *Barbados Life* magazine?

(A) It comes out every other month.
(B) It has readers outside of Barbados.
(C) It has photo contests for each issue.
(D) It sponsors Barbadian festivals.

192. In the announcement, the word "run" in
paragraph 3, line 3, is closest in meaning to

(A) edit
(B) oversee
(C) evaluate
(D) print

193. What most likely is NOT true about Ida
Serrano?

(A) She submitted 10 or fewer images.
(B) Her income does not come from
photography.
(C) Her entry was received after February
15.
(D) She is a current resident of Barbados.

194. What is suggested about one of
Ms. Serrano's photos?

(A) It will be featured on a T-shirt design.
(B) It was taken during a tour of a garden.
(C) It was entered in two different
categories.
(D) It will be recognized with a cash award.

195. What does Mr. Marlin ask Ms. Serrano to
do?

(A) Give permission for her name to be
published
(B) Create a list of other suitable prizes as
substitutes
(C) Direct future inquiries to another
department
(D) Confirm her home address for a mailing

Birley City News   **March 20**

New manager has new marketing plans for Birley Hotel

By Sarah Cozzi, Business Writer

Located on Frontage Road, which separates Dahlman and Henley Counties, the 200-year-old Birley Hotel is surrounded by shaded gardens and offers a relaxing stay for guests.

During my visit, facility manager Monica Hu told me she has ambitious marketing plans for the hotel, which is owned by local entrepreneur Dan Crosby. Mr. Crosby hired her late last year to allow him to focus more on his growing, three-year-old café business.

As we talked, I mentioned that the hotel's Web site did not fully represent the facility's luxurious amenities. She smiled as she picked up a tablet device and pointed out a page on the newly-redesigned site showcasing images of each beautifully-decorated guest room. She then discussed her efforts to promote the hotel as a launch point for exploring Henley County, which boasts many attractions but receives far fewer visitors than Dahlman County. She says the hotel's new brochures encourage visitors to "experience Henley County."

Ms. Hu said she also plans to rework the Birley's dinner menu to include options to "match every budget." Currently, its gift shop sells artisanal herbs and spices created by Mr. Crosby.

Birley City News   March 24

Exploring Henley County

By Jim Skandar, Travel Columnist

Birley City—Recently, I stayed at the Birley Hotel and explored the charming attractions of Henley County. The hotel's manager put me in contact with Brian Kuzo, president of the Henley County Tourist Association (HCTA), and he guided my daylong tour of the county. It began with a delicious breakfast at Lite Bistro, one of several highly-rated restaurants located near the hotel. We then stopped at Grayley Town, a famous arts community, and toured Paxton Park historical village. The highlight of the trip was a narrated cruise down Paxton Canal in an open-air barge. Mr. Kuzo showed great enthusiasm for the region, and I highly recommend seeing its many sights.

www.birleyhotel.com/home

Stay at the Birley Hotel—and experience Henley County

Relax
Learn about our services

Stay
View our rooms

Eat
See our meal menus

Discover
Explore nearby attractions

*The Birley Hotel welcomes group events. A large conference room, with a projector and speaker system, is available for rental. The hotel also features charging stations for electric bikes and cars, which are free to guests and $15 for non-guests.

---

196. What most likely is true about the Birley Hotel?

(A) It has recently increased its occupancy rates.
(B) It is decorated with vintage furniture.
(C) It offered a discounted stay to a columnist.
(D) It sells food-related products made by its owner.

197. Which section of the Web site did Ms. Hu show Ms. Cozzi?

(A) Relax
(B) Stay
(C) Eat
(D) Discover

198. What is implied about Mr. Kuzo?

(A) He was referred by Ms. Hu to a columnist.
(B) He hosted a meal at one of Mr. Crosby's cafés.
(C) He spoke to Ms. Cozzi during a sightseeing trip.
(D) He designed a brochure for the Birley Hotel.

199. What is indicated about Henley County?

(A) It receives more tourists than Dahlman County.
(B) It was settled before Dahlman County.
(C) Its visitors can take boat tours.
(D) Its parks were expanded recently.

200. What does the hotel offer guests at no charge?

(A) Use of audiovisual equipment
(B) Workshops on plant care techniques
(C) Charging facilities for electric vehicles
(D) Laundering of some types of clothing

Stop! This is the end of the test. If you finish before time is called, you may go back to Parts 5, 6, and 7 and check your work.

RC

TEST 9

READING TEST

In the Reading test, you will read a variety of texts and answer several different types of reading comprehension questions. The entire Reading test will last 75 minutes. There are three parts, and directions are given for each part. You are encouraged to answer as many questions as possible within the time allowed.

You must mark your answers on the separate answer sheet. Do not write your answers in your test book.

PART 5

Directions: A word or phrase is missing in each of the sentences below. Four answer choices are given below each sentence. Select the best answer to complete the sentence. Then mark the letter (A), (B), (C), or (D) on your answer sheet.

---

101. Providing excellent support to customers is ------- with Woshett's online chat platform.

(A) simply
(B) simple
(C) simplify
(D) simplifying

102. With its affordability and straightforward design, the Cruiser 10 sewing machine is a great choice for ------- sewers.

(A) durable
(B) wealthy
(C) casual
(D) fresh

103. Meese, Inc. expects sales of its hair care products to improve when it ------- their prices next month.

(A) will lower
(B) lowers
(C) had lowered
(D) is lowered

104. The candidate said it was the prospect of frequent international travel that caused him to ------- the promotion to manager.

(A) retreat
(B) withhold
(C) enroll
(D) decline

105. While it represented a personal record, Ms. Polk's score was not high ------- to qualify her for the national competition.

(A) anyway
(B) enough
(C) much
(D) up

106. All of the department's fall courses will take place as initially scheduled ------- "Ethics in Nursing", which has been moved to Tuesday evenings.

(A) except
(B) on
(C) for
(D) during

107. Mr. Wellington has requested a hotel adjacent to the conference center for ------- and two coworkers.

(A) he
(B) his own
(C) himself
(D) his

108. Because of the office's open floor plan, employees must use unoccupied meeting rooms to hold ------- phone conversations.

(A) privately
(B) privacy
(C) private
(D) privatized

109. In order to maintain your wooden furniture, Hilge Home recommends ------- rubbing coconut oil into its surface.

(A) carelessly
(B) occasionally
(C) unexpectedly
(D) recently

110. The studio reluctantly allowed the director to cast Mel Frazier, ------- is better known for his television work, as the star of her film.

(A) someone
(B) whoever
(C) who
(D) that

111. Company regulations state that shift supervisors have the ------- to assign tasks to employees.

(A) amenity
(B) adjustment
(C) intention
(D) authority

112. Apontle's poorly designed mobile app requires users to ------- enter their log-in information each time they open it.

(A) repeatedly
(B) repetition
(C) repetitive
(D) repeat

113. Many participants in Pittman Group's survey of urban consumers preferred name-brand products ------- generic ones.

(A) just as
(B) down to
(C) over
(D) toward

114. After several years of operating under restricted budgets, we have become accustomed to ------- unnecessary expenses.

(A) avoid
(B) avoided
(C) avoidance
(D) avoiding

115. Because of rumors that it has security issues, passengers are ------- to use the metro system's payment card.

(A) critical
(B) sensitive
(C) unsuitable
(D) hesitant

116. Mr. Bailey's latest book offers readers interested in real estate investment practical ------- on entering the field.

(A) guide
(B) guidance
(C) guidable
(D) guiding

117. Corporate policies must be easy for staff to understand and ------- enforced by management.

(A) consistently
(B) relatively
(C) shortly
(D) supposedly

118. ------- her session drew almost 30 people, Ms. Sato endeavored to speak individually with each at least once.

(A) Nevertheless
(B) Although
(C) Prior to
(D) Apart from

119. Building ample bike parking facilities is just one of the ------- Stounville has taken to promote cycling among the public.

(A) indicators
(B) objectives
(C) measures
(D) terms

120. Members of the Osborne Opera Supporters Club receive ------- access to discounts on tickets and merchandise.

(A) exclusive
(B) excludes
(C) exclude
(D) exclusively

GO ON TO THE NEXT PAGE

121. Ever since we began advertising in *Enterprising Now*, business travelers ------- our hotel in large numbers.

(A) visited
(B) were visiting
(C) would have visited
(D) have been visiting

122. Ms. Philips has built a strong relationship with her team at the Beijing branch ------- their cultural differences.

(A) on behalf of
(B) in addition to
(C) notwithstanding
(D) in exchange for

123. The ------- of workshops to a full day will enable each one to cover significantly more information.

(A) lengthening
(B) lengthiest
(C) lengthen
(D) length

124. Choosing to specialize in wedding planning may ------- to be one of the best decisions Vohan Events has made.

(A) unite
(B) prove
(C) envision
(D) strive

125. ------- Zinte Apparel decides not to have us run its marketing campaign, this quarter is still on track to be one of our most successful ever.

(A) Upon
(B) As soon as
(C) In order that
(D) Even if

126. It is actually easier to reach Caswell Waterfall by Summers Road than by the ------- traveled Highway 24.

(A) more frequent
(B) most frequent
(C) most frequently
(D) more frequently

127. Patrons of Mason Café are ------- to connect to our wireless Internet service using the password on their receipt.

(A) possible
(B) welcome
(C) suggested
(D) beneficial

128. Consultants have recommended that the store's loyalty program ------- to offer more immediate and tangible rewards.

(A) be redesigned
(B) was to redesign
(C) was redesigned
(D) will be redesigning

129. The electronic time tracking system notifies supervisors when workers are ------- reach their weekly limit of working hours.

(A) nearly
(B) close to
(C) about to
(D) within

130. Frigigo's refrigerated trucks ensure that food items do not undergo dangerous ------- in temperature during delivery.

(A) fluctuations
(B) boundaries
(C) sensations
(D) standards

Directions: Read the texts that follow. A word, phrase, or sentence is missing in parts of each text. Four answer choices for each question are given below the text. Select the best answer to complete the text. Then mark the letter (A), (B), (C), or (D) on your answer sheet.

Questions 131-134 refer to the following e-mail.

From: <accounts@final-tally.com>

To: Tonya Bell

Subject: End of Free Trial

Date: February 7

Dear Ms. Bell,

Your free trial of Final Tally ------- to end on February 10. That means that you have just 3 days
                                 131.

left of comprehensive cloud-based accounting solutions. We hope that Final Tally has helped

you not just organize your small business's day-to-day finances but also understand its -------
                                                                                         132.

financial situation. If you would like to keep using Final Tally, please <u>log in to your account</u> and

become a paid subscriber.

If you do not buy a subscription, you will have 60 days to retrieve any materials you are storing

in Final Tally. -------, all data associated with your account will be deleted. Also, if there is a
                133.

particular reason you end up deciding not to subscribe, please <u>let us know</u>. -------.
                                                                                 134.

Thanks,

The Final Tally Team

131. (A) is scheduled
(B) was scheduled
(C) has scheduled
(D) scheduled

132. (A) preliminary
(B) assorted
(C) overall
(D) foremost

133. (A) Meanwhile
(B) However
(C) Therefore
(D) Afterward

134. (A) We have been eagerly awaiting your reply.
(B) We are always looking for ways to improve.
(C) We have several options that may be
appropriate.
(D) We love to share praise with the rest of our team.

GO ON TO THE NEXT PAGE

Questions 135-138 refer to the following instructions.

Instructions for Fingerprinting

Clear impressions of your fingers and thumbs are necessary in order to confirm that you are eligible for a long-term visa. ------- your own fingerprints, you will need a black ink pad. Roll a

135.

single finger on the ink pad so that it becomes evenly coated in ink. Find the box on the background check form that ------- to that finger. Press one side of the finger into it and roll

136.

toward the other side of the finger, maintaining an even amount of pressure. Repeat the procedure for all other fingers. You may attempt to retake unclear impressions only if there is sufficient space ------- in the appropriate box. -------.

137.   138.

---

135. (A) Take
(B) To take
(C) Having taken
(D) The taking of

136. (A) devotes
(B) designates
(C) corresponds
(D) consents

137. (A) remained
(B) remaining
(C) remainder
(D) remains

138. (A) Doing so would cause serious imperfections in the fingerprint.
(B) You will not need to be fingerprinted again until shortly before that date.
(C) Finally, allow the participant to thoroughly wipe his or her hands off.
(D) Otherwise, please start the process over with a new copy of the form.

Questions 139-142 refer to the following memo.

From: Jerry Moore
To: All employees
Re: Accounting area

Hi everyone,

Following the recent remodel, many employees have been choosing to pass through the accountants' area in order to go from the front entrance to the break room or vice versa. I understand that this way is the ------, but this practice cannot be allowed to continue. The
139.
accountants have reported that they find it very distracting. ------. On my advice, they have tried
140.
locking the door and directly asking the employees who do this to stop, but ------ effort has
141.
succeeded. Therefore, building maintenance has given its permission to block off the door between the accounting area and the break room with heavy furniture. This memo is intended to notify you all that from tomorrow, the door will be absolutely unusable. Please adjust your ------ accordingly.
142.

Jerry Moore
Head of Human Resources

---

139. (A) convenient
(B) convenience
(C) most convenient
(D) more conveniently

140. (A) If you are having a similar problem, we can speak to management together.
(B) The break room would be a better place for such a conversation anyway.
(C) Please knock first to give them some warning that you are approaching.
(D) More importantly, they need to be able to work on confidential materials freely.

141. (A) this
(B) any
(C) their
(D) neither

142. (A) routes
(B) priorities
(C) estimates
(D) greetings

GO ON TO THE NEXT PAGE

Test 9

Lewitts Episode of *On The Case* To Air

LEWITTS (October 2)—An episode of the television drama *On The Case* that was shot ------- in
143.
Lewitts will be broadcast on NBO tonight at nine.

The show stars Farida Abboud and Henry Bryant as detectives who travel around the country
solving crimes. In tonight's episode, they visit the ------- town of Marndale to investigate a
144.
disappearance.

Several locations around Lewitts, including the courthouse, Kelley Park, and Butler General
Store, were chosen to embody the places imagined by the show's staff. -------. As usual, though,
145.
the beginning and end of the episode were shot on sets in Dromery City.

Town official Albert Cheong said he hopes that the broadcast attracts the ------- of other
146.
productions: "We would welcome more film and television projects."

---

143. (A) primarily
(B) highly
(C) overly
(D) exclusively

144. (A) authentic
(B) fictional
(C) adjacent
(D) diverse

145. (A) All other sites require a permit from
Lewitts's government.
(B) Residents should expect traffic disruptions
in these areas.
(C) The scenes were filmed over a one-week
period in August.
(D) So far, the episode has been well-received
by critics and viewers.

146. (A) attendant
(B) most attentive
(C) attention
(D) attending

PART 7

Directions: In this part you will read a selection of texts, such as magazine and newspaper articles, e-mails, and instant messages. Each text or set of texts is followed by several questions. Select the best answer for each question and mark the letter (A), (B), (C), or (D) on your answer sheet.

Questions 147-148 refer to the following Web page.

www.leampter.com/order

The Leampter Company

Order Summary

Please review your order before completing it.

Ship to: University of Bowmoss
         Maintenance Department
         c/o Derrick McGuire
         1660 University Ave.
         Bowmoss, MS 38637

Payment method: Credit card ending in 0455
Billing address: *Same as shipping*
Shipping preference: Standard Ground Shipping

Product	Quantity	Unit Price	Total
Medium-strength trash bags (box of 200)	5	$25.00	$125.00
13-watt fluorescent light bulbs (box of 12)	1	$4.20	$4.20
12-volt cordless drill	1	$129.00	$129.00
Chemical-resistant rubber gloves (box of 10)	2	$10.40	$20.80
		Shipping	$24.99
		Total	$303.99

Promotional code: _____

Place Order

147. What kind of business most likely is the Leampter Company?

(A) A furniture store
(B) A hardware retailer
(C) An office supplies distributor
(D) An auto parts manufacturer

148. What information has Mr. McGuire NOT provided?

(A) Where the order should be sent
(B) How the goods should be shipped
(C) What he will use to make a payment
(D) Why he is eligible for a discount

Questions 149-150 refer to the following online chat discussion.

Judy Klein [2:14 P.M.]
Eric, I'm glad I caught you online. I ran into a problem processing your travel reimbursement request this morning.

Eric Holland [2:15 P.M.]
Hi, Judy. What was the issue?

Judy Klein [2:16 P.M.]
Sorry, but could you give me a second? I thought I had the form right here, but I've been working on a few other files since then.

Eric Holland [2:16 P.M.]
Sure.

Judy Klein [2:19 P.M.]
OK, here we are. In the "Miscellaneous" section, you listed a $24.38 charge on May 25, but I can't read your handwriting in the description box. Do you remember what you wrote there? It looks like it starts with an "h".

Eric Holland [2:20 P.M.]
Hmm. I'll come over to your desk.

Judy Klein [2:21 P.M.]
Oh, that would be great. See you in a minute.

149. What is suggested about Ms. Klein?
(A) She is often interrupted by questions from colleagues.
(B) She sometimes has trouble opening a software program.
(C) She retrieved some pages from a printer before the chat.
(D) She is searching for some paperwork during part of the chat.

150. At 2:20 P.M., what does Mr. Holland imply when he writes, "I'll come over to your desk"?
(A) He needs a request to be processed quickly.
(B) He prefers to submit a physical copy of a form.
(C) He cannot recall how he spent some funds.
(D) He is offering to demonstrate a procedure.

Questions 151-152 refer to the following article.

A New Way to Get News

(October 15)—For more than 70 years, the Boldwin Times has been Boldwin citizens' preferred source of daily news. These days, however, people want to learn about news events as they happen, not once a day. For this reason, we released the Boldwin Times app this morning as an even more convenient alternative to our Web site.

With our app, readers can get the same in-depth local coverage and insightful analyses of regional and national news that they have come to expect from our print and online editions. However, they can also use its customizable notifications feature to receive alerts about breaking news stories that are of interest to them. The app's content is free for the first month and just $4.99 per month after that. Visit any major app store today to download it.

151. What is the purpose of the article?

(A) To advertise a digital product
(B) To inform about a local trend
(C) To summarize a company's history
(D) To announce the launch of a new column

152. What is indicated about the *Boldwin Times?*

(A) It used to be the most popular publication in the region.
(B) It is famous for its business news coverage.
(C) There is more than one way to access its content.
(D) Many of its readers live outside of Boldwin.

GO ON TO THE NEXT PAGE

Enjoy both dinner and a movie at Hasley Cinema!

Funfare Hall, Hasley Cinema's new dine-in theater, is open for business! Ticketholders to all screenings in the hall can enjoy not just popcorn but also less traditional movie fare like hamburgers and pizza. — [1] —. Our waiters will take your order and serve the food at your seat, which is extra-wide and equipped with a retractable tray table. Funfare Hall's unique dining-and-viewing experience is an exciting addition to the cinema that the *Billegant Herald* has already called "the top choice for film enthusiasts in Billegant". — [2] —.

Special events at Hasley Cinema in March:

<u>Director's Screening of *Southerland*</u>: Come to Funfare Hall on March 19 to see the thoughtful new drama before its wide release. — [3] —. After the screening, director Tanesha Robson will discuss the film and take questions from the audience.

<u>Kids Tuesdays</u>: Every Tuesday morning in March, parents can bring kids under six years old to screenings of child-friendly movies for just $5 per adult and $2 per child. — [4] —.

---

153. What is NOT mentioned about Funfare Hall?

(A) It is the site of an upcoming preview screening.
(B) Its patrons can order a variety of foods.
(C) It was reviewed in a newspaper.
(D) Its seating is spacious.

154. What is indicated about a weekly event in March?

(A) It is intended for groups of schoolchildren.
(B) Its ticket prices are lower for some viewers.
(C) Its schedule includes an interactive discussion.
(D) It offers an opportunity to see older films.

155. In which of the positions marked [1], [2], [3], and [4] does the following sentence best belong?

"And all of this is available at the touch of a button—even while the film is playing!"

(A) [1]
(B) [2]
(C) [3]
(D) [4]

Questions 156-158 refer to the following customer review.

www.tradespeoplereview.com

Home >> Cities >> Omaha >> Plumbers >> Fulton Plumbing

Reviewed by: Harper Quintero   Posted: March 22

My friend had a bathroom renovation done by Chad Fulton and his team, and she recommended the business to me. When I discovered that water was dripping from my kitchen faucet even when it was turned all the way off, I contacted Fulton Plumbing to resolve the issue. The representative I spoke to was able to provide an estimate over the phone, and it was an affordable price. But what I want to emphasize is how quickly the workers arrived—just twenty minutes after I made the call! This is definitely the best thing about the service, even though it wasn't really necessary in my case because my issue was unlikely to cause water damage. But I can see how those in emergency situations would really appreciate it. Anyway, Mr. Fulton and the employee accompanying him carried out the work quickly and professionally. I certainly recommend Fulton Plumbing.

156. Why did Ms. Quintero hire Fulton Plumbing?

(A) To improve a home's water pressure
(B) To have a faulty tap repaired
(C) To renovate a bathroom
(D) To hook up a kitchen appliance

157. What aspect of Fulton Plumbing does Ms. Quintero provide the most detail on?

(A) Its variety of service options
(B) Its employees' attitudes
(C) Its work fees
(D) Its response time

158. What is implied about the service Fulton Plumbing provided?

(A) It is the company's specialty.
(B) Ms. Quintero did not regard it as urgently needed.
(C) Ms. Quintero had obtained it from another provider before.
(D) It included a consultation visit.

GO ON TO THE NEXT PAGE

Master of Greenery

Does your office use plants to create a nurturing work environment? Or is there only a potted fern sitting at the foot of the receptionist's desk, with the rest of the decorations composed of boring paintings?

Unfortunately, most offices miss out on the joys of a vibrant assortment of flora because they are concerned that it will not be easy to keep the plants alive. Did you know that there are many plant species that are extremely resilient and don't need fancy soil or frequent watering, though?

Let Donna recommend which plants to buy and how to arrange them to maximize the desired effects. When she redesigns your office with a thoughtful selection of plants that require little upkeep, you'll be amazed at the resulting improvements in staff morale and productivity. Call Donna today at (990) 555-0107 to get started.

159. According to the advertisement, why do most offices choose not to have many plants?

(A) They are expensive to buy.
(B) They give off strong smells.
(C) They create a low-energy atmosphere.
(D) They seem difficult to care for properly.

160. What type of service is being advertised?

(A) Regular on-site plant tending
(B) Advice on decorating with plants
(C) Lessons on how to grow plants
(D) Disposal of unwanted plants

From:	Douglas McCoy
To:	Itsumi Wakimoto
Subject:	Trial results
Date:	January 28
Attachment:	📎 Report

Hi Ms. Wakimoto,

I just received the report on the trial of our new safety measure, and the results are clear: conducting a job hazard analysis (JHA) before construction begins has a positive effect on keeping projects on track and reducing cost. The full report is attached, but I'll summarize the key points here.

We implemented the measure on three projects—Robinson Tower, Sparks Apartments, and Bryant Market—over the past two years, and had Broseley Consulting analyze and compare those projects to our other projects that took place in the same period. Because of the injuries and other problems that the JHA prevented, Robinson Tower and Bryant Market were completed 8% and 11% faster and cost 6% and 10% less than similar projects, respectively. Sparks Apartments was merely average in both categories, but considering that it faced major problems due to unseasonable regional weather, this is excellent. For comparison, the Hubert Building, which ran into similar issues, was 15% more behind schedule and cost 13% more than average.

Remember, the initial time and money spent to conduct the JHA is *already* factored into this data. It seems pretty clear to me that we should implement this process on all projects as soon as possible. When you're ready, why don't we meet to talk about how to present this idea to the other departments? Let me know.

Sincerely,

Doug

---

161. What measure was most likely tested in the trial?

(A) Immediately investigating incidents of injury
(B) Studying potential dangers to workers ahead of time
(C) Encouraging workers to suggest safety improvements
(D) Requiring additional qualifications for certain positions

162. What is indicated about the trial?

(A) It lasted longer than initially planned.
(B) It involved an external company.
(C) Its findings were unexpected.
(D) Its data will be released publicly.

163. Which project was completed the most successfully?

(A) Robinson Tower
(B) Sparks Apartments
(C) Bryant Market
(D) The Hubert Building

164. What does Mr. McCoy suggest doing?

(A) Creating a promotional strategy
(B) Researching service providers
(C) Double-checking some calculations
(D) Streamlining an implementation process

GO ON TO THE NEXT PAGE

MEMO

To: Jem Fashion Directors
From: Larry May, Supply and Control Manager
Date: October 2
Re: Operational updates

As you know, it has been a busy year for us in the Jem Fashion operations department. We have overseen the opening of five new manufacturing hubs, and I am pleased to announce that all five are now fully operational. Goods are being produced at a rapid rate in line with the targets we set last year.

However, I have concerns about one particular area of our business. After liaising with the customer services team, it became clear to me that our goods are not being delivered within the timeframe promised to our customers. I personally conducted investigations into this and discovered the delivery company we currently use has an insufficient number of vehicles to meet our demands. This has led to a backlog of orders and many customer complaints.

Therefore, I propose meeting with the head of the delivery firm to discuss the terms of our contract with them. We need to hold them accountable for this problem and demand changes to the document as necessary. If you have any concerns about or suggestions for taking this step, please call me at extension 553 or e-mail me at larry.may@jem-fashion.com.

Larry

---

165. What is stated about Jem Fashion?

(A) It achieved record profits last year.
(B) It has reorganized a department.
(C) It has launched a new product line.
(D) It recently underwent an expansion.

166. What problem does Mr. May mention?

(A) Orders are not being completed on time.
(B) A manufacturing facility is not yet operational.
(C) Merchandise has been found to be defective.
(D) Delivery vehicles are frequently breaking down.

167. What does Mr. May propose that Jem Fashion do?

(A) Replace an account manager
(B) Revise a complaints procedure
(C) Renegotiate an agreement
(D) Make a public apology

GO ON TO THE NEXT PAGE

Test 9

Goodwin Place Condominium Association

9070 Bradley Street
Abentel, ON N0G 1Y0

18 August

Julio Salazar
Unit 503

Dear Mr. Salazar,

Greetings from the Goodwin Place Condominium Association. We are writing to officially inform you of an addition to our condominium bylaws. From 1 September, unit owners will no longer be allowed to let any part of their unit for short-term rental (less than six months). — [1] —. You may be familiar with this practice as "using Owillo.com," but this ban applies to short-term rentals set up through any channels, even offline ones.

As you are likely aware, this addition is the result of a formal vote among association members following months of discussion. As such, it is legally binding for all members, and violating the rule even a single time will result in a substantial fine. — [2] —. For details, see the full text of the rule (Article 9, Section B, Clause 12), which is enclosed.

We hope that those among you who voted against the ban will keep in mind the considerable benefits of not allowing short-term rental. First, it will eliminate the security issues created by a constant stream of non-residents coming and going from our grounds. — [3] —. Moreover, it will preserve the spirit of Goodwin Place as a community of friendly neighbors.

To confirm that you understand this change, please sign the enclosed form and return it to the association office by 31 August. — [4] —. Note that refusal to sign does not exempt you from the rule.

Sincerely,

Courtney Graham

President
Goodwin Place Condominium Association
Encl.

---

168. What most likely can people use Owillo. com to do?

(A) Arrange paid stays on their property
(B) Communicate with their neighbors
(C) Report issues with common spaces
(D) View estimated values of homes in their area

169. What does the letter come with?

(A) A form for casting a vote
(B) A timeline for some maintenance work
(C) A collection of statistics
(D) An excerpt from a set of regulations

170. What is suggested about some residents of Goodwin Place?

(A) They requested a safety inspection.
(B) They expressed opposition to a proposal.
(C) They have incurred some financial penalties.
(D) They would like to make alterations to their units.

171. In which of the positions marked [1], [2], [3], and [4] does the following sentence best belong?

"Multiple violations will provoke legal action by the association."

(A) [1]
(B) [2]
(C) [3]
(D) [4]

Test 9

GO ON TO THE NEXT PAGE

Questions 172-175 refer to the following online chat discussion.

| Brather Public Library | Staff Chat — ☐ X |

Clifton Sanders [10:19 A.M.]

Hey, Amanda and Jeffrey. I'm going through the comment cards that we got from book club participants this past week, and there's an issue I think you should know about.

Amanda Thomas [10:20 A.M.]

What is it, Clifton?

Clifton Sanders [10:22 A.M.]

More than half of the participants of the Classics Club wrote something like, "The leader isn't doing a good job of moderating the discussion." It seems that Sabrina—the leader of that group—lets one of the participants talk too much.

Amanda Thomas [10:23 A.M.]

Ah, yes, that's the group that Doyle is in this year. He's one of the library's regular book club participants, and he tends to dominate the conversation if the leader isn't assertive.

Jeffrey Shim [10:24 A.M.]

Oh, Doyle! It's too bad that Sabrina has to deal with him her first time leading a club.

Clifton Sanders [10:25 A.M.]

Should I just give her a summary of the feedback as usual, or does this require some kind of special response?

Amanda Thomas [10:26 A.M.]

We should do something about it. I'll sit down with her and give her some tips for balancing the participants' contributions better. But I need to run to a meeting right now. Is there anything else, Clifton?

Jeffrey Shim [10:27 A.M.]

I have a pretty good relationship with Sabrina, and I've had to lead a group with Doyle in it before. Maybe I should be the one to speak with her.

Amanda Thomas [10:28 A.M.]

Sure, Jeffrey. That sounds good.

Clifton Sanders [10:29 A.M.]

Thanks, Jeffrey. OK, talk to you both later.

172. What are the writers discussing?

(A) Advertisements for an upcoming event
(B) Book selections for a reading club
(C) Evaluations of a library program
(D) Inefficiencies in an automated process

173. What is indicated about Sabrina?

(A) She is new to a role.
(B) She is an aspiring author.
(C) She is an unpaid volunteer.
(D) She is free to take on an assignment.

174. At 10:26 A.M., what does Ms. Thomas mean when she writes, "Is there anything else, Clifton?"

(A) She hopes there is an alternative way to resolve a problem.
(B) She does not have enough information to make a decision.
(C) She is concerned that she has forgotten about a task.
(D) She wants to know if it is acceptable to end the chat.

175. What does Mr. Shim state that he has experience with?

(A) Handling a difficult patron
(B) Providing training on a skill
(C) Giving tours of a building
(D) Editing a type of writing

GO ON TO THE NEXT PAGE

Montara Campground

Information on Camping Facilities

Montara Campground is an excellent lodging option for visitors to Montara National Park. Its team of rangers is always ready to recommend hiking trails, fishing spots, and fun activities—and even answer questions about their iconic flat hats! Restroom and shower facilities at the campground are shared among all campers, and the following campsites are available for rent (fire pit included with all sites):

  -Pioneer ($15/night): Space for one tent and one vehicle

  -Adventurer ($20/night): Space for one tent and one vehicle (picnic table included)

  -Explorer ($18/night): Space for one motor home

  -Pathfinder ($26/night): Space for one motor home (water and electricity included)

Please note that demand is high in early March, when the park first opens for the season, and on national holidays, so advance booking is strongly advised.

To make a booking at Montara Campground, visit www.campingmontara.gov.

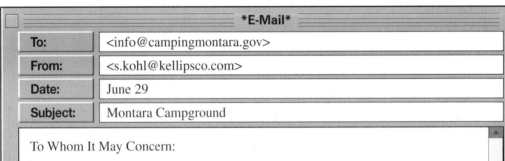

E-Mail	
To:	<info@campingmontara.gov>
From:	<s.kohl@kellipsco.com>
Date:	June 29
Subject:	Montara Campground

To Whom It May Concern:

I recently stayed at Montara Campground for one week. Although the site itself was lovely, I was disappointed with the amenities for motor homes. From the second day of our stay until the end of the week, the electricity for our campsite didn't work. Because of this, I believe we should only be charged the rate for motor home sites without water and electricity, and I'd like the difference to be sent back to me. The park ranger on duty, Chet Rinehart, was very kind, and he gave me this e-mail address so that I could get in touch with someone to help me. You can reach me by replying to this e-mail.

Thank you,

Shannon Kohl

176. In the information, the word "shared" in paragraph 1, line 4, is closest in meaning to

(A) divided
(B) discussed
(C) made known
(D) used in common

177. What is implied about Montara National Park?

(A) It is located in a region with a wet climate.
(B) It receives more visitors than any other national park.
(C) It is closed for part of the year.
(D) It has recently hired more park rangers.

178. Why did Ms. Kohl write the e-mail?

(A) To suggest revising a description
(B) To request a partial refund
(C) To explain a negative review
(D) To check the status of a complaint

179. What type of campsite did Ms. Kohl most likely reserve?

(A) Pioneer
(B) Adventurer
(C) Explorer
(D) Pathfinder

180. What is indicated about Mr. Rinehart?

(A) He wears a special type of headgear at work.
(B) He recommended moving to a different campsite.
(C) He had temporary access to a fire pit.
(D) He leads hikes on a famous mountain.

GO ON TO THE NEXT PAGE

Test 9

Association of Retail Pharmacy Managers (ARPM) 11th Annual Conference
Schedule for: Day 2 – December 4

8:00–9:00 A.M.	Shuttle service from designated hotels	
9:15–9:30 A.M.	Remarks by Anita Morrison, ARPM Executive Vice President	Main Auditorium
9:30 – 10:45 A.M.	Morning Session 1 "Refining Your Sales and Marketing Strategy" *Drew Espino, Consultant, Caruso Pharmaceutical Solutions*	Main Auditorium
11:00 A.M.– 12:15 P.M.	Morning Session 2 "Is It Time to Upgrade Your Point-of-Sale Technology?" *Kelly Powell, Editor, 'Retail Pharmacy Today' Web site*	Main Auditorium
12:30–2:00 P.M.	Lunch Buffet	South Hall
2:00–3:15 P.M.	Afternoon Session 1 "Effective Staff Training on Patient Care" *Marshall Holloway, Manager, Allsworth Pharmacy*	Main Auditorium
3:30–4:45 P.M.	Afternoon Session 2 "Get Ready: Future Trends in Retail Pharmacy" *Radka Bielik, Professor, Paxon University College of Pharmacy*	Main Auditorium
5:00–8:00 P.M.	Closing Banquet	Grand Ballroom

• See www.arpm-conf.com for information about each speaker and their session.
• The last half hour of each session will be reserved for audience Q&A.
• Refreshments will be available outside the auditorium during the morning and afternoon breaks.

Notice

For personal reasons, Marshall Holloway will be unable to join us today to give his scheduled session, "Effective Staff Training on Patient Care." Sarah Hughes, our standby speaker and the ARPM's chief operating officer, will lead a replacement session. In a presentation entitled "How to Find and Eliminate Inefficiency," she will describe her five-step system for identifying and addressing issues that waste pharmacies' time and money. Attendees who feel strongly inconvenienced by this change and would prefer financial compensation over attending Ms. Hughes's presentation must make this request at the registration desk before the session begins.

In addition, conference center management has informed us that the South Hall's catering fridge failed last night, spoiling much of the food that would have been served at lunch today. Please use the attached voucher to purchase lunch at a nearby restaurant instead. Tonight's dinner event will go forward as planned.

We apologize deeply for these inconveniences and ask for your understanding.

–Organizers of the ARPM 11th Annual Conference

181. What is most likely true about the conference?

(A) It takes place over a two-day period.
(B) Its venue has accommodations on site.
(C) It will be recorded and broadcast online.
(D) It is mainly attended by academics.

182. According to the conference schedule, what can conference attendees do?

(A) Bring certain beverages into the auditorium
(B) Test new types of retail equipment
(C) Ask questions at the end of each session
(D) Reveal their reactions to conference content electronically

183. By what time must attendees ask to be reimbursed for an inconvenience?

(A) 9:30 A.M.
(B) 11:00 A.M.
(C) 12:30 P.M.
(D) 2:00 P.M.

184. What is suggested about Ms. Hughes?

(A) She prepared a talk in case of an emergency.
(B) She will use another speaker's materials.
(C) She will finish at a later time than scheduled.
(D) She spoke at a previous ARPM conference.

185. What caused the second problem mentioned in the notice?

(A) A mistake in a catering order
(B) A malfunctioning appliance
(C) Poor behavior by ARPM members
(D) Unplanned road work on a nearby street

GO ON TO THE NEXT PAGE

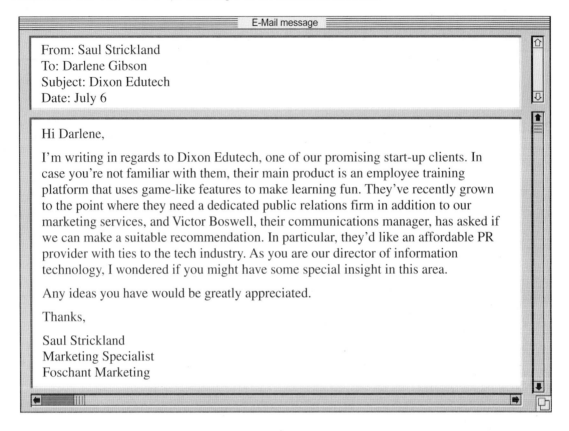

E-Mail message

From: Saul Strickland
To: Darlene Gibson
Subject: Dixon Edutech
Date: July 6

Hi Darlene,

I'm writing in regards to Dixon Edutech, one of our promising start-up clients. In case you're not familiar with them, their main product is an employee training platform that uses game-like features to make learning fun. They've recently grown to the point where they need a dedicated public relations firm in addition to our marketing services, and Victor Boswell, their communications manager, has asked if we can make a suitable recommendation. In particular, they'd like an affordable PR provider with ties to the tech industry. As you are our director of information technology, I wondered if you might have some special insight in this area.

Any ideas you have would be greatly appreciated.

Thanks,

Saul Strickland
Marketing Specialist
Foschant Marketing

LUNEDAY PARTNERS

Public Relations Services

Whether your company is just starting out or is an established business, Luneday Partners is ready to provide you with smart, cutting-edge service. We will take the time to understand your brand, challenges, and goals in order to craft a unique and effective public relations strategy for you.

Here are a few more reasons to choose Luneday Partners:

- Our wide range of services include everything from copywriting to event support.
- We use advanced digital tools to give you valuable data about how your brand is perceived.
- We have special connections in several fields, including real estate, technology, and finance.

Visit us at www.luneday.com to see testimonials from our many satisfied clients.

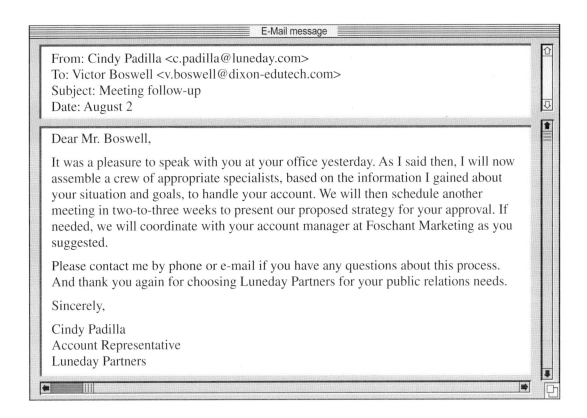

E-Mail message

From: Cindy Padilla <c.padilla@luneday.com>
To: Victor Boswell <v.boswell@dixon-edutech.com>
Subject: Meeting follow-up
Date: August 2

Dear Mr. Boswell,

It was a pleasure to speak with you at your office yesterday. As I said then, I will now assemble a crew of appropriate specialists, based on the information I gained about your situation and goals, to handle your account. We will then schedule another meeting in two-to-three weeks to present our proposed strategy for your approval. If needed, we will coordinate with your account manager at Foschant Marketing as you suggested.

Please contact me by phone or e-mail if you have any questions about this process. And thank you again for choosing Luneday Partners for your public relations needs.

Sincerely,

Cindy Padilla
Account Representative
Luneday Partners

---

186. What is the purpose of the first e-mail?

(A) To ask for assistance with a client inquiry
(B) To introduce a staff training resource
(C) To report a difficulty with a contractor
(D) To express concern about the scope of an endeavor

187. Why most likely would Ms. Gibson recommend Luneday Partners to Mr. Strickland?

(A) Its price range
(B) Its technological tools
(C) Its connections in another industry
(D) Its services for live events

188. According to the advertisement, what is available on Luneday Partners' Web site?

(A) Appointment reservation forms
(B) Data on current trends in its field
(C) Positive feedback about its work
(D) Profiles of its top executives

189. Whom did Ms. Padilla meet with on August 1 ?

(A) A sales representative at Dixon Edutech
(B) The communications manager at Dixon Edutech
(C) The director of information technology at Foschant Marketing
(D) A marketing specialist at Foschant Marketing

190. What does Ms. Padilla indicate she will do next?

(A) Schedule a presentation meeting
(B) Update a strategy proposal
(C) Set a project budget
(D) Form an account team

GO ON TO THE NEXT PAGE

Test 9

Arts in Rellsdale

By Shane Weller

RELLSDALE (September 10)—Just weeks after its children's summer classes came to an end, the Rellsdale Community Center has begun planning another exciting activity. The 32nd Annual Rellsdale Community Art Show will be held in its auditorium during the week of October 22–28.

The event began 32 years ago when Grant Lindsey, a local watercolor painter, invited his friends to join him in exhibiting their paintings in a small show. It has since grown into a chance for all of Rellsdale's professional and amateur visual artists to display their talents.

In its current form, the art show features a contest judged by a committee led by Tina Jordan, the community center's director, and including Adnan Khalif, an art historian at Malker University. Also, most of the artwork in the show is for sale. Twenty-five percent of the proceeds of each sale goes toward funding the upkeep of the center's buildings and grounds.

Hye-Ran Kyeong, the center's vice director of recreation and the show's organizer, urges citizens of all ages, backgrounds, and artistic disciplines to consider exhibiting. Those interested should visit www.rellsdaleart.com for instructions.

32nd ANNUAL RELLSDALE COMMUNITY ART SHOW

Welcome to the Rellsdale Community Art Show!
The Rellsdale Community Center is glad you have joined us
to celebrate the artistic gifts of our community.

Schedule of the Opening Night Reception

5 P.M.– Doors open
6 P.M.– Provision of refreshments donated by Rellsdale
        Supermarket
7 P.M.– Welcoming remarks and announcement of contest
        results by the head of the judging committee
9 P.M.– Doors close

Other helpful information:

✦ To locate a certain work of art, see the full list of entries ordered alphabetically by artist on pages 3 and 4.
✦ To inquire about purchasing a piece, please speak promptly with a member of our staff. Remember, sales are first come, first served!

Page 1

```
╔══════════════════ E-Mail message ══════════════════╗
║ ┌─────────┬──────────────────────────────────────┐ ║
║ │ From:   │ Samuel Mayhew                         │ ║
║ ├─────────┼──────────────────────────────────────┤ ║
║ │ To:     │ Eulalia Prosser                       │ ║
║ ├─────────┼──────────────────────────────────────┤ ║
║ │ Subject:│ Inquiry                               │ ║
║ ├─────────┼──────────────────────────────────────┤ ║
║ │ Date:   │ November 4                            │ ║
║ └─────────┴──────────────────────────────────────┘ ║
```

Dear Ms. Prosser,

Hello. My friend Anne Watson bought the wooden sculpture you exhibited in the Rellsdale Community Arts Show. I think it's gorgeous, and I would love to have one like it for my office. So I got your e-mail address from the business card that came with Anne's purchase. Could you write me back and let me know whether you have other pieces for sale? Thank you.

Sincerely,

Samuel Mayhew

191. What is one purpose of the article?

(A) To describe the success of a fund-raising effort
(B) To publicize the accomplishments of local artists
(C) To invite people to participate in a community event
(D) To announce a new offering at a community center

192. How will some collected funds be used?

(A) To maintain a facility
(B) To hold classes for youth
(C) To publish a history book
(D) To reward a contest winner

193. According to the brochure page, how is a list of artwork organized?

(A) By the type of art
(B) By the title of the artwork
(C) By the location of the artwork
(D) By the name of the creator

194. Who spoke publicly on October 22 ?

(A) Mr. Lindsey
(B) Ms. Jordan
(C) Mr. Khalif
(D) Ms. Kyeong

195. What is most likely true about Ms. Prosser?

(A) She was mentioned on another page of the brochure.
(B) She contributed refreshments to a gathering.
(C) She received an e-mail from Ms. Watson.
(D) She is an amateur visual artist living in Rellsdale.

GO ON TO THE NEXT PAGE

Questions 196-200 refer to the following job advertisement, meeting notes, and article.

SUMMER LEGAL INTERN

Huane Associates, a growing presence in the field of commercial law in the Gilvey area, is offering a legal internship from June 1 through July 31.
The intern will perform legal research and analysis, draft a variety of legal documents, attend client meetings, and complete special projects, all with the benefit of direction and feedback from seasoned attorneys.

Requirements

- Current law student who has completed at least one year of law school
- Able to work 30 hours per week at firm's office in Waterfront District

Preferred qualifications

- Familiarity with local, state, and federal commercial law
- Proficiency in legal research platforms such as Rolento

To apply, e-mail the following documents to marlon.terry@huanelegal.com by March 31: a one-page cover letter, your résumé, your law school transcript, and a writing sample of between three and five pages.

Internship Documentation – Biweekly Meeting Notes	
Date: Wed., July 8 **Intern:** Renée Walters **Supervisor:** Marlon Terry	
Reflections on previous projects/ experiences	• Analysis of online retailer tax laws: Marlon gave general feedback and suggestions for improving "Summary" section • Meeting with Sovaughn Shoes: In response to Renée's question, Marlon discussed options for handling surprising requests from clients
Updates on ongoing projects	• Blog post on history of non-disclosure agreements: Renée reported difficulty working with Rolento; Marlon scheduled training session for July 10 at 1 P.M. • Drafting of employment contract for Marquitta Café: Renée has been unable to schedule necessary meeting with Jeannie Wilkerson; Marlon will contact Jeannie about this
New assignments	• Drafting of operating agreement for Blair-Logue, LLC: Tentatively due July 15; Renée should refer to resources in internal network's "Operating Agreements" file

Saying Goodbye to Huane Associates' First Intern

By Akira Chinen   Posted Tuesday, July 28

Renée Walters' internship at our firm will be coming to a close at the end of this week. Ms. Walters has spent the past two months working on a variety of tasks under the supervision of associate Marlon Terry. You may have seen Ms. Walters attending meetings with Mr. Terry or read her blog post on non-disclosure agreements.

As she finished up a draft of an operating agreement yesterday, Ms. Walters told me that the practical experience she has gotten here has been very valuable. She also said she was especially thankful to Mr. Terry for his thoughtful mentorship.

For his part, Mr. Terry said that he has really enjoyed supervising Ms. Walters because he has "seen her grow so much even in this short time." He expressed hopes that the internship program would take place again next summer with even more student participants.

All members of the firm are invited to a goodbye party for Ms. Walters at 4 P.M. on Friday in Conference Room A.

---

196. What does the job advertisement NOT ask applicants to submit?

(A) A record of school performance
(B) A letter of professional reference
(C) A list of career experiences
(D) Evidence of writing skills

197. What do the meeting notes indicate Ms. Walters had trouble with?

(A) Arranging a meeting with an executive
(B) Understanding some printed feedback
(C) Commuting to a certain neighborhood
(D) Using an electronic research tool

198. In the article, the word "under" in paragraph 1, line 2, is closest in meaning to

(A) having as her title
(B) concealed by
(C) subject to
(D) less than

199. What is suggested about Ms. Walters?

(A) She uploaded a document to a network folder.
(B) She took Mr. Terry's advice for dealing with a client.
(C) The deadline for one of her projects was postponed.
(D) A special training session for her did not take place.

200. According to the article, how does Mr. Terry want to change the internship program?

(A) By increasing the number of positions
(B) By extending its duration
(C) By having more employees involved
(D) By giving participants more responsibilities

Test 9

Stop! This is the end of the test. If you finish before time is called, you may go back to Parts 5, 6, and 7 and check your work.

TEST 10

READING TEST

In the Reading test, you will read a variety of texts and answer several different types of reading comprehension questions. The entire Reading test will last 75 minutes. There are three parts, and directions are given for each part. You are encouraged to answer as many questions as possible within the time allowed.

You must mark your answers on the separate answer sheet. Do not write your answers in your test book.

PART 5

Directions: A word or phrase is missing in each of the sentences below. Four answer choices are given below each sentence. Select the best answer to complete the sentence. Then mark the letter (A), (B), (C), or (D) on your answer sheet.

---

101. The caterers have been instructed to serve additional ------- of the dessert upon request only.

(A) guests
(B) menus
(C) recipes
(D) portions

102. Mr. Hayes has been using tax software to prepare ------- income tax report for years.

(A) he
(B) him
(C) his own
(D) himself

103. All entries must be signed and submitted on or ------- February 11 to be considered.

(A) within
(B) until
(C) before
(D) from

104. ------- more graduates would apply for its specialist positions, Colep Farms agreed to host field trips for university agricultural classes.

(A) If
(B) Even
(C) So that
(D) As soon as

105. One way that grocery chains are addressing the environmental problems ------- with delivery services is by using reusable packaging.

(A) associated
(B) associate
(C) associating
(D) associations

106. The construction noise from the building next door was so loud that we could ------- hear our coworkers speak.

(A) still
(B) hardly
(C) finally
(D) ever

107. The enthusiastic ------- of the band's new album by audiences has been a surprise to critics.

(A) receipt
(B) received
(C) recipient
(D) reception

108. Several candidates interviewed for the receptionist position, ------- of whom impressed the hiring committee.

(A) none
(B) nobody
(C) those
(D) both

276

109. The project leader is responsible for ------- the members of the team of any updates to the plan.
(A) coordinating
(B) notifying
(C) recruiting
(D) crediting

110. Yarroll Bank provides loans to ------- small business owners at attractive interest rates.
(A) relative
(B) aspiring
(C) unprecedented
(D) customary

111. Once the air conditioning units -------, one employee on each floor should be assigned to monitor their use.
(A) were installed
(B) installed
(C) install
(D) are installed

112. The laboratory may have been contaminated with a hazardous chemical substance and has ------- been sterilized.
(A) since
(B) so
(C) yet
(D) enough

113. The panel's moderator was praised for ------- maneuvering the discussion through some difficult topics.
(A) skills
(B) skilled
(C) skillful
(D) skillfully

114. Sales representatives at Bigor Communications earn a flat commission ------- $100 for each cable package sold.
(A) about
(B) of
(C) over
(D) toward

115. Travel ------- will only be processed upon return from a trip and are contingent on managerial approval.
(A) reimbursing
(B) reimbursement
(C) reimbursements
(D) reimbursed

116. ------- our longstanding relationship with Garston Tech, it is no surprise that it will play an important part in developing our new apps.
(A) Given
(B) Notwithstanding
(C) Beyond
(D) In place of

117. Bunod Hotel patrons are encouraged to call the front desk ------- they require service.
(A) that
(B) whether
(C) anytime
(D) as though

118. Clinical trials have shown that the drug can treat symptoms that have proven ------- to other medications.
(A) resistant
(B) resisting
(C) resistibly
(D) resistible

119. Although it was not popular during her lifetime, Ms. Chang's unique style of design ------- considerable influence over later generations of architects.
(A) invested
(B) conferred
(C) dominated
(D) exerted

GO ON TO THE NEXT PAGE

120. In general, customers struggle with making decisions when ------- too many options to choose from.

(A) offers
(B) offered
(C) offering
(D) offer

121. Sorgan latex paint should be used only ------- a coat of Sorgan-brand primer has been applied to the bare surface.

(A) as much as
(B) after
(C) over
(D) in case

122. Specialty Health and Cosmetics Mart presents a satisfying ------- of wellness products in a small, well-organized space.

(A) array
(B) substitute
(C) expectation
(D) outcome

123. ------- among the reasons Franklin Bookstore purchased this software was its effectiveness at keeping data secure.

(A) Primary
(B) Informative
(C) Productive
(D) Selective

124. Ms. Nakano is ------- the hardest-working executive at Shibata Engineering.

(A) reputation
(B) reputable
(C) reputing
(D) reputedly

125. The popularity of the outdoor summer exhibition "Rock Art" has led the parks department to look into whether it can be made -------.

(A) feasible
(B) mandatory
(C) permanent
(D) abundant

126. If the prototype for our newest V2 coffee maker had received high marks from product testers, Techmart ------- to enter into a long-term contract with us.

(A) decided
(B) can decide
(C) would have decided
(D) would have been decided

127. Wait times at Skyspear Airlines' service counters have been cut in half ------- the self-check-in kiosks it recently introduced.

(A) wherever
(B) together with
(C) while
(D) thanks to

128. Some conference participants were displeased that organizers scheduled the only two workshops on statistics to take place -------.

(A) identically
(B) simultaneously
(C) intentionally
(D) adversely

129. The photographers whose pictures are used on the blog are not named, ------- do they receive compensation for their contributions.

(A) nor
(B) rather
(C) except
(D) although

130. The next task assigned to the interim accountant is to ------- the system by which research projects are funded.

(A) grant
(B) overhaul
(C) deduct
(D) experiment

PART 6

Directions: Read the texts that follow. A word, phrase, or sentence is missing in parts of each text. Four answer choices for each question are given below the text. Select the best answer to complete the text. Then mark the letter (A), (B), (C), or (D) on your answer sheet.

Questions 131-134 refer to the following e-mail.

From: Theresa Yates

To: Irma Sims

Subject: Gryell Toys Project Team

Date: September 2

Hi Irma,

As you requested, I thought about which of the senior engineers should replace me as head of the Gryell Toys team when I retire. While Karen could probably do the job if needed, Trevor is my recommendation. Karen's grasp of engineering may be ------- , but she doesn't always
131.
communicate clearly, and communication is very important in managing. In contrast, Trevor ------- his decent engineering know-how with outstanding interpersonal skills. In my
132.
opinion, he ------- an excellent project team leader.
133.

Please let me know if you need any more information to make your decision, or if you would like to discuss my recommendation in person. ------- .
134.

- Theresa

---

131. (A) superior
(B) urgent
(C) maximum
(D) eager

132. (A) prioritizes
(B) amplifies
(C) assesses
(D) designates

133. (A) is
(B) would be
(C) has been
(D) would have been

134. (A) And thank you again for this exciting opportunity.
(B) I have no particular preference, so choose whichever you like.
(C) I will be in-office all week, wrapping up my assignments.
(D) There are only a few more minor points to cover.

Questions 135-138 refer to the following press release.

Melapin Symphony
Media Relations Office

Beginning in May, the Melapin Symphony will play and livestream a monthly special concert in a program called "Share the Music".

The program has been made possible by a grant from the Okafor Foundation, an organization dedicated to increasing access to music. ------. Share the Music is mainly intended for people
              135.
with mobility issues, but it will be open to all members of the public.

The concerts will be viewable for free through a page on the symphony's Web site, www.

melapinsymphony.com, ------ they take place. ------, visitors may be required to create and
                     136.   137.
log in through a member account in order to access the page.

Symphony members and officials are pleased to be collaborating with the Okafor Foundation.

Daiki Sano, its director, said, "The opportunity to share our music with more people is ------.
                                                                                      138.
We are very grateful."

---

135. (A) Its other activities include music camps for children with disabilities.
(B) The funding will even enable the concerts to be streamed over the Internet.
(C) Later, wheelchair spaces were also added to Melapin Symphony Hall.
(D) Before now, no patrons were permitted backstage during performances.

136. (A) meanwhile
(B) unless
(C) as
(D) then

137. (A) Namely
(B) However
(C) Likewise
(D) Instead

138. (A) honored
(B) to honor
(C) an honor
(D) honoring

Questions 139-142 refer to the following letter.

11 May

Shaheena Singh
83 Bowfield Street
Benningham, UK
BN4 7DA

Dear Ms. Singh,

I recently received your letter in which you described the poor condition of the pavement on your street and the flat tyre you suffered ------- the uneven paving slabs. As you pointed out in **139.** your letter, the roads and pavements in your neighbourhood have been in desperate need of repair for quite some time. -------. **140.**

Beginning on 18 May, work crews will remove and reinstall all paving slabs on Bowfield Street and several other streets in the area. They will also fix the potholes in the roads that many motorists complained about at the community meeting in March. I hope this will come as good news to you and your fellow constituents ------- in the area. **141.**

Please accept my apologies for the incident with your car. I am confident that the planned work will prevent any similar ------- from occurring in the future. **142.**

Sincerely,

Mike Duke
City Councillor

---

139. (A) by
(B) following
(C) during
(D) due to

140. (A) I am proud to announce that the work is finally complete.
(B) Unfortunately, street repairs are not within our budget this year.
(C) Please know that I am committed to rectifying the situation.
(D) We will consider your proposal and attempt to find a solution.

141. (A) reside
(B) residing
(C) residents
(D) residential

142. (A) inaccuracies
(B) misunderstandings
(C) cancelations
(D) accidents

GO ON TO THE NEXT PAGE

Questions 143-146 refer to the following advertisement.

Diamond Sewing

308 Third Street, Lawrence, 555-0184

www.diamondsewing.com

Diamond Sewing has been helping the people of Lawrence look ------- in their clothes for over
                                                                        143.
10 years. Whether it is because your size has changed or a new purchase doesn't quite fit right,

our sewing specialists are always ready to make the alterations you need. -------.
                                                                              144.

We ------- specialize in wedding gowns, tuxedoes, and other formalwear. Hundreds of brides
      145.
and grooms have walked down the aisle in clothing altered by Diamond Sewing.

Do you have clothing that is frayed, worn or ripped? We also provide expert ------- services!
                                                                                146.
Come see us for a free consultation before you throw away that beloved pair of jeans or vintage

jacket. We are open Monday through Friday, 9 A.M. to 5 P.M., and 9 A.M. to 12 P.M. on

Saturdays.

---

143. (A) stuns
　　　(B) stunned
　　　(C) stunning
　　　(D) stunningly

144. (A) A well-fitting suit is essential for today's
　　　　　business professional.
　　　(B) Orders can even be placed entirely
　　　　　online through our Web site.
　　　(C) Simply choose from among our
　　　　　collection of design templates.
　　　(D) We can shorten pants, put darts in
　　　　　shirts, and much more.

145. (A) ideally
　　　(B) recently
　　　(C) exceedingly
　　　(D) particularly

146. (A) mending
　　　(B) manufacturing
　　　(C) laundering
　　　(D) styling

Directions: In this part you will read a selection of texts, such as magazine and newspaper articles, e-mails, and instant messages. Each text or set of texts is followed by several questions. Select the best answer for each question and mark the letter (A), (B), (C), or (D) on your answer sheet.

Questions 147-148 refer to the following notice.

NOTICE

We believe the monitor on this stationary bicycle was shattered by a person who used it while also holding hand weights. We cannot be sure, because our security cameras only show that the person who likely did it was a non-member that followed a member into our center. Please do not allow other people to enter the building with you. If someone asks you to do this, claiming they have lost or forgotten their card, tell them to wait outside while you alert the front desk. Thank you.

—Hounsler Fitness Center Management

147. Where would the notice most likely appear?

(A) On some damaged machinery
(B) Outside of a building entrance
(C) Next to some training weights
(D) Behind a reception area

148. What are readers of the notice asked to do?

(A) Avoid blocking security cameras
(B) Use one type of equipment at a time
(C) Report the loss of their cards immediately
(D) Refrain from letting others into a facility

GO ON TO THE NEXT PAGE

Questions 149-150 refer to the following text-message chain.

Alex White, 3:09 P.M.
Bratislava, I'm sorry to bother you on your day off, but I have a quick question. We're almost out of gloves. Didn't you order some last week?

Bratislava Kovac, 3:11 P.M.
Oh yes, they came in yesterday, but I didn't have the chance to unpack them. They're in a box on my desk.

Alex White, 3:13 P.M.
Yes, I see them. Thanks! We had a couple of extra walk-in patients today, so we've gone through gloves faster than expected.

Bratislava Kovac, 3:14 P.M.
Got it. I'm going to need a record of how many you take and who they're for, though.

Alex White, 3:16 P.M.
Oh, can I just tell you on Monday? I'm already back at Reception.

Bratislava Kovac, 3:17 P.M.
Sorry, but that's a bit too far off. Could you just write it on a sticky note and put it on my door? I'd rather not risk either of us forgetting.

Alex White, 3:18 P.M.
Sure, I'll do that. Thanks again, Bratislava.

149. What is probably true about Ms. Kovac?

(A) She used up some supplies.
(B) She does not have a private office.
(C) She has gone out on an errand.
(D) She is not currently on duty.

150. At 3:17 P.M., what does Ms. Kovac mean when she writes, "that's a bit too far off"?

(A) She is arguing that a figure has been miscalculated.
(B) She is criticizing a modification to a document.
(C) She is refusing to seek out a location.
(D) She is opposing a suggestion to delay a task.

Questions 151-153 refer to the following consent form.

Ticard, Inc.

Market Research Participation Consent Form

Thank you for agreeing to participate in this study of men aged 18 to 34. You will be shown two versions of a television advertisement for a facial razor and asked for your opinions on each. The entire process will take approximately 30 minutes.

Please read the items below and write your initials in the adjacent boxes to indicate your agreement to each.

- I consent to the audio recording of my responses during the study and the use of these recordings, with my identifying information removed, internally by Ticard. ☐

- I understand that I may stop my participation in the study at any time by informing the researchers of my wish to do so. ☐

- Afterward, I will not speak about or create any physical or digital materials about the contents of this study. ☐

- I have asked the researchers any questions I have about this study. ☐

Participant name: _____   Signature: _____

Date: _____

---

151. What will participants do for the study?

(A) Try out a product
(B) Compare two designs
(C) Describe their habits
(D) Watch some video clips

152. According to the form, what will happen after the study?

(A) The data will be anonymized.
(B) Some recordings will be destroyed.
(C) A follow-up questionnaire will be sent out.
(D) The researchers will answer participants' questions.

153. What must the participants agree to do?

(A) Speak honestly about their opinions
(B) Keep information about the study confidential
(C) Disclose their participation in any previous studies
(D) Retain a copy of the form for a period of time

GO ON TO THE NEXT PAGE

Questions 154-155 refer to the following e-mail.

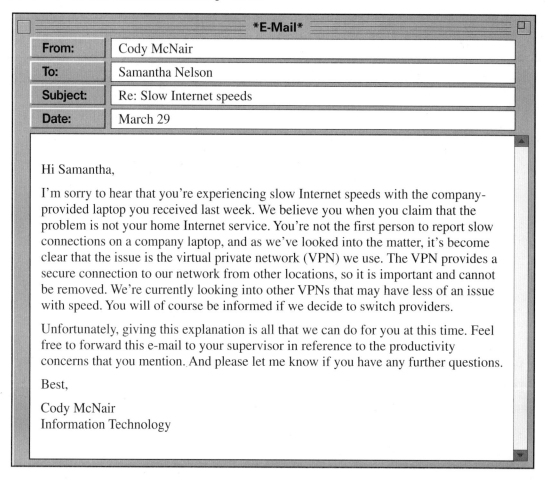

From:	Cody McNair
To:	Samantha Nelson
Subject:	Re: Slow Internet speeds
Date:	March 29

Hi Samantha,

I'm sorry to hear that you're experiencing slow Internet speeds with the company-provided laptop you received last week. We believe you when you claim that the problem is not your home Internet service. You're not the first person to report slow connections on a company laptop, and as we've looked into the matter, it's become clear that the issue is the virtual private network (VPN) we use. The VPN provides a secure connection to our network from other locations, so it is important and cannot be removed. We're currently looking into other VPNs that may have less of an issue with speed. You will of course be informed if we decide to switch providers.

Unfortunately, giving this explanation is all that we can do for you at this time. Feel free to forward this e-mail to your supervisor in reference to the productivity concerns that you mention. And please let me know if you have any further questions.

Best,

Cody McNair
Information Technology

---

154. What is most likely true about Ms. Nelson?

(A) She is not authorized to access part of a network.
(B) She asked to have some equipment replaced.
(C) She did not read an instruction manual.
(D) She is currently working remotely.

155. What does Mr. McNair give Ms. Nelson permission to do?

(A) Uninstall a program from a laptop
(B) Share his message with another person
(C) Contact him at home if an issue reoccurs
(D) Use an alternative to an approved provider

Blizzard Hockey

Press Conference

Blizzard management is excited to offer you the opportunity to meet the person tasked with leading the team to victory in their new home. Dolores Ikeda, owner of the Blizzard, is hosting a press conference to introduce the team's new general manager. The press conference will consist of a speech by Ms. Ikeda, a speech by the new general manager, a question-and-answer session, and a photo opportunity.

WHERE: Shallard Arena Press Room (1st floor, near North Entrance)
Space will be limited, so bring press credentials to ensure entry.

WHEN: Wednesday, June 8, at 11 A.M.
Please be present and seated by 10:45.

CONTACT: Rex Welch, Blizzard Media Relations Manager
rex.welch@blizzard-hockey.com

---

156. What will be announced at the press conference?

(A) The relocation of a hockey team
(B) The appointment of a sports executive
(C) A contract with a professional athlete
(D) Plans for building a new playing space

157. What is suggested about the press conference?

(A) Priority admission will be given to journalists.
(B) There will be a chance to tour a facility.
(C) Mr. Welch will speak after Ms. Ikeda.
(D) Promotional gifts will be handed out.

GO ON TO THE NEXT PAGE

Test 10

Questions 158-160 refer to the following letter.

December 7

Dixonette Hotel
1520 Sunset Street
Vancouver, BC V54 1R9

Dear sir or madam,

I stayed at your hotel during my visit to Vancouver on December 2–4, and I would like to share with you a memorable experience that I had. — [1] —.

On the last day of my stay, I was about to drive my rental car to the airport when I found that its battery had died. I contacted the rental car company, but their representative said that they would not be able to send assistance for two hours. — [2] —. Fortunately, I had this conversation on my mobile phone in the lobby, and Delray Scott, a member of your front desk staff, overheard it. He offered to jump-start my rental car using his own vehicle and cables. — [3] —. I gratefully accepted, and his cheerful and efficient work allowed me to arrive at the airport on time.

While I was satisfied with many aspects of your establishment, it was this act of kindness that I found most impressive. Mr. Scott deserves to be rewarded for being willing to use his valuable supplementary abilities to help out a guest in need. — [4] —. I hope that you have some kind of policy in place for this.

Sincerely,

Travis Quinn

---

158. What is the main purpose of the letter?

(A) To suggest an additional service
(B) To complain about a facility
(C) To convey praise for a worker
(D) To ask about the details of a policy

159. What did Mr. Scott most likely do on December 4 ?

(A) Left his assigned work station for a short time
(B) Charged a mobile device in a private area
(C) Asked a guest to move a parked vehicle
(D) Looked up some information on an airport Web site

160. In which of the positions marked [1], [2], [3], and [4] does the following sentence best belong?

"This could have caused me to miss my flight."

(A) [1]
(B) [2]
(C) [3]
(D) [4]

Questions 161-163 refer to the following job posting.

Job title: Route Salesperson (part-time)   **Company name**: Rotunno's, Inc.

Job location: Stockton area, California   **Job posted**: 10 days ago

Details: Rotunno's is a family-owned food manufacturer specializing in snacks aimed at health-conscious consumers. All of our products are made from at least 80% natural ingredients. We are committed to making our business a healthy and enjoyable place to work for our more than 1,100 employees. Last year, Rotunno's, Inc. was presented with a "Workplace Well-being" award from the Stockton Business Association (SBA).

The route salesperson is responsible for delivering Rotunno's products to grocery stores in a specific area. Other essential duties include conducting inventory checks and monitoring the stocking of store shelves with the company's products. Strong communication skills are a must, as regular interaction with store managers is necessary to provide the most suitable mix of Rotunno's products.

The successful candidate will drive a 22-foot delivery truck over the assigned route. While on duty, the employee will also use a tablet computer to input inventory data. The assigned work hours are from 4 P.M. to 10 P.M., Thursday to Sunday (24 hours per week).

To apply for the position, visit www.rotunnos.com/jobs and follow the instructions to upload your résumé. In order to qualify for an interview, candidates must achieve a certain score in a basic computer proficiency test that requires about 20 minutes to take.

---

161. What is NOT stated about Rotunno's, Inc.?

(A) Its products are made from mostly natural ingredients.
(B) It has been recognized by a business group.
(C) It regularly posts multiple job openings.
(D) It employs over 1,100 people.

162. What is mentioned as a duty of the advertised position?

(A) Acquiring new business clients
(B) Setting up displays at trade shows
(C) Entering data into a portable device
(D) Providing updates to the holder's supervisor

163. What are job candidates required to do?

(A) Promise to protect confidential information
(B) Submit copies of professional licenses
(C) Perform well in a phone interview
(D) Demonstrate technical skills

GO ON TO THE NEXT PAGE

Harris & Kwon Group

Harris & Kwon Group provides high-quality language services in English and Korean for reasonable prices. Located in the heart of Seoul, we have assisted domestic, overseas, and international companies of all sizes in bridging gaps in communication.

Our services include translation of printed and digital materials, transcription of video and audio clips, and interpretation for in-person meetings and large events. We also rent out audio systems that can ensure the smooth transmission of interpretations to up to 300 participants.

Automated translation and interpretation software still regularly makes errors that can cause serious confusion, while the expertise of professional translators/interpreters is unreliable, even among those with a degree in the field. That is why Harris & Kwon Group only employs language specialists who grew up using both English and Korean with native fluency. We guarantee that our output will not just be error-free, but also capture and sensitively convey cultural nuances.

Visit our Web site, www.hkgroup.co.kr, to learn more about our process and read testimonials from satisfied clients. If you would then like to discuss hiring Harris & Kwon Group for a project, use the convenient form in the "Contact" section. We are happy to provide a reliable quote for the cost of our services up front. Also, if you are inquiring on behalf of an organization that serves the public good, ask about our special rates for nonprofits.

164. What is NOT listed as a service that Harris & Kwon Group provides?

(A) Lending of specialized equipment
(B) Conversion of the language of a text
(C) Making a written copy of audio materials
(D) Advising on cultural differences in business

165. What is mentioned as a characteristic of Harris & Kwon Group's employees?

(A) Substantial career experience
(B) A completely bilingual upbringing
(C) Serious academic study of a subject
(D) Extensive training on a technology

166. What is implied about Harris & Kwon Group?

(A) It has branches in more than one country.
(B) It specializes in serving companies in a certain field.
(C) It gives a discount to clients whose work benefits society.
(D) It recently increased its number of employees.

167. According to the advertisement, what can Harris & Kwon Group do for its new customers?

(A) Supply a price estimate in advance
(B) Research the terminology of their industry
(C) Provide personal references from executives
(D) Create a customized work process

GO ON TO THE NEXT PAGE

Guy Wallace, 11:24 A.M. Hi, everyone. I'm sorry to bother you, but I was wondering where to get images to post on our Web site. I need some for the latest post I'm putting on our blog.

Jerry Grant, 11:25 A.M. Sorry, I don't know.

Sania Najjar, 11:26 A.M. I think Mark used Photofield to download stock photos. Didn't he give you the log-in information for that site?

Guy Wallace, 11:26 A.M. Let me check.

Guy Wallace, 11:28 A.M. Ah, yes, I see it! Thank you, Sania.

Peter Chen, 11:29 A.M. How are you finding it filling in for Mark, Guy?

Guy Wallace, 11:30 A.M. It's tough. There have been a lot of experiences like this, where the information needed to do his work isn't available or isn't labeled clearly.

Peter Chen, 11:31 A.M. I had the same issues when I took over Robin's position last year. We really should be documenting our job processes more clearly. It's in the company handbook, after all.

Guy Wallace, 11:32 A.M. Oh, really? I had no idea.

Peter Chen, 11:33 A.M. Most employees aren't aware of it. I'm going to speak to Amy about encouraging everyone to set aside time to create documentation.

Jerry Grant, 11:34 A.M. That's a great idea. And please don't feel hesitant to ask us questions, Guy. It's better than guessing and making a mistake.

Guy Wallace, 11:35 A.M. Thank you. I appreciate that.

168. At 11:28 A.M., what does Mr. Wallace report finding?

(A) A file of digital images
(B) A draft of an online article
(C) A user name and password
(D) A comment under a blog post

169. What is suggested about Mr. Wallace?

(A) He is temporarily handling a colleague's duties.
(B) He is a newly hired employee.
(C) He recently returned from a leave of absence.
(D) He was not previously aware of an internal Web site.

170. At 11:31 A.M., what does Mr. Chen mean when he writes, "It's in the company handbook, after all"?

(A) He is instructing Mr. Wallace to seek out some information.
(B) He is explaining why he is not allowed to assist Mr. Wallace with a task.
(C) He is emphasizing the importance of a work responsibility.
(D) He is suggesting that a company policy is outdated.

171. What does Mr. Wallace thank Mr. Grant for?

(A) Confirming the accuracy of some directions
(B) Sharing the location of some documentation
(C) Forgiving him for misunderstanding an assignment
(D) Reassuring him about potentially causing inconvenience

GO ON TO THE NEXT PAGE

Test 10

District News Tribune   *October 22*

Three businesses in the Vine Heights district—Barksdale Bakery, Triollo Grill, and Raley's Laundromat—have closed recently. Barksdale Bakery, a regional chain that also has a location in Balboa Shopping Mall, closed its Vine Heights location on October 9. Company spokesperson Brenda Chiu said it "had become difficult to compete" in the area, as a number of neighborhood coffee shops have been expanding their offerings of baked goods. — [1] —.

Triollo Grill, a Mexican-Japanese fusion restaurant, has been closed for two weeks, and a "space available" sign now hangs on its door. The popular eatery had been operating at 56 Dew Street. — [2] —. Its owner, Antonio Cruz, said he will reopen his establishment in a larger space near Alvin Park.

Raley's Laundromat closed last week. It offered customers self-service, coin-operated laundry machines, along with laundry soap vending machines. "With all the recent development, the neighborhood is changing," said owner Dolores Raley. "The new apartment buildings, such as the Deltonne, are equipped with in-unit washers and dryers. So demand for our services is decreasing." She added that, as part of a trend, several local laundromats are being converted into restaurants. — [3] —.

Ms. Raley moved her business to 17 Butler Avenue, where she has also started to offer commercial laundry services. — [4] —. Only one self-service laundry establishment, Laundry Breeze, still exists in the Vine Heights district.

The district is also left with only one eatery, Tampico Burrito, that serves Mexican food, while a food truck, Ivy's Quick Bites, offers its only Japanese food.

---

172. What is NOT suggested about the Vine Heights district?

(A) It is a competitive market for bakeries.
(B) It now has several coin-operated laundry services.
(C) It has newly-built housing.
(D) It is served by mobile food facilities.

173. What is indicated about Triollo Grill?

(A) It had recently changed ownership.
(B) It was famous for its coffee drinks.
(C) It has not gone completely out of business.
(D) It was a district's first fusion restaurant.

174. Which establishment is outside of the Vine Heights district?

(A) Balboa Shopping Mall
(B) Deltonne
(C) Laundry Breeze
(D) Tampico Burrito

175. In which of the positions marked [1], [2], [3], and [4] does the following sentence best belong?

"Indeed, an Italian bistro will soon move into her facility's empty space."

(A) [1]
(B) [2]
(C) [3]
(D) [4]

GO ON TO THE NEXT PAGE

Autumn Classes at the Artesia Institute

Classes begin the week of September 25. Each class will meet on the same day each week for eight sessions. Class fees include all necessary materials. Students are charged 80% of the class fee for second/third/fourth classes within the autumn term.

Class/Price	Description	Day/Time of Sessions
Room Life Drawing ($285)	Recommended for intermediate artists, this class will have a different live model each week.	Tuesdays/6:30 P.M.–7:30 P.M. Wednesdays/7:00 P.M.–8:00 P.M. Thursdays/6:30 P.M.–7:30 P.M.
Pottery ($300)	Students will learn wheel-throwing techniques to make bowls, vases, and more. All levels welcome.	Mondays/6:30 P.M.–8:30 P.M. Thursdays/6:30 P.M.–8:30 P.M.
Watercolor Painting ($260)	Intended for beginners, this class teaches basic watercolor techniques with a focus on landscape painting.	Mondays/6:00 P.M.–7:00 P.M. Wednesdays/6:00 P.M.–7:00 P.M. Thursdays/7:00 P.M.–8:00 P.M.
Screen Printing ($280)	Learn the steps of screen printing to make your own T-shirts. Designed for beginners, this class has never been offered before.	Tuesdays/6:30 P.M.–8:00 P.M.

To register for classes, or for more detailed information, visit www.artesiainst.com/autumn. The registration deadline is September 12. Early registration is highly recommended.

To:	Cynthia Lopez <c.lopez@artesiainst.com>
From:	Tae-Woo Park <t.park@artesiainst.com>
Date:	November 22
Subject:	Feedback survey

Dear Cynthia,

I have finished compiling the answers from the feedback survey we distributed to students on the last day of class. We had overwhelmingly positive reviews for your class, and all of the students stated that they would recommend it to others. Because of the popularity of your teaching, I don't think two classes per term is enough. If possible, I'd like you to teach an additional class for the winter term, a matter we can discuss further at the staff dinner this Friday. It will be somewhere within walking distance to the institute, and it's tentatively scheduled for 7 P.M. Pablo is making the arrangements, so please let him know if you will attend alone or with your spouse.

Thanks for your hard work!

Tae-Woo

176. How can students get a discount?

(A) By recommending the institute to friends
(B) By paying the full fee in advance
(C) By meeting an early registration deadline
(D) By enrolling in more than one class

177. What is true about the autumn classes?

(A) Two are suitable for students with a moderate level of ability.
(B) Two are being held for the first time.
(C) One is taught by a different instructor each week.
(D) One has shorter single-day sessions than all of the others.

178. Which class does Ms. Lopez most likely teach?

(A) Room Life Drawing
(B) Pottery
(C) Watercolor Painting
(D) Screen Printing

179. What does Mr. Park want Ms. Lopez to do?

(A) Train a newly hired instructor
(B) Review some survey results
(C) Increase her working hours
(D) Request supplies for the next term

180. What information does Pablo need regarding a dinner?

(A) Whether attendees have food allergies
(B) Which time is most convenient
(C) Which restaurant is preferred
(D) Whether a guest will be brought

GO ON TO THE NEXT PAGE

EyeChat

Mobile Version 3.0

Top User Reviews

Kerry Lucas ★★★★⯪ (4.5 stars)

Eyechat is great for keeping in touch with family and friends from anywhere. I've tried several of the video chat apps available on Allivanta, and this is the best one. I just wish that it would let you customize or hide the menu—its color hurts my eyes.

Dominick Frazier ★★★★☆ (4 stars)

I'm glad that Eyechat is offering "invisible" status again, but the range of emoticons is still really limited. It should allow other companies to make emoticons for its platform, like Spangler does.

Chien Nguyen ★☆☆☆☆ (1 star)

It doesn't let you use Mooth to add money to your account, even though that's much safer than handing over your credit card information. I will be uninstalling.

Yolanda Castillo ★★★★☆ (4 stars)

Please let users stop this app from starting automatically! My Titus phone doesn't have great battery life, and EyeChat makes it run out even more quickly. Otherwise, I have no complaints. Reliable video and sound quality.

Platformula Releases EyeChat Version 3.1 for Mobile

By Adriana Russell, April 8, 10:35 A.M.

Earlier this week, Platformula launched the newest version of video chat app EyeChat for mobile devices. Version 3.1 features a simplified menu that can be hidden to allow more space for video. It also supports greater integration, allowing users to charge their account through Mooth and import contacts from StarMail. The update notice from Platformula even boasts that Eyechat now allows users to buy emoticons from third-party developers, though these do not seem to exist yet. In addition, one popular feature from the desktop version of EyeChat, screen-sharing, has finally been made available in the mobile version.

Platformula bought EyeChat's developer from its founder, Gus Danielson, three years ago. The first update that the company spearheaded, 2.0, was met with strong criticism from users. Several of the preexisting features that were removed from that version, such as the ability to set the user status to "invisible", were restored in 3.0.

Online reviews of version 3.1 have been positive so far. Platformula is expected to update the mobile version of EyeChat Business next.

181. What does Mr. Nguyen indicate that he is concerned about?

(A) The security of his financial information
(B) The unhealthfulness of an online activity
(C) The increasing cost of a chat service
(D) The difficulty of deleting a mobile app

182. What is mentioned as a competitor of EyeChat?

(A) Allivanta
(B) Spangler
(C) Mooth
(D) Titus

183. What is implied about Mr. Frazier?

(A) Part of his review refers to the desktop version of EyeChat.
(B) He has experience with version 2.0 of EyeChat.
(C) His work is the primary reason that he uses EyeChat.
(D) He paid to download EyeChat.

184. Whose suggestion was NOT adopted in the updated version of EyeChat?

(A) Ms. Lucas's
(B) Mr. Frazier's
(C) Mr. Ngyuen's
(D) Ms. Castillo's

185. What is mentioned about Platformula?

(A) It was founded three years ago.
(B) It used to be headed by Mr. Danielson.
(C) It is not the original creator of EyeChat.
(D) It outsourced some development work.

GO ON TO THE NEXT PAGE

Test 10

Questions 186-190 refer to the following e-mails and property listing.

From:	Eduardo West
To:	Susan Barker
Subject:	Listing
Date:	January 16

Hi Susan,

After the meeting the other day, you mentioned that you'd be willing to look over the description I wrote for my Mowery Building listing. Here it is:

Professional office space available in Mowery Building. Corner location with open central area plus three rooms (one with sink), two single-stall bathrooms, and storage closet. Equipped with dedicated heating and cooling system, stain-resistant carpeting. Elevator access. Receives natural light throughout the day!

Then I'll add our usual paragraph about the Mowery Building. What do you think? I'd appreciate any advice you can give as a senior agent.

Thanks,
Eduardo

---

www.property-finder.com/commercial/9320

416 Floyd Avenue (Mowery Building), 2nd Floor

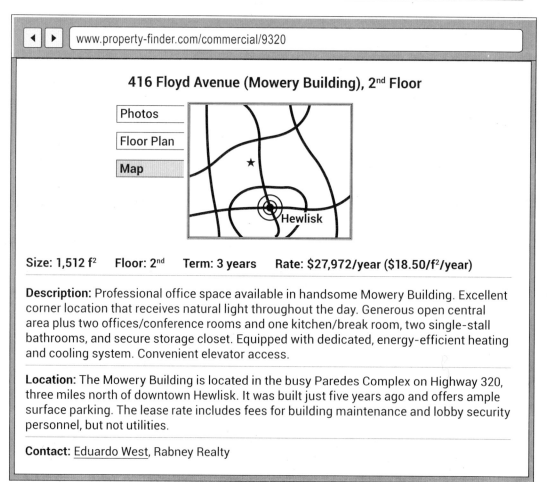

Photos
Floor Plan
Map

Size: 1,512 f²   **Floor: 2nd**   **Term: 3 years**   **Rate: $27,972/year ($18.50/f²/year)**

Description: Professional office space available in handsome Mowery Building. Excellent corner location that receives natural light throughout the day. Generous open central area plus two offices/conference rooms and one kitchen/break room, two single-stall bathrooms, and secure storage closet. Equipped with dedicated, energy-efficient heating and cooling system. Convenient elevator access.

Location: The Mowery Building is located in the busy Paredes Complex on Highway 320, three miles north of downtown Hewlisk. It was built just five years ago and offers ample surface parking. The lease rate includes fees for building maintenance and lobby security personnel, but not utilities.

Contact: Eduardo West, Rabney Realty

From:	Darlene Bullard
To:	Amir Ramdani
Subject:	Potential office space
Date:	January 19

Hi Amir,

I know that you liked the Gilbardo Street office that I showed you on Monday, but I've just learned about a new space that might be an even better fit for your business. It's a second-floor corner space in the Mowery Building that gets a lot of light. It's larger than the Gilbardo Street office, but the price per square foot is the same. The Gilbardo Street office is a little closer to downtown, but since the Mowery Building is right next to the highway, there won't be a big difference in convenience. And the Mowery office has a shorter lease term, so if you don't like it, you won't have to stay there long.

I really think you should take a look at this new space. Let me know if you're interested, and I can schedule a viewing.

Regards,

Darlene

186. What is suggested about Ms. Barker?

(A) She is Mr. West's current supervisor.
(B) She has more work experience than Mr. West.
(C) She wrote a description of an office building.
(D) She gave an assignment at a meeting.

187. What is mentioned in the first draft but NOT in the published description of the space?

(A) A third enclosed space
(B) The type of flooring
(C) The security system
(D) Exposure to some light

188. What would a tenant in the Mowery Building most likely need to pay extra for?

(A) Usage of water infrastructure
(B) Repairs to a temperature control system
(C) Access to an outdoor parking area
(D) Security services at the building entrance

189. Who most likely is Ms. Bullard?

(A) Mr. Ramdani's business partner
(B) Mr. Ramdani's legal advisor
(C) Mr. Ramdani's real estate agent
(D) Mr. Ramdani's administrative assistant

190. What can be concluded about the Gilbardo Street office?

(A) It has more than 1,500 square feet of space.
(B) It is more than 3 miles from central Hewlisk.
(C) It requires a lease term of over 5 years.
(D) It costs less than $28,000 per year.

Test 10

GO ON TO THE NEXT PAGE

Corlingdale History Museum

Major Exhibitions

Wood, Steel, and Concrete Find out the fascinating stories behind Corlingdale buildings ranging from small houses and storefronts to factories and skyscrapers.	***Ms. Collins's Library*** This look into the life of Deanna Collins, Corlingdale native and writer of the *Kiera Smith* series, is sure to delight her fans— even the ones who have grown up.
50 Years of Fur Created for the recent fiftieth anniversary of the Corlingdale Zoo, this exhibition traces the history of the facility and its amazing creatures.	***Over the Mountains*** You may not have heard of Nicolas Vicario, but you'll never forget his name once you see his beautiful paintings of the nearby Trueheart Mountains.

Notes

• We welcome groups, but please make a reservation 24 hours in advance if you plan to bring more than eight people. This can be done with our online reservation system at www.corlingdalehistory.com.

• Guided tours are only available in English, but self-guided audio tours are available in several other languages.

E-Mail message	
From:	<verag@corlingdalehistory.com>
To:	<chiranjeevi.somchai@ben-mail.net>
Subject:	RE: A visit today?
Date:	July 15

Dear Mr. Somchai,

Thank you for letting us know about your visit this afternoon. While we do usually require groups like yours to give us at least one day's notice before arrival, we will luckily be able to accommodate you this time.

Since you mentioned the *Over the Mountains* exhibition that is normally located on our third floor, I have to warn you it is currently on loan to the Meehan Museum in the United Kingdom. There is related merchandise available in our first-floor gift shop, but if the exhibition is the main attraction for your group, you should consider rescheduling your visit for August, when it will be on display here again.

If you decide to come anyway, we will look forward to seeing you this afternoon.

Best,

Vera Gordan
Operations Manager
Corlingdale History Museum

Sorry!

The exhibition normally housed in this space is currently on loan to London's Meehan Museum. It is scheduled to reopen here on August 1. Ask our information desk how your party can get free admission if you would like to return to see it then. We apologize for the inconvenience.

- Corlingdale History Museum staff

191. According to the brochure, what is the subject of a major exhibit?

(A) Textile manufacturing
(B) A children's book author
(C) Paintings of a city
(D) Local wildlife

192. What is probably true about Mr. Somchai's group?

(A) It consists of more than eight individuals.
(B) Some of its members are relatives of an artist.
(C) Some of its members do not speak English.
(D) It will receive a personal guided tour.

193. What does Ms. Gordan recommend to Mr. Somchai?

(A) Making a reservation for a performance
(B) Buying some limited-edition goods
(C) Contacting an overseas organization
(D) Touring the museum on a later date

194. On what floor of Corlingdale History Museum is the notice most likely posted?

(A) The first floor
(B) The second floor
(C) The third floor
(D) The fourth floor

195. In the notice, the word "party" in paragraph 1, line 4, is closest in meaning to

(A) celebration
(B) collection of people
(C) participation
(D) time off

Test 10

Questions 196-200 refer to the following Web page, e-mail, and article.

http://www.shalkon.gov/council/foster

Arlene Foster
Representative of District 4 (district map)

Though in her first term with the city council, Arlene has spent her entire career in public service. She was raised and attended university in Zantry. After graduating with a degree in political science, she first worked at a nonprofit organization based in Venkins that promotes the building of affordable housing. She then moved to Shalkon to become part of former council member Mitchell Blair's staff. In her time in that role, she assisted with projects such as the SETIP package of tax incentives for making environmentally-friendly improvements to residential and commercial properties.

Since joining the council, Arlene has focused on improving traffic congestion issues across Shalkon, including by planning the widening of Young Avenue. She is dedicated to maintaining open lines of communication with her constituents and reserves Tuesday mornings and Thursday afternoons exclusively for meetings with the public.

Committees:	Transportation	Contact Information
	Budget Review	

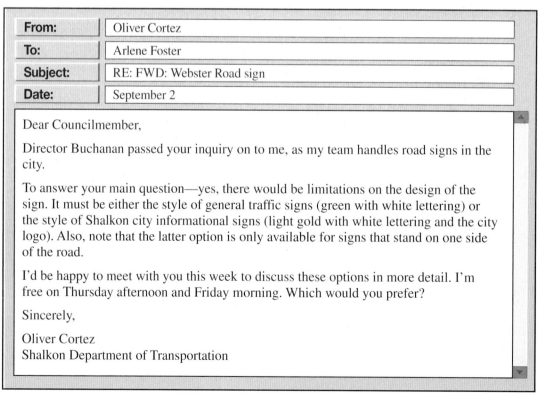

From:	Oliver Cortez
To:	Arlene Foster
Subject:	RE: FWD: Webster Road sign
Date:	September 2

Dear Councilmember,

Director Buchanan passed your inquiry on to me, as my team handles road signs in the city.

To answer your main question—yes, there would be limitations on the design of the sign. It must be either the style of general traffic signs (green with white lettering) or the style of Shalkon city informational signs (light gold with white lettering and the city logo). Also, note that the latter option is only available for signs that stand on one side of the road.

I'd be happy to meet with you this week to discuss these options in more detail. I'm free on Thursday afternoon and Friday morning. Which would you prefer?

Sincerely,

Oliver Cortez
Shalkon Department of Transportation

City Names Stretch of Webster Road after Cummings

(September 29)—A section of Webster Road between Coleman Street and Young Avenue has been co-named in honor of Frances Cummings, Shalkon's first female mayor.

Shalkon city council member Arlene Foster, who proposed the tribute, gathered with members of the late Mayor Cummings's family and others near the intersection of Webster Road and Coleman Street yesterday for a small unveiling ceremony.

The crowd cheered as a tarp was pulled off a new sign bridge that spans Webster Road and proclaims the subsequent half-mile of road to be "Frances Cummings Way". This section of road was chosen because of its proximity to Talmage Park, which Mayor Cummings famously revitalized during her tenure in office.

Council member Foster and Edmund Cummings, Mayor Cummings's son, gave speeches highlighting the mayor's positive impact on Shalkon.

196. What does the Web page state about Ms. Foster?

(A) She is not a native of Shalkon.
(B) She has been elected multiple times.
(C) She owns property on Young Avenue.
(D) She does not work in the field her degree is in.

197. When did Mr. Cortez and Ms. Foster most likely meet?

(A) On a Thursday morning
(B) On a Thursday afternoon
(C) On a Friday morning
(D) On a Friday afternoon

198. In the e-mail, the word "passed" in paragraph 1, line 1, is closest in meaning to

(A) relayed
(B) enacted
(C) declined
(D) surpassed

199. What is most likely true about the finished sign?

(A) It features a city symbol.
(B) It is visible from the entrance to a park.
(C) It is located outside of a city's limits.
(D) Its background is green.

200. What did Ms. Foster speak about on September 28 ?

(A) The future of a scientific endeavor
(B) The accomplishments of a local politician
(C) The importance of environmental conservation
(D) The unique characteristics of a neighborhood

Stop! This is the end of the test. If you finish before time is called, you may go back to Parts 5, 6, and 7 and check your work.

ANSWER SHEET

YBM 실전토익 RC 1000

수험번호

응시일자 : 20   년   월   일

성명 한글 / 한자 / 영자

Test 01 (Part 5~7)

Answer bubbles for questions 101–200.

Test 02 (Part 5~7)

Answer bubbles for questions 101–200.

ANSWER SHEET

YBM 실전토익 RC 1000

수험번호

응시일자 : 20   년   월   일

성명

한글	
한자	
영자	

Test 03 (Part 5~7)

101 102 103 104 105 106 107 108 109 110 111 112 113 114 115 116 117 118 119 120
121 122 123 124 125 126 127 128 129 130 131 132 133 134 135 136 137 138 139 140
141 142 143 144 145 146 147 148 149 150 151 152 153 154 155 156 157 158 159 160
161 162 163 164 165 166 167 168 169 170 171 172 173 174 175 176 177 178 179 180
181 182 183 184 185 186 187 188 189 190 191 192 193 194 195 196 197 198 199 200

Test 04 (Part 5~7)

101 102 103 104 105 106 107 108 109 110 111 112 113 114 115 116 117 118 119 120
121 122 123 124 125 126 127 128 129 130 131 132 133 134 135 136 137 138 139 140
141 142 143 144 145 146 147 148 149 150 151 152 153 154 155 156 157 158 159 160
161 162 163 164 165 166 167 168 169 170 171 172 173 174 175 176 177 178 179 180
181 182 183 184 185 186 187 188 189 190 191 192 193 194 195 196 197 198 199 200

ANSWER SHEET

YBM 실전토익 RC 1000

수험번호

응시일자 : 20   년   월   일

성명 한글 / 한자 / 영자

Test 05 (Part 5~7)

101~120, 121~140, 141~160, 161~180, 181~200

Test 06 (Part 5~7)

101~120, 121~140, 141~160, 161~180, 181~200

ANSWER SHEET

YBM 실전토익 RC 1000

수험번호

응시일자 : 20   년   월   일

성	한 글
명	한 자
	영 자

Test 07 (Part 5~7)

101 102 103 104 105 106 107 108 109 110 111 112 113 114 115 116 117 118 119 120

121 122 123 124 125 126 127 128 129 130 131 132 133 134 135 136 137 138 139 140

141 142 143 144 145 146 147 148 149 150 151 152 153 154 155 156 157 158 159 160

161 162 163 164 165 166 167 168 169 170 171 172 173 174 175 176 177 178 179 180

181 182 183 184 185 186 187 188 189 190 191 192 193 194 195 196 197 198 199 200

Test 08 (Part 5~7)

101 102 103 104 105 106 107 108 109 110 111 112 113 114 115 116 117 118 119 120

121 122 123 124 125 126 127 128 129 130 131 132 133 134 135 136 137 138 139 140

141 142 143 144 145 146 147 148 149 150 151 152 153 154 155 156 157 158 159 160

161 162 163 164 165 166 167 168 169 170 171 172 173 174 175 176 177 178 179 180

181 182 183 184 185 186 187 188 189 190 191 192 193 194 195 196 197 198 199 200

ANSWER SHEET

YBM 실전토익 RC 1000

수험번호

응시일자 : 20   년   월   일

성명	한글
	한자
	영자

Test 09 (Part 5~7)

101 102 103 104 105 106 107 108 109 110 111 112 113 114 115 116 117 118 119 120
121 122 123 124 125 126 127 128 129 130 131 132 133 134 135 136 137 138 139 140
141 142 143 144 145 146 147 148 149 150 151 152 153 154 155 156 157 158 159 160
161 162 163 164 165 166 167 168 169 170 171 172 173 174 175 176 177 178 179 180
181 182 183 184 185 186 187 188 189 190 191 192 193 194 195 196 197 198 199 200

Test 10 (Part 5~7)

101 102 103 104 105 106 107 108 109 110 111 112 113 114 115 116 117 118 119 120
121 122 123 124 125 126 127 128 129 130 131 132 133 134 135 136 137 138 139 140
141 142 143 144 145 146 147 148 149 150 151 152 153 154 155 156 157 158 159 160
161 162 163 164 165 166 167 168 169 170 171 172 173 174 175 176 177 178 179 180
181 182 183 184 185 186 187 188 189 190 191 192 193 194 195 196 197 198 199 200

ANSWER SHEET

YBM 실전토익 RC 1000

수험번호

응시일자 : 20   년   월   일

성명	한글
	한자
	영자

Test 09 (Part 5~7)

101 ~ 120, 121 ~ 140, 141 ~ 160, 161 ~ 180, 181 ~ 200

Test 10 (Part 5~7)

101 ~ 120, 121 ~ 140, 141 ~ 160, 161 ~ 180, 181 ~ 200

YBM 실전토익 RC1000

3

만점 대비
ALL NEW

정답 및 해설

YBM
실전토익
RC 1000
3

YBM

101 (C)	102 (D)	103 (B)	104 (A)	105 (C)
106 (D)	107 (A)	108 (A)	109 (B)	110 (C)
111 (A)	112 (B)	113 (D)	114 (B)	115 (A)
116 (B)	117 (C)	118 (D)	119 (C)	120 (D)
121 (D)	122 (C)	123 (A)	124 (D)	125 (D)
126 (C)	127 (C)	128 (B)	129 (D)	130 (B)
131 (B)	132 (D)	133 (A)	134 (B)	135 (C)
136 (C)	137 (A)	138 (B)	139 (D)	140 (C)
141 (B)	142 (D)	143 (D)	144 (A)	145 (D)
146 (B)	147 (C)	148 (A)	149 (B)	150 (C)
151 (D)	152 (A)	153 (D)	154 (C)	155 (B)
156 (B)	157 (D)	158 (B)	159 (D)	160 (D)
161 (D)	162 (A)	163 (B)	164 (C)	165 (A)
166 (D)	167 (B)	168 (C)	169 (D)	170 (B)
171 (D)	172 (C)	173 (B)	174 (C)	175 (D)
176 (A)	177 (D)	178 (C)	179 (B)	180 (A)
181 (A)	182 (D)	183 (A)	184 (C)	185 (D)
186 (C)	187 (B)	188 (D)	189 (D)	190 (A)
191 (C)	192 (B)	193 (C)	194 (B)	195 (B)
196 (D)	197 (B)	198 (A)	199 (C)	200 (C)

PART 5

101 동사 어휘 [고난도]

해설 빈칸은 명사 concern과 동격 관계를 이루는 that절의 동사 자리이므로, 우려를 표할 만한(expressed concern) 상황을 나타내는 동사가 들어가야 자연스럽다. 따라서 '조직력이 부족하다'라는 의미를 완성하는 (C) lacks(~가 부족하다)가 정답이다.

번역 아데어리 씨는 추천된 후보자가 해당 직책에 요구되는 조직력이 부족하다며 우려를 표했다.

어휘 express 표현하다   concern 걱정, 우려   proposed 추천된   candidate 후보자   required 요구되는, 필요한   organizational 조직적인, 체계적인   fail 실패하다   struggle 애쓰다   limit 제한하다

102 명사 자리 _ 동사의 목적어 _ 어휘

해설 빈칸은 동사 hired의 목적어 역할을 하는 명사 자리로, 고용의 대상을 나타내는 (C) contractor(하청업체) 혹은 (D) contractors(하청업체들) 중 하나가 들어가야 한다. 가산명사는 앞에 한정사가 붙지 않을 경우 복수형으로 쓰여야 하므로, (D) contractors가 정답이 된다.

번역 레이빌 공공사업부는 호숫가를 청소하기 위해 지역 하청업체들을 고용했다.

어휘 hire 고용하다   lakeside 호숫가   contract 계약(서); 계약하다

103 상관접속사 [고난도]

해설 문맥상 원문(the original text)과 번역(your translation) 모두 제출물에 포함되어야 한다는 내용이 되어야 자연스러우므로, 두 명사구를 연결하는 상관접속사 (B) as well as(~뿐만 아니라 ~도)가 정답이다. (A) along은 '~를 따라서'라는 뜻의 전치사로 쓰일 수 있지만 의미상 어

색하며, (C) altogether와 (D) also는 부사로 구조상 빈칸에 들어갈 수 없다.

번역 번역 원고 제출물에는 원문과 번역이 모두 포함되어야 한다.

어휘 submission 제출(물)   translated 번역된   original 원래의

104 전치사 자리 _ 어휘

해설 명사구 a temporary problem을 목적어로 취하는 자리로, 보기에서 전치사인 (A) Apart from과 (C) Instead of 중 하나를 선택해야 한다. 문맥상 '일시적인 문제를 제외하고는 계획대로 진행되었다'라는 내용이 되어야 자연스러우므로, (A) Apart from(~을 제외하면, ~ 이외에)이 정답이다. (C) Instead of는 '~대신에'라는 뜻이므로 적절하지 않다. 부사 (B) After all과 상관접속사 (D) Not only는 구조상 빈칸에 들어갈 수 없다.

번역 스피커 시스템에 일시적 문제가 생긴 것만 제외하면, 제품 출시 행사는 계획대로 진행되었다.

어휘 temporary 일시적인   product launch 제품 출시   go 진행되다, ~으로 되다   after all 결국에는, 어쨌든

105 대명사 어휘

해설 빈칸은 so that이 이끄는 절에서 동사 borrow의 목적어 역할을 하는 자리이다. 문맥상 대출 대상인 the books를 가리키는 대명사가 들어가야 하므로, (C) them이 정답이다.

번역 다른 이용자들이 자유롭게 책을 빌릴 수 있도록 명시된 날짜까지 도서관에 반납하세요.

어휘 indicated 명시된, 지정된   so that A can B A가 B할 수 있도록   patron 이용자, 손님   borrow 빌리다   freely 자유롭게

106 동사 어휘

해설 빈칸은 동사 will reduce의 주어 역할을 하는 동명사 자리로, 명사구 this drug를 목적어로 취한다. 문맥상 약효를 떨어뜨리는(reduce its effectiveness) 행위를 나타내는 단어가 들어가야 한다. 따라서 '강한 빛이나 열에 약을 노출시키는 것'이라는 내용을 완성하는 (D) Exposing이 정답이다. 참고로 expose는 '노출시키다, 드러내다'라는 뜻으로 전치사 to와 어울려 쓰인다.

번역 이 약을 강한 빛이나 열에 노출시키면 약효가 떨어질 것이다.

어휘 reduce 떨어뜨리다   effectiveness 효과   consume 소비하다   handle 다루다   allow 허락하다

107 부사 자리 _ 어휘 [고난도]

해설 빈칸 없이도 완전한 문장으로, 보기 중 적절한 부사를 선택해야 한다. 문맥상 '용지가 떨어지거나 그 외 다른 사유로 작동할 수 없으면'이라는 내용이 되어야 자연스럽다. 따라서 or와 함께 '그 외 다른 (방식으로)'라는 뜻을 나타내는 (A) otherwise가 정답이다. (B) however(아무리 ~해도)는 정도를 나타내는 형용사를 수식하고, (D) anymore(더 이상, 이제는)는 주로 절 끝에 위치하므로, 빈칸에 적절하지 않다.

번역 기계에 용지가 떨어지거나 그 외에 다른 사유로 작동할 수 없으면 표시 화면에 알림이 나타난다.

어휘 **be unable to** ~할 수 없다 **function** 작동하다 **notification** 알림, 통지 **appear** 나타나다

108 명사 어휘

해설 빈칸은 동사 may be extended의 주어 자리로, 문맥상 양식을 작성해 연장 가능한 대상을 나타내는 명사가 들어가야 한다. 따라서 '보증 기간'이라는 의미의 (A) warranty가 정답이다.

번역 밈엑스 스마트폰의 보증 기간은 온라인 양식을 작성해 연장할 수 있다.

어휘 **extend** 연장하다 **fill out** 작성하다 **lifespan** 수명 **vendor** 판매회사

109 대명사 자리 _ 수 일치

해설 빈칸은 주격 관계대명사 who가 이끄는 절의 수식을 받고 있으므로, 동사 enters와 수가 일치하는 대명사가 들어가야 한다. 따라서 단수형인 (B) everyone이 정답이다. 참고로, (A) those와 (D) many는 복수형 동사와 쓰여야 한다.

번역 참여율을 높이기 위해, 사진 공모전에 참가한 모든 사람이 약소한 선물을 받게 될 것이다.

어휘 **boost** 늘리다 **participation** 참여, 참가 **receive** 받다

110 전치사 어휘 고난도

해설 빈칸에는 동사 is being directed와 동명사구 developing new vehicles를 적절히 연결하는 전치사가 들어가야 한다. 문맥상 신차 개발(developing new vehicles)에 재원(financial resources)이 쓰인다는 내용이 되어야 자연스러우므로, '~로, ~에'라는 의미의 (C) towards가 정답이다.

번역 엘티스 자동차 사의 재원 대부분은 신차 개발에 쓰이고 있다.

어휘 **bulk** (~의) 대부분 **direct** ~로 보내다, (~를 향하여) 쓰다 **vehicle** 차 **besides** ~ 외에, ~에 더하여; 게다가, 또한

111 형용사 자리 _ 명사 수식 _ 어휘

해설 빈칸은 명사 means를 수식하는 형용사 자리로, 통신 수단(means of communication)의 특성을 적절히 묘사하는 형용사가 들어가야 한다. 따라서 '믿음직한, 신뢰할 수 있는'이라는 의미의 (A) reliable이 정답이다. (B) reliably는 부사, (C) reliability는 명사로 품사상 빈칸에 들어갈 수 없고, (D) reliant는 '의지하는'이라는 뜻으로 문맥상 어색하다.

번역 산악 지형일지라도 송신탑은 공원 관리원들에게 믿음직한 통신 수단을 제공할 것이다.

어휘 **radio tower** 송신탑 **park ranger** 공원 관리원 **mountainous** 산이 많은, 산악의 **terrain** 지형, 지역

112 부사 자리 _ 동사 수식

해설 빈칸은 원급 비교 구문 「as ~ as possible」에서 동사 Arrange를 수식하는 부사 자리이다. 따라서 '촘촘하게'라는 의미의 (B) densely가 정답이

다. (A) densest는 형용사의 최상급, (C) density는 명사, (D) denser는 형용사의 비교급으로 품사상 빈칸에 들어갈 수 없다.

번역 수족관 바닥에 식물을 가능한 한 촘촘하게 배치해 물고기에게 이상적인 환경을 만드세요.

어휘 **arrange** 배치하다 **ideal** 이상적인 **environment** 환경 **density** 밀도

113 형용사 어휘 고난도

해설 제조업의 기술 발전(technological advancements)이 가격(prices)에 미친 영향을 묘사하는 형용사가 들어가야 자연스러우므로, '더 좋은, 더 나은'이라는 의미의 (D) better가 정답이다. 참고로, better prices는 더 나은 가격, 즉 소비자의 입장에서 더 저렴한 가격을 뜻한다.

번역 뮤어 씨는 제조업의 기술 발전이 더 저렴한 소비자 가격으로 이어졌다고 주장한다.

어휘 **argue** 주장하다 **advancement** 발전 **manufacturing** 제조(업) **consumer** 소비자 **comparable** 비슷한, 비교할 만한 **market price** 시세

114 동사 어형 _ 분사구문

해설 빈칸은 명사구 its rivals를 목적어로 취하면서 앞에 온 완전한 절을 수식하는 분사 자리이다. 따라서 능동의 의미를 내포한 현재분사 (B) surprising(놀라게 하는)이 정답이다. (A) surprised도 분사로 볼 수 있지만, 수동의 의미를 나타내며 목적어를 취할 수 없으므로 빈칸에 들어갈 수 없다.

번역 그렐프 사는 어제 기자회견을 열고 사업 확장 계획을 발표해 광산업계 경쟁업체들을 놀라게 했다.

어휘 **press conference** 기자회견 **expand** (사업 등을) 확장하다, 확장되다 **rival** 경쟁 상대 **mining industry** 광산업(계)

115 부사 어휘 고난도

해설 식당의 가장 인기 있는 음식(Brenford Grill's most popular dish)인 치즈버거가 광고에 등장(featured in advertisements)하는 방식을 적절히 묘사하는 부사가 들어가야 하므로, '두드러지게, 눈에 띄게'라는 의미의 (A) prominently가 정답이다.

번역 브렌포드 그릴에서 가장 인기 있는 음식인 코린의 칠리 치즈버거는 식당 광고에 두드러지게 등장한다.

어휘 **feature** 특별히 포함하다, 등장시키다 **inadvertently** 우연히 **rapidly** 빨리 **respectively** 각각

116 명사 어휘

해설 형용사 scientific의 수식을 받는 명사를 선택하는 문제이다. '하이얼 헬스 사의 주장(claims)에는 과학적인 근거가 없다'라는 내용이 되어야 자연스러우므로, '입증, 확인'이라는 의미의 (B) verification이 정답이다.

번역 아로마테라피 오일의 이점에 대한 하이얼 헬스 사의 주장은 과학적으로 입증되지 않았다.

어휘 claim 주장; 주장하다 benefit 이점 result 결과 experiment 실험 excuse 변명, 구실

117 부사절 접속사

해설 빈칸은 완전한 절(mobile advertising is more suited to niche products)을 이끄는 접속사 자리이다. 콤마 앞뒤의 절이 서로 다른 두 가지 광고 방식을 비교하고 있으므로, '~ 반면에'라는 의미의 부사절 접속사 (C) whereas가 정답이다. (D) only if는 '~해야만'이라는 뜻으로 문맥상 어색하고, (A) in spite of와 (B) contrary to는 전치사로 완전한 절을 이끌 수 없다.

번역 텔레비전 광고는 표적시장이 넓은 제품에 적합한 반면, 모바일 광고는 틈새시장 제품에 더 적합하다.

어휘 appropriate for ~에 적합한 target market 표적시장(일정한 고객군) suited 적합한 niche product (특정 고객층을 대상으로 하는) 틈새시장 제품 in spite of ~에도 불구하고 contrary to ~과 반대로

118 to부정사 _ 형용사적 용법

해설 빈칸은 명사구 the secondary storage closet을 목적어로 취하면서 앞에 있는 명사 proposal(동사 details의 목적어)을 수식하는 역할을 한다. 따라서 형용사 역할을 할 수 있는 to부정사 (D) to convert가 정답이다. (A) will convert와 (C) was converted는 본동사, (B) conversion은 명사로 품사상 빈칸에 들어갈 수 없다.

번역 이 메모에는 보조 창고 공간을 작은 회의 공간으로 전환하자는 우리의 제안이 상세히 적혀 있다.

어휘 memo 메모, (특정 주제에 대한) 제안서[보고서] detail 상세히 열거하다 secondary 보조의 storage closet 수납[창고] 공간 convert A into B A를 B로 전환시키다[개조하다]

119 동사 어휘

해설 빈칸이 포함된 절(as long as ~ their work)은 근무자들이 수염을 기를 수 있는 조건을 나타낸다. 문맥상 '업무에 지장을 주지 않는 한'이라는 내용이 되어야 자연스러우므로, 전치사 with와 함께 '~에 지장을 주다, ~를 방해하다'라는 의미를 완성하는 자동사 (C) interfere가 정답이다. (A) affect(~에 영향을 미치다), (B) disrupt(~를 방해하다)는 타동사로 전치사 없이 바로 목적어가 와야 하고, (D) compromise는 '타협하다'라는 뜻의 자동사로, with와 쓰일 수 있지만 이 경우 뒤에 사람이 온다.

번역 조립 라인 근무자들은 업무에 지장을 주지 않는 한 수염을 기를 수 있다.

어휘 assembly 조립 facial hair 수염 as long as ~하는 한

120 형용사 자리 _ 목적격 보어

해설 빈칸은 「found + 목적어(the written training materials) + 목적격 보어」의 구조에서 목적어를 보충 설명하는 자리로, more와 함께 비교급 표현을 완성하는 형용사가 들어가야 한다. 따라서 '유익한'이라는 의미의 형용사 (D) informative가 정답이다. 현재분사인 (A) informing도 형용사 역할을 할 수 있지만, '(~에게) 정보를 주는, 통지하는'이라는 의미를 나타

내며 보통 목적어를 취하므로 빈칸에는 적절하지 않다. (B) information은 명사, (C) informatively는 부사로 품사상 빈칸에 들어갈 수 없다.

번역 조사 결과에 따르면, 인턴들은 동영상보다 서면 교육 자료가 더 유익하다고 생각했다.

어휘 material 자료 inform 정보를 주다, 알리다

121 부사절 접속사 _ 어휘

해설 빈칸은 완전한 절(their official identification cards are issued)을 이끄는 접속사 자리로, 빈칸이 이끄는 절이 앞에 있는 주절을 수식하고 있다. 문맥상 '공식 신분증이 발급될 때까지 임시 배지를 착용해야 할 것이다'라는 내용이 되어야 자연스러우므로, '~까지'라는 뜻의 부사절 접속사 (D) until이 정답이다. (C) as though는 '마치 ~인 것처럼'이라는 뜻이므로 빈칸에는 적절하지 않다. 참고로, (A) whether는 부사절 접속사로 쓰일 경우 or (not)을 동반해야 하고, (B) rather than(~라기 보다는)은 상관접속사로 쓰일 수 있으나 해당 문장의 빈칸에 들어가서 두 개의 완전한 절을 이어줄 수는 없다.

번역 신입사원들은 공식 신분증이 발급될 때까지 임시 배지를 착용하라는 요청을 받을 것이다.

어휘 be asked to ~할 것을 요청 받다, ~해야 한다 temporary 임시의 official 공식적인 identification card 신분증 issue 발급하다

122 동사 어형 _ 태 고난도

해설 빈칸은 주어 education의 동사 자리이다. '드러나다, 부상하다'라는 의미의 자동사인 emerge는 수동태로 쓰일 수 없으므로, 능동태 동사인 (C) is emerging이 정답이 된다. (A) emerging은 동명사/현재분사로 본동사 자리에 들어갈 수 없다.

번역 페리 씨의 지칠 줄 모르는 캠페인 활동 덕분에 교육이 시의회 선거의 핵심 쟁점으로 부상하고 있다.

어휘 thanks to ~덕분에 tireless 지칠 줄 모르는 council 의회 election 선거

123 명사 어휘

해설 빈칸은 동사 gives의 직접 목적어 역할을 하는 명사 자리로, to work hard의 수식을 받는다. 성과급 제도(The commission system)가 영업사원들(sales associates)에게 주는 것을 나타내는 명사가 들어가야 하므로, '열심히 일할 동기'라는 의미를 완성하는 (A) incentive(동기, 자극)가 정답이다.

번역 성과급 제도는 영업사원들이 열심히 일하도록 강력한 동기를 부여한다.

어휘 commissiom 수수료, 성과급 sales associate 영업사원 satisfaction 만족 supervision 감독 approach 접근(법)

124 부사 자리 _ 전치사구 수식 고난도

해설 빈칸은 자동사 caters 뒤에서 전치사구 to 이하를 수식하는 부사 자리이다. 따라서 '특히, 구체적으로'라는 의미의 부사 (D) specifically가 정답이다. (A) specify는 동사, (B) specific은 형용사, (C) specified는 동사/과거분사로 품사상 빈칸에 들어갈 수 없다.

번역 이름에서 암시하듯, "초보자용 화법"은 특히 이 기술을 전혀 공부해 본 적이 없는 사람들을 위한 것이다.

어휘 suggest 암시하다, 시사하다 cater to ~의 수요에 응하다, 충족시키다 craft 기술, 공예 specify 구체화하다 specific 구체적인

125 형용사 어휘 고난도

해설 빈칸은 주어 The technical support department's budget의 주격 보어 자리로 no longer와 to cover의 수식을 받는다. 문맥상 '기술지원과의 예산(budget)이 더 이상 인건비(staffing expenses)를 감당할 만큼 충분하지 않다'는 내용이 되어야 자연스러우므로, '충분한'이라는 의미의 (D) sufficient가 정답이다. 참고로, '~할 만큼 예산이 많지 않다'는 뜻을 나타내려면 형용사 big 혹은 large를 쓰고 뒤에 enough를 붙여야 한다.

번역 기술지원과의 예산은 더 이상 인건비를 감당할 만큼 충분하지 않다.

어휘 budget 예산 staffing expense 인건비 vital 필수적인 plentiful 풍부한 accustomed 익숙한

126 부사 어휘

해설 수동태 동사 are being distributed를 적절히 수식하는 부사를 선택하는 문제이다. 팀원들에게 업무(tasks)가 분배되는 방식을 나타내는 부사가 빈칸에 들어가야 자연스러우므로, '균등하게, 고르게'라는 의미의 (C) evenly가 정답이다.

번역 태스코 소프트웨어는 관리자가 반드시 팀원들에게 업무를 고르게 분배할 수 있도록 도와준다.

어휘 ensure 반드시 ~하게 하다 distribute 분배하다 briefly 짧게 loosely 느슨하게, 막연히 newly 새롭게

127 명사 자리 _ 동사의 목적어 _ 어휘

해설 빈칸은 동사 include의 목적어 역할을 하는 명사 자리로, 전치사구 of any required import and export documents의 수식을 받는다. 따라서 보기에서 명사인 (A) supplies(비품, 공급품), (B) supplier(공급업체), (C) supplying(공급, 제공) 중 하나를 선택해야 한다. 서비스(services)에 포함될 만한 것은 '수출입 서류 제공'이므로 (C) supplying이 정답이다. 참고로, supplying 대신에 supply(단수형 불가산명사)가 쓰일 수도 있다.

번역 당사 서비스에는 필요한 수출입 서류 제공이 포함된다.

어휘 required 필요한 import 수입 export 수출 supply 공급하다; 공급 (행위), 공급품 supplier 공급업체

128 전치사 어휘

해설 빈칸은 명사구 the guidance of seasoned attorneys를 목적어로 취하는 전치사 자리이다. 문맥상 '법대생에게 숙련된 변호사의 지도 하에 배울 수 있는 기회를 준다'라는 내용이 되어야 자연스러우므로, '~아래, ~하에'라는 의미의 (B) under이 정답이다.

번역 호건 앤 파트너스의 인턴십 프로그램은 법대생들에게 숙련된 변호사의 지도 하에 배울 수 있는 기회를 제공한다.

어휘 guidance 지도 seasoned 숙련된, 노련한 attorney 변호사

129 동사 어형 _ 시제 _ 가정법 과거완료

해설 If절의 동사가 had arrived로 과거와 반대되는 상황(도착했었다면)을 가정하고 있으므로, 해당 문장이 가정법 과거완료 구문임을 알 수 있다. 가정법 과거완료 구문은 「If+주어+had+p.p. ~, 주어+조동사 과거형 +have+p.p. ~.」의 구조로 쓰이므로, (B) could have attended가 정답이다.

번역 마드리드발 비행기가 제시간에 도착했다면 마틴 씨는 학회의 환영회에 참석할 수 있었을 것이다.

어휘 on time 제시간에 attend 참석하다 conference 회의, 학회 reception 연회

130 명사 어휘

해설 빈칸은 동사 has reduced의 목적어 역할을 하는 명사 자리로, 전치사구 on its flagship snack bars의 수식을 받는다. 신제품의 성공(The success of its new line of beverages) 덕분에 주요 수익처에 대한 의존도가 감소했다는 내용이 되어야 자연스러우므로, '의존도'라는 의미의 (B) dependence가 정답이다. 참고로, dependence는 전치사 on/ upon과 자주 쓰인다.

번역 새로운 음료 제품군이 성공하면서 주요 수익처인 스낵바에 대한 젠비아 사의 의존도가 감소했다.

어휘 reduce 줄이다, 감소시키다 flagship 주력하는, 주요한 revenue 수익 expertise 전문지식 perspective 관점 shortage 부족

PART 6

131-134 웹페이지

www.vegashift.com

베가시프트

베가시프트는 식당, 상점, 기타 교대근무 기반 업체들을 대상으로 교대근무 교환을 용이하게 할 수 있게 신속하고 간편한 방법을 제공하는 모바일 앱입니다. 직원들이 원치 않는 근무시간을 동료들에게 **131직접** 제안하면 동료들은 이를 받아들일지 말지 선택할 수 있습니다. 이렇게 하면 직원들은 상사에게 불편을 주지 않고 근무시간의 유연성을 높일 수 있습니다. **132동시에**, 베가시프트는 경영진이 일정에 대한 통제권을 유지할 수 있도록 합니다. 관리자는 모든 교환을 승인 받게끔 하여 근무자가 **133허용된** 시간보다 더 많이 일하는 경우가 생기지 않도록 할 수 있습니다. 또한 이 앱은 직원들의 시급 차이로 인해 발생할 수 있는 추가 비용에 대해서 경영진에게 알림을 보내줄 수도 있습니다.

당사는 베가시프트의 품질에 자신이 있기에 기업들에게 한 달 내내 무료로 사용할 수 있는 기회를 드립니다. **134아래에 정보를 입력하여 오늘 바로 무료 체험판을 시작해 보세요.**

어휘 shift 교대근무(시간, 조) facilitate 용이하게 하다, 촉진하다 enable ~할 수 있게 하다 increase 높이다 flexibility 유연성, 탄력성 inconvenience 불편하게 하다 supervisor 상사, 관리자 management 경영진, 관리진 retain 유지하다 approve 승인하다 alert A to B A에게 B에 대해 알리다 confident 자신 있는

131 부사 자리_동사 수식

해설 빈칸은 동사 offer를 수식하는 부사 자리이므로, (B) directly(직접, 바로)가 정답이다. (A) directs는 동사, (C) directing은 동명사/현재분사, (D) direction은 명사로 품사상 빈칸에 들어갈 수 없다.

어휘 direct 지시하다, ~로 향하다 direction 방향, 지시

132 접속부사　　　　　　　　　　고난도

해설 빈칸 앞 문장에서는 직원들에게 주어지는 재량(This enables employees to increase the flexibility of their working hours)을, 빈칸 뒤에서 경영진의 통제권(VegaShift allows management to retain control of the schedule)을 언급하고 있다. 이 두 가지 모두 베가시프트의 특징이자 장점이므로, '동시에'라는 의미의 (D) At the same time이 정답이다.

어휘 as a result 결과로 in other words 달리 말하면 on the contrary 반대로

133 형용사 어휘

해설 빈칸이 포함된 절(so that ~ hours)은 모든 근무시간 교환을 승인 받게끔 하는 목적을 나타낸다. 따라서 '허용된 시간보다 더 많이 일하는 경우가 없도록'이라는 내용이 되어야 자연스러우므로, '허용된'이라는 의미의 (A) permitted가 정답이다.

어휘 shortened 짧아진 preferred 선호되는 extra 추가의

134 문맥에 맞는 문장 고르기　　　　고난도

번역 (A) 〈테크 Z〉가 당사를 업계 최고의 고용주로 선정한 이유를 알아보세요.
(B) 아래로 정보를 입력하여 오늘 바로 무료 체험판을 시작해 보세요.
(C) 전체 제품 목록을 보시려면 "제공품"을 클릭하세요.
(D) 추가 기술 지원은 1-800-555-0184로 전화하시면 됩니다.

해설 빈칸 앞 문장에서 베가시프트를 한 달 내내 무료로 사용할 수 있는 기회를 준다(we give businesses the chance to use it for a whole month at no cost)고 했으므로, 빈칸에도 이 기회와 관련된 내용이 이어져야 문맥상 자연스럽다. 따라서 이용 방법을 언급한 (B)가 정답이다.

어휘 employer 회사, 고용주 trial 시용, 체험(판) offering 제공하는 것, 제공품 additional 추가의 available 이용할 수 있는

135-138 기사

레이노 전국과학축제 개최 예정

레이노(12월 11일)—국립과학기술부(NDST)는 레이노 시가 6월에 제2회 연례 전국과학축제를 개최한다고 발표했다.

NDST 대변인 아이작 호지스는 이 영예를 차지하려는 **135경쟁**이 치열했지만 "급성장하는 농업과학 및 생명공학 산업" 때문에 레이노가 선정되었다고 말했다. 그는 또한 시에 최근에 기술 분야 신생기업을 위한 '레이노 300' 단지를 조성한 사실도 언급했다. **136그곳에 임차업체로 입주하는 기업들은 특별한 재정 지원과 조언을 받는다.**

국립과학축제는 국가의 과학적 성취와 프로젝트를 선보이는 일주일간의 행사다. 일반인들에게 최첨단 개념을 소개하는 강의와 모든 연령대를 대상으로 한 전시, **137흥미진진한** 시연 등이 펼쳐진다. 첫 번째 축제는 오글스비에서 **138열렸다.**

어휘 announce 발표하다 host 개최하다 annual 연례의 fierce 치열한, 맹렬한 agricultural 농업의 biotechnology 생명공학 industry 산업, 업계 recent 최근의 establishment 조성, 설립 start-up 신생기업 achievement 업적, 성취 cutting-edge 최첨단의 exhibition 전시(회) demonstration 시연

135 명사 어휘

해설 빈칸은 was fierce의 주어 역할을 하는 명사 자리로, 전치사구 for the honor의 수식을 받는다. 국립과학축제 개최라는 영예를 차지하기 위한 경쟁이 치열했다는 내용이 되어야 자연스러우므로, '경쟁'이라는 의미의 (C) competition이 정답이다.

어휘 selection 선정(된 것) opportunity 기회 recommendation 추천

136 문맥에 맞는 문장 고르기　　　　고난도

번역 (A) 그곳에 체류를 원하는 방문객들은 빨리 예약해야 한다.
(B) 그는 시 정부 재직 시 그런 프로젝트 몇 가지를 추진했다.
(C) 그곳에 임차업체로 입주하는 기업들은 특별한 재정 지원과 조언을 받는다.
(D) 그곳의 공사로 축제 기간 동안 교통 문제가 야기될 것이라는 우려가 있다.

해설 빈칸 앞 문장에서 최근 시에서 기술 분야 신생기업을 위한 '레이노 300' 단지를 조성했다(the city's recent establishment of the Reyno 300 complex for technology start-ups)고 했으므로, 빈칸에는 조성된 단지와 관련된 부연 설명이 이어져야 문맥상 자연스럽다. 따라서 (C)가 정답이다.

어휘 initiate 추진[시작]하다 accepted 받아들여진 tenant 임차인[업체] concern 우려 construction 공사, 건설 cause 야기하다

137 형용사 자리_명사 수식_어휘

해설 빈칸은 lectures 및 exhibitions와 더불어 features의 목적어 역할을 하는 명사 demonstrations를 수식하는 형용사 자리이다. 따라서 보기에서 분사형 형용사 (A) fascinating과 (C) fascinated 중 하나를 선택해야 하는데, 시연(demonstrations)은 흥미를 유발하는 주체이므로, 능동의 의미를 내포한 현재분사형 형용사 (A) fascinating(흥미진진한)이 정답이 된다. (B) fascinatingly는 부사, (D) fascinates는 동사로 품사상 빈칸에 들어갈 수 없다.

어휘 fascinate 마음을 사로잡다

138 동사 어형_시제

해설 빈칸은 주어 The first one의 동사 자리로, 전치사구 in Oglesby의 수식을 받는다. 여기서 one은 National Science Festival을 가리키는데, 첫 번째 단락에서 레이노 시가 제2회 연례 전국과학축제를 개최한다(the city of Reyno will host the second annual National Science Festival)고 했으므로, 제1회 축제(the first one)는 이미 개최되었음을 알 수 있다. 따라서 수동태 과거동사인 (B) was held가 정답이다.

139-142 이메일

발신: 패트릭 홀브룩
수신: 도서관 서비스 직원
제목: 동료 평가
날짜: 11월 15일
첨부 파일: 평가 양식

여러분 안녕하세요,

연간 직원 인사 고과가 다음 달에 걸쳐 실시될 예정입니다. 이전처럼, 평가는 제가 하지만 도서관 서비스 부서 내 동료들**139에게서** 받은 의견을 포함할 겁니다. 이 의견을 취합하기 위해, 여러분 각자 첨부 파일에 있는 평가 양식을 작성해서 제게 회신해 주셨으면 합니다. 부서의 모든 구성원에 대해 하나씩 **140작성하세요.** **141설문지 양식은 변경되지 않았습니다.** 지난번과 마찬가지로 먼저 다양한 분야에서 동료의 성과를 평가한 다음, 답변에 대해 설명하고 상세히 기술하는 단락을 쓰도록 요청 받을 것입니다. 다만 올해에는 후자에 각별히 신경 써 주실 것을 당부합니다. 사려 깊은 의견이 동료들에게 **142상당히** 도움이 될 수 있다는 점 기억하세요.

패트릭 홀브룩
도서관 서비스 부국장

어휘 performance evaluation 인사 고과, 성과 평가 conduct 수행하다 peer 동료 fill out 작성하다 rate 평가하다, 점수를 매기다 a range of 다양한 explain 설명하다 expand on ~에 대해 상세히 기술하다 urge 권고[촉구]하다 latter 후자의 thoughtful 사려 깊은 benefit 도움[혜택]이 되다

139 전치사 어휘

해설 동사 include의 목적어 역할을 하는 input과 명사구 your peers를 적절히 연결하는 전치사가 들어가야 한다. '동료들에게서 받은 의견을 포함한다'라는 내용이 되어야 자연스러우므로, '~로부터'라는 의미로 출처를 나타내는 (A) from이 정답이다.

140 동사 어휘

해설 명사구 one(=evaluation form) for every member of the department를 목적어로 취하는 동사를 선택하는 문제이다. 앞서 모든 평가서들을 작성해(fill out) 회신해 달라고 했으므로, 빈칸에도 '작성하다'라는 의미의 동사가 들어가야 문맥상 자연스럽다. 따라서 (C) complete가 정답이다.

어휘 grant 주다 compile 집계하다, 편찬하다 attend 참석하다

141 문맥에 맞는 문장 고르기 [고난도]

번역 (A) 설문조사서는 도서관 이용객들에게도 배포되었습니다.
(B) 설문지 양식은 변경되지 않았습니다.
(C) 매 검토 시 툰 국장이 참석할 예정입니다.
(D) 여러분이 칸 몇 개를 비워둔 듯합니다.

해설 빈칸 앞 문장에서 모든 직원의 평가서를 작성해달라(Please complete one for every member of the department)고 요청했고, 뒤에서는

지난번과 같은(Like last time) 방법으로 작성해달라고 설명하고 있다. 따라서 빈칸에도 직원 평가서 양식 작성과 관련된 내용이 들어가야 문맥상 자연스러우므로, (B)가 정답이다.

어휘 survey 설문조사(서) distribute 배포하다 patron 이용객 questionnaire 설문지 blank 빈

142 부사 자리 _ 동사 수식

해설 빈칸이 「주어(thoughtful feedback)+동사(can benefit)+목적어(your peers)」의 완전한 절 뒤에 있으므로, 동사 benefit을 수식하는 부사가 들어가야 한다. 따라서 (D) considerably(상당히)가 정답이다. (A) consider와 (B) considers는 동사, (C) considerable은 형용사로 품사상 빈칸에 들어갈 수 없다.

어휘 consider 고려하다 considerable 상당한

143-146 공지

고객님들께 알립니다

종이와 잉크 같은 원자재 가격 상승으로 인해, 휠러 인쇄소는 2월 1일자로 인쇄 서비스 가격을 인상하기로 결정했습니다. **143그래픽 디자인 서비스의 가격은 그대로 유지됩니다.**

이는 5년 만에 처음 실시되는 **144조정**입니다. 고객님들을 배려하는 마음에서 미루어 왔으나, 앞서 언급된 경제적인 요인으로 인해 이제는 어쩔 수 없게 되었습니다. 저희가 앞으로 계속 최고의 서비스를 제공할 수 있으려면 가격 **145인상**이 필요합니다.

가격표 게시판은 2월 1일에 변경사항을 반영해 수정될 예정이며, 착오를 방지하고자 직원들이 모든 인쇄 서비스의 가격을 미리 명시하도록 할 것입니다. 이 사안에 대한 문의는 매니저인 루시아 자이지에게 **146하시면 됩니다.** 이해해 주시면 감사하겠습니다.

어휘 due to ~ 때문에 increase 인상, 상승 raw material 원자재 raise 인상하다 delay 지연시키다, 미루다 respect 존중, 경의 unavoidable 어쩔 수 없는 abovementioned 앞서 언급된, 상기된 factor 요인 top-notch 최고의 encourage 독려하다, 권고하다 state 알리다, 명시하다 upfront 미리, 솔직히 avoid 피하다, 방지하다 misunderstanding 착오, 오해

143 문맥에 맞는 문장 고르기

번역 (A) 저희는 다른 어떤 디지털 파일 형식도 받을 수 없습니다.
(B) 정규 영업시간은 2월 8일에 재개됩니다.
(C) 포장재를 인쇄하시려면 할로웨이 지점을 방문하세요.
(D) 그래픽 디자인 서비스의 가격은 그대로 유지됩니다.

해설 빈칸 앞 문장에서 원자재 가격 상승으로 인해 인쇄 서비스 가격을 인상하기로 결정했다(Wheeler Printing Shop has decided to raise the prices of our printing services)고 했으므로, 빈칸에도 서비스 가격과 관련된 내용이 이어지는 것이 문맥상 자연스럽다. 따라서 (D)가 정답이다.

어휘 resume 재개되다 material 재료 remain 여전히 ~이다

144 명사 어휘

해설 빈칸은 문장의 주격 보어 역할을 하는 명사 자리로, 주어 This와 동격 관계를 이룬다. This가 가리키는 것은 일부 서비스 가격의 변동이므로, 빈칸에는 이러한 변경을 나타내는 명사가 들어가야 자연스럽다. 따라서 '조정'이라는 의미의 (A) adjustment가 정답이다.

어휘 expenditure 지출 departure 출발 error 오류

145 동명사 자리 _ 주어

해설 빈칸은 our prices를 목적어로 취하며 문장에서 주어 역할을 하는 준동사 자리이다. 문맥상 '가격을 인상하는 것'이라는 내용이 되어야 하므로, (D) Raising이 정답이다. (A) Having raised는 이미 가격을 인상했다는 완료의 의미를 나타내므로 빈칸에 적절하지 않고, (C) To be raised는 수동형으로 목적어를 취할 수 없으므로 빈칸에 들어갈 수 없다.

146 동사 어형 _ 태 _ 시제

해설 주어인 Questions는 담당자에게 보내지는 대상이므로, 타동사 address (보내다, ~에게 이야기하다)가 수동태로 쓰여야 한다. 또한 '문의는 루시아 자이저에게 하면 된다'라는 일반적인 안내 사항을 나타내야 하므로, 조동사가 포함된 (B) can be addressed가 정답이 된다. 현재완료 수동태인 (A) have been addressed는 문맥상 어색하며, (C) are addressing과 (D) will be addressing은 능동태 동사로 빈칸에 들어갈 수 없다.

147 세부 사항

번역 정보문에 따르면 멤버십 종류에 따라 다른 것은?
(A) 게스트가 머무를 수 있는 시간
(B) 허용된 게스트 수
(C) 게스트를 데려오는 비용
(D) 게스트에게 요구되는 자격요건

해설 초반부에서 플래티넘 멤버십 소지자는 일정 게스트를 스카이 라운지에 무료로 동반할 수 있지만(Platinum Membership holders may bring two guests ~ into the Sky Lounge at no cost), 골드 멤버십 소지자는 1인당 25달러의 수수료를 지불해야 같은 혜택을 누릴 수 있다(Gold Membership holders may do the same for a fee of $25 per person)고 했으므로, (C)가 정답이다.

어휘 amount 양 qualification 자격요건

148 세부 사항

번역 스카이 라운지에 입장한 게스트가 해야 하는 것은?
(A) 인도자와 함께 있기
(B) 신분증 착용
(C) 지정된 구역에 짐 두기
(D) 편의시설 이용료 지불

해설 중반부에서 게스트는 머무는 동안 입장을 허가한 회원과 동행해야 한다(Guests must be accompanied by the admitting member for the duration of their visit)고 했으므로, (A)가 정답이다.

어휘 identification 신분(증) designated 지정된

> ▶▶ **Paraphrasing** 지문의 **be accompanied by the admitting member** → 정답의 **Remain with an escort**

PART 7

147-148 정보문

하월 항공

하월 스카이 라운지 게스트 규정

스카이 라운지 회원은 하월 항공의 당일 항공권 소지자를 라운지 게스트로 데려올 수 있습니다. **147**플래티넘 멤버십 소지자는 게스트 2인, 또는 배우자 1인 및 21세 미만의 자녀를 스카이 라운지에 무료로 동반할 수 있으며, 골드 멤버십 소지자는 1인당 25달러의 수수료를 지불하면 같은 혜택을 누릴 수 있습니다. **148**게스트는 머무는 동안 입장을 허가한 회원과 동행해야 합니다. 이들은 또한 복장, 행동, 라운지 편의시설 이용에 관한 스카이 라운지 규정에 따라야 합니다.

어휘 policy 규정, 정책 holder 소지자 spouse 배우자 at no cost 무료로 accompany 동반하다 admit (입장을) 허가하다, 들어가게 하다 duration 기간 be subject to ~의 적용을 받다, ~의 지배를 받다 attire 복장 behavior 행동 amenities 편의시설, (편의를 위한) 비치품

149-150 이메일

발신: 나타샤 에이커스
수신: 새철튼 달리기 동호회
제목: 3월 행사
날짜: 2월 28일

안녕하세요, 주자 여러분! 날씨가 점점 따뜻해지기 시작하니 정말 좋지 않나요? 곧 녹음이 무성해질 테고, 출전을 하면 이를 감탄하며 바라볼 수 있을 겁니다.

3월에 동호회에서 진행될 상황은 다음과 같습니다.

- 주변 행사 알림: 스프랫 시 마라톤. 자세한 사항은 아래와 같습니다. **149**전날 밤 시내까지 카풀로 가고 싶다면 경기 등록 마감일까지 제게 연락하세요.
  - 날짜: 3월 30일
  - 장소: 스프랫
  - 코스 길이: 26.2마일
  - **149**등록 마감일: 3월 16일
  - 웹사이트: www.sprattcitymarathon.com

- 매주 일요일 오전 10시(7마일 코스)와 수요일 오후 7시(5마일 코스) 코스몬 공원에서 열리는 단체 달리기는 계속됩니다. **150**제가 취소나 기타 변경사항을 문자 메시지로 통보할 수 있도록 잊지 마시고 동호회 웹사이트에서 사전 등록해 주세요.

코스에서 만나요!

– 나타샤

어휘 greenery 녹수, 녹음 admire 감탄하다 outing (스포츠)
출전, 소풍 registration 등록 in advance 미리 notification
통보 cancellation 취소

149 세부 사항

번역 스프랫까지 교통편을 함께 이용하려면 며칠까지 에이커스 씨에게 연락해야 하
는가?
(A) 2월 28일
(B) 3월 16일
(C) 3월 29일
(D) 3월 30일

해설 에이커스 씨는 세 번째 단락에서 스프랫 시 마라톤에 대해 공지하며, 카
풀을 하고 싶으면 경기 등록 마감일까지 자신에게 연락하라(If you're
interested in carpooling ~ contact me by the race registration deadline)고 했다. 그 아래를 보면 등록 마감일(Registration
deadline)이 3월 16일이라고 나와있으므로, (B)가 정답이다.

▶▶ Paraphrasing 지문의 carpooling
→ 질문의 sharing transportation

150 세부 사항

번역 에이커스 씨는 수신자들에게 무엇을 하라고 상기시키는가?
(A) 일요일마다 그녀에게 문자메시지 보내기
(B) 단체 달리기 전 준비운동 하기
(C) 등록해서 행사 관련 최신 정보 받기
(D) 코스 경로 미리 익히기

해설 네 번째 단락에서 수신자들에게 취소나 기타 변경사항을 문자 메시지
로 통보할 수 있게 동호회 웹사이트에서 사전 등록하라(Remember to
sign up in advance on the club Web site ~ to send you text
message notifications about cancellations or other changes)
고 했으므로, (C)가 정답이다.

▶▶ Paraphrasing 지문의 sign up → 정답의 Register
지문의 text message notifications about
cancellations or other changes
→ 정답의 updates about events

151-153 이메일

발신: 〈service@hildytea.com〉
수신: 로잘린드 버크 〈roz.burke@pow-mail.com〉
제목: 알림
날짜: 12월 8일

버크 씨께,

힐디 티 박스는 지난 1년 동안 고객님께서 저희의 선물 서비스 이용에 만족하셨
기를 바랍니다. ¹⁵¹12월 이후에도 매달 고품질 잎차 패키지를 계속 받으시려면
이 페이지를 방문해 청구 정보를 입력하세요. 상품 가격과 배송비는 월 14달러
에 불과하며 3개월, 6개월, 1년 이용권을 선택하실 수 있습니다. ¹⁵²아울러, 기
존 이용자인 고객님께서는 갱신 기념 특별 선물로 차를 한 번에 12시간까지 따뜻
하게 유지할 수 있는 프레일 브랜드의 여행용 머그컵을 받으실 수 있습니다. 현재
이용권이 만료되면 이 제공품은 무효화 된다는 점 유의하세요.

¹⁵³문의 사항이 있으시면 이 이메일로 회신하시면 됩니다. 저나 다른 직원이 24
시간 이내에 응답하겠습니다.

엘모어 스탠리
고객서비스부
힐디 티 박스

어휘 satisfied 만족한 subscription 구독, 이용(권) loose leaf
tea 잎차 billing 청구서(발송) existing 기존의 be eligible
for ~의 대상이다, ~의 자격이 되다 renewal 갱신 invalid 무효인
current 현재의 run out 만기가 되다

151 주제 / 목적

번역 버크 씨에게 이메일을 보낸 이유는?
(A) 그녀가 힐디 티 박스에 대해 불만을 제기했다.
(B) 그녀가 친구에게 힐디 티 박스를 추천했다.
(C) 신제품이 나왔다.
(D) 그녀의 서비스 이용 기간이 곧 끝난다.

해설 첫 번째 단락에서 12월 이후에도 매달 고품질 잎차 패키지를 계속 받으
려면 링크해 준 페이지를 방문해 청구 정보를 입력하라(To continue
receiving a monthly package of high-quality loose leaf teas
after December, please visit this page and enter your billing
information)고 하고 있으므로, 서비스 이용 기간 만료를 알리기 위한 이
메일임을 알 수 있다. 따라서 (D)가 정답이다.

어휘 refer A to B A에게 B를 추천[소개]하다, A를 B에 보내다

152 세부 사항

번역 스탠리 씨가 버크 씨에게 제공하는 것은?
(A) 음료 용기
(B) 겨울철 의류
(C) 1년간 무료 배송
(D) 판촉 행사 사전 통지

해설 첫 번째 단락 후반부에서 버크 씨가 기존 구독자라서 갱신 시 특별 선물
을 받을 수 있다(as an existing subscriber, you are eligible for a
special renewal gift)고 한 후, 그 선물이 여행용 머그컵(travel mug)
이라며 부연 설명을 했으므로, (A)가 정답이다.

어휘 apparel 의류 sales promotion 판촉 행사

▶▶ Paraphrasing 지문의 travel mug
→ 정답의 drinking container

153 문장 삽입

번역 [1], [2], [3], [4]로 표시된 곳 중에서 다음 문장이 가장 적합한 곳은?
"저나 다른 직원이 24시간 이내에 응답하겠습니다."
(A) [1]
(B) [2]
(C) [3]
(D) [4]

해설 주어진 문장에서 '저나 다른 직원이 24시간 이내에 응답하겠다(I or
another representative will respond within 24 hours)'고 했으므
로, 앞에서 먼저 응답이 필요한 상황이 언급되어야 한다. [4] 앞에서 문의

TEST 1 **9**

사항이 있으면 이 이메일로 회신하면 된다(If you have any questions, simply reply to this e-mail)고 했으므로, (D)가 정답이다.

어휘 representative (담당) 직원

154-155 온라인 채팅

알렉스 콜린스 (오전 9시 2분)
머세이디즈, 잠깐 물어볼 게 있어요. 154새 노트북 구매 요청 건은 어떻게 되고 있나요? 지금쯤이면 처리될 줄 알았는데요.

머세이디즈 버치 (오전 9시 3분)
안녕하세요, 알렉스. 제 이메일 못 받았나요? 154IT부서에서 다른 모델을 추천하고 있어요. 변경을 승인해 주시면 요청 처리를 마무리할 수 있어요.

알렉스 콜린스 (오전 9시 7분)
아, 그렇군요. 음, 그들이 추천하는 모델이 제가 요청한 것보다 더 무거운 것 같아요. 155그런데 제가 종종 노트북을 공사 현장에 가지고 다녀야 하니까 가벼운 모델로 하는 게 중요해요.

머세이디즈 버치 (오전 9시 8분)
그렇다면 변경에 반대할 수 있어요. 해당 상황을 설명하는 짧은 글을 써주면 제가 요청서에 첨부할게요.

알렉스 콜린스 (오전 9시 8분)
그런 방법이 있다니 다행이네요. 그렇게 할게요. 고마워요.

어휘 purchase 구매; 구매하다 request 요청; 요청하다 process 처리하다 recommend 추천하다 approve 승인하다 construction site 공사 현장 lightweight 가벼운 oppose 반대하다 paragraph 짧은 글, 단락 append 첨부하다, 덧붙이다

154 의도 파악

번역 오전 9시 3분에 버치 씨가 "제 이메일 못 받았나요?"라고 쓴 의도는?
(A) 그녀의 이메일에 지연에 대한 설명이 있다.
(B) 그녀의 이메일에 처리 종결 통지가 있다.
(C) 그녀의 이메일에 정책 변경사항이 기술되어 있다.
(D) 그녀의 이메일에서 직원 전보를 알린다.

해설 콜린스 씨가 오전 9시 2분 메시지에서 새 노트북 구매 요청 건의 진행 상황을 물었는데, 이에 대해 버치 씨가 '제 이메일 못 받았나요?(Didn't you get my e-mail?)'라며 반문한 후, IT부에서 다른 모델을 추천하고 있는데 이 변경을 승인해 주면 요청 처리를 마무리할 수 있다(Once you approve the change, we can finish processing the request)고 관련 내용을 설명했다. 이를 통해 처리가 지연되는 이유가 이메일에 언급되어 있음을 추론할 수 있으므로, (A)가 정답이다.

어휘 conclusion 종결 describe 기술하다 transfer 전보

155 세부 사항

번역 콜린스 씨가 업무상 자주 해야 한다고 말한 것은?
(A) 교육 실시
(B) 현장 방문
(C) 설득력 있는 글쓰기
(D) 개인용 전자장비 연구

해설 콜린스 씨가 오전 9시 7분 메시지에서 종종 노트북을 공사 현장에 가지고 다녀야 한다(I often have to carry my laptop around construction sites)고 했으므로, 업무상 현장 방문을 자주 해야 한다는 것을 알 수 있다. 따라서 (B)가 정답이다.

어휘 carry out 실시하다 persuasive 설득력 있는

▶▶ **Paraphrasing** 지문의 construction sites
→ 정답의 work sites

156-157 공지

샌들링 아파트 주민 여러분께 알립니다

지난 몇 달 동안 아파트 관리사무소로 배송되는 입주자 소포 물량이 감당할 수 없을 정도로 증가했습니다. 그 결과 직원 업무량 과다, 시설 내 공간 축소, 여러 건의 소포 분실 사고가 발생했습니다. 156따라서 10월 1일 월요일부터는 사무소에서 입주자 소포 배송을 받지 않겠습니다. 시일을 충분히 두고 사전 통지하니 이를 활용해 해당 날짜 또는 그 이후에 도착할 가능성이 있는 소포에 대해서는 다른 방안들을 마련해 두십시오. 157여러분이 거주하는 건물 현관에서 배송 받거나 사서함, 직장 등 제3의 장소에서 받는 방법이 이에 해당합니다.

– 샌들링 아파트 관리소

어휘 tenant 입주자, 세입자 deliver 배송하다 capacity 능력, 수용력 excessive 과도한 reduced 감소한 facility 시설 incident 사건 take advantage of ~을 이용하다 ample advance notice 시일을 충분히 두고 하는 통지 arrangement 준비, 방안

156 주제 / 목적

번역 아파트 주민들에게 주로 통보되고 있는 것은?
(A) 입주자 회의 개최
(B) 수령 서비스 폐지
(C) 편의시설 설치
(D) 일부 상품 분실

해설 초반부에서 증가하는 소포 물량에 따른 문제점을 언급한 후, 중반부에서 10월 1일 월요일부터 사무소에서 입주자 소포 배송을 받지 않겠다(the office will no longer accept delivery of packages for tenants from Monday, October 1)고 했으므로, (B)가 정답이다.

어휘 elimination 폐지 misplacement 분실, (엉뚱한 곳에 두어) 찾지 못함

▶▶ **Paraphrasing** 지문의 **no longer accept delivery of packages** → 정답의 **The elimination of a receiving service**

157 추론 / 암시　　　　　고난도

번역 샌들링 아파트에 관해 암시된 것은?
(A) 사무실은 주말마다 문을 닫는다.
(B) 곧 새로운 관리자가 맡는다.
(C) 최근 직원 수를 줄였다.
(D) 건물이 여러 동이다.

해설 공지 후반부를 보면, 주민들이 거주하는 건물 현관에서 배송을 받는 방안
을 언급하며 'your building'이라고 지칭했으므로, 관리사무소와 주민들
의 거주지가 서로 다른 건물에 있음을 추론할 수 있다. 따라서 건물이 두
동 이상임을 알 수 있으므로, (D)가 정답이다.

어휘 recently 최근 reduce 줄이다 occupy 차지하다, 사용[거주]하다
multiple 다수의, 두 개 이상의

158-160 회람

발신: 세인 맥스웰

수신: 전 직원

주제: 알림

날짜: 5월 8일

골드윈 출판사가 전 직원에게 창의력을 발휘할 수 있는 기회를 주는 시기가 되
었습니다. **158/159**당사의 다양한 스페인어 교육 솔루션에 추가할 만한 혁신적인
제안을 또 한 번 찾고 있습니다. 책, 플래시 카드, 보드 게임 등 당사가 이미 제공
하고 있는 유형의 제품 또는 상당히 비슷한 제품 모두 환영합니다.

당사는 귀중한 기여가 색다른 출처에서 나올 수 있다고 믿기에 전 분야 직원들
이 참여하도록 독려하고 있습니다. **159**지난해 회계과의 로이스 에드워즈가 제안
한 책이 출판되었을 뿐만 아니라 매우 잘 팔리기도 했습니다. 새로운 아이디어가
떠오르면 잠시 정규 업무를 제쳐두고 제안서를 작성해 주세요.

직원 한 명당 제안서를 2개까지 제출할 수 있습니다. **160**구체적인 제안서 양
식은 없지만, 제품 및 표적시장에 대한 상세한 설명이 포함되어야 합니다. 그
러나 제출물의 양을 저희가 감당할 수 있도록, 길이는 한 페이지가 넘지 않게
써주길 부탁합니다. 5월 19일 금요일까지 제 비서 이반 브릭스에게 ivan@
goldwinpublishing.com으로 보내주세요.

어휘 creativity 창의력 seek 구하다, 찾다 innovative 혁신적인
addition 추가(된 것) reasonably 상당히 similar to ~와 비슷한
valuable 귀중한 contribution 기여, 공헌 unconventional
색다른, 관습에 얽매이지 않는 be encouraged to ~하도록 독려 받다
participate 참여하다 temporarily 잠시 put aside 제쳐두다
submit 제출하다 specific 구체적인, 특정한 description 설명
submission 제출(물) manageable 감당할 만한, 관리 가능한

158 세부 사항

번역 맥스웰 씨가 회람 수신자들에게 제출하라고 요청하는 것은?
(A) 기존 제품에 대한 평가
(B) 잠재적인 신제품 후보 아이디어
(C) 제품 개발팀에 합류하겠다는 지원서
(D) 제품 개발 절차를 개선하기 위한 제안

해설 첫 번째 단락에서 회사의 다양한 스페인어 교육 솔루션에 추가할 만한 혁
신적인 제안을 또 한 번 찾고 있다(We are again seeking proposals
for innovative additions to our range of Spanish language
education solutions)고 한 후, 제안서를 제출해 달라고 요청하고 있다.
따라서 (B)가 정답이다.

어휘 potential 가능한, 잠재적인 improve 개선[향상]하다

▶▶ **Paraphrasing** 지문의 **proposals for innovative additions**
→ 정답의 **Ideas for potential new products**

159 추론 / 암시

고난도

번역 에드워즈 씨의 책은 누구를 대상으로 삼았겠는가?
(A) 보드게임 팬
(B) 아마추어 요리사
(C) 언어 학습자
(D) 회계학과 학생

해설 두 번째 단락에서 지난해 회계과의 로이스 에드워즈가 제안한 책이 출판
되었다(Last year, Lois Edwards in the accounting department
suggested a book that ~ was published)고 했는데, 첫 번째 단락
을 보면 골드윈 출판사가 다양한 스페인어 교육 솔루션(our range of
Spanish language education solutions)을 제공하고 있음을 알 수
있다. 따라서 골드윈 출판사의 직원인 에드워즈 씨가 제안한 책도 언어 학
습자를 위한 제품이라고 추론할 수 있으므로, (C)가 정답이다.

160 사실 관계 확인

번역 제출물에 관해 알 수 있는 것은?
(A) 두 사람에게 보내야 한다.
(B) 1년에 두 번 접수한다.
(C) 길이는 최대 2페이지다.
(D) 두 가지 정보가 포함되어야 한다.

해설 마지막 단락에서 제출되는 제안서에는 제품 및 표적시장에 대한 상세한 설
명이 포함되어야 한다(they should include a detailed description
of the product and its target market)고 했으므로, 두 가지 정보가
있어야 함을 알 수 있다. 따라서 (D)가 정답이다.

▶▶ **Paraphrasing** 지문의 **a detailed description of the**
product and its target market
→ 정답의 **two pieces of information**

161-164 웹페이지

www.shopslam.com/hiring/faq

숍슬램 채용 관련 자주 묻는 질문

161즐거운 근무환경과 탁월한 직원 복리후생 때문에, 매년 수천 명이 숍슬램 팀
의 일원이 되고자 관심을 표합니다. 당사 채용 담당자들은 접수되는 모든 문의에
응답할 수 없어 자주 하는 질문과 답변 몇 가지를 이 페이지에 모았습니다.

1. 두 가지 이상 직무에 지원할 수 있나요?
허용됩니다. **163**그러나 가장 적합한 직위에 집중하실 것을 적극 권고합니다.

1622. 채용 과정에서 장애인을 위한 편의를 제공하나요?
당사는 수화통역사, 시외에서 오는 면접 대상자를 위한 휠체어 출입 가능 호텔 등
의 편의를 기꺼이 제공해 드립니다. 선택사항인 "편의 지원 요청 양식"을 작성해
기타 지원 자료에 포함하세요.

1643. 불합격 시 알려주나요?
지원서가 많이 접수되는 관계로 합격자 분들께만 채용 절차에 따른 전형별 결과
를 보내드릴 수 있습니다.

4. 불합격된 후 같은 직무에 다시 지원해도 되나요?
됩니다. 하지만 기술직이라면 그렇게 하시기 전에 추가 경력을 많이 쌓도록 하
세요.

161 추론 / 암시

번역 숍슬램에 대해 가장 사실인 것은?
(A) 해마다 수천 명을 채용한다.
(B) 대학 캠퍼스에 채용 담당자들을 보낸다.
(C) 일부 기술직은 자격 요건이 낮다.
(D) 좋은 회사로 정평이 나 있다.

해설 첫 번째 단락에서 즐거운 근무환경과 탁월한 직원 복리후생 때문에 매년 수천 명이 숍슬램 팀의 일원이 되고자 관심을 표현한다(Due to our exciting work environment and excellent employee benefits, thousands of people each year express interest in becoming part of the Shopslam team)고 했으므로, 숍슬램이 좋은 회사로 정평이 나 있음을 추론할 수 있다. 따라서 (D)가 정답이다. 참고로, 수천 명이 지원에 관심을 표현한다고 했지만 채용된다는 내용은 언급되지 않았으므로 (A)는 정답이 될 수 없다.

어휘 annually 해마다 requirement 자격 요건 reputation 정평, 명성

162 사실 관계 확인   고난도

번역 장애인을 위한 편의의 예로 언급된 것은?
(A) 대면 소통 지원
(B) 큰 글자로 되어 있는 양식
(C) 쉽게 접근할 수 있는 면접 장소
(D) 서류를 작성하기 위한 추가 시간

해설 2번 질문에 대한 답변에서 숍슬램이 수화통역사를 제공한다(We are happy to offer accommodations such as sign language interpreters)고 했으므로, (A)가 정답이다. 참고로, 시외에서 오는 면접 대상자를 위해 휠체어 출입이 가능한 호텔(wheelchair-accessible hotels for interviewees coming from out of town)은 제공한다고 했지만, 면접 장소에 대한 언급은 없었으므로 (C)는 정답이 될 수 없다.

어휘 in-person 대면의, 직접 하는

163 세부 사항

번역 웹페이지에 따르면 구직자가 해야 할 일은?
(A) 웹페이지에서 채용 최신 정보 확인하기
(B) 하나의 공석에 노력을 쏟기
(C) 지원 자료에 작업 샘플 포함하기
(D) 자주 묻는 면접 질문 목록 검토하기

해설 1번 질문에 대한 답변에서 구직자에게 가장 적합한 직위에 집중할 것을 적극 권고한다(we strongly recommend that you focus on the position for which you are best qualified)고 했으므로, (B)가 정답이다.

어휘 concentrate 집중하다 effort 노력

▶▶ Paraphrasing 지문의 focus on the position for which you are best qualified
→ 정답의 Concentrate their efforts on a single opening

164 사실 관계 확인   고난도

번역 긍정적인 답변을 받지 못한 질문은?
(A) 1
(B) 2
(C) 3
(D) 4

해설 불합격 시 알려주는지(Will you notify me if my application is rejected?) 묻는 3번 질문의 답변에서 합격자에게만 전형별 결과를 보낼 수 있다(we are only able to send updates about the hiring process to successful candidates)고 했으므로, 불합격 시 통보를 받지 못한다는 것을 알 수 있다. 따라서 (C)가 정답이다.

어휘 affirmative 긍정적인

165-168 문자 메시지

린 플레밍 [오후 1시 45분]
조니, 아직 슈퍼마켓이에요?
존 리베라 [오후 1시 47분]
아뇨, 돌아가는 길이에요. 문자에 답하려고 길가에 차를 세웠어요. 왜 물어보는 거예요?
린 플레밍 [오후 1시 48분]
¹⁶⁵5시에 오는 손님들을 위해 로즈룸을 청소하고 있었는데 청소용품 몇 가지가 떨어졌어요. ¹⁶⁶돌아가서 좀 사다 주실래요? 불편하겠지만요.
존 리베라 [오후 1시 49분]
음, 저 내시마트 바로 옆이에요.
린 플레밍 [오후 1시 50분]
¹⁶⁶아, 그러면 괜찮겠네요! 종이 타월과 창문 세정제가 필요해요.
존 리베라 [오후 1시 51분]
정말요? ¹⁶⁷종이 타월이 다 떨어졌다고요? 바로 지난주에 12팩을 샀는데요.
린 플레밍 [오후 1시 52분]
예, 지난 주말에 라일락 스위트에 머물렀던 어린이 동반 가족이 흘린 걸 치우느라 많이 썼더라고요. 이번에는 24팩을 사는 게 어때요? 그럼 한동안 쓰겠죠.
존 리베라 [오후 1시 53분]
예, 알겠어요. 30분 뒤에 돌아갈게요.
린 플레밍 [오후 1시 53분]
좋아요. ¹⁶⁸이번 구매건도 영수증 받는 거 잊지 마세요.
어휘 pull over 차를 세우다 run out of ~이 떨어지다 inconvenient 불편한 spill 엎지른 것; 엎지르다 purchase 구매(품)

165 추론 / 암시

번역　필자들은 어디에서 일하겠는가?
(A) 작은 호텔
(B) 조경업체
(C) 청소업체
(D) 교육기관

해설　플레밍 씨가 오후 1시 48분 메시지에서 5시에 오는 손님들을 위해 로즈룸을 청소하고 있었다(I was just cleaning up the Rose Room for the guests who are coming at five)고 했으므로, 필자들이 숙박 업소에서 일한다고 추론할 수 있다. 따라서 (A)가 정답이다.

166 의도 파악

번역　오후 1시 49분에 리베라 씨가 "저 내시마트 바로 옆이에요."라고 쓴 의도는?
(A) 이동이 빨리 진행되고 있다.
(B) 내시마트에서 물건을 살 수 있을 것이다.
(C) 플레밍 씨가 데리러 오기 바란다.
(D) 플레밍 씨가 있는 위치에서 그를 볼 수 있을 것이다.

해설　플레밍 씨가 오후 1시 48분 메시지에서 슈퍼마켓에 돌아가서 청소용품을 좀 사다 줄 것(Would you mind going back and picking some up?)을 요청했는데, 이에 대해 리베라 씨가 '저 내시마트 바로 옆이에요(I am right by Nash Mart)'라고 응답했다. 그러자 플레밍 씨가 '그러면 괜찮겠네요!(that would work!)'라고 한 후 필요한 물품을 이야기한 것으로 보아, 리베라 씨가 내시마트에서 청소용품 구매가 가능하다는 의도로 한 말임을 알 수 있다. 따라서 (B)가 정답이다.

167 추론 / 암시

번역　리베라 씨를 놀라게 한 것은?
(A) 자신이 임무를 수행하도록 선택되었다는 것
(B) 플레밍 씨가 문제점을 알고 있다는 것
(C) 사건이 발생한 지 꼬박 일주일이 지났다는 것
(D) 일부 비품을 다 썼다는 것

해설　리베라 씨가 오후 1시 51분 메시지에서 종이 타월이 다 떨어진 것(We're out of paper towels?)에 대해 놀라움을 표한 후, 바로 지난주에 12팩을 샀다(I bought a 12-pack just last week)며 자신이 놀란 이유를 덧붙였다. 따라서 리베라 씨가 종이 타월이 빨리 소진되었다는 사실에 놀랐음을 추론할 수 있으므로, (D)가 정답이다.

어휘　occur 발생하다　use up ~을 다 쓰다

▸▸ Paraphrasing　지문의 out of paper towels → 정답의 some supplies have been used up

168 세부 사항

번역　플레밍 씨가 리베라 씨에게 상기시킨 일은?
(A) 차량에 연료 넣기
(B) 액체 흘리지 않기
(C) 결제 증명서 받기
(D) 동료에게 통지하기

해설　플레밍 씨가 오후 1시 53분 메시지에서 이번 구매건에 대한 영수증도 받아야 한다(Don't forget to get a receipt for this purchase too)고 한 번 더 상기시켰으므로, (C)가 정답이다.

어휘　fuel 연료　liquid 액체　proof 증명(서)

▸▸ Paraphrasing　지문의 get a receipt for this purchase → 정답의 Receive proof of a payment

169-171 이메일

발신: 윌리 반스 〈w.barnes@mclerdon.com〉
수신: 아라셀리 디아즈 〈araceli@hevneymanufacturing.com〉
제목: 요청
날짜: 4월 28일

디아즈 씨께,

제 이름은 윌리 반스이며, 맥러든 사의 마케팅 전문가입니다. [169]헤브니 매뉴팩처링과 같은 고객사들의 꾸준한 성원에 힘입어 성장한 덕분에, 저희 부서가 올해 초 개설되었습니다. [170]귀사의 거래처 관리인인 퀸 씨는 저희 맥러든 직원들이 영광스럽게도 5년 가까이 헤브니 공장 부지를 경비하고 있다고 말했습니다.

[171]제 소개에 덧붙여 한 가지 요청을 드리고자 이 글을 씁니다. 제가 지금 맥러든 웹사이트에 고객사 로고를 추가하고 있는데 귀사의 로고도 포함시켰으면 합니다. 이는 보통 귀사와 당사 간 서비스 계약으로 승인되는 사안이지만, 계약서 작성 당시 저희의 마케팅 전문지식이 부족해 이러한 조항이 포함되지 않았습니다. 이 요청에 동의하신다면, 귀사가 현재 사용하고 있는 선명한 로고 이미지를 150픽셀 x 150픽셀 크기로 주시기만 하면 됩니다. 하지만 저희가 귀사의 로고를 표시하지 않는 편을 원하신다면 주저 없이 제게 알려주시기 바랍니다.

맥러든은 다시 한 번 귀사의 거래에 감사드립니다. 곧 연락 주시기 바랍니다.

윌리 반스
맥러든 사

어휘　establish 개설[설립]하다　fuel ~에 활기를 불어넣다　loyal 꾸준한, 충실한　patronage 이용, 애용　account manager 거래처 (영업) 관리자　premises 부지　in addition to ~에 덧붙여　currently 현재　normally 보통, 일반적으로　authorize 승인하다　agreement 계약(서)　expertise 전문지식　contract 계약(서)　provision 조항　prefer 선호하다　hesitate 주저하다

169 추론 / 암시

번역　반스 씨에 관해 암시된 것은?
(A) 퀸 씨가 그의 매니저다.
(B) 계약서 초안 작성을 도왔다.
(C) 최근에 생긴 직책을 맡고 있다.
(D) 헤브니 매뉴팩처링의 웹사이트를 방문했다.

해설　첫 번째 단락에서 반스 씨가 헤브니 매뉴팩처링과 같은 고객사들의 꾸준한 성원에 힘입어 성장한 덕분에 자신의 부서가 올해 초 개설되었다(My department was established earlier this year thanks to growth fueled by the loyal patronage of clients)고 했으므로, 그가 새로 생긴 직책을 맡고 있음을 추론할 수 있다. 따라서 (C)가 정답이다.

어휘　draft 초안을 작성하다

170 추론 / 암시

`고난도`

번역 맥러든 사는 고객들을 위해 무엇을 하겠는가?
(A) 마케팅 캠페인 실시
(B) 보안요원 제공
(C) 공장 설비 보수
(D) 법률 조언 제공

해설 첫 번째 단락에서 맥러든 직원들이 5년 가까이 헤브니 공장 부지를 경비하고 있다(McLerdon staff have had the honor of guarding Hevney's factory premises for nearly five years now)고 했으므로, 맥러든 사가 보안·경비 업체라는 것을 추론할 수 있다. 따라서 (B)가 정답이다.

어휘 repair 보수하다 equipment 설비

171 세부 사항

번역 반스 씨가 디아즈 씨에게 요청한 것은?
(A) 고객 추천서
(B) 서명한 계약서 사본
(C) 기계 치수 확인
(D) 이미지 사용 허가

해설 두 번째 단락에서 반스 씨는 요청할 사항이 있어 글을 쓰고 있다(I am writing to make a request)고 한 후, 디아즈 씨의 회사 로고를 맥러든 웹사이트에 포함시키고 싶다(I ~ would like to include your company's (logo))고 했다. 따라서 (D)가 정답이다.

어휘 testimonial 추천서 confirmation 확인 dimension 치수 permission 허가

172-175 기사

팟캐스트 업계에 파문을 일으킨 〈도레타〉

필립 너트센

소설가 도레타 워스의 삶을 연대순으로 기록한 8부작 오디오 팟캐스트인 〈도레타〉의 팬들은 곧 비슷한 작품을 많이 듣게 될 것이다. 〈도레타〉의 성공에 고무되어 제작사인 엘지오르 미디어와 몇몇 다른 팟캐스트 거물들이 역사상 흥미로운 사건과 인물들을 그린 팟캐스트 대본을 제작하게 되었다.

172팟캐스트 업계 분석업체인 캐스트아이에 따르면 상위 10개 팟캐스트의 대다수는 보통 시사 또는 인터뷰 프로그램이라고 한다. 그렇기 때문에 〈도레타〉가 주류에 편입되는 인기를 얻은 성과는 특히 강렬한 인상을 준다. **172이 프로그램은 역사 소설 팟캐스트로, 프로 배우들이 연기를 펼치는 대본과 음향 효과, 그리고 음악으로 구성되었다.** 그럼에도 불구하고, 방송 두 달 만에 캐스트아이 순위

목록 4위에 올랐다. **173아직도 엘지오르 웹사이트에는 이 프로그램에 대한 토론 게시판이 활발하며, 종영 직후 출연자들이 했던 축약판 공연은 다섯 차례 매진을 기록했다.**

일각에서는 〈도레타〉가 가진 차별성이 장벽이 아닌 인기의 원인이라는 추측도 나왔다. 그러나 캐스트아이 분석가 신시아 마이어스는 동의하지 않는다. 그녀는 "따지고 보면, 〈도레타〉는 최초의 역사 소설 팟캐스트가 아니었다"고 말했다. "**174우리가 한 조사에 따르면, 프로그램 극본 및 연기의 우수성이 청취자들에게 통했던 겁니다.**"

그래도 업계에서는 이제 비슷한 프로젝트를 들을 청취자가 생겼다고 보고 있다. **175엘지오르는 내년에 또 다른 역사 소설 팟캐스트를 제작하기 위해 〈도레타〉의 창작자 켄트 멀리건에게 거액의 계약을 제안했다. 그 회사 대변인은 그것이 코빗 대교 건설을 다룰 것이라고 말했다.** 한편 렌스턴 스튜디오는 다음 달 마천드 팬더스가 챔피언에 오른 시즌을 상세히 다룬 팟캐스트 〈1955〉를 선보일 예정이며, 캐리어버 라디오는 머렐 대 탤버트 법정 소송 사건을 그린 프로그램을 현재 제작 중이라고 밝혔다.

어휘 stir 파문 chronicle 연대순으로 기록하다 similar 비슷한 offering 제공물, 작품 inspire 고무하다 scripted 대본[원고]으로 된 depict 그리다, 묘사하다 analytics 분석 majority 다수 achievement 업적 mainstream 주류, 대세 popularity 인기 make an impression 인상을 남기다 feature 특별히 포함하다, ~가 특징이다 score 음악, 악보 reach 도달하다 active 활발한 discussion board 토론 게시판 performance 공연, 연기 abridged 축약된, 요약된 shortly after ~ 직후 speculate 추측[짐작]하다 distinctness 차별성 barrier 장벽 indicate 보여주다, 시사하다 appeal 관심을 끌다, 매력적으로 다가가다 audience 청중, 청취자 lucrative 수익성이 좋은, 유리한 deal 계약, 거래 meanwhile 한편 release 출시하다, 공개하다 court case 법정 소송 사건

---

172 사실 관계 확인

번역 〈도레타〉에 관해 알 수 있는 것은?
(A) 베스트셀러를 토대로 했다.
(B) 더 많은 에피소드가 방송되리라 예상되었다.
(C) 다른 인기 팟캐스트와 장르가 달랐다.
(D) 제작사가 만든 첫 프로그램이었다.

해설 두 번째 단락에서 상위 10개 팟캐스트의 대다수가 보통 시사 또는 인터뷰 프로그램(the majority of the top ten most popular podcasts are usually current events or interview shows)이라고 했는데, 〈도레타〉는 역사소설 팟캐스트(As a historical fiction podcast)이므로, 다른 인기 팟캐스트와 장르가 다르다는 것을 알 수 있다. 따라서 (C)가 정답이다.

173 추론 / 암시

번역 〈도레타〉 팬들은 엘지오르 미디어 웹사이트에서 무엇을 할 수 있겠는가?
(A) 테마 상품 구매
(B) 서로에게 메시지 게시
(C) 신상에 관한 사실 읽기
(D) 공연 사진 보기

해설 두 번째 단락에서 아직도 엘지오르 웹사이트에는 〈도레타〉에 대한 토론 게시판이 활발하다(The show still has an active discussion board on Elgior's Web site)고 했으므로, 서로에게 메시지를 게시할 수 있다고 추론할 수 있다. 따라서 (B)가 정답이다.

▸▸ **Paraphrasing** 지문의 an active discussion board
→ 정답의 Post messages to each other

174 세부 사항

번역 마이어스 씨는 무엇에 관해 전문가 의견을 제시하는가?
(A) 〈도레타〉의 성공 원인
(B) 〈도레타〉의 역사적 정확성
(C) 캐스트아이 순위의 신뢰도
(D) 엘지오르 미디어의 미래 전망

해설 세 번째 단락에서 마이어스 씨는 자신들의 조사에 따르면 프로그램 극본 및 연기의 우수성이 청취자들에게 통한 것(Our research indicates that it was the excellence of the show's writing and performances that appealed to listeners)이라며 〈도레타〉의 인기 원인을 제시했다. 따라서 (A)가 정답이다.

어휘 accuracy 정확성 reliability 신뢰도 prospect 전망

175 문장 삽입 〔고난도〕

번역 [1], [2], [3], [4]로 표시된 곳 중에서 다음 문장이 가장 적합한 곳은?
"그 회사 대변인은 그것이 코빗 대교 건설을 다룰 것이라고 말했다."
(A) [1]
(B) [2]
(C) [3]
(D) [4]

해설 주어진 문장에서 그것이 코빗 대교 건설을 다룰 것(it would deal with the building of Corbitt Bridge)이라고 했으므로, 앞에서 먼저 대명사 it이 가리키는 대상이 언급되어야 한다. [4] 앞에서 엘지오르가 내년에 또 다른 역사소설 팟캐스트를 제작하기 위해 〈도레타〉의 창작자에게 거액의 계약을 제안했다(Elgior offered ~ Doretta's creator, a lucrative deal to develop another historical fiction podcast next year)며 it이 가리키는 구체적인 대상(another historical fiction podcast)을 밝혔으므로, (D)가 정답이다.

176-180 이메일 + 웹페이지

발신: 남연희
수신: 연구팀
제목: 워크숍
날짜: 1월 30일

모두 안녕하세요,

새로운 데이터 시각화 소프트웨어인 슬린뷰에 대해 대부분 들어보셨을 겁니다. 개발사인 바젠 테크가 다음 달 이곳에서 교육 워크숍을 열 예정입니다. ¹⁷⁸8시간 수업에 1인당 불과 40달러로, 거액을 투자해 구입하기 전에 슬린뷰에 대해 알아볼 수 있는 좋은 기회가 될 것입니다. ^{176/178}팀원 2명을 보내 워크숍에 참석하게 해서 슬린뷰 도입이 파눈 농업 컨설팅에 도움이 되는지 판단해 보려고 합니다.

워크숍에 대한 정보는 이 페이지에서 찾을 수 있습니다. 근처 식당에서의 점심값을 우리가 지불하겠지만, 그레노리 호텔로 가는 교통편은 각자 마련해서 오전 8시까지 그곳에 도착해야 합니다.

¹⁷⁶관심이 있으면, 오늘 중으로 이 이메일로 회신해 자신이 가야 하는 ¹⁷⁷근거를 간략히 적어 보내세요. ¹⁷⁹내일 선정된 사람들에게 통지하고 제 비서가 전화로 신청하게끔 하겠습니다.

– 연희

어휘 visualization 시각화 become familiar with ~에 익숙해지다, ~를 알게 되다 invest 투자하다 purchase 구매하다 attend 참석하다 determine 판단하다, 결정하다 benefit 도움이 되다 agricultural 농업의 adopt 도입[채택]하다 coordinate 마련[준비]하다 transportation 교통(편) argument 논거, 주장 notify 통지하다

---

http://www.vazenttech.com

소개	제품	뉴스	연락처

온타리오에서 열리는 1일 슬린뷰 워크숍

바젠 테크가 온타리오 소재의 기업과 개인에 한해 슬린뷰 기본기를 배우고 싶은 분들을 초청하오니, 2월 중 주 곳곳에서 개최될 4개의 입문 워크숍 중 하나에 참여해 보세요. ¹⁸⁰저희 전문 강사들이 슬린뷰의 다양한 기능을 시연한 후 실습을 통해 참가자들에게 소프트웨어 사용 기회를 드립니다. 이 활동에 사용할 수 있는 컴퓨터 수와 참가자 수가 일치해야 하므로, 인원이 20명으로 제한된다는 점에 유의하세요.

워크숍은 오전 8시부터 오후 5시까지 진행되며, 점심시간은 1시간입니다. ¹⁷⁸비용은 1인당 55달러이고, 온타리오 비즈니스 협회에 기업 혹은 개인 회원으로 가입되어 있는 분들은 40달러입니다. 간식과 물이 제공되지만 참가자는 직접 점심을 싸오거나 근처에서 구입해야 합니다.

위치 및 날짜:

웨스트 토론토 (신들리 컨벤션 센터)	2월 17일
이스트 토론토 (허노트 플라자)	2월 19일
오타와 (그레노리 호텔)	2월 21일
해밀턴 (블레인스 대학교)	2월 24일

¹⁷⁹등록하시려면 여기를 클릭하세요.

어휘 individual 개인 introductory 입문의 province (행정 단위) 주 expert 전문적인; 전문가 instructor 강사 demonstrate 시연하다 feature 기능, 특징 participant 참가자 hands-on exercise 실습 cap 상한[한도]을 정하다 corporate 기업의

176 추론 / 암시

번역 남 씨는 누구이겠는가?
(A) 팀장
(B) 소프트웨어 개발자
(C) 보좌관
(D) 프리랜서 행사 코디네이터

해설 이메일의 첫 번째 단락에서 남 씨가 팀원 2명을 보내 워크숍에 참석하게

할 것(I'd like to send two members of the team to attend the workshop)이라고 한 후, 마지막 단락에서 참석하고 싶다면 본인에게 회신하라(respond to this e-mail)고 했으므로, 남 씨가 팀장이라고 추론할 수 있다. 따라서 (A)가 정답이다.

177 동의어 찾기

번역 이메일에서 3번째 단락 2행의 "arguments"와 의미상 가장 가까운 것은?
(A) 절차
(B) 태도
(C) 논란
(D) 이유

해설 'arguments'가 포함된 부분은 '자신이 가야 하는 근거를 간략히 적어 이메일로 회신하세요'라는 의미로 해석되는데, 여기서 argument는 '근거, 주장'이라는 뜻으로 쓰였다. 따라서 '이유, 근거'라는 의미의 (D) reasons가 정답이다.

178 연계 고난도

번역 파논 농업 컨설팅에 관해 암시된 것은?
(A) 토론토 서부에 있다.
(B) 직원이 기술교육을 받을 수 있도록 정기적으로 대금을 지불한다.
(C) 온타리오 비즈니스 협회 소속이다.
(D) 최근 새로운 데이터 수집 기법을 도입했다.

해설 이메일의 첫 번째 단락에서 팀원 2명을 워크숍에 참가하게 하여 슬린뷰 도입이 파논 농업 컨설팅에 도움이 되는지 판단할 것(I'd like ~ two members of the team to attend the workshop and determine if it would benefit Fannon Agricultural Consulting to adopt Slinview)이라고 한 후, 참가 비용이 1인당 40달러(At just $40 per person)라고 했는데, 웹페이지의 두 번째 단락을 보면 온타리오 비즈니스 협회의 기업 혹은 개인 회원일 시 워크숍 비용이 40달러(The cost is ~ $40 for those with corporate or individual memberships in the Ontario Business Association)라고 되어 있다. 따라서 1인당 40달러를 지불할 예정인 파논 농업 컨설팅은 온타리오 비즈니스 협회 소속이라고 추론할 수 있으므로, (C)가 정답이다.

179 연계 고난도

번역 남 씨가 제공한 워크숍 세부 사항 중 웹페이지 정보와 다른 것은?
(A) 도착하라고 권한 시간
(B) 설명한 등록 방법
(C) 참가자들이 식사하리라 예상한 장소
(D) 교육에 소요될 거라고 한 시간

해설 이메일의 마지막 단락에서 남 씨는 자신의 비서가 전화로 신청하게끔 하겠다(I'll ~ have my assistant call to sign them up)고 했지만, 웹페이지의 하단에는 '등록하려면 여기를 클릭하세요(Click here to register)'라고 되어 있다. 따라서 (B)가 정답이다.

어휘 describe 설명하다 attribute ~의 특징으로 알다[생각하다]

180 세부 사항

번역 웹페이지에 따르면, 워크숍 참가자의 수가 제한된 이유는 무엇인가?
(A) 참가자가 소프트웨어 사용을 연습할 수 있도록 하기 위해
(B) 장소 접근이 어려워지는 것을 방지하기 위해
(C) 참가자가 강사와 대화할 수 있도록 하기 위해
(D) 독점적인 경험에 대한 관심을 유발하기 위해

해설 웹페이지의 첫 번째 단락에서 전문 강사들이 슬린뷰의 다양한 기능을 시연한 후 실습을 통해 참가자들에게 소프트웨어 사용 기회를 준다(Our expert instructors will ~ give participants the chance to try out the software through hands-on exercises)고 한 후, 해당 활동에 사용할 수 있는 컴퓨터 수와 참가자 수가 일치해야 하므로 인원이 20명으로 제한된다(the number of participants is capped ~ to match the number of computers available for this activity)고 했다. 따라서 (A)가 정답이다.

어휘 venue (행사 등의) 장소 access 접근하다 generate 유발하다 exclusive 독점적인, 특권층의

▸▸ Paraphrasing 지문의 capped → 질문의 limited
지문의 try out the software through hands-on exercises → 정답의 practice using the software

181-185 기사 + 이메일

슈레이더 사회교육원, 원격 업무 수료증 제공

슈레이더 시티 (12월 1일)—슈레이더 대학 사회교육원이 "원격 업무 능력 수료증" 발급을 시작한다고 발표했다.

대학에서 운영하는 이 사회교육원은 슈레이더 전역에 있는 사무실의 네트워크 역할을 하며, 평생교육 수업과 기타 프로그램을 통한 지식 공유를 담당한다. 181/185사회교육원장 어윈 히라노 박사는 이 프로그램의 목표가 할 일이 충분하지 않은 지방 거주자들에게 기회를 주는 것이라고 말했다: "그들이 어쩔 수 없이 도시로 이주해야 한다고 생각하는 대신, 공동체의 일부로 남아 생계를 유지할 수 있었으면 합니다."

학생들의 편의를 위해 이 프로그램은 전적으로 온라인을 통해 운영될 예정이다. 히라노 박사는 "사람들에게 필요한 것은 컴퓨터, 중간 정도의 컴퓨터 사용능력, 그리고 원활한 인터넷 연결뿐입니다"라고 설명했다. 그는 마케팅이나 그래픽 디자인 같은 분야의 경력이 도움이 된다고 하면서도 "고객 서비스 담당자처럼 이전 근무 경력이 거의 필요 없는 원격 업무 직종이 있습니다"라고 말했다.

이 5주짜리 프로그램은 특정 지방 거주자들에게 무료로 제공되며, 원격 업무에 필요한 기술 도구와 직무 역량을 가르치는 과정을 중심으로 한다. 182과정이 끝나고 수료증 소지자들이 구직 활동을 시작하면 진로 상담사를 만날 수 있게 된다.

184예비 학생이라면 1월 2일 개강하는 첫 학기는 12월 26일까지, 3월 3일 시작하는 학기는 2월 24일까지 등록해야 한다. 프로그램에 대한 자세한 내용은 www.extension.shrader.edu/rwpc에서 확인할 수 있다.

어휘 extension 사회교육원, 개방대학 certificate 수료증 remote 원격의 proficiency 능력, 숙달도 be charged with ~를 책임 맡고 있다 continuing education 평생교육 dean 학장 opportunity 기회 underemployed 할 일이 충분하지 않은, 능력 이하의 일을 하는 rural 지방의, 시골의 make a living 생계를 유지하다 be forced to 어쩔 수 없이 ~하다 convenience 편의

administer 운영하다 entirely 전적으로 moderate 중간의,
적당한 computer literacy 컴퓨터 사용능력 representative
담당자, 직원 previous 이전의 have access to ~를 이용할 수 있다
potential 예비의, 잠재적인 inaugural 첫 번째의

발신: 트레이시 번 〈tracy.byrne@obr-mail.com〉
수신: 〈editor@shraderherald.com〉
제목: 슈레이더의 원격 업무 능력 수료증
날짜: 11월 7일

편집장님께,

약 1년 전, 귀하의 신문사에서 슈레이더 대학 사회교육원의 원격 업무 교육 프로그램에 대해 보도했습니다. **184저는 첫 학기에 학생으로 등록했고, 수료증을 딴 지 2주 만에 원격 업무 일자리를 얻었으며 지금도 계속 일하고 있습니다.** 저와 같은 학기에 참가한 다른 사람들도 대부분 비슷한 경험을 했습니다.

그래서 최근에 그 프로그램을 더 이상 이용할 수 없는 것 같아서 무척 놀랐습니다. 프로그램 웹페이지가 없어졌더군요. **185히라노 박사님은 대학을 떠나셨고, 제가 그 분의 후임자에게 프로그램에 관한 이메일을 보냈는데 답장을 받지 못했습니다. 183기자들 중 누군가가 이 문제를 조사해 봐 줄 수 있을까요?** 지역민이라면 그토록 성공적인 프로그램이 중단된 이유를 알 자격이 있다고 생각합니다.

이 문제에 대해 관심을 가져주시면 감사하겠습니다.

트레이시 번

어휘 take down 치우다, 없애다 successor 후임자 deserve
~할 자격이 되다 initiative 프로그램, 계획 discontinue 중단하다

181 세부 사항

번역 프로그램은 어떤 사람들을 위한 것인가?
(A) 인구 밀도가 낮은 지역에 사는 사람
(B) 가족을 돌볼 책임이 있는 사람
(C) 대학 학위가 없는 사람
(D) 예전에 특정 업계에서 일했던 사람

해설 기사의 두 번째 단락에서 이 프로그램의 목표가 할 일이 충분하지 않은 지방 거주자들에게 기회를 주는 것(the goal of this program is to give opportunities to underemployed people in rural areas)이라고 했으므로, 인구밀도가 낮은 지역에 사는 사람들을 위한 프로그램임을 알 수 있다. 따라서 (A)가 정답이다.

어휘 density 밀도 responsibility 책임 previously 예전에
industry 업계

▸▸ Paraphrasing   지문의 underemployed people in rural
areas → 정답의 People in areas with low
population density

182 사실 관계 확인

번역 기사에서 프로그램 강좌에 관해 언급한 것은?
(A) 내용에는 기말고사가 포함되어 있다.
(B) 일부 학생은 수업료가 인하된다.
(C) 일부 수업은 대학 사회교육원 사무실에서 진행한다.
(D) 졸업생은 구직 활동 지원을 받을 수 있다.

해설 기사의 네 번째 단락에서 과정이 끝나고 수료증 소지자들이 구직 활동을 시작하면 진로 상담사를 만날 수 있게 된다(Once the course ends, certificate-holders will have access to a career coach as they launch their job search)고 했으므로, 수료생이 구직 활동에 도움을 받을 수 있다는 것을 알 수 있다. 따라서 (D)가 정답이다.

▸▸ Paraphrasing   지문의 have access to a career coach as
they launch their job search
→ 정답의 get job seeking assistance

183 주제 / 목적

번역 이메일의 목적은?
(A) 프로그램 현황에 대한 조사 요청
(B) 프로그램 기획 변경에 대한 불만 제기
(C) 다른 예비 학생들에게 프로그램 추천
(D) 프로그램을 홍보한 간행물에 감사 표현

해설 이메일의 두 번째 단락에서 기자들 중 누군가가 원격 업무 교육 프로그램 관련 문제를 조사해 줄 수 있는지(Could one of your reporters look into this issue?)고 묻고 있으므로, 프로그램 현황에 대한 조사를 요청하는 이메일임을 알 수 있다. 따라서 (A)가 정답이다.

어휘 investigation 조사 status 현황 publication 간행(물)

▸▸ Paraphrasing   지문의 look into this issue
→ 정답의 an investigation into the
program's status

184 연계

번역 번 씨는 1월 2일에 무엇을 했겠는가?
(A) 기사를 보았다.
(B) 등록을 완료했다.
(C) 교육 과정을 시작했다.
(D) 수료증을 받았다.

해설 이메일의 첫 번째 단락에서 번 씨는 자신이 첫 학기에 학생으로 등록했다(I signed up to be a student in its first session)고 했는데, 기사의 마지막 단락을 보면 1월 2일에 첫 학기가 개강한다(the inaugural session, which will begin classes on January 2)고 나와 있으므로, 번 씨가 이 날 교육 과정을 시작했다고 추론할 수 있다. 따라서 (C)가 정답이다.

어휘 enrollment 등록

▸▸ Paraphrasing   지문의 begin classes
→ 정답의 Started her course

185 연계   고난도

번역 슈레이더 대학 사회교육원에 대해 암시된 것은?
(A) 번 씨의 현재 고용주다.
(B) 번 씨에게 한 약속을 이행하지 않았다.
(C) 더 이상 온라인에 존재하지 않는다.
(D) 신임 원장이 부임했다.

해설 이메일의 두 번째 단락에서 히라노 박사가 대학을 떠났고, 그의 후임자에게 프로그램에 관한 이메일을 보냈다(Dr. Hirano has left the university ~ I sent an e-mail to his successor about the program)고 했는데, 기사의 두 번째 단락을 보면 히라노 박사가 사회교육원장(The extension's dean, Dr. Irwin Hirano)이라고 소개되어 있다. 따라서 슈레이더 대학 사회교육원에 히라노 박사를 대신하는 원장이 새로 부임했다는 것을 추론할 수 있으므로, (D)가 정답이다. 참고로, 원격 업무 교육 프로그램 사이트가 없어진 것이지 사회교육원의 사이트가 없어진 것은 아니므로, (C)는 정답이 될 수 없다.

어휘 fulfill 이행하다 presence 존재

186-190 웹페이지 + 웹페이지 + 이메일

www.locetopumpkinfair.com/participate/music/

음악 그룹 구함!

라이브 음악은 로체토 호박 축제에서 빠질 수 없는 부분입니다. 186그래서 저희는 해마다 기획사에 연락해 몇 개의 주요 그룹을 예약하고 있지만, 자리 대부분을 유망한 소규모 그룹을 위해 187남겨 두고자 합니다. 만약 건전한 팝, 록, 또는 R&B 음악을 연주한다면, 이번이 수백 혹은 수천 명의 청중 앞에서 공연할 수 있는 기회가 될 수 있습니다. 지원하시려면 music@locetopumpkinfair.com으로 짤막한 아티스트/밴드 약력(50~100단어)과 공연 동영상 파일 2개를 제출하세요. 오디오 파일은 받지 않으며, 동영상은 청중 앞에서 공연하는 모습을 보여주는 것으로 보내주기를 권장합니다. 제출 마감일은 7월 31일 오후 5시입니다. 189로체토 카운티에 소재한 그룹은 대면 오디션을 요청 받을 수도 있습니다. 최종 결정은 8월 말까지 내릴 예정입니다.

어휘 act (음악) 공연자[그룹], 공연 vital 빠질 수 없는, 중요한 fair 축제, 박람회 up-and-coming 유망한, 떠오르는 family-friendly 건전한, 가족끼리 즐기기 좋은 biography 약력, 전기 submission 제출(물)

---

www.locetopumpkinfair.com/music/lineups/sat

10월 19일 토요일 출연진

자세한 정보를 보시려면 해당 그룹의 이름을 클릭하세요.

1904:30–5:10 P.M. 오퍼레이터즈
5:30–6:10 P.M. 실버 스타피쉬
6:30–7:10 P.M. 자넷 앤 더 재머스
7:30–8:30 P.M. 록 갬빗

← 10월 18일 금요일   10월 20일 일요일 →

발신: ⟨music@locetopumpkinfair.com⟩
수신: 로라 고든 ⟨lora.g@pmt-mail.com⟩
제목: 로체토 호박 축제
날짜: 9월 23일

고든 씨께,

18810월 19일 로체토 호박 축제에서 공연 예정이었던 밴드들 중 하나가 예기치 않게 빠지게 되어 귀하의 밴드에게 그 자리를 대신할 기회를 드리고 싶습니다. 189앞서 이메일에서 언급했듯이, 다른 음악위원회 위원들과 저는 헤어핀스의 오

디션이 인상 깊었고, 애초에 자리를 제공하지 못해 아쉬웠습니다. 이번 공석에 관해 연락하는 그룹은 귀하의 밴드가 처음입니다.

190오후 4시 30분부터 40분 세트로 연주하게 되며, 보수는 300달러입니다. 헤어핀스에게 그날 다른 일이 있을 수도 있다는 점 이해하므로, 저희의 제안을 밴드 동료들과 의논 후 결정해서 알려주시기 바랍니다. 내일 업무 시간이 끝나기 전까지 연락을 주셔야 합니다.

감사합니다.

웬델 폭스
로체토 호박 축제 음악위원회

어휘 drop out 중도에 빠지다 unexpectedly 예기치 않게 committee 위원회 impressed 감명 받은 initially 애초에 engagement 업무, 약속

186 사실 관계 확인

번역 첫 번째 웹페이지에서 신청 절차에 관해 명시된 것은?
(A) 절차가 전년보다 더 간단하다.
(B) 절차를 설명하는 동영상 지침이 있다.
(C) 일부 밴드는 그 절차를 거치지 않는다.
(D) 지원자가 대금을 내야 한다.

해설 첫 번째 웹페이지의 제목이 '음악 그룹 구함(Musical acts wanted)'이지만, 초반부에서 축제를 위해 해마다 기획사에 연락해 몇 개의 주요 그룹은 예약한다(we book a few major acts each year by reaching out to their agents)고 했으므로, 일부 밴드는 공연 참가 신청 절차를 거치지 않는다는 것을 알 수 있다. 따라서 (C)가 정답이다.

187 동의어 찾기   고난도

번역 첫 번째 웹페이지에서 1번째 단락 2행의 "reserve"와 의미상 가장 가까운 것은?
(A) 소유하다
(B) 따로 두다
(C) 인수하다
(D) 행사하다

해설 'reserve'가 포함된 부분은 '자리 대부분을 유망한 소규모 그룹을 위해 남겨 두고자 한다'라는 의미로 해석되는데, 여기서 'reserve'는 '따로 남겨[잡아] 두다'라는 뜻으로 쓰였다. 따라서 '따로 두다'라는 의미의 (B) set aside가 정답이다.

188 주제 / 목적

번역 이메일의 목적은?
(A) 고든 씨에게 기회를 알리기 위해
(B) 제안 조건을 수정하기 위해
(C) 준비에 대한 지침을 주기 위해
(D) 고든 씨에게 어떤 문제에 대해 경고하기 위해

해설 이메일의 첫 번째 단락에서 로체토 호박 축제에서 공연 예정이었던 밴드들 중 하나가 예기치 않게 빠지게 되어 고든 씨의 밴드에게 그 자리를 대신할 기회를 주고 싶다(One of the bands scheduled to perform at the Loceto Pumpkin Fair ~ has dropped out unexpectedly, and

18

we would like to offer your band the chance to take its place)
고 했으므로, 공연 기회를 알리기 위한 이메일임을 알 수 있다. 따라서 (A)
가 정답이다.

▶▶ **Paraphrasing**　지문의 **chance** → 정답의 **opportunity**

189 연계

번역　헤어핀스에 관해 가장 사실에 가까운 것은?
(A) R&B 음악을 연주한다.
(B) 7월 31일 공연했다.
(C) 전문 에이전트가 대리한다.
(D) 멤버들이 로체토 카운티에 거주한다.

해설　이메일의 첫 번째 단락에서 헤어핀스의 오디션이 인상 깊었다(the other
members of the music committee and I were very impressed
by the Hairpins' audition)고 했는데, 첫 번째 웹페이지의 하단을 보
면 로체토 카운티에 소재한 그룹은 대면 오디션을 요청 받을 수도 있다
(Selected acts based in Loceto County may then be asked to
audition in person)고 나와 있다. 따라서 헤어핀스의 멤버들이 로체토
카운티에 거주한다고 추론할 수 있으므로, (D)가 정답이다.

190 연계

번역　10월 19일에 공연하지 않는 밴드는?
(A) 오퍼레이터즈
(B) 실버 스타피쉬
(C) 자넷 앤 더 재머스
(D) 록 갬빗

해설　이메일의 두 번째 단락에서 10월 19일에 고든 씨의 밴드가 축제에 참여할
경우 오후 4시 30분부터 40분 세트로 연주하게 될 것(You would play
a 40-minute set starting at 4:30 P.M.)이라고 했는데, 두 번째 웹페
이지의 출연진(Lineup for Saturday, October 19)을 보면 원래 오후
4시 30분부터 5시 10분까지 공연하기로 했던 그룹이 오퍼레이터즈(The
Operators)임을 알 수 있다. 따라서 (A)가 정답이다.

191-195 광고 + 이메일 + 고지서

벨커 사이언스의 고효율 배기 후드

거의 모든 종류의 실험실에는 과학자들이 유해 가스를 배출하는 화학물질로 안
전하게 작업할 수 있도록 배기 후드가 필요합니다. 안타깝게도 배기 후드는 가
장 에너지가 소모가 큰 실험실 장비에 속하기도 합니다. 그래서 벨커 사이언스
는 다양한 고효율 배기 후드를 만들었습니다. 191(A)/(B)각각에는 정교한 제어
기와 3단 속도의 송풍기가 있어 함께 후드의 공기 흐름 사용량을 줄여 에너지 필
요량도 줄일 수 있습니다. 191(D)또한 특수 모터는 기존의 구형 모터보다 에너
지를 적게 소모합니다. 193후드는 2피트, 4피트, 6피트, 8피트 모델로 구입할
수 있으며, 안정성과 유용성을 최대화하기 위한 세로형 안전유리창도 특별히 포
함되어 있습니다.

지금 바로 www.belkerscience.com을 방문해 이들 제품 및 기타 혁신적인
제품에 대해 자세히 알아보세요.

어휘　efficiency 효율(성)　fume hood 배기 후드　laboratory
실험실, 연구소　hazardous 유해한　unfortunately 안타깝게도
sophisticated 정교한　blower 송풍기　airflow 기류
requirement 필요 조건, 필요량　in addition 또한　feature 특별히
포함하다, ~가 특징이다　vertical 수직의, 세로의　sash 새시, 창틀)
usability 유용성, 편리함

발신: 린다 머피 〈l.murphy@simonroylabs.com〉
수신: 자브릴 나세르 〈j.nasser@simonroylabs.com〉
날짜: 2월 2일
제목: 배기 후드 교체

안녕하세요 자브릴,

요청하신 대로 지난주 무역박람회에서 실험실 비용을 절약할 수 있는 방법을 찾
으며 192보냈는데요. 벨커 사이언스의 부스에서 본 것이 가장 인상 깊었
어요. 그들의 고효율 배기 후드가 우리가 찾는 바로 그 제품 같아요. 우리 배기
후드는 모두 10년이 넘었으니 교체하면 분명 에너지 요금이 눈에 띄게 낮아질
거예요. 194게다가 그쪽 영업사원이 말하길, 우리의 에너지 공급업체인 와이즈웨
이가 5월 내내 "EE"(에너지 효율) 할인을 제공하고 있으니 서둘러 업그레이드하
면 최대 500달러를 할인 받을 수 있다더군요.

www.belkerscience.com/fumehoods/he에서 다양한 모델을 볼 수 있어
요. 193이번에 변경해서 현재 쓰는 4피트짜리 후드보다 한 치수 높은 걸 써야 한
다고 생각하지만, 예산에 따라 결정된다는 건 알고 있어요.

추천한 게 도움이 되었으면 좋겠어요!

– 린다

어휘　trade fair 무역박람회　replace 교체하다　result in
(결과가) ~이 되다　noticeably 눈에 띄게　provider 공급[제공]업체
rebate 할인, 환불　take advantage of ~을 이용하다　depend
on ~에 따라 결정되다, ~에 달려 있다　budget 예산

와이즈웨이 에너지

사이먼로이 실험실　　　　　　　　　　계정 번호:4018532
콜 가 540번지　　　　　　　　　　　　납부액: 648.86달러
크로펜드, 콜로라도 80022　　　　　　　납부일: 7월 22일

에너지 고지서

194청구 기간: 6월 1일–6월 30일
에너지 사용량: 7,348 킬로와트　　　　과거 사용량
미터기 번호: 8231004248　　　　　　　– 이전 청구 기간: 8,011 킬로와트
계측 날짜: 6월 30일　　　　　　　　　– 195전년 동기간: 8,104 킬로와트
요금 유형: 상업

청구 유형	요금	총액
에너지	킬로와트당 0.12달러	881.76달러
배급	킬로와트당 0.032달러	235.14달러
시스템 이용	월 7달러	7달러
194EE 할인	−500달러 (1회)	−500달러

	소계	623.9달러
	세금 (4.0퍼센트)	24.96달러
	총계	**648.86달러**

결제 옵션은 뒷면을 보세요→

어휘 **account** 계정, 거래처 **distribution** 배급, 유통

191 사실 관계 확인

번역 배기 후드 부품 중 에너지 효율을 높이는 것으로 설명되지 않은 것은?
(A) 제어기
(B) 송풍기
(C) 창
(D) 모터

해설 광고 첫 번째 단락의 '각각에는 정교한 제어기와 3단의 속도 송풍기가 있어 함께 후드의 공기 흐름 사용량을 줄여 에너지 필요량도 줄일 수 있다(Each has a sophisticated controller and three-speed blower that together can reduce the hood's airflow usage and thus its energy requirements)'에서 (A)와 (B)를, '특수 모터는 기존의 구형 모터보다 에너지를 적게 소모한다(the special motor uses less energy than a traditional motor)'에서 (D)를 확인할 수 있다. 창은 안전성 및 유용성을 최대화하기 위한 부품으로 언급되었으므로, (C)가 정답이다.

▶ **Paraphrasing** 지문의 **reduce ~ its energy requirements / uses less energy**
→ 질문의 **increasing energy efficiency**

192 동의어 찾기

번역 이메일에서 1번째 단락 1행의 "spent"와 의미상 가장 가까운 것은?
(A) 기여했다
(B) 시간을 보냈다
(C) 지불했다
(D) 분명히 말했다

해설 'spent'가 포함된 부분은 '실험실 비용을 절약할 수 있는 방법을 찾으며 보냈다(I spent last week's trade fair looking for ways for the lab to save money)'는 의미로 해석되는데, 여기서 spent는 '(시간을) 보냈다, 사용했다'라는 뜻으로 쓰였다. 따라서 '시간을 보냈다'라는 의미의 (B) passed가 정답이다.

193 연계

번역 머피 씨는 어떤 크기의 배기 후드를 구매하자고 제안하는가?
(A) 2피트
(B) 4피트
(C) 6피트
(D) 8피트

해설 이메일의 두 번째 단락에서 머피 씨는 이번에 후드를 변경해서 현재 쓰는 4피트짜리 보다 한 치수 높은 걸 써야 한다고 생각한다(I think we should take advantage of the change to move up a size from our current 4-foot hoods)며 자신의 의견을 밝혔는데, 광고의 첫 번

째 단락에서 후드는 2피트, 4피트, 6피트, 8피트 모델로 구입할 수 있다(Available in 2-foot, 4-foot, 6-foot, and 8-foot models)고 나와 있다. 따라서 한 치수가 큰 (C) 6피트가 정답이다.

194 연계

번역 할인 프로그램에 관해 암시된 것은?
(A) 연장되었다.
(B) 최대 금액이 인상되었다.
(C) 현재 2개 기관에서 제공하고 있다.
(D) 명칭이 변경되었다.

해설 이메일의 첫 번째 단락에서 에너지 공급업체인 와이즌웨이가 5월까지 "EE"(에너지 효율) 할인을 제공하고 있다(Wisenway, our energy provider, is offering an "EE"(energy efficiency) rebate through May)고 했는데, 고지서를 보면 청구 기간(Billing period)이 6월 1일부터 6월 30일까지(June 1 – June 30)임에도 불구하고 EE 할인(EE Rebate)을 받았다는 것을 확인할 수 있다. 따라서 할인 제공 기간이 연장되었다고 추론할 수 있으므로, (A)가 정답이다.

어휘 **extend** 연장하다 **organization** 기관

195 사실 관계 확인

번역 고지서에서 사이먼로이 연구소에 관해 명시된 것은?
(A) 현재 고지서는 다음 청구 기간이 끝날 무렵에 지불해야 한다.
(B) 적어도 1년 이상 와이즌웨이 에너지 고객이었다.
(C) 에너지 비용은 은행 계좌에서 자동 인출된다.
(D) 모든 정규 에너지 요금은 에너지 사용량에 따라 달라진다.

해설 고지서 오른쪽 상단에서 전년 동기간(This billing period last year)의 사용량을 보여주고 있으므로, 사이먼로이 연구소가 적어도 1년 이상 와이즌웨이 에너지의 고객이었음을 알 수 있다. 따라서 (B)가 정답이다.

어휘 **due** 지불해야 하는 **withdraw** 인출하다

196-200 광고 + 이메일 + 이메일

플리킹어 코퍼렛 다이닝 서비스
www.delicious-fcds.com

플리킹어 코퍼렛 다이닝 서비스(FCDS)가 버밍엄 지역에서 기업 구내식당 1위 사업자가 된 것은 우수한 품질을 향한 노력과 다양하게 제공하는 유연한 서비스 때문입니다. [197(B)]당사는 구내식당 신설을 기획하거나, 사내 공급자로부터 기존 시설을 인수하여 효율성을 높일 수도 있습니다. [197(D)]원하시면 오전 6시부터 오후 10시까지 식사를 제공할 수 있습니다. [197(C)]환경 문제를 염려하는 사업장을 위해 지역 납품업체에서 조달한 식품만으로 만든 요리로 구성된 메뉴안을 제공합니다. 무엇보다도, 맛있고 영양가 있는 식사 및 간식을 보장합니다. [196]당사 웹사이트를 방문해 요리사들이 일하는 장면을 비롯해 더 많은 정보와 자료를 확인해 보세요.

어휘 **corporate dining** 회사에서 직원들에게 제공하는 식음료(서비스) **operator** 사업자, 운영자 **dedication** 전념, 헌신 **excellence** 우수함, 탁월함 **range** 다양성, 범위 **flexible** 유연한, 탄력적인 **take over** 인수하다 **existing** 기존의 **in-house** 사내의 **efficiency** 효율성 **environmental** 환경의 **concern** 우려 (사항), 관심(사) **regional** 지역의 **supplier** 납품업체 **nutritious** 영양가 있는 **footage** 장면

발신: 로널드 셔바 ‹r.scherba@wibbenslogistics.com›

수신: ‹inquiries@delicious-fcds.com›

제목: 문의

날짜: 1월 14일

안녕하세요,

제 이름은 로널드 셔바이며, 위벤스 로지스틱스의 총무부 부장입니다. 199저희는 시내 중심가에 있는 작은 회사로 60명 정도의 직원이 있습니다. 직원 구내식당을 운영할 새로운 서비스 업체를 찾고 있는데, 최근 귀사의 광고를 인상 깊게 보아 이메일을 씁니다. 197(C)/(D)현재 서비스 제공업체는 친환경 메뉴안이나 심야 서비스를 제공하지 않는데, 저희 직원들이 해외 거래처 담당자들과 소통하기 위해 특이한 시간대에 근무하므로 특히 후자가 필요합니다.

그래도 주된 관심사는 식사의 질과 고객 서비스 같은 기본적인 문제들입니다. 198그래서 현재 귀사가 운영하고 있는 구내식당 한 곳을 둘러보고 싶습니다. 이렇게 하면 계약을 협상하기 전에 귀사의 서비스가 당사 사업장에 적합한지 판단하는 데 도움이 될 것입니다. 이러한 자리를 마련해 주실 수 있을까요? 이 이메일에 회신해서 알려 주세요.

로널드 셔바

총무부장

위벤스 로지스틱스

어휘 administrative services departmet 총무부 operate 운영하다 recent 최근의 environmentally-friendly 친환경적인 fit 적합한 것 negotiate 협상하다

발신: ‹inquiries@delicious-fcds.com›

수신: 도로시 하겐 ‹dorothy.hagen@delicious-fcds.com›

제목: 전달: 문의

날짜: 1월 14일

안녕하세요 도로시,

아래 전달된 메시지는 오늘 아침 위벤스 로지스틱스의 셔바 씨라는 분이 보낸 문의 사항인데, 조짐이 좋은 것 같아요. 199회사 규모가 당신이 관리하는 다른 고객사와 비슷해서 당신에게 배정하고 싶어요. 200그런데 이메일을 보시면 아시겠지만 셔바 씨가 특이한 요청을 한 가지 했어요. 오후 2시에 제 사무실로 와서 최선의 대처법에 대해 논의해볼까요? 1시 30분까지 회신이 없으면 회사 메시지 서비스를 통해 연락할게요.

고마워요.

빈센트 포터

어휘 promising 유망한, 조짐이 좋은 account 위탁 업무, 거래(처) assign 배정하다 handle 다루다, 대처하다

---

196 세부 사항

번역 광고에 따르면 FCDS 웹사이트 방문자들이 할 수 있는 것은?
(A) 현재 고객의 의견 읽기
(B) 다양한 샘플 메뉴안 보기
(C) 회사 납품업체 목록 보기
(D) 식사 준비 동영상 보기

해설 광고의 후반부에서 FCDS 웹사이트를 방문해 요리사들이 일하는 장면을 비롯해 더 많은 정보와 자료를 확인해 보라(Visit our Web site for more information and resources, including footage of our chefs at work)고 제안했으므로, (D)가 정답이다.

▸▸ Paraphrasing   지문의 footage of our chefs at work
→ 정답의 videos of meals being prepared

---

197 연계 [고난도]

번역 광고에 언급된 서비스 중 셔바 씨가 문의하지 않은 것은?
(A) 특별 행사 음식 공급
(B) 구내식당 건설 계획
(C) 현지에서 조달한 식품 프로그램
(D) 연장된 서비스 시간

해설 보기 중 광고에서 언급된 서비스는 구내식당 신설(We can plan the creation of a new cafeteria), 현지 식품을 조달해 만든 식단(we offer menu plans with dishes made only with foods from regional suppliers), 연장된 서비스 시간(If desired, we can serve meals from 6 A.M. to 10 P.M.)이다. 첫 번째 이메일의 첫 단락을 보면, 셔바 씨는 현재 서비스 제공업체가 친환경 메뉴안이나 심야 서비스를 제공하지 않는다(Our current provider doesn't offer environmentally-friendly menu plans or late-night service)며 우회적으로 (C)와 (D)에 대해 문의했다. 기존 서비스 업체를 변경하고 싶어서 연락한 것이지 식당을 신설하고자 문의한 것은 아니므로, (B)가 정답이다. 참고로, (A)는 광고에서 언급된 서비스가 아니므로 우선적으로 제외되어야 할 오답이다.

어휘 occasion 행사, 경우 construction 공사, 건설

▸▸ Paraphrasing   지문의 menu plans with dishes made only with foods from regional suppliers
→ 보기 (C)의 A locally-sourced food program
지문의 serve meals from 6 A.M. to 10 P.M.
→ 보기 (D)의 Extended serving hours

---

198 세부 사항

번역 셔바 씨가 계획하고 싶어 하는 것은?
(A) 급식 시설 방문
(B) FCDS 직원과 전화회의
(C) 정보가 담긴 자료 배송
(D) 두 급식 업체 간의 협업

해설 첫 번째 이메일의 두 번째 단락에서 셔바 씨가 현재 FCDS에서 운영하고 있는 구내식당 한 곳을 둘러보고 싶다(I would like to tour one of the cafeterias you currently manage)고 했으므로, (A)가 정답이다.

어휘 conference call 전화회의 collaboration 협업

▸▸ Paraphrasing   지문의 tour one of the cafeterias
→ 정답의 A visit to a food service facility

199 연계

번역 하겐 씨에 관해 가장 사실에 가까운 것은?
(A) 특정 시가지에 있는 모든 고객사를 관리한다.
(B) 인맥 교류 행사에서 셔바 씨를 만났다.
(C) 소규모 기업을 상대한 경험이 있다.
(D) 해외 거래처 전문이다.

해설 두 번째 이메일의 초반부에서 포터 씨는 셔바 씨의 회사 규모가 하겐 씨가 관리하는 다른 거래처와 비슷하다(the company's scale is similar to that of the other clients whose accounts you manage)고 했는데, 첫 번째 이메일의 첫 단락을 보면 셔바 씨의 회사가 60명 정도가 일하는 작은 회사(We're a small firm of about 60 people)라고 나와 있다. 따라서 하겐 씨가 소규모 기업을 상대한 경험이 있다고 추론할 수 있으므로, (C)가 정답이다.

어휘 district 구역 specialize in ~를 전문으로 하다

200 세부 사항

번역 하겐 씨가 포터 씨 사무실로 오라고 요청 받은 이유는?
(A) 연구 결과를 발표하기 위해
(B) 다른 직원에게 업무 배정하는 일을 돕기 위해
(C) 요청에 대한 대응 전략을 논의하기 위해
(D) 소프트웨어 문제를 해결하기 위해

해설 두 번째 이메일의 중반부에서 포터 씨는 셔바 씨가 특이한 요청을 했다(Mr. Scherba makes an unusual request)며 하겐 씨에게 자신의 사무실로 와서 최선의 대처법에 대해 논의하자(Could you come to my office ~ to talk about the best way to handle it?)고 제안했으므로, (C)가 정답이다.

어휘 present 발표하다, 제시하다 strategy 전략 resolve 해결하다

▶▶ Paraphrasing 지문의 talk about the best way to handle it(an unusual request)
→ 정답의 discuss strategies for responding to a request

22

TEST 2

101 (D)	102 (C)	103 (A)	104 (C)	105 (B)
106 (A)	107 (D)	108 (B)	109 (A)	110 (C)
111 (D)	112 (B)	113 (A)	114 (B)	115 (D)
116 (A)	117 (D)	118 (D)	119 (D)	120 (C)
121 (B)	122 (C)	123 (D)	124 (A)	125 (C)
126 (A)	127 (A)	128 (D)	129 (B)	130 (C)
131 (B)	132 (D)	133 (A)	134 (D)	135 (B)
136 (D)	137 (C)	138 (A)	139 (D)	140 (D)
141 (A)	142 (C)	143 (C)	144 (B)	145 (B)
146 (B)	147 (C)	148 (D)	149 (D)	150 (A)
151 (D)	152 (A)	153 (B)	154 (C)	155 (B)
156 (C)	157 (D)	158 (B)	159 (D)	160 (C)
161 (C)	162 (A)	163 (C)	164 (D)	165 (A)
166 (B)	167 (A)	168 (A)	169 (D)	170 (A)
171 (B)	172 (B)	173 (A)	174 (C)	175 (D)
176 (B)	177 (A)	178 (B)	179 (C)	180 (D)
181 (B)	182 (A)	183 (D)	184 (D)	185 (C)
186 (D)	187 (C)	188 (B)	189 (B)	190 (B)
191 (D)	192 (A)	193 (C)	194 (D)	195 (C)
196 (A)	197 (B)	198 (C)	199 (D)	200 (B)

PART 5

101 동사 어형 _ 수 일치 _ 능동태

해설 빈칸은 주어 Authorities의 동사 자리로, a warning을 목적어로 취한다. 따라서 Authorities와 수가 일치하는 능동태 동사 (D) have issued가 정답이다.

번역 당국은 최근 폭풍우로 인한 열악한 도로 환경에 대해 운전자들에게 경보를 발령했다.

어휘 authorities 당국 issue 발령하다, 발급하다

102 부사 자리 _ 최상급 강조　　[고난도]

해설 빈칸 없이도 「주어(Ben Johnson)+be동사(was)+보어(one of the most influential photographers)」 구조를 이루는 완전한 문장이다. 따라서 보기 중 부사만이 빈칸에 들어갈 수 있으므로, (C) easily가 정답이다. 여기서 easily는 '의심할 여지 없이, 단연코'라는 뜻으로 쓰여 최상급 표현을 강조한다.

번역 벤 존슨은 단연코 그해 가장 영향력 있는 사진 작가 중 한 명이었다.

어휘 influential 영향력 있는 photographer 사진 작가

103 전치사 자리 _ 어휘

해설 동명사 turning과 어울리는 전치사를 선택하는 문제이다. '공터를 작은 놀이터 또는 텃밭용 대지로 바꿀 것'이라는 내용이 되어야 자연스러우므로, '~로'라는 의미의 (A) into가 정답이다.

번역 시는 공터를 작은 놀이터 또는 공동체 텃밭으로 바꿀 것을 검토하고 있다.

어휘 consider 고려하다, 검토하다 vacant 비어 있는 plot 대지, 땅 조각

104 인칭대명사의 격 _ 목적격

해설 빈칸이 전치사 to의 목적어 역할을 하는 자리이므로, 보기에서 재귀대명사 (A) herself, 소유대명사 (B) hers, 목적격 인칭대명사 (C) her 중 하나를 선택해야 한다. 문맥상 청중의 질문을 받는 대상은 Ms. Huff이므로, Ms. Huff를 대신하는 (C) her가 정답이다. 해당 절의 주어가 the audience이므로, (A) herself는 빈칸에 들어갈 수 없다.

번역 허프 씨의 강의는 가장 논란이 많은 주제를 다루었기 때문에 청중은 질문 대부분을 그녀에게 했다.

어휘 lecture 강의 deal with ~을 다루다 controversial 논란이 많은 direct 보내다, ~에게 하다 majority 대부분

105 전치사 어휘

해설 자동사 appears와 명사구 lists of banks를 적절히 연결하는 전치사를 선택하는 문제이다. 주어인 Collis Group이 은행 목록에 등장한다는 내용이므로, '~ (위)에'라는 의미로 list와 어울려 쓰이는 (B) on이 정답이다.

번역 콜리스 그룹은 고객 만족도가 가장 높은 은행 목록에 자주 등장한다.

어휘 regularly 자주, 정기적으로 customer satisfaction 고객 만족(도)

106 부사 어휘　　[고난도]

해설 동사구 have closed the paper drawers를 적절히 수식하는 부사를 선택하는 문제이다. 문맥상 용지 서랍을 닫은 정도 또는 방법을 묘사하는 부사가 들어가야 자연스러우므로, '단단히, 안전하게'라는 의미의 (A) securely가 정답이다.

번역 프린터를 작동하기 전에 용지 서랍을 꽉 닫았는지 확인하세요.

어휘 attempt to ~하려고 하다 operate 작동하다 widely 널리 hardly 거의 ~않다 strictly 엄격히

107 부사 자리 _ 동사 수식

해설 was timed(시기가 맞춰졌다)를 수식하는 부사 자리이므로, '전략적으로'라는 의미의 (D) strategically가 정답이다. (A) strategy는 명사, (B) strategized는 동사/과거분사, (C) strategic은 형용사로 품사상 빈칸에 들어갈 수 없다.

번역 휴가철 쇼핑 시즌이 시작될 때 스위프트플레이 게임기가 출시되도록 전략적으로 시기를 맞췄다.

어휘 release 출시 time 시기를 맞추다 occur 일어나다 strategy 전략

108 부사 자리 _ 어휘　　[고난도]

해설 빈칸에는 '상근직 및 시간제 근로자 모두'라는 의미를 나타내는 부사가 들어가야 하므로, (B) alike가 정답이다. alike는 「A and B」 구조 뒤에 쓰일 경우 'A와 B 모두에게 똑같이'라는 뜻을 나타낸다. 참고로, (C) both는 「A and B」 앞에 오거나, 복수형 목적격 대명사 뒤에 와야 한다.

번역 탄력 근무제는 상근직 및 시간제 근로자 모두에게 점점 더 지지를 받고 있다.

어휘 flexible 탄력적인, 유연한 working arrangements 작업 방식, 근무 시간 조정 increasingly 점점 더 favor 찬성하다, 지지하다

109 명사 자리 _ 복합명사 [고난도]

해설 빈칸은 deadline과 복합명사를 이루어 동명사 requesting의 목적어 역할을 하는 명사 자리로, deadline 앞에 있는 부정관사 a와 수가 일치해야 한다. 따라서 deadline과 함께 '기한 연장'이라는 의미를 완성하는 단수 명사 (A) extension이 정답이다.

번역 신중한 심의 끝에, 기한 연장을 요청한 마쉬 씨의 사유가 미흡하다는 판결이 내려졌다.

어휘 consideration 고려, 심의 insufficient 미흡한 extension (기간의) 연장 extend 연장하다 extendable 연장할 수 있는

110 명사 어휘 [고난도]

해설 빈칸은 동사 provide의 목적어 역할을 하는 명사 자리로, 전치사구 of their qualifications의 수식을 받는다. 예시로 언급된 졸업장 (diplomas), 수료증(certificates) 등은 지원자들의 자격(qualifications)을 증명하기 위해 제공하는 수단이므로, '증빙, 증거'라는 의미의 (C) evidence가 정답이다.

번역 지원자는 졸업장, 수료증 등의 형태로 자격을 증빙하라는 요청을 받을 수 있습니다.

어휘 qualification 자격 diploma 졸업장 certificate 자격증, 증명서 access 접근 renewal 갱신 compensation 보상

111 동사 어휘

해설 목적어 the company 및 전치사구 of a change in their home address와 어울리는 동사를 선택하는 문제이다. 「동사 A of B」 구조로 쓰여 '회사에 주소 변경을 알리다'라는 의미가 되어야 하므로, '알리다, 통지하다'라는 뜻의 (D) inform이 정답이다. 참고로, 전치사 자리에는 of 대신 about이 올 수도 있다.

번역 알론타 어소시에이츠는 직원들에게 집 주소 변경 사항을 회사에 알리라고 요구한다.

어휘 note 지적하다 reveal 드러내다 educate 교육하다

112 명사절 접속사 _ 어휘 [고난도]

해설 빈칸은 주어가 없는 불완전한 절(draws readers to the *Willard Daily News*)을 이끄는 접속사 자리로, 빈칸이 이끄는 절이 동사 is의 주어 역할을 한다. 따라서 명사절 접속사가 들어가야 하는데, 해당 명사절이 주격 보어 역할을 하는 our commitment(헌신, 전념)와 동격 관계를 이루어야 하므로, '~라는 것'이라는 의미의 (B) What이 정답이다. (D) Whoever도 명사절 접속사로 쓰일 수 있지만, '~하는 사람은 누구든'이라는 뜻으로 문맥상 빈칸에 적절하지 않다.

번역 〈윌러드 데일리 뉴스〉로 독자들을 끌어들이는 것은 공정하고 정직한 보도에 대한 당사의 헌신입니다.

어휘 draw (사람의 마음을) 끌다 fair 공정한

113 부사 어휘 _ 비교급 강조

해설 비교급 부사인 better를 강조할 수 있는 부사가 들어가야 하므로, better와 함께 '훨씬 더 좋은'이라는 의미를 완성하는 (A) far가 정답이다. 참고로, far 외에 much, even, still, a lot 등도 비교급을 강조할 수 있다. (B) so와 (C) very는 원급을 수식하는 부사이다.

번역 베일리 스튜디오의 신작 코미디는 영화 산업 분석가들이 예측한 것보다 훨씬 더 좋은 흥행 성적을 거두었다.

어휘 box office 흥행 성적 analyst 분석가 predict 예측하다

114 동명사 _ 동사의 주어

해설 명사구 the construction permit application을 목적어로 취하면서 동사 took의 주어 역할을 하는 준동사 자리이다. 따라서 동명사인 (B) Preparing이 정답이다. 명사인 (C) Preparation은 목적어를 취할 수 없으므로 빈칸에 들어갈 수 없다.

번역 건축 허가 신청서 준비는 그 도급업체가 예상했던 것보다 오래 걸렸다.

어휘 permit 허가(증) application 신청(서) contractor 도급업체, 건축업체 anticipate 예상하다

115 동사 어형 _ 시제

해설 빈칸은 부사절 접속사 while이 이끄는 절에서 주어 the representative의 동사 역할을 하므로, 단수 명사와 수가 일치하는 (A) described, (B) has described, (D) is describing 중 하나를 선택해야 한다. 주절에 조동사 should가 쓰여 연수생들이 일반적으로 지녀야 할 태도를 나타내고 있으므로, 빈칸에는 '~하는 동안에'라는 의미를 완성하는 현재진행형 (D) is describing이 들어가야 자연스럽다.

번역 오리엔테이션에서 연수생들은 본사 직원이 당사 기업 가치를 설명하는 동안 주의 깊게 들어야 한다.

어휘 attentively 주의 깊게 representative 직원, 대표 headquarters 본사 corporate 기업의 value 가치 describe 설명하다

116 전치사 어휘

해설 빈칸 앞에 온 절과 명사구 its inconvenient placement를 적절히 연결해 주는 전치사를 선택하는 문제이다. 부스가 불편한 위치에 있었지만 관람객들이 많이 찾아왔다는 내용의 문장이므로, '~에도 불구하고'라는 의미의 (A) despite가 정답이다.

번역 바우프트 소프트웨어 부스는 전시장 뒤편 구석에 있어 불편했지만 관람객으로 북적댔다.

어휘 crowded 북적대는 inconvenient 불편한 placement 배치 exhibition 전시

117 부사 자리 _ 과거분사 수식

해설 분사구문(upgraded with the latest hardware)을 이끄는 과거분사 upgraded를 수식하는 부사 자리이므로, '자주'라는 의미의 (D) Frequently 가 정답이다. (A) Frequent는 형용사/동사, (B) Frequenting은 동명사/현재분사, (C) Frequency는 명사로 품사상 답이 될 수 없다.

번역 당사 데이터 센터는 최신 하드웨어로 자주 업그레이드되어 안전하고 안정적으로 데이터를 저장합니다.

어휘 reliable 믿음직한 frequent 자주 일어나는; 자주 다니다
frequency 빈도, 빈번

118 형용사 어휘

해설 concluded(완료된)와 함께 명사 projects를 수식하는 형용사 자리이다. 따라서 빈칸에도 프로젝트의 진행 상황을 묘사하는 형용사가 들어가야 자연스러우므로, '진행 중인'이라는 의미의 (D) ongoing이 정답이다.

번역 당신의 부서에서 작성하게 될 연말 보고서에는 완료된 프로젝트와 진행 중인 프로젝트 모두에 대한 개요가 포함되어야 합니다.

어휘 summary 개요, 요약 multiple 여러 개의, 한 개 이상의
ambitious 야심 찬 tailored 맞춤의

119 형용사 자리 _ 명사 수식 _ 최상급

해설 소유격 Jennings Winter Recreation Area's와 함께 명사 season을 수식하는 형용사 자리이므로, 보기에서 형용사의 최상급인 (B) shortest와 비교급인 (C) shorter 중 하나를 선택해야 한다. 빈칸 뒤를 보면 시간의 범위를 나타내는 전치사구 of the past fifteen years 또한 season을 수식하고 있으므로, 빈칸에는 최상급 표현이 들어가야 문맥상 자연스럽다. 따라서 (B) shortest가 정답이다.

번역 온화한 날씨 때문에 이번이 제닝스 겨울 휴양지에서 지난 15년 중 가장 짧은 시즌이 될 듯하다.

어휘 due to ~ 때문에

120 명사 어휘

해설 energy와 복합명사를 이루어 동사 has been successfully reduced의 주어 역할을 하는 명사 자리이다. 따라서 빈칸에는 전자제품 전원 끄기 캠페인을 통해 감소될 수 있는 것을 나타내는 명사가 들어가야 자연스러우므로, energy와 함께 '에너지 소비량'이라는 의미를 완성하는 (C) consumption이 정답이다.

번역 야간에 쓰지 않는 전자제품 전원 끄기 캠페인을 통해 사무실 에너지 소비량이 성공적으로 감소했다.

어휘 reduce 줄이다 idle 쓰지 않는, 가동되지 않는 transition 전환
efficiency 효율 awareness 인식

121 명사 자리 _ 전치사의 목적어 _ 어휘   고난도

해설 빈칸은 전치사 to의 목적어 역할을 하는 명사 자리로, 이메일 알림을 받는 대상이 들어가야 한다. 빈칸 앞에 한정사가 없으므로 복수형 사람 명사인 (B) recruits(신입 사원들)가 정답이다.

번역 곧 있을 일련의 교육에 관한 이메일 알림이 신입 사원들에게 발송되었다.

어휘 notification 알림 upcoming 곧 있을, 다가오는 training
session 교육 (과정) recruiter 모집자, 채용 담당자 recruit
모집하다; 신입사원

122 형용사 어휘

해설 빈칸은 명사 amount를 수식하는 형용사 자리로, 쇠고기 1파운드(one pound of ground beef)를 대체하는 채식 대용품(a vegetarian substitute)의 양을 적절히 묘사하는 형용사가 들어가야 한다. 따라서 '동등한, ~에 상당하는'이라는 의미의 (C) equivalent가 정답이다.

번역 조리법에는 다진 쇠고기 1파운드가 필요하지만, 이는 익힌 렌틸콩 같은 동량의 채식 대용품으로 대체할 수 있다.

어휘 ground 다진, 갈은 (grind의 과거분사) replace 대체하다
vegetarian 채식의 substitute 대용품 existing 기존의
accountable ~할 책임이 있는 overall 종합적인

123 대명사 어휘

해설 전치사 with의 목적어 역할을 하는 (대)명사 자리이다. 주어인 The business world와 the academic community가 서로 협력하도록 장려해야 한다는 내용이 되어야 자연스러우므로, '서로'라는 의미의 (D) one another가 정답이다. 참고로, (A) other는 단독으로 쓰일 경우 대명사 역할을 할 수 없고, (B) which(어떤 사람, 어느 것)와 (C) itself(그것 자신, 그것 자체)는 의미상 적절하지 않다.

번역 재계와 학계가 서로 협력해 실용적인 연구에 참여하도록 장려해야 한다.

어휘 encourage A to B A가 B하도록 장려하다 collaborate with
~와 협력하다 engage in ~에 참여하다 practical 실용적인

124 동사 어휘

해설 to부정사(to supply)와 어울려 쓰이는 동사를 선택하는 문제이다. 실속 있고 연비가 좋은 상용 차량을 공급하기 위한 회사의 의지를 나타내는 동사가 들어가야 자연스러우므로, to부정사와 함께 '~하기 위해 노력하다'라는 의미를 완성하는 (A) strives가 정답이다.

번역 목시스 모터스는 운송업체들에게 실속 있고 연비가 좋은 상용 차량을 공급하기 위해 노력하고 있다.

어휘 transportation provider 운송재[업체] economical 실속 있는, 경제적인 fuel-efficient 연비가 좋은 commercial 상용의
conform 따르다, 순응하다 discontinue 중단하다 specialize
전문으로 하다

125 명사 어휘

해설 빈칸은 동사 verifies의 목적어 역할을 하는 명사 자리로, 소유격 applicants'의 수식을 받는다. 따라서 실기 시험(a practical exam)을 통해 검증하려는 지원자의 자질을 나타내는 명사가 들어가야 자연스러우므로, '능숙도, 실력'이라는 의미의 (C) proficiency가 정답이다.

번역 자격증 취득 과정의 마지막 단계는 응시자들의 머리 스타일링 실력을 검증하는 실기 시험이다.

어휘 licensing 자격, 면허(취득) process 과정 verify 검증하다
applicant 응시자, 수험생 insight 통찰력 privilege 특권
compliance 준수

126 전치사 어휘

해설 동명사구 joining Keller Fox Ltd.와 뒤따르는 절을 자연스럽게 연결하는 전치사를 선택하는 문제이다. 켈러 폭스 사에 입사하기 전에 코티스 호텔에 근무했다는 내용이 되어야 자연스러우므로, '~ 전에'라는 의미의 (A) Prior to가 정답이다.

번역 장 씨는 켈러 폭스 사에 입사하기 전 코티스 호텔의 영업 부서장이었다.

어휘 compared to ~에 비해 ever since 그 이래 줄곧 according to ~에 따르면

127 동사 어형 _ 시제 〔고난도〕

해설 빈칸은 that절의 주어 the technicians 뒤에 오는 동사 자리로, 전치사구 by this time tomorrow의 수식을 받는다. 따라서 미래의 특정 시점(this time tomorrow)까지 완료될 상황을 나타내는 미래완료시제 (A) will have finished가 정답이다.

번역 IT 이사는 기술자들이 내일 이 시간까지 시스템 수리를 마칠 것이라고 우리에게 장담했다.

어휘 assure 장담하다, 확약하다 repair 수리

128 전치사 자리

해설 빈칸이 동사 released의 목적어 역할을 하는 명사 a statement와 또 다른 명사구 his spokesperson 사이에 있으므로, 빈칸에는 전치사가 들어가야 한다. 문맥을 살펴보면 '대변인을 통해 성명을 발표했다'라는 내용이 되어야 자연스러우므로, '~을 통해'라는 의미의 전치사 (D) through가 정답이다.

번역 이스턴 씨는 언론에 직접 말하는 대신 대변인을 통해 성명을 발표했다.

어휘 release 발표하다 statement 성명 directly 직접 press 언론 officially 공식적으로 announce 발표하다, 선언하다

129 동사 어휘 〔고난도〕

해설 문맥상 두 법원(the Sparks and Corgan courts)을 한 건물에(in a new building) 통합하자고 제안했다는 내용이 되어야 자연스러우므로, and와 함께 'A와 B를 통합하다, 합병하다'라는 의미를 완성하는 (B) consolidating이 정답이다.

번역 위원회는 스파크스 법원과 코건 법원을 서부 코건에 들어설 새 건물에 통합하자고 제안했다.

어휘 committee 위원회 expedite 촉진하다 delegate 위임하다 waive 면제하다

130 등위접속사

해설 빈칸이 전치사 in의 목적어 역할을 하는 동명사구 determining your business objectives와 evaluating your progress 사이에 있으므로, 빈칸에는 두 동명사구를 연결하는 등위/상관접속사 또는 evaluating your progress를 목적어로 취하는 전치사가 들어갈 수 있다. 문맥상 '사업 목표를 결정하는 것'과 '진행 상황을 평가하는 것' 모두에 도움을 준다는 내용이 되어야 자연스러우므로, (C) and가 정답이다.

번역 분쉬 컨설팅의 전략 기획 서비스는 사업 목표 결정과 목표 달성을 위한 진행 상황 평가에도 도움이 될 것이다.

어휘 determine 결정하다 objective 목표 evaluate 평가하다 achieve 달성하다 yet 그렇지만 beside ~ 옆에, ~에 비해 in regard to ~에 관해서는

PART 6

131-134 편지

2월 25일

다이애나 타운센드
로빈 로 407번지
버켓, 메인 04007

타운센드 씨께,

골드 노선 일부 구간과 평행하는 급행 열차 노선 건설안을 논의할 주민 회의에 귀하를 초대합니다. 회의는 3월 18일 목요일 오후 6시부터 8시까지 파월라 주민센터 대강당에서 열립니다. ¹³¹**센터는 버켓 2번가 150번지에 있습니다.**

동봉물에 자세히 설명되어 ¹³²**있듯**, 급행 노선은 버켓에서 그렌햄 중앙역까지 두 번 만 정차하며 운행합니다. 그러므로 도심을 ¹³³**더 빨리** 오갈 수 있게 됩니다.

이번 회의는 버켓 주민들이 제안서에 대해 의견을 제시할 수 있는 기회가 될 것입니다. 의사 일정에는 교통 관계자들에 의해 ¹³⁴**진행되는** 발표와 질의응답 시간이 포함됩니다.

귀하께서 참석하시길 바랍니다.

게리 머피
그렌햄 지역 교통국 국장
동봉

어휘 hereby 이로써 parallel 평행의; 평행하다 describe 설명하다 enclosure 동봉(물) enable 가능하게 하다 agenda 안건[의제], 의사 일정 input 의견 transit 교통 (체계) official 관계자, 공무원

131 문맥에 맞는 문장 고르기

번역 (A) 아쉽게도 이 날짜는 제 일정에 맞지 않습니다.
(B) 센터는 버켓 2번가 150번지에 있습니다.
(C) 그때쯤이면 공사가 거의 끝나리라 예상합니다.
(D) 수정된 제안서 초안을 준비해서 오세요.

해설 빈칸 앞에서 노선 건설안을 논의할 주민 회의에 타운센드 씨를 초대하며, 이 회의가 3월 18일 목요일 오후 6시부터 8시까지 파월라 주민센터 대강당에서 열린다(The meeting will be held in the auditorium of the Powlar Community Center from 6 to 8 P.M. on Thursday, March 18)고 했으므로, 회의 일정 및 장소와 관련된 부연 설명이 이어지는 것이 문맥상 자연스럽다. 따라서 회의 장소(the Powlar Community Center)를 안내한 (B)가 정답이다.

어휘 unfortunately 아쉽게도 suit 맞다 nearly 거의 revised 수정된 draft 초안

132 부사절 접속사 자리 _ 어휘

해설 빈칸이 부사절에서 축약된 분사구문 described in detail in the enclosure 앞에 있으므로, 보기에서 부사절 접속사로 쓰일 수 있는 (C) Until과 (D) As 중 하나를 선택해야 한다. 문맥상 '동봉물에 자세히 설명되어 있는 대로'라는 내용이 되어야 자연스러우므로, 과거분사와 함께 '~된 대로'라는 의미를 완성하는 (D) As가 정답이다.

133 형용사 어휘　　　　　　　　　　고난도

해설 해당 문장의 주어 it이 the express line을 대신하므로, 빈칸에는 급행 열차 노선이 도심을 오가는 여정(journeys)에 미치는 영향을 적절히 묘사하는 형용사가 들어가야 한다. 따라서 '더 빠른'이라는 의미의 (A) swifter가 정답이다.

어휘 swift 빠른　cozy 아늑한　scenic 경치가 좋은　cheap 저렴한

134 동사 어형 _ 과거분사

해설 빈칸은 명사 presentation을 뒤에서 수식하는 준동사 자리이다. 발표는 교통 관계자들에 의해(by transit officials) 진행되는 것이므로, 수동의 의미를 내포한 과거분사 (D) conducted가 정답이다.

어휘 conduct 수행[진행]하다

135-138 이메일

발신: 그웬돌린 램지
수신: 자원봉사자 전원
제목: 규정
날짜: 12월 16일

린디 패션 박물관 자원봉사자들께,

저는 최근에 한 자원봉사자 안내원이 전시관 투어 ¹³⁵중에 잘못된 정보를 제공하는 것을 우연히 들었습니다. 이런 일은 하지 마십시오. 대답할 수 없는 질문을 받으면 난처할 수도 있다는 점 이해합니다. ¹³⁶그렇기는 하지만, 그 상황에서 올바른 대응은 방문객을 교육 담당자에게 안내하는 것입니다. ¹³⁷그들을 만날 수 없다면 방문객은 나중에 info@lfm.org.nz로 이메일을 보내면 됩니다. 문제가 재발하지 않도록 스스로 그 답을 익히는 것도 현명한 방법이 되겠습니다.

제가 목격한 사건이 일회성 실수인지 아니면 널리 퍼진 문제의 일부¹³⁸인지 분명하지 않으므로 이 규정을 여러분 모두에게 자세히 설명하고 싶었습니다. 간략하게 회신해 이 이메일을 읽고 이해했다는 것을 확인해 주시기 바랍니다.

고맙습니다.

그웬돌린 램지
자원봉사자 담당
린디 패션 박물관

어휘 overhear 우연히 듣다　incorrect 잘못된, 부정확한　embarrassing 난처한　direct ~에게 보내다, 돌리다　prevent A from ~ing A가 ~하는 것을 방지하다　recur 재발하다

spell out 자세히 설명하다　policy 정책, 규정　witness 목격하다　widespread 널리 퍼진　briefly 간략하게　confirm 확인하다, 확인해 주다

135 전치사 자리 _ 어휘

해설 명사구 a tour of our exhibits를 목적어로 취하는 전치사 자리이므로, (A) like와 (B) during 중 하나를 선택해야 한다. 문맥상 '전시관 투어 중에 잘못된 정보를 제공하는 것'이라는 내용이 되어야 자연스러우므로, '~ 중에, ~ 동안'이라는 의미의 (B) during이 정답이다. (C) though와 (D) while은 접속사이므로 빈칸에 들어갈 수 없다.

136 접속부사　　　　　　　　　　고난도

해설 빈칸 앞 문장에서 대답할 수 없는 질문을 받으면 난처할 수도 있다는 점 이해한다(I understand that ~ embarrassing to be asked a question that you can't answer)고 했는데, 뒤 문장에서는 그 상황에서의 올바른 대응 방법(the correct response in that situation)을 제시하고 있다. 따라서 문맥상 '이해는 하지만 이렇게 해야 한다'라는 흐름이 되어야 자연스러우므로, '그렇기는 하지만, 그럼에도 불구하고'라는 의미의 (D) Nevertheless가 정답이다.

어휘 likewise 마찬가지로　on the contrary 반대로　more importantly 더 중요하게는

137 문맥에 맞는 문장 고르기

번역 (A) 그들은 행사 일정에 대한 개요를 제공할 수 있을 것입니다.
(B) 박물관은 화요일에서 일요일 오전 10시부터 오후 6시까지 엽니다.
(C) 그들을 만날 수 없다면 방문객은 나중에 info@lfm.org.nz로 이메일을 보내면 됩니다.
(D) 우리는 언제든 투어를 이끌 자원봉사자를 추가로 모집하고자 합니다.

해설 빈칸 앞 문장에서 질문에 답할 수 없는 난처한 상황의 올바른 대응은 방문객을 교육 담당자에게 안내하는 것(to direct the visitor to our educational staff)이라고 했고, 뒤 문장에서는 다른 방안(to learn the answer yourself to prevent the problem from recurring)을 제시하고 있다. 따라서 빈칸에도 대응 방법에 관련된 내용이 들어가야 자연스러우므로, 첫 번째 방법에 대해 부연 설명을 하는 (C)가 정답이다. 참고로, 여기서 they는 our educational staff를 가리킨다.

어휘 overview 개요　unavailable 만날 수 없는　additional 추가의

138 명사절 접속사

해설 빈칸은 완전한 절(the incident ~ was a one-time mistake or part of a widespread problem)을 이끌어 it의 진주어 역할을 하는 명사절 접속사 자리이다. a one-time mistake와 part of a widespread problem를 연결하는 or와 어울려 '~인지 아닌지'라는 의미를 나타내는 접속사가 들어가야 하므로, (A) whether가 정답이다. (D) when도 완전한 절을 이끌 수 있지만 문맥상 빈칸에 적절하지 않고, (B) based on은 전치사, (C) after all은 부사로 품사상 빈칸에 들어갈 수 없다.

139-142 정보문

사린타 스튜디오에서 주문해 주셔서 감사합니다!

동봉된 초는 고급 재료로 만든 수제품입니다. 최상의 효과를 보시려면 심지를 1/8인치 길이로 다듬어 ¹³⁹**두세요**. 또한 윗면이 울퉁불퉁해지는 것을 방지하기 위해 매번 왁스 맨 윗층이 완전히 녹을 때까지 태우실 것을 권합니다.

어떤 이유든 구매품에 불만이 있으시면 주저 없이 저희에게 연락하세요. ¹⁴⁰**반품이나 교환을 해드릴 뿐만 아니라 도움이 되는 조언도 드리겠습니다**. 수십 년간 저희가 쌓아 온 향기 관련 전문지식을 마음껏 활용하세요. 고객님께 기꺼이 다른 ¹⁴¹**향**을 추천하거나 맞춤 향도 만들어 드리겠습니다. 저희에게 sarinta@pexo-market.com으로 이메일 주시거나 정규 영업 시간에 (864) 555-0192로 전화 주시면 됩니다.

반면 사린타 초가 마음에 드신다면 ¹⁴²**다른 사람들에게** 알려 주세요! www.pexo-market.com/sarinta에서 저희 스튜디오에 대해 긍정적인 후기를 남기실 수 있습니다. 보내주시는 성원에 진심으로 감사 드리겠습니다.

> 어휘 ingredient 재료 wick 심지 trim 다듬다 melt 녹다 be displeased with ~에 불만이 있다 purchase 구매(품) hesitate to ~하기를 주저하다 decade 10년 fragrance 향기 expertise 전문지식 at one's disposal 마음대로 쓸 수 있는 customized 맞춤의 reach 연락하다, 닿다 positive 긍정적인 appreciate 감사하다, 환영하다 support 지지, 성원

139 동사 어형 _ 명령문

해설 빈칸 앞에 주어가 없고 빈칸 뒤에 「목적어(its wick) + 목적격 보어 (trimmed)」가 있으므로, 해당 문장이 주어 You가 생략된 명령문임을 알 수 있다. 따라서 동사원형 (D) Keep이 정답이다.

140 문맥에 맞는 문장 고르기

번역 (A) 현재 사린타 스튜디오는 오프라인 매장을 운영하지 않습니다.
(B) 당사 소셜 미디어 계정은 신제품 사진으로 자주 업데이트됩니다.
(C) 다음 주문 시 쿠폰 코드 "MYSARINTA"를 입력하여 15퍼센트 할인을 받으세요.
(D) 반품이나 교환을 해드릴 뿐만 아니라 도움이 되는 조언도 드리겠습니다.

해설 빈칸 앞 문장에서 구매품에 불만이 있으면 주저 없이 연락하라(If you are displeased with your purchase ~ don't hesitate to contact us)고 했고, 뒤에서는 향기에 관한 자신들의 전문지식을 마음껏 활용하라 (Our decades of fragrance expertise are at your disposal)고 했다. 따라서 빈칸에는 불만에 따른 조치와 관련된 내용이 들어가야 자연스러우므로, (D)가 정답이다.

어휘 at present 현재 operate 운영하다

141 명사 어휘

해설 앞에서 향기에 관한 자신들의 전문지식을 마음껏 활용하라(Our decades of fragrance expertise are at your disposal)고 조언했으므로, 빈칸에 들어갈 추천(recommend) 대상 역시 향기(fragrance)와 관련된 것이어야 한다. 따라서 '향(기)'라는 의미의 (A) scent가 정답이다.

어휘 texture 감촉, 질감

142 대명사 어휘

해설 「let + 목적어 + 목적격 보어(know)」 구조에서 목적어 역할을 하는 명사 자리로, 문맥상 '제품이 마음에 들 경우 후기를 남겨 다른 사람들에게 알려 주세요'라는 내용이 되어야 자연스럽다. 따라서 불특정한 타인을 가리키는 부정대명사 (C) others(다른 사람들)가 정답이다.

143-146 회람

수신: 펭글러 사 전 직원
주제: 라우즈 커머셜 서비스

당사의 최근 성공담을 공유하기 위해 글을 씁니다.

유지 보수 서비스 공급업체인 라우즈 커머셜 서비스는 한때 서류 작업에 문제가 있었습니다. 이 업체의 서비스 방문 보고서 양식은 길었고 잃어버리기가 쉬웠습니다. 기술자가 매번 방문 후 양식을 수기로 ¹⁴³**작성하는 데** 소비한 시간에도 비용을 지불하는 것에 대해 고객들은 불만을 토로했고, 한편 업체 측에서는 분실된 양식 때문에 서비스 청구서를 정확하게 발행하는 데 있어서 종종 어려움을 겪었습니다.

다행히, 라우즈 사는 태블릿 컴퓨터를 구입해 펭글러 비즈니스를 사용하기 시작했습니다. 기술자들은 ¹⁴⁴**이제** 잘 정리된 공유 폴더에 자동 저장되는 전자 양식을 작성합니다.

라우즈 사의 서비스 사업 감독관은 "귀사 덕분에 우리 기술자들의 생산성이 훨씬 높아졌습니다. ¹⁴⁵**그리고 마찬가지로 중요한 것은, 더 이상 비용을 적게 청구하는 것으로 인한 손해를 보지 않는다는 겁니다.**"라고 우리에게 말했습니다. 이러한 이점 덕분에 그 업체는 불과 1년 만에 투자금을 ¹⁴⁶**회수했습니다**.

우리 펭글러 사가 라우즈 커머셜 서비스에 이러한 도움을 제공했다는 점을 자랑스럽게 생각합니다. 앞으로도 계속 노력해 주시기 바랍니다.

한건우
최고 경영자

> 어휘 maintenance 유지 repair 보수 paperwork 서류 작업 misplace 잃어버리다, 엉뚱한 곳에 두다 fill out ~을 작성하다 well-organized 잘 정돈된 supervisor 감독관, 관리자 productive 생산적인 benefit 이점 investment 투자(금) assistance 도움

143 동사 어형 _ 동명사 `고난도`

해설 앞에 목적격 관계대명사(that/which)가 생략된 관계사절(technicians spent ------- them by hand)이 선행사 time을 수식하여 '양식(them)을 수기로 작성하는 데 소비한 시간'이라는 의미를 나타내고 있다. 따라서 「spent + 목적어(time) + (in) + 동명사구」 구조가 변형된 것이라 볼 수 있으므로, (C) completing이 정답이다. 참고로, spend는 「spend + 목적어 + on + 명사」 구조로 쓰이기도 하지만 (A) on completion은 them을 목적어로 취할 수 없기 때문에 빈칸에 들어갈 수 없다.

144 부사 어휘

해설 앞에서 라우즈 사가 태블릿 컴퓨터를 구입해 펭글러 비즈니스를 사용하기 시작했다고 했으므로, 빈칸을 포함한 문장은 구입 이후 변화한 현재의 상황(fill out)을 묘사해야 자연스럽다. 따라서 '이제, 지금'이라는 의미의 (A) now가 정답이다. 참고로 (B) then은 '그 때, 그 다음에'라는 의미로,

과거나 미래의 특정 시점, 혹은 일의 순서를 나타낸다.

어휘 rarely 드물게

145 문맥에 맞는 문장 고르기 〈고난도〉

번역 (A) 당사는 배관, 전기 및 건물 보수 전문가들을 고용합니다.
(B) 그리고 마찬가지로 중요한 것은, 더 이상 비용을 적게 청구하는 것으로 인한 손해를 보지 않는다는 겁니다.
(C) 당사가 고객들의 데이터를 안전하게 보관하고 있다는 점을 알아 주셨으면 합니다.
(D) 사실, 우리는 현재 그러한 가능성을 탐색하고 있습니다.

해설 빈칸 앞 문장에서 펭글러 사의 제품(Pengler Business)이 미친 긍정적인 영향(You've made it possible for our technicians to be much more productive)을 설명했고, 뒤 문장에서는 '이러한 이점들(these benefits)'이라고 지칭하며 다수의 이점이 있음을 드러냈다. 따라서 빈칸에 제품의 또 다른 이점이 언급되어야 문맥상 자연스러우므로, (B)가 정답이다.

어휘 underbilling (비용) 과소 청구 explore 탐색하다 possibility 가능성

146 동사 어휘 〈고난도〉

해설 빈칸은 its investment를 목적어로 취하는 동사 자리로, in just one year의 수식을 받는다. 앞서 언급된 이점들 덕분에(Thanks to these benefits) 불과 1년만에 제품에 투자했던 금액을 회수했다는 내용이 되어야 자연스러우므로, '회수했다, 회복했다'라는 의미의 (B) recovered가 정답이다.

어휘 reserve 따로 남기다 maintain 유지하다 encourage 독려하다

PART 7

147-148 이메일

발신: 로웰 도슨
수신: 안드레아 힉스
제목: 부동산
날짜: 9월 9일

안녕하세요 안드레아,

어제 약속에 대해 좀 더 생각해 봤는데, 제가 깨달은 걸 공유하고 싶어요. 당신이 보여준 부동산들이 제 예산과 소요 면적에 맞는데도 제가 마음에 안 들어 했던 것 기억하세요? 음, 문제는 자연광이 부족하다는 거였어요. [148]제 법률사무소를 개업하게 될 사무실 공간에서 시간을 많이 보낼 거라서, 햇살이 있으면 긍정적인 기분을 유지하는 데 도움이 될 거예요. [147]그래서 다음 약속 때는 햇빛이 많이 들어오는 창문이 있는 곳을 보여주세요.

고마워요,

로웰

어휘 appointment 약속 realization 깨달음, 자각 property 부동산, 재산 budget 예산 requirement 요건 positive 긍정적인

147 주제 / 목적

번역 도슨 씨가 이메일을 보낸 이유는?
(A) 선택 확정
(B) 예산 문의
(C) 상세사항 제공
(D) 약속 잡기

해설 이메일 전반에서 이전에 봤던 부동산들의 문제점을 언급한 후, 후반부에서 다음 약속 때는 햇빛이 많이 들어오는 창문이 있는 곳을 보여 달라(at our next appointment, please show me places with windows that let in a lot of sunlight)고 요청했으므로, 상세사항을 제공하기 위한 이메일임을 알 수 있다. 따라서 (C)가 정답이다.

어휘 specification 상세사항, 명세, 사양

148 추론 / 암시

번역 도슨 씨에 관해 암시된 것은?
(A) 곧 야외에서 많은 시간을 보낼 것이다.
(B) 조명 설비를 개선하고 싶어 한다.
(C) 재산법에 대해 염려하고 있다.
(D) 창업할 계획이다.

해설 이메일의 중반부에서 도슨 씨는 자신의 법률사무소를 개업하기로 한 사무실에서 시간을 많이 보낼 것(I'm going to be spending long hours in the office I choose to open my law firm in)이라고 했으므로, 창업할 계획임을 추론할 수 있다. 따라서 (D)가 정답이다.

▶▶ Paraphrasing 지문의 **open my law firm**
→ 정답의 **start his own business**

149-150 정보문

폭스헤드 바위

[149]폭스헤드 바위는 이 지점 맞은편 오르막에서 볼 수 있는 커다란 암석입니다. 여우 머리와 닮아 이런 이름이 붙었으며 공원에서 가장 유명한 지질학적 특징 중 하나입니다. 27피트인 이 구조물은 수백만 년 동안 침식 같은 자연 현상으로 형성된 사암으로 이루어져 있습니다.

[150]폭스헤드 바위는 등산로 다른 지점에서도 보이지만, 이곳이 등산객들에게 최고의 사진을 찍을 수 있는 기회를 제공합니다. 주변 지반이 가파르고 바위가 많으므로 등산로에서 벗어나 바위에 접근하려고 하지 마십시오. 감사합니다.

룬데스 국립공원

어휘 visible 보이는 rise 오르막 opposite 맞은편의 resemblance 닮음 geological 지질학의 erosion 침식 trail 등산로, 오솔길 approach 접근하다 surround 둘러싸다 steep 가파른

149 추론 / 암시 〈고난도〉

번역 정보문은 어디에서 보이겠는가?
(A) 박물관 전시장
(B) 공원 안내책자
(C) 제품 라벨
(D) 옥외 표지판

해설 첫 번째 단락에서 폭스헤드 바위가 이 지점 맞은편 오르막에서 볼 수 있는 커다란 암석(Foxhead Rock is the large rock formation visible on the rise opposite this point)이라고 설명하고 있으므로, 야외 표지판에서 볼 수 있는 정보문이라고 추론할 수 있다. 따라서 (D)가 정답이다.

150 세부 사항

번역 정보문은 독자들이 무엇을 할 수 있다고 제시하는가?
(A) 사진 찍기
(B) 전시품 만지기
(C) 기념품 사기
(D) 투어 등록하기

해설 두 번째 단락을 보면 정보문이 게시된 곳에서 최고의 폭스헤드 바위 사진을 찍을 수 있다(this spot offers hikers the best photo opportunity)고 되어 있으므로, (A)가 정답이다.

▶▶ Paraphrasing 지문의 the best photo opportunity
→ 정답의 Take photographs

151-152 문자 메시지

허먼 아더롬 [오후 3시 2분]
151라이언 씨, 당신이 우리에게 데려온 지원자와 영상 채팅을 하려는데 응답이 없네요.

엘리너 라이언 [오후 3시 3분]
매튜 캐스퍼? 데이터 입력직 지원자요?

허먼 아더롬 [오후 3시 3분]
맞아요.

엘리너 라이언 [오후 3시 4분]
죄송해요. 제가 그 사람한테 확인해 볼게요.

엘리너 라이언 [오후 3시 5분]
착오가 있는 게 틀림없어요. 온라인 상태라고 하는데요.

허먼 아더롬 [오후 3시 6분]
정보를 확인해 봅시다. '챗리치'라는 프로그램을 이용해 전화하고 있는데, 사용자 이름이 'matthew_kasper' 맞죠?

엘리너 라이언 [오후 3시 7분]
152실은 제 자료에 의하면 'matthew.kasper'예요. 그걸로 한번 해보세요.

허먼 아더롬 [오후 3시 9분]
알겠어요. 이제 전화가 걸리네요. 고마워요. 나중에 전화해서 면접이 어땠는지 알려 드릴게요.

어휘 candidate 지원자, 후보자 respond to ~에 응답하다 attempt 시도, 노력 misunderstanding 착오 confirm 확인하다 material 자료

151 추론 / 암시

번역 라이언 씨는 누구이겠는가?
(A) 컴퓨터 기술자
(B) 정치부 기자
(C) 행사 기획자
(D) 채용담당자

해설 아더롬 씨가 오후 3시 2분 메시지에서 라이언 씨가 데려온 지원자와 영상 채팅을 시도했지만 응답이 없다(the candidate you brought to us isn't responding to my attempts to video chat with him)고 했으므로, 라이언 씨가 채용과 관련된 일을 한다고 추론할 수 있다. 따라서 (D)가 정답이다.

152 의도 파악

번역 오후 3시 7분에 라이언 씨가 "그걸로 한번 해보세요"라고 쓸 때 권하는 것은?
(A) 다른 연락처 정보 사용
(B) 소프트웨어 프로그램 다시 시작하기
(C) 일부 교육용 자료 읽기
(D) 컴퓨터 디스플레이 설정 변경

해설 사용자 이름(matthew_kasper)을 확인하는 아더롬 씨의 질문에, 라이언 씨가 자신의 자료에 있는 사용자 이름(it's "matthew.kasper", according to my materials)을 알려준 후, '그걸로 한번 해보세요(Try that)'라며 권유했으므로, (A)가 정답이다.

153-154 웹페이지

http://www.scheelerexpress.com/rail

셸러 익스프레스 철도 서비스

철도는 대량의 화물을 옮기는 탁월한 수단이 될 수 있습니다. 다른 주요 지상 운송 수단인 트럭 운송과 비교할 때, 철도는 느리고 편의성이 떨어질 수 있지만 더 안전하고 환경에 덜 해롭습니다. 153철도는 정기적으로 대량 화물을 장거리 운송해야 하는 사업체에 가장 적합합니다.

153셸러 익스프레스의 운송 전문가들은 철도 운송이 귀사에 적합한지 조언해 드릴 수 있습니다. 만약 그렇다고 판단하신다면, 이용하시는 경로에 있는 다양한 철도회사의 복잡한 시스템을 알아보시는 데 도움을 드리겠습니다. 154저희는 주요 업체들 모두와 관계를 유지하고 있으므로 그들의 끊임없이 변하는 기술에 대한 최신 정보를 알고 있습니다.

시작하시려면 지금 바로 연락하세요.

어휘 freight 화물 compare 비교하다 convenient 편리한 environment 환경 suited 적합한 distance 거리 on a regular basis 정기적으로 transportation 운송, 교통 expert 전문가 navigate 알아보다, 이해하다 operator 운영자[업체] stay up-to-date on ~에 대한 최신 정보를 꿰고 있다 constantly 끊임없이

153 추론 / 암시

번역 누구를 대상으로 하는 웹페이지인가?
(A) 통근하는 직원
(B) 화물을 운송하는 회사
(C) 특정 지역을 찾는 관광객
(D) 수리 서비스를 받으려는 열차 운영자

해설 첫 번째 단락에서 철도는 대량 화물을 장거리 운송해야 하는 사업체에 가장 적합하다(It is best suited to businesses that need to transport large amounts of freight over a long distance)고 한 후 다음 단락에서 '셀러 익스프레스의 운송 전문가들은 철도 운송이 귀사에 적합한지 조언해 드릴 수 있습니다'라고 했다. 따라서 화물을 운송하는 회사를 대상으로 하는 웹페이지라고 볼 수 있으므로, (B)가 정답이다.

어휘 commute 통근하다 cargo 화물

▶ **Paraphrasing** 지문의 businesses that need to transport large amounts of freight → 정답의 Companies shipping cargo

154 세부 사항 〔고난도〕

번역 웹페이지에 따르면 셀러 익스프레스의 한 가지 장점은?
(A) 장시간 운영이 가능하다.
(B) 첨단 기술을 사용한다.
(C) 다른 회사들과 관계를 맺고 있다.
(D) 철도 노선을 전용으로 사용하고 있다.

해설 두 번째 단락에서 셀러 익스프레스가 주요 업체들 모두와 관계를 유지하고 있어 그들의 끊임없이 변하는 기술에 대한 최신 정보를 알고 있다(We maintain relationships with all major operators, ~ to stay up-to-date on their constantly changing technology)고 했으므로, (C)가 정답이다.

어휘 employ 사용하다 advanced 고급의, 발전된 exclusive 전용의, 독점적인

▶ **Paraphrasing** 지문의 maintain relationships with all major operators → 정답의 has connections with other companies

155-157 이메일

발신: 재터스 하드웨어
수신: 월리스 글로버
제목: 발표
날짜: 11월 1일

소중한 고객님께,

¹⁵⁵유감스럽게도 재터스 하드웨어가 재터스 포인트 프로그램 중단을 발표하게 되었습니다. 지난 8년 동안 재터스 포인트는 고객님들이 저희 제품을 할인 받을 수 있는 좋은 방법이었습니다. ¹⁵⁶아쉽게도 프로그램을 운영하는 비용이 커져서 이를 계속 제공하는 것이 더 이상 타당하지 않게 되었습니다. 오늘부터 이 프로그램에 신규 신청을 받지 않겠습니다. 다만 기존 참여자는 11월 30일까지 재터스 포인터를 계속 적립해 1월 31일까지 쓰실 수 있도록 하겠습니다. ¹⁵⁷남은 포인트를 어떻게 사용할지 결정할 때 두 번째 마감일을 염두에 두세요. 앞으로 해당 사항을 상기시키는 이메일도 주기적으로 보내 드리겠습니다.

재터스 하드웨어의 단골 고객이 되어 주신 점 늘 감사드립니다.

대릴 하몬, CEO
재터스 하드웨어

어휘 hardware 철물 discontinuation 중단 unfortunately 아쉽게도 accept 받다 existing 기존의 accrue 적립하다 remaining 남은 periodic 주기적인 reminder 일깨우는 것, 상기시키는 것

155 주제 / 목적 〔고난도〕

번역 이메일이 수신자에게 통지하는 것은?
(A) 소매점 폐점
(B) 고객 보상 프로그램 종료
(C) 임원 교체
(D) 철물 제품 회수

해설 이메일의 초반부에서 재터스 하드웨어가 재터스 포인트 프로그램 중단을 발표하게 되었다(Zaters Hardware is sorry to announce the discontinuation of our Zaters Points program)고 한 후, 이메일 전반에서 포인트 적립/사용 프로그램 중단과 관련된 설명을 이어가고 있다. 따라서 (B)가 정답이다.

어휘 replacement 교체 recall 회수, 리콜

▶ **Paraphrasing** 지문의 the discontinuation of our Zaters Points program → 정답의 The end of a loyalty program

156 세부 사항

번역 이메일에 따르면 그렇게 결정한 이유는?
(A) 보안 문제
(B) 법적 분쟁
(C) 재정적 고려
(D) 업체 구조조정

해설 이메일의 중반부에서 프로그램을 운영하는 비용이 커져서 계속 제공하는 것이 더 이상 타당하지 않게 되었다(the cost of running the program has grown to the point where it no longer makes sense to continue offering it)며 프로그램의 종료 이유를 밝혔으므로, (C)가 정답이다.

어휘 dispute 분쟁 restructuring 구조조정

▶ **Paraphrasing** 지문의 the cost of running the program has grown → 정답의 Financial considerations

157 세부 사항

번역 수신자들이 요청 받은 일은?
(A) 양식 작성하기
(B) 향후 이메일 기다리기
(C) 두 가지 선택사항 중에서 선택하기
(D) 날짜 기억하기

해설 이메일의 후반부에서 남은 포인트를 어떻게 사용할지 결정할 때 두 번째 마감일(1월 31일)을 염두에 두라(Please keep the latter deadline in mind)고 했으므로, (D)가 정답이다.

▶▶ Paraphrasing 지문의 **keep the latter deadline in mind**
→ 정답의 **Remember a date**

158-160 웹페이지

http://www.olimmer.com/purchase/step2

2단계: 구독을 선택하세요

가르자 씨, 올림머에 계정을 만들어 주셔서 감사합니다. ¹⁵⁸이제 얼마나 오랫동안 저희의 방대한 템플릿, 테마 및 그래픽 시리즈를 이용해 귀하의 고객을 위한 최고의 온라인 콘텐츠를 만드실지 결정하실 차례입니다. 다음 정보를 검토하고 페이지 하단의 드롭다운 메뉴에서 원하시는 구독 옵션을 선택하세요.

가격:

• 3개월 구독료 (90달러) • 1년 구독료 (270달러)
• 6개월 구독료 (160달러) • 2년 구독료 (410달러)

보시다시피, 저희는 장기 구독을 아주 좋은 가격에 제시합니다. 2년 구독료는 하루 0.56달러에 불과하며, 이는 3개월 구독료인 하루 0.98달러의 겨우 절반 정도에 해당합니다. 사실 이 3개월 구독료도 적정한 수준입니다. ¹⁵⁹6개월 구독료와 1년 구독료도 각각 하루 0.88달러와 0.73달러로 아주 좋은 옵션입니다.

결제:

결제는 월 또는 년 단위로 가능합니다. 첫 번째 결제는 즉시 해주셔야 합니다. 저희는 신용카드와 직불카드를 받습니다. 다음 화면에서 결제 세부 정보를 제공하라는 요청을 받으실 겁니다.

¹⁶⁰구독 기간 변경:

언제든지 무료로 할 수 있습니다. 즉시 청구서 발송 주기가 새롭게 시작되고, 첫 번째 청구서에는 이전 구독에서 사용되지 않은 기간에 대한 공제액이 포함됩니다.

구독: [¹⁵⁹1년 ▼]   [다음 ▶]

어휘 subscription 구독(료) template 템플릿, 견본 first-rate 최고의 barely 겨우 reasonable (가격이) 적정한 respectively 각각 due 지불해야 하는 immediately 즉시 debit card 직불카드 at no charge 무료로 credit 공제액 previous 이전의

158 추론 / 암시

번역 올림머는 누구를 대상으로 하겠는가?
(A) 프리랜서 회계사
(B) 웹 디자이너
(C) 사서
(D) 기자

해설 첫 번째 단락에서 얼마나 오랫동안 올림머의 방대한 템플릿, 테마 및 그래픽 시리즈를 이용해 고객을 위한 최고의 온라인 콘텐츠를 만들지 결정하라(to decide how long you want to be able to access our vast library of templates, themes, and graphics to make first-rate online content for your clients)고 했으므로, 올림머가 웹 디자이너를 대상으로 하는 사이트임을 추론할 수 있다. 따라서 (B)가 정답이다.

159 세부 사항

번역 가르자 씨는 구독료로 하루에 얼마를 지불할 것인가?
(A) 0.56달러
(B) 0.73달러
(C) 0.88달러
(D) 0.98달러

해설 웹페이지 하단의 구독(Subscription) 옵션에서 가르자 씨가 1년 구독(1-year)을 선택한 것을 확인할 수 있는데, 세 번째 단락을 보면 1년 구독료가 하루 0.73달러(Our 6-month and 1-year subscriptions are ~ at $0.88 and $0.73 per day, respectively)라고 나와 있다. 따라서 (B)가 정답이다.

160 사실 관계 확인

번역 올림머 구독에 관해 언급된 것은?
(A) 언제든지 취소할 수 있다.
(B) 가격에 따라 이용 가능한 서비스가 다르다.
(C) 다른 구독 옵션으로 전환 시 수수료가 없다.
(D) 월 단위로 지불해야 한다.

해설 구독 기간 변경(Changing your subscription term)에 대해 안내한 부분에서 언제든지 무료로 할 수 있다(This can be done at any time at no charge)고 했으므로, (C)가 정답이다. 결제는 월 또는 년 단위로 가능하다(Payments can be made monthly or yearly)고 했으므로 (D)는 정답이 될 수 없다.

어휘 cancel 취소하다 reflect 반영하다 access 이용(권) on a monthly basis 월 단위로

▶▶ Paraphrasing 지문의 **Changing your subscription term**
→ 정답의 **switching from one to another**
지문의 **no charge** → 정답의 **no fee**

161-163 회람

수신: 전 직원
발신: 다이앤 에릭슨
주제: 탄력시간제

최근 탄력근무제 관련 프래스크의 정책에 대해 직원들 사이에 다소 혼선이 있다는 점을 알게 되었습니다. 저는 이 문제를 명확히 하기 위해 다음과 같이 직원 사규를 다시 작성했습니다.

"프래스크 상근직 직원은 매주 40시간씩 사무실에서 일해야 한다. 단, 탄력시간제가 승인된 직원은 월요일부터 금요일까지 오전 7시에서 오후 8시 사이의 시간을 조합해 근무함으로써 이 요건을 충족할 수 있다. ¹⁶¹탄력시간제는 직무상 특정 시간에 사무실에 있을 필요가 없는 직원만 이용할 수 있다. 탄력시간제를 하려면 직원은 관리자의 승인을 받아야 한다. ¹⁶³업무상 필요 또는 직원 성과 문제로 탄력시간제의 특례는 언제든지 철회될 수 있다. 어느 경우든 해당 직원의 관리자는 상황을 명확히 설명하고 변경사항을 그 직원에게 사전 통지해야 한다."

¹⁶²만약 탄력시간제로 근무할 자격이 된다고 생각하고 그렇게 하고 싶다면, 일정 제안서를 작성하는 일부터 해야 하며 이후 관리자와 만나서 논의해야 합니다. 탄력시간제 요청서를 인사부로 직접 가져오지 마십시오. 그러나 이 정책에 대한 일반적인 문의는 저희 인사부의 존 버로우스(내선 72, john.burrows@prask.com)에게 하시면 됩니다.

다이앤 에릭슨
인사부 이사

어휘 flexible 탄력 있는, 유연한 recently 최근 come to one's attention 알게 되다 confusion 혼선 with regard to ~에 대해 employee handbook 직원 사규 clarify 명확히 하다 approve 승인하다 fulfill 충족하다 requirement 요구 조건 specific 특정한 managerial 관리자의 privilege 특혜 revoke 철회하다 eligible 자격이 있는

161 사실 관계 확인 　　　　　　　　　　 고난도

번역 프래스크의 탄력시간제 정책에 관해 알 수 있는 것은?
(A) 주말 근무를 허용한다.
(B) 최근에 시행되었다.
(C) 일부 직원을 배제한다.
(D) 직원들에게 인기가 있다.

해설 두 번째 단락에서 탄력시간제는 직무상 특정 시간에 사무실에 있을 필요가 없는 직원만 이용할 수 있다(Flextime is only available to employees whose job duties do not require them to be in the office at specific times)고 했으므로, 그 외 직원은 이용이 제한된다는 것을 알 수 있다. 따라서 (C)가 정답이다.

어휘 implement 시행하다 exclude 배제하다

162 세부 사항 　　　　　　　　　　 고난도

번역 회람에 따르면 탄력시간제 근무에 관심 있는 직원이 먼저 해야 하는 일은?
(A) 원하는 근무시간 결정
(B) 관리자에게 허가 요청
(C) 인사부에 요청서 제출
(D) 긍정적인 인사 고과 획득

해설 마지막 단락에서 탄력시간제로 근무하고 싶다면 일정 제안서를 작성하는 일부터 해야 한다(you should begin by creating a proposed schedule)고 했으므로, (A)가 정답이다.

어휘 performance (업무) 수행 evaluation 평가

▶ Paraphrasing 지문의 creating a proposed schedule → 정답의 Determine their desired working hours

163 문장 삽입

번역 [1], [2], [3], [4]로 표시된 곳 중에서 다음 문장이 가장 적합한 곳은?
"어느 경우든 해당 직원의 관리자는 상황을 명확히 설명하고 변경사항을 그 직원에게 사전 통지해야 한다."
(A) [1]
(B) [2]
(C) [3]
(D) [4]

해설 주어진 문장이 '어느 경우든(In either case)'이라는 표현으로 시작하므로 앞에서 먼저 관리자의 조치(the employee's manager should clearly explain ~ the change)가 필요한 두 가지 경우가 언급되어야 한다. [3] 앞에서 업무상 필요 또는 직원 성과 문제로 탄력시간제의 특혜는 언제든지 철회될 수 있다(The privilege of working flextime

---

may be revoked ~ due to business needs or employee performance issues)며 구체적인 두 경우를 명시했으므로, (C)가 정답이다.

164-167 문자 메시지

라나 노턴 [오전 11시 54분] 여러분 안녕하세요. 시간이 오래 걸리는 병원 진료 중이라 오늘 오후 1시 에어로빅 수업은 못 가르칠 것 같아요. ^{164/165}경모가 모두에게 문자를 보내서 여러분 중 누가 저 대신 할 수 있는지 알아보라고 했어요.
헨리 러셀 [오전 11시 54분] 그러고 싶지만, 그 시간에 전 한창 필라테스 수업 중일 거예요.
케냐 헌트 [오전 11시 55분] 전 오늘 예정된 수업을 끝냈어요. 좀 자세히 설명해 주실래요?
라나 노턴 [오전 11시 55분] ^{166(A)/(C)}3번 스튜디오에서 1시부터 1시 50분까지 이어지는 저강도 댄스 중심 수업이에요. 어떤 장비도 필요 없고, 학생들은 대체로 연세가 지긋하신 여성분들이에요.
케냐 헌트 [오전 11시 56분] ¹⁶⁵알겠어요. 할 만 하겠네요. 제가 할게요. 주로 어떤 음악을 트나요?
전경모 [오전 11시 57분] 고마워요, 케냐. ^{166(D)}정규 수강생들에게 문자를 보내서 다른 강사가 수업을 진행한다고 알릴게요.
라나 노턴 [오전 11시 58분] ¹⁶⁷몇 주 전에 녹화한 수업 영상이 있어요. 그걸 보면 어떤 음악을 트는지, 우리가 보통 어떤 동작을 하는지 감이 잡힐 거예요. ¹⁶⁷이메일 주소가 어떻게 되죠?
케냐 헌트 [오전 11시 58분] kenya.hunt@pnb-mail.com. 고마워요! 정말 도움이 될 거예요.
라나 노턴 [오전 11시 59분] 뭘요, 대신하겠다고 자원해 줘서 고마워요! 더 궁금한 게 있으면 알려 주세요. 나머지 진료 시간에 주기적으로 핸드폰을 확인할 수 있을 거예요.

어휘 appointment 약속, (진료) 예약 intensity 강도 equipment 장비 doable 할 수 있는 attendee 출석자; 수강생 substitute 대신하다 periodically 주기적으로

164 세부 사항

번역 노턴 씨가 다른 참석자들에게 메시지를 보내는 이유는?
(A) 부탁하려고
(B) 행사를 홍보하려고
(C) 상황에 대해 사과하려고
(D) 일정을 발표하려고

해설 노턴 씨가 오전 11시 54분 메시지에서 누가 자신의 수업을 대신할 수 있는지 알아보기 위해(to see if one of you could do it for me) 문자를 보낸다고 했으므로, 수업을 부탁하기 위해 메시지를 보냈음을 알 수 있다. 따라서 (A)가 정답이다.

165 의도 파악

번역 오전 11시 56분에 헌트 씨가 "제가 할게요"라고 쓴 의미는?
(A) 강습 기회를 수락하고 있다.
(B) 물건을 옮기는 일에 자원하고 있다.
(C) 몇 가지 장비를 보유하고 싶어 한다.
(D) 새로운 기술을 습득하는 데 관심이 있다.

해설 노턴 씨가 오전 11시 54분 메시지에서 누가 자신의 수업을 대신할 수 있는지 알아보기 위해(to see if one of you could do it for me) 문자를 보낸다고 했는데, 수업 설명을 듣고 난 후 헌트 씨가 할 만 하겠다(that sounds doable)며 본인이 대신 가르치겠다고 응답한 것이다. 따라서 (A)가 정답이다.

166 사실 관계 확인

번역 오후 1시 수업에 대해 알 수 없는 것은?
(A) 1시간이 안 걸린다.
(B) 사전에 등록이 필요하다.
(C) 비교적 쉬운 운동으로 이루어진다.
(D) 일부 사람들이 정기적으로 참석한다.

해설 노턴 씨가 쓴 오전 11시 55분 메시지 '1시부터 1시 50분까지 이어지는 저강도 댄스 중심 수업이다(It's a low-intensity, dance-centered class that runs from 1 to 1:50)'에서 (A)와 (C)를, 전 씨가 쓴 오전 11시 57분 메시지의 '정규 수강생들에게 문자를 보내서 알리도록 하겠다(I'll send out a text to let the regular attendees know)'에서 (D)를 확인할 수 있다. 따라서 언급되지 않은 (B)가 정답이다.

어휘 relatively 비교적 routinely 정기적으로

▶▶ Paraphrasing 지문의 runs from 1 to 1:50
→ 보기 (A)의 lasts for less than an hour

지문의 low-intensity
→ 보기 (C)의 relatively easy

지문의 the regular attendees
→ 보기 (D)의 attended routinely by some people

167 추론 / 암시

번역 노턴 씨는 헌트 씨에게 무엇을 이메일로 보내겠는가?
(A) 동영상
(B) 노래 목록
(C) 등록 용지
(D) 인근 지도

해설 노턴 씨가 오전 11시 59분 메시지에서 녹화한 수업 영상이 있다(I actually have a video of the class that I recorded)고 한 후, 헌트 씨의 이메일 주소(What is your e-mail address?)를 물었으므로, (A)가 정답이다.

▶▶ Paraphrasing 지문의 a video of the class that I recorded
→ 정답의 A video clip

168-171 편지

클레어 필즈
홀트 가 390번지
4C24+8G 브리지타운

3월 18일

루디즈
필립 로 2090번지
3CV4+9Q 브리지타운

담당자 귀하:

제 이름은 클레어 필즈고, 가게 단골이에요. [168]전 가게의 아이스 모카를 좋아하고, 서비스도 훌륭하다고 생각해요. [169]하지만 휠체어 사용자로서 접근성 문제가 있다는 것을 알려 드리고 싶어요. 서비스 카운터가 상당히 높아요. 바닥에서 150센티미터 정도 떨어져 있는 것 같아요. 카운터 위에 놓인 것들도 안 보이고 그 위로 손을 뻗으려면 애를 써야 하며, 심지어 메뉴를 보는 데 카운터가 시야를 방해해요.

카운터를 교체하려면 큰 비용이 들어갈 것이니 그렇게 하라고 요청드리는 건 아니에요. [170]그보다는, 브리지타운의 다른 지역에 새 지점을 여신다고 들어서 이렇게 편지를 써요. 휠체어를 편하게 사용할 수 있는 시설을 갖추는 것도 고려해 보시면 좋겠어요. [171]또한 바베이도스 장애인 지원 공단(BDA)에 문의해 접근이 용이한 설계에 대해 조언을 더 구하시는 게 어떨까 해요. 웹사이트는 www.bda.bb예요.

시간 내서 편지를 읽어 주셔서 감사하며, 행운을 빌어요! 지역 사업체가 번창하는 걸 보면 언제나 신나요!

클레어 필즈

어휘 frequent customer 단골 accessibility 접근(용이)성
struggle 애쓰다 obstruct 방해하다 replace 교체하다
disability 장애 authority 공사[공단]

168 추론 / 암시

번역 루디즈는 어떤 업체인가?
(A) 카페
(B) 미용실
(C) 꽃가게
(D) 의류매장

해설 첫 번째 단락에서 필즈 씨가 가게의 아이스 모카를 좋아한다(I love your iced mochas)고 했으므로, 루디즈가 카페임을 추론할 수 있다. 따라서 (A)가 정답이다.

169 세부 사항

번역 필즈 씨는 어떤 문제를 설명하고 있는가?
(A) 출입구가 너무 좁다.
(B) 간판 글씨가 너무 작다.
(C) 일부 바닥이 너무 울퉁불퉁하다.
(D) 가구 하나가 너무 높다.

해설 첫 번째 단락에서 휠체어 사용자로서 접근성 문제가 있다(as a wheelchair user, there is an accessibility issue)고 한 후, 서비스 카운터가 상당히 높다(Your service counter is quite high)는 구체적

인 문제점을 언급했다. 따라서 (D)가 정답이다.

▶▶ Paraphrasing 지문의 **Your service counter is quite high**
→ 정답의 **A piece of furniture is too tall**

170 사실 관계 확인

번역 루디즈에 관해 알 수 있는 것은?
(A) 현재 확장하고 있다.
(B) 특이한 서비스를 제공한다.
(C) 장애인을 고용한다.
(D) 세계적인 체인점이다.

해설 두 번째 단락에서 브리지타운의 다른 지역에 새 지점을 연다고 들었다(I heard that you are opening new locations in other areas of Bridgetown)고 했으므로, 루디즈가 지금 확장 중임을 알 수 있다. 따라서 (A)가 정답이다.

어휘 currently 현재 expand 확장하다

▶▶ Paraphrasing 지문의 **opening new locations**
→ 정답의 **expanding**

171 세부 사항

번역 필즈 씨가 BDA에 연락하라고 권하는 이유는?
(A) 점검 일정 잡기
(B) 추가 정보 받기
(C) 재정지원 신청
(D) 어려움 보고

해설 두 번째 단락에서 필즈 씨가 BDA에 문의해 접근이 용이한 설계에 대해 조언을 더 구할 것을 제안한다(I suggest contacting the ~ (BDA) for more tips on accessible design)고 했으므로, (B)가 정답이다.

▶▶ Paraphrasing 지문의 **for more tips**
→ 정답의 **To receive further information**

172-175 기사

에바슨 농부들의 청원서, 주의회에 제출되다

스카벨 (9월 8일)—[174]오늘, 주의회 의원인 나오미 블랙은 에바슨 지역 농부들이 용수 사용권을 줄이려는 정부 계획에 반대해 작성한 청원서를 제출했다.

용수 사용권은 소지자에게 특정한 대량의 지하수를 사용하도록 허가한다. [172]정부의 감축 계획으로 농업에 종사하는 용수 사용권 소지자에게 허가되는 물 양이 향후 5년간 10퍼센트 감소할 예정이다. 이는 가뭄이 증가하는 지역을 방지하기 위한 방안으로 에바슨 수자원 및 농업 대책 위원회(EWAT)에 의해 고안되었다.

앨빈 브룩스 EWAT 회장은 "모두가 적응해야 한다"고 말했다. "주정부는 이미 공원 잔디를 돌 자갈로 대체하는 등 조치를 통해 자체 물 사용량을 줄였습니다. 이 면세제는 농민들이 물을 더 효율적으로 사용하도록 독려할 것입니다."

그러나 농민들은 이번 감축으로 인해 토지 가치가 부당하게 떨어지고 지역경제가 피해를 입을 것이라며 불만을 토로한다. 에바슨 농민협회(EFA) 대표이자 청원서를 작성한 사람 중 한 명인 코트니 그랜트는 "우리는 이미 물을 효율적으로 사용하고 있어요. 감축안은 그저 우리의 생산량을 줄이기만 하겠죠"라고 말했다.

[173]EWAT 위원들과 EFA 회원들은 지난달 감축안 발표 직후 열린 공청회에서 이 안에 대해 논의했지만 상호 수용 가능한 타협점을 찾지 못했다. 이어 협회는 "책임 있는 수자원 관리를 위한 청원"을 작성해 배포했다.

[175]청원서는 주정부가 대신 추가 상수원 발굴이나 개발에 투자해야 한다고 제안한다. 그것은 2주 동안 1,000개가 넘는 서명을 받았다. 이제 청원서가 공식적으로 주의회에 제출되었으므로 해당 의회 위원회에 회부되어 심사를 받게 될 것이다.

어휘 petition 청원(서) introduce (의회 등에) 제출하다 parliament 의회 submit 제출하다 protest 반대하다 reduce 줄이다 authorize 허가하다 groundwater 지하수 shrink 줄이다 agricultural 농업의 be entitled to ~에 대한 자격을 받다 combat 방지하다 adjust 적응하다 gravel 자갈 efficiently 효율적으로 unfairly 부당하게 devalue 가치를 떨어트리다. 평가 절하하다 output 생산량 representative 위원, 대표 mutually 상호간에 acceptable 수용 가능한 compromise 타협 circulate 배포하다, 돌리다 responsible 책임 있는 water resources 수자원 refer 회부하다 appropriate 적절한, 해당하는

172 세부 사항 〔고난도〕

번역 EWAT가 하자고 제안하는 것은?
(A) 물 절약 기술에 보조금 지원하기
(B) 영농 활동에 물을 적게 할당하기
(C) 용수 사용권 자격 강화하기
(D) 공공 재산에 물 절약형 조경 이용하기

해설 두 번째 단락에서 정부의 감축 계획으로 농업에 종사하는 용수 사용권 소지자에게 허가되는 물 양이 감소할 예정(The government's reduction plan would slowly shrink the amount of water that licence-holders in the agricultural industry are entitled to)이라고 한 후, 이는 가뭄이 증가하는 지역을 방지하기 위한 방안으로 에바슨 수자원 및 농업 대책 위원회(EWAT)에 의해 고안되었다(It was developed by the Evarson Water and Ariculture Taskforce (EWAT))고 했다. 따라서 (B)가 정답이다.

어휘 subsidize 보조금을 지원하다 allocate 할당하다 qualification 자격 conserve 절약하다 property 재산

▶▶ Paraphrasing 지문의 **shrink the amount of water that licence-holders in the agricultural industry are entitled to**
→ 정답의 **Allocating less water to farming efforts**

173 추론 / 암시 〔고난도〕

번역 EWAT의 계획안에 관해 암시된 것은?
(A) EFA의 의견을 받지 않고 고안되었다.
(B) 몇 년 연기된 후에 시행될 예정이다.
(C) 다른 주들에서 발의된 제안과 비슷하다.
(D) 대규모 국비 투자가 필요할 것이다.

해설 다섯 번째 단락에서 EWAT 위원들과 EFA 회원들이 감축안 발표 '직후' 열린 공청회에서 이 안에 대해 논의했다(EWAT representatives and EFA members discussed the plan ~ soon after its announce-ment)고 했으므로, EWAT의 계획안이 EFA의 의견을 받지 않고 고안되었음을 추론할 수 있다. 따라서 (A)가 정답이다.

Test 2

어휘 input 의견 implement 시행하다

174 추론 / 암시

번역 블랙 씨는 누구이겠는가?
(A) 대학교수
(B) 농산물 재배자
(C) 지역 정치인
(D) 환경운동가

해설 첫 번째 단락에서 주의회 의원인 나오미 블랙이 에바슨 지역 농부들이 작성한 청원서를 제출했다(member of State Parliament Naomi Black submitted a petition created by farmers in the Evarson area)고 했으므로, 블랙 씨가 지역 정치인임을 알 수 있다. 따라서 (C)가 정답이다.

어휘 produce 농산물

▶▶ Paraphrasing   지문의 member of State Parliament
→ 정답의 regional politician

175 문장 삽입

번역 [1], [2], [3], [4]로 표시된 곳 중에서 다음 문장이 가장 적합한 곳은?
"그것은 2주 동안 1,000개가 넘는 서명을 받았다."
(A) [1]
(B) [2]
(C) [3]
(D) [4]

해설 주어진 문장에서 '그것은 2주 동안 1,000개가 넘는 서명을 받았다(It garnered more than 1,000 signatures in two weeks)'라고 했으므로, 앞에서 먼저 It이 가리키는 대상이 언급되어야 한다. [4] 앞에서 '청원서(The petition)'를 언급하며 서명을 받는 대상을 명시했으므로, (D)가 정답이다.

어휘 garner 얻다, 모으다

176-180 차트 + 이메일

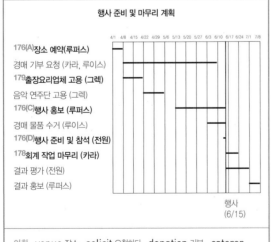

어휘 venue 장소 solicit 요청하다 donation 기부 caterer 출장요리업체 evaluate 평가하다

발신: ¹⁷⁸카라 그리핀
수신: 루이스 로드리게스
제목: 희소식
¹⁷⁹날짜 : 4월 24일

안녕하세요 루이스,

¹⁷⁷오늘 아침 팔콘 갤러리에서 보브로바 씨와 회의를 했는데, 좋은 소식이 있어요. 그가 가브리엘 서시의 그림을 기증하기로 했어요! 그림은 거의 500달러의 가치가 있으므로 꽤 높은 가격에 입찰이 들어올 수 있어요. ¹⁸⁰보브로바 씨는 펠릭스 숲을 사랑하신다고 해요. 그래서 우리의 보존 활동을 기꺼이 돕겠다고 하신 거예요.

그런데 작품을 어떻게 수령하고 운반할지 당신이 그와 미리 이야기해야 해요. 제 생각엔 그 일이 힘들 거 같거든요. ¹⁷⁸만약 포장이나 운송 서비스를 이용해야 한다면 영수증과 다른 서류들을 반드시 보관하세요. 행사 후에 회계 처리할 때 필요할 거예요.

일은 어떻게 돼 가요? 놀이공원에선 연락이 왔나요? 그곳 입장권은 가족들에게 아주 매력적일 거예요.

¹⁷⁹그리고 또, 보니까 그레이 첫 번째 마감일을 지키지 않았더군요. 왜 그랬는지 아세요? 당신이 그 사람 옆에 앉으니까 무슨 얘기를 들었을지도 모른다 싶어서 물어봐요.

－카라

어휘 bid 입찰(가) conservation (자연) 보존 effort (특정 목적을 달성하기 위한) 활동, 노력 in advance 미리 transport 운반하다 admission 입장

176 사실 관계 확인

번역 차트에 따르면 루퍼스가 맡지 않은 일은?
(A) 장소 예약
(B) 급식 업체 고용
(C) 행사 홍보
(D) 장소 준비

해설 차트의 '장소 예약(Reserve venue (Rufus))'에서 (A)를, '행사 홍보(Advertise event (Rufus))'에서 (C)를 확인할 수 있고, '행사 준비 및 참석(Set up and attend event (All))'은 모두에게 해당되는 일이니 (D) 역시 루퍼스가 맡은 업무로 볼 수 있다. 하지만 '출장요리업체 고용(Hire caterer)'은 그렉(Greg)이 맡은 일이므로 (B)가 정답이다.

어휘 publicize 홍보하다

▶▶ Paraphrasing   지문의 Reserve venue
→ 보기 (A)의 Reserving a site
지문의 Hire caterer
→ 정답의 Hiring a food provider
지문의 Advertise event
→ 보기 (C)의 Publicizing the event
지문의 Set up ~ event
→ 보기 (D)의 Setting up a venue (Set up event에 포함)

177 세부 사항

그리핀 씨는 무엇을 기증 받기로 했는가?
- (A) 예술작품
- (B) 갤러리 투어
- (C) 일련의 회화 수업
- (D) 화가와의 식사

해설 이메일의 첫 번째 단락에서 그리핀 씨는 팔콘 갤러리에서 보브로바 씨와 회의(my meeting with Mr. Bobrova at Falcon Gallery)를 했고 그에게 그림을 기증받기로 했다(he agreed to donate a Gabrielle Searcy painting)는 소식을 전했다. 따라서 (A)가 정답이다.

▶▶ Paraphrasing 지문의 painting → 정답의 artwork

178 연계

고난도

번역 이메일에 언급된 서류가 필요한 사람은 누구이겠는가?
- (A) 루퍼스
- (B) 그리핀 씨
- (C) 그렉
- (D) 서시 씨

해설 이메일의 두 번째 단락에서 로드리게즈 씨에게 영수증과 다른 서류들을 반드시 보관할 것(you keep the receipts and any other paperwork)을 요청한 후, 행사 후 회계 처리할 때 필요할 것(We'll need them for accounting purposes after the event)이라는 이유를 덧붙였다. 차트를 보면, 회계 작업 마무리(Complete accounting tasks (Kara)) 업무가 이메일 발신자인 카라 그리핀 씨 담당임을 확인할 수 있으므로, (B)가 정답이다.

179 연계

번역 그렉이 맞추지 못한 마감일은?
- (A) 4월 8일
- (B) 4월 15일
- (C) 4월 22일
- (D) 5월 6일

해설 이메일의 네 번째 단락에서 그렉이 첫 번째 마감일을 지키지 않았다(Greg hasn't met his first deadline)고 했는데, 차트를 보면 그렉의 첫 번째 임무인 '출장요리업체 고용(Hire caterer (Greg))' 마감일이 4월 22임을 알 수 있다. 따라서 (C)가 정답이다.

▶▶ Paraphrasing 지문의 hasn't met → 질문의 fail to meet

180 추론 / 암시

번역 이메일에서 기획 중인 행사에 관해 암시된 것은?
- (A) 일정을 다시 잡아야 했다.
- (B) 참석자를 위한 특별한 교통수단이 필요할 것이다.
- (C) 연예계의 후원을 받고 있다.
- (D) 환경을 위한 활동에 도움이 될 것이다.

해설 이메일의 첫 번째 단락에서 보브로바 씨가 펠릭스 숲을 사랑하기 때문에 자신들의 보존 활동을 기꺼이 도와주는 것(Mr. Bobrova loves Felix Forest, so he was very happy to help with our conservation efforts)이라고 했으므로, 기획 중인 행사가 환경 보호 활동의 일환임을 추론할 수 있다. 따라서 (D)가 정답이다.

어휘 benefit 도움이 되다 cause 대의, (특정 목적을 위한) 운동

▶▶ Paraphrasing 지문의 help with our conservation efforts
→ 정답의 benefit an environmental cause

181-185 청구서 + 이메일

청구서

브렌단 예체바리아 서비스

사서함 10392
토론토 온타리오 M4N 3P6
647-555-0129
www.brendanechevarria.com

청구서 번호: 62
작업 기간: 1월 1일~1월 31일
발행일: 2월 1일
기한: 3월 2일

고객: 발도라 온라인
아만다 아오키 귀하
리치먼드 가 780번지
토론토 온타리오 M6J 1B9
416-555-0105

서비스	요금	총액
181웨라 사 확장에 관한 300단어 뉴스 기사	단어당 0.3달러	90달러
181경영 기법에 관한 450단어 정보성 기사	단어당 0.5달러	225달러
고객과 30분 통화	15분에 5달러	10달러
183450단어 기사 수정	183단어당 0.1달러	45달러
	총액:	370달러

결제는 상기 실제 주소로 수표를 보내시거나 위즈페이를 통해 payment@brendanechevarria.com으로 지불 하시면 됩니다.

거래해 주셔서 감사합니다!

어휘 date due 기한 expansion 확장 informative 정보를 제공하는 revision 수정 physical 실제의, 물리적인

발신: 브렌단 예체바리아 〈contact@brendanechevarria.com〉
수신: 아만다 아오키 〈amanda.aoki@baldora.com〉
제목: 회신: 질문
날짜: 2월 5일

아만다에게,

182이번 달 제 청구서에 대한 질문에 기꺼이 대답해 드릴게요. 183첫째, 올해 재작성 작업료가 올랐다는 말은 맞아요. 놀라셨다면 죄송하지만, 제가 12월에 전임자에게 보낸 요금표에 새 작업료가 기재되어 있고, 전임자가 이에 동의했었습니다. 이를 확인하실 수 있도록 이메일로 184주고 받은 내용을 따로 전달할게요. 제 생각엔 그가 회사 파일에서 제 정보를 수정하는 걸 깜빡한 것 같아요.

182다른 예비 기고가를 추천해 달라는 요청에 대해 답변 드리면, 당신이 관심 가질 만한 사람을 알고 있어요. 185그녀의 이름은 멜로디 소프로, 예전에 〈요크빌 헤럴드〉에 있을 때 제 동료였는데 최근에 프리랜서 과학 기자가 됐죠. 그녀는 단순하고 매력적인 문체를 갖고 있어요. 〈헤럴드〉 웹사이트에 실린 그녀의 예전 기사를 보면 아실 수 있을 거예요. 만약 연락하고 싶다는 생각이 드시면, 그녀의 이메일 주소인 m.thorpe@vct-mail.com으로 하시면 됩니다.

더 궁금하신 점이나 용건이 있으시면 알려 주세요. 다른 언급이 없으시면 현재 쓰고 있는 250단어 뉴스 기사를 계속 작업하겠습니다.

브렌단

어휘 predecessor 전임자 separately 따로 potential 예비의, 잠재적인 contributor 기고가

181 세부 사항

번역 에체바리아 씨가 1월에 발도라 온라인을 위해 쓴 내용은?
(A) 스포츠
(B) 정치
(C) 경제
(D) 연예

해설 청구서 내역에서 에체바리아 씨가 제공한 서비스(Service) 목록을 보면, '웨라 사 확장에 관한 300단어 뉴스 기사(300-word news article on Werra, Inc. expansion)'와 '경영 기법에 관한 450단어 정보성 기사 (450-word informative article on management skills)'라는 경제 관련 기사를 작성한 것을 알 수 있다. 따라서 (C)가 정답이다.

182 주제 / 목적

번역 이메일의 목적은?
(A) 고객 문의에 답변
(B) 결제 관련 문제 보고
(C) 프로젝트 변경 논의
(D) 청구 실수에 대해 사과

해설 이메일의 첫 번째 단락에서는 이번 달 청구서에 대한 아오키 씨의 질문 (your question about my invoice for this month)에 대해, 두 번째 단락에서는 다른 예비 기고가를 추천해 달라는 아오키 씨의 요청(your request to recommend other potential contributors)에 대해 답변하고 있다. 따라서 (A)가 정답이다.

183 연계

번역 에체바리아 씨가 최근 바뀌었다고 말한 요금은?
(A) 단어당 0.3달러
(B) 단어당 0.5달러
(C) 15분에 5달러
(D) 단어당 0.1달러

해설 이메일의 첫 번째 단락에서 에체바리아 씨의 재작성 작업료가 올해 올랐다(my rewriting rate increased this year)고 했는데, 청구서 내역을 보면 재작성과 관련된 서비스는 '450단어 기사 수정(Revision of 450-word article)'으로, 이에 해당하는 작업료가 단어당 0.1달러임을 알 수 있다. 따라서 (D)가 정답이다.

184 동의어 찾기 〔고난도〕

번역 이메일에서 1번째 단락 4행의 "exchange"와 의미상 가장 가까운 것은?
(A) 무역
(B) 시장
(C) 전환
(D) 서신

해설 'exchange'가 포함된 부분은 '이메일로 주고 받은 내용을 따로 전달하겠다(I'll forward you the e-mail exchange separately)'라는 의미로 해석된다. 따라서 '서신 (교환)'이라는 의미의 (D) correspondence가 정답이다.

185 사실 관계 확인 〔고난도〕

번역 이메일에서 소프 씨에 대해 알 수 있는 것은?
(A) 에체바리아 씨의 고객 중 한 명이다.
(B) 과학 분야 학위를 갖고 있다.
(C) 더 이상 상근직 고용주가 없다.
(D) 웹사이트 광고에 응했다.

해설 이메일의 두 번째 단락에서 소프 씨가 최근에 프리랜서 과학 기자가 됐다(Her name is Melody Thrope ~ who recently became a freelance science writer)고 했으므로, (C)가 정답이다.

어휘 degree 학위 field 분야 employer 고용주, 회사

▶▶ **Paraphrasing** 지문의 became a freelance science writer → 정답의 no longer has a full-time employer

186-190 이메일 + 양식 + 메모

발신: 에드 패짓
수신: 로즈 테이트
제목: 사무실 장식
날짜: 9월 30일
첨부: 사무실_장식_요청서

테이트 씨께,

런스포드 앤 어소시에이츠에 오신 것을 환영합니다! 제 이름은 에드 패짓이며, 귀하가 쓰실 층의 사무실 관리자입니다. 업무를 시작한 후에는 매우 바빠지실테니, 지금 새 사무실을 위해 쇼핑을 시작하시는 것이 좋을 듯 합니다. 사무실 장식 규정은 다음과 같습니다:

－ 개인 사무실이 있는 직원(이하 "사무실보유자"라고 한다)은 고객에게 좋은 인상을 주기 위해 1개월 이내에 사무실을 꾸며야 한다.
－ 188채용이나 승진 시, 새로운 사무실보유자는 사무실 장식에 1000달러까지 지출할 수 있다.
－ 사무실 관리자에게 전자 '사무실 장식 요청서' 양식을 제출해 구매를 요청할 수 있다.
－ 188현재 또는 이후에 추가 자금을 지출한다는 요청은 반드시 사무실보유자의 매니저에게 승인을 받아야 한다.
－ 장식은 고상하고 187직업상 적절해야 한다.
－ 190업무에 지장을 줄 수 있는 경우에 대비해 인근 사무실보유자에게 장식 작업을 미리 공지해야 한다.

186(A)참고로, 귀하의 사무실은 대략 길이 10피트, 너비 10피트 크기입니다. 186(B)/(C)또한 방문하신 적이 있으니 기억하시겠지만, 사무실은 회색 대리석 바닥이며 책상, 작은 소파, 책장이 이미 있습니다. 물론 원하시면 어떤 물품이든 교체할 수 있습니다.

이 이메일에 필요한 양식을 첨부했습니다. 이 내용에 대해 궁금한 점이 있으면 알려 주세요.

에드

어휘 administrator 관리자 policy 규정 hereafter 이후로 impression 인상 promotion 승진 additional 추가의 approve 승인하다 tasteful 고상한 disturb 방해하다 for reference 참고로 contain 포함하다

사무실 장식 요청

이름: 로즈 테이트 채용/승진 발표일: 10월 4일
직함: 선임 회계사 사무실 번호: 305

품목 명세	판매자	웹페이지 링크	수량	(대략) 총 가격*
책상용 의자	맬로린	www.mallorin.com/4024	1	235달러
189아트 프린트	니콜 판	189없음	1	175달러
안락의자	본 홈즈	www.bohnhomes.com/3421	2	210달러
작은 탁자	본 홈즈	www.bohnhomes.com/0257	1	65달러
코트 걸이	본 홈즈	www.bohnhomes.com/6369	1	40달러
			188견적 총액:	725달러

제출일: 10월 6일 제출처: 에드 패짓

*가격 견적에는 배송/배달/설치 예상 비용이 포함되어야 한다.

어휘 effective date 발표일, 유효기일 quantity 수량 approx. 대략 (= approximate(ly)) estimated 견적의, 예상되는

안녕하세요 오드리,

190오늘 오전에 제 사무실에서 장식 작업이 있다는 걸 알려드리고 싶었어요. 특별히 불편한 시간이 있다면 말해 주세요. 왜냐하면 시간을 어느 정도는 조절할 수 있거든요.

고마워요,
로즈

어휘 inconvenient 불편한 flexibility 융통성, 유연성

---

186 사실 관계 확인

번역 패짓 씨가 테이트 씨의 사무실에 대해 제공하지 않은 정보는?
(A) 치수
(B) 기존 내용물
(C) 바닥재
(D) 위치

해설 이메일 세 번째 단락에서 '사무실이 대략 길이 10피트, 너비 10피트 크기이다(your office is roughly 10 feet long by 10 feet wide)'라며 (A) 관련 정보를, '사무실은 회색 대리석 바닥에 책상, 작은 소파, 책장이 이미 있다(it has grey marble floors and already contains a desk, a small sofa, and a bookcase)'라며 (B)와 (C) 관련 정보를 제공하고 있다. 따라서 언급되지 않은 (D)가 정답이다.

▶▶ Paraphrasing 지문의 roughly 10 feet long by 10 feet wide
→ 보기 (A)의 dimensions

지문의 already contains a desk, a small sofa, and a bookcase
→ 보기 (B)의 existing contents

지문의 grey marble floors
→ 보기 (C)의 flooring material

187 동의어 찾기

번역 이메일에서 6번째 단락 1행의 "professional"과 의미상 가장 가까운 것은?
(A) 돈을 받는
(B) 튼튼한
(C) 업무에 적합한
(D) 공손한

해설 'professional'이 포함된 문장은 '장식은 고상하고 직업상 적절해야 한다(Decorations must be tasteful and professional)'라는 의미로 해석되는데, 여기서 professional은 '직업상 적절한'이라는 뜻으로 쓰였다. 따라서 '업무에 적합한'이라는 의미의 (C) appropriate for business가 정답이다.

188 연계 고난도

번역 테이트 씨의 요청에 관해 암시된 것은?
(A) 매니저의 승인이 필요 없다.
(B) 일부 중고 가구의 교체품이 포함된다.
(C) 권고보다 늦게 제출되었다.
(D) 이미 한 차례 수정되었다.

해설 테이트 씨의 사무실 장식 요청서(Office Decoration Request)를 보면 견적 총액(Estimated Total)이 725달러임을 확인할 수 있다. 이메일의 세 번째 단락에서 채용이나 승진 시 새로운 사무실보유자는 사무실 장식에 1000달러까지 지출할 수 있다(Upon hiring or promotion, new officeholders may spend up to $1000 on office decoration)고 했고, 다섯 번째 단락에서 추가 자금을 지출한다는 요청은 반드시 사무실보유자의 매니저에게 승인을 받아야 한다(Requests to spend any additional funds ~ must be approved by the officeholder's manager)고 했으므로, 견적 총액이 1000달러 미만인 테이트 씨는 별도로 매니저의 승인을 받을 필요가 없음을 추론할 수 있다. 따라서 (A)가 정답이다.

189 사실 관계 확인 고난도

번역 양식에 기재된 상품에 대해 알 수 있는 것은?
(A) 그중 하나는 맞춤으로 제작될 예정이다.
(B) 모두 온라인에서 판매되는 것은 아니다.
(C) 일부는 중고품이다.
(D) 모두 같은 제조사에서 만들어졌다.

해설 사무실 장식 요청서(Office Decoration Request)의 표를 보면, 웹페이지 링크(Web page link)가 '없음(Not available)'으로 표시된 품목이 있으므로, (B)가 정답이다.

어휘 customized 맞춤의

190 연계

번역 오드리에 관해 암시된 것은?
(A) 오전에는 일하지 않는다.
(B) 사무실이 테이트 씨 사무실 근처에 있다.
(C) 정비 감독관이다.
(D) 직함이 패짓 씨와 같다.

해설 메모에서 테이트 씨는 오드리에게 자신의 사무실에서 장식 작업이 있다는 걸 알려주고 싶다(I just wanted to let you know that I need to do some decorating in my office)고 했는데, 이메일의 일곱 번째 단락을 보면 사무실 장식을 할 경우 인근 사무실보유자에게 미리 공지해야 한다(Nearby officeholders should be notified of decorating activities in advance)고 되어 있으므로, 오드리의 사무실이 테이트 씨 사무실 근처에 있음을 추론할 수 있다. 따라서 (B)가 정답이다.

어휘 maintenance 정비

191-195 기사 + 웹페이지 + 웹페이지

해멜, 벨론 스프링스에서 남우주연상 수상

벨론 스프링스(5월 17일)—일요일 밤 열린 시상식에서 벨론 스프링스 영화제 심사위원단은 베테랑 배우 크리스토퍼 해멜에게 최우수 남우주연상을 수여했다. 이 영화제에서 경쟁한 22편의 독립영화와 수많은 연기자들 중에서 선정된 다른 주요 수상자로는 〈바람 속의 외침〉(최우수 작품상)과 실비아 마티스(〈전진〉에서 맡은 역으로 여우주연상)가 있다.

해멜 씨는 〈우리의 울타리〉에서 보인 뛰어난 연기로 수상했다. **193**비토미르 홈우드가 감독하고 펠리샤 칼슨과 함께 주연을 맡은 〈우리의 울타리〉는 은퇴한 시애틀 트럭 운전사(해멜 씨)의 조용한 삶이 한 예술가(칼슨 씨)와 그녀의 어린 딸이 옆집으로 이사를 오며 방해받게 되는 이야기를 그린다. 이 감동적인 영화는 관객들이 가장 좋아한 영화였고 RTY 필름이 늦여름 미국 전역에 배급하기로 한 영화로 선정되었다.

192이 상은 연달아 실망스러운 흥행 성적을 내고 난 약 10년 전부터 주요 스튜디오 제작 영화에 출연을 중단했던 해멜 씨에게는 활동 복귀를 의미할 수도 있다. 그는 그때 이후 연극 작품과 작은 영화에 꾸준히 출연했지만, 〈우리의 울타리〉가 널리 인정을 받은 첫 번째 작품이다.

191벨론 극장 무대에 올라 한 수상 소감에서 해멜 씨는 홈우드 씨와 칼슨 씨, 영화제 심사위원들에게 감사를 표한 뒤 이렇게 끝맺었다. "두 번째 기회를 받은 것 같아요. 믿을 수가 없어요."

어휘 independent film 독립 영화   countless 수많은   compete 경쟁하다   costar 함께 주연으로 출연하다   interrupt 방해하다, 중단하다   moving 감동적인   distribution 배급   represent 상징하다, 나타내다   decade 10년   disappointing 실망스러운   box-office 흥행 성적   steadily 꾸준히   production 작품   widespread 광범위한   recognition 인정, 표창

http://www.all-about-movies.com/053809

홈	최근 개봉작	편집자 추천	연락처

영화에 관한 모든 것

〈우리의 울타리〉
장르: 드라마, 코미디, 가족
개봉일: 8월 31일 (전국)

상영 시간: 125분
감독: 비토미르 홈우드
195각본: 에보니 프랜시스
음악: 코리 깁슨

줄거리: 어떤 노인이 새로 온 이웃으로부터 뜻하지 않게 인생의 교훈을 얻는다.

193기타 정보: 토론토에서 촬영. 더 보기
주요 출연자:

크리스토퍼 해멜 …… 테렌스 존스		이본 파크 ………… 에바 웹	
펠리샤 칼슨 ………… 바네사 웹		라울 알비조 ……… 마르코	

전체 출연자 및 작업팀 보기

어휘 release 개봉   wide (영화가) 전국에서 개봉되는   unexpected 뜻하지 않은   trivia 사소한[기타] 정보

http://www.all-about-movies.com/053809/reviews

홈	최근 개봉작	편집자 추천	연락처

영화에 관한 모든 것

후기: 〈우리의 울타리〉

"코미디라기보다는 드라마" ★★★☆☆
194이 영화를 보러 간 이유는 TV 광고가 정말 재미있어 보였기 때문인데, 어떤 부분에서는 꽤 슬펐어요. 그래도 긍정적으로 평가할 수 있을 것 같아요. 출연진들은 대단했어요.
실비아 플로레스, 9월 3일

"전부 훌륭해요!" ★★★★☆
195크리스토퍼 해멜이 분명 영화제 상을 받을만 하지만, 전 에보니 프랜시스가 이 영화의 진정한 인재라고 생각해요. 전 꼭 그녀의 작품을 더 찾아 볼 거예요.
커트 스튜어트, 9월 1일

어휘 definitely 분명   earn (그럴 만한 자질이 되어서) 받다

191 세부 사항

번역 기사가 영화제에 관해 제공하는 정보는?
(A) 심사위원단 대표
(B) 진행 시간
(C) 개최 횟수
(D) 시상식 장소

해설 기사의 마지막 단락에서 벨론 극장 무대에 올라 한 수상 소감에서 해멜 씨는 홈우드 씨와 칼슨 씨, 영화제 심사위원들에게 감사를 표했다(During his acceptance speech onstage at the Vellon Theater, Mr. Hammell thanked ~ the festival jury)고 했으므로, 시상식 장소가 벨론 극장임을 알 수 있다. 따라서 (D)가 정답이다.

192 추론 / 암시   고난도

번역 기사는 해멜 씨가 최근 몇 년간 어떤 일을 했다고 암시하는가?
(A) 독립영화에 출연해 연기했다.
(B) 영화 제작자로 일했다.
(C) 연극 프로그램에서 학생들을 가르쳤다.
(D) 모금운동에 참여했다.

Test 2

해설 기사의 세 번째 단락에서 하멜 씨가 약 10년 전 주요 스튜디오 제작 영화에 출연을 중단했다고 한 후, 이후 연극 작품과 작은 영화에 꾸준히 출연했지만 〈우리의 울타리〉가 널리 인정을 받은 첫 번째 작품(He has worked steadily in theater productions and smaller films since that time ~ recognition)이라고 했다. 따라서 하멜 씨가 최근 몇 년간 독립영화에 출연했음을 알 수 있으므로, (A)가 정답이다.

193 연계

번역 〈우리의 울타리〉에 관해 사실인 것은?
(A) 전국 개봉이 지연되었다.
(B) 영화제가 끝난 후 단축되었다.
(C) 이야기가 벌어지는 곳에서 촬영되지 않았다.
(D) 포스터가 RTY 필름의 승인을 받지 않았다.

해설 기사의 두 번째 단락에서 〈우리의 울타리〉가 은퇴한 시애틀 트럭 운전사(해멜 씨)의 조용한 삶이 한 예술가(칼슨 씨)와 그녀의 어린 딸이 옆집으로 이사를 오며 방해받게 되는 이야기를 그린다(Our Fence tells the story of a retired Seattle truck driver who finds his quiet life interrupted ~ next door)고 했는데, 첫 번째 웹페이지의 기타 정보(Trivia) 부분을 보면 영화가 토론토에서 촬영(Filmed in Toronto)되었음을 알 수 있다. 따라서 (C)가 정답이다.

194 세부 사항

번역 플로레스 씨가 〈우리 울타리〉를 보기로 결심한 이유는?
(A) 긍정적인 관객 후기를 읽었다.
(B) 출연진 중 한 사람의 팬이다.
(C) 주제에 대해 더 알고 싶었다.
(D) 홍보물이 마음에 들었다.

해설 두 번째 웹페이지의 첫 번째 후기에서 플로레스 씨는 TV 광고가 정말 재미있어 보여서 영화를 보러 갔다(I went to see this movie because the TV commercials for it made it look really fun)고 밝혔으므로, (D)가 정답이다.

어휘 promotional materials 홍보물

▶▶ Paraphrasing 지문의 TV commercials for it
→ 정답의 its promotional materials

195 연계 고난도

번역 스튜어트 씨가 〈우리의 울타리〉에서 가장 높이 평가한 것은?
(A) 연기
(B) 감독
(C) 각본
(D) 음악

해설 두 번째 웹페이지의 두 번째 후기에서 스튜어트 씨는 에보니 프랜시스가 이 영화의 진정한 인재라고 생각한다(I think Ebony Francis is the real talent involved in this film)고 했는데, 첫 번째 웹페이지를 보면 에보니 프랜시스가 각본을 쓴 사람(Written by: Ebony Francis)임을 확인할 수 있다. 따라서 (C)가 정답이다.

어휘 appreciate 평가[인정]하다

196-200 웹페이지 + 보증서 + 이메일

http://www.gwi-insulation.com/services/sprayfoaminsulation

홈	서비스	고객 추천글	당사 정보

스프레이 폼 단열재

스프레이 폼 단열재는 가정용 단열재 중 최고가 유형이지만, 또한 더위와 추위에 맞서는 가장 강력한 방벽을 만들기도 합니다. **196당사 고객들은 설치 후 가정용 에너지 요금이 50퍼센트 이상 줄어들었다고 말했습니다.** 폼은 오픈 셀과 클로즈드 셀 두 가지 유형으로 나옵니다. 오픈 셀 폼은 저렴하고 닿기 어려운 모서리를 채우는 데 더 좋은 반면, 클로즈드 셀 폼은 극한의 온도에 맞서 더 좋은 보호막을 제공합니다. **197마틴 카운티 내에서는 두 유형 모두 자격증을 소지한 전문가가 도포해야 하며, 시에서 발급하는 작업 허가증의 경우 보벳 시에서만 요구됩니다.** 신청 절차가 하루 이상 걸리는 경우는 드뭅니다.

GWI의 스프레이 폼 단열 서비스에 대해 자세히 알아보시려면 555-0173으로 전화 또는 services@gwi-insulation.com으로 이메일을 보내세요.

어휘 testimonial 추천하는 글 insulation 단열(재) barrier 방벽, 장벽 installation 설치 open cell 개방형 (연질) closed cell 폐쇄형 (경질) protection 보호 extreme 극한의 temperature 온도 apply 도포하다, 칠하다 licensed 자격증[면허증]을 소지한 expert 전문가 permit 허가증 rarely 거의 ~하지 않는

GWI 인슐레이션

보증서

작업 정보
197GWI 인슐레이션은 소유주 앨버트 맥키의 요청에 따라 보벳 시 브루어 가 450번지에 위치한 집의 다락방에 오픈 셀 단열 폼을 설치했다.

보증 범위
GWI 인슐레이션은 설치 당시 불량품이나 잘못된 작업으로 발생하는 모든 단열재 문제에 대해 무상으로 노무와 물품을 제공해 수리한다.

198이 보증서는 구조물의 수명이 다할 때까지 유효하며 구조물의 소유권과 함께 양도될 수 있다.

제외 사항
다음 경우 GWI 인슐레이션은 단열재 문제에 대해 책임을 지지 않는다.
1. 주택 소유자 또는 다른 회사에 의해 단열재나 그 주변이 변경 또는 대체되었다.
2. 강풍, 폭우, 기타 자연현상으로 파손되었다.
3. 단열재가 부착된 표면이 구조물의 토대 혹은 벽체의 붕괴나 이동에 의해 파손되었다.
1994. 단열재가 부착된 표면에 곰팡이가 생겼거나 자연적으로 노후되었다.

릴리언 틸
GWI 인슐레이션 사장

어휘 warranty 보증(서) attic 다락(방) labor 노무 at no charge 무료로 defective 결함이 있는 valid 유효한 transfer 양도하다 responsible for ~에 책임을 지는 alter 변경하다 occurrence 현상, 발생 collapse 붕괴 mildew 흰곰팡이 mold 곰팡이

맥키 씨께,

[199]GWI 인슐래이션은 귀하가 곰팡이 문제로 다락방에 있는 기둥과 판자 일부를 교체해야 한다는 사실을 [200]알게 되어 유감스러웠습니다. [199]아쉽게도 이 상황은 보증에서 명백히 제외되는 경우에 속하므로, 귀하의 다락방 단열 시공 작업에 대한 비용을 저희 쪽에서 청구해야 합니다. 참고하시라고 보증서를 스캔해서 첨부했습니다.

설치했던 단열재의 수리 또는 교체를 위해 당사를 고용하고 싶으신지 알려주세요. 무료는 아닐지라도 좋은 가격을 제시해 드리겠습니다.

데릭 설리번
GWI 인슐레이션

어휘 beam 기둥 explicitly 명백히 exclude 제외하다 for reference 참고용으로

196 세부 사항

번역 웹페이지에 따르면 GWI 인슐레이션 고객들은 무엇을 보고했는가?
(A) 에너지 비용 절감
(B) 실내 공기질 개선
(C) 소음 공해 감소
(D) 구조물 강도 증가

해설 웹페이지의 첫 번째 단락에서 GWI 인슐레이션 고객들이 단열재 설치 후 가정용 에너지 요금이 50퍼센트 이상 줄어들었다고 말했다(Our customers have told us that their home energy bills dropped 50% or more after its installation)고 했으므로, (A)가 정답이다.

어휘 pollution 공해 structural 구조적인, 구조물의

▶▶ Paraphrasing 지문의 their home energy bills dropped 50% or more → 정답의 Lower energy costs

197 연계

번역 맥키 씨의 집에서 한 작업에 관해 암시된 것은?
(A) 지하공간에서 진행되었다.
(B) 시 정부의 허가를 받고 진행되었다.
(C) 더 비싼 유형의 스프레이 폼이 사용되었다.
(D) 완공하는 데 하루 이상 걸렸다.

해설 보증서의 작업 정보(Work Information) 부분을 보면 GWI 인슐레이션에서 앨버트 맥키의 요청에 따라 보벳 시 브루어 가 450번지에 위치한 집의 다락에 오픈 셀 단열 폼을 설치했다(GWI Insulation installed ~ located at 450 Brewer Street, Vorvett, at the request of its owner, Albert Mackie)고 했는데, 웹페이지의 첫 번째 단락에서 시에서 발급하는 작업 허가증은 보벳 시에서만 필요하다(a city permit for the work is only required in Vorvett)고 했다. 따라서 보벳 시에 있는 맥키 씨의 집이 시 정부의 허가를 받고 작업했음을 추론할 수 있으므로, (B)가 정답이다.

▶▶ Paraphrasing 지문의 a city permit
→ 정답의 a city government's permission

198 사실 관계 확인 [고난도]

번역 보증서에 관해 언급된 것은?
(A) 만기일이 있다.
(B) 맥키 씨는 이를 받기 위해 추가 비용을 지불했다.
(C) 맥키 씨가 집을 팔더라도 여전히 유효할 것이다.
(D) 수리에 필요한 제품 비용은 포함되지 않는다.

해설 보증서의 보증 범위(Coverage)를 보면, 보증서는 구조물의 수명이 다할 때까지 유효하며 구조물의 소유권과 함께 양도될 수 있다(This warranty is valid throughout the life of the structure and can be transferred along with the ownership of the structure)고 했으므로, (C)가 정답이다.

어휘 expiration 만기

▶▶ Paraphrasing 지문의 can be transferred along with the ownership of the structure
→ 정답의 still be valid even if Mr. Mackie sells the house

199 연계

번역 설리번 씨가 보증서에서 언급하는 제외 사항은?
(A) 1번 제외 사항
(B) 2번 제외 사항
(C) 3번 제외 사항
(D) 4번 제외 사항

해설 이메일의 첫 번째 단락에서 맥키 씨가 곰팡이 문제로 다락방에 있는 기둥과 판자 일부를 교체해야 한다(you will need to replace some ~ because of mold issues)는 사실을 알게 되어 유감스럽다고 한 후, 이 상황은 보증에서 명백히 제외되는 경우에 속한다(this situation is one of those explicitly excluded from your warranty)고 했다. 보증서를 보면, 이메일에서 언급된 경우는 4번 제외 사항인 '단열재가 부착된 표면에 곰팡이가 생겼거나 자연적으로 노후되었다(The surface to which it has been attached is suffering from mildew, mold, or natural aging)'에 해당하므로, (D)가 정답이다.

▶▶ Paraphrasing 지문의 one of those explicitly excluded from your warranty
→ 질문의 exclusion in the warranty

200 동의어 찾기

번역 이메일에서 1번째 단락 1행의 "learn"과 의미상 가장 가까운 것은?
(A) 숙달하다
(B) 알게 되다
(C) 외우다
(D) 경험하다

해설 'learn'이 포함된 부분은 '교체해야 한다는 사실을 알게 되어 유감이다(We ~ were sorry to learn that you will need to replace)'라는 뜻으로 해석되므로, '알게 되다, 발견하다'라는 의미의 (B) discover가 정답이다.

TEST 3

101 (A)	102 (B)	103 (B)	104 (C)	105 (A)
106 (B)	107 (C)	108 (D)	109 (C)	110 (D)
111 (A)	112 (D)	113 (A)	114 (B)	115 (D)
116 (A)	117 (D)	118 (B)	119 (D)	120 (C)
121 (D)	122 (C)	123 (A)	124 (B)	125 (D)
126 (C)	127 (B)	128 (A)	129 (C)	130 (B)
131 (C)	132 (B)	133 (A)	134 (C)	135 (A)
136 (D)	137 (C)	138 (A)	139 (D)	140 (B)
141 (C)	142 (D)	143 (B)	144 (A)	145 (B)
146 (D)	147 (D)	148 (A)	149 (D)	150 (A)
151 (B)	152 (D)	153 (D)	154 (C)	155 (C)
156 (A)	157 (D)	158 (A)	159 (D)	160 (D)
161 (B)	162 (D)	163 (A)	164 (C)	165 (D)
166 (A)	167 (A)	168 (A)	169 (D)	170 (C)
171 (B)	172 (B)	173 (D)	174 (B)	175 (C)
176 (C)	177 (A)	178 (D)	179 (C)	180 (C)
181 (D)	182 (D)	183 (B)	184 (B)	185 (C)
186 (D)	187 (A)	188 (B)	189 (D)	190 (C)
191 (C)	192 (D)	193 (B)	194 (D)	195 (A)
196 (B)	197 (C)	198 (C)	199 (A)	200 (D)

PART 5

101 부사 어휘

해설 현재완료시제를 이루는 has regretted를 가장 적절히 수식하는 부사를 선택하는 문제이다. 문맥상 '전공을 바꾼 것을 후회한 적이 없다'라는 내용이 되어야 자연스러우므로, '결코 ~않다'라는 의미의 (A) never가 정답이다. 참고로, (C) very는 부사로 쓰일 경우 형용사나 부사를 수식하며, 동사를 수식하지 못한다. (B) enough는 '충분히', (D) less는 '덜하게'라는 뜻으로, 동사 수식 시 동사 뒤에 와야 한다.

번역 이디스 스탠리는 대학 전공을 재무학에서 공학으로 바꾼 것을 결코 후회한 적이 없다고 말한다.

어휘 regret 후회하다 switch 바꾸다 major 전공

102 부사 자리 _ 동명사 수식

해설 more ~ than necessary와 함께 동명사구 closing the copy machine's lid를 수식하는 부사 자리이므로, '세게, 강력히'라는 의미의 (B) forcefully가 정답이다. (A) forceful은 형용사, (C) forcing은 동명사/현재분사, (D) force는 명사/동사로 품사상 빈칸에 들어갈 수 없다.

번역 사용자는 복사기 뚜껑을 필요 이상으로 세게 닫지 않도록 해야 한다.

어휘 avoid -ing ~하지 않도록 하다 lid 뚜껑 necessary 필요한 forceful 강력한

103 인칭대명사의 격 _ 목적격 [고난도]

해설 빈칸은 that절의 동사 would enable의 목적어 자리이다. 문맥상 커리어코치를 고용하는 것(hiring the career coach)이 Mr. Hawkins로 하여금 목표를 추구할 수 있게 해줄 것이라 희망했다는 내용이 되어야 하므로, Mr. Hawkins를 대신하는 목적격 대명사 (B) him이 정답이다. that절의 주어와 목적어가 같은 대상이 아니므로 재귀대명사 (A) himself는 정답이 될 수 없고, (C) his를 소유대명사로 보더라도 '그의 것'이라고 지칭할 만한 대상이 나오지 않았으므로 빈칸에는 적절하지 않다.

번역 호킨스 씨는 커리어코치를 고용하면 특정 목표들을 추구할 수 있으리라 희망했다.

어휘 career coach (진로 계획 등을 돕는) 커리어코치 enable ~할 수 있게 하다 pursue 추구하다

104 전치사 어휘

해설 무료 배달이 제공되는 장소(locations)와 거리의 범위를 나타내는 명사구 five miles of its store를 적절히 연결하는 전치사를 선택해야 한다. 따라서 '~ 이내에, ~ 안에'라는 의미의 (C) within이 정답이다.

번역 케사다 그릴은 매장에서 5마일 이내에 있는 장소까지는 무료 배달을 제공하지만, 더 긴 이동 거리에는 비교적 높은 수수료를 부과한다.

어휘 delivery 배달 charge 부과하다 relatively 비교적, 상대적으로

105 동사 어형 _ 태

해설 주어인 Seasonal sporting equipment and other infrequently used items의 동사 자리이다. 스포츠 장비와 어쩌다 쓰이는 물품들은 지하실에 보관되는 대상이므로, 수동태 동사인 (A) can be stored가 정답이다. 나머지 보기는 능동태 동사이므로 빈칸에 들어갈 수 없다.

번역 계절 스포츠 장비와 어쩌다 쓰이는 그 밖의 물품들은 아파트 단지 지하실에 보관 가능하다.

어휘 equipment 장비 infrequently 어쩌다, 드물게 complex 단지 basement 지하(실) store 보관하다

106 동사 어형 _ 동명사

해설 빈칸은 명사 responsibility를 목적어로 취하면서 전치사 after의 목적어 역할을 하는 자리이므로, 동명사가 들어가야 한다. 따라서 (B) assuming이 정답이다. (A) assumes, (C) assumed, (D) assume은 주어가 있어야 하므로, 빈칸에 들어갈 수 없다.

번역 공장 운영에 대한 책임을 맡은 지 단 몇 주 만에 제닝스 씨는 효율성을 높이는 변화를 만들기 시작했다.

어휘 responsibility 책임 operation 운영, 작업 increase 높이다 efficiency 효율성 assume (책임 등을) 맡다

107 부사 자리 _ 전치사구 수식 [고난도]

해설 문맥상 on time이 주격 보어 역할을 하므로, 빈칸에는 are on time을 수식하는 부사가 들어가야 한다. 따라서 '대체로, 일반적으로'라는 의미의 (C) generally가 정답이다. (A) general은 형용사, (B) generalized는 동사/과거분사, (D) generalizing은 동명사/현재분사로 품사상 빈칸에 들어갈 수 없다.

번역 연구에 따르면, 아침 출근 시간을 제외하고 시내버스는 대체로 하루 종일 제시간에 맞춰 운행된다.

어휘 be on time 시간을 잘 지키다 exception 예외 generalize
일반화하다

108 형용사 어휘

해설 빈칸은 가주어 it(=that절)을 보충 설명하는 형용사 자리이다. 확실히
입증될 수는 없지만 어떤 물건이 음식 준비에 사용되었을 것(that the
object was used in preparing food)이라고 생각한다는 내용이 되어
야 자연스러우므로, 가능성을 나타내는 (D) probable(사실일 것 같은, 있
음 직한)이 정답이다.

번역 비록 확실히 입증될 수는 없지만, 고고학자들은 그 물건이 음식을 준비하는
데 사용되었을 것이라고 생각한다.

어휘 conclusively 단정적으로, 확실히 prove 입증[증명]하다
archaeologist 고고학자 actual 실제의 functional 기능적인
usual 보통의, 흔히 있는

109 인칭대명사의 격 _ 목적격

해설 전치사 of의 목적어 역할을 하는 자리로, 보기에서 소유대명사
(A) theirs, 목적격 (C) them, 재귀대명사 (D) themselves 중 하나
를 선택해야 한다. 해당 절에서 few of ------가 were popular with
critics upon release의 주어 역할을 하는데, 발간 당시 인기가 거의 없
었던 것은 '몬타노 씨의 책'이므로, Mr. Montano's books를 대신하는
(C) them이 정답이 된다.

번역 몬타노 씨의 책을 좋아하는 오늘날의 팬들은 출간 당시 비평가들에게 인기 있
던 책이 거의 없었다는 사실을 알면 놀랄지도 모른다.

어휘 critic 비평가 release 출시, 발간

110 형용사 자리 _ 주격 보어 _ 어휘   고난도

해설 2형식 동사 remains 뒤에서 주어인 Ms. Diaz를 보충 설명하는 자
리이다. 따라서 형용사 (A) respectful, 형용사 역할을 할 수 있는
(B) respecting과 (D) respected 중 하나를 선택해야 한다. 디아즈 씨
는 투자자들 사이(among investers)에서 존경을 받는 대상이므로, 수동
의 의미를 내포한 과거분사 (D) respected가 정답이 된다.

번역 최근 주스 바 프랜차이즈가 실패했음에도 불구하고, 디아즈 씨는 디아즈 카페
로 일찍이 성공을 거둔 덕분에 여전히 투자자들 사이에서 존경 받고 있다.

어휘 in spite of ~에도 불구하고 recent 최근의 investor 투자자
respectful 존경심을 보이는, 공손한 respect 존경하다

111 부사 어휘   고난도

해설 주격 보어인 형용사 popular를 수식하는 부사 자리이다. 인기의 정도
를 묘사하는 단어가 들어가야 자연스러우므로, '이 정도로, 이렇게'라는
의미의 (A) this가 정답이다. 참고로, (B) high와 (D) much는 형용사
popular를 수식할 수 없고, (C) how는 형용사를 수식할 수 있긴 하지만
뒤에 절이 와야 한다.

번역 로스탄 빌딩은 오랫동안 헨트빌의 랜드마크로 여겨져 왔지만, 이렇게까지 인
기가 많았던 적은 없었다.

어휘 consider 여기다, 고려하다 landmark 랜드마크, 주요 지형지물

112 명사 자리 _ 전치사의 목적어 _ 어휘

해설 전치사 in의 목적어 역할을 하는 명사 자리로, 빈칸을 포함한 전치사구 in
the ------- of Leskett Avenue가 동사 proceed를 수식하고 있다. 두
도로의 교차점에서 재포장 작업을 시작해 레스켓 가 방향으로 진행할 것이
라는 내용이 되어야 자연스러우므로, '방향'이라는 의미의 (D) direction
이 정답이다.

번역 메이플 가 재포장 작업을 맡은 작업반은 힉스 로와 만나는 교차점에서 시작해
레스켓 가 방향으로 진행할 것이다.

어휘 resurface 재포장하다 intersection 교차점 proceed 진행하다
director 감독 direct 직접적인; 지시하다

113 부사절 접속사 _ 어휘

해설 완전한 절(the Boyce Eagles have reached the final round ~
several times)을 이끌어 콤마 뒤 주절을 수식하는 부사절 접속사 자리
이다. 따라서 보기에서 부사절 접속사인 (A) While과 (C) Whenever
중 하나를 선택해야 한다. 여러 번 워스컵 결승에 올랐지만 최종적으로 우
승한 적은 없다는 내용이므로, '~이긴 하지만, ~인 반면에'라는 의미의
(A) While이 정답이다. (C) Whenever는 '~할 때마다'라는 뜻으로 문맥
상 적절하지 않고, (B) Even은 형용사/부사/동사, (D) Despite는 전치사
로 완전한 절을 이끌 수 없다.

번역 보이스 이글스는 여러 번 워스컵 결승에 올랐지만 아직 우승은 하지 못했다.

어휘 reach 도달하다 manage 해내다

114 형용사 자리   고난도

해설 「how + 주어(people) + 동사(have) ~」 구조의 명사절에서 people을 뒤
에서 수식하는 형용사 자리로, 전치사구 to strong leadership과 이어
져야 한다. 사람들은 강력한 리더십에 호응하는 주체이므로, '호응하는,
반응하는'이라는 의미로 전치사 to와 함께 쓰이는 (B) responsive가 정
답이다. 참고로, responsive 앞에 주격 관계대명사와 be 동사가 생략
된 것으로 볼 수 있다. (A) respond는 동사, (C) responsively는 부사,
(D) responded는 동사/과거분사로 품사상 빈칸에 들어갈 수 없다.

번역 〈조직심리학〉에 실린 백 박사의 논문은 강력한 리더십에 호응하는 사람들이
어떻게 수평 구조의 직장에서 어려움을 겪는지 설명한다.

어휘 organizational 조직의 psychology 심리(학) horizontally
수평으로 respond 호응하다, 반응하다 responsively 호응하며

115 to부정사 _ 「to + 동사원형」

해설 빈칸 앞에 완전한 절이 왔고 뒤에 동사원형 abide가 있으며, 해당 부분
이 '준수하는 데 동의'라는 뜻을 나타낸다. 따라서 to부정사의 (D) to가 정
답이다. (A) with, (B) through, (C) regarding은 모두 전치사로 뒤에
(동)명사가 와야 한다.

번역 서명은 이 계약서의 조건을 준수하는 데 동의한다는 것을 의미한다.

어휘 signature 서명 indicate 의미하다, 나타내다 abide by 준수하다
terms (계약) 조건 contract 계약(서)

116 동사 어형_태_수 일치

해설 복수 주어인 special bins의 동사 자리로, 빈칸에는 복수 동사가 들어가야 한다. 쓰레기통(bins)은 비치되는 대상이므로, 수동태 복수 동사인 (A) have been placed가 정답이다.

번역 오늘부로 다 쓴 건전지 폐기를 위한 특별 쓰레기통이 시의 모든 공공 도서관 앞에 비치되었다.

어휘 as of ~부로 bin 쓰레기통 disposal 폐기

117 전치사 어휘

해설 명사구 the latest market report와 뒤에 오는 절을 적절히 연결하는 전치사를 선택하는 문제이다. '최근에 나온 시장 보고서'는 화장품 산업 (cosmetics industry)이 성장할 것이라는 전망이 언급된 출처이므로, '~에 따르면'이라는 의미의 (D) According to가 정답이다.

번역 최근에 나온 시장 보고서에 따르면, 화장품 산업은 소득 수준 상승에 힘입어 계속 성장할 것이다.

어휘 cosmetics 화장품 industry 산업, 업계 continue to 계속 ~하다 expand 성장하다 thanks to ~에 힘입어 growth 상승, 성장 income 소득 except for ~을 제외하고 in addition to ~에 더하여

118 동사 어휘

해설 빈칸은 주어 Our negotiator의 동사 자리로, 「동사＋목적어(Silmond Software)＋목적격 보어(to discount its service)」의 5형식 구조로 쓰일 수 있는 동사가 들어가야 한다. 또한 문맥상 실몬드 소프트웨어의 서비스 할인을 이끌어 내기 위한 협상가의 역할을 나타내는 동사여야 하므로, '~를 설득하여 ~하게 하다, 납득시키다'라는 의미의 (B) persuaded가 정답이다.

번역 우리 측 협상가는 실몬드 소프트웨어를 설득해 긍정적인 고객 추천글을 받는 대가로 서비스를 할인해 주도록 만들었다.

어휘 negotiator 협상가 in exchange for ~의 대가로 testimonial 추천글 argue 주장하다 assure 장담하다 settle 해결하다

119 주격 보어 자리_과거분사

해설 빈칸은 that절의 동사 is 뒤에서 주어 telecommuting을 설명하는 주격 보어 자리로, 명사 또는 형용사가 들어갈 수 있다. 재택근무(tele-commuting)는 허용되는 대상이므로, 수동의 의미를 내포한 과거분사 (D) permitted(허용된)가 정답이 된다. (A) permit은 명사로 쓰일 경우 '허가증'이라는 뜻의 가산 명사가 되고, (C) permission은 '허락'이라는 의미로 telecommuting과 동격 관계를 이루지 않으므로 빈칸에 적절하지 않다.

번역 제랄트 사 직원들은 재택근무가 허용되고 온라인 일정 시스템을 통해 매우 쉽게 일정을 정할 수 있다는 것에 고마워한다.

어휘 appreciate 고마워하다, 환영하다 telecommuting 재택근무 via ~을 통해 arrange 준비하다, 정하다

120 명사 어휘

해설 과거분사 reduced와 전치사구 of heart disease의 수식을 받는 명사

자리로, '차를 많이 마시는 사람이 심장병에 걸릴 위험이 적다'라는 내용이 되어야 자연스럽다. 따라서 '위험, 위험 요소'라는 의미의 (C) risk가 정답이다.

번역 차를 자주 마시는 사람은 심장병에 걸릴 위험이 적다는 증거가 있다.

어휘 evidence 증거 regular 잦은 reduce 줄이다 disease 병 treatment 치료 progress 진전 risk 위험 (요소) diagnosis 진단

121 부사 어휘 [고난도]

해설 동사 offered를 수식하는 자리이므로, 고객의 항의에 대해 호텔 매니저가 해결책을 제시하는 태도 또는 방식을 적절히 묘사하는 부사가 들어가야 한다. 따라서 '흔쾌히, 선뜻'이라는 의미의 (D) readily가 정답이다.

번역 우리 직원이 그 문제에 대해 항의하자 호텔 매니저는 그녀를 더 좋은 방으로 업그레이드해 주겠다고 흔쾌히 제의했다.

어휘 complain 항의[불평]하다 greatly 대단히 collectively 통틀어 randomly 무작위로

122 명사 자리_to부정사의 목적어 [고난도]

해설 가산명사 passenger 앞에 한정사가 없으므로, 빈칸에는 passenger와 복합명사를 이루어 to ensure의 목적어 역할을 하는 명사가 들어가야 한다. 따라서 '안락함, 편안함'이라는 의미의 불가산명사 (C) comfort가 정답이다. (A) comforting은 동명사/분사, (B) comfortable은 형용사, (D) comfortably는 부사로 품사상 빈칸에 들어갈 수 없다.

번역 에어 프리메라는 승객의 안락함을 보장하기 위해 항공기에 더 넓어진 다리 공간을 제공하기 시작할 것이다.

어휘 increased 늘어난 leg room 다리를 뻗는 공간 comfortable 안락한 comfort 안락함; 안락하게 하다

123 형용사 어휘 [고난도]

해설 「to make＋목적어(the medical industry's pricing)＋목적격 보어」 구조에서 목적격 보어 역할을 하는 형용사 자리이다. 해당 부분이 병원비를 온라인으로 공표하도록 한 법의 취지를 설명해야 하므로, '의료산업의 가격 책정이 더 투명해지게끔 만들기 위해'라는 내용이 되어야 자연스럽다. 따라서 '투명한, 명료한'이라는 의미의 (A) transparent가 정답이다.

번역 병원비를 온라인으로 공표하도록 한 법은 의료산업의 가격 책정을 환자들에게 더 투명하게 공개하기 위한 것이다.

어휘 publish 공표하다 be intended to ~하도록 의도되다 patient 환자 equivalent 동등한 adequate 적절한 knowledgeable 박식한

124 명사 어휘

해설 소감 발표의 기회(the opportunity to make remarks)는 수상이 전제되어야 하므로, 빈칸이 포함된 부분은 '상을 받으며'라는 내용이 되어야 자연스럽다. 따라서 전치사 in 및 of와 함께 '~을 수락하는'이라는 의미를 완성하는 (B) acceptance가 정답이다.

번역 연회 동안 레일터 상 수상자는 소개된 후 상을 받으며 소감을 말할 기회를 얻는다.

어휘 recipient 수상자 opportunity 기회 make remarks 말하다
honor 상, 영예 reaction 반응 gratitude 감사 analysis 분석

125 동사 어휘　고난도

해설 주어인 they(=Our training courses)의 동사 자리로, 빈칸에는 전치사 with와 어울려 쓰이는 자동사가 들어가야 한다. 문맥상 교육 과정은 특정 요건(requirements)에 부합해야 하므로, with와 함께 '~에 부합하다, ~와 (취지를) 나란히 하다'라는 의미를 완성하는 (D) align이 정답이다. 참고로, align은 '일직선으로 하다, 조정하다'라는 의미의 타동사로도 쓰인다. (A) collaborate도 with와 어울려 쓰이는 자동사이지만, '~와 협업 하다'라는 뜻으로 문맥상 적절하지 않다.

번역 당사 교육 과정은 인력 요건에 부합하도록 계속 업데이트된다.

어휘 constantly 계속 requirement 요건 workforce 인력 collaborate 협업하다 implement 시행하다 equip 장비를 갖추다

126 관계대명사 _ 주격

해설 주어가 없는 불완전한 절(displays pictures taken by the trade show's attendees)을 이끄는 접속사 자리로, 빈칸이 이끄는 절이 명 사구 a video screen을 수식한다. 따라서 빈칸에는 사물 명사(video screen)를 대신하는 주격 관계대명사가 들어가야 하므로, (C) that이 정답이다. (A) whose는 소유격 관계대명사로 뒤에 명사가 와야 하고, (B) just는 부사/형용사, (D) of는 전치사로 절을 이끌 수 없다.

번역 프로스트 애그리컬처의 부스에는 무역 박람회 참석자들이 찍은 사진들을 보여 주는 영상 스크린이 있다.

어휘 agriculture 농업 feature 특별히 포함하다, 특징을 이루다 attendee 참석자

127 명사 어휘　고난도

해설 동사구 must demonstrate의 목적어 역할을 하는 명사 자리이다. 따라 서 빈칸에는 개인정보를 처리하는 데 있어서(in handling the private information) 인사 담당자가 보여주어야 하는 자세를 나타내는 단어가 들어가야 자연스러우므로, '신중함, 분별'이라는 의미의 (B) discretion이 정답이다.

번역 인사 담당자는 동료의 개인정보를 처리하는 데 있어서 신중함을 보여야 한다.

어휘 demonstrate 보여주다 handle 처리하다 prosperity 번영 consensus 합의 aspiration 열망

128 명사 자리 _ 전치사의 목적어 _ 어휘

해설 명사 language와 함께 복합명사를 이루어 전치사 of의 목적어 역할을 하 는 명사 자리이다. 프로그램이 50시간 동안 제공할 만한 것은 '언어 교육' 이므로, (A) instruction(교육, 가르침)이 정답이다.

번역 일본 체류에 대비해 JFLT 프로그램은 참가자들에게 50시간의 일본어 교육 을 제공한다.

어휘 in preparation for ~에 대비해 participant 참가자 instructed 교육을 받은 instructive 교육적인, 유익한 instructor 강사

129 동사 어휘　고난도

해설 명사 construction을 목적어로 취하는 동사 자리로, 공사 과정과 연관 된 동사가 들어가야 한다. 문맥상 필요한 승인을 모두 받으면(when all necessary approvals have been obtained) 공사를 시작할 것이 라는 내용이 되어야 자연스러우므로, '시작하다, 개시하다'라는 의미의 (C) commence가 정답이다.

번역 고인스 사는 필요한 승인을 모두 받으면 건물 공사를 시작할 것이다.

어휘 construction 공사 approval 승인 obtain 얻다 redeem 보완하다 exercise 행사하다 maneuver 조종하다

130 형용사 어휘　고난도

해설 명사 effect를 수식하는 형용사 자리로, 수익 감소(The decrease in Sparont's revenues)라는 결과(effect)를 적절히 묘사하는 단어가 들어 가야 한다. 수익 감소는 주력 상품의 수요 감소(a drop in demand for ~ its chief product)에 따라 자연스럽게 일어난 결과이므로, '불가피한, 당연한'이라는 의미의 (B) inevitable이 정답이다.

번역 스파론트의 수익 감소는 주력 제품인 디지털 카메라의 수요 감소에 따른 불가 피한 결과다.

어휘 decrease 감소 revenue 수익 effect 결과, 영향 demand 수요 scarce 부족한 competent 유능한 cooperative 협동하는

PART 6

131-134 기사

1,000번째 주간 정원 청소 행사 여는 그라운즈워크

비영리 단체인 그라운즈워크가 이번 주 토요일인 9월 8일에 슐러 파크에서 1,000번째 주간 정원 청소 행사를 연다.

그라운즈워크는 지역 환경보호 활동가들에 의해 ¹³¹설립된 이후 멜린 카운티 주민들의 자연 사랑 정신을 고취하기 위해 노력해왔다. ¹³²이 단체에서 거의 매 주 주말 슐러 파크에 ¹³²보내는 열정적인 자원봉사자들이 이러한 활동의 중심 이 된다. 공원 직원들의 감독 하에 그들은 19년 넘게 쓰레기를 줍고 식물 관리 업무를 돕고 있다. 이 단체는 또한 정기적으로 모든 연령대를 대상으로 도보 여 행 및 자연과 관련된 주제의 수업을 진행한다.

그라운즈워크는 토요일 청소 이후 파티를 열어 이 ¹³³중요한 시점을 기념할 계 획이다. ¹³⁴거기에는 음악, 가족용 게임, 다과 등이 포함된다. 참석하고 싶은 사 람은 웹사이트 www.groundswork.org을 방문해 더 자세한 정보를 얻을 수 있다.

어휘 nonprofit 비영리의 organization 단체 conservationist 환경보호 활동가, 환경보존 운동가 strive to ~하려고 노력하다 promote 고취하다 resident 주민 enthusiastic 열성적인 effort (특정 목적을 위한) 활동, 노력 oversee 감독[관리]하다 trash 쓰레기 celebrate 기념하다 attend 참석하다

131 (동)명사 어휘

해설 빈칸은 소유격 Its(=Groundsworks's) 및 전치사구 by a group of local conservationists의 수식을 받는 (동)명사 자리이다. 뒤에 언급된 활동 내용(Groundswork has strived to promote a love of nature among ~ residents)으로 미루어 보아, 해당 부분은 '그라운즈워크의 설립 이래'라는 내용이 되어야 자연스럽다. 따라서 '설립, 창립'을 뜻하는 (C) founding이 정답이다.

어휘 grant 주다 achieve 달성하다 join 합류하다

132 관계대명사의 생략 [고난도]

해설 The enthusiastic volunteers ~ every weekend가 주어, are가 동사, a major part 이하가 보어인 문장으로, 빈칸부터 every weekend까지가 volunteers를 수식하는 형용사 역할을 하고 있다. 따라서 본동사 역할을 하는 (A) have been sent 및 (D) are sending을 제외하고, 목적격 관계대명사가 생략된 (B) it sends와 주격 관계대명사로 시작하는 (C) that send 중 하나를 선택해야 한다. 타동사인 send 뒤에 목적어가 아닌 전치사 to가 왔으며, 그라운즈워크가 공원에 자원봉사자들을 보낸다는 내용이 되어야 하므로, (B) it sends가 정답이 된다.

133 명사 어휘 [고난도]

해설 빈칸은 to celebrate의 목적어 역할을 하는 명사 자리이다. 기사의 제목 및 초반부에서 주간 정원 청소 행사가 1,000번째에 달했다고 했으므로, 그라운즈워크에서 파티를 열어 이 업적을 기념하려는 것임을 알 수 있다. 따라서 '중요한 시점, 획기적인 사건'이라는 의미의 (A) milestone이 정답이다.

어휘 acquisition 인수 improvement 개선 decision 결정

134 문맥에 맞는 문장 고르기

번역 (A) 입회 신청은 1년 내내 받는다.
(B) 사실 모든 공원 행사에는 청소 계획이 제출되어야 한다.
(C) 거기에는 음악, 가족용 게임, 다과 등이 포함된다.
(D) 찬 시장은 소셜 미디어에 축하까지 올렸다.

해설 빈칸 앞 문장에서 그라운즈워크가 토요일 청소 이후 기념 파티를 열 계획(Groundswork plans to celebrate the milestone with a party after Saturday's clean-up)이라고 했고, 뒤에서 파티 관련 정보를 얻는 방법(Those interested in attending should visit its Web site ~ for more information)을 제시했으므로, 빈칸에도 파티와 관련된 내용이 들어가야 문맥상 자연스럽다. 따라서 (C)가 정답이다. 참고로, (C)의 It은 a party를 대신한다.

어휘 application 신청 submit 제출하다 refreshments 다과 congratulatory 축하하는

135-138 이메일

발신: 이마니 잭슨
수신: 토비 오르테가
제목: 접수담당자 지원자

날짜: 4월 2일
첨부 파일: 지원자 스프레드시트

안녕하세요 토비,

기억하시겠지만 접수담당자 지원 기간이 지난주 금요일에 끝났어요. 50명이 넘는 사람들의 이력서를 받았다는 소식을 전하게 되어 기쁘네요! 135그 구직 웹사이트에 광고를 올린 게 확실히 효과가 있었어요.

아무튼 당신이 말한 요건에 따라 후보군을 좁혔고, 첨부된 스프레드시트에 유망 후보 상위 10명에 대해 136설명이 되어 있어요. 시간 있을 때 파일을 137검토하고 면접하고 싶은 사람을 고르세요. 138가능하면 광고에 명시된 일정표를 지켜 이번 주부터 전화를 거는 게 좋을 것 같아요.

더 필요한 게 있으면 알려 주세요.

이마니

어휘 job candidate 구직자 narrow down 좁히다 in accordance with ~에 따라 requirement 요건 specify (구체적으로) 말하다, 명시하다 prospect 유망한 후보자

135 문맥에 맞는 문장 고르기

번역 (A) 그 구직 웹사이트에 광고를 올린 게 확실히 효과가 있었어요.
(B) 그런데 그게 저희가 귀하의 지원서에 즉시 응답할 수 없었던 이유예요.
(C) 어쨌든 4월 말까지 10개의 공석을 모두 채우는 게 그리 어렵지 않을 것 같아요.
(D) 다음 주에 마크가 시간이 있어서 하나하나 검토하는 일을 도와준다니 다행이에요.

해설 빈칸 앞 문장에서 50명이 넘는 사람들의 이력서를 받았다는 소식을 전하게 되어 기쁘다(I'm happy to report that we received résumés from more than 50 people)고 했으므로, 빈칸에 이와 관련된 내용이 이어져야 자연스럽다. 따라서 많은 이력서를 받게 된 경위를 설명한 (A)가 정답이다. (D)도 이력서와 관련된 내용이기는 하나, 바로 뒷부분에서 후보군을 좁혔다고 했으므로 정답이 될 수 없다.

어휘 make a difference 차이를 만들다, 효과가 있다 promptly 즉시

136 동사 어형 _ 태

해설 주어 the top ten prospects의 동사 자리이므로, 본동사인 (A) have described와 (D) are described 중 하나를 선택해야 한다. 유망 후보 상위 10명은 스프레드시트에 설명되는 대상이므로, 수동태 동사 (D) are described가 정답이다.

어휘 describe 설명하다, 묘사하다

137 동사 어휘

해설 문맥상 유망 후보 상위 10명 중 면접하고 싶은 사람을 고르기(choose the people you would like to interview) 전에 해야 할 행동을 나타내는 동사가 빈칸에 들어가야 한다. 따라서 '파일을 검토하다'라는 의미를 완성하는 (C) look over가 정답이다.

어휘 pass up 거절하다, (기회를) 놓치다 call for 요구하다 turn around 돌다, 회전시키다

138 접속부사

해설 빈칸 앞 문장에서 면접하고 싶은 사람을 선택해달라(choose the people you would like to interview)고 요청했고, 뒤에서는 광고에 명시된 일정표를 지키는 게 좋을 것 같다(we should follow the timetable stated in the ad)고 제안했다. 따라서 빈칸에는 요청과 관련된 제안을 할 때 쓰이는 표현이 들어가야 자연스러우므로, '가능하면'이라는 의미의 (A) If possible이 정답이다.

어휘 instead 대신 therefore 그러므로 in particular 특히

139-142 편지

로릴 카운티 유료도로청
메인 가 430번지, 칼슨, 버지니아 22432

4월 10일
멜바 그레이브스
프랭클린 레인 108번지
칼슨, 버지니아 22433

그레이브스 씨께,

귀하 명의로 등록된 차량이 4월 2일에 냅 유료도로를 사용했으므로 이 편지를 받으시는 겁니다. 차량이 로릴 카운티의 전자 요금 징수 시스템(ETCS)에 등록되어 있지 않아, 이 행위는 카운티 법률을 위반입니다. 동봉된 **139청구서**를 참조하세요. 여기에 청구된 금액은 5월 2일까지 지불되어야 합니다. **140그때**까지 대금이 납부되지 않으면 경우 추가 요금이 부과된다는 점에 유의하세요.

또한 추후에 다시 유료도로를 이용하실 것 같으면, ETCS에 등록하시기를 적극 권장합니다. **141상기 주소로 저희 사무실에 방문하시면 할 수 있습니다.** 등록은 무료이며 이런 문제가 **142더** 발생하는 것을 방지할 것입니다.

착오로 이 통지를 받았다고 생각하면 이 페이지 뒷면의 지침에 따라 이의를 제기하세요.

동봉

어휘 toll road 유료도로 register 등록하다 enroll 등록하다 violation 위반 enclosed 동봉된 requested 요청된, 청구된 charge 부과하다 additional 추가의 suggest 제안하다 prevent 방지하다 in error 착오로, 실수로 instruction 지침 dispute 이의를 제기하다

---

139 명사 어휘

해설 과거분사 enclosed의 수식을 받는 명사 자리이다. 카운티 법률을 위반(a violation of county law)하여 발급되었으며 금액(The amount requested on it)이 명시되어 있고 편지에 동봉할 만한 서류를 나타내는 단어가 빈칸에 들어가야 하므로, '청구서, 송장'이라는 의미의 (A) invoice가 정답이다.

어휘 photograph 사진 manual 설명서 license 면허(증)

140 (대)명사 어휘 [고난도]

해설 대금이 납부되지 않으면(if your payment has not been received) 추가 요금이 부과된다는 내용이므로, 빈칸이 포함된 전치사구는 앞 문장에서 언급한 지불 기한(May 2)을 대신하는 시간 표현이 되어야 자연스럽다. 따라서 '그때'라는 의미의 (B) then이 정답이다.

141 문맥에 맞는 문장 고르기

번역 (A) 통행료 징수금은 도로 유지 작업에 쓰입니다.
(B) 그것은 기타 인근 지역의 교통 체증도 완화시켰습니다.
(C) 상기 주소로 저희 사무실에 방문하시면 할 수 있습니다.
(D) 차량 내 장치는 매번 전자신호를 전송합니다.

해설 빈칸 앞 문장에서 ETCS에 등록하기를 적극 권장한다(we strongly suggest that you enroll in the ETCS)고 했고, 뒤 문장에서는 등록이 무료(Enrollment is free)라고 했으므로, 빈칸에도 ETCS 등록과 관련된 내용이 들어가야 문맥상 자연스럽다. 따라서 등록 방법(by visiting our office at the address above)을 언급한 (C)가 정답이다.

어휘 upkeep 유지(비) congestion 체증 transmit 전송하다

142 형용사 어휘 [고난도]

해설 명사 issues를 적절히 수식하는 형용사를 선택하는 문제이다. 앞에서 언급한 ETCS 등록(you enroll in the ETCS) 목적은 비슷한 문제(issues of this sort)가 추가로 발생하는 것을 방지하기 위함이므로, '더 이상의, 추가의'라는 의미의 (D) further가 정답이다.

어휘 total 총, 전체의 identical 똑같은 valuable 귀중한

143-146 정보문

정보 검증

기고자가 전문가가 아닐 수도 있는 오픈 소스 온라인 백과사전으로서, 칼훈 과학 백과사전은 정보 검증을 **143중요하게** 생각합니다. 기고자들은 백과사전 항목에 추가하는 **144모든** 내용의 출처를 명시해야 합니다. 이렇게 하려면 각주 링크를 텍스트 내 관련 부분에 첨부하고 연결된 각주에 필요한 모든 정보를 제공하십시오. (각주 형식에 대한 자세한 내용은 이 페이지를 참조) 출처는 신뢰할 수 있고 전문가에 의해 출간된 것이어야 합니다. **145학술지 논문과 교과서 등이 이상적인 예입니다.** 이러한 출처를 언급한 각주가 첨부되지 않은 내용은 **146삭제되어야** 합니다. 삭제 이유는 다른 사람이 확인할 수 있도록 해당 항목의 토론 페이지에서 설명되어야 합니다. 마지막으로, 신뢰할 수 있는 출처들 간에 서로 내용이 다를 경우, 기고자는 모든 측면의 입장에 대해 중립적으로 설명해야 합니다.

어휘 verification 검증 open-source 오픈 소스, 무상으로 공개된 encyclopedia 백과사전 contributor 기고자 expert 전문가 specify 명시하다 append 첨부[추가]하다 footnote 각주 relevant 관련 있는 reliable 믿을 수 있는 accompany 첨부하다 cite (인용의) 출처를 밝히다, 언급하다 removal 삭제 trustworthy 신뢰할 수 있는 neutral 중립적인 account 설명, 기술

143 부사 자리 _ 동사 수식

해설 빈칸이 「주어(Calhoun Science Encyclopedia)+동사(takes)+ 목적어(the verification of information)」의 완전한 절 뒤에 있으므로, 빈칸에는 동사 takes를 수식하는 부사가 들어가야 한다. 따라서 '심각하게, 중요하게'라는 의미의 (B) seriously가 정답이다. 참고로, 여기서 take는 '(특정 방식으로) 생각하다, 받아들이다'라는 뜻을 나타내며, 목적어 뒤에 주로 부사나 전치사구를 동반한다. (A) serious와 (D) more serious는 형용사, (C) seriousness는 명사로 품사상 빈칸에 들어갈 수 없다.

144 한정사 어휘

해설 문맥상 '백과사전 항목에 추가하는 모든 내용의 출처를 명시해야 한다'라는 내용이 되어야 자연스러우므로, '어떤 ~라도(=무엇이든), 모든'이라는 의미의 (A) any가 정답이다.

145 문맥에 맞는 문장 고르기　　고난도

번역 (A) 후자의 주장은 추가 검증이 필요합니다.
(B) 학술지 논문과 교과서 등이 이상적인 예입니다.
(C) 그렇지 않으면, 인용문은 출판 저작권을 침해할 수 있습니다.
(D) 여기에는 제목, 저자, 출판사 및 날짜가 포함됩니다.

해설 앞 문장에서 출처는 신뢰할 수 있고 전문가에 의해 출판된 것이어야 한다(Sources must be reliable and professionally published)고 했고, 뒤에서는 이러한 출처를 언급한 각주가 포함되지 않은 내용(Content that is not accompanied by a footnote citing such a source)을 언급했으므로, 빈칸에는 이러한 출처에 대한 부연 설명이 들어가야 자연스럽다. 따라서 유효한 출처의 구체적인 예를 제시한 (B)가 정답이다.

어휘 quotation 인용(문)

146 동사 어휘

해설 주어인 Content that is not accompanied by a footnote citing such a source를 보충 설명하는 과거분사를 선택하는 문제이다. 뒤에서 해당 항목의 토론 페이지에 삭제 이유(The reason for the removal)가 설명되어야 한다고 했으므로, '이러한 출처를 언급한 각주가 첨부되지 않은 내용'은 삭제 대상임을 알 수 있다. 따라서 '삭제되는'이라는 의미의 과거분사 (D) deleted가 정답이다.

어휘 highlight 강조하다　reorganize 재편성하다　condense 압축하다

PART 7

147-148 공지

> **가로수 전지작업 공지**
>
> 6월 28~29일 오전 8시에서 오후 5시 사이에 거리에 있는 나무들을 전지할 예정입니다. 거리 위 13피트 이하, 보도 위 8피트 이하의 높이에 매달린 나뭇가지들은 다듬거나 제거될 것입니다.

> [147]도튼 공원부는 나무들의 구조적 안정성을 높이고 가지가 부러지면서 발생할 지 모르는 손상으로부터 나무들을 보호하기 위해 정기적으로 도시 공원 및 인근 거리에서 이 작업을 수행합니다. [148]해당 작업이 적절하게 이루어지도록 공인된 나무 관리 전문가가 작업반을 감독합니다.
>
> 이들 날짜에는 사유 차도나 다른 거리에 주차하여 해당 거리를 비워주세요. 또한 전지 기계에서 발생하는 시끄러운 소음과 관련해 양해를 구합니다.

어휘 trim 전지하다, 다듬다　remove 제거하다　regularly 정기적으로　perform 수행하다　adjacent 인근의, 인접한　structural 구조적인　stability 안정성　certified 공인된　professional 전문가; 전문가의　supervise 감독하다, 관리하다　properly 적절하게　automobile 자동차　driveway 사유 차도, (차고까지의) 진입로

147 세부 사항

번역 나무를 다듬는 이유는?
(A) 주민의 자동차를 보호하기 위해
(B) 전선 손상을 방지하기 위해
(C) 나무의 외관을 개선하기 위해
(D) 나무의 건강을 유지하기 위해

해설 두 번째 단락에서 도튼 공원부는 나무들의 구조적 안정성을 높이고 가지가 부러지면서 발생할 지 모르는 손상으로부터 나무들을 보호하기 위해 전지 작업을 수행한다(The Dawston Parks Department regularly performs this work(=trimming) ~ in order to improve the trees' structural stability and protect them from damage)고 했으므로, (D)가 정답이다.

어휘 prevent 방지하다　appearance 외관

▸▸ **Paraphrasing** 지문의 improve the trees' structural stability and protect them from damage → 정답의 maintain their well-being

148 세부 사항

번역 공지에 따르면 시는 어떻게 작업이 잘되도록 할 것인가?
(A) 전문가가 감독하도록 해서
(B) 시민들의 의견을 수용해서
(C) 여러 작업반을 보내서
(D) 특수한 기계를 사용해서

해설 두 번째 단락에서 공인된 나무 관리 전문가가 작업이 적절하게 이루어지도록 작업반을 감독한다(A certified tree care professional supervises our crew to make certain that the work is done properly)고 했으므로, (A)가 정답이다.

어휘 expert 전문가　incorporate 수용하다, 포함하다

▸▸ **Paraphrasing** 지문의 make certain that the work is done properly → 질문의 ensure the work is done well

지문의 A certified tree care professional supervises our crew → 정답의 having an expert monitor it

149-150 영수증

```
                배리 서점 4호점
                  퍼 가 47번지
            센트럴시티, 일리노이 61087
                   555-0161

149(C)매장 번호: 4      계산대 번호: 3      계산원: 케이트 G.
149(B)카드: 배리 고객보상 클럽 회원        만료: 5월 11일

책: 〈뭄바이의 유산〉                        26달러
   10% 회원카드 할인(-2.6)           → 23.4달러

잡지: 〈월간 영화〉                          7달러
   10% 회원카드 할인(-0.7)            → 6.3달러

                          판매 소계      29.7달러

고객 특별 주문 #1127            * 추후 매장에서 수령
                               * 알림 방법: 문자 메시지

책: 〈대담한 건축〉                          34달러
150판촉 2848 - 50% 할인(-17)        → 17달러
   10% 회원카드 할인(-1.7)          → 15.3달러

                        특별 주문 소계    15.3달러

                          총액          45달러
                          현금 지불       50달러
                          거스름          5달러

149(D)매장 내 카페를 방문하세요 – 정규 매장 영업시간에 문을 엽니다
구입 날짜/시간: 3월 7일 오후 4시 9분
```

어휘 register (금전) 등록기, 계산대 expire 만료되다 heritage 유산 bold 대담한 architecture 건축 purchase 구매(품)

---

149 사실 관계 확인

번역 배리 서점에 관해 영수증에서 알 수 없는 것은?
(A) 한정된 기간 동안만 반품을 받는다.
(B) 고객보상 프로그램이 있다.
(C) 매장이 두 개 이상이다.
(D) 카페를 운영하고 있다.

해설 영수증 상단의 '카드: 배리 고객보상 클럽 회원(Card: Barry's Loyalty Club Member)'에서 (B)를, '매장 번호: 4(Store number: 4)'에서 (C)를, 하단의 '매장 내 카페를 방문하세요(Visit our in-store café)'에서 (D)를 확인할 수 있다. 따라서 언급되지 않은 (A)가 정답이다.

▶▶ Paraphrasing   지문의 Barry's Loyalty Club Member
→ 보기 (B)의 a customer loyalty program
지문의 Store number: 4
→ 보기 (C)의 It has more than one store
지문의 our in-store café
→ 보기 (D)의 It ~ operates a café

---

150 사실 관계 확인

번역 영수증에 따르면 〈대담한 건축〉에 관해 사실인 것은?
(A) 온라인에서만 구매할 수 있다.
(B) 판촉의 일환이었다.
(C) 전화로 주문되었다.
(D) 직원 추천이었다.

해설 특별 주문 항목인 〈대담한 건축〉(Book: *Bold Architecture*) 아래에 '판촉 2848 - 50% 할인(Promotion 2848 - 50% off)'이라고 표시되어 있으므로, (B)가 정답이다.

어휘 recommendation 추천

▶▶ Paraphrasing   지문의 Promotion 2848 - 50% off
→ 정답의 a sales promotion

151-152 문자 메시지

조디 로드리게스 (오후 1시 43분) 그래디, 지금 공사 현장에 있어요?
그래디 웹 (오후 1시 44분) 예, 북쪽 편에 와서 전기팀과 얘기하고 있어요. 무슨 일이죠?
조디 로드리게스 (오후 1시 44분) RBX80을 올려 보내도 괜찮은지 확인하고 싶어서요.
그래디 웹 (오후 1시 45분) RBX80이요? 151미안하지만 그게 뭔지 모르겠어요.
조디 로드리게스 (오후 1시 46분) 오, 새로운 기술이에요. 카메라가 장착된 드론 항공기예요. 그걸 건물 외부 주변으로 날려 지금까지 올려놓은 벽에 문제가 없는지 확인할 거예요.
그래디 웹 (오후 1시 47분) 아, 그렇군요. 괜찮을 거예요. 152하지만 보려고 하는 층에서 작업하고 있는 팀에게 미리 알려 주세요. 특히 높은 층이요. 그들을 놀라게 하면 위험할지도 몰라요.
조디 로드리게스 (오후 1시 48분) 지금 팀장들에게 단체 문자를 보낼게요.

어휘 construction site 공사 현장 equipped with ~을 장착한 advance notice 사전통보, 미리 알림 especially 특히

---

151 의도 파악

번역 오후 1시 46분에 로드리게스 씨가 "새로운 기술이에요"라고 쓸 때 의미하는 것은?
(A) 그녀는 RBX80이 잘 작동한다고 장담할 수 없다.
(B) 웹 씨가 RBX80에 대해 잘 모르는 것을 이해할 수 있다.
(C) 오늘은 과거에 발생한 문제를 피할 것이다.
(D) 그녀의 팀은 절차를 준비할 시간이 필요할 것이다.

해설 웹 씨가 오후 1시 45분 메시지에서 RBX80이 뭔지 모르겠다(I don't know what that is)고 했는데, 이에 대해 로드리게스 씨가 '새로운 기술이에요(it's a new technology)'라고 응답한 것이므로, 웹 씨가 RBX80에 대해 모를만 하다는 의도로 쓴 메시지임을 알 수 있다. 따라서 (B)가 정답이다.

어휘 unfamiliarity 잘 모름, 생소함 understandable 이해할 수 있는 occur 발생하다 avoid 피하다 procedure 절차

152 추론 / 암시

번역 건설 중인 건물에 관해 암시된 것은?
(A) 둥근 모양이다.
(B) 벽돌 벽이 있다.
(C) 공항에 있다.
(D) 높을 것이다.

해설 웹 씨가 오후 1시 47분 메시지에서 드론을 날리려면 각 층에서 작업하고 있는 팀에게 미리 알리라(please give advance notice to the teams that are working on any of the floors)고 한 후, '특히 높은 층(especially the high ones)'에 그래야 한다며 한 번 더 강조했다. 따라서 건설 중인 건물이 높다는 것을 추론할 수 있으므로, (D)가 정답이다.

153-154 광고

> **포랜스 컴퍼니**
> 알림: 블루 스카이 라인 인사 카드
>
> [153]루퍼스 포랜스가 70여년 전 라이프스타일 잡지를 발행하기 위해 포랜스 컴퍼니를 시작했을 때, 그는 어떻게 될지 상상하지 못했습니다. 루퍼스는 인쇄기를 통해 추가로 수익을 얻기 위해 인사 카드를 만들기 시작했습니다. [153]그러나 잡지 담당 아티스트들이 디자인한 카드는 순식간에 성공을 거두었고, 루퍼스는 곧 오로지 카드에만 집중하기로 결정했습니다. 이후 포랜스 컴퍼니는 국내에서 아름답고 사려 깊은 인사 카드를 제공하는 가장 신뢰 받는 곳 중 하나가 되었습니다.
>
> 이제, 포랜스 컴퍼니는 자랑스럽게도 카탈로그에 새로운 카드 라인을 추가합니다: 바로 블루 스카이 라인입니다. [154]블루 스카이 카드는 일상생활에서 사랑, 응원, 우정이 담긴 진심 어린 메시지를 전하기 위한 것입니다. 카드의 단순하고 매력적인 스타일은 보내는 사람의 말에 초점을 맞추도록 디자인되었습니다. [154]생일이나 휴일을 기다리는 대신에, 지금 당장 주변 사람들에게 당신의 마음을 알리세요. 오늘 주요 문구점을 방문해 블루 스카이 라인을 둘러보세요.

어휘 earn 얻다 profit 수익 printing press 인쇄기 instant 순식간의, 즉각적인 exclusively 오로지, 독점적으로 trusted 신뢰 받는 thoughtful 사려 깊은 heartfelt 진심 어린 stationery 문구(류)

153 사실 관계 확인 [고난도]

번역 포랜스 컴퍼니에 대해 언급된 것은?
(A) 여전히 포랜스 집안이 소유하고 있다.
(B) 직원 70명으로 시작했다.
(C) 인쇄 광고로 성공했다.
(D) 예전에는 다른 종류의 제품을 만들었다.

해설 첫 번째 단락에서 루퍼스 포랜스가 라이프스타일 잡지를 발행하기 위해 회사를 설립(When Rufus Forance started The Forance Company ~ to publish a lifestyle magazine)한 후 잡지 이외에 카드도 제작하기 시작했다고 했고, 이후 잡지 담당 아티스트들이 디자인한 카드가 순식간에 성공을 거두어서 오로지 카드에만 집중하기로 결정했다(the cards ~ were an instant success, and Rufus soon decided to focus exclusively on them)고 했다. 따라서 포랜스 컴퍼니가 예전에는 카드가 아닌 잡지를 발행했음을 알 수 있으므로, (D)가 정답이다.

154 세부 사항

번역 블루 스카이 라인은 고객이 무엇을 할 수 있도록 고안되었는가?
(A) 인사 카드 디자인 주문 제작하기
(B) 특별한 날 이외에 호의를 표현하기
(C) 온라인으로 긍정적인 메시지 보내기
(D) 구매를 통해 현지 아티스트 지원하기

해설 두 번째 단락에서 블루 스카이 카드는 일상생활에서 사랑, 응원, 우정이 담긴 진심 어린 메시지를 전하기 위한 것이라고 한 후, 생일이나 휴일을 기다리는 대신에 지금 당장 주변 사람들에게 마음을 알리라(Instead of waiting for a birthday or holiday, let people know you care about them right now)고 권유했으므로, (B)가 정답이다.

어휘 customize 주문[맞춤] 제작하다 occasion (특정한) 때, 행사 positive 긍정적인 electronically 전자로, 온라인으로 purchase 구매(품)

▶▶ **Paraphrasing** 지문의 let people know you care about them → 정답의 Express goodwill
지문의 Instead of waiting for a birthday or holiday
→ 정답의 outside of special occasions

155-157 이메일

> 발신: 사이먼 버지스
> 수신: 바이올라 맥도날드
> 제목: 회신: 문의
> 날짜: 7월 30일
>
> 맥도날드 씨에게
>
> 롤렌트 스마트 유리에 대한 문의 감사합니다. 고객님 글로 보아 당사의 RC-2 유리가 고객님 프로젝트에 안성맞춤이라고 생각합니다. [155]투명한 설정으로 하면 고객님 건물에 있다고 묘사하신 어둡고 비좁은 느낌을 없애고, 불투명한 "반투명" 설정으로 하면 회의실, 복사실 등에서 현재 누리고 계신 것과 똑같이 사생활이 보장될 것입니다.
>
> 또한 저는 비용에 관한 고객님의 우려도 해소할 수 있습니다. [156]스마트 유리는 설정을 바꾸려면 전력이 필요하지만 둘 중 한 설정을 유지하는 데는 전기가 필요 없습니다. 만족을 표하는 많은 고객님들 중 아무도 스마트 유리가 공과금에 큰 영향을 끼쳤다고 하지 않았습니다.
>
> [157]기꺼이 현장을 방문해 RC-2 유리에 대한 정보를 더 많이 드리고 프로젝트에 가장 적합한 활용법을 제안하고 싶습니다. 관심 있으시면 이 이메일로 회신 또는 555-0196으로 전화하세요.
>
> 사이먼 버지스
> 영업사원, 롤렌트 사

어휘 fit 적합한 것: 적합한 transparent 투명한 eliminate 제거하다 cramped 비좁은 opaque 불투명한 frosted 반투명인 currently 현재 address 해결(하려고) 하다 concern 우려 significant 큰 impact 영향 utility bill 공과금

155 추론 / 암시

번역 맥도날드 씨는 무엇을 계획하고 있겠는가?
(A) 건물 건축
(B) 차량 설계 개선
(C) 사무실 개조
(D) 실외 전시품 만들기

해설 버지스 씨가 첫 번째 단락에서 맥도날드 씨에게 스마트 유리의 투명한 설정이 건물에 미치는 영향(In its transparent setting, it will eliminate the dark, cramped feeling you describe your building as having)과 불투명한 "반투명" 설정이 회의실, 복사실 등에 미치는 영향(in its opaque "frosted" setting, it will provide your conference rooms, copy rooms, etc.)을 설명했으므로, 맥도날드 씨가 유리창 변경과 같은 사무실 개조를 계획하고 있다고 추론할 수 있다. 따라서 (C)가 정답이다.

156 세부 사항 고난도

번역 버지스 씨가 맥도날드 씨를 안심시키려고 스마트 유리에 관해 쓴 것은?
(A) 에너지를 많이 소모하지 않는다.
(B) 설치비가 비싸지 않다.
(C) 청결 유지가 어렵지 않다.
(D) 쉽게 깨지지 않는다.

해설 두 번째 단락에서 버지스 씨는 스마트 유리의 설정을 바꾸려면 전력이 필요하지만 둘 중 한 설정을 유지하는 데는 전기가 필요 없다(Though smart glass does require electric power to switch settings, it does not need electricity to maintain either setting)고 한 후 공과금에 큰 영향을 미치지 않는다고 강조했다. 따라서 (A)가 정답이다.

157 세부 사항 고난도

번역 버지스 씨가 맥도날드 씨에게 제안하는 것은?
(A) 추천서
(B) 상담
(C) 시연
(D) 할인

해설 마지막 단락에서 버지스 씨는 자신이 기꺼이 현장을 방문해 더 많은 정보를 제공하고 프로젝트에 가장 적합한 활용법을 제안하고 싶다(I would be happy to visit your site to provide more information ~ and suggestions on its best use in your project)고 했다. 따라서 (B)가 정답이다.

▶▶ Paraphrasing 지문의 visit your site to provide more information ~ and suggestions on its best use in your project
→ 정답의 consultation

158-160 공지

손턴 버거, 레이크사이드 지점

공지

158직원 워크숍이 다음 주 화요일 오전 9시부터 오후 12시까지 열릴 예정입니다. 연공서열에 관계없이 전 직원 의무 사항이므로 그 시간 동안 식당은 문을 닫

습니다. 선약이 있다면 직속상사에게 연락해 적절한 조치를 취하십시오.

워크숍 리더는 카렌 다우닝입니다. 159그녀는 우리 식당의 위생 수준 유지에 대해 이야기할 것입니다. 다우닝 씨는 이미 전국 각 지점에서 이 워크숍을 진행했으며 최신 규정과 연구 등 최신 정보에 정통합니다. 여러분에게 유익한 날이 되리라 확신합니다.

여러분 모두 이 행사에 자동으로 사전 등록되었습니다. 160이 날은 유니폼이 필요 없습니다. 하지만 회사에서 용인될 만한 비지니스 캐주얼 복장으로 입으셨으면 합니다. 직원 사규의 관련 조항을 참조하십시오.

어휘 be due to ~할 예정이다 mandatory 의무인 regardless of ~에 관계없이 seniority level 연공서열 prior 사전의 commitment 약속, 책무 line manager 직속상관 appropriate 적절한 arrangement 처리 (방식), 준비 hygiene 위생 up to date 최신 정보에 정통한 regulation 규정 informative 유익한 employee handbook 직원 사규

158 주제 / 목적

번역 공지에서 발표하는 것은?
(A) 교육 행사
(B) 일자리
(C) 시설 점검
(D) 새로운 복장 규정

해설 첫 번째 단락에서 직원 워크숍이 다음 주 화요일 오전 9시부터 오후 12시까지 열릴 예정(Our staff workshop is due to take place next Tuesday from 9 A.M. to 12 P.M.)이라고 한 후, 공지 전반에서 직원 교육 관련 설명을 이어가고 있다. 따라서 (A)가 정답이다.

어휘 inspection 점검 code 규정

▶▶ Paraphrasing 지문의 Our staff workshop
→ 정답의 A training event

159 사실 관계 확인

번역 다우닝 씨에 관해 알 수 있는 것은?
(A) 최근에 경영진으로 승진했다.
(B) 식당 영업을 지켜볼 것이다.
(C) 몇 가지 회사 규정을 제안했다.
(D) 식품위생 전문가다.

해설 두 번째 단락에서 다우닝 씨가 식당의 위생 수준 유지에 대해 이야기할 것(She will be talking about maintaining hygiene standards at our restaurant)이라고 한 후, 그녀가 최신 규정과 연구 등 최신 정보에 정통하다(Ms. Downing ~ is up to date with the latest regulations and research)는 부연 설명을 했다. 따라서 다우닝 씨가 식품위생 전문가임을 알 수 있으므로, (D)가 정답이다.

160 문장 삽입

번역 [1], [2], [3], [4]로 표시된 곳 중에서 다음 문장이 가장 적합한 곳은?
"하지만 회사에서 용인될 만한 비지니스 캐주얼 복장으로 입으셨으면 합니다."
(A) [1]
(B) [2]
(C) [3]
(D) [4]

해설 주어진 문장에서 '하지만 회사에서 용인될 만한 비지니스 캐주얼 복장으로 입었으면 한다(we expect you to wear company-recognized business casual clothing)'며 복장에 대한 조건을 덧붙였으므로, 이 앞에 자유 복장에 대한 내용이 언급되어야 한다. [4] 앞에서 '이 날은 유니폼이 필요 없다(Uniforms are not required for this day)'고 했으므로, 이 뒤에 해당 문장이 들어가야 자연스럽다. 따라서 (D)가 정답이다.

어휘 recognize 인정하다, 용인하다

161-163 계약서

레오파드 자동차

본인은 재직 기간 동안 레오파드 자동차의 기밀 정보를 접할 수 있습니다. 162(A)/(B)/(D)여기에는 자동차 및 제조 장비의 기술 사양, 사업 관행, 회사 계획, 시장조사 데이터, 판매 및 수익 정보, 보안 절차에 대한 세부 사항이 포함되지만 이에 국한되지는 않습니다. 이 범주에는 레오파드 자동차에서 근무하면서 본인이 직접 개발한 정보와 자료도 포함됨을 알고 있습니다.

161본인은 레오파드 자동차에 재직 기간 동안 또는 퇴사 후 경쟁업체, 언론인, 일반인을 포함한 제3자에게 해당 정보를 공개하지 않겠습니다.

163재직 기간이 끝나면 본인은 즉시 회사에 모든 실물 보안 인증서, 회사에서 지급한 기기 등을 반납하고 회사 시스템의 모든 비밀번호를 제공하겠습니다.

본인은 개인 보관용으로 이 문서를 한 부 제공받았습니다.

서명: 제레미 풀턴

직함: 제조 관리자

날짜: 11월 19일

어휘 employment 근무, 고용 be exposed to ~에 노출되다, 접하다 confidential 기밀의 specification 사양 manufacturing 제조 practice 관행 revenue 수익 procedure 절차 disclose 공개하다 competitor 경쟁업체 immediately 즉시 credential 인증서, 증명서 company-issued 회사에서 지급한 device 기기

161 추론 / 암시 고난도

번역 계약서에 관해 암시된 것은?
(A) 회사 대표의 서명도 받아야 한다.
(B) 풀턴 씨의 재직 기간 이후까지 효력이 연장된다.
(C) 사업장에서 가지고 나올 수 없다.
(D) 풀턴 씨의 요청으로 수정되었다.

해설 두 번째 단락에 재직 기간 동안 또는 퇴사 후 제3자에게 회사 관련 정보를 공개하지 않겠다(I will not disclose such information to third parties ~ during or following my employment at Leopard Automotive)는 내용이 명시되어 있으므로, 계약서의 효력이 풀턴 씨의 재직 기간 이후까지 연장된다고 추론할 수 있다. 따라서 (B)가 정답이다.

어휘 representative 대표 extend 연장되다 premise 구내 remove 제거하다, 가지고 나오다 modify 수정하다

▸▸ Paraphrasing 지문의 following my employment → 정답의 past Mr. Fulton's period of employment

162 사실 관계 확인

번역 기밀 정보로 언급되지 않은 것은?
(A) 소비자 연구 결과
(B) 회사 수익
(C) 공급업체 이름
(D) 차량 사양

해설 첫 번째 단락의 '여기에(기밀 정보에) 자동차 및 제조 장비의 기술 사양, 사업 관행, 회사 계획, 시장조사 데이터, 판매 및 수익 정보, 보안 절차에 대한 세부 사항이 포함되지만 이에 국한되지는 않는다(This includes but is not limited to technical specifications of automobiles and manufacturing equipment ~ data from market research, sales and revenue information, and details about security procedures)'에서 (A), (B), (D)를 확인할 수 있다. 따라서 언급되지 않은 (C)가 정답이다.

▸▸ Paraphrasing 지문의 data from market research → 보기 (A)의 Results of consumer studies
지문의 revenue → 보기 (B)의 earnings
지문의 automobiles → 보기 (D)의 Vehicle

163 세부 사항

번역 계약서에 명시된 것은?
(A) 풀턴 씨가 직장을 그만둘 때 해야 할 일
(B) 위반 시 풀턴 씨가 받을 처벌
(C) 풀턴 씨가 정보를 공유할 수 있는 사람
(D) 풀턴 씨가 회사에서 지급한 기기를 사용하는 방법

해설 세 번째 단락에 재직 기간이 끝나면 해야 할 일들(At the end of my employment period, I will immediately return to the company all physical security credentials and company-issued devices, and supply all passwords to company systems)이 명시되어 있으므로, (A)가 정답이다.

어휘 violate 위반하다

▸▸ Paraphrasing 지문의 At the end of my employment period → 정답의 upon leaving his job

164-167 이메일

수신: 루이스 앤더슨

발신: 제시 리드

제목: 패널 토론 초대

날짜: 6월 18일

앤더슨 씨께,

안녕하세요. 제 이름은 제시 리드로, IT 헬스링크 주최자 중 한 명입니다. 167IT 헬스링크는 해마다 수백 명의 의료 서비스 제공자, 기업가, 투자자, 정부 대표 등이 모여 의료 정보 기술을 주제로 토론하는 영국에서 가장 흥미진진한 회의로 손꼽힙니다. 사흘간의 행사 동안 참가자들은 인맥을 쌓고 실용적인 팁을 공유하며 중요한 아이디어를 놓고 토론합니다. 저희는 지금 10월 5~7일 런던 피오레 홀에서 열리는 올해 회의에 모실 강연자와 토론자를 찾고 있습니다.

제가 귀하께 연락드리게 된 관련 세션은 "차세대 보건 의료 기술"이라는 제목의 한 시간짜리 패널 토론입니다. 이미 클라이브 미나모어, 콰메 오벵, 로건 노윅, 앤드류 얼 등 업계에서 가장 혁신적인 젊은 지성 4인이 참여하기로 했습니다. ¹⁶⁴그러나 금방 깨달으셨겠지만, 이 집단에 뭔가 빠진 게 있는데 바로 여성의 관점입니다. ¹⁶⁵따라서 저는 제가 아는 사람들에게 추천을 요청했고, 해롤드 커비 씨가 지난해 헬스 리버풀에서 귀하의 강연에 매우 감명 받았다고 말했습니다. 온라인에 있는 동영상을 보고, 저 역시 그렇게 되었습니다. 귀하가 패널에 참여해서 창의적인 생각을 참석자들과 공유해 주신다면 영광이겠습니다.

¹⁶⁶만약 관심이 있으시면, 지금 단계에서 하실 일은 동의한다는 답변과 함께 웹사이트에 올릴 증명사진과 공식 직함을 이메일로 회신만 하시면 됩니다. 이번 달 말까지 행사의 모든 세부사항을 담은 담화 참여 계약서를 보내겠습니다. 아니면 이와 관련해 궁금하신 사항 또는 우려되시는 부분이 있으면 이 이메일로 회신하거나 업무시간 중 020 7043 5214번으로 전화 주셔도 됩니다.

연락 기다리겠습니다.

제시 리드

어휘 organizer 주최자 entrepreneur 기업가 annually 해마다 particular 특정한 engage 끌어들이다 innovative 혁신적인 mind 인재, 지성인 participate 참석하다 realize 깨닫다 immediately 금방 female 여성의 perspective 관점 recommendation 추천 impressed 감명 받은 attendee 참석자 affirmative 동의하는, 긍정적인 professional headshot 증명사진 (직업상 적절한 얼굴 사진) alternatively 아니면, 대신에

164 사실 관계 확인

번역 패널 토론에 관해 언급된 것은?
(A) 10월 7일에 열린다.
(B) 커비 씨가 사회를 볼 것이다.
(C) 현재로서는 여성이 포함되지 않을 예정이다.
(D) 이전 회의들의 일부였다.

해설 두 번째 단락에서 패널 참석자들을 나열한 후 여성의 관점이 빠졌다(there is something missing from that group—a female perspective)고 했으므로, 현재 패널 토론에 여성이 포함되지 않았다는 것을 알 수 있다. 따라서 (C)가 정답이다.

어휘 moderate 사회를 보다, 중재하다

▶▶ Paraphrasing 지문의 missing from that group—a female perspective
→ 정답의 not currently scheduled to include any women

165 세부 사항

번역 리드 씨가 앤더슨 씨에 대해 알게 된 경위는?
(A) 강연에 참석해서
(B) 신문을 읽어서
(C) 인터넷을 검색해서
(D) 추천을 받아서

해설 두 번째 단락에서 리드 씨는 본인이 아는 사람들에게 추천을 요청했다(I asked around my network for recommendations)고 한 후, 커비 씨가 앤더슨 씨를 추천한 경위(Harold Kirby said he was very impressed with your speech)를 설명했다. 따라서 (D)가 정답이다.

어휘 referral 추천(서)

▶▶ Paraphrasing 지문의 recommendations
→ 정답의 referral

166 세부 사항

번역 앤더슨 씨가 참가하고 싶다면 우선 제공해야 하는 것은?
(A) 자신의 사진
(B) 서명한 계약서
(C) 수수료 견적서
(D) 제안된 주제

해설 네 번째 단락에서 만약 패널로 참가하고 싶다면 동의한다는 답변과 함께 웹사이트에 올릴 증명사진과 공식 직함을 이메일로 회신하면 된다(If you are interested, all ~ is respond to this e-mail with your affirmative answer and, for our Web site, a professional headshot and your official job title)고 했으므로, (A)가 정답이다.

▶▶ Paraphrasing 지문의 If you are interested
→ 질문의 If she wants to participate
지문의 a professional headshot
→ 정답의 A photograph of herself

167 문장 삽입

번역 [1], [2], [3], [4]로 표시된 곳 중에서 다음 문장이 가장 적합한 곳은?
"사흘간의 행사 동안 참가자들은 인맥을 쌓고 실용적인 팁을 공유하며 중요한 아이디어를 놓고 토론합니다."
(A) [1]
(B) [2]
(C) [3]
(D) [4]

해설 주어진 문장에서 행사 기간과 참가자들이 행사에서 하는 일(participants form connections, share practical tips, and discuss big ideas)을 나열하고 있으므로, 앞에서 먼저 사흘간 진행되는 구체적인 행사가 언급되어야 한다. [1] 앞에서 IT 헬스링크가 의료 정보 기술을 주제로 토론하는 영국에서 가장 흥미진진한 회의로 손꼽힌다(IT Healthlink has become one of the UK's most exciting conferences on information technology in healthcare)라며 특정 행사를 소개했으므로, (A)가 정답이다.

168-171 온라인 기사

오클랜드 경제 뉴스

(2월 19일)—크리스틴 레드먼은 최근 그녀가 가장 좋아하는 커피숍에서 주문한 아이스 라떼 값을 낼 수 없었다—현금이 넉넉한데도 말이다. "그로부터 몇 주 전에 전자 결제로 전환했더군요." 레드먼 씨는 설명했다. "그런데 그날 직불카드를 깜박하고 안 가져간 거예요. 난처했죠."

¹⁶⁸/¹⁶⁹해당 커피숍인 실리즈 빈즈는 매장에서 현금 결제를 중단한 뉴질랜드의 여러 소매점 중 하나이다. 이러한 추세를 지지하는 사람들은 전자결제가 더 빠른 거래, 오류 없는 기록 관리, 비위생적일 수도 있는 지폐와 동전 취급 감소와 같은 장점이 있다고 말한다. 실리즈 빈즈 대변인 샤론 라이트는 "솔직히 쉬운 선택이었다"고 말했다.

그러나 소비자들은 미심쩍어 한다. 종이돈 대신 카드와 앱을 사용하는 방향으로 꾸준히 바뀌어 왔지만 여전히 많은 사람들이 현금 사용을 선호하거나 최소한 현금을 사용할 선택권이 있었으면 한다. "제게는 사생활 문제예요. ¹⁶⁹제가 무엇을 사는지 카드사가 전부 아는 게 싫어서 현금 없는 매장에는 가지 않을 겁니다." 오클랜드 주민 채드 윌리엄스는 말했다.

¹⁷⁰미국에서는 비슷한 소비자 저항으로 인해 일부 시 정부가 업체들이 현금 없는 매장으로 전환하는 것을 금지했다. 소매업 분석가인 정상욱은 그런 일이 여기에서도 일어날 수 있지만 당장은 아니라고 보고 있다. "지금은 현금 없는 매장이 몇 군데밖에 없어서 크게 불편하지는 않을 겁니다. 하지만 많은 매장이 바뀌기 시작하면 우리도 역풍을 맞을 수 있어요."

¹⁷¹현금 없는 매장에 가보신 적이 있나요? 댓글로 이야기해 주세요! (댓글을 달려면 〈오클랜드 트리뷴〉 계정을 만들어야 한다는 점 유의하세요)

어휘 recently 최근 plenty of 많은 electronic payment 전자 결제 debit card 직불카드 embarrassing 난처한 retailer 소매점, 소매업 accept (결제 수단으로) 받아들이다 supporter 지지자 benefit 장점 transaction 거래 potentially 잠재적으로 unsanitary 비위생적인 convinced 확신하는 steady 꾸준한 cashless 현금이 없는 consumer 소비자 resistance 저항 prohibit 금지하다 inconvenience 불편 backlash 역풍, 반발

168 주제 / 목적

번역 무엇에 관한 기사인가?
(A) 소매 결제 방법의 추세
(B) 커피숍 체인의 확장
(C) 시 조례안
(D) 고객과 상점 간의 갈등

해설 두 번째 단락에서 실리즈 빈즈가 매장에서 현금 결제를 중단한 뉴질랜드의 여러 소매점 중 하나(The coffee shop, Seeley's Beans, is one of several New Zealand retailers that have stopped accepting cash at their stores)라고 한 후, 기사 전반에서 전자 결제의 장단점과 변화하는 결제 방법의 추세에 대한 설명을 이어가고 있으므로, (A)가 정답이다.

어휘 ordinance 조례 dispute 갈등, 분쟁

169 추론 / 암시

번역 윌리엄스 씨에 관해 암시된 것은?
(A) 금융계에서 일한다.
(B) 실리즈 빈즈 같은 카페를 이용하지 않을 것이다.
(C) 2월 초 레드먼 씨와 이야기했다.
(D) 지역 정치인이 되고 싶어한다.

해설 세 번째 단락에 나온 인터뷰 내용에서 윌리엄스 씨는 자신이 무엇을 사는지 카드사가 전부 아는 게 싫어서 현금 없는 매장에는 가지 않을 것(I wouldn't go to a cashless store, because I don't like the credit card company knowing everything I buy)이라고 했는데, 두 번째 단락을 보면 실리즈 빈즈가 매장에서 현금 결제를 중단한 뉴질랜드의 여러 소매점 중 하나(Seeley's Beans, is one of several New Zealand retailers that have stopped accepting cash at their stores)라고 되어 있다. 따라서 윌리엄스 씨가 실리즈 빈즈와 같은 카페를 이용하지 않을 것으로 추론할 수 있으므로, (B)가 정답이다.

어휘 patronize (자주) 이용하다

170 사실 관계 확인 고난도

번역 기사에서 다른 나라를 언급하는 이유는?
(A) 경영 관행의 기원을 설명하기 위해
(B) 기업의 구조를 강조하기 위해
(C) 어떤 상황의 잠재적 결과를 소개하기 위해
(D) 지역의 성과에 대한 자부심을 표현하기 위해

해설 네 번째 단락에서 현금 없는 매장을 향한 소비자 저항으로 미국의 일부 시 정부가 취한 조치(Similar consumer resistance has led some city governments in the United States to prohibit businesses from going cashless)를 소개한 후, 이에 대한 소매업 분석가의 의견, 즉 오클랜드에서도 그런 일이 일어날 수 있다는 예측(Retail analyst Sang-Wook Jung believes that could happen here as well, but not right away)을 덧붙였다. 따라서 (C)가 정답이다.

어휘 outcome 결과 achievement 성과

171 세부 사항

번역 기사 독자들이 권유 받은 행동은?
(A) 기사 업데이트 수신 신청
(B) 관련 경험에 대한 논의
(C) 비슷한 글의 목록 보기
(D) 사실에 관한 오류 보고하기

해설 기사 말미에 독자들에게 현금 없는 매장에 가본 적이 있는지(Have you visited a cashless store?) 물은 후, 댓글로 이야기해 줄 것(Tell us about it in the comment!)을 독려했으므로, (B)가 정답이다.

어휘 relevant 관련된 factual 사실의

▶▶ Paraphrasing 지문의 Tell us about it → 정답의 Discuss any relevant experiences

172-175 온라인 채팅

모니카 디트리히 [오후 2시 11분]
기쁜 소식이에요! ¹⁷²라모나 엔터프라이즈 직원이 마침내 저와 인터뷰하는 데 동의했어요!

타오 호우 [오후 2시 12분]
대단해요! ¹⁷³우리 독자들이 업계에서 가장 빠르게 성장하고 있는 소프트웨어 회사로 손꼽히는 곳에 대해 알게 되면 아주 좋아할 거예요. 거긴 언제 가세요?

모니카 디트리히 [오후 2시 14분]
다음 주 월요일 오후 2시예요. 그래서 준비할 시간도 별로 없고, 배정된 시간도 1시간뿐이지만 얻을 수 있는 만큼 얻어내죠.

록산느 토로 [오후 2시 16분]
¹⁷⁴자크, 모니카랑 같이 가서 사진 찍을 시간 있어요?

모니카 디트리히 [오후 2시 17분]
¹⁷⁴실은 사무실에는 저 혼자만 들어갈 수 있어요. 회사에서 자체 사진을 제공하고 싶다고 얘기했어요.

자크 파브로 [오후 2시 18분]
유감이네요. 그들의 사무실을 보고 싶은데 말이죠. 직원들이 작업공간을 개인에 맞게 꾸밀 수 있어서 러닝머신이 있는 스탠딩 책상부터 등받이를 젖힐 수 있는 의자까지 다 있다고 들었어요.

모니카 디트리히 [오후 2시 19분]

그게 사실인지 꼭 알려줄게요!

록산느 토로 [오후 2시 22분]

173/175이번 달 호 시간에 맞춰 기사를 준비해 주실래요? 175마감일은 3월 18일, 라모나 엔터프라이즈를 방문한 뒤 이틀 만이에요.

모니카 디트리히 [오후 2시 23분]

그건 좀 아닌 것 같아요.

타오 호우 [오후 2시 24분]

175동의해요. 품질이 최우선이어야 하죠.

어휘 **representative** 직원 **insight** 이해, 통찰 **fastest-growing** 가장 빠르게 성장하는 **supply** 제공하다 **personalize** 개인에게 맞추다 **treadmill** 러닝머신 **recliner chair** 등받이를 젖힐 수 있는 의자 **priority** 우선 사항

172 추론 / 암시 〔고난도〕

번역 디트리히 씨에 관해 암시된 것은?
(A) 라모나 엔터프라이즈에서 일한 적이 있다.
(B) 라모나 엔터프라이즈에 여러 번 요청했다.
(C) 라모나 엔터프라이즈 웹사이트를 정기적으로 확인한다.
(D) 라모나 엔터프라이즈에 판매를 확정했다.

해설 디트리히 씨가 오후 2시 11분 메시지에서 라모나 엔터프라이즈 직원이 자신과 인터뷰하는 데 동의했다(A representative from Ramona Enterprises has finally agreed to do an interview with me)는 소식을 전하며 '마침내(finally)'라는 표현을 사용했으므로, 디트리히 씨가 라모나 엔터프라이즈에 여러 번 인터뷰 요청을 했을 것으로 추론할 수 있다. 따라서 (B)가 정답이다.

173 추론 / 암시

번역 글쓴이들은 어디에서 일하겠는가?
(A) 기술 회사
(B) 뉴스 방송국
(C) 채용 대행사
(D) 잡지 출판사

해설 호우 씨가 오후 2시 12분 메시지에서 독자들(Our readers)을 언급했고, 토로 씨가 오후 2시 22분 메시지에서 이번 달 호 시간에 맞춰 기사를 준비할 것(Will you have the article ready in time for this month's issue?)을 요청했으므로, 글쓴이들이 잡지 출판사에서 근무한다고 추론할 수 있다. 따라서 (D)가 정답이다.

174 세부 사항

번역 파브로 씨가 디트리히 씨와 동행하지 못하는 이유는?
(A) 너무 멀리 있어서 제시간에 도착하지 못한다.
(B) 접근 권한이 부여되지 않았다.
(C) 다른 일로 바쁘다.
(D) 임무를 수행할 자격이 없다.

해설 토로 씨가 오후 2시 16분 메시지에서 파브르 씨에게 디트리히 씨와 같이 라모나 엔터프라이즈에 가서 사진 찍을 시간 있는지(are you free to go with Monica and take pictures?) 물었는데, 이에 디트리히 씨가 사무실에는 본인만 들어갈 수 있다(I'm the only one who will be allowed in the offices)고 말했다. 따라서 파브르 씨는 접근 권한이 없어서 디트리히 씨와 동행할 수 없는 것이므로, (B)가 정답이다.

어휘 **grant** 부여하다 **qualified** 자격이 되는

▸▸ **Paraphrasing** 지문의 go with → 질문의 accompany
지문의 be allowed in the offices
→ 정답의 been granted access

175 의도 파악

번역 오후 2시 23분, 디트리히 씨가 "그건 좀 아닌 것 같아요"라고 쓸 때 의미하는 것은?
(A) 절차를 감독할 계획이다.
(B) 직접 만나는 것을 선호한다.
(C) 일에 더 많은 시간을 원한다.
(D) 회사 정책이 현명하지 않다고 생각한다.

해설 토로 씨가 오후 2시 22분 메시지에서 이번 달 호 시간에 맞춰 기사를 준비해 줄 수 있는지(Will you have the article ready in time for this month's issue?) 물어본 후, 마감일이 라모나 엔터프라이즈를 방문한 뒤 이틀 만(The deadline is ~ just two days after you visit Ramona Enterprises)이라고 덧붙였다. 이에 대해 디트리히 씨가 '그건 좀 아닌 것 같아요(I don't think that's a good idea)'라고 응답했고 호우 씨도 이 말에 동의한다며 품질이 가장 중요하다고 했으므로, 둘 다 작업 시간이 이틀 이상 필요하다고 생각하고 있음을 알 수 있다. 따라서 (C)가 정답이다.

어휘 **in-person** 직접

176-180 이메일 + 기사

발신: 메건 대너
수신: 리링 양
제목: 요청
날짜: 9월 3일
첨부: 7개 파일

양 교수님께,

안녕하세요! 잘 지내고 계시길 바랍니다. 지난 여름 제가 졸업할 당시 교수님께서 하셨던 제안을 받아들이고자 메일을 드립니다. 176특히, 제가 이번에 퀸즐랜드 영 디자이너 공모전에 참가하기로 결정했는데, 제출하기 전에 제 출품작을 검토해 주셨으면 합니다.

이미 그 공모전에 대해 잘 아실 수도 있겠지만, 혹시 모르니 간략히 설명 드리겠습니다. 공모전은 재능 있는 젊은 디자이너들을 지원하고자 퀸즐랜드 패션위원회에서 주최합니다. 1781등 수상자는 위원회 연감에서 특집으로 다뤄지지만, 저는 5위 안에만 들었으면 합니다. 이 다섯 명 모두 위원회 연례 패션쇼 초대장을 받기 때문입니다. 출품작의 경우, 참가자들은 3개의 컬렉션을 제출해야 합니다. 각 컬렉션은 지원자가 선택한 창의적인 콘셉트로 연결된 3가지 의류 디자인 스케치로 구성됩니다.

177(C)/(D) 그래서 제가 선택한 창의적 컨셉트에 대한 설명과 스케치를 보내 드립니다. **177(B)** 또한 참고하시라고 심사기준을 열거한 문서도 포함했습니다. 바쁘시겠지만 9월 10일 이전까지 이 자료들을 보시고 생각나는 의견을 공유해주시면 정말 감사하겠습니다. 어떤 도움을 주시든, 미리 감사드립니다.

메건

어휘 in particular 특히 submission 출품(작) organis[z]e 주최하다, 조직하다 council 의회, 위원회 entry 출품작 contestant (대회 등의) 참가자, 경쟁자 applicant 지원자 accompany 동반[수반]하다 criteria 기준 (criterion의 복수형) for reference 참고로

퀸즐랜드 영 디자이너 공모전 수상자 발표

브리즈번(12월 12일) — **179** 퀸즐랜드 패션위원회(QFC)가 어제 젊은 패션 디자이너들을 위한 제4차 연례 공모전 우승자를 발표했다. 샌드페이스 어패럴의 구매 보조직에 종사하며 최근 윌버트 대학을 졸업한 재클린 애벗 씨가 500명에 가까운 참가자 중 1위를 차지했다.

QFC에는 디자이너, 타 업계 종사자, 투자자 등 3,000여 명의 회원이 있으며 퀸즐랜드 영 디자이너 공모전 심사위원단은 호주 동부 패션계의 최고 저명인사들로 구성돼 있다.

'신선한', '반영', '비행'의 개념을 구현한 애벗 씨의 디자인 출품작은 고전적인 스타일을 독창적으로 해석해 심사위원들에게 깊은 인상을 남겼다. 심사위원장이자 QFC 이사회 회원인 게리 오델 씨는 "애벗 씨의 옷과 액세서리는 매혹적이어서 오래 볼수록 더 복합적입니다. 우리는 그녀가 이 업계에서 **180** 밝은 미래를 가지고 있다고 생각합니다."

178 애벗 씨와 더불어, 상위권 입상자인 제다 라이언, 헤이든 노, 메건 대너, 케빈 네일러 씨도 위원회로부터 다양한 지원 서비스를 받게 된다.

어휘 reveal 밝히다 assistant buyer (직급이 낮은) 구매 업무 담당 직원 apparel 의류 graduate 졸업생 consist of ~로 구성되다 embody 구현하다 impress 깊은 인상을 남기다 interpretation 해석 a range of 다양한

---

176 주제 / 목적

번역 이메일이 발송된 이유는?
(A) 요건에 대한 설명을 요청하기 위해
(B) 공모전에 응모하라는 제안에 응하기 위해
(C) 일부 출품 자료에 대한 의견을 요청하기 위해
(D) 마감일에 대해 다시 한번 알리기 위해

해설 이메일의 첫 번째 단락에서 자신의 공모전 출품작을 검토해 주기를 바란다(I'm hoping that you'll review my submission before I turn it in)고 했으므로, 출품작에 대한 의견을 요청하기 위한 이메일임을 알 수 있다. 따라서 (C)가 정답이다.

어휘 clarification 설명 requirement 요건 reminder 상기시키는 것

▸▸ **Paraphrasing** 지문의 **my submission**
→ 정답의 **some entry materials**

---

177 사실 관계 확인

번역 이메일에 첨부되지 않은 것은?
(A) 문서의 샘플 양식
(B) 평가 기준 목록
(C) 디자인 콘셉트에 대한 설명
(D) 패션 아이템의 스케치

해설 이메일 마지막 단락에서 자신이 선택한 창의적 콘셉트에 대한 설명과 스케치를 보낸다(I'm sending you my sketches and the accompanying explanations of the creative concepts)고 한 후, 심사기준을 열거한 문서도 포함했다(I've also included a document listing the judging criteria)고 했으므로, (B), (C), (D)가 이메일에 첨부되었음을 알 수 있다. 따라서 언급되지 않은 (A)가 정답이다.

어휘 template 템플릿, 견본 evaluation 평가

▸▸ **Paraphrasing** 지문의 **a document listing the judging criteria → 보기 (B)의 A list of some evaluation standards**

지문의 **the accompanying explanations of the creative concepts → 보기 (C)의 Descriptions of design concepts**

지문의 **sketches → 보기 (D)의 Drawings of fashion items**

---

178 연계 　고난도

번역 대너 씨에 대해 암시된 것은?
(A) QFC에서 인턴십을 마쳤다.
(B) 연간 간행물에 홍보될 것이다.
(C) 윌버트 대학교 교수에게 이메일을 썼다.
(D) 패션 행사에 참석할 수 있는 입장권을 받을 것이다.

해설 이메일의 두 번째 단락에서 대너 씨는 5위 안에만 들었으면 좋겠다고 한 후, 이 다섯 명 모두 연례 패션쇼 초대장을 받을 수 있기 때문(as all of them come with an invitation to the council's yearly fashion show)이라는 말을 덧붙였다. 기사의 마지막 단락을 보면 대너 씨가 상위 5명의 수상자 중 한 명(Ms. Abbot, as well as top runners-up Jedda Ryan, Hayden Noe, Megan Danner, and Kevin Naylor)임을 알 수 있으므로, (D)가 정답이다.

▸▸ **Paraphrasing** 지문의 **come with → 질문의 receive**

지문의 **an invitation to the council's yearly fashion show → 정답의 a pass to a fashion event**

---

179 사실 관계 확인 　고난도

번역 기사에 따르면 QFC에 대한 설명으로 옳은 것은?
(A) 회원은 500여 명이다.
(B) 이사회는 오델 씨가 의장을 맡고 있다.
(C) 이전에 3차례 대회를 개최한 적이 있다.
(D) 샌드페이스 어패럴과 제휴하고 있다.

해설 기사의 첫 번째 단락에서 QFC가 어제 젊은 패션 디자이너들을 위한 제4차 연례 공모전 우승자를 발표했다(QFC revealed the winner of its fourth annual contest for young fashion designers yesterday)고 했으므로, QFC가 이전에 3차례 같은 대회를 개최했다는 것을 알 수 있다. 따라서 (C)가 정답이다. 참고로, QFC에는 3,000여 명의 회원이 있다(The QFC has over 3,000 members)고 했고, 오델 씨는 QFC 이사회 회원(Gary Odell, ~ a member of the QFC board)으로 소개되었으며, 샌드페이스 어페럴은 애벗 씨의 근무처(Jacquelyn Abbot, an assistant buyer at Sandpace Apparel)로 언급되었으므로, (A), (B), (D)는 오답이다.

180 동의어 찾기

번역 기사에서 3번째 단락 9행의 "bright"와 의미상 가장 가까운 것은?
(A) 화창한
(B) 쾌활한
(C) 유망한
(D) 영리한

해설 'bright'가 포함된 부분은 '그녀가 이 업계에서 밝은 미래를 가지고 있다(she has a bright future in this industry)'라는 의미로 해석된다. 따라서 '유망한, 촉망되는'이라는 의미의 (C) promising이 정답이다.

181-185 회의 안건 + 이메일

손우드 월례 시의회 회의
손우드 주민센터 105호실
2월 10일 화요일 오후 7시

181(C)출석: 시의원 12명 중 10명 / 불출석: 패트릭 추, 타마라 월튼

1월 회의록이 낭독되고 승인되었다.

분과별 보고:
  181(A)재무과: 3월 운영비 요청 승인
  공원여가과: 공원 개선 보조금 설명

공개 프레젠테이션: 랜들 파크 보조금 사용처 제안
  –리처드 디진, 전 시의원: 피크닉 탁자가 여러 개 있고 지붕이 있는 피크닉 쉼터 구축
  –183로레나 팔레르모, 손우드 주민: 조깅하는 사람들이 공원에서 운동할 수 있도록 아스팔트 길 추가
  –비어 카마스, 손우드 주민: 축구장 주변에 울타리 친 농구장 설치
  –181(B)헤더 볼린, 네이처 나우 자선단체 대표: 공원 외관 개선을 위해 꽃밭 만들기

심의: 시의원들은 다양한 제안의 장점에 대해 토론했다.

다음 회의(3월 13일): 182회의는 공원 개선 보조금을 투표에 부칠 것이다. 이례적으로 많은 참석자가 몰릴 것으로 예상돼 회의는 본관 강당에서 열릴 예정이다.

어휘 attendance 출석 absent 결석한 minutes 회의록 approve 승인하다 operating expense 운영비 improvement 개선 grant 보조금 shelter 쉼터 install 설치하다 enhance 개선하다, 강화하다 appearance 외관 debate 토론하다 merit 장점 auditorium 강당 predict 예상하다

수신: 루이스 넛슨 〈lknutson@thornwood.gov〉
발신: 빅토리아 피카드 〈vpickard@thornwood.gov〉
날짜: 3월 15일
제목: 랜들 파크 프로젝트

안녕하세요 루이스,

랜들 파크를 위한 프로젝트를 선정했으니 계획에 착수해야 해요. 184저는 이번 주 중으로 공원여가과 위원장 및 부위원장과 자리를 함께 했으면 해요. 그런 자리를 마련해 주실 수 있나요? 183조깅로가 어디에 설치될지 정확한 지도를 구해야 해요.

일단 잠정안이 마련되면 프로젝트를 알리고 건설회사들로부터 입찰을 받을 수 있어요. 저는 이 프로젝트가 우리가 받은 보조금을 아주 훌륭하게 사용하는 것이라고 믿어요. 185하지만 그 과정이 시민들이 기대하는 것보다 훨씬 더 길어질까 봐 걱정이에요. 늦여름까지 준비되게끔 하고 싶다면 서둘러야 해요.

진행 상황을 계속 알려 주세요.

고마워요!

빅토리아

어휘 arrange 준비하다, 마련하다 accurate 정확한 tentative 잠정적인 bid 입찰 lengthy 오랜, 장황한

181 사실 관계 확인 　고난도

번역 2월 회의에 관해 알 수 없는 것은?
(A) 월 예산이 승인되었다.
(B) 한 자선단체 대표가 발표를 했다.
(C) 의원 과반수가 출석했다.
(D) 다음 회의 장소를 놓고 논쟁이 있었다.

해설 회의 안건에 적힌 분과별 보고(Department Reports) 내용의 '재무과: 3월 운영비 요청 승인(Finance: Request for March's operating expenses approved)'에서 (A)를, 공개 프레젠테이션(Public Presentations) 목록의 '헤더 볼린, 네이처 나우 자선단체 대표(Heather Bolin, president of the Nature Now charity)'에서 (B)를, 상단의 '출석: 시의원 12명 중 10명(Attendance: 10 out of 12 council members)'에서 (C)를 확인할 수 있다. 따라서 언급되지 않은 (D)가 정답이다.

어휘 majority 과반수 debate 논쟁, 토론 venue 장소

▶ Paraphrasing 　지문의 March's operating expenses → 보기 (A)의 A monthly budget
지문의 president of the ~ charity → 보기 (B)의 A charity representative
지문의 Attendance: 10 out of 12 council members → 보기 (C)의 The majority of council members were present

182 추론 / 암시 　고난도

번역 회의 안건이 공원 개선 보조금 투표에 관해 암시하는 것은?
(A) 일부 시의원은 참석하지 않을 것이다.
(B) 2월에 열리기로 되어 있었다.
(C) 현지 시청자들에게 방송될 것이다.
(D) 대중의 관심을 많이 끌 것으로 예상되었다.

58

해설 회의 안건 하단에 다음 회의를 공지한 부분을 보면, 공원 개선 보조금을 투표에 부칠 것(The council will vote on the park improvement grant)이라고 한 후, 이례적으로 많은 참석자가 몰릴 것으로 예상돼 회의는 본관 강당에서 열릴 예정(The meeting will be held in the main auditorium because unusually large attendance is predicted)이라고 되어 있다. 따라서 (D)가 정답이다.

▸▸ Paraphrasing 지문의 **unusually large attendance is predicted**
→ 정답의 **It was expected to attract a lot of public interest**

183 연계

번역 누구의 제안이 채택되었나?
(A) 디진 씨
(B) 팔레르모 씨
(C) 카마스 씨
(D) 볼린 씨

해설 이메일의 첫 번째 단락에서 최종 선정된 랜들 파크 프로젝트를 위해 조깅로가 어디에 설치될지 정확한 지도를 구해야 한다(We need to get an accurate map of where the jogging path will be installed)고 했는데, 회의 안건의 공개 프레젠테이션(Public Presentations) 목록을 보면 팔레르모 씨가 조깅로를 추가하자는 제안(Lorena Palermo, Thornwood resident: adding an asphalt path that joggers can use to exercise in the park)을 했다고 나와 있다. 따라서 (B)가 정답이다.

184 세부 사항

번역 넛슨 씨가 이번 주에 부탁 받은 일은?
(A) 자원봉사자 교육
(B) 회의 준비
(C) 건설회사에 연락
(D) 광고 게재

해설 이메일의 첫 번째 단락에서 피카드 씨가 이번 주 중으로 공원여가위원회 위원장 및 부위원장과 자리를 함께 했으면 한다(I would like to sit down with the director and assistant director ~ sometime this week)며 그런 자리를 마련해 줄 수 있는지(could you arrange that?) 넛슨 씨에게 문의했으므로, (B)가 정답이다.

▸▸ Paraphrasing 지문의 **arrange that**
→ 정답의 **Set up a meeting**

185 사실 관계 확인

번역 피카드 씨가 공원 개선 프로젝트에 관해 언급한 것은?
(A) 보조금 단체가 프로젝트 계획을 승인하지 않을 수도 있다.
(B) 이용 가능한 자금을 프로젝트에 전부 사용하지는 않을 것이다.
(C) 그녀는 프로젝트의 소요 기간을 걱정한다.
(D) 프로젝트가 계절 축제에 방해가 될 수 있다.

해설 이메일의 두 번째 단락에서 피카드 씨는 조깅로를 추가하는 과정이 시민들이 기대하는 것보다 훨씬 더 길어질까 봐 걱정(I'm worried that the process will be much lengthier than citizens expect)이라고 했으므로, (C)가 정답이다.

어휘 duration (지속되는) 기간 disrupt 방해하다

▸▸ Paraphrasing 지문의 **worried that the process will be much lengthier**
→ 정답의 **concerned about its duration**

186-190 웹페이지 + 이메일 + 이메일

www.bernlakeoutfitters.com

| 홈 | 직원 | 배 | 추천글 | 연락처 |

번 레이크 아웃피터스

번 레이크 아웃피터스 온라인 홈에 오신 것을 환영합니다! 파올로 가스파는 10년 전 자신의 개인용 카약인 리틀 러쉬를 주말에 친구들에게 빌려주기 시작하면서 번 레이크 아웃피터스를 개업했습니다. **186/188당사는 '스피릿 오브 더 레이크'라고 부르는 50미터짜리 요트를 올해 초 구입함으로써, 이제 이 지역 어느 회사보다 많은 배를 보유하게 되었습니다.** 골든 블레이즈 고속 모터보트 한 척으로 속도감 있는 수상스포츠에 참여하기 원하시든, 노로 젓는 보트인 콰이어트 리플에서 친구 몇 명과 낚시를 하며 오후 시간을 보내기 원하시든 간에, 당사는 모든 고객의 요구를 충족할 수 있습니다.

***이 지역에 머무르신다면 저희가 숙소 문제를 도와드리겠습니다. **190저희의 오랜 파트너 호텔인 라구나 로지에서 할인을 받게 해드릴 수 있습니다.**

어휘 outfitter 여행[캠핑]용품점 purchase 구입 watercraft 배(들) aquatic 물과 관련된 lodging 숙소

발신: 〈chloeblosser@sod.ch〉
수신: 〈paolo@bernlakeoutfitters.com〉
제목: 문의
날짜: 1월 15일

안녕하세요,

스위스 치과의사 협회를 대표해 이메일을 드립니다. **187연례 회의가 6월에 번 레이크 근처에서 열릴 예정인데, 제가 폐회식 만찬을 준비하고 있거든요. **188긴장을 풀고 함께 즐기는 비공식 행사이므로 호수 위에서 하면 근사하겠다고 생각했어요. 40명 정도 될 거예요. 이렇게 많은 사람이 탈 만큼 큰 배가 있나요?**

또한 숙소에 대한 조언도 해 주시면 좋겠습니다.

감사합니다.

클로에 블로저
스위스 치과의사 협회

어휘 dentist 치과의사 annual 연례의 informal 비공식의 accommodation 숙소

발신: 〈paolo@bernlakeoutfitters.com〉
수신: 〈chloeblosser@sod.ch〉
제목: 회신: 문의
날짜: 1월 15일

블로저 씨께,

연락 주셔서 감사합니다!

저희 업체에는 분명 고객님의 요구에 딱 맞는 보트가 있습니다. 6월 중 언제 그 보트가 필요할 지 정확한 날짜를 알려주시겠습니까?

190숙소에 관한 문의에 **189**대해서 답변 드리면, 해당 기간에 라구나 로지에 공실이 있다고 알고 있습니다. 하지만 브랜뉴 선셋 호텔이 좀 더 저렴한 선택일 수도 있습니다. 그곳에 아직 예약이 다 차지 않았다면 말이죠. 어떤 숙소를 정하시는 지에 따라 저희가 할인된 가격으로 예약해 드릴 수 있을 것 같으니, 결정 사항을 알려 주세요.

파올로 가스파

어휘 opening 공실, 공석 pricey 값비싼

186 사실 관계 확인

번역 번 레이크 아웃피터스의 특별한 특징으로 언급된 것은?
(A) 연혁 기간
(B) 보트 임대료
(C) 위치의 편리함
(D) 소유한 보트 수

해설 웹페이지 전반부에서 번 레이크 아웃피터스가 올해 초 50미터짜리 요트를 구입함으로써 지역 어느 회사보다 많은 배를 보유하게 되었다(with the purchase of a 50-meter yacht ~ we have the most watercraft of any company in the area)고 했으므로, (D)가 정답이다.

▸▸ Paraphrasing   지문의 we have the most watercraft
→ 정답의 The number of boats it owns

187 세부 사항

번역 블로저 씨가 번 레이크 지역을 방문하는 이유는?
(A) 전문가 모임에 참석하기 위해
(B) 해외 휴가를 가기 위해
(C) 일련의 스포츠 경기를 관람하기 위해
(D) 과학 연구를 수행하기 위해

해설 첫 번째 이메일의 첫 번째 단락에서 블로저 씨는 치과의사 협회 연례 회의가 번 레이크 근처에서 열릴 예정(Our annual conference will be held close to Bern Lake)이라고 한 후, 자신이 폐회식 만찬을 준비한다(I'm in charge of organizing the closing dinner)고 했다. 따라서 (A)가 정답이다.

어휘 gathering 모임

▸▸ Paraphrasing   지문의 conference → 정답의 gathering

188 연계

번역 블로저 씨는 어떤 보트를 추천 받겠는가?
(A) 리틀 러쉬
(B) 스피릿 오브 더 레이크
(C) 골든 블레이즈
(D) 콰이어트 리플

해설 첫 번째 이메일의 첫 번째 단락에서 블로저 씨는 자신이 준비하는 폐회식 만찬이 긴장을 풀고 함께 즐기는 비공식 행사(It will be an informal event for us to unwind at and have fun together)라고 설명한 후, 참가 인원이 40명 정도 될 것(There will be about 40 of us)이라고 덧붙였다. 웹페이지의 첫 번째 단락을 보면, '리틀 러쉬'는 가스파 씨의 개인 카약(his personal kayak), '스피릿 오브 더 레이크'는 50미터짜리 요트(a 50-meter yacht), '골든 블레이즈'는 속도감 있는 수상 스포츠(fast-paced aquatic sports)에 적합한 고속 모터보트(speedboat), '콰이어트 리플'은 친구 몇 명과 낚시를 할 경우(fishing with a few friends)에 적합한 노 젓는 보트(rowboat)임을 알 수 있다. 따라서 대규모 인원 수용이 가능하며 편안하게 시간을 보내는 데 적합한 '스피릿 오브 더 레이크'를 추천 받게 될 것이라고 볼 수 있으므로, (B)가 정답이다.

189 동의어 찾기   고난도

번역 두 번째 이메일에서 3번째 단락 1행의 "goes"와 의미상 가장 가까운 것은?
(A) 이용 가능하다
(B) 관련되다
(C) 기능하다
(D) 출발하다

해설 'goes'가 포함된 부분은 '숙박 시설에 관한 문의에 대해서(As far as your inquiry about accommodations goes)'라는 의미로 해석되는데, 여기서 goes는 as far as와 함께 '~에 관한 한, ~에 대해서는'이라는 뜻으로 쓰였다. 따라서 '관련되다'라는 의미의 (B) is concerned가 정답이다.

190 연계   고난도

번역 가스파 씨가 번 레이크 아웃피터스의 파트너 호텔에 관해 언급한 것은?
(A) 비교적 저렴하다.
(B) 최근에 다시 문을 열었다.
(C) 현재 6월 예약이 비어 있다.
(D) 내부에 식당이 있다.

해설 웹페이지 하단에서 번 레이크 지역에 머무를 경우 번 레이크 아웃피터스의 오랜 파트너 호텔인 라구나 로지에서 할인을 받게 해줄 수 있다(We can get you a discounted rate at our longtime partner hotel, the Laguna Lodge)고 했는데, 두 번째 이메일의 두 번째 단락을 보면 블로저 씨가 방문할 기간(6월)에 라구나 로지에 공실이 있다(I know that the Laguna Lodge has some openings for that time frame)고 했으므로, (C)가 정답이다.

▸▸ Paraphrasing   지문의 the Laguna Lodge has some openings for that time frame
→ 정답의 It currently has vacancies for June

191-195 기사 + 이메일 + 주문서

더 나은 세상 만들기

(8월 4일)—기업의 사회적 책임이 전 세계 소비자들에게 더욱 중요해지고 있지만, 일부 기업은 사회 환원 활동이 어려울 수도 있다는 사실을 깨닫고 있다.

핀플래시는 지난해 채리티 모니터(자선 활동/단체 평가) 리포트가 영향력이 부족하다는 이유로 자사의 주요 자선 활동 파트너 사이에 D등급을 주는 바람에 곤혹을 치렀다. **193**마찬가지로, 던 갤러웨이는 회계 절차에 대한 의견 차이로 최근 비영리 예술 단체와의 관계를 정리했다.

191이것이 피터 간디가 기업의 기부 활동을 최대한 쉽고 효율적이게 만드는 영리 기업 기블러를 창업한 이유이다.

"우리는 모든 일을 합니다." 간디 씨가 말한다. "**191**기업들이 후원할 자선 활동을 선택하도록 돕고, 평판이 좋은 자선단체나 비영리단체와 연결해 주며, 기부 활동의 제반 사항을 관리하고, 홍보 수단을 제공합니다."

사업을 시작한 이래로 2년 동안 기블러는 100여 개 기업에 서비스를 제공해 왔으며, 고객들이 다양한 자선 활동에 약 300만 달러를 기부한 것으로 추산한다.

이처럼 성공을 거둔 가운데 간디 씨는 리카드 페이퍼 사가 가장 자랑스럽다고 말한다. "우리는 그들이 판매하는 거의 모든 문구용품에 대해, 나무 한 그루씩 심어지는 프로그램을 입안했습니다. 지금까지 5만 6천 그루의 나무가 심어졌을 뿐만 아니라, 이 프로그램의 홍보를 통해 리카드의 매출이 10퍼센트 **192**상승했습니다. 이것이 우리가 모든 고객사와 파트너 조직에게 바라는 상호 이익 관계입니다."

어휘 corporate 기업의 responsibility 책임 giving back 환원 embarrassed 곤혹스러운, 당황한 charity 자선(단체) similarly 마찬가지로 nonprofit 비영리인 disagreement 의견 차이[충돌], 이견 for-profit 영리의 cause (사람들이) 지지[후원]하는 대상, 명분 reputable 평판이 좋은 donation 기부 logistics 실행 계획[작업], (특정 활동에 필요한) 제반 사항[작업] publicity 홍보 estimate 추산하다 stationery 문구 mutually beneficial 상호 이익이 되는

발신: 사무엘 아카기 〈samuel.akagi@giveler.com〉
수신: 자넬 혼 〈janelle.hawn@weatherfordpro.com〉
제목: 예비 파트너들
날짜: 8월 24일
첨부: 비영리 검토

자넬에게,

어제 만나 봬서 반가웠어요. 그때 약속했듯이, 기업을 파트너 자선단체나 비영리단체에 연결하는 과정을 정리한 개요를 지금 보내드립니다. **193**던 갤러웨이처럼 차질을 겪지 않을까 걱정된다고 하셨는데, 이 개요가 그 걱정을 덜어주리라 생각합니다.

덧붙여 저희가 웨더포드 프로에 적합하다고 생각하는 몇 가지 단체를 적어드립니다:

– 키르히너 재단 – 어린이들을 위한 무료 농촌 여름 캠프 운영
– 그린 나우! – 국립공원을 확대하도록 정부에 로비
– **195**위드로우 협회 – 다양한 서식지의 멸종 위기 동물 보호
– 미션 클린 – 해변과 바다에서 쓰레기 제거

더 자세히 알아보실 수 있도록 각 단체의 이름에 웹사이트가 연결되어 있습니다. 궁금한 점이 생기시거나 선택할 준비가 되시면 이메일 또는 전화번호 555-0186으로 연락하십시오.

사무엘 아카기
고객 계정 관리자

어휘 overview 개요 relieve (고통이나 걱정을) 덜다 setback 차질 fit 적합한 것 rural 농촌의, 시골의 expand 확장하다 endangered 멸종위기에 처한 habitat 서식지 remove 제거하다 garbage 쓰레기

---

http://www.weatherfordpro.com

| 홈 | 제품 | 홍보 | 정보 |

웨더포드 프로

배송 정보: 빅토리아 콜
　　　　　 그리핀 로 340번지
　　　　　 푸에블로, 콜로라도 81008

청구지 주소: 배송지와 동일 ☑
결제 방법: 페이라이트
계정: vicky100@efr-mail.com

제품 번호	명세	수량	가격
H2420	**194**트레일 마스터 백팩 – 진청	1	59.99달러
R4371	**194**오니빈 트레킹 슈즈 – 사이즈 10	1	89.99 달러
		소계	149.98 달러
		세금	10.5 달러
		총액	160.48 달러

알고 계셨나요? **195**웨더포드 프로는 세전 매출액의 5퍼센트를 위드로우 협회에 전달합니다! 저희가 7.50달러를 기부할 수 있도록 지금 당장 "주문 완료"를 클릭하세요.

주문 완료

어휘 description 명세 pre-tax 세전

---

191 주제 / 목적

번역 기사의 목적은?
(A) 일부 기업의 잘못을 살피기 위해
(B) 지역 기업가를 소개하기 위해
(C) 기업의 서비스를 홍보하기 위해
(D) 소비자에게 특정한 선택을 촉구하기 위해

해설 기사의 세 번째 단락에서 기업의 기부 활동을 돕는 영리 기업 기블러(Giveler, a for-profit company that tries to make corporate giving as easy and efficient as possible)가 창업된 사실을 알린 후, 네 번째 단락에서 기블러가 제공하는 서비스(We help businesses choose a cause to support, connect them with a reputable charity or nonprofit organization, handle the donation logistics, and supply publicity tools)를 소개했다. 따라서 (C)가 정답이다.

어휘 profile (인물 등을) 소개하다 entrepreneur 기업가

192 동의어 찾기

번역 기사에서 6번째 단락 7행의 "bump"와 의미상 가장 가까운 것은?
(A) 어려움
(B) 충돌
(C) 기회
(D) 증가

해설 'bump'가 포함된 부분은 '이 프로그램의 홍보를 통해 리카드의 매출이 10퍼센트 상승했다(the publicity from the program has led to a 10% bump in Rickard's sales)'라는 의미로 해석되는데, 여기서 bump는 '상승'이라는 뜻으로 쓰였다. 따라서 '증가'라는 의미의 (D) increase가 정답이다.

193 연계　　　　　　　　　　　　[고난도]

번역 혼 씨에 관해 암시된 것은?
(A) 홍보 방법이 간단해야 한다고 생각한다.
(B) 금융 분쟁에 휘말리는 것을 피하고 싶어 한다.
(C) 예비 파트너 조직의 효율성에 대해 걱정하고 있다.
(D) 우발적으로 법을 어길까 봐 염려한다.

해설 이메일의 첫 번째 단락에서 아카기 씨는 혼 씨가 던 갤러웨이처럼 차질을 겪을까 걱정된다고 한 말(the concerns you mentioned about experiencing the same setback as Dunne Galloway)을 언급했는데, 기사의 두 번째 단락을 보면 던 갤러웨이가 회계 절차에 대한 의견 차이로 최근 비영리 예술 단체와 관계를 정리했다(Dunne Galloway recently ended its relationship with an arts nonprofit because of a disagreement over accounting processes)고 나와 있다. 따라서 혼 씨가 금융 분쟁에 휘말리는 것을 피하고 싶어 한다고 추론할 수 있으므로, (B)가 정답이다.

어휘 publicity 홍보　be engaged in ~에 휘말리다　effectiveness 효율성　potential 예비의　accidentally 우발적으로

▶▶ **Paraphrasing**　지문의 experiencing
→ 정답의 becoming engaged in
지문의 a disagreement over accounting processes → 정답의 a financial dispute

194 세부 사항

번역 콜 씨가 웨더포드 프로에서 주문하는 것은?
(A) 자전거 장비
(B) 캠핑용품
(C) 낚시 장비
(D) 등산용 부대용품

해설 주문서의 명세(Description) 목록에서 콜 씨가 등산용품인 '트레일 마스터 백팩(Trail Master Backpack)'과 '오니빈 트레킹 슈즈(Onivin Trekking Shoes)'를 주문했음을 확인할 수 있으므로, (D)가 정답이다.

195 연계

번역 웨더포드 프로는 어떤 활동을 지원하기로 했는가?
(A) 희귀 동물을 멸종에서 구하기
(B) 아이들이 야외에서 시간을 보낼 수 있도록 하기
(C) 자연 분야에 대한 정부 정책에 영향력 행사하기
(D) 해안 서식지에서 쓰레기 치우기

해설 주문서 하단에서 웨더포드 프로가 세전 매출액의 5퍼센트를 위드로우 협회에 전달한다(Weatherford Pro passes on 5% of each pre-tax sale to the Withrow Society)고 했는데, 이메일의 두 번째 단락을 보면 위드로우 협회가 다양한 서식지에서 멸종 위기 동물 보호하는 단체(Withrow Society - Protects endangered animals in a variety of habitats)임을 확인할 수 있다. 따라서 (A)가 정답이다.

어휘 extinction 멸종

▶▶ **Paraphrasing**　지문의 Protects endangered animals → 정답의 Saving rare animals from extinction

196-200 웹페이지 + 이메일 + 이메일

http://www.kurgess.com/packages

홈	정보	패키지	연락처

196커지스 프로퍼티 매니지먼트는 주택, 아파트 또는 콘도 관리에 있어 각기 다른 레벨로 관여하는 다양한 패키지를 제공합니다. 어느 것을 선택하시든, 귀하의 부동산을 관리하는 일에 헌신하는 전담 전문가들에 의해 모든 서비스가 수행됨을 확신하실 수 있습니다.

- 브론즈 – 서비스에는 부동산 보여주기, 임대 신청 처리, 신용 및 신원 조회, 임차계약서 서명, 보증금 수금 등이 포함됩니다.
  비용: 월 임대료의 100퍼센트 (1회)

- 실버 – 브론즈 패키지의 모든 서비스와 월세 수금.
  비용: 월 임대료의 4퍼센트 (매월)

- **198**골드 – 실버 패키지의 모든 서비스와 유지보수 및 수리 서비스.
  196비용: 월 임대료의 6퍼센트 (매월)

- 골드 플러스 – 골드 패키지의 모든 서비스. 하지만 3개 이상의 부동산을 관리하도록 커지스를 고용하는 사람들에게는 할인가로 제공됨.
  비용: 각 부동산에 대해 월 임대료의 5퍼센트 (매월)

어휘 property management 부동산 관리　a range of 다양한　represent 반영하다, 나타내다　involvement 관여, 참여　perform 수행하다　dedicated 전담하는　committed to ~에 헌신하는　tenancy agreement 임차계약서　deposit 보증금　maintenance 유지보수　repair 수리

발신: 렉스 캠벨 <rex@kurgess.com>
수신: 도라 맥러플린 <d.mclaughlin@rui-mail.com>
제목: 희소식
날짜: 3월 21일
첨부: 신청서, 신원 조회, 신용 조회, 계약서

맥러플린 씨에게,

헤니스버그 페리 로 682번지에 있는 고객님의 부동산에 적합한 세입자를 찾았다는 것을 알려드리게 되어 기쁩니다. 그의 신용과 신원을 아주 철저하게 조사했습니다. 정독하실 수 있도록 그 결과를 첨부합니다. **197**보다시피 아이제이어 프리처드는 고등학교 교사로서 안정된 직업과 재정 능력이 있습니다. 또한 물론 고객님께서 명시한 모든 부동산 사용 조건에 기꺼이 동의하겠다고 합니다.

프리처드 씨는 4월 14일 토요일에 1년 임대를 시작하고 싶어합니다. ²⁰⁰저희가 제공해 드린 정보가 만족스러우시면 계약서를 출력하여 서명한 후 가능한 한 빨리 등기 우편으로 제 사무실로 보내주세요. 감사합니다.

렉스 캠벨
고객관리 담당
커지스 프로퍼티 매니지먼트
²⁰⁰헤니스버그 지점

어휘 background check 신원조회 suitable 적합한 tenant 세입자 carry out 수행하다 thoroughness 철저함 perusal 정독, 숙독 history 이력 financial responsibility 재정 책임 terms 조건 specify 명시하다 certified mail 배달 증명 우편, 등기 우편

발신: 도라 맥러플린 <d.mclaughlin@rui-mail.com>
수신: 렉스 캠벨 <rex@kurgess.com>
제목: 회신: 희소식
날짜: 3월 22일

캠벨 씨께,

프리처드 씨가 좋은 세입자가 되리라 생각합니다. ²⁰⁰요청하신 대로 할게요. ¹⁹⁹계약이 체결되면 프리처드 씨가 입주하기 전에 또 어떤 일을 해야 하나요?

그리고 집을 보여주고 후보들을 심사하느라 애써 주셔서 정말 감사합니다. 아시다시피, 제가 실레넌으로 이사 올 때는 오래된 집을 부동산 관리 회사의 손에 맡기는 것이 불안했어요. 히미터면 팔기로 결정할 뻔 했죠. 하지만 지금까지 귀사의 서비스 덕분에 팔지 않아 다행이라고 생각해요. ¹⁹⁸제 마음에 평화를 주는 만큼 약속대로 프리처드 씨의 월세에서 6퍼센트를 회사에 기꺼이 지불하죠.

감사합니다.

도라 맥러플린

어휘 screen 확인하여 가려내다 nervous 불안한 afford 제공하다

196 추론 / 암시

번역 커지스 프로퍼티 매니지먼트에 관해 암시된 것은?
(A) 유지보수 서비스 일부를 외주에 맡긴다.
(B) 주거용 부동산만 취급한다.
(C) 보증금 선불을 요구한다.
(D) 3년 지난 고객은 할인해 준다.

해설 웹페이지의 첫 번째 단락에서 커지스 프로퍼티 매니지먼트는 주택, 아파트 또는 콘도 관리에 있어 다양한 패키지를 제공한다(Kurgess Property Management offers a range of packages ~ in the management of your house, apartment, or condominium)고 했으므로, 주거용 부동산만 취급한다고 추론할 수 있다. 따라서 (B)가 정답이다.

어휘 outsource 외주에 맡기다

▸▸ Paraphrasing   지문의 your house, apartment, or condominium
→ 정답의 residential properties

197 사실 관계 확인

번역 프리처드 씨의 긍정적인 특징으로 언급되는 것은?
(A) 주택 소유 이력
(B) 변경 가능한 입주일
(C) 안정된 직업
(D) 반려동물 없음

해설 첫 번째 이메일의 첫 번째 단락에서 프리처드 씨가 고등학교 교사로서 안정된 직업과 재정 능력이 있다(Isaiah Pritchard has a steady job as a high school teacher and a history of financial responsibility)는 점을 긍정적인 특징으로 언급했으므로, (C)가 정답이다.

▸▸ Paraphrasing   지문의 a steady job as a high school teacher → 정답의 A stable career

198 연계

번역 맥러플린 씨는 어떤 서비스 패키지를 선택하겠는가?
(A) 브론즈
(B) 실버
(C) 골드
(D) 골드 플러스

해설 두 번째 이메일의 두 번째 단락에서 맥러플린 씨는 약속대로 프리처드 씨의 월세에서 6퍼센트를 회사에 기꺼이 지불하겠다(I will be more than happy to pay your company the promised 6% of Mr. Pritchard's monthly fee)고 했는데, 웹페이지를 보면 월 임대료의 6퍼센트(6% of the monthly rental fee)를 지불하는 패키지는 '골드(Gold)' 서비스임을 알 수 있다. 따라서 (C)가 정답이다.

199 세부 사항

번역 맥러플린 씨가 질문하는 것은?
(A) 과정의 일부 단계
(B) 계약 변경 사항
(C) 추천 이유
(D) 업무 담당자

해설 두 번째 이메일의 첫 번째 단락에서 맥러플린 씨가 계약이 체결되면 프리처드 씨가 입주하기 전에 또 어떤 일을 해야 하는지(Once the contract is signed, what else needs to happen before Mr. Pritchard can move in?)를 질문하고 있으므로, (A)가 정답이다.

200 연계   고난도

번역 맥러플린 씨에 관해 암시된 것은?
(A) 커지스 프로퍼티 매니지먼트의 사무실을 방문할 것이다.
(B) 4월 14일까지 현재의 집에서 이사를 나갈 것이다.
(C) 캠벨 씨의 직장으로 전화할 것이다.
(D) 헤니스버그로 서류를 보낼 것이다.

해설 첫 번째 이메일의 두 번째 단락에서 캠벨 씨는 맥러플린 씨에게 계약서를 출력하여 서명한 후 자신의 사무실로 보내달라(please print out the contract, sign it, and send it to my office)고 요청했는데, 메일 하단을 보면 캠벨 씨의 사무실이 헤니스버그에 있음(Hennisberg Branch)을 알 수 있다. 두 번째 이메일의 첫 번째 단락을 보면 맥러플린 씨가 요청대로 하겠다(I will do as you asked)고 응답했으므로, 그녀가 헤니스버그로 서류를 보낼 것이라 추론할 수 있다. 따라서 (D)가 정답이다.

TEST 4

101 (D)	**102** (A)	**103** (B)	**104** (C)	**105** (C)
106 (B)	**107** (C)	**108** (D)	**109** (B)	**110** (A)
111 (D)	**112** (B)	**113** (D)	**114** (A)	**115** (C)
116 (A)	**117** (B)	**118** (B)	**119** (D)	**120** (C)
121 (B)	**122** (A)	**123** (A)	**124** (D)	**125** (C)
126 (C)	**127** (B)	**128** (C)	**129** (A)	**130** (D)
131 (D)	**132** (C)	**133** (B)	**134** (B)	**135** (C)
136 (D)	**137** (A)	**138** (D)	**139** (A)	**140** (B)
141 (C)	**142** (C)	**143** (B)	**144** (A)	**145** (A)
146 (D)	**147** (B)	**148** (C)	**149** (A)	**150** (D)
151 (C)	**152** (D)	**153** (B)	**154** (A)	**155** (B)
156 (D)	**157** (B)	**158** (D)	**159** (A)	**160** (C)
161 (B)	**162** (D)	**163** (D)	**164** (A)	**165** (B)
166 (A)	**167** (C)	**168** (B)	**169** (C)	**170** (A)
171 (D)	**172** (C)	**173** (D)	**174** (B)	**175** (C)
176 (A)	**177** (D)	**178** (D)	**179** (D)	**180** (A)
181 (B)	**182** (D)	**183** (A)	**184** (C)	**185** (C)
186 (D)	**187** (C)	**188** (B)	**189** (B)	**190** (A)
191 (D)	**192** (A)	**193** (A)	**194** (D)	**195** (B)
196 (A)	**197** (D)	**198** (C)	**199** (A)	**200** (C)

PART 5

101 부사 자리 _ 전치사구 수식

해설 빈칸 없이도 「주어(she)+동사(was)+보어(in control of the situation)」 구조의 완전한 절을 이루고 있으며, 문맥상 in control of the situation(상황을 통제하는)을 수식하는 부사가 들어가야 자연스럽다. 따라서 '완전히, 충분히'라는 의미의 (D) fully가 정답이다.

번역 CEO는 이메일에서 주주들에게 자신이 상황을 완전히 통제하고 있다고 단언했다.

어휘 assure 단언하다, 확약하다   shareholder 주주   fill in 채우다, 대신하다, 알려주다

102 인칭대명사의 격 _ 주격

해설 빈칸은 what이 이끄는 명사절에서 동사 had learned의 주어 역할을 하는 자리이므로, 주격 인칭대명사 (A) we가 정답이다. 참고로, we는 Mr. Moss and I를 대신한다.

번역 모스 씨와 나는 회의에 참석했고 돌아오자마자 거기서 알게 된 것을 나머지 팀원들과 공유했다.

어휘 attend 참석하다   conference 회의, 학회   rest 나머지   upon -ing ~하자마자

103 동사 어휘

해설 주어 Train conductors와 폭우 시 해야 하는 행위를 설명하는 to부정사구(to reduce the machines' speed)를 자연스럽게 연결하는 과거분사를 선택해야 한다. 열차 차장은 속도를 줄이도록 지시 받는 대상이므로,

are와 함께 '지시를 받는다'라는 수동의 의미를 완성하는 (B) instructed가 정답이다. 참고로, refer to의 to는 전치사이다.

번역 열차 차장은 폭우 시 기계의 속도를 줄이도록 지시 받는다.

어휘 conductor 차장   reduce 줄이다   examine 조사하다, 검사하다   refer to 참조하다, 언급하다   fix 고치다

104 형용사 자리 _ 명사 수식

해설 빈칸이 to부정사의 동사원형 overlook과 명사 effects 사이에 있으므로, effect를 수식하는 형용사나 effect와 복합명사를 이루는 명사가 들어갈 수 있다. 문맥상 간과하지 말라고 권고하는 대상은 '이로운 효과'가 되어야 자연스러우므로, '이로운, 유익한'이라는 의미의 형용사인 (C) beneficial이 정답이다.

번역 마에다 씨는 독자들에게 소셜 미디어 활용의 이로운 효과를 간과하지 말라고 강력히 권고한다.

어휘 urge (강력히) 권고하다, 촉구하다   overlook 간과하다   effect 효과   benefit 이득, 이점; 득을 보다

105 명사 어휘

해설 registration과 함께 복합명사를 이루어 동사 will last의 주어 역할을 하는 명사를 선택하는 문제이다. '영업일을 기준으로 총 10일 동안 지속된다'는 특정 기간과 관련된 설명이므로, registration과 함께 '등록 기간'이라는 의미를 완성하는 (C) period가 정답이다.

번역 우리 수업의 등록 기간은 영업일을 기준으로 총 10일 동안 지속될 것이다.

어휘 registration 등록   last 지속하다[되다]   requirement 요건   administrator 관리자   form 양식

106 동사 어형 _ 수 일치 _ 태

해설 빈칸은 복수 주어인 The recent improvements의 동사 자리로, 명사구 its popularity를 목적어로 취한다. 따라서 능동태 복수 동사인 (B) have enhanced가 정답이다.

번역 최근 월튼 볼룸이 개선되면서 공식 행사장소로 인기가 높아졌다.

어휘 recent 최근의   improvement 개선   ballroom 무도회장   popularity 인기   venue 장소   enhance 높이다

107 전치사 어휘　　　　　[고난도]

해설 동사원형 drive와 명사구 the Botanic Garden Café를 자연스럽게 연결하는 전치사를 선택하는 문제이다. 식물원 카페는 엘름 가에서 좌회전을 하기 전에 지나가는 장소이므로, '~를 지나'라는 의미의 (C) past가 정답이다. 참고로, (A) between은 '~사이에'라는 의미로 식물원 카페와 다른 장소가 함께 와야 하고, (D) through는 '~을 관통하여'라는 의미로 상황에 적합하지 않다.

번역 무료 주차장을 이용하고자 하는 고객들은 식물원 카페를 지나 엘름 가에서 좌회전해야 한다.

어휘 botanic 식물의

108 명사 자리 _ to부정사의 목적어 _ 어휘

해설 빈칸은 dance와 복합명사를 이루어 to photograph의 목적어 역할을 하는 명사 자리로, 형용사 daylong(하루 걸리는, 온종일 계속되는)의 수식을 받는다. 따라서 기간을 나타내는 표현과 어울리는 단어가 들어가야 하므로, '경연대회'라는 의미의 (D) competition이 정답이다.

번역 예이츠 씨는 전국지를 위해 하루 동안 열리는 엠버그의 댄스 경연대회 사진을 촬영하는 데 동의했다.

어휘 photograph 사진; 사진을 촬영하다 national 전국적인, 국가의 compete 경쟁하다 competitor 경쟁자

109 형용사 어휘

해설 전치사 for와 관용적으로 함께 쓰이는 형용사를 선택하는 문제이다. Mr. Staley가 관리자로서 프로젝트 결과(outcome)에 대해 책임진다는 내용이 되어야 자연스러우므로, (B) accountable(~을 책임지는)이 정답이다. 참고로, (D) obliged도 for와 쓰일 수 있지만 '~에 감사하는'이라는 의미로 문맥상 빈칸에 적절하지 않고, (A) confident는 of/about, (C) sensible은 of와 어울려 쓰인다.

번역 관리자로서 스테일리 씨는 건축 프로젝트의 결과를 책임진다.

어휘 outcome 결과 confident 확신하는, 자신하는 sensible 분별 있는, ~를 의식하고 있는

110 대명사 어휘 _ 수 일치 고난도

해설 be동사 are의 주어 역할을 하는 명사 자리이므로, 보기에서 are와 수가 일치하는 (A) few와 (D) many 중 하나를 선택해야 한다. 소프트웨어가 널리 사용되고 있지만(Although Warron's spreadsheet software is widely used) 특수 기능을 아는 사람들은 별로 없다는 내용이 되어야 자연스러우므로, 부정의 의미를 나타내는 (A) few(거의 없는)가 정답이다.

번역 워런의 스프레드시트 소프트웨어는 널리 사용되고 있지만, 이 소프트웨어의 특수 기능을 아는 사람은 거의 없다.

어휘 widely 널리 be aware of ~을 알다 specialty function 특수 기능

111 접속사 자리 _ 어휘

해설 빈칸은 완전한 두 절을 이어주는 접속사 자리로, 등위 접속사나 부사절 접속사가 들어갈 수 있다. 문맥을 살펴보면, '예약이 꽉 찬 것(Cobb Buffet is booked solid)'이 원인, '다른 장소를 찾아야 하는 것(you will need to find a different site)'은 결과를 나타내므로, 원인과 결과를 연결해주는 등위 접속사 (D) so(그래서)가 정답이다. 참고로, (B) then은 부사/명사/형용사로 절을 이끌 수 없다.

번역 콥 뷔페는 12월에 예약이 꽉 차 있으므로 송년회를 위해 다른 장소를 찾아야 할 것이다.

어휘 booked solid 예약이 꽉 찬 site 장소 banquet 연회

112 형용사 자리 _ 주격 보어

해설 빈칸은 be동사의 주격 보어 역할을 하는 자리로, 명사 또는 형용사가 들어갈 수 있다. Angul Timepieces가 창의적인 마케팅을 시도하기 위

해 애니메이션 광고를 제작할 예정이라는 내용이 되어야 자연스러우므로, be와 함께 '창의적이다'라는 의미를 완성하는 (B) creative(창의적인)가 정답이다. (A) creatively는 부사로 품사상 빈칸에 들어갈 수 없고, (C) creators(창작자들)와 (D) creations(창작품들)는 주어와 수가 일치하지 않으며 문맥상 어색하므로 정답이 될 수 없다.

번역 앤굴 타임피시즈는 창의적인 마케팅을 시도하기 위해 일련의 애니메이션 광고를 제작할 예정이다.

어휘 timepiece 시계 advertisement 광고 in an attempt to ~하려고 시도하기 위해

113 부사절 접속사 자리 _ 복합관계부사 고난도

해설 빈칸 뒤 형용사 busy를 수식하는 동시에 절(they may be)을 이끄는 접속사 자리이다. 따라서 부사절을 이끌며 '아무리 ~해도'라는 의미를 나타내는 복합관계부사 (D) however가 정답이다. 참고로, however는 '하지만, 그러나'라는 뜻의 접속부사로도 쓰인다. (A) very는 부사/형용사, (B) even은 형용사/부사/동사, (C) likewise는 부사로 절을 이끌 수 없으므로 빈칸에 들어갈 수 없다.

번역 접수 담당자는 아무리 바빠도 즉시 전화를 받아야 한다.

어휘 necessary 필요한 receptionist 접수 담당자 promptly 즉시 likewise 마찬가지로, 게다가

114 부사 자리 _ to부정사 수식

해설 전치사구 before its deadline과 함께 to부정사구(in order to finish the budget report)를 수식하는 부사 자리이므로, '성공적으로, 제대로'라는 의미의 (A) successfully가 정답이다. (B) succeeded는 동사/과거분사, (C) successful은 형용사, (D) success는 명사로 품사상 빈칸에 들어갈 수 없다.

번역 마감일 전에 예산 보고서를 제대로 끝내려면 우즈 씨는 도움이 필요할 것이다.

어휘 require 필요하다 assistance 도움 budget 예산

115 명사 어휘

해설 to enable의 목적어 역할을 하는 명사 자리로, faster와 of our products의 수식을 받는다. 빈칸을 포함한 to부정사구가 창고를 건설한 목적을 설명하고 있으므로, 문맥상 '해당 지역에서 더 빠른 유통을 가능하게 하기 위해'라는 내용이 되어야 자연스럽다. 따라서 '유통, 분배'라는 의미의 (C) distribution이 정답이다.

번역 프랭클린 창고는 해당 지역에서 우리 제품을 더 빨리 유통시키기 위해 건설되었다.

어휘 region 지역 proximity 근접 destination 목적지 fulfillment 실현, 달성

116 동사 어휘 고난도

해설 빈칸을 포함한 now that 부사절은 시장이 재개장(reopen)하기 전 상황을 설명하고 있다. 시장 운영권을 둘러싼 시와의 분쟁(a dispute with the city over the market's operating license)이 해결되어 재개장이 가능해진 것이라고 볼 수 있으므로, '해결했다'라는 의미의 (A) settled 가 정답이다.

번역 조카비아 시장 운영위원들이 시장 운영권을 둘러싼 시와의 분쟁을 해결했으므로, 시장은 다시 문을 열 것이다.

어휘 organizer 운영위원, 창립위원   dispute 분쟁   resign 사퇴하다
convey 전달하다   elect 선출하다

117 관계대명사 _ 소유격

해설 빈칸은 뒤에 오는 절(achievements ~ included winning a "Most Valuable Player" award)을 이끌어 주어인 Luigi Mancini를 보충 설명한다. 따라서 관계사절을 이끌 수 있는 소유격 관계대명사 (B) whose와 주격 관계대명사 (C) who 중 하나를 선택해야 하는데, Luigi Mancini와 빈칸 뒤에 온 명사 achievements가 소유 관계를 나타내므로, (B) whose가 정답이 된다. 명사절/부사절 접속사인 (A) whichever가 이끄는 절은 선행사를 수식하거나 보충 설명할 수 없고, (D) his는 소유격/소유대명사로 절을 이끌 수 없다.

번역 선수로서 'MVP' 상을 받는 등의 업적이 있는 루이지 만시니가 아드서 레이번즈 감독으로 채용되었다.

어휘 achievement 업적   include 포함하다   coach 지도하다

118 형용사 어휘

해설 명사 size를 수식하는 형용사 자리로, 휴대성(portability)이 있는 공기청정기의 크기를 묘사하는 형용사가 들어가야 자연스럽다. 따라서 '작은, 소형의'이라는 의미의 (B) compact가 정답이다.

번역 일부 사무실은 작은 크기와 휴대성 때문에 호라이즌 공기청정기를 선호한다.

어휘 air purifier 공기청정기   portability 휴대성   brief 짧은
demanding 힘든   authentic 진짜인

119 동사 어형 _ to부정사 _ 부사적 용법   고난도

해설 The services ~ on the go까지가 주어, include가 동사, digital check-in이 목적어인 문장으로, 목적격 관계대명사(that/which)가 생략된 절(Sephat Hotel offers ~ on the go)이 주어인 services를 수식하고 있다. 빈칸이 포함된 관계사절에 이미 동사(offers)가 있으므로, 빈칸에는 the needs를 목적어로 취하는 준동사가 들어가야 한다. 따라서 to부정사 형태인 (D) to accommodate가 정답이다.

번역 세팟 호텔이 바쁜 여행객들의 요구에 부응하기 위해 제공하는 서비스에는 디지털 체크인이 포함된다.

어휘 on the go 매우 바쁜, 자주 움직이는   accommodate (요구에) 부응하다, 수용하다

120 명사 자리 _ 동사의 목적어   고난도

해설 to부정사 to allow의 목적어 역할을 하는 명사 자리로, 형용사 easy와 전치사구 to essential items의 수식을 받는다. 따라서 '접근, 이용'이라는 의미의 (C) access가 정답이다. (A) accesses는 동사, (B) accessing은 현재분사/동명사, (D) accessed는 동사/과거분사로 품사상 빈칸에 들어갈 수 없다. 참고로, access는 불가산명사 혹은 타동사로 쓰인다.

번역 잠바디-Z 백팩에는 옆 주머니가 있어 물병이나 간식 같은 필수품들을 쉽게 꺼낼 수 있다.

어휘 essential 필수적인

121 명사 어휘   고난도

해설 빈칸은 동사 does not specify의 목적어 역할을 하는 명사 자리로, 전치사구 of breaking this rule의 수식을 받는다. 문맥상 사규에 특정 행위를 금지한다는 규정은 있지만(While the staff handbook prohibits smartphone use on the job) 이를 어길 시 어떤 처분을 받게 되는지 명시되어 있지 않다는 내용이 되어야 자연스럽다. 따라서 '이 규정을 어긴 결과'라는 의미를 완성하는 (B) consequences(결과)가 정답이다.

번역 직원 사규에는 근무 중 스마트폰 사용을 금지하고 있지만, 이 규정을 어긴 결과가 어떨지는 명시하지 않고 있다.

어휘 staff handbook 직원 사규   prohibit 금지하다   on the job 근무 중에   specify 명시하다   offender 위반자   alternative 대안
objective 목표

122 부사 어휘

해설 동사구 does not share customer data를 가장 적절히 수식하는 부사를 선택하는 문제이다. 울리오가 자사의 앱을 통해 수집한 정보를 내부적으로는 사용하지만 제3자와 공유하지는 않는다(does not share)는 내용이 되어야 자연스러우므로, '외부에, 대외적으로'라는 의미의 (A) externally가 정답이다.

번역 울리오는 모바일 앱을 통해 수집한 정보를 이용해 자체 서비스를 개선하지만, 고객 데이터를 외부와 공유하지는 않는다.

어휘 improve 개선하다   inaccurately 부정확하게   meticulously 꼼꼼하게   originally 원래

123 전치사 어휘   고난도

해설 기간을 나타내는 명사(a month)를 목적어로 취하는 전치사 자리이다. 문맥상 '시장이 거의 한 달 만에 모습을 드러냈다'라는 내용이 되어야 자연스러우므로, first와 함께 '~만에 처음으로'라는 의미를 완성하는 (A) in이 정답이다.

번역 시장은 그 집회에 참석함으로써 거의 한 달 만에 처음으로 공식 석상에 모습을 드러냈다.

어휘 attendance 출석, 참석   gathering 모임, 집회   mark ~를 나타내다, 의미하다

124 동사 어휘 _ 동명사

해설 전치사 to와 어울려 쓰이는 자동사를 선택하는 문제이다. 빈칸 이하가 capable of의 목적어 역할을 하고 있으므로, 빈칸에는 자발적인 학습자(self-motivated learners)가 새로운 환경(new circumstances)에서 보여주는 능력을 나타내는 단어가 들어가야 자연스럽다. 따라서 to와 함께 '~에 적응하는 것'이라는 의미를 완성하는 (D) adapting이 정답이다. 참고로, adapt는 '조정하다'라는 뜻의 타동사로도 쓰일 수 있다. 타동사/자동사인 (B) converting도 to와 어울려 쓰이지만, '전환하다[되다]'라는 의미로 문맥상 적절하지 않다.

번역 스토건 에듀케이션의 언어 프로그램은 새로운 환경에 적응할 수 있는 자발적인 학습자를 배출한다.

어휘 self-motivated 스스로 동기를 부여하는, 자발적인   cooperate 협조하다   address 다루다, 보내다

125 동사 어형 _ 분사 _ 명사 수식

해설 all of the merchandise부터 store까지가 주어, is placed가 동사인 절에서 merchandise를 수식하는 자리이므로, 형용사와 같은 역할을 하는 to부정사 또는 분사가 들어갈 수 있다. 따라서 '가게에서 판매되고 있는'이라는 의미를 완성하는 (C) being sold가 정답이다. (A) are selling, (B) will sell, (D) have sold는 모두 본동사 역할을 하므로 빈칸에 들어갈 수 없다.

번역 재고 담당자의 업무 중 하나는 매장에서 판매되고 있는 모든 상품이 반드시 올바른 선반에 놓이도록 하는 것이다.

어휘 merchandise 상품

126 부사 어휘

해설 비교급 형용사 lower를 가장 적절히 수식하는 부사를 선택하는 문제이다. 월 공과금(Our monthly utility bills)이 줄어든 정도를 묘사하는 부사가 빈칸에 들어가야 자연스러우므로, '상당히'라는 의미의 (C) substantially가 정답이다. 참고로, (D) extremely(극도로)는 very처럼 원급 형용사 및 부사를 강조하므로, 빈칸에 적합하지 않다.

번역 우리 월 공과금은 새로운 온도 제어 시스템이 설치된 이후로 상당히 낮아졌다.

어휘 utility bill (가스, 수도 같은) 공과금 temperature 온도 install 설치하다 deeply 깊이 forcefully 힘차게

127 명사절 접속사

해설 빈칸은 완전한 절(standard procedures are being properly followed)을 이끄는 접속사 자리로, 빈칸이 이끄는 절이 동명사 investigating의 목적어 역할을 한다. 따라서 빈칸에는 명사절 접속사가 들어가야 하므로, '~인지 (아닌지)'라는 의미의 (B) whether가 정답이다. (A) into는 전치사, (C) before는 전치사/부사절 접속사, (D) any는 한정사/대명사로 품사상 빈칸에 들어갈 수 없다.

번역 옥 씨는 표준절차가 제대로 준수되고 있는지 점검하는 임무를 맡았다.

어휘 task 과업을 맡기다 investigate 점검하다 procedure 절차 properly 제대로

128 형용사 자리 _ 목적격 보어 고난도

해설 「동사(will make)＋목적어(Blundell's economy)＋목적격 보어」의 5형식 구조에서 비교급 표현 less와 함께 Blundell's economy를 보충 설명하는 형용사 자리이다. 따라서 (C) reliant(의존하는)와 (D) reliable(믿을 만한) 중 하나를 선택해야 하는데, 문맥상 전치사 on과 쓰여 '제조업에 덜 의존하게 만들 것이다'라는 의미를 완성하는 형용사가 필요하므로, (C) reliant가 정답이다.

번역 콜센터 단지가 조성되면 블룬델의 경제는 제조업에 덜 의존하게 될 것이다.

어휘 establishment 조성 manufacturing 제조(업) reliance 의존 rely 의존하다

129 동사 어휘 고난도

해설 냉장고가 고장 났던 돌발 상황(when the refrigeration unit suddenly broke down)에서 출장 요리사들(the party's caterers)이 대처했던 방식을 나타내는 동사가 빈칸에 들어가야 자연스럽다. 따라서 '임시변통으로 마련하다, 즉석에서 하다'라는 의미의 (A) improvise가 정답이다.

번역 파티의 출장 요리사들은 세심하게 준비했지만 냉장고가 갑자기 고장 나자 임시변통으로 음식을 마련할 수밖에 없었다.

어휘 caterer 출장 요리사 be forced to ~할 수밖에 없다 refrigeration 냉장 designate 지정하다 condense 압축하다 attain 이루다

130 명사 자리 _ 복합명사 고난도

해설 단수가산명사 employee 앞에 한정사가 없으므로, 빈칸에는 employee와 복합명사를 이루는 복수명사 또는 불가산명사가 들어가야 한다. 따라서 '개성, 특성'이라는 의미의 불가산명사 (D) individuality가 정답이다. (A) individual은 단수가산명사/형용사, (B) individually는 부사, (C) individualized는 동사/과거분사로 품사상 빈칸에 들어갈 수 없다.

번역 모텔 컨설팅의 리더십 세미나 중 가장 인기 있는 세미나는 경영자들에게 직원들의 개성을 존중하면서 팀워크를 기르는 법을 가르친다.

어휘 foster 기르다, 촉진하다 individual 개인; 개인의 individually 개별로 individualized 개별화된

PART 6

131-134 기사

3월 3일 주간

〈시티 뉴스 타임즈〉

131유명한 요리사 데이비드 후우의 새로운 레스토랑인 퓨전 푸드의 개업식이 큰 기대를 모으고 있는 가운데, 3월 13일 목요일 오후 5시에 열릴 예정이다. 이 행사에서는 테이프 커팅식과 별미가 무료로 제공되는 연회가 **132**열릴 예정이다.

후우 씨는 24년 동안 경력을 쌓으면서 이 지역에서 가장 유명하고 인기 있는 요리사로 손꼽히게 되었다. **133**퓨전 푸드는 그의 두 번째 레스토랑이다. 첫 번째 식당인 카페 웨스트 24는 지난해 초에 문을 열어 아주 좋은 평가를 받았고 시내에서 식사하는 손님들에게 계속 해서 인기 있는 선택지가 되고 있다. 후우 씨는 자신의 식당을 운영하기 **134**전에 3번가에 있는 지안마티 비스트로에서 10년 동안 주방장으로 일했다.

퓨전 푸드는 조던 가 3402번지에 있다. 3월 14일부터는 화요일부터 일요일까지 문을 열어 점심과 저녁을 제공한다. 메뉴는 이미 온라인으로 확인 가능하며, www.fusion-food.com에서 볼 수 있다.

어휘 highly anticipated 크게 기대를 모으는 ceremony 식, 의식 reception 연회 complimentary 무료의 delicacy 별미[진미] prominent 유명한 eatery 식당 decade 10년

131 형용사 어휘 고난도

해설 chef David Huu를 적절히 묘사하는 수식어를 선택하는 문제이다. 두 번째 단락에서 후우 씨를 지역에서 가장 유명하고 인기 있는 요리사(Mr. Huu has become one of the region's most prominent and popular chefs)로 설명하고 있으므로, 빈칸에도 비슷한 의미를 나타내는 단어가 들어가야 자연스럽다. 따라서 '유명한'이라는 의미의 (D) noted가

정답이다.

어휘 **aspiring** 장차 ~가 되려는, 포부가 큰　**visiting** 방문하는　**retired** 은퇴한

---

132 동사 어형 _ 시제 _ be to부정사

해설　앞 문장에서 개업식이 3월 13일 목요일 오후 5시에 열릴 예정(The highly anticipated grand opening of Fusion Foods ~ is scheduled for Thursday, March 13 at 5 P.M.)이라고 했으므로, 빈칸에도 미래를 나타내는 동사가 들어가야 한다. 따라서 예정된 일을 이야기할 때 쓰이는 「be＋to부정사」 형태의 (C) is to feature가 정답이다. 미래 완료 시제인 (D) will have featured는 미래의 어느 시점까지 특정 행위가 완료됨을 나타내므로, 문맥상 빈칸에는 적절하지 않다.

어휘　**feature** ~를 특별히 포함하다, ~를 특징으로 하다, 선보이다

---

133 문맥에 맞는 문장 고르기

번역　(A) 그는 현재 그곳에서 요리법 강좌를 가르친다.
　　　(B) 퓨전 푸드는 그의 두 번째 레스토랑이다.
　　　(C) 퓨전 푸드는 곧 주인이 바뀔지도 모른다.
　　　(D) 그는 또한 영업시간을 연장할 계획이다.

해설　빈칸 앞 문장에서 후우 씨가 24년 동안 경력을 쌓으면서 이 지역에서 가장 유명하고 인기 있는 요리사로 손꼽히게 되었다(During his 24-year career, Mr. Huu has become one of the region's most prominent and popular chefs)고 했고, 뒤에서는 후우 씨의 첫 번째 식당인 카페 웨스트 24(His first eatery, Café West 24)와 식당 개업 전의 경력을 역순으로 나열하고 있다. 따라서 빈칸에는 후우 씨의 최근 상황과 관련된 내용이 들어가야 문맥상 자연스러우므로, 두 번째 식당으로 개업할 퓨전 푸드를 언급한 (B)가 정답이다. (A)도 현재와 관련된 내용이지만, 후우 씨가 강좌를 가르치는 '그곳(there)'이 어디인지 알 수 없으며 뒤따르는 문장과 어울리지 않으므로 정답이 될 수 없다.

어휘　**culinary art** 요리법　**extend** 연장하다

---

134 전치사 자리

해설　빈칸에는 동명사구를 목적어로 취하는 전치사, 혹은 부사절에서 주어＋be동사가 생략된 분사구를 이끄는 일부 접속사가 들어갈 수 있다. 지안마티 비스트로에서 주방장으로 일한 것은 자신의 식당을 운영하기 전에 있었던 일이므로, '~ 전에'라는 의미의 (B) Prior to가 정답이다. 부사절 접속사 (A) As soon as 뒤에는 분사가 올 수 없으며, 접속부사인 (C) Afterward와 (D) In addition은 (동)명사를 목적어로 취할 수 없으므로 빈칸에 들어갈 수 없다.

어휘　**afterward** 이후　**in addition** 덧붙여

135-138 이메일

수신: ⟨customerservice@romerouniforms.com⟩
발신: ⟨natasha.maxwell@odn-mail.com⟩
제목: 유니폼 로고
날짜: 11월 25일
첨부: 사자_이미지

안녕하세요,

제가 지도하는 유소년 농구팀을 위한 맞춤형 유니폼을 주문하기 위해 웹사이트를 이용하려고 하는데, 웹사이트가 135**제대로** 작동하지 않는 것 같습니다. 저희는 라이온즈 팀인데요, 한 팀원의 부모님께서 로고로 사용할 사자 이미지를 디자인해 주셨습니다. 136**아쉽게도**, 이미지를 사이트에 올리면 유니폼 미리보기 이미지 상에서 일그러져 보이네요. 여러 가지 이미지 크기와 가능한 모든 파일 형식을 시도해 보았지만, 문제는 137**그대롭니다**. 그래서 이미지를 이 이메일에 첨부해서 보냅니다. 138**무엇이 문제인지 알아내 주셨으면 합니다**. 이게 문제가 되는 건지는 모르겠지만, 저희는 에메랄드 그린 바탕에 흰 다이아몬드가 있는 '위너 다이아몬드 덩크' 유니폼 스타일을 선택했습니다.

감사합니다.

나타샤 맥스웰

어휘　**customized** 맞춤형의　**distorted** 일그러진, 왜곡된　**preview** 미리 보기　**different** 다양한, 여러 가지의　**attachment** 첨부(파일)　**matter** 중요하다, 문제가 되다

---

135 부사 자리 _ 현재분사 수식

해설　자동사로 쓰인 현재분사 working을 수식하는 부사 자리이므로, '제대로, 적절히'라는 의미의 (C) correctly가 정답이다. (A) corrected는 동사/과거분사, (B) correct는 동사/형용사, (D) corrections는 명사로 품사상 빈칸에 들어갈 수 없다.

어휘　**correct** 정정하다; 올바른　**correction** 정정(한 것)

---

136 접속부사

해설　빈칸 앞에서 로고로 사용할 사자 이미지 디자인이 완성되었다(one ~ designed an image of a lion that we plan to use as our logo)고 했는데, 뒤에서는 이를 사이트에 올리면 유니폼 미리보기 이미지 상에서 일그러져 보인다(when we upload it to your site, it looks distorted in the uniform preview image)고 했다. 따라서 빈칸에는 계획에 방해가 되는 문제점을 언급할 때 쓰이는 접속부사가 들어가야 자연스러우므로, '아쉽게도'라는 의미의 (D) Unfortunately가 정답이다.

어휘　**instead** 대신　**namely** 즉　**similarly** 마찬가지로

---

137 동사 어휘

해설　빈칸이 포함된 절은 이미지가 일그러져 보이는 문제를 해결하기 위해 시도한 노력(We've tried different image sizes and all of the possible file types)과 상반되는 결과를 나타낸다. 따라서 '문제가 지속되다'라는 의미를 완성하는 (A) persists가 정답이다.

어휘　**reside** 거주하다　**determine** 결정하다　**assert** 주장하다

---

138 문맥에 맞는 문장 고르기　고난도

번역　(A) 그것의 매력에 대해 솔직한 의견을 들려주세요.
　　　(B) 어쨌든 제 사무실에 직접 들르시지 않아도 될 겁니다.
　　　(C) 그것을 로고 디자인 밑바탕으로 사용해 주셨으면 합니다.
　　　(D) 무엇이 문제인지 알아내 주셨으면 합니다.

해설　빈칸 앞에서 이미지가 일그러져 보이는 문제가 지속되어 이미지를 이메일에 첨부해서 보낸다(So, I'm sending you the image as an attachment to this e-mail)고 했고, 뒤에서는 문제의 원인이 되었을지 모르는 유니폼 스타일(we've chosen the "Winner Diamond Dunk" uniform style)을 언급하고 있다. 따라서 빈칸에는 문제 해결을 요청하는 내용이 들어가야 자연스러우므로, (D)가 정답이다.

어휘 **in person** 직접 **after all** 어쨌든, 결국 **figure out** 알아내다

139-142 웹페이지

http://www.russontmining.com/careers/tp

수습직원 프로그램

수습직원 프로그램은 최근에 대학을 졸업한 졸업생들에게 흥미진진한 진로 기회일 **139뿐 아니라** 루손트 마이닝 사가 미래의 리더를 양성할 수 있는 중요한 방법이기도 합니다. 저희는 다양한 분야에서 유망한 청년들을 선발해 루손트 팀의 귀중한 일원이 되는 데 필요한 도구와 지식을 제공합니다. 12개월에 걸친 프로그램 기간 동안 수습직원들은 캐나다 전역의 루손트 현장을 방문해 각 직원 및 임원과 이야기를 나눕니다. **140그들은 주요 프로젝트에 참여할 기회까지 얻습니다.** 숙소, 식사, 넉넉한 생활비가 제공됩니다. 이 프로그램을 성공적으로 수료하는 수습직원들은 루손트에서 본인의 자질 및 관심사에 가장 **141적합한** 분야에 정규직으로 일할 자격을 얻게 됩니다.

수습직원이 되는 방법을 알고 싶으세요? **142지원** 절차에 대해 알아보려면 여기를 클릭하세요.

어휘 **career opportunity** 진로 기회 **university graduate** 대학교 졸업생 **cultivate** 양성하다 **promising** 유망한 **a variety of** 다양한 **field** 분야 **valuable** 귀중한, 소중한 **executive** 임원 **generous** 넉넉한 **living stipend** 생활비 **completion** 수료 **entitle** 자격[권리]를 주다 **qualification** 자격, 자질

139 상관접속사

해설 빈칸에는 and와 함께 상관접속사를 이루어 an exciting career opportunity for recent university graduates와 an important way for Russont Mining Co. to cultivate our future leaders를 연결하는 단어가 들어가야 하므로, (A) both가 정답이다. 상관접속사 'both A and B'는 'A와 B 둘 다, A뿐만 아니라 B도'라는 의미로 쓰인다. 참고로 (C) either는 or와 함께 'either A or B'의 상관접속사를 이루어 'A 또는 B'라는 의미를 나타낸다.

어휘 **intended** 의도된

140 문맥에 맞는 문장 고르기 고난도

번역 (A) 특히 그들은 소통 능력이 탁월해야 합니다.
(B) 그들은 주요 프로젝트에 참여할 기회까지 얻습니다.
(C) 예를 들어, 당사의 현직 운영 부사장은 대학원생입니다.
(D) 이 기간 동안 수시로 제출물을 검토할 예정입니다.

해설 빈칸 앞 문장에서 수습직원들에게 주어지는 기회(trainees travel to Russont sites across Canada and speak with employees and executives at all levels)를, 뒤 문장에서는 수습직원들에게 제공되는 혜택(Room, board, and a generous living stipend are provided)을 설명하고 있으므로, 빈칸에도 수습직원들에게 주어지는 기회나 혜택과 관련된 내용이 들어가야 자연스럽다. 따라서 (B)가 정답이다.

어휘 **in particular** 특히 **graduate** 대학원생 **submission** 제출(물) **on a rolling basis** 수시로

141 형용사 자리 _ 주격 보어 _ 어휘 고난도

해설 빈칸은 which 관계사절의 주어 their qualifications and interests를 보충 설명하는 주격 보어 자리로, 부사 best의 수식을 받으며 전치사 to와 어울리는 분사형 형용사가 들어갈 수 있다. 따라서 '적합한'이라는 의미의 (C) suited가 정답이다. 참고로, suited는 for와도 어울려 쓰인다. 형용사인 (D) suitable도 '적합한'이라는 의미이지만, 전치사 for와 함께 쓰이며, best가 아닌 most의 수식을 받아야 한다.

142 명사 어휘

해설 '절차'라는 뜻의 process와 함께 복합명사를 이루는 명사를 선택하는 문제이다. 앞에서 수습직원이 되는 방법을 알고 싶은지(Would you like to find out how to become a trainee?) 묻고 있으므로, 이 절차는 수습직원이 되기 위한 과정과 관련된 것이어야 한다. 따라서 '지원 절차'라는 의미를 완성하는 (C) application이 정답이다.

어휘 **development** 개발 **appraisal** 평가 **procurement** 조달, 입수

143-146 공지

온라인 뱅킹 고객에게 알림:

1월 1일부터 메인트 은행은 기본 설정으로 전자 계좌 내역서를 제공할 예정입니다. 이 날짜 이후에는 종이 내역서를 받고 싶다고 특별히 당사에 통지하지 **143않는** 한 더 이상 우편으로 종이 내역서를 받을 수 없습니다. 온라인 뱅킹 계좌에 로그인해 '설정' 탭을 열고 '계속 종이 내역서 수신'을 선택하면 그렇게 하실 수 있습니다.

전자 내역서는 계좌 페이지의 '입출금 내역서' 탭에서 이용할 수 있습니다. 저희는 매달 내역서가 나오면 이메일 **144통지**를 보내겠습니다. **145이 메시지는 고객의 개인정보를 보호하도록 고안되었습니다.** 이름과 계좌 번호의 마지막 네 자리만 기재됩니다. 계좌와 연결된 이메일 주소를 항상 업데이트해 두세요. 이렇게 하면 메인트 은행에서 보내는 이 메시지들뿐만 아니라 기타 중요 메시지들도 확실히 **146전달**될 것입니다.

어휘 **account statement** 계좌 (입출금) 내역서[명세서] **electronically** 전자로, 온라인으로 **by default** 기본값[설정]으로, 자동적으로 **specifically** 특별히 **mention** 언급[거론]하다, 기재하다 **associated with** ~와 연결된 **ensure** 보장하다, 확실히 ~하게 하다

143 부사절 접속사 자리 _ 어휘

해설 두 완전한 절을 이어주는 접속사 자리로, 빈칸이 이끄는 절이 앞에 있는 주절을 수식하고 있다. 따라서 보기 중 적절한 접속사를 선택해야 하는데, 문맥을 살펴보면 해당 부사절이 조건(you specifically inform us that you wish to (receive paper statements in the mail))을 나타내고 있고 주절은 이 조건이 이행되지 않을 시 발생하는 결과(you will no longer receive paper statements in mail)를 설명하고 있다. 따라서 '~하지 않으면'이라는 의미의 부사절 접속사인 (B) unless가 정답이다. (C) besides는 전치사/부사로 완전한 절을 이끌 수 없다.

144 명사 자리 _ 동사의 직접목적어 _ 복합명사 [고난도]

해설 명사 e-mail과 함께 복합명사를 이루어 동사구 will send의 직접목적어 역할을 하는 명사 자리이므로, e-mail과 함께 '이메일 통지'라는 의미를 완성하는 (A) notification이 정답이다. (C) notified를 과거분사로 볼 경우 앞에 「주격 관계대명사(which) + be동사(is)」가 생략된 형태로 빈칸에 들어갈 수 있지만, e-mail은 통지 받는 대상(사람)이 아니므로 문맥상 적절하지 않다. (B) notifying은 동명사/현재분사로 뒤에 통지 받는 대상(사람)이 목적어로 와야 하므로 구조상 불가능하고, 형용사인 (D) notifiable은 '통지해야 할'이라는 뜻이므로 빈칸에 적합하지 않다.

145 문맥상 맞는 문장 고르기 [고난도]

번역 (A) 이 메시지는 고객의 개인정보를 보호하도록 고안되었습니다.
(B) 공동 계좌 보유자에게도 절차는 동일합니다.
(C) 명세서에는 최근 거래 내역이 모두 나열되어 있습니다.
(D) 현재 이 날짜는 온라인으로 변경할 수 없습니다.

해설 빈칸 앞 문장에서 이메일 통지를 보내겠다(We will send you an e-mail notification)고 했고, 뒤 문장에서 이름과 계좌 번호의 마지막 네 자리만 기재된다(It will only mention your name and the last four digits of your account number)고 했으므로, 빈칸에도 이메일 통지와 관련된 내용이 들어가야 자연스럽다. 따라서 이메일에 개인정보의 일부만 기재되는 이유를 언급한 (A)가 정답이다.

어휘 transaction 거래

146 명사 어휘

해설 동사 ensure의 목적어 역할을 하는 명사 자리로, 전치사구 of these and other important messages from Meypt Bank의 수식을 받는다. 앞에서 계좌와 연결된 이메일 주소를 항상 업데이트해 두라(Please keep the e-mail address associated with your account updated at all times)고 요청했으므로, 빈칸에는 이메일 업데이트가 보장하는(ensure) 사항을 나타내는 명사가 들어가야 자연스럽다. 따라서 '메시지의 전달'이라는 의미를 완성하는 (D) delivery가 정답이다.

어휘 clarity 명확성 deletion 삭제 relevance 타당성

PART 7

147-148 쿠폰

혼스 힐 묘목장
봄맞이 할인!

147**4월 14일부터 4월 23일 사이에 이 쿠폰을 혼스 힐 묘목장에 가져오시면 모든 식물은 25퍼센트, 도기는 15퍼센트 할인을 받을 수 있습니다.** 집이나 사업체를 위해 아름다운 꽃, 관목, 그리고 나무까지 놀라운 가격에 구입해 새해에 처음 맞는 따뜻한 날씨를 기념해 보세요. 148**모든 구매품에 대해 상시 저가 요금으로 배송 및 식재 지원 서비스를 받으실 수 있습니다.**

어휘 nursery 묘목장 bush 관목 planting 식재, 식목 assistance 지원, 도움 purchase 구매(품)

147 사실 관계 확인

번역 판촉 할인에 관해 알 수 있는 것은?
(A) 식물 무료 나눔이 포함된다.
(B) 다양한 품목에 적용된다.
(C) 묘목장의 오랜 고객들에게 보답한다.
(D) 쇼핑객들은 일정 금액의 돈을 써야 한다.

해설 쿠폰의 초반부에서 모든 식물과 도기를 할인 받을 수 있다(to get 25% off all plants and 15% off all pottery)고 했으므로, 할인이 적용되는 품목이 다양함을 알 수 있다. 따라서 (B)가 정답이다.

어휘 involve 포함하다, 수반하다 multiple 다수의, 두 개 이상의 reward 보상[보답]하다

▶▶ Paraphrasing 지문의 all plants and ~ all pottery
→ 정답의 multiple types of items

148 추론 / 암시 [고난도]

번역 혼스 힐 묘목장에 관해 암시된 것은?
(A) 옥외 가구도 구비하고 있다.
(B) 일주일에 하루 휴무한다.
(C) 출장 서비스를 제공한다.
(D) 주로 다른 사업체에 서비스를 제공한다.

해설 쿠폰의 후반부에서 모든 구매품에 대해 상시 저가 요금으로 배송 및 식재 지원 서비스를 받을 수 있다(Delivery and planting assistance for our everyday low fees will be available)고 했으므로, 혼스 힐 묘목장이 식물을 배송해주고 식재도 도와주는 출장 서비스를 제공한다고 추론할 수 있다. 따라서 (C)가 정답이다.

어휘 stock (판매용 상품을) 구비하다 off-site 외부의, 사외의

▶▶ Paraphrasing 지문의 Delivery and planting assistance
→ 정답의 some off-site services

149-150 문자 메시지

자마르 리처드슨 [오후 6시 14분]
안녕하세요, 아미나. 방금 올해 열리는 대학 재정지원 전문가 회의에 참석하기로 승인 받았는데, 당신이 거기서 발표하신다는 걸 알게 되었어요. 우리 거기 있는 동안 만나는 게 어때요?

아미나 은디아예 [오후 6시 28분]
안녕하세요, 자마르. 그럼요, 만나서 회포를 풀고 싶네요. 149**떠난 지 2년 됐죠?** 믿을 수가 없어요. 149**당신이 우리의 신입 학생 상담사로 있었던 게 마치 어제 같아요.**

자마르 리처드슨 [오후 6시 31분]
그러게 말이에요! 제 비행기는 목요일 7시쯤 도착해요. 우리 만나서 늦은 저녁을 함께 할까요?

아미나 은디아예 [오후 6시 33분]
음. 150**토요일 점심은 어때요?** 목요일 저녁은 발표 준비를 하는 데 쓰고 싶어요.

자마르 리처드슨 [오후 6시 34분]
그럼 되겠네요.

아미나 은디아예 [오후 6시 35분]

좋아요. 그 전에 마주치지 못하면 금요일에 다시 문자 해서 자세한 사항을 정하기로 해요.

> 어휘 approve 승인하다 catch up 회포를 풀다 run into 마주치다, 우연히 만나다

149 추론 / 암시

번역 리처드슨 씨는 누구이겠는가?
  (A) 은디아예 씨의 예전 동료
  (B) 은디아예 씨의 공동발표자
  (C) 대학생
  (D) 회의 주최자

해설 은디아예 씨는 오후 6시 28분 메시지에서 리처드슨 씨가 떠난 지 2년 됐다는 것을 확인(It's been two years since you left, right?)한 후, '우리의 새 학생 상담사로 있었던 게 마치 어제 같아요(It seems like only yesterday that you were our newest student counselor)'라고 했다. 따라서 리처드슨 씨가 은디아예 씨의 예전 동료였음을 추론할 수 있으므로, (A)가 정답이다.

150 의도 파악

번역 오후 6시 34분에 리처드슨 씨가 "그럼 되겠네요"라고 쓴 의미는?
  (A) 준비를 어느 정도 하는 것이 유용하리라 생각한다.
  (B) 일부 장비가 신뢰할 만하다고 생각한다.
  (C) 기꺼이 도와줄 의향이 있다.
  (D) 아마 제안된 시간에 만날 수 있을 것이다.

해설 은디아예 씨가 오후 6시 33분 메시지에서 목요일 저녁에는 발표 준비를 하고 싶으니 토요일 점심에 만나는 게 어떠냐(How about lunch on Saturday?)고 제안했는데, 이에 대해 리처드슨 씨가 '그럼 되겠네요(That should work)'라고 긍정의 응답을 한 것이므로, (D)가 정답이다.

151-152 이메일

발신: ⟨lester.knight@eorp.com⟩
수신: ⟨benita.garza@niy-mail.com⟩
제목: 다가오는 약속
날짜: 1월 2일
첨부: 정보

가르자 씨께,

1월 17일 오후 2시에 저와 만나기로 약속해 주셔서 감사합니다. **151**저는 세심한 자금 관리와 현명한 투자를 통해 고객님이 목표를 달성하실 수 있게 도와 드릴 기회를 갖게 되어 매우 기쁩니다. 그 목표가 자택 구매이든지, 자녀의 대학 등록금 마련이든지, 아니면 그 외 무엇이든지 말입니다.

첫 만남을 최대한 생산적인 자리로 만들기 위해서, 고객님의 수입, 자산, 부채 등에 관한 정보를 갖고 오실 필요가 있습니다. **152**이 이메일에 첨부된 내용을 검토해 필요한 모든 문서를 확인해 보십시오. 제 사무실로 오시기 전에 제게 문의할

거리를 생각하고 적어두시는 것도 좋습니다.

만나 뵙기를 고대합니다.

레스터 나이트

> 어휘 make an appointment 약속을 잡다 achieve 달성하다
money management 자금 관리 investing 투자(하는 행위)
productive 생산적인 asset 자산 debt 부채, 빚 full range of
모든, 전체의 paperwork 서류

151 추론 / 암시

번역 나이트 씨의 직업은 무엇이겠는가?
  (A) 부동산 중개업자
  (B) 과외 교사
  (C) 재무 설계사
  (D) 채용 담당자

해설 첫 번째 단락에서 나이트 씨는 자신이 세심한 자금 관리와 현명한 투자를 통해 고객이 목표를 달성하게끔 도와줄 수 있다(to help you achieve your goals ~ through careful money management and smart investing)고 했으므로, 나이트 씨가 재정 관리에 조언을 해주는 사람, 즉 재무 설계사임을 추론할 수 있다. 따라서 (C)가 정답이다.

152 세부 사항

번역 나이트 씨에 따르면, 첨부물의 목적은?
  (A) 사무실 위치 설명
  (B) 지급 요청의 당위성 주장
  (C) 제안 세부내용 요약
  (D) 필요한 문서 목록 제공

해설 두 번째 단락에서 이메일에 첨부된 내용을 검토해 첫 만남에 가져와야 하는 모든 서류를 확인해 보라(Please review the attachment to this e-mail to see the full range of paperwork that will be necessary)고 권유했으므로, (D)가 정답이다.

어휘 describe 설명하다 justify 당위성을 주장하다 summarize
요약하다 required 요구되는, 필요한

▸▸ Paraphrasing 지문의 the full range of paperwork that
will be necessary
→ 정답의 a list of required documents

153-155 공지

고시

3월 6일: 도널리 시는 4월부터 용수 배급 시스템 일부를 개선할 계획이다. **154/155**도시의 현재 수요에 비해 부족한 크기의 강관은 고밀도 플라스틱 배관으로 교체될 예정이다. 나머지 배관에도 밸브를 추가해 송수관 파손에 따른 용수 손실을 제한할 것이다. 도시 평가 결과 이 사업이 지역 습지에 영향을 미칠 수 있다고 판단되었다. **153**따라서 주민들에게 환경 및 안전에 대한 우려를 표명할 수 있는 기회를 제공하기 위해 이를 고시한다. 평가 결과가 담긴 사업 파일은 시청 수자원부에서 공개 열람할 수 있다. 사업에 대한 의견은 3월 27일까지 같은 장소에서 제출할 수 있다.

153 주제 / 목적

번역 공지를 쓴 이유는?
(A) 사업 기회를 발표하려고
(B) 제안에 대한 의견을 구하려고
(C) 주민들에게 서비스 중단을 미리 알리려고
(D) 사업에 대한 오해를 바로잡으려고

해설 초반에 용수 배급 시스템 개선의 일환으로 배수관을 교체할 계획이라고 한 후, 중반부에서 주민들에게 환경 및 안전에 대한 우려를 표명할 수 있는 기회를 제공하기 위해(in order to provide residents with an opportunity to express their environmental and safety concerns) 이를 고시한다고 했다. 따라서 (B)가 정답이다.

어휘 caution 경고하다, 미리 주의를 주다 interruption 중단 correct 정정하다

▸▸ Paraphrasing 지문의 in order to provide residents
with an opportunity to express their
environmental and safety concerns
→ 정답의 To seek feedback on a proposal

154 추론 / 암시 고난도

번역 도널리에 관해 암시된 것은?
(A) 물 사용량이 증가했다.
(B) 비교적 건조한 지역에 위치한다.
(C) 시 공무원들이 공청회를 열 예정이다.
(D) 식수의 품질을 평가했다.

해설 초반부에서 도시의 현재 수요에 비해 부족한 크기의 강관이 교체될 예정(Steel pipes of insufficient size for the city's current needs will be replaced)이라고 했으므로, 물 사용량이 예전보다 증가했음을 추론할 수 있다. 따라서 (A)가 정답이다.

155 문장 삽입 고난도

번역 [1], [2], [3], [4]로 표시된 곳 중에서 다음 문장이 가장 적합한 곳은?
"나머지 배관에도 밸브를 추가해 송수관 파손에 따른 용수 손실을 제한할 것이다."
(A) [1]
(B) [2]
(C) [3]
(D) [4]

해설 주어진 문장에서 나머지 배관에도 밸브가 추가된다(Valves will also be added to the remaining pipes)고 했으므로, 앞에서 먼저 기존 배관에 대한 변경 사항이 언급되어야 한다. [2] 앞에서 강관이 고밀도 플라스틱 배관으로 교체된다(Steel pipes ~ be replaced with high-density plastic pipes)고 했으므로, 이 뒤에 주어진 문장이 들어가야 자연스럽다. 따라서 (B)가 정답이다.

156-157 안내문

나보스 어소시에이츠

156전자레인지를 사용하기 전에 읽으세요!

1. 156심한 냄새가 날 수도 있는 음식(예: 생선)을 데우기 위해 전자레인지를 사용하지 마십시오.

2. 접시를 뚜껑이나 키친타월로 덮어서 전자레인지 안에 음식물이 튀지 않도록 합니다.

3. 전자레인지에 음식물이 튀거나 떨어지면 즉시 깨끗이 씻어내십시오. 청소용품은 싱크대 밑에 있습니다.

4. 157전자레인지에 문제가 생기면 이제 사무장이 아닌 정비팀의 토니 미첼(내선 32번)에게 보고해야 합니다.

156 주제 / 목적

번역 안내문의 목적은?
(A) 편의 시설의 특징 홍보
(B) 위험에 대해 경고
(C) 절차 설명
(D) 일련의 규칙 공표

해설 제목에서 '전자레인지를 사용하기 전에 읽으세요!(Please read before using the microwave!)'라고 한 후, 1번부터 사용시 주의사항들을 나열하고 있으므로, (D)가 정답이다.

어휘 feature 특징, 기능 amenity 편의 시설 issue 공표[발표]하다

157 추론 / 암시 고난도

번역 미첼 씨의 직무에 관해 가장 사실에 가까운 것은?
(A) 편람에 명시되어 있다.
(B) 최근에 늘었다.
(C) 주로 청소 작업으로 이루어져 있다.
(D) 사무장들과 소통하는 일이 포함된다.

해설 4번 주의사항에서 전자레인지에 문제가 생기면 이제 사무장이 아닌 정비팀 토니 미첼에게 보고해야 한다(Any problems with the microwave should now be reported to Tony Mitchell in Maintenance ~ not an office administrator)고 했으므로, 그의 직무가 늘어났음을 추론할 수 있다. 따라서 (B)가 정답이다.

어휘 specify 명시하다 consist of ~로 이루어져 있다

158-160 이메일

발신: 스콧 팸
수신: 자원봉사자 목록
제목: 먼섹 도서 전시회
날짜: 8월 7일

안녕하세요, 자원봉사자 여러분!

먼섹 도서 전시회 조직위원회를 대표해, 여러분 모두를 이 멋진 행사의 진행을 책임지고 있는 팀으로 맞이하고자 합니다.

¹⁵⁸여러분은 이달 중으로 본인이 속한 특정 분야(예: 출품자 지원, 교통 등)의 관리자로부터 출근 장소 같은 세부사항이 명시된 이메일을 받게 됩니다만, 제가 먼저 몇 가지 일반적인 조언과 정보를 공유하겠습니다.

¹⁵⁹모든 자원봉사자는 편한 신발을 신는 것은 물론, 혹시 필요할 때를 대비해 자외선 차단제를 갖고 오는 것이 좋겠습니다. 또한 혼디나 컨벤션 센터는 대형 행사장이므로, 근무시간을 제대로 맞추려면 15분 일찍 도착하도록 계획을 세워야 합니다.

전시회에서 무슨 일을 하든, 일단 '자원봉사자' 배지를 달게 되면 손님을 돕는 일이 우선이 되어야 합니다. ¹⁶⁰입구에서 받게 될 '전시회 참가자 가이드' 책자를 살펴보고 손님들이 편의 시설을 찾는 데 도움이 될 수 있도록 하세요. 대답할 수 없는 질문을 받으면 문의한 사람을 가장 가까운 안내소로 안내하세요.

전시회에서 만나요!

스콧 팸
자원봉사자 수석 코디네이터

어휘 **on behalf of** ~을 대표하여 **organizing committee** 조직위원회 **responsible for** ~을 맡은 **supervisor** 관리자 **particular** 특정한 **exhibitor** 출품자[사] **assistance** 도움, 지원 **transportation** 교통 **specify** 명시하다 **report** 출근 보고를 하다 **shift** (교대) 근무시간, 근무조 **recommend** 권고하다 **comfortable** 편안한 **venue** 장소, 행사장 **ensure** 보장하다, ~하게 하다 **priority** 우선 사항 **convenience facility** 편의 시설

158 세부 사항

번역 팸 씨는 향후 이메일에 어떤 정보가 제공된다고 말하는가?
(A) 교육 과정 날짜
(B) 유니폼 요건
(C) 교통비
(D) 근무 장소

해설 두 번째 단락에서 이달 중으로 본인이 속한 특정 분야(예: 출품자 지원, 교통 등)의 관리자로부터 출근 장소 같은 세부사항이 명시된 이메일을 받게 된다(You'll receive an e-mail later this month from the supervisor of your particular area that specifies details such as where to report for your shift)고 했으므로, (D)가 정답이다.

▶▶ Paraphrasing 지문의 **an e-mail later this month**
→ 질문의 **a future e-mail**

지문의 **where to report for your shift**
→ 정답의 **Some work sites**

159 추론 / 암시 고난도

번역 자원봉사자들에 관해 암시된 것은?
(A) 일부는 실외에 배치될 것이다.
(B) 각 활동 영역에 15명이 있을 것이다.
(C) 전시회 입구에서 배지를 받을 것이다.
(D) 무료 숙박을 받을 자격이 된다.

해설 세 번째 단락에서 혹시 필요할 때를 대비해 자외선 차단제를 갖고 오는 것이 좋겠다(We recommend that all volunteers ~ bring sunscreen just in case it is needed)고 권고했으므로, 자원봉사자들 중 일부는 실외에 배치될 것으로 추론할 수 있다. 따라서 (A)가 정답이다.

어휘 **be entitled to** ~을 받을 자격이 되다

160 세부 사항

번역 자원봉사자들은 전시회에 관해 어떻게 배우도록 권고되는가?
(A) 관리자에게 물어봐서
(B) 도보로 탐색해서
(C) 출판물을 읽어서
(D) 안내소를 방문해서

해설 네 번째 단락에서 입구에서 받게 될 '전시회 참가자 가이드' 책자를 살펴보고 손님들이 편의 시설을 찾는 데 도움이 될 수 있도록 하라(Please take a look at the "Fairgoers Guide" booklet ~ so that you can help them find convenience facilities)고 했으므로, (C)가 정답이다.

어휘 **publication** 출판(물)

▶▶ Paraphrasing 지문의 **take a look at the "Fairgoers Guide" booklet** → 정답의 **reading a publication**

161-163 기사

흥분과 논란이 관광청 공모전을 휩싸다

해스펜튼 관광청이 최근 행사인 '#마이해스펜튼 공모전'으로 파문을 일으키고 있다. 이 공모전은 해스펜튼의 모습을 가장 잘 담은 짧은 영상을 만든 사람에게 1,000달러를 지급한다. 동영상은 소셜 미디어 플랫폼인 샤우트스터에 게시되어야 하고 '#마이해스펜튼'으로 해쉬태그가 달려야 한다. 각 동영상이 받는 '좋아요' 수와 관광청 위원들이 제출하는 투표를 합산해 우승자가 결정된다.

¹⁶²이 공모전은 관광청에서 가장 최근 임명된 위원이자 유일하게 35세 이하인 엘라 포르테가 생각해냈다. 포르테 씨는 어제 전화 통화에서 이 공모전이 "기술과 해스펜튼의 가장 위대한 자원인 사람을 모두 활용한다"고 말했다. 확실히 샤우트스터 이용자들은 공모전에 열광했다. ¹⁶¹지금까지 80개 가까운 동영상이 올라와 총 1만 개가 넘는 '좋아요'를 얻었다.

하지만 모두가 공모전에 만족하는 것은 아니다. ¹⁶³지난주 시의회 회의에서 지역 식당 주인 어니스트 매튜스는 관광청이 근본적으로 샤우트스터를 사용하지 않는 사람의 생각을 무시하고 있다고 불평했다. 그는 "제 고객은 대부분 어르신들인데, 샤우트스터를 사용하는 사람이 아무도 없습니다"라고 말했다. "이번 공모전에서 보여지는 해스펜튼의 측면은 너무 좁아요." 이에 대해 후아니타 파딜라 의원은 향후 홍보 활동에서는 다양한 참여 방법을 고려할 것을 관광청에 촉구하겠다고 말했다.

>> Paraphrasing 지문의 the board was essentially ignoring the ideas of anyone who does not use Shoutster → 정답의 it excludes some residents' perspectives

161 세부 사항

번역 공모전은 현재 어떤 단계인가?
(A) 아직 시작되지 않았다.
(B) 출품작들이 제출되고 있다.
(C) 관광청이 투표하고 있다.
(D) 우승자가 선정되었다.

해설 두 번째 단락에서 지금까지 80개 가까운 동영상이 올라왔다(Nearly 80 videos have been posted so far)고 했으므로, 현재는 출품작이 제출되는 단계임을 알 수 있다. 따라서 (B)가 정답이다.

>> Paraphrasing 지문의 have been ~ so far
→ 질문의 currently
지문의 Nearly 80 videos have been posted → 정답의 Entries are being submitted

162 사실 관계 확인

번역 포르테 씨에 관해 언급된 것은?
(A) 시의회 회의에 출석했다.
(B) 샤우트스터에 개인 계정을 갖고 있다.
(C) 짧은 홍보 영상에 출연했다.
(D) 조직의 최연소 구성원이다.

해설 두 번째 단락에서 포르테 씨가 관광청에서 가장 최근 임명된 위원이자 유일하게 35세 이하(the board's newest member as well as its only one under 35)인 사람이라고 했으므로, 조직의 최연소 구성원임을 알 수 있다. 따라서 (D)가 정답이다.

>> Paraphrasing 지문의 its only one under 35
→ 정답의 the youngest member of an organization

163 세부 사항

번역 매튜스 씨가 공모전에서 싫어하는 것은?
(A) 관광청이 결과에 영향을 미칠 수 있다는 점
(B) 일부 주민의 관점을 배제한다는 점
(C) 과거에 성공하지 못했다는 점
(D) 시 입장에서 보았을 때 비용이 많이 든다는 점

해설 마지막 단락에서 지역 식당 주인 매튜스 씨가 관광청이 샤우트스터를 사용하지 않는 사람의 생각을 무시하고 있다고 불평했다(local restaurant owner Ernest Mathews complained that the board was essentially ignoring the ideas of anyone who does not use Shoutster)고 했으므로, (B)가 정답이다.

164-167 온라인 채팅

셀레나 호바스, 오후 3시 49분
164월크 머티리얼 핸들링의 컨설턴트가 오늘 아침에 와서 푸크빌 창고 재설계에 대한 아이디어를 발표했죠? 어땠어요?
에이미 캐롤, 오후 3시 50분
그녀의 제안들은 대부분 훌륭했어요. 165(D)예를 들어, 출입구 근처에 구역을 하나 만들어서 고객들이 가장 자주 주문하는 자재를 소량으로 모아두라고 권유했어요. 그렇게 하면 가져오는 시간이 단축될 거예요.
셀레나 호바스, 오후 3시 50분
좋은 생각인 것 같네요. 165(A)우리가 짐작했던 것처럼 팰릿 랙에 투자해야 한다고 생각하던가요?
에이미 캐롤, 오후 3시 51분
165(A)네, 하지만 아까 말한 그 특별 전면 구역만요. 나머지 재고품은 바닥에 계속 쌓아두면 돼요.
로널드 에구치, 오후 3시 51분
165(C)그렇지만 그녀는 우리가 스캔 가능한 라벨로 위치 찾기 시스템을 시행해야 한다고도 말했어요.
셀레나 호바스, 오후 3시 52분
166음, 비싸겠네요. 하지만 효율성을 개선할 가능성이 크다고 확신해요.
에이미 캐롤, 오후 3시 53분
우리 생각도 그래요. 생산성 향상을 통해 시스템 비용을 회수하는 데 얼마나 걸리는지 물었더니 어떤 공급업체를 선택하느냐에 따라 다르다고 하더군요.
로널드 에구치, 오후 3시 54분
창고 한 곳이 아니라 여러 군데에 시스템을 도입하면 흔쾌히 할인해 줄 공급업체를 찾고 있어요.
셀레나 호바스, 오후 3시 55분
167다른 곳에 시스템을 실행하기 전에 우선 한 곳에만 해보기로 할 지도 몰라요. 하지만 흥미로운 생각이네요. 알아보고 알려주세요.

164 주제 / 목적

번역 호바스 씨가 온라인 채팅을 시작한 이유는?
(A) 회의 결과를 알아보려고
(B) 문서의 내용을 명확히 설명하려고
(C) 점검 준비사항을 논의하려고
(D) 발표에 대한 자신의 의견을 공유하려고

해설 호바스 씨는 오후 3시 49분에 메시지를 보내 웰크 머티리얼 핸들링의 컨설턴트가 푸크빌 창고 재설계에 대한 아이디어를 발표했는지 확인(The consultant from Welk Material Handling came ~ to present her ideas for redesigning the Pookville warehouse, right?)한 후, 어땠는지(What did you think?) 다른 사람들에게 의견을 물었다. 따라서 (A)가 정답이다.

어휘 clarify 명확하게 하다, 분명히 말하다 arrangement 준비(사항) inspection 점검

165 사실 관계 확인

번역 컨설턴트가 권고한 사항이 아닌 것은?
(A) 시설물 한 부분에 받침대 설치하기
(B) 바닥에 선을 칠해 통로 크기 표시하기
(C) 전자 장치로 읽을 수 있는 스티커 사용하기
(D) 인기 있는 재고품에는 더 쉽게 접근할 수 있게 하기

해설 오후 3시 50분 메시지에서 컨설턴트가 팰릿 랙에 투자해야 한다고 생각했는지(Did she think we'll need to invest in pallet racks?) 묻는 호바스 씨의 질문에 캐롤 씨가 특별 전면 구역만 그렇다(Yes, but only for that special front area)고 응답한 부분에서 (A)를 확인할 수 있다. 그리고 에구치 씨의 오후 3시 51분 메시지 중 '그녀는 우리가 스캔 가능한 라벨로 위치 찾기 시스템을 시행해야 한다고도 말했어요(she also said we should implement a location-finding system with scannable labels)'에서 (C)를, 캐롤 씨의 오후 3시 50분 메시지 중 '출입구 근처에 구역을 하나 만들어서 고객들이 가장 자주 주문하는 자재를 소량으로 모아두라고 권유했어요(she recommended setting up an area near the entrance that would have small quantities of the materials that customers order most frequently)'에서 (D)를 확인할 수 있다. 따라서 언급되지 않은 (B)가 정답이다.

어휘 install 설치하다 aisle 통로 accessible 접근하기 쉬운

▶ Paraphrasing 지문의 invest in pallet racks
→ 보기 (A)의 Installing racks
지문의 for that special front area
→ 보기 (A)의 in one part of a facility
지문의 scannable labels
→ 보기 (C)의 stickers that can be read electronically
지문의 setting up an area near the entrance
→ 보기 (D)의 Make ~ more accessible
지문의 the materials that customers order most frequently
→ 보기 (D)의 popular types of stock

166 의도 파악

번역 오후 3시 53분에 캐롤 씨가 "우리 생각도 그래요"라고 쓸 때 의미하는 것은?
(A) 그녀와 에구치 씨는 어떤 아이디어에 대해 복잡한 심경이다.
(B) 그녀와 에구치 씨는 어떤 결과에 혼란스러워 한다.
(C) 창고의 생산고가 실망스러울 정도로 낮다.
(D) 사업 예산을 늘리면 안 된다.

해설 호바스 씨가 오후 3시 52분 메시지에서 위치 찾기 시스템을 시행하는 것에 대해 비싸겠다(that sounds expensive)고 한 후, 효율성을 개선할 수 있는 가능성이 크다고 확신한다(I'm sure it has a huge potential to improve our efficiency)며 자신이 생각하는 부정적 측면과 긍정적 측면 모두를 언급했다. 이에 대해 캐롤 씨가 '우리 생각도 그래요(Our thoughts exactly)'라며 응답했으므로, 그녀와 에구치 씨도 위치 찾기 시스템 시행을 고민하고 있음을 알 수 있다. 따라서 (A)가 정답이다.

167 세부 사항

번역 호바스 씨에 따르면, 채팅 참여자들의 회사가 무엇을 선택하겠는가?
(A) 푸크빌에 새 지점 개설
(B) 시스템의 일부 기능을 맞춤형으로 설정
(C) 제도를 소규모로 실시
(D) 오래된 상품 할인

해설 호바스 씨가 오후 3시 55분 메시지에서 다른 곳에 시스템을 시행하기 전에 우선 한 곳에서만 해보기로 할 지도 모른다(we may decide to try out the system in one location before implementing it in the others)고 했으므로, (C)가 정답이다.

어휘 customize 맞춤형으로 설정하다 scheme 제도, 계획 merchandise 상품

▶ Paraphrasing 지문의 try out the system in one location
→ 정답의 Conduct a small-scale test of a scheme

168-171 웹페이지

http://www.allstons.com/corporate

올스톤즈 >> 기업 문의

[168]40년이 넘는 기간 동안, 올스톤즈는 모든 체육 활동에 맞는 최고 품질의 의류와 신발을 고객님들께 제공해 드리기 위해 전력을 기울여왔습니다. 오늘날 당사는 국내에서 가장 인기 있고 흥미로운 제품들을 대표하는 판매업체 수백 곳과 거래 관계를 유지하고 있습니다. 하지만, 당사는 지금도 '올스톤즈'의 기치 아래 판매할 새로운 브랜드와 스타일을 찾고 있습니다. 당사는 대규모의 충성 고객층과 신속하고 신뢰할 수 있는 대금 지급 일정을 자랑합니다. [170]그 대가로 당사가 판매업체에 요구하는 것은 상품 포장 및 트럭 배송 시 당사의 합리적인 기준을 준수하는 것뿐입니다. 당사에 판매업체로 입점하는 방법에 대해 문의하시려면 (809) 555-0162로 전화하거나 vendors@allstons.com으로 이메일을 보내세요. 선별된 기존 판매업체들의 추천 글을 기꺼이 제공해 드리겠습니다.

[169/171]또한, 올스톤즈는 미국 중서부 지역 전역에서 신규 매장을 열 수 있는 예비 입지를 계속 검토하고 있습니다. 매장 최소 면적 요건은 일반적으로 15,000 제곱피트입니다. [171]적합한 상업용 부동산을 소유하고 있으며 당사에 임대건을 논의하고 싶으시면 (809) 555-0160으로 시카고 본사에 전화해 주세요.

어휘 committed 전력을 기울이는, 헌신하는 apparel 의류
athletic 체육의, 운동 선수용의 vendor 판매업체 represent
대표하다, 나타내다 under the "A" banner "A"의 기치 아래, ~의
일부로 (= under the banner of A) boast 자랑하다 dependable
신뢰할 수 있는 reasonable 합리적인 merchandise 상품
establish a relationship 관계를 맺다[정립하다] testimonial
추천 글 existing 기존의 constantly 계속 suitable 적합한
commercial 상업의 property 부동산

168 추론 / 암시

번역 올스톤즈는 어떤 사업체이겠는가?
(A) 건강식품 공급업체
(B) 스포츠 의류 매장
(C) 헬스장 체인
(D) 행사 기획사

해설 첫 번째 단락에서 올스톤즈가 모든 체육 활동에 맞는 최고 품질의 의류
와 신발을 고객들에게 제공하기 위해 전력을 기울여 왔다(Allston's has
been committed to giving our customers the best selection of
quality apparel and footwear for every athletic activity)고 했으
므로, 올스톤즈가 스포츠 의류 매장이라고 추론할 수 있다. 따라서 (B)가
정답이다.

▸▸ Paraphrasing 지문의 quality apparel ~ for every athletic
activity
→ 정답의 sports clothing

169 추론 / 암시

번역 올스톤즈에 관해 암시된 것은?
(A) 최근에 본사를 이전했다.
(B) 곧 이름을 바꿀 것이다.
(C) 확장을 시도하고 있다.
(D) 지역 무역박람회에 참석한다.

해설 두 번째 단락에서 올스톤즈가 신규 매장을 열 수 있는 예비 입지를 계속 검
토하고 있다(Allston's is constantly reviewing potential locations
for opening new stores)고 했으므로, 올스톤즈가 사업을 확장하려 한
다고 추론할 수 있다. 따라서 (C)가 정답이다.

어휘 expand (사업을) 확장하다, 확장되다

▸▸ Paraphrasing 지문의 opening new stores
→ 정답의 expand

170 세부 사항

번역 웹페이지에 따르면, 기존의 모든 판매업체는 무엇을 해야 하는가?
(A) 회사 방침에 따라 품목 포장
(B) 요청 시 추천 글 제공
(C) 트럭에 올스톤즈 로고 게시
(D) 친환경적으로 운영한다는 점 입증하기

해설 첫 번째 단락에서 올스톤즈가 판매업체에 요구하는 것은 상품 포장 및
트럭 배송 시 자사의 합리적인 기준을 준수하는 것뿐(we merely ask
vendors to follow our reasonable standards for merchandise
packing and truck deliveries)이라고 했으므로, (A)가 정답이다.

▸▸ Paraphrasing 지문의 follow our reasonable standards
for merchandise packing
→ 정답의 Pack items according to
company policies

171 문장 삽입

번역 [1], [2], [3], [4]로 표시된 곳 중에서 다음 문장이 가장 적합한 곳은?
"매장 최소 면적 요건은 일반적으로 15,000제곱피트입니다."
(A) [1]
(B) [2]
(C) [3]
(D) [4]

해설 주어진 문장에서 매장 최소 면적 요건을 제시하고 있으므로, 앞에서 먼
저 요건을 제시한 이유와 배경이 언급되어야 한다. [4] 앞에서 신규 매장
을 열 수 있는 예비 입지를 계속 검토하고 있다(Allston's is constantly
reviewing potential locations for opening new stores)고 했고,
뒤에서는 적합한 상업용 부동산(a suitable commercial property)을
보유하고 있다면 연락해 달라고 요청했으므로, 이 사이에 주어진 문장이
들어가야 자연스럽다. 따라서 (D)가 정답이다.

172-175 회람

수신: 관리자들
발신: 신준태
주제: 직원 처우
날짜: 7월 20일

다들 아시다시피, **175눌런 씨께서 올해 저를 눌런 소프트웨어의 첫 정규직 인사
담당자로 채용하셨습니다.** 제 직무 중 하나는 직원의 관점으로 전반적인 상황을
보는 것인데, 이제 여기 온 지 몇 달이 되었으니 몇 가지 개선안을 생각해보았습니
다. **172더 큰 기업으로 성장하고자 하는 중소 기업으로서, 우수한 직원을 유치
하고 근속하게 하는 근무 환경을 제공하는 것이 중요합니다.**

한 가지 중요한 고려사항은 업무량입니다. **173(B)직원들과 주기적으로 확인해서
표준 주당 근무시간 내에 업무를 끝낼 수 있도록 해야 합니다.** 174만약 여러분 부
서의 업무가 과중해지면, 눌런 씨 및 저와 함께 회의를 잡아서 인원 충원에 관해
논의하길 바랍니다.

**173(C)마찬가지로, 직원들이 필요할 때 편하게 병가를 내고 할당된 휴가 일수를
전부 사용할 수 있어야 합니다.** 이는 직원의 건강과 사기를 지키는 중요한 방법
입니다.

**173(A)마지막으로, 직원들이 성과 목표를 달성하는 한, 각자의 근무 시간에 어느
정도 융통성을 발휘할 수 있게 하세요.** 아직 원격근무를 지원할 수는 없지만 최
소한 직원들이 적절한 선에서 자신의 일정을 관리할 수 있도록 힘을 실어줄 수
있습니다.

눌런 씨와 저, 그리고 여러분 모두 목요일 오전 10시에 만나 이 회람 내용에 대
해 논의하도록 하겠습니다. **175눌런 씨는 이미 제 권고안을 승인했으므로 이에
대해 논쟁할 자리는 아니라는 점 유의하시기 바랍니다.** 대신, 어떻게 하면 이것이
을 최대치로 달성할 지에 집중할 예정입니다. 감사합니다.

어휘 treatment 처우 overall 전반적인 perspective 관점 improvement 개선 workload 업무량 workweek 주당 근무시간 workload 업무량 similarly 마찬가지로 allotment 할당 morale 사기 flexibility 융통성 performance 성과 remote work 원격근무 empower 힘을 싣다 within reason 적절한 선에서, 온당한 범위 내에서 recommendation 권고(안) debate 논쟁하다

172 사실 관계 확인

번역 눌런 소프트웨어에 관해 알 수 있는 것은?
(A) 최근 새로운 사무실을 열었다.
(B) 설립된 지 채 1년이 안 됐다.
(C) 직원이 많지 않다.
(D) 주주들을 만족시켜야 한다.

해설 첫 번째 단락에서 눌런 소프트웨어가 더 큰 기업으로 성장하고자 하는 중소 기업(As a small business that hopes to grow into a larger one)이라고 했으므로, 직원이 많지 않다는 것을 알 수 있다. 따라서 (C)가 정답이다.

어휘 found 설립하다 shareholder 주주

▶▶ Paraphrasing   지문의 **a small business**
→ 정답의 **It does not have many employees**

173 사실 관계 확인   고난도

번역 직원 처우 개선 방안으로 언급되지 않은 것은?
(A) 조정 가능한 근무 시간
(B) 합리적인 업무량
(C) 쉬운 휴가 사용
(D) 구내 건강 프로그램

해설 네 번째 단락의 '각자의 근무 시간에 어느 정도 융통성을 발휘할 수 있게 할 것(allow employees some flexibility in their hours)'에서 (A)를, 두 번째 단락의 '표준 주당 근무시간 내에 업무를 끝낼 수 있도록 할 것(ensure that their tasks can be completed in a standard workweek)'에서 (B)를, 세 번째 단락의 '편하게 병가를 내고 할당된 휴가 일수를 전부 사용할 수 있어야 할 것(employees should feel comfortable taking sick time when needed and using their full allotment of vacation days)'에서 (C)를 확인할 수 있다. 따라서 언급되지 않은 (D)가 정답이다.

어휘 adjustable 조정 가능한 reasonable 합리적인

▶▶ Paraphrasing   지문의 **allow employees some flexibility in their hours**
→ 보기 (A)의 **Adjustable working hours**

지문의 **their tasks can be completed in a standard workweek**
→ 보기 (B)의 **A reasonable workload**

지문의 **feel comfortable taking sick time ~ vacation days**
→ 보기 (C)의 **Easy usage of leave time**

174 세부 사항   고난도

번역 회람에 따르면, 수신자들이 신 씨와 회의 일정을 잡아야 하는 이유는?
(A) 그의 생각에 반대를 표명하려고
(B) 인력 충원을 제안하려고
(C) 성과급을 권고하려고
(D) 직원의 원격 근무를 허가 받으려고

해설 두 번째 단락에서 신 씨는 인원 충원에 관해 논의하려면 자신과 회의를 잡아야 한다(please set up a meeting with ~ me to discuss adding more personnel)고 했으므로, (B)가 정답이다.

어휘 opposition 반대 performance-based bonus 성과급 permission 허가, 승인

▶▶ Paraphrasing   지문의 **set up a meeting**
→ 질문의 **schedule a meeting**

지문의 **to discuss adding more personnel**
→ 정답의 **To propose hiring more workers**

175 추론 / 암시

번역 신 씨가 회람에 있는 권고안에 관해 암시하는 것은?
(A) 전 직원에게 공지될 것이다.
(B) 과학 연구의 뒷받침을 받는다.
(C) 기업 소유주의 지지를 받는다.
(D) 경쟁업체에 의해 채택되었다.

해설 마지막 단락에서 신 씨는 눌런 씨가 이미 자신의 권고안을 승인했다(Ms. Noolan has already given her approval to my recommendations)고 했으므로, (C)가 정답이다. 참고로, 첫 단락에서 눌런 씨가 신 씨를 채용했다고 한 것으로 보아 눌런 씨가 최종 결정권자(기업 소유주)임을 알 수 있다.

어휘 endorse 지지하다 adopt 채택하다 competitor 경쟁업체

▶▶ Paraphrasing   지문의 **Ms. Noolan has already given her approval** → 정답의 **endorsed by the business's owner**

176-180 웹페이지 + 이메일

www.orosco-pac.org/fscs

오로스코 공연 예술 센터

무료 가을 콘서트 시리즈

176 9월부터 11월까지 매주 목요일 저녁, 센터는 가장 오붓한 공연 공간인 어빈 원형극장에서 무료 공연을 선보입니다. 다양한 장르를 보여주도록 치밀하게 기획된 이번 시리즈는 기성 음악가들을 만나고 흥미진진한 신진 음악가들을 발견할 수 있는 절호의 기회입니다.

공연은 오후 7시에 시작합니다. 180 예약은 10인 이상만 가능합니다. 기타 모든 참석자들은 콘서트 시작 전 충분한 시간을 두고 매표소에 줄을 서서 표를 확보하기를 권합니다.

다가오는 콘서트 (전체 일정)

10월 19일 에밀리아 베르나우어: 177(D) 저명한 콘서트 피아니스트 로만 허프 씨가 "클래식 피아노의 차세대 스타"라고 칭한 베르나우어 씨가 프랑스 작곡가들의 작품을 연주합니다.

10월 26일	그린 클리프 트리오: ^{177(B)}재즈음악 아카데미의 권위 있는 "올해의 앨범" 상을 받은 그룹이 연주하는 피아노, 더블 베이스, 드럼의 부드러운 조화를 감상해 보세요.
11월 2일	조니와 농부들: 전설적인 포크 밴드가 10년 만에 처음으로 헬름스페드를 방문합니다! ^{177(A)}와서 "부러진 밴조"를 비롯한 베스트셀러 앨범 히트곡들을 들어보세요.
¹⁷⁹11월 9일	오로스코 오페라단: 바로 이곳 헬름스페드 출신의 실력파 가수들이 이탈리아어와 영어로 된 다양한 오페라의 유명 아리아 및 듀엣곡을 공연합니다.

더 자세한 정보는 555-0180으로 전화하거나, 소셜 미디어에서 저희를 팔로우해 과거 콘서트 사진을 보고 다가오는 콘서트에 대한 알림 메시지를 받으세요.

어휘 amphitheater 원형극장 intimate 아늑한 represent 대표하다, 보여주다 established 기성의, (이미 자리를 잡아) 인정받는 renowned 저명한 recital 연주회 prestigious 권위 있는 decade 10년 aria 아리아, 오페라의 독창 부분 reminder 알림 메시지, 상기시켜 주는 것

발신: 엘로이즈 플린

수신: 트리나 맥기

제목: 회신: 무료 가을 콘서트

날짜: 10월 10일

트리나에게

¹⁷⁸그래자, 나도 너랑 그 콘서트에 가고 싶어. ¹⁷⁹오로스코 공연 예술 센터에서 오페라를 무료로 볼 수 있다니 믿을 수가 없는 걸! 난 거기에 한 번도 가본 적이 없고, 정말 좋다고 들었거든. 넌 항상 도시에서 일어나는 가장 흥미로운 행사들에 대해 알고 있는 것 같아—언젠가 비결이 뭔지 알려줘야 해! ¹⁸⁰그리고 아니, 표는 내가 처리해도 돼. 넌 목요일에 일을 하니까. 우리 둘뿐인 거 맞지?

– 엘로이즈

어휘 wouldn't mind -ing ~하는 것을 개의치 않다 handle 처리하다

---

176 사실 관계 확인

번역 오로스코 공연 예술 센터에 관해 알 수 있는 것은?
(A) 두 개 이상의 무대가 있다.
(B) 다양한 건축양식을 보인다.
(C) 소셜 미디어 계정에 인터뷰를 올린다.
(D) 10세 미만 어린이가 일부 행사에 참석하도록 허용한다.

해설 웹페이지의 첫 번째 단락에서 어빈 원형극장을 설명하며 최상급 표현(its most intimate performance space)을 사용한 것으로 보아, 어빈 원형극장 이외에 다른 무대도 있음을 알 수 있다. 따라서 (A)가 정답이다.

---

177 사실 관계 확인   고난도

번역 웹페이지에서 열거된 공연자들의 성과로 언급되지 않은 것은?
(A) 앨범 다수 판매
(B) 주요 상 수상
(C) 전 세계에서 공연
(D) 유명한 음악가로부터의 찬사

해설 웹페이지의 '다가오는 콘서트(Upcoming Concerts)' 목록 중 조니와 농부들(Johnny and The Farmers)의 베스트셀러 앨범 히트곡들을 들어보라(listen to ~ hits from its bestselling records)고 권유한 부분에서 (A)를, 그린 클리프 트리오(The Green Cliff Trio)가 권위 있는 '올해의 앨범' 상(prestigious "Album of the Year" honor)을 받은 그룹이라고 소개한 부분에서 (B)를, 저명한 콘서트 피아니스트가 에밀리아 베르나우어 씨를 '클래식 피아노의 차세대 스타'라고 불렀다(Ms. Bernauer, called "the next big star in classical piano" by renowned concert pianist Roman Huff)고 설명한 부분에서 (D)를 확인할 수 있다. 따라서 언급되지 않은 (C)가 정답이다.

어휘 acclaim 칭찬, 찬사

▶ Paraphrasing 지문의 its bestselling records
→ 보기 (A)의 Selling many albums
지문의 its prestigious "Album of the Year" honor → 보기 (B)의 a major award
지문의 called "the next big star in classical piano" by renowned concert pianist → 보기 (D)의 Receiving acclaim from a famous musician

---

178 주제 / 목적

번역 이메일을 쓴 이유는?
(A) 일부 계획의 변경을 요청하려고
(B) 완료된 예약에 대한 문의에 답변하려고
(C) 예약이 이루어졌음을 확인하려고
(D) 친절한 초대에 응하려고

해설 이메일 초반부에서 플린 씨는 긍정(Sure)의 응답을 한 후, 맥기 씨와 함께 콘서트에 가고 싶다(I would love to go to the concert with you)며 한번 더 수락 의사를 밝혔으므로, 맥기 씨의 콘서트 초대에 응하기 위해 쓴 이메일임을 알 수 있다. 따라서 (D)가 정답이다.

---

179 연계

번역 플린 씨는 언제 콘서트를 보려고 하는가?
(A) 10월 19일
(B) 10월 26일
(C) 11월 2일
(D) 11월 9일

해설 이메일 초반부에서 플린 씨가 오로스코 공연 예술 센터에서 오페라를 무료로 볼 수 있다니 믿을 수 없다(I can't believe we'll be able to see opera singing in the Orosco Performing Arts Center for free!)고 했으므로, 그녀가 맥기 씨와 함께 오페라 공연을 볼 것으로 추론할 수 있다. 웹페이지의 콘서트(Upcoming Concerts) 일정을 보면, 오로스코 오페라단(Orosco Opera Company)의 오페라 공연(Talented singers from right here in Helmsped will perform famous arias and duets from various operas)은 11월 9일로 예정되어 있으므로, (D)가 정답이다.

180 연계

번역 플린 씨는 무엇을 하겠는가?
(A) 공연 당일 일찍 도착하기
(B) 공연 예술 센터 매표소로 전화하기
(C) 특정 날짜에 온라인 절차 밟기
(D) 관광 관련 모바일 앱 다운로드하기

해설 이메일 후반부에서 플린 씨는 자신이 표를 처리해도 된다(I wouldn't mind handling the tickets)고 한 후 맥기 씨와 둘만 간다는 것(It will just be the two of us, right?)을 확인했는데, 웹페이지의 두 번째 단락을 보면 예약은 10인 이상만 가능하며 기타 모든 참석자들은 콘서트 시작 전 충분한 시간을 두고 매표소에 줄을 서서 표를 확보하기를 권한다(All other attendees are encouraged to line up at the box office well before the concert in order to secure their tickets)고 되어 있다. 따라서 플린 씨가 공연 당일 일찍 도착해서 매표소에서 표를 받을 예정임을 추론할 수 있으므로, (A)가 정답이다.

▶ **Paraphrasing** 지문의 line up at the box office well before the concert
→ 정답의 Arrive early on the day of the performance

181-185 기사 + 독자 편지

(2월 7일)—데놀드 시에 웨이마르 편의점이 온다.

181(A)시 경제개발위원회(EDC)는 4,600제곱피트의 편의점을 건설하겠다는 웨이마르의 계획을 만장일치로 승인했다. 이곳에는 12개의 주유기 위에 기와를 올린 덮개를 설치할 예정이다. **181(D)**7번 도로 근처의 마일든 가에 있는 공터에 지어질 예정이며 주 7일 24시간 영업한다.

182회사가 매장을 운영하려면 시의 소음 및 교통량 감소 규정을 준수해야 한다. 무엇보다 새벽 1시부터 5시 사이에는 휘발유를 제외하고는 대형트럭으로 배송을 받을 수 없다. 또한 트럭이 마일든 가에서 매장으로 접근할 수 없기 때문에 웨이마르는 매장의 반입 구역으로 통하는 전용 도로를 건설할 예정이다.

승인은 회사 소속 교통 기술자들의 발표가 포함된 공청회가 열린 후에 이루어졌다. 참석한 주민들은 지지와 반대가 뒤섞인 목소리를 냈다. **183**마일든 가 400번지에 사는 베티 팀파노는 동네에 편의점이 생기는 건 좋지만 인근 라모나 길에 교통량이 늘어나는 건 걱정스럽다고 말했다. 그 증거로 그녀는 출퇴근 시간 자신의 차창에서 촬영한 디지털 영상을 보여줬다. 영상은 브룩 가 인근의 라모나 길에 차량 정체가 심한 모습을 보여줬다.

181(C)반면 주민인 스티브 그로식은 매장이 퇴근 후 "빠르고 따뜻한 요깃거리"를 제공할 것이므로 환영한다고 말했다. 현재 가장 가까운 편의점은 약 3킬로미터 떨어진 로렐 가에 있는 웨이스볼드 플러스 매장이다.

어휘 unanimously 만장일치로 approve 승인하다 feature (특별히) 포함하다, 선보이다 vacant 비어 있는 comply with ~을 준수하다 reduction 감소 regulation 규정 exception 예외 attendance 참석 voice 목소리를 내다, 의견을 내다 support 지지 opposition 반대 evidence 증거 congestion 체증

편집장님께,

184평생 데놀드 시에 거주한 주민으로서, 건설 예정인 웨이마르 편의점과 관련된 2월 7일 보도에 감사 드립니다. 그러나 기사에 일부 잘못된 정보가 담겨 있었습니다. **183**제가 공청회에서 공개한 디지털 동영상은 제 거주지가 있는 거리의 교통 혼잡을 녹화한 것이었습니다.

또한, 시민 두 사람이 매장의 현대적인 디자인에 대해 우려를 표했다는 점도 알려드리고 싶습니다. 저는 우리 도시만의 독특한 건축적 특징을 **185**유지하도록 노력해야 한다는 그들의 의견에 동의합니다. 가능하다면 새 건물들이 우리의 유서 깊은 구조물들과 조화를 이루는 것이 좋겠습니다.

다시 한 번 보도에 감사 드립니다.

베티 팀파노

어휘 lifelong 평생의 grateful 감사해 하는 contain 포함하다 present 제시하다, 보여주다 retain 유지하다 distinctive 독특한 architectural 건축의 blend in with ~와 어울리다

181 사실 관계 확인 [고난도]

번역 건설 예정인 편의점에 관해 사실이 아닌 것은?
(A) 덮개가 있는 주유 구역이 있을 것이다.
(B) 이른 아침에는 휘발유를 팔지 않을 것이다.
(C) 조리된 음식을 제공할 것이다.
(D) 비어 있는 땅에 건설될 것이다.

해설 기사 첫 번째 단락의 '12개의 주유기 위에 기와를 올린 덮개를 설치할 예정이다(which will feature a tiled canopy above its 12 gas pumps)'에서 (A)를, 마지막 단락의 '퇴근 후 "빠르고 따뜻한 요깃거리"를 제공할 것이다(it would provide a "quick, warm bite to eat" after work)'에서 (C)를, 첫 번째 단락의 '공터에 조성된다(It will be built on a plot of vacant land)'에서 (D)를 확인할 수 있다. 따라서 언급되지 않은 (B)가 정답이다.

▶ **Paraphrasing** 지문의 feature a tiled canopy above its 12 gas pumps
→ 보기 (A)의 have a covered fueling area
지문의 provide a "quick, warm bite to eat"
→ 보기 (C)의 offer cooked food selections
지문의 built on a plot of vacant land
→ 보기 (D)의 constructed on empty land

182 사실 관계 확인

번역 데놀드 시에 관해 언급된 것은?
(A) 넓은 창고 지구로 유명하다.
(B) 해마다 열리는 엔지니어링 회의 장소이다.
(C) 다른 편의점이 3개 있다.
(D) 교통량을 줄이기 위한 정책을 시행해 왔다.

해설 기사의 두 번째 단락에서 회사가 편의점 매장을 운영하려면 데놀드 시의 소음 및 교통량 감소 규정을 준수해야 한다(the company will have to comply with the city's noise and traffic reduction regulations)고 했으므로, 데놀드 시가 교통량을 줄이기 위한 정책을 시행 중임을 알 수 있다. 따라서 (D)가 정답이다.

어휘 implement 시행하다 decrease 줄이다

> **Paraphrasing** 지문의 traffic reduction regulations
> → 정답의 policies to decrease traffic

183 연계 <u>고난도</u>

번역 팀파노 씨가 공청회를 위해 동영상을 촬영한 장소는 어디였겠는가?
(A) 마일든 가
(B) 라모나 길
(C) 브룩 가
(D) 로렐 가

해설 편지의 첫 번째 단락에서 팀파노 씨는 공청회에서 공개한 디지털 동영상이 자신의 거주지가 있는 거리의 교통 혼잡을 녹화한 것(The digital video I presented at the public meeting was a recording of congested traffic on my street of residence)이라며 기사의 잘못된 정보(라모나 길)를 정정했다. 기사의 세 번째 단락을 보면 팀파노 씨가 마일든 가 400번지에 산다(Betty Timpano, who lives on the 400 block of Milden Drive)고 나와 있으므로, 팀파노 씨가 동영상을 촬영한 장소는 마일든 가라고 추론할 수 있다. 따라서 (A)가 정답이다.

184 사실 관계 확인

번역 독자 편지에서 팀파노 씨에 관해 알 수 있는 것은?
(A) 지역 사학자다.
(B) 현대 건축을 선호한다.
(C) 데놀드 시 밖에서 산 적이 없다.
(D) 웨이마르 편의점에 가본 적이 있다.

해설 편지의 첫 번째 단락에서 팀파노 씨가 본인을 평생 데놀드 시에 거주한 주민(a lifelong resident of Denold City)이라고 소개했으므로, (C)가 정답이다.

> **Paraphrasing** 지문의 a lifelong resident of Denold City
> → 정답의 She has never lived outside of Denold City

185 동의어 찾기

번역 독자 편지에서 2번째 단락 2행의 "retain"과 의미상 가장 가까운 것은?
(A) 임명하다
(B) 숨기다
(C) 보존하다
(D) 제한하다

해설 'retain'이 포함된 부분은 '도시만의 독특한 건축적 특징을 유지하도록 노력해야 한다(we must try to retain our city's distinctive architectural character)'라는 의미로 해석되는데, 여기서 retain은 '유지하다, 간직하다'라는 뜻으로 쓰였다. 따라서 (C) preserve가 정답이다.

186-190 제안서 + 광고 + 고객 후기

민타나 스파

판촉 제안서

판매 사원 조지프 바럼 제출
9월 2일

프로모션 형태: 모든 서비스 15퍼센트 할인

[187]대상 고객: 간호사

날짜/기간: 계속 진행, 가능한 한 빨리 시작

장점:

- 신규 고객 집단. 스트레스가 높지만 항상 보수가 좋지는 않은 직업에 종사하는 자로서, 간호사들은 우리 서비스에서 크게 도움을 받을 수 있지만 정가는 버겁다고 생각할 수도 있다.
- 대중을 상대로 자사 이미지 개선

[186]난제:

- 시행 문제. [186]우리 직원이 참가자들의 자격증을 주의 깊게 확인하고 할인 대상에 서비스만 포함된다는 점을 기억해야 할 것이다.

어휘 sales assistant 판매 사원 benefit 도움을 받다
affordable (가격이) 감당할 수 있는 logistical 시행[실행]의, 실행에 필요한 준비 사항과 관련된 credential 자격증

민타나 스파가 의료진을 지원합니다!

민타나 스파는 생명을 구하고 매일 의료 서비스를 제공하는 것이 힘든 일이라는 점을 알고 있습니다. [187]그래서 11월 1일부터 간호사, 구급의료대원, 응급의료기술자 분들께 모든 서비스를 15퍼센트 할인해 드립니다.* [189]여기에는 긴장을 풀어주는 마사지, 상쾌함을 선사하는 안면 및 신체 관리, 몸과 마음을 정화하는 사우나 시간 등이 포함되며, 심지어 사우나는 적외선을 사용해 독소를 해독하는 땀을 빼주고 순환을 개선해 주는 새로운 적외선 사우나 박스에서 이루어집니다! 이는 약소하지만 우리 사회의 건강을 지키는 영웅들에게 감사를 표하는 저희의 방식입니다.

민타나 스파는 브루너의 휘트콤 로 1200번지에 있습니다. 예약 없이 방문하시는 분들도 받지만, 일정이 자주 꽉 차므로 예약하시는 것이 좋습니다. 자세한 정보는 555-0122로 전화하세요.

*적격한 재직 증명서가 필요합니다. 스파 상품권이나 제품에는 할인을 이용할 수 없다는 점 유의하세요.

어휘 paramedic 구급의료대원 emergency 응급 refreshing 상쾌하게 하는 treatment 치료(법), 관리(법) cleansing 정화하는 infrared 적외선의 induce 유도[유발]하다 detoxify 해독하다 circulation 순환 walk-in 예약 없이 방문하는 사람 proof 증명(서) eligible 적격인 employment 고용, 취업 gift certificate 상품권 merchandise 상품, 제품

http://www.brunerbusinessreviews.com/mintanaspa

브루너 업체 후기

민타나 스파 최신 후기:

"어제 하루 휴가를 냈기 때문에 새로 생긴 간호사 대상 할인 혜택을 이용하기 위해 이른 오후에 방문했어요. 평일치고 꽤 붐볐는데, 운이 좋게도 예약을 안 하고 갔지만 **188거절 당하지** 않았어요. 그래도 직원들이 서두르라고 재촉하는 분위기는 결코 느끼지 못했어요. **190모두 배려심이 깊었고 그날 손님이 저 하나뿐인 것처럼 대했어요. 가장 고마웠던 점이죠.** **189하지만 블루베리 추출물로 한 얼굴 마사지 효과는 오늘 아침이 되자 사라졌고, 사우나 박스는 긴장을 풀어줬지만 온욕보다 별로 나을 게 없었어요.** 이 스파에 다시 가긴 하겠지만 다음엔 다른 서비스를 받아 볼 것 같아요."

작성자 테이사 코인, 11월 12일

어휘 take advantage of 이용하다 attentive 배려하는, 세심한 appreciate 감사히 여기다 extract 추출물 facial 안면 마사지; 안면의

---

186 사실 관계 확인

번역 제안서에서 예측되는 판촉의 어려움으로 언급된 것은?
(A) 잠재적 참여자가 알도록 유도
(B) 대규모 신규 고객 접대
(C) 충분한 수익률 유지
(D) 참가자의 자격 평가

해설 제안서에 언급된 난제(Challenges) 부분에서 시행 시 직원이 참가자들의 자격증을 주의 깊게 확인해야 할 것(Our staff would have to carefully check the credentials of participants)이라고 했으므로, (D)가 정답이다.

어휘 patron 고객 sufficient 충분한 evaluate 평가하다 qualification 자격

▸▸ Paraphrasing 지문의 Challenges
→ 질문의 a potential difficulty
지문의 carefully check the credentials of participants → 정답의 Evaluating participants' qualifications

187 연계

번역 제안서와 광고의 판촉이 다른 점은?
(A) 할인 규모
(B) 이용 가능한 기간
(C) 자격이 되는 대상자
(D) 적용될 수 있는 구매품

해설 제안서에서는 대상 고객이 간호사(Target Customer: Nurses)라고 했는데, 광고의 첫 번째 단락을 보면 간호사, 구급의료대원, 응급의료 기술자에게 모든 서비스를 15퍼센트 할인해 준다(we will offer a 15% discount on all of our services to nurses, paramedics, and emergency medical technicians)고 나와 있다. 따라서 할인 혜택 대상자가 더 다양해졌다는 것을 알 수 있으므로, (C)가 정답이다.

---

188 동의어 찾기 [고난도]

번역 고객 후기에서 1번째 단락 3행의 "turned away"와 의미상 가장 가까운 것은?
(A) 묵살된
(B) 거부된
(C) 방지된
(D) 폐기된

해설 'turned away'를 포함한 부분은 '운이 좋게도 예약을 안 하고 갔지만 거절 당하지 않았다(I was lucky that I didn't get turned away for not having an appointment)'는 의미로 해석되는데, 여기서 turned away는 '거절된, 돌려보내진'이라는 뜻으로 쓰였다. 따라서 '거부된'이라는 의미의 (B) rejected가 정답이다.

189 연계 [고난도]

번역 코인 씨에 관해 암시된 것은?
(A) 판촉 첫날에 방문했다.
(B) 광선 요법을 받았다.
(C) 민타나 스파에서 가장 인기 있는 서비스를 시도해봤다.
(D) 광고에 나온 전화번호로 전화했다.

해설 고객 후기 후반부에서 코인 씨는 사우나 박스가 긴장을 풀어줬지만 온욕보다 별로 나을 게 없었다(the sauna pod, while relaxing, wasn't much better than a hot bath)고 평가했는데, 광고를 보면 사우나 박스가 적외선을 사용한다(in our new infrared sauna pods, which use infrared light)고 나와 있다. 따라서 코인 씨가 광선 요법을 받았다고 추론할 수 있으므로, (B)가 정답이다.

190 세부 사항

번역 코인 씨는 민타나 스파의 어떤 점을 특히 좋아했는가?
(A) 배려 깊은 고객 서비스
(B) 고급스러운 실내장식
(C) 절차의 효율성
(D) 공간 배치에 따른 사생활 보호

해설 고객 후기 중반부에서 코인 씨는 직원들 모두 배려심이 깊었고 손님이 본인 한 명뿐인 것처럼 대했다(Everyone was very attentive and treated me like I was the only customer that day)고 한 후, 이것이 가장 고마웠던 점(I appreciated the most)이라고 덧붙였다. 따라서 (A)가 정답이다.

어휘 considerate 배려 깊은 effectiveness 효율성 afford 제공하다

▸▸ Paraphrasing 지문의 appreciated the most
→ 질문의 especially like
지문의 very attentive and treated me like I was the only customer that day
→ 정답의 considerate customer service

191-195 기사 + 이메일 + 보고서 발췌

콥쇼에서 아랍어 시험 실시 예정

글 실라 라이드노어

콥쇼 (5월 13일)—미국인의 영어 외 언어 능력 향상을 위한 활동에 전념하는 비영리 단체 국립외국어협회(NFLA)가 콥쇼에서 아랍어 능력 시험을 시행할 예정이다. 아랍어능력시험(TOCIA)은 오는 7월부터 연 2회 실시된다.

NFLA 관계자인 켄 리드는 쉽게 **191내린** 결정이었다고 말한다. "콥쇼 지역에서 수험생들이 많이 온다는 것을 알아냈죠." 그는 이것이 콥쇼 대학의 아랍어 프로그램 덕분이라고 믿고 있다. **195그는 또한 이 프로그램이 시험을 감독할 자격을 갖춘 지역민을 배출한다고 말한다.** 이 업무는 언어에 대한 지식이 어느 정도 있어야 한다.

TOCIA는 50분짜리 듣기 영역과 70분짜리 독해 영역으로 구성되어 있다. **193첫 시험은 이 대학의 덕켓 강당에서 열릴 예정이지만**, 리드 씨는 수험생이 150명을 넘길 경우 다른 장소도 추가될 수 있다고 말한다. 등록은 40달러이며, 6월 4일 오후 5시까지 www.nfla.org/tocia에서 완료해야 한다.

> **어휘** **non-profit** 비영리의 **commit** 전념하다, 헌신하다 **proficiency** 능력 **administer** (시험을) 실시[시행]하다, 집행하다 **supply** 공급하다 **qualified to** ~할 자격을 갖춘 **consist of** ~로 구성되다 **venue** 장소 **registration** 등록

발신: NFLA
수신: 브라이언트 페이지
제목: TOCIA
날짜: 6월 11일

페이지 씨께,

192아랍어 능력 시험에 등록해주셔서 감사합니다. 다음 정보를 확인해 주시기 바랍니다.

1. 시험 일시: 7월 3일 오후 1시
   유의 사항: 수험생은 상기 시작 시간 최소 30분 전에 시험장에 도착해야 합니다.
2. **193장소: 콥쇼 대학 게이니 빌딩 (컬리지 길 350 N.) 203호실 (지도)**
3. 구비 서류: 정부에서 발급한 사진이 있는 신분증

응시 절차에 대한 자세한 내용은 이 페이지를 참고하세요.

> **어휘** **stated** 명시된, 기재된 **photo identification** 사진이 있는 신분증

아랍어능력 시험(TOCIA)
시험 절차 준수사항 보고서

시험장: 콥쇼 대학 덕켓 강당
시험일: 7월 3일
195시험 감독: 사반나 키넌

각 항목 옆에 있는 상자에 체크해 관련 절차가 실행되었음을 표시하세요. **194표시하지 않은 상자가 있다면 그 이유에 대한 자세한 설명을 이 보고서에 첨부해야 합니다.**

- 시험 시작 30분 전 후로는 현장에 수험생 출입이 허용되지 않았다. ☑
- 모든 수험생의 신분이 확인되었다. ☑
- **194수험생들이 가져온 개인용 전자제품은 모두 현장에서 떨어진 곳에 보관되었다.** ☐
- 수험생들은 시험 전 필수 서식을 모두 작성했다. ☑

> **어휘** **observance** 준수 **procedure** 절차 **relevant** 관련 있는 **append** 첨부하다 **verify** 확인하다 **fill out** 작성하다

---

191 동의어 찾기

번역 기사에서 2번째 단락 2행의 "reach"와 의미상 가장 가까운 것은?
(A) 뻗다
(B) 달성하다
(C) 연락하다
(D) 하다

해설 'reach'가 포함된 부분은 '쉽게 내린 결정이었다(the decision was an easy one to reach)'라는 의미로 해석되는데, 여기서 reach는 decision과 함께 '결정에 이르다, 결정을 내리다'라는 뜻으로 쓰였다. 따라서 decision과 함께 '결정하다'라는 의미를 완성하는 (D) make가 정답이다.

192 주제 / 목적

번역 페이지 씨에게 이메일이 발송된 이유는?
(A) 시험 준비를 시키기 위해
(B) 등록을 마치도록 요청하기 위해
(C) 학습 서비스를 광고하기 위해
(D) 문의에 응하기 위해

해설 이메일의 첫 번째 단락에서 아랍어 능력 시험에 등록해 주어 감사하다(Thank you for signing up to take the Test of Competency in Arabic)고 한 후, 관련 정보를 검토하라(Please review the following information)고 요청했으므로, 페이지 씨에게 시험 준비와 관련된 정보를 알리기 위한 이메일임을 알 수 있다. 따라서 (A)가 정답이다.

193 연계 [고난도]

번역 TOCIA에 관해 암시된 것은?
(A) 150명 이상이 콥쇼에서 응시하기 위해 등록했다.
(B) 시험 영역 사이에 30분의 휴식시간이 있다.
(C) 보통 주말에 시행된다.
(D) NFLA 웹사이트에 연습용 문제가 있다.

해설 기사의 마지막 단락에서 첫 시험은 대학의 덕켓 강당에서 열릴 예정이지만 수험생이 150명을 넘길 경우 다른 장소도 추가될 수 있다(The first exam will be held in the university's Duckett Auditorium, though ~ other venues may be added if there are over 150 test-takers)고 했는데, 이메일의 시험 관련 정보를 보면 페이지 씨의 시험 장소(Site)가 콥쇼 대학의 게이니 빌딩(University of Cobshaw, Gainey Building)이라고 되어 있다. 따라서 150명 이상이 시험에 등록했다고 추론할 수 있으므로, (A)가 정답이다.

194 추론 / 암시

번역 보고서에 첨부된 자료에 무슨 설명이 있겠는가?
(A) 마지막 수험생이 도착한 시간
(B) 수험생들이 신분을 증명한 방식
(C) 수험생이 시험 전에 작성한 서류
(D) 시험 시간에 수험생들의 소지품이 보관된 장소

해설 보고서 발췌본 두 번째 단락에서 시행 절차 항목 중 표시하지 않은 상자가 있다면 그 이유에 대한 자세한 설명을 보고서에 첨부해야 한다(If any box is left unmarked, a full explanation of the reason must be appended to this report)고 했는데, 수험생들의 개인용 전자제품 보관 장소를 명시한 세 번째 항목(All personal electronics brought by test-takers were stored away from the site) 옆 상자가 비어 있다. 따라서 (D)가 정답이다.

▶▶ Paraphrasing 지문의 a full explanation of the reason must be appended → 질문의 be explained in an attachment

지문의 All personal electronics brought by test-takers were stored → 정답의 test-takers' belongings were kept

195 연계
고난도

번역 키넌 씨에 관해 가장 사실에 가까운 것은?
(A) 6월에 연수에 참가했다.
(B) 아랍어 능력을 갖추고 있다.
(C) 라이드노 씨가 인터뷰했다.
(D) 콥쇼 대학의 교수다.

해설 보고서 발췌본을 보면 키넌 씨가 시험 감독(Test Administrator: Savanna Keenan)임을 확인할 수 있는데, 기사의 두 번째 단락에서 아랍어 시험 감독 업무를 하려면 언어에 대한 지식이 어느 정도 있어야 한다(to administer the test, as such work requires some knowledge of the language)고 했으므로, 그녀가 아랍어 능력을 갖추고 있다고 추론할 수 있다. 따라서 (B)가 정답이다.

▶▶ Paraphrasing 지문의 some knowledge of the language → 정답의 some Arabic language skills

196-200 이메일 + 웹페이지 + 이메일

수신: 닉 버로우즈 〈nickborrows1@renseed.com〉
발신: 바네사 캐슬 〈vanessacastle@renseed.com〉
날짜: 4월 20일
제목: 샌디에이고
첨부: 프레젠테이션 수정본

안녕하세요 닉,

다음 주 샌디에이고에서 할 발표 슬라이드에서 수정된 사항을 알려주려고요. ¹⁹⁶그래프와 대차대조표는 그대로 두었지만, 제품 사진을 조금 더 크고 선명하게 만들었어요. ¹⁹⁷또 슬라이드에 들어간 텍스트 관련해서도 메모를 좀 했지만, 일단 당신에게 얘기하지 않고 수정하고 싶지는 않았어요. 제 생각을 별도의 파일로 보낼게요.

그리고, 우리 비행기 예약도 해야 해요. 거기 가는 방법으로는, 우리가 선호하는 항공사에서 네 가지 옵션을 이용할 수 있어요. ¹⁹⁸당신은 어떨지 모르지만, 저는 그곳에 저녁에 도착하는 항공편을 택하고 싶어요. 그러면 하루 중 대부분을 여기 사무실에서 준비하는 데 쓸 수 있고, 또 제시간에 도착해서 좀 쉴 수도 있을 거예요. 동의하시면 오늘 퇴근하기 전에 예약할게요.

알려주세요.

– 바네사

어휘 sharp 선명한 alter 변경하다, 수정하다 separate 별도의, 분리된 preferred 선호되는 carrier 항공사

---

www.lightningair.com/departures/april28/query83789

라이트닝 항공 – 미국 전역에 저가 항공편 매일 운항!

출발일: 4월 28일
출발 공항: 샌프란시스코
도착 공항: 샌디에이고

○ 항공편 번호: L106   출발: 오전 4시 30분   도착: 오전 6시
○ 항공편 번호: L982   출발: 오전 11시   도착: 오후 12시 30분
○ 항공편 번호: L392   출발: 오후 1시   도착: 오후 2시 30분
○ ¹⁹⁸항공편 번호: L720   출발: 오후 5시 45분   도착: 오후 7시 15분

중요사항: ¹⁹⁹3시간 미만 비행에는 이코노미 클래스 승객을 위한 무료 기내식 서비스를 폐지했습니다. 해당 승객은 추가 비용으로 식사를 구입할 수 있습니다. 비즈니스 클래스 승객은 여전히 이 식사를 무료로 이용할 수 있습니다. 클럽 클래스 승객은 식사와 더불어 본인이 선택한 음료를 무제한으로 받습니다. 프리미엄 클래스 승객은 클럽 클래스와 동일한 혜택을 받으며, 라이트닝 항공 전용 라운지에도 입장할 수 있습니다.

다음 페이지 ▶

어휘 eliminate 폐지하다 complimentary 무료의 purchase 구입하다 additional cost 추가 비용 entitled to ~를 받을 자격이 있는 unlimited 무제한의 exclusive 전용의

수신: 바네사 캐슬 〈vanessacastle@renseed.com〉
출처: 닉 버로우즈 〈nickborrows1@renseed.com〉
날짜: 4월 22일
제목: 회신: 샌디에이고

안녕하세요 바네사,

이메일 줘서 고맙고, 발표 슬라이드에 쏟은 노고에도 감사 드려요.

제가 지금 회사 신용카드를 갖고 있어요. 그래서 바로 당신이 원하는 비행기표와 30일에 돌아오는 표를 구했어요. ¹⁹⁹기내식을 사려고 돈을 조금 더 내야 했지만, 가격이 괜찮은 편이었어요.

²⁰⁰괜찮다면 지금 제가 주로 도심에서 이용하는 호텔에 예약할게요. 호텔에 무료 셔틀버스가 있어서 공항에서 호텔까지 가는 교통편을 예약하지 않아도 될 거예요. 그곳에는 발표 슬라이드를 출력할 수 있는 근사한 비즈니스 센터도 있어요. 괜찮겠어요?

닉

Test 4

어휘 reasonable 가격이 적당한 reservation 예약
transportation 교통(편)

196 세부 사항

번역 캐슬 씨는 이미지들을 어떻게 했는가?
(A) 이미지들을 더 잘 보이게 만들었다.
(B) 이미지들을 다른 파일에 넣었다.
(C) 이미지들에 문구를 추가했다.
(D) 이미지들에서 결함을 제거했다.

해설 첫 번째 이메일의 첫 단락에서 제품 사진을 조금 더 크고 선명하게 만들었다(I've made the pictures of our products a little bigger and sharper)고 했으므로, (A)가 정답이다.

어휘 visible 보이는 flaw 결함

▶▶ Paraphrasing 지문의 made the pictures of our products a little bigger and sharper
→ 정답의 made them more visible

197 세부 사항

번역 캐슬 씨가 버로우즈 씨에게 보내겠다고 약속한 것은?
(A) 예약 확인
(B) 여행 옵션에 대한 세부 정보
(C) 발표 녹음 파일
(D) 일부 글을 수정하기 위한 제안

해설 첫 번째 이메일의 첫 단락에서 캐슬 씨는 버로우즈 씨에게 얘기하지 않고 슬라이드에 들어간 텍스트를 수정하고 싶지 않았다(I didn't want to alter it without talking to you first)고 한 후, 자신이 생각한 바를 별도의 파일로 보내겠다(I'll send my ideas in a separate file)고 했다. 따라서 (D)가 정답이다.

▶▶ Paraphrasing 지문의 ideas → 정답의 Suggestions
지문의 alter → 정답의 revising

198 연계

번역 캐슬 씨가 선호하는 항공편은?
(A) L982
(B) L106
(C) L720
(D) L392

해설 첫 번째 이메일의 두 번째 단락에서 캐슬 씨는 저녁에 도착하는 항공편을 택하고 싶다(I'd like to take the one that gets us there in the evening)고 했는데, 웹페이지에 나온 항공편 중 저녁에 도착하는 (Arrival: 7:15 P.M.) 것은 L720이므로, (C)가 정답이다.

199 연계

번역 버로우즈 씨는 어떤 등급의 항공권을 구매했겠는가?
(A) 이코노미 클래스
(B) 클럽 클래스
(C) 비즈니스 클래스
(D) 프리미엄 클래스

해설 두 번째 이메일의 첫 단락에서 버로우즈 씨는 기내식을 사기 위해 돈을 조금 더 내야 했다(I had to pay a little extra to get in-flight meals for us)고 했는데, 웹페이지의 중요사항 부분(Important note)을 보면 이코노미 클래스 승객을 위한 무료 기내식 서비스가 폐지되어 식사를 하려면 추가 비용을 내야 한다(We have eliminated our complimentary meal service for economy class passengers ~ purchase a meal for an additional cost)고 되어 있다. 따라서 버로우즈 씨가 이코노미 클래스로 예약했다고 추론할 수 있으므로, (A)가 정답이다.

200 사실 관계 확인

번역 버로우즈 씨는 다음에 무엇을 하겠다고 하는가?
(A) 비용 환급 신청
(B) 육상 교통편 준비
(C) 숙박시설 예약
(D) 컴퓨터 스크린샷 인쇄

해설 두 번째 이메일의 마지막 단락에서 버로우즈 씨가 자신이 도심에서 주로 이용하는 호텔에 예약하겠다(I'll make reservations now at the hotel I usually use in the city center)고 했으므로, (C)가 정답이다.

어휘 reimbursement 환급 expense 비용 accommodation 숙박시설

▶▶ Paraphrasing 지문의 make reservations ~ at the hotel
→ 정답의 Book some accommodations

TEST 5

101 (B)	**102** (D)	**103** (A)	**104** (C)	**105** (B)
106 (D)	**107** (C)	**108** (D)	**109** (A)	**110** (D)
111 (B)	**112** (D)	**113** (A)	**114** (C)	**115** (C)
116 (B)	**117** (D)	**118** (A)	**119** (A)	**120** (B)
121 (C)	**122** (A)	**123** (C)	**124** (A)	**125** (C)
126 (B)	**127** (D)	**128** (B)	**129** (A)	**130** (B)
131 (B)	**132** (A)	**133** (C)	**134** (B)	**135** (D)
136 (B)	**137** (A)	**138** (D)	**139** (A)	**140** (D)
141 (C)	**142** (C)	**143** (C)	**144** (A)	**145** (B)
146 (C)	**147** (C)	**148** (D)	**149** (D)	**150** (A)
151 (B)	**152** (A)	**153** (C)	**154** (B)	**155** (A)
156 (D)	**157** (C)	**158** (C)	**159** (C)	**160** (B)
161 (B)	**162** (B)	**163** (C)	**164** (C)	**165** (D)
166 (A)	**167** (C)	**168** (D)	**169** (B)	**170** (B)
171 (A)	**172** (C)	**173** (D)	**174** (A)	**175** (C)
176 (A)	**177** (D)	**178** (D)	**179** (B)	**180** (B)
181 (B)	**182** (C)	**183** (D)	**184** (A)	**185** (C)
186 (C)	**187** (D)	**188** (B)	**189** (B)	**190** (C)
191 (D)	**192** (C)	**193** (B)	**194** (A)	**195** (A)
196 (C)	**197** (B)	**198** (D)	**199** (B)	**200** (D)

PART 5

101 명사 어휘

해설 각 직원의 인사고과(performance review)에 따라 달라지는 보상 중에서 양이나 액수(amount)로 수치화 할 수 있는 명사가 빈칸에 들어가야 하므로, '성과급, 상여금'이라는 의미의 (B) bonus가 정답이다.

번역 각 직원의 성과급 액수는 인사고과를 토대로 결정된다.

어휘 workstation 사무실 컴퓨터, 작업 장소 promotion 승진

102 명사 자리 _ 동사의 목적어   [고난도]

해설 동사 issued의 목적어 역할을 하는 명사 자리로, 형용사 firm과 전치사구 of rumors의 수식을 받는다. 따라서 '부인, 거부'라는 의미의 명사인 (D) denial이 정답이다. (A) deny와 (B) denies는 동사, (C) denied는 동사/과거분사로 품사상 빈칸에 들어갈 수 없다.

번역 길리스 광업그룹은 최고경영자 교체를 계획하고 있다는 소문들에 대해 단호하게 부인하는 입장을 발표했다.

어휘 issue 발표하다, 발급하다 firm 단호한 replace 교체하다 deny 부인하다

103 전치사 어휘   [고난도]

해설 명사구 a minimal additional charge를 목적어로 취하는 전치사 자리로, 빈칸을 포함한 전치사구가 콤마 뒤에 오는 절을 수식한다. 추가 비용은 삽화 제작(our design professionals can produce eye-catching illustrations)의 대가로 받는 것이므로, 교환의 대상을 나타내는 (A) For (~와 교환으로, ~에)가 정답이다.

번역 소액의 추가 비용에 당사의 디자인 전문가들이 귀사의 홍보물에 추가할 수 있도록 눈길을 사로잡는 삽화를 제작해 드립니다.

어휘 minimal 최소한의, 아주 적은 additional 추가의 charge 요금, 비용 eye-catching 눈길을 사로잡는 promotional 홍보의

104 동사 어휘

해설 빈칸은 명사구 a considerable amount of effort를 목적어로 취하는 동사 자리로, 전치사구 into maintaining its reputation과 어울려 쓰이는 단어가 들어가야 한다. 따라서 '명성을 유지하는 데 상당한 노력을 쏟는다'라는 내용을 완성하는 (C) puts(마음·정신 등을 쏟다)가 정답이다. 참고로, (B) spends(쓰다, 들이다)는 effort를 목적어로 취할 경우 전치사 on/in과 함께 쓰이므로 빈칸에는 적합하지 않다.

번역 펠런트 호텔은 스타일이 멋지고 안락하다는 명성을 유지하기 위해 상당한 노력을 기울인다.

어휘 considerable 상당한 maintain 유지하다 reputation 명성, 평판

105 부사 어휘

해설 요리 준비 시간을 단축하는 방법(One way to shorten the preparation time)에 대해 설명하는 문장이므로, 빈칸이 포함된 that 관계사절은 시간 단축에 도움이 되는 양배추(cabbage)의 상태를 적절히 묘사해야 한다. 따라서 has been cut into strips와 함께 '이미 잘게 썰린'이라는 의미를 완성하는 (B) already(이미, 벌써)가 정답이다. 양배추가 썰려 있다는 '완료' 상태를 나타내기 때문에 (A) sometimes와 (D) since는 어울리지 않고, (C) finally는 '마침내, 마지막으로'라는 뜻이므로 문맥상 적합하지 않다.

번역 이 요리를 준비하는 시간을 단축하는 한 가지 방법은 이미 잘게 썰어 놓은 양배추를 사는 것이다.

어휘 preparation 준비 dish 요리 strip 가느다란 조각

106 인칭대명사의 격 _ 소유격

해설 전치사 for의 목적어 역할을 하는 명사구 skilled and careful work를 한정 수식하는 자리이므로, 소유격 인칭대명사 (D) their가 정답이다.

번역 창고 관리인은 능숙하고 세심하게 작업한 스프링클러 설치팀을 칭찬했다.

어휘 praise A for B B한 것에 대해 A를 칭찬하다 installation 설치 skilled 능숙한

107 동사 어형 _ 시제

해설 주어 The Galaxxania Plus navigation device의 동사 자리로, 보기에서 본동사 역할을 할 수 있는 (C) activates와 (D) activated 중 하나를 선택해야 한다. 뒤에 오는 시간 부사절(as soon as the vehicle is started)의 동사가 현재시제이므로, 빈칸에는 미래 또는 현재시제 동사가 들어갈 수 있다. 따라서 (C) activates가 정답이다. 참고로, activate는 '활성화 시키다' 외에도 '활성화 되다'라는 의미로 쓰일 수 있다.

번역 운전자를 위한 갤럭시아니아 플러스 내비게이션 장치는 차량 시동이 걸리는 즉시 자동으로 작동한다.

어휘 vehicle 차량 activation 작동, 활성화 activator 활성체

108 부사 자리 _ 동사 수식

해설 자동사 vary(다양하다)를 수식하는 부사 자리이므로, '널리, 매우'라는 의미의 (D) widely가 정답이다. 참고로, (A) wide는 부사로 쓰일 경우 '활짝, 완전히'라는 뜻으로 주로 물리적인 정도(eg. open wide)를 나타낸다.

번역 대학 보건 서비스에 관한 최근의 학생 설문조사 응답이 매우 다양하다.

어휘 response 반응 widen 넓히다

109 명사 자리 _ to부정사의 목적어 _ 어휘

해설 to increase의 목적어 역할을 하는 명사 자리로, 전치사구 of some sectors의 수식을 받는다. 따라서 일부 부문에 있어서 늘리거나 강화할 수 있는 대상을 나타내는 단어가 들어가야 하므로, '감독'이라는 의미의 (A) supervision이 정답이다. (C) supervisors도 명사이지만 증가의 대상이 될 수 있는 것은 감독관들의 수나 비율이므로 문맥상 적절하지 않다. (B) supervised는 동사/과거분사, (D) supervises는 동사로 품사상 빈칸에 들어갈 수 없다.

번역 더들리 씨의 기사는 통신 산업의 일부 부문에 대한 감독을 강화하라고 당국에 요구하고 있다.

어휘 call on 요구하다 authority 당국 increase 강화하다 supervise 감독하다 supervisor 감독관, 관리자

110 부사절 접속사 _ 어휘

해설 빈칸 뒤 완전한 절(Ms. Weaver is gone)을 이끄는 접속사 자리이므로, 보기에서 (C) so that과 (D) when 중 하나를 선택해야 한다. 부점장인 플로레스 씨가 매장을 책임지는 것은 위버 씨가 없을 때 발생하는 일이므로, 상황이나 조건을 나타내는 (D) when(~할 때, ~하면)이 정답이 된다. (A) during(~동안)은 전치사이고, (B) if not(그렇지 않으면)은 접속부사의 역할을 하므로 절을 이끌 수 없다.

번역 위버 씨가 없을 때는 부점장인 플로레스 씨가 매장을 책임진다.

어휘 be in charge of ~을 책임지다

111 동사 어휘

해설 꾸준히 높은 고객 만족도(Our consistently high customer satisfaction ratings)는 품질의 우수성(excellent quality of our product line)을 나타내는 지표라고 볼 수 있으므로, '나타내다, 반영하다'라는 의미의 (B) reflect가 정답이다.

번역 고객 만족도 등급이 꾸준히 높다는 것은 우리 제품군의 품질이 우수하다는 것을 나타낸다.

어휘 consistently 꾸준히 customer satisfaction 고객 만족도 transmit 전달하다 deliver 배송하다 arrange 정리하다, 준비하다

112 전치사 어휘

해설 명사구 the major regions of the world를 목적어로 취하는 전치사 자리로, 빈칸을 포함한 전치사구는 과거분사 spread를 수식한다. 12개의 연구소가 세계 주요 지역 곳곳에 퍼져 있다는 내용이 되어야 자연스러우므로, '~에 걸쳐, ~ 도처에'라는 의미의 (D) across가 정답이다. (A) between은 '~사이에, 중간에'라는 뜻으로 빈칸에 어울리지 않는다.

번역 한다하르 케미칼즈 사는 세계 주요 지역에 걸쳐 12개의 연구소를 갖고 있다.

어휘 chemicals 화학 약품 laboratory 실험실, 연구소 spread 퍼지다 region 지역

113 부사 자리 _ 형용사 수식

해설 Nishioka Industrial's leadership이 주어, is가 동사, 형용사 supportive가 보어인 완전한 문장으로, '회사의 지도부가 직원들의 노력을 지원하고 있다'라는 의미를 나타낸다. 따라서 빈칸에는 supportive를 수식하는 부사가 들어가야 자연스러우므로, '열렬히, 열광적으로'라는 뜻의 (A) enthusiastically가 정답이다.

번역 니시오카 인더스트리얼의 지도부는 환경친화적인 세제를 개발하기 위한 직원들의 노력을 열렬히 지원하고 있다.

어휘 industrial 생산 업체; 산업의 leadership (집합적으로) 지도부, 리더십 supportive 지원[지지]하는 environmentally-friendly 환경친화적인 detergent 세제 enthusiasm 열정 enthusiastic 열정적인 enthusiast 열정적인 사람

114 주어 자리 _ 대명사

해설 동사 has been leaving의 주어 역할을 하는 (대)명사 자리이므로, '누군가'라는 뜻의 (C) someone이 정답이다. (A) who와 (B) whoever가 평서문의 주어 자리에 쓰일 경우 명사절을 이끌게 되므로 빈칸에는 적합하지 않다. (D) one another는 대명사이지만 '서로'라는 의미로 주어 자리에는 들어갈 수 없다.

번역 관리인에 따르면 누군가 휴게실 싱크대에 씻지 않은 접시를 놓아둔다고 한다.

어휘 janitor (건물) 관리인 break room 휴게실

115 부사 어휘

해설 전치사구 over a long period of time과 함께 to develop을 적절히 수식하는 부사를 선택하는 문제이다. 앞에서 외국어 숙달은 빨리 이루어지는 과정이 아니라고(not a fast process) 했으므로, 해당 부분은 '실력 향상에 오랜 시간이 걸리는 것이 정상이다'라는 내용이 되어야 자연스럽다. 따라서 '점차, 서서히'라는 의미의 (C) gradually가 정답이다.

번역 외국어 숙달은 빨리 이루어지는 과정이 아니며, 오랜 시간에 걸쳐 점차 실력이 느는 것이 보통이다.

어휘 normal 보통인 hurriedly 황급히, 서둘러서 affirmatively 긍정적으로, 확정적으로 reluctantly 마지못해, 주저하며

116 형용사 자리 _ 명사 수식

해설 주어가 the person, 동사가 may work인 문장으로, 빈칸부터 supplies까지가 person을 수식하고 있다. 따라서 빈칸에는 형용사가 들어가야 하므로, for와 함께 '~를 담당하는'이라는 의미를 완성하는 (B) responsible이

정답이다. 참고로, person과 responsible 사이에 「주격 관계대명사 who/that + be동사 is」가 생략된 것으로 볼 수 있다. (A) responsibly는 부사, (C) responsibility 및 (D) responsibilities는 명사로 품사상 빈칸에 들어갈 수 없다.

번역 일부 중소기업에서는 물품 주문 담당자가 경리부나 재무부에서 일하기도 한다.

어휘 supplies 물품 accounting 회계, 경리 responsibly 책임감 있게 responsibility 책임, 책무

117 형용사 어휘 　고난도

해설 명사 search를 수식하는 형용사 자리로, 완벽한 연기자를 찾기 위한(to find the perfect performer) 작업의 특성을 적절히 묘사하는 단어가 들어가야 한다. 따라서 '광범위한, 폭넓은'이라는 의미로 조사의 범위를 나타내는 (D) extensive가 정답이다.

번역 배역 담당자는 그 영화의 주연을 맡을 완벽한 연기자를 찾기 위해 광범위한 조사를 실시했다.

어휘 conduct 실시하다 performer 연기자 starring role 주연 absolute 절대적인 eligible 자격이 있는 exhausted 다 써버린

118 부사 자리 _ 동사 수식

해설 자동사 participated와 전치사구 in the city's campaign 사이에서 participated를 수식하는 부사 자리이므로, '자발적으로'라는 의미의 (A) voluntarily가 정답이다. (B) voluntary는 형용사, (C) volunteers는 명사/동사, (D) volunteering은 동명사/현재분사로 품사상 빈칸에 들어갈 수 없다.

번역 시의 물 사용 줄이기 캠페인에 엄청난 수의 시민이 자발적으로 참여했다.

어휘 extraordinary 비상한, 엄청나게 많은 participate 참여하다 reduce 줄이다 voluntary 자발적인 volunteer 자원봉사자; 자원하다

119 전치사 어휘

해설 명사구 its materials' delicacy and high value를 목적어로 취하는 전치사를 선택하는 문제이다. 자료가 훼손되기 쉽고 가치가 높다는 점은 접근권이 도서관 직원들에게만 제한되는(access ~ is limited to library staff only) 이유가 되므로, '~ 때문에'라는 의미의 (A) Because of가 정답이다.

번역 희귀 서적 컬렉션의 자료는 훼손되기 쉽고 굉장히 귀중하기 때문에 도서관 직원들만 접근할 수 있다.

어휘 delicacy 연약함, 훼손되기 쉬움 access 접근(권) rare 희귀한 along with ~와 함께 in spite of ~에도 불구하고 regardless of ~와 상관없이

120 동사 어형 _ 태 _ 수 일치 　고난도

해설 단수명사 a review를 수식하는 주격 관계대명사절(that ~ durability)의 동사 자리로, the differences를 목적어로 취한다. 따라서 빈칸에는 a review와 수가 일치하는 능동태 단수동사가 들어가야 하므로, (B) analyzes가 정답이다. 조깅 용품(jogging accessories)을 선행사로 착각하지 않도록 유의해야 한다.

번역 이번 주 호에는 조깅 용품들의 기능성과 가격, 내구성 차이를 상세히 분석한 평가가 실려 있다.

어휘 functionality 기능성 durability 내구성 analyze 분석하다

121 명사 어휘 　고난도

해설 케이시 가가 유명해진 이유를 설명하는 문장이므로, 빈칸이 포함된 전치사구(for ~ start-ups)는 '기술 신생기업이 고도로 밀집해 있어서'라는 내용이 되어야 문맥상 자연스럽다. 따라서 '밀집, 집중'이라는 의미의 (C) concentration이 정답이다.

번역 케이시 가는 기술 신생기업이 고도로 밀집해 유명해졌다.

어휘 start-up 신생기업 position 위치, 지위 standard 표준, 기준 attendance 참석

122 명사 자리 _ 동사의 목적어 _ 복합명사

해설 빈칸은 sales와 복합 명사를 이루어 동사 practice의 목적어 역할을 한다. 따라서 연습 대상을 나타내는 명사가 들어가야 하므로, '발표'라는 의미의 (A) presentation이 정답이다.

번역 고객 방문에 앞서 우리가 제품 소개 발표를 연습할 수 있도록 3번 회의실을 예약하세요.

어휘 sales presentation 제품 소개 발표, 영업을 위한 발표 reserve 예약하다 in advance of ~에 앞서 presentable 소개할 수 있는, 받아들여질 만한 presenter 진행자, 발표자 present 발표하다, 수여하다

123 동사 어휘 　고난도

해설 「주어(Submitting this application)+동사+목적어(you)+목적격 보어(to accept a loan from Masple Bank)」 구조의 문장으로, 신청서를 제출했다고 해서 반드시 은행으로부터 대출을 받아야 하는 것은 아니라는 내용이 되어야 자연스럽다. 따라서 '의무를 지우다, 강요하다'라는 뜻의 (C) obligate가 정답이다. 나머지 동사는 의미상 적절하지 않을 뿐만 아니라, 구조상으로도 빈칸에 들어갈 수 없다. 참고로, '반드시 ~하게 하다'라는 뜻의 (A) ensure의 경우 3형식(직접목적어) 혹은 4형식(간접목적어 + 직접목적어)으로 쓰인다.

번역 이 신청서를 제출한다고 해서 반드시 매스플 은행으로부터 대출을 받아야 하는 것은 아니다.

어휘 application 신청(서) relieve 완화하다 expedite 신속히 처리하다

124 부사절 접속사 _ 어휘

해설 빈칸 뒤 완전한 절(construction of the condominiums is complete)을 이끄는 접속사 자리이므로, 보기에서 (A) Now that과 (D) In order that 중 하나를 선택해야 한다. 문맥상 콘도 건설이 완료되어 잠재 구매자들에게 공개될 수 있다는 내용이 되어야 자연스러우므로, '~이므로'라는 의미의 (A) Now that이 정답이다. 참고로, (C) Whatever는 뒤에 불완전한 절이 나와야 하고, (B) Throughout은 전치사로 절을 이끌 수 없다.

번역 콘도 건설이 완료되었으므로, 잠재 구매자들에게 공개될 수 있다.

어휘 exhibit 전시하다, 공개하다 prospective 잠재적인 throughout
∼ 내내 in order that ∼하기 위하여

125 명사 어휘 　　　　　　　　　　　　　고난도

해설 should be discussed (and approved)의 주어 역할을 하는 명사 자리
로, 전치사구 to the logo design의 수식을 받는다. 따라서 빈칸에는 로
고 디자인과 관련해 협의 및 승인되어야 할 사항을 나타내는 단어가 들어
가야 하므로, '수정, 변경'이라는 의미의 (C) modifications가 정답이다.
참고로, '∼에 대한 수정'이라는 뜻으로 쓰이는 modification, change,
revision은 주로 전치사 to를 동반한다. 의미상 (A) proposals,
(B) concepts 도 가능할 것 같지만 전치사 to와 쓰이지 않으므로 빈칸에
는 부적합하다.

번역 로고 디자인을 수정하려면 저작권 전문가와 사전에 협의해 왕 씨의 승인을 받
아야 한다.

어휘 expert 전문가 approve 승인하다 proposal (for) 제안
concept (of) 개념, 발상 necessity 필수품

126 동사 어형 _ to부정사 _ 목적격 보어

해설 「urge + 목적어(medical personnel) + 목적격 보어」의 구조에서 목적
격 보어 역할을 하는 자리이다. '설득하다, 강력히 권고하다'라는 의미의
urge는 5형식으로 쓰일 경우 to부정사를 목적격 보어로 취하므로, (B) to
take가 정답이다.

번역 환자의 안위를 위해, 모롤병원은 의료진에게 필요시에는 병가를 내라고 강력
히 권고한다.

어휘 for the sake of ∼을 위해, ∼를 생각해서 sick leave 병가

127 부사 자리 _ 어휘 　　　　　　　　　　　　고난도

해설 빈칸이 be동사 was와 명사구 the only route 사이에 있으므로, 부사 또
는 the only route를 목적어로 취하는 전치사가 들어갈 수 있다. 문맥을
살펴보면, 주어인 Raynor Highway와 the only route가 동격 관계이
며 완전한 2형식 구조를 이루고 있음을 알 수 있다. 따라서 보기 중 부사를
선택해야 하는데, 레이너 고속도로가 해안 도시들 사이의 유일한 길이었던
상황은 과거(was)이므로, '한때'라는 의미의 (D) once가 정답이 된다.

번역 멋진 바다 경치를 자랑하는 레이너 고속도로는 한때 해안 도시인 오트리와 램
보트 사이의 유일한 길이었다.

어휘 boast 자랑하다 scenic view 멋진 경치 coastal 해안의

128 동사 어형 _ 태 _ 시제

해설 주어 production과 어울리는 동사 형태를 선택하는 문제이다. 생산
(production)은 지연되는 대상이며, 과거부터 현재까지의 횟수를 나타내
는 표현(Several times in the past year)이 문장을 수식하고 있으므
로, 수동태 현재완료 동사인 (B) has been delayed가 정답이 된다.

번역 지난 1년 사이 몇 차례 네트샬드 공장의 생산은 쉽게 예방할 수 있는 기계 고
장으로 지연되었다.

어휘 preventable 예방할 수 있는 breakdown 고장

129 형용사 어휘 　　　　　　　　　　　　　　고난도

해설 부사 financially의 수식을 받아 주어 it(=the company)을 보충 설명하
는 자리이다. 빈칸이 포함된 that절은 회사가 감사를 받아(undergo an
audit) 증명해야(prove) 하는 사항을 나타내고 있다. 따라서 '재정적으로
건전한'이라는 의미를 완성하는 (A) sound(건전한, 견실한)가 정답이다.
참고로, 주절에 요청·제안의 동사 request가 쓰였으므로 that절의 동사
는 「(should) + 동사원형(undergo)」 형태가 된다.

번역 발터스 주식회사의 투자자들은 감사를 받아 재정적으로 건전하다는 것을 증명
하라고 회사에 요구하고 있다.

어휘 investor 투자자 undergo 받다 audit (회계) 감사 equivalent
동등한 feasible 실현 가능한 detailed 상세한

130 부사 어휘 　　　　　　　　　　　　　　　고난도

해설 손님들의 주의가 산만해지지 않도록(to avoid distracting guests'
attention) 테이블을 치우는(clear tables) 방식을 적절히 묘사하는 부
사가 빈칸에 들어가야 한다. 따라서 '조심스럽게, 신중하게'라는 의미의
(B) discreetly가 정답이다.

번역 식사가 끝나면, 하콘 케이터링 직원들은 연설이나 기타 행사에서 손님들의 주
의가 산만해지지 않도록 조심스럽게 테이블을 치울 것이다.

어휘 distract one's attention 주의를 산만하게 만들다 accurately
정확하게 persistently 끈질기게 luxuriously 호화롭게

PART 6

131-134 공지

> ### 중요 고객 공지 사항
>
> 델둔스 바겐 스토어는 1월 13일 월요일, 재고 및 컴퓨터 업데이트를 위해 문
> 을 닫습니다. 이로 인해 발생할 수 있는 불편에 대해 사과 드리며, 양해해 주
> 시는 점 미리 감사 드립니다. 정상 영업시간에 재고 처리와 **131연관된** 모든 업
> 무를 직원들이 처리할 수 없는 경우가 가끔 있습니다. **132따라서, 저희로서**
> **는 하루 휴점하는 것이 유일한 방법입니다.** 월요일에는 **133비교적** 쇼핑객이 적
> 기 때문에 이날 이 중요 업무를 처리하기로 했습니다. 월요일은 보통 일주일 중
> **134가장 한산한** 날입니다. 매장은 1월 14일 화요일 오전 9시 정각에 다시 문
> 을 엽니다. 감사합니다.

> 어휘 inventory 재고 apologize for ∼에 대해 사과하다
> inconvenience 불편함 patience 참을성, 인내 processing 처리
> promptly 정각에, 지체 없이

131 형용사 자리 _ 분사

해설 빈칸은 전치사구 to inventory processing과 함께 명사 task를 수식하
는 자리로, 형용사 또는 분사가 들어갈 수 있다. 따라서 '재고 처리와 연관
된 모든 업무'라는 내용을 완성하는 (B) related(∼와 연관된, 관계가 있
는)가 정답이 된다. 참고로, related는 과거분사형 형용사로서 전치사 to
와 함께 쓰인다.

어휘 relate 관련시키다 relation 관계, 관련성, 친지 relatively
비교적으로, 상대적으로

132 문맥에 맞는 문장 고르기

번역 (A) 따라서, 저희로서는 하루 휴점하는 것이 유일한 방법입니다.
(B) 그 소프트웨어 프로그램은 새롭게 추가된 것입니다.
(C) 하지만 여전히 대부분은 아직 온라인에서 이용할 수 있습니다.
(D) 고객 서비스 데스크에 도움을 요청하세요.

해설 빈칸 앞 문장에서 정상 영업시간에 모든 업무를 처리할 수 없는 경우가 가끔 있다(it is not possible for our staff to handle every task ~ during normal opening hours)는 문제점을 언급했고, 뒤 문장에서는 월요일에 쇼핑객이 적기 때문에 이날 해당 업무를 처리하기로 했다(We chose to take care of these important business functions on this day because we have ~ few shoppers on Mondays)며 월요일을 선택한 이유를 밝혔다. 따라서 빈칸에는 문제 해결을 위한 휴점일 지정과 관련된 내용이 들어가야 자연스러우므로, (A)가 정답이다.

어휘 addition 추가된 것 assistance 도움

133 부사 어휘 고난도

해설 형용사 few 를 수식하는 부사 자리이다. 일주일 중 월요일을 휴점일로 선택(We chose ~ this day)한 이유에 대해 설명하는 부분이므로, '다른 요일에 비해 상대적으로 쇼핑객이 적기 때문'이라는 내용이 되어야 자연스럽다. 따라서 '비교적, 상대적으로'라는 의미의 (C) comparatively가 정답이다. 참고로, (B) considerably가 빈칸에 들어가려면 뒤에 비교 표현이 와야 한다.

어휘 solely 오직 considerably 상당히 regularly 주기적으로

134 형용사 어휘

해설 주어 It(=Monday)과 동격 관계를 이루는 day of the week을 수식하는 자리이다. 앞에서 다른 요일에 비해 월요일에 쇼핑객이 적다고 했으므로, 해당 문장도 이와 유사한 내용이 되어야 한다. 따라서 '일주일 중 가장 한산한 날'이라는 의미를 완성하는 (B) slowest가 정답이다. slow가 '한산한, 저조한' 이라는 뜻으로도 쓰인다는 것을 알아두자.

135-138 이메일

발신: 더글러스 베일리
수신: 〈totycontest@inspiriteach.com〉
제목: 케리 윌킨슨 추천
날짜: 11월 26일

담당자님께:

저는 인스피리티치 '올해의 선생님' 후보로 케리 윌킨슨을 추천합니다. ¹³⁵웹사이트에는 획기적인 면과 친절함에 보상하고자 한다고 되어 있는데요. 윌킨슨 씨는 윙크필드 중학교에서 5년 동안 함께 일해온 제 동료로, 저는 윌킨슨 씨보다 이러한 자질들을 더 잘 보여주는 ¹³⁶교육자는 상상할 수 없습니다.

윌킨슨 씨는 6학년 학급을 위한 수업 계획에서 끝없는 창의력을 보여줍니다. 예를 들어, 그녀는 최근 ¹³⁷저널리즘 단원을 진행하며 학교의 기술적 역량을 탁월

하게 활용했습니다. 그녀가 가르치는 학생들은 학교에 관한 뉴스 방송을 기획하고, 촬영, 편집했습니다.

윌킨슨 씨는 인정이 넘치는 사람이기도 합니다. 그녀는 아무리 다루기 어려운 학생이라도 이해심을 발휘합니다. ¹³⁸실제로, 그녀는 동료들의 귀감이 되는 인내심과 친절함으로 반항적인 행동에 대처하는 능력을 보여줍니다.

윌킨슨 씨를 올해의 선생님으로 적극 고려해 주셨으면 하는 마음으로 글을 마무리합니다.

더글러스 베일리

어휘 endorse 지지하다, 추천하다 nomination 후보 지명 representative 나타내는, 대표하는 demonstrate 보여주다 capability 역량 compassionate 인정 많은 disruptive 지장을 주는, 반항적인 behavior 행동 inspiration 귀감, 영감

135 문맥에 맞는 문장 고르기 고난도

번역 (A) 그녀는 그 캠페인에 헌신한 것으로 표창을 받을 만합니다.
(B) 저는 인스피리티치의 활동을 전적으로 지지합니다.
(C) 제 이메일을 적합한 담당자 또는 위원회에 전달해 주세요.
(D) 웹사이트에는 획기적인 면과 친절함에 보상하고자 한다고 되어 있는데요.

해설 빈칸 앞 문장에서 '올해의 선생님' 후보로 케리 윌킨슨을 추천한다(I would like to endorse Kerri Wilkinson's nomination for ~ "Teacher of the Year" award)고 했고, 뒤 문장에서는 윌킨슨 씨보다 이러한 자질들을 더 잘 보여주는 교육자는 상상할 수 없다(I cannot imagine an educator more representative of these qualities)고 했으므로, 빈칸에는 후보가 지녀야 하는 자질들에 대한 내용이 들어가야 한다. 따라서 획기적인 면과 친절함(innovation and caring)을 언급한 (D)가 정답이다.

어휘 deserve 자격이 되다 recognition 인정, 표창 dedication 헌신 wholehearted 전적인, 마음을 다한 appropriate 적합한 reward 보상[보답]하다

136 명사 자리 _ 동사의 목적어 고난도

해설 빈칸은 동사구 cannot imagine의 목적어 역할을 하는 명사 자리로, 형용사구 more representative of these qualities의 수식을 받는다. 따라서 '교육자'라는 의미의 (B) an educator가 정답이다. 참고로, 빈칸 뒤에 「주격 관계대명사 who/that + be동사 is」가 생략된 것으로 볼 수 있다.

137 명사 어휘

해설 빈칸은 전치사 on과 함께 unit을 수식하는 명사 자리로, 단원(unit)의 주제를 나타낸다. 뒤 문장에서 학생들이 학교에 관한 뉴스 방송을 기획하고, 촬영, 편집했다(Her students planned, filmed, and edited a newscast about the school)고 했으므로, 해당 단원이 언론 활동과 관련된 것임을 알 수 있다. 따라서 (A) journalism이 정답이다.

어휘 geography 지리 economics 경제학 government 정치 체제, 정부

138 접속부사

해설 앞 문장에서 윌킨스 씨가 아무리 다루기 어려운 학생이라도 이해심을 발휘한다(She shows nothing but understanding toward even our most difficult students)고 했고, 빈칸 뒤에서는 그녀가 인내심과 친절함으로 반항적인 행동에 대처한다(she is able to handle disruptive behavior with patience and kindness)며 앞서 언급한 자질에 대해 부연 설명을 했다. 따라서 빈칸에는 설명을 덧붙일 때 쓰이는 접속부사가 들어가야 자연스러우므로, '실제로'라는 의미의 (B) In fact가 정답이다.

어휘 At first 처음에는 Otherwise 그렇지 않으면 Nevertheless 그럼에도 불구하고

139-142 정보문

비에라고 호텔들에게 요구되는 사항

비에라고에 등재된다는 것은 다양한 책임이 따르는 특권입니다. 가장 중요한 책임은 손님들이 쾌적하게 머물게끔 하는 것[139]이지만, 당사는 회원 호텔들이 다음과 같은 조치를 통해 비에라고의 명성을 유지하는 데 도움을 주었으면 합니다.

첫째, 비에라고를 통해 들어오는 호텔에 관한 모든 문의에, 심지어 호텔에 수용할 수 없는 투숙객이 한 문의라도, 신속하게 응답하십시오. 다음으로, 비에라고를 통해 예약이 접수된 후에는 반드시 필요한 경우가 아니면 취소하지 마십시오. [140]손님들의 여행 계획이 여러분에게 달려 있다는 점 명심하십시오. 마지막으로, 건물을 잘 관리하고 투숙객 후기에 언급된 문제들을 [141]해결해 비에라고에서 높은 평점을 받도록 노력하십시오.

비에라고는 이 영역을(응답 속도, 취소율, 투숙객 평점)에서 각 회원 호텔의 실적을 추적해 일정 수준 이하로 떨어지는 호텔에 불이익을 줄 수 있습니다. 이를 방지하려면 계정 페이지를 통해 이 데이터를 직접 [142]점검해 주십시오.

어휘 requirement 요구 사항 privilege 특혜 responsibility 책임 uphold 유지하다 reputation 명성, 평판 property 건물, 부동산 performance 실적 responsiveness 대응성, 응답 속도 impose 부과하다

---

139 부사절 접속사 자리

해설 완전한 절(the key one is to provide guests with a pleasant stay)을 이끄는 접속사 자리로, 보기에서 (A) While과 (C) Whether 중 하나를 선택해야 한다. 문맥을 살펴보면, 빈칸이 이끄는 절에서 가장 중요한 책임을 설명한 후, 뒤에 오는 절에 추가적으로 지켜 주었으면 하는 기타 주요 사항을 덧붙이고 있다. 따라서 한 측면과 다른 측면을 연결할 때 쓰이는 (A) While(~이지만, ~인 한편)이 정답이 된다. (C) Whether는 부사절 접속사로 쓰일 경우 or (not)을 동반해야 하므로 빈칸에 들어갈 수 없다. (B) Regarding(~에 관해)은 전치사, (D) Besides(~외에; 게다가)는 전치사/부사이므로 절을 이끌 수 없다.

140 문맥에 맞는 문장 고르기

번역 (A) 프런트 데스크에서 실물 사본 제공할 수 있습니다.
(B) 일부 호텔은 비에라고에 광고해도 이득을 보지 못할 수도 있습니다.
(C) 대부분의 예약에서는, 세면용품과 수건일 것입니다.
(D) 손님들의 여행 계획이 여러분에게 달려 있다는 점 명심하십시오.

해설 빈칸 앞 문장에서 비에라고를 통해 예약이 접수된 후에는 반드시 필요한 경우가 아니면 취소하지 말라(after a booking has been made through VieraGo, do not cancel it unless it is absolutely necessary)고 했고, 뒤에서는 마지막 당부 사항(Finally, please try to achieve a high rating on VieraGo ~ guest reviews)을 언급했다. 따라서 빈칸에는 예약 취소와 관련된 내용이나 또 다른 당부 사항이 들어가야 자연스러우므로, (D)가 정답이다.

어휘 benefit (~에서) 득을 보다 toiletry 세면용품 depend on ~에 달려 있다

141 동사 어형 _ 동명사 _ 전치사의 목적어

해설 빈칸은 taking good care of your property와 병렬 구조(both A and B)를 이루어 전치사 by의 목적어 역할을 하는 동명사 자리이다. 따라서 (C) resolving이 정답이다.

어휘 resolve 해결하다

142 동사 어휘 _ 동명사

해설 앞 문장에서 고객 응대 관련(responsiveness, cancelation rate, and guest ratings) 부문의 실적이 일정 수준 이하로 떨어지는 호텔에 불이익을 줄 수 있다고 했으므로, 빈칸이 포함된 부분은 이를 방지하기 위한(To avoid this) 방법을 설명해야 한다. 따라서 '(실적) 데이터 점검'이라는 의미를 완성하는 (C) monitoring이 정답이다.

어휘 supply 공급하다 revise 수정하다 save 절약하다

143-146 보도자료

즉시 보도용

연락처: publicrelations@pearron.com

토론토 (10월 22일)—제약 회사 피어런 사가 웜플러 캐피털과 계약을 체결했다고 발표했다. 계약 조건에 따라 웜플러 캐피털은 피어런의 소수 지분을 7,200만 캐나다달러에 매입했고, [143]그렇게 함으로써 피어런의 성장 전략을 실행하기 위한 자금을 지원하게 되었다.

피어런 주주들은 [144]이 획기적인 거래를 지지한다. 주주들은 이 거래로 회사가 앞으로 몇 년 안에 크게 사업을 확장할 수 [145]있을 것이라고 굳게 믿는다.

피어런은 다양한 피부, 머리카락, 손발톱 질환을 위한 약을 개발하고 상용화한다. [146]제품으로는 손발톱 감염 치료에 사용되는 크림인 트라바린 등이 있다. 앞으로 회사는 환자의 필요와 안전을 최우선으로 하는 엄격한 개발 과정을 개선하는 데 주력할 예정이다. 또한 회사는 캐나다 전역의 의료 사업자에게 자사의 약을 판매하는 전담 판매 인력을 증원할 예정이다.

어휘 immediate 즉시의 release 공개, 보도 pharmaceutical 제약의 purchase 매입하다 stake 지분 shareholder 주주 landmark 획기적인 것 firmly 굳게 expand (사업을) 확장하다, 확장되다 significantly 크게 commercialize 상용화하다

---

medication 약   condition 질환, 문제   refine 개선하다, 다듬다
rigorous 엄격한   prioritize 최우선으로 하다   build up 증원하다,
확립하다   dedicated 전담하는   provider (서비스 등의) 제공자

143 부사 어휘   고난도

해설   앞에 나온 절과 뒤따르는 분사 구문을 의미상 자연스럽게 연결하는 부사를
선택하는 문제이다. 피어런의 성장 전략을 실행하기 위한 자금을 지원하게
된 것(providing funding to realize Pearron's growth strategy)
은 피어런의 소수 지분을 매입(Wompler Capital has purchased a
minority stake in Pearron)한 결과라고 볼 수 있다. 따라서 '그렇게
함으로써, 그로 인해'라는 의미의 (C) thereby가 정답이다. 콤마 다음에
「thereby doing something」 구조로 쓰이며, 분사 구문이 결과를 나타
낸다는 것을 알아 두자. (B) instead도 같은 구조로 쓰일 수 있지만 '(앞에
언급된 것) 대신 ~하며'라는 뜻을 나타내므로 빈칸에는 적절하지 않다.

144 한정사 _ 지시형용사

해설   빈칸이 수식하는 획기적인 거래(landmark deal)는 첫 단락에 나온 피
어런 사와 웜플러 캐피털 간의 계약(Pharmaceutical firm Pearron,
Inc. ~ the signing of a deal with Wompler Capital)을 의미한다.
따라서 앞서 언급된 것을 가리킬 때 쓰이는 (A) this가 정답이다.

145 동사 어형 _ 시제

해설   빈칸은 that절의 동사 자리로, 미래를 나타내는 전치사구 in the coming
years의 수식을 받는다. 따라서 미래시제 동사인 (B) will allow가 정
답이다. 단순현재 시제는 현재 혹은 예정된 가까운 미래를 나타내므로
(A) allows는 정답이 될 수 없다.

146 문맥에 맞는 문장 고르기

번역   (A) 많은 환자들은 여전히 대체요법보다 전통 의학을 선호한다.
(B) 기계들은 전국 각지의 병실에서 찾을 수 있다.
(C) 제품으로는 손발톱 감염 치료에 사용되는 크림인 트라바린 등이 있다.
(D) 진행 중인 임상시험의 초기 결과는 전망이 밝다.

해설   빈칸 앞 문장에서 피어런이 다양한 질환을 위한 약을 개발하고 상용화한
다(Pearron develops and commercializes medications for a
variety of skin, hair, and nail conditions)고 했고, 뒤에서는 회사의
제약 개발 과정과 관련된 미래 계획을 소개했으므로, 빈칸에는 피어런의
현 상황을 묘사한 문장이 들어가야 자연스럽다. 따라서 피어런의 제약품
(medications → its products)을 예시로 든 (C)가 정답이다. 빈칸 앞뒤
에 진행 중인 임상시험(ongoing clinical trial)과 관련된 내용은 언급되
지 않았으므로, (D)는 적합하지 않다.

어휘   conventional 전통적인   alternative 대체의   remedy 치료법
infection 감염   clinical trial 임상시험   promising 전망이 밝은

PART 7

147-148 광고

스완 스페이스

스완 스페이스는 개인과 중소기업을 대상으로 편안한 첨단기술 근무 환경을 제
공합니다. 당사 시설은 함께 일할 수 있는 자율적인 라운지 공간부터 전용 회의
공간이 있는 개인 사무실까지 다양한 옵션을 제공합니다. 모든 회원이 이용할
수 있는 편의시설은 다음과 같습니다.

• 무료 고속 무선 인터넷 및 프린터, 스캐너, 파쇄기 사용
• 무료 음료와 상품이 넉넉하게 구비된 자판기가 있는 주방과 휴게실
• 147소포 수신 서비스 및 좋은 인상을 줄 수 있는 당사의 하이랜드 지구 주소
(바니 가 3100번지)를 업무용 우편물에 사용하는 것

자세히 알고 싶으세요? 1485월 3일 열리는 다음 번 스완 스페이스 공개 환영회
에 참석해 당사 직원, 현재 회원 및 링클리 업계의 다른 선두주자들과 만나세요.
아니면 평일 오전 8시에서 오후 6시 사이에 당사를 방문해 개인적으로 둘러보
시거나 www.swannspace.com을 방문하시면 됩니다.

어휘   comfortable 편안한   environment 환경   facility 시설
range from A to B (범위가) A에서 B에 이르다   flexible 융통성
있는, 탄력 있는   dedicated 전용의   amenity 편의시설   shredder
파쇄기   well-stocked 상품이 넉넉하게 구비된   impressive
인상적인, 강한[좋은] 인상을 주는   alternatively 아니면, 또는

147 사실 관계 확인

번역   스완 스페이스에 관해 알 수 있는 것은?
(A) 주로 창의 산업 종사자를 대상으로 서비스를 제공한다.
(B) 회원에게 기술 지원 서비스를 제공한다.
(C) 유명한 동네에 있다.
(D) 회원들은 운동 기기를 이용할 수 있다.

해설   두 번째 단락의 세 번째 항목에서 스완 스페이스 건물이 좋은 인상을 주
는 하이랜드 지구에 주소를 두고 있다(our building's impressive
Highlands District address)고 했으므로, (C)가 정답이다. 회원이 인
터넷이나 사무용 기기를 이용할 수 있게 해주지만, 이에 대한 기술 지원 서
비스를 제공하는지는 확인할 수 없으므로 (B)는 정답이 될 수 없다.

어휘   cater 서비스를 제공하다   prestigious 명성이 있는, 고급의

▸▸ Paraphrasing   지문의 impressive Highlands District
address → 정답의 located in a prestigious
neighborhood

148 세부 사항

번역   스완 스페이스는 5월 3일에 무엇을 할 것인가?
(A) 월세 인상
(B) 시설 견학 안내
(C) 새 임원 환영
(D) 인맥을 쌓을 수 있는 행사 주최

해설   마지막 단락에서 5월 3일에 열리는 스완 스페이스 공개 환영회에 참석해
회사 직원, 현재 회원 및 링클리 업계의 다른 선두주자들과 만나보라(Join
~ Swann Space Open Reception on May 3 to connect with

us, our current members, and other leaders of the Linkley business community)고 권하고 있으므로, (D)가 정답이다.

어휘 executive 임원

▶▶ Paraphrasing
지문의 to connect with us, our current members, and other leaders of the Linkley business community
→ 정답의 networking

지문의 Swann Space Open Reception
→ 정답의 event

149-150 이메일

발신: 에이지 후루타
수신: 질 베넷
제목: 배송품 포장
날짜: 4월 3일

안녕하세요 질,

고객 서비스부에서 말하길, 식료품 배송 고객들이 고기 포장 건으로 연락했다고 하세요. 듣자 하니 고기가 우리의 기본 포장재(랩으로 씌운 스티로폼 접시)로만 포장된 걸 걱정한다고 해요. 149이들은 이 포장재가 잘못돼 육즙이 샐 경우에 대비해 한 번 더 포장하여 다른 제품에 박테리아가 생기지 않도록 했으면 한대요.

150현재로서는 실제로 기본 포장재가 잘못됐다는 보고는 받지 못했으므로 반드시 개선해야 할지 확신은 없어요. 하지만 적어도 이러한 고객들의 바람에 부응할 방법을 강구해야 한다고 생각해요. 추가 포장 옵션과 여기에 드는 비용, 환경에 미치는 영향을 조사해 주시겠어요? 이번 달 말까지 간략한 조사 결과를 보고해 주세요.

고마워요.

에이지

어휘 grocery 식료품 apparently 듣자 하니 concerned 걱정하는 foam tray 스티로폼 접시 stretchable film 랩 layer 겹, 층 leak 새다 convinced 확신하는, 설득된 accommodate 부응하다, 수용하다 impact 영향 involved in ~와 관련된 finding (조사) 결과

149 세부 사항

고난도

번역 고객이 걱정하는 것은?
(A) 재활용이 안 되는 포장재 사용
(B) 안전하지 않은 수준으로 상승하는 고기 온도
(C) 직원이 배송용기를 조심스럽게 다루지 않는 것
(D) 식품이 교차 오염되는 것

해설 첫 번째 단락에서 포장재가 잘못돼 육즙이 샐 경우에 대비해 한 번 더 포장하여 다른 제품에 박테리아가 생기지 않도록 했으면 한다(They would like another layer to be added to protect the other products from bacteria in case this packaging fails and the meat's juices leak)는 고객의 의견을 전했으므로, (D)가 정답이다.

어휘 temperature 온도 contaminate 오염시키다

150 추론 / 암시

고난도

번역 에이지 씨가 포장재의 변경 가능성에 관해 암시하는 것은?
(A) 필요 없을 수도 있다.
(B) 서서히 도입해야 한다.
(C) 베넷 씨의 승인이 필요하다.
(D) 직원들이 좋아하지 않을 것이다.

해설 두 번째 단락에서 에이지 씨는 실제로 기본 포장이 잘못됐다는 보고는 받지 못했으므로 반드시 개선해야 할지 확신은 없다(I'm not convinced that it has to be upgraded)고 했다. 따라서 (A)가 정답이다.

▶▶ Paraphrasing
지문의 be upgraded
→ 질문의 change

지문의 I'm not convinced
→ 정답의 It may not be necessary

151-152 정보문

하드나 시 주민 소식지

하드나 시 원예 클럽(HCGC)

새 시즌을 시작하니 와서 저희와 함께 하세요! 올해 첫 회의가 3월 13일 월요일 오후 7시에 기존 행사장인 하드나 주민센터에서 열립니다. 패트릭 레트와 지나 루가 '꿀벌이 원예가를 돕는 방법'에 대한 강연 및 시연에 나섭니다. 이들은 하드나 시 양봉가협회 회원으로, 꿀벌이 환경에 주는 이점을 대중에게 알리는 데 전념하고 있습니다. 강의에는 벌을 끌어들이는 정원 설계에 관한 값진 조언도 포함됩니다. 이 프로그램은 대화식으로 진행되므로 질문을 준비해 오세요.

151다음 주 월요일에 새로운 얼굴들을 많이 볼 수 있었으면 합니다. HCGC 개인 회원비는 연간 20달러이며 회원 가입 양식은 회의에서 얻을 수 있습니다. 152앞으로 있을 현장 학습, 식물 판매 및 자원봉사 활동을 포함한 전체 일정표는 온라인 www.hcgc.org에서 확인할 수 있습니다.

어휘 venue 장소, 행사장 demonstration 시연 beekeeper 양봉가 be committed to ~에 전념하다 benefit 이점, 혜택 interactive 상호 작용의, 대화식의 individual 개인의 complete 전체의

151 주제 / 목적

번역 정보문의 한 가지 목적은?
(A) 장소 변경 발표
(B) 클럽 신규 회원 모집
(C) 이전 강의에 대한 의견 구하기
(D) 지역 환경 문제 강조

해설 첫 번째 단락에서 올해의 첫 회의를 공지한 후, 두 번째 단락에서 다음 주 월요일에 새로운 얼굴들을 많이 볼 수 있었으면 한다(We hope to see a lot of new faces next Monday)며 회원 가입과 관련된 설명(An individual membership to the HCGC costs $20 per year, and membership registration forms will be available at the meeting)을 이어 가고 있다. 따라서 (B)가 정답이다.

어휘 recruit 모집하다 previous 이전의 highlight 강조하다

▶▶ Paraphrasing
지문의 a lot of new faces
→ 정답의 new members

152 세부 사항

번역 정보문에 따르면 HCGC 웹사이트에서 이용할 수 있는 것은?
(A) 행사 일정
(B) 회원 가입 신청서
(C) 도시 지도
(D) 토론 포럼

해설 두 번째 단락에서 현장 학습, 식물 판매 및 자원봉사 활동을 포함한 전체 일정표는 온라인에서 확인할 수 있다(A complete calendar of our upcoming field trips, plant sales, and volunteer activities can be found online)고 했으므로, (A)가 정답이다.

▶▶ Paraphrasing 지문의 can be found online
→ 질문의 available on the HCGC Web site
지문의 A complete calendar of our upcoming field trips, plant sales, and volunteer activities
→ 정답의 A schedule of events

153-154 문자 메시지

제프 크리스, 오후 3시 22분
에이미, 라벨 부착기 하나에 문제가 생겼어요. 라벨이 삐뚤삐뚤하게 나와요.

에이미 모라, 오후 3시 23분
공급 장치 부분을 청소해 보세요. 더러울 수도 있으니까요. ¹⁵³아직도 공장 작업 현장에 있나요?

제프 크리스, 오후 3시 24분
¹⁵³예, 지금 여기 있어요. ¹⁵⁴이 장비 담당 서비스 기술자가 누군지 아세요? 실은 청소한 지 얼마 안 되었거든요.

에이미 모라, 오후 3시 24분
좋은 질문이군요. ¹⁵⁴다시 연락할게요.

제프 크리스, 오후 3시 25분
아, 그렇다면 굳이 필요 없어요. 제조사의 기술지원 상담전화를 이용해 볼게요.

어휘 issue 문제 crooked 삐뚤삐뚤한 feeder 공급 장치 equipment 장비 manufacturer 제조사

153 추론 / 암시

번역 크리스 씨는 어디에 있겠는가?
(A) 생산 공장
(B) 인쇄소
(C) 건물 로비
(D) 컴퓨터 매장

해설 모라 씨가 오후 3시 23분 메시지에서 크리스 씨에게 아직도 공장 작업 현장에 있는지(Are you still down on the factory floor?) 물었는데, 이에 대해 크리스 씨가 그렇다(Yes, I'm down here now)고 대답했다. 따라서 (A)가 정답이다.

▶▶ Paraphrasing 지문의 on the factory floor
→ 정답의 In a production plant

154 의도 파악 [고난도]

번역 오후 3시 24분에 모라 씨가 "좋은 질문이군요"라고 쓴 의미는?
(A) 크리스 씨가 중요한 문제를 지적했다.
(B) 수리를 위해 누구에게 연락해야 할지 확실하지 않다.
(C) 기계가 오작동한 이유를 모른다.
(D) 크리스 씨가 그녀에게 급한 일을 일깨워줬다.

해설 크리스 씨가 오후 3시 24분 메시지에서 라벨 기계 담당 서비스 기술자가 누군지 아는지(Do you know who the service technician is for this equipment?) 물었는데, 이에 대해 모라 씨가 '좋은 질문이군요(Good question)'라고 한 후, 질문에 답하지 않고 다시 연락하겠다(Let me get back to you)고 했다. 따라서 모라 씨도 수리 담당 기술자가 누구인지 모른다고 추론할 수 있으므로, (B)가 정답이다.

어휘 malfunction 오작동하다 urgent 급한

155-157 계약서 발췌

8. 행위 규범

¹⁵⁵박람회는 본래 지식 공유의 장으로 기획되었으므로, 전시업체 및 해당 직원들은 엑스포 현장에서 판매, 주문 접수 등을 하지 않는다. 마찬가지로, 계약된 전시 공간에는 어떠한 가격도 표시하지 않는다.

행사장 전역에서 관람객의 자유로운 ¹⁵⁶이동을 유도하기 위해, 전시업체들은 계약된 전시공간 외부에 직원이나 자료를 배치하지 않는다. 마찬가지로, 직원이나 자료를 공간 내 배치할 때는 통로를 메우지 말고 참석자들을 안쪽으로 끌어들이도록 해야 한다.

모든 참석자들과 마찬가지로, 전시업체 직원들은 공식 엑스포 참가자격증을 차고 항상 비즈니스 정장 또는 비즈니스 캐주얼 복장을 적절히 갖추어야 한다.

¹⁵⁷전시업체가 관여하는 시연이나 기타 활동은 85데시벨 이상의 소음을 발생시키면 안 된다.

박람회 공식 종료 전에 전시품을 해체하거나 짐을 싸는 것을 금지한다.

어휘 code 규범, 규칙 conduct 행위 exposition 전시회, 박람회 primarily 주로, 본래 representative 직원 engage in ~를 하다, ~에 관여하다 similarly 마찬가지로 display 표시하다, 전시하다 contracted 계약된 exhibition 전시 encourage 장려하다, 유도하다 exhibitor 전시업체, 출품자 placement 배치 arrange 배치하다 credential 자격증, 신용 증명서 appropriately 적절히 generate 발생시키다 dismantle 해체하다

155 사실 관계 확인

번역 박람회에 관해 언급된 것은?
(A) 목적은 교육이다.
(B) 여러 동의 건물을 차지한다.
(C) 이전에 개최된 적이 있다.
(D) 언론인들은 무료다.

해설 첫 번째 단락에서 박람회는 본래 지식 공유의 장으로 기획되었다(the exposition is primarily intended as a venue for the sharing of knowledge)고 했으므로, (A)가 정답이다.

156 동의어 찾기   `고난도`

번역 2번째 단락 1행의 "flow"와 의미상 가장 가까운 것은?

(A) 순서
(B) 방향
(C) 수량
(D) 순환

해설 'flow'가 포함된 부분은 '관람객의 자유로운 이동을 유도하기 위해(In order to encourage the free flow of visitors)'라는 의미로 해석되는데, 여기서 flow는 '이동, 흐름'이라는 뜻으로 쓰였다. 따라서 '순환, 유통'이라는 의미의 (D) circulation이 정답이다.

157 사실 관계 확인

번역 발췌문에서 전시업체에 관해 명시한 것은?

(A) 사용할 수 있는 전기의 양
(B) 배포 가능한 유인물의 종류
(C) 낼 수 있는 소리의 크기
(D) 파견 가능한 직원 수

해설 네 번째 단락에서 전시업체가 관여하는 시연이나 기타 활동은 85데시벨 이상의 소음을 발생시키면 안 된다(Any demonstrations or other activities engaged in by the exhibitor will not generate a noise of greater than 85 decibels)고 했으므로, (C)가 정답이다.

어휘 handout 유인물 distribute 배포하다

158-161 기사

지역 경제

(9월 13일)—**158**카인렌 슈퍼스토어 개점을 불과 2주 앞두고, 베이커트 상인회 (BMA)가 소비자를 상대로 지역 업체 지원을 독려하는 운동을 시작했다. 적어도 30개 가게가 "베이커트산을 구매합시다"라고 적힌 팻말을 앞유리창에 걸었다.

159전국의 다른 카인렌 매장들과 마찬가지로, 18만 제곱피트의 땅 위에 펼쳐진 베이커트 지점 신규 매장은 식료품, 의류, 전자제품을 판매하고 원예용품 센터와 사진 현상실을 자랑할 예정이다. **161(D)**평면 규모가 이처럼 거대했기 때문에, 토드 로 부지 인근의 식물과 야생동물에 미칠 수 있는 피해에 대한 공공 검토를 받아야 했다.

당시 BMA는 신규 매장이 다른 **160**영역, 즉 지역 상권에 미치는 영향을 고려하도록 시의회에 압력을 넣어 개발을 저지하는 데 거의 성공했다. **161(C)**BMA는 카인렌 때문에 소규모 소매업체들이 폐업할 것이며, 따라서 장기적으로 지역사회가 약화될 것이라고 주장했다.

161(A)그러나 의회는 매장이 시민들을 위해 새로운 일자리를 창출하고, 시민들이 유명할 정도로 저렴한 체인점의 가격을 누릴 수 있으므로 궁극적으로 베이커트에 이로울 것이라는 카인렌 측의 주장에 더 설득되었다.

BMA 회장이자 베이커트 스포팅 굿즈의 사장인 로라 콤스톡은 "베이커트산을 구매합시다" 캠페인은 "단지 사람들에게 쇼핑하기 전에 생각하라고 하는 것뿐"이라면서 "필요하다고 생각되는 한" 계속하겠다고 덧붙였다.

어휘 initiative 계획, (특정 목적을 달성하기 위한) 운동 location 지점 boast 자랑하다 photo developing 사진 현상 massiveness 거대함 be subject to ~의 대상이다, ~에 달려있다 potential 가능성이 있는, 잠재적인 block 막다, 저지하다 press 압박하다, 압력을 넣다 commerce 상업 retailer 소매업체 out of business 폐업한 in the long term 장기적으로 persuade 설득하다 ultimately 궁극적으로

158 주제 / 목적   `고난도`

번역 기사를 쓴 이유는?

(A) 지역 소매업체가 주도하는 캠페인을 알리기 위해
(B) 전국적 기업의 역사를 설명하기 위해
(C) 신규 매장 개점 기념식을 설명하기 위해
(D) 시의회 회의에 시민을 초청하기 위해

해설 첫 번째 단락에서 베이커트 상인회가 소비자를 상대로 지역 업체 지원을 독려하는 운동을 시작했다(the Bakert Merchants Association (BMA) has begun an initiative that encourages consumers to support local businesses)고 한 후, 이 운동이 시작된 계기와 취지를 소개하고 있다. 따라서 (A)가 정답이다.

159 세부 사항

번역 기사에 따르면 카인렌 슈퍼스토어를 방문하는 사람들이 할 수 있는 것은?

(A) 인물 사진 찍기
(B) 처방 약품 조제
(C) 조경용품 구매
(D) 식당에서 식사하기

해설 두 번째 단락에서 전국의 다른 카인렌 매장들과 마찬가지로 베이커트 지점 신규 매장이 식료품, 의류, 전자제품을 판매하고 원예용품 센터와 사진 현상실을 자랑할 예정(Like other Cainlen locations across the nation, the new Bakert store will ~ boast a garden supply center and a photo developing lab)이라고 했다. 따라서 (C)가 정답이다. 참고로, 사진 현상실에서 인물 사진 촬영이 가능한 것은 아니므로, (A)는 정답이 될 수 없다.

어휘 portrait 인물 사진, 초상(화) prescription 처방(전)

160 동의어 찾기

번역 3번째 단락 3행의 "area"와 의미상 가장 가까운 것은?
(A) 크기
(B) 영역
(C) 거리
(D) 지방

해설 'area'가 포함된 부분은 '다른 영역, 즉 지역 상권에 미치는 효과(its effects in another area—that of local commerce)'라는 의미로 해석되는데, 여기서 area는 영역, 분야라는 뜻으로 쓰였다. 따라서 '지역, 분야'라는 의미의 (B) field가 정답이다.

161 사실 관계 확인   고난도

번역 카인렌 슈퍼스토어 신규 매장이 미칠 수 있는 영향으로 언급되지 않은 것은?
(A) 고용 기회 증가
(B) 새로운 유형의 제품 구입 가능
(C) 타 사업장의 폐업
(D) 환경 훼손

해설 네 번째 단락의 '시민들을 위해 새로운 일자리를 창출하여 베이커트에 이로울 것이다(the store would ~ benefit Bakert by creating new jobs for its citizens)'에서 (A)를, 세 번째 단락의 '카인렌 때문에 소규모 소매업체들이 폐업할 것이다(Cainlen would put smaller retailers out of business)'에서 (C)를, 두 번째 단락의 '부지 인근의 식물과 야생동물에 미칠 수 있는 피해에 대한 공공 검토를 받아야 했다(its construction was subject to public review regarding potential harm to plants and wildlife near its site)'에서 (D)를 확인할 수 있다. 따라서 언급되지 않은 (B)가 정답이다.

▶ **Paraphrasing**   지문의 **creating new jobs for its citizens** → 보기 (A)의 **An increase in employment opportunities**

지문의 **put smaller retailers out of business** → 보기 (C)의 **The closing of other businesses**

지문의 **potential harm to plants and wildlife** → 보기 (D)의 **Damage to the environment**

162-164 편지

몰셔 대학교   음악과
                                         오타와, 온타리오 K1A 4H9

동창생, 친구들께:

¹⁶⁴몰셔 대학은 티노르 예술재단(TAF)이 운영하는 '음악 나누기' 프로그램 덕분에 지난 1년간 새로운 피아노를 사용할 수 있었습니다. 그것은 우리 과에 고품질의 악기를 매년 무료로 아낌없이 공급합니다. ¹⁶²이제, 프로그램의 일환으로 저희는 엄선된 피아노들을 일반인이 구매할 수 있게 제공하고자 합니다.

구매 가능한 악기에는 선도적인 제조업체가 만든 그랜드 피아노, 수형 피아노, 디지털 피아노 등이 포함됩니다. 대부분 아직 보증기간이 남아 있으며, 구매 시 현장에서 배송 서비스 등록이 가능합니다.

악기를 보고 구입하시려면 2월 10일 토요일 오후 2시에서 6시 사이에 예술의 전당을 방문하십시오. 예약은 필요 없습니다. 예술의 전당은 1번가와 2번가 사이 캔비 로에 있습니다. ¹⁶³근처에 노상 주차를 하실 경우 어디든 시간당 2달러의 요금이 적용됩니다. 아니면, 전당 주차장에서 유료 주차를 이용할 수 있습니다. 찾아오시는 길은 www.arts-center.org를 참조하십시오.

¹⁶²모든 악기 수익금의 일부는 TAF에 반환되어 '음악 나누기' 프로그램을 유지하는 데 쓰이며, 이는 우리 과의 수준 높은 음악 지도 역량에 중요한 역할을 합니다.

폴 렘케
임시 학장, 음악과
몰셔 대학교

어휘 operate 운영하다   a selection of 엄선된   purchase 구매: 구매하다   instrument 악기, 도구   leading 선도적인   manufacturer 제조업체   warranty 보증(기간), 보증서   arrangement 준비, 주선   vicinity 근처, 인근   directions 길 안내   portion 일부   proceed 수익   instruction 지도, 교육   interim 임시의

162 주제 / 목적

번역 편지의 주요 목적은?
(A) 학과 신입 직원 환영
(B) 모금을 위한 판매 세부사항 알리기
(C) 기부자의 기여에 감사하기
(D) 프로그램 확대 발표

해설 첫 번째 단락에서 '음악 나누기' 프로그램의 일환으로, 프로그램에서 사용되었던 피아노를 엄선하여 일반인이 구매할 수 있게 하고자 한다(we are offering a selection of the pianos to the public for purchase)고 한 후, 구매 방법을 설명했다. 또한 마지막 단락에서 모든 악기 수익금의 일부는 TAF에 반환되어 '음악 나누기' 프로그램을 유지하는 데 쓰인다(A portion of the proceeds from each instrument is returned to the TAF to maintain Giving Music)고 했으므로, 악기 판매가 모금을 위한 것임을 알 수 있다. 따라서 (B)가 정답이다.

어휘 contribution 기여   expansion 확대

163 추론 / 암시

번역 예술의 전당에 관해 암시된 것은?
(A) 보통 주말에는 문을 닫는다.
(B) 출입구가 둘 이상이다.
(C) 인근에 무료 주차장이 없다.
(D) TAF의 자원봉사자들로 운영된다.

해설 세 번째 단락을 보면 전당 근처에서 노상 주차를 할 경우 어디든 시간당 2달러의 요금이 적용되며(A $2-per-hour rate applies to all street parking in the vicinity), 전당 주차장에서 유료 주차를 이용할 수도 있다(paid parking is available in the center's garage)고 되어 있다. 따라서 인근에 무료 주차 공간이 없다고 추론할 수 있으므로, (C)가 정답이다.

▶ **Paraphrasing**   지문의 **in the vicinity** → 정답의 **nearby**

164 문장 삽입

번역 [1], [2], [3], [4]로 표시된 곳 중에서 다음 문장이 가장 적합한 곳은?
"그것은 우리 과에 고품질의 악기를 매년 무료로 아낌없이 공급합니다."
(A) [1]
(B) [2]
(C) [3]
(D) [4]

해설 주어진 문장의 주어인 대명사 It이 대신하는 악기 공급처가 먼저 언급되어야 한다. [1] 앞에서 TAF가 운영하는 '음악 나누기' 프로그램 덕분에 지난 1년간 학교에서 새로운 피아노들을 사용할 수 있었다(Molsher University has had the use of new pianos for the past year thanks to the "Giving Music" program operated by ~ TAF)며 누가 악기를 공급하는지 구체적으로 밝혔으므로, (A)가 정답이다.

165-167 보고서 요약

파지노 직원 만족도 조사 보고서

개요

타요나 컨설팅 서비스는 파지노 직원들의 직무 만족도를 측정하기 위해 설문조사를 실시했다. ¹⁶⁶**데이터는 주로 설문조사 플랫폼인 제스트서베이를 활용해 수집했다.** 직원들은 회사 경영, 직무, 직원 복리후생 등의 요소에 대한 만족도를 수치로 평가하도록 요구 받았다. 이 보고서 부록에는 질문 목록과 수집된 데이터에 대한 상세한 분석이 포함되어 있다. 답변에 관해 기꺼이 추가로 논의하겠다는 의사를 밝힌 직원들을 대상으로 4차례의 보충 면접이 진행됐다. 이 직원들의 사생활을 보호하기 위해 이 보고서에는 면접에 관해 상세히 기술하지 않았다.

조사 결과는 직원들이 직업의 대부분 측면, 특히 급여에 만족하고 있다는 점을 보여준다. 이번 조사에서 부정적인 평가가 많이 나온 부분은 직원에 대한 지원뿐이다. ¹⁶⁵**직원들이 통화 중 문제가 생기면, 종종 고객의 전화를 매니저에게 연결하도록 지시 받는 것으로 보인다.** 이때 직원은 향후 어떻게 해당 문제를 해결할 수 있을지 배우지 않는다. 직원들은 이런 상황에 답답함을 토로했다. ¹⁶⁷**따라서 이 보고서는 정기적인 교육을 통해 반복되는 문제에 잘 대처하는 방법을 직원들에게 가르치라고 제안한다.**

어휘 executive summary (회사 경영 보고서 등의) 개요
measure 재다, 측정하다 numerically 수치로 rate 평가하다
factor 요소 employee benefits 직원 복리후생 analysis
분석 appendix (appendices) 부록 supplementary 보충하는
conduct 시행[실시]하다 willingness 기꺼이 할 의향 aspect 측면
encounter 접하다 frustration 답답함 recurring 반복되는

165 추론 / 암시

번역 설문조사 참여자는 누구이겠는가?
(A) 소매점 점원
(B) 은행 창구직원
(C) 승무원
(D) 콜센터 직원

해설 두 번째 단락에서 직원들이 통화 중 문제가 생기면 종종 고객의 전화를 매니저에게 연결하도록 지시 받는다(when employees encounter a problem during a call, they are often directed to connect the customer to a manager)고 했으므로, 직원 만족도 설문조사의 참여자가 콜센터 직원이라고 추론할 수 있다. 따라서 (D)가 정답이다.

166 세부 사항

번역 설문조사 데이터는 주로 어떻게 얻었는가?
(A) 특화된 소프트웨어를 통해
(B) 개별 면접을 통해
(C) 종이 설문지를 통해
(D) 포커스 그룹 토론을 통해

해설 첫 번째 단락에서 데이터는 주로 설문조사 플랫폼인 제스트서베이를 활용해 수집했다(Data was primarily collected with the use of the survey platform ZestSurvey)고 했으므로, (A)가 정답이다.

어휘 questionnaire 설문지 focus group 포커스 그룹(여론조사 등을 위해 각계각층에서 뽑은 집단)

▸▸ **Paraphrasing** 지문의 **primarily collected**
→ 질문의 **mainly obtained**
지문의 **with the use of the survey platform ZestSurvey** → 정답의 **Through specialized software**

167 세부 사항

번역 보고서는 무엇을 하라고 권고하는가?
(A) 까다로운 고객에 대한 서비스 중단
(B) 직원 보상 인상
(C) 직원에게 지속적인 지침 제공
(D) 감독자에게 덜 엄격하게 관리하라고 지시

해설 두 번째 단락에서 정기적인 교육을 통해 반복되는 문제에 잘 대처하는 방법을 직원들에게 가르치라고 제안한다(this report proposes that regular training sessions be held to teach employees how to successfully deal with recurring problems)고 했으므로, (C)가 정답이다.

어휘 discontinue 중단하다 compensation 보상

▸▸ **Paraphrasing** 지문의 **proposes** → 질문의 **recommend**
지문의 **regular training sessions be held to teach employees** → 정답의 **Providing ongoing instruction to staff**

168-171 온라인 채팅

대니카 페이 [오전 11시 2분]
¹⁶⁸인탁, 어떤 로펌에서 방금 우리 웹사이트를 통해 아이비 책상 여섯 개를 주문했어요. 호두나무 재고가 부족하다는 건 알고 있어요. 그래서 예상 배송 날짜를 알려주기 전에 확인하려고요.

이인탁 [오전 11시 3분]
여섯 개 책상을 제작하기에는 호두나무가 모자라요. ¹⁷⁰책상 세 개는 한 달 더 지연될 거예요.

대니카 페이 [오전 11시 4분]
음, 이 고객을 잃고 싶지 않은데요. 아이비 책상을 다른 나무로 만들어서 제안하면 어떨까요?

이인탁 [오전 11시 4분]
흠. 벤트를 데려올게요. 그 팀에서 만드니까요.

이인탁 [오전 11시 5분]

169벤트, 아이비 책상을 만드는 데 사용할 수 있는 다른 나무가 있나요? 호두나무가 거의 다 떨어졌어요.

벤트 달 [오전 11시 7분]

169참나무라면 될 거예요. 이것도 단단한 나무고, 색도 비슷해요.

대니카 페이 [오전 11시 8분]

170만약 참나무를 사용하면 주문품을 평소처럼 4주 안에 배송할 수 있을까요?

이인탁 [오전 11시 8분]

170예. 참나무는 많아요.

대니카 페이 [오전 11시 9분]

훨씬 낫네요. 그 로펌에 그렇게 하고 싶은지 물어볼게요.

이인탁 [오전 11시 10분]

171그러세요. 하지만 대형 호두나무 제품 페이지에 '주문 밀림' 배너를 추가해야 할 거예요. 고객마다 전부 주문제작을 해줄 순 없으니까요.

어휘 law firm 로펌, 법률 사무소 estimated 예상되는 alternative 다른, 대안의 similar 비슷한 plenty of 많은 backordered 주문이 밀린 custom order 주문제작

168 세부 사항

번역 채팅 참여자의 회사가 제조하는 것은?
(A) 포장재
(B) 자동차 부품
(C) 의류
(D) 가구

해설 페이 씨가 오전 11시 2분 메시지에서 한 로펌이 방금 회사 웹사이트를 통해 아이비 책상 여섯 개를 주문했다(a law firm just ordered six Ivy desks through our Web site)고 했으므로, 가구 제조업체임을 알 수 있다. 따라서 (D)가 정답이다.

169 세부 사항

번역 달 씨가 확인해준 것은?
(A) 배색이 결정되었다.
(B) 제품을 다른 소재로 만들 수 있다.
(C) 그녀의 팀은 제조 공정을 이해한다.
(D) 그녀의 다음 달 일정은 아직 다 차지 않았다.

해설 이 씨가 오전 11시 5분 메시지에서 달 씨에게 아이비 책상을 만드는 데 사용할 수 있는 다른 나무가 있는지(are there any alternative woods that you could use to make the Ivy desk?) 문의했는데, 달 씨가 참나무(Oak would work)를 대안으로 제시하며 긍정의 응답을 했다. 따라서 (B)가 정답이다.

어휘 color scheme 색체 조합, 배색 material 소재, 재료 process 과정, 공정

▶▶ Paraphrasing 지문의 any alternative woods
→ 정답의 another material

170 의도 파악

번역 오전 11시 9분에 페이 씨가 "훨씬 낫네요"라고 쓴 의도는?
(A) 새로운 샘플 물품이 더 매력 있다.
(B) 생산시간이 단축되는 것이 더 낫다.
(C) 고객이 가격 인하에 고마워할 것이다.
(D) 주문품은 육로로 운송해야 한다.

해설 이 씨가 오전 11시 3분 메시지에서 호두 나무로 제작할 경우 책상 세 개가 한 달 더 지연될 것(Three of the desks would be delayed by an extra month)이라는 문제를 언급했고, 이후 페이 씨는 오전 11시 8분 메시지에서 호두나무 대신 참나무를 사용하면 주문품을 평소처럼 4주 안에 배송할 수 있을지(If we use that, could the order be shipped within the usual four weeks?) 문의했다. 이에 대해 이 씨가 그렇다고 하자 페이 씨가 그 편이 훨씬 낫다(That's much better)고 한 것이므로, 그녀가 생산시간이 지연되지 않는 쪽을 선호한다고 추론할 수 있다. 따라서 (B)가 정답이다.

어휘 attractive 매력적인 preferable 더 나은, 선호되는 appreciate 감사하다, 환영하다

171 세부 사항

번역 이 씨가 페이 씨에게 권하는 일은?
(A) 회사 웹사이트 업데이트하기
(B) 협상 철회
(C) 매장에 광고 걸기
(D) 일부 상품의 디자인에 특징 추가

해설 이 씨가 오전 11시 10분 마지막 메시지에서 대형 호두나무 제품 페이지에 '주문 밀림' 배너를 추가해야 한다(you should probably add "backordered" banners to the pages of our larger walnut products)고 했으므로, 웹사이트 업데이트를 권하고 있음을 알 수 있다. 따라서 (A)가 정답이다.

어휘 withdraw 철회하다 feature 특징

▶▶ Paraphrasing 지문의 add "backordered" banners to the pages
→ 정답의 Update a company Web site

172-175 기사

갤트우드 토박이, 앤트렐 극장 복원해 개관

갤트우드 (6월 22일)—갤트우드 토박이 주드 래글런은 아주 힘든 복원 작업 끝에 앤트렐 극장이 〈꿈꾸는 듯한 1년〉이라는 공연으로 가을에 재개관한다고 말한다.

로켓 가 카페에서 한 인터뷰에서 래글런 씨는 극장을 복원하자는 생각에 20년 만에 갤트우드로 돌아오게 되었다고 말한다. 그는 라티메프 극장에서 관리자로 일하던 중, 2년 전 가족 방문 때 앤트렐 극장이 곧 문을 닫는다는 사실을 알게 됐다.

그는 "충격이었다"고 말한다. 그는 젊은 시절, 4번가와 니콜스 대로가 만나는 모퉁이에 자리잡은 이 오래된 극장을 굉장히 좋아했다. 173그는 이렇게 회상한다. "카든 길에 있는 우리 집에서 걸어오곤 했어요. 거기서 〈유리 깃발〉을 보고 감동받아 극장에서 일하게 됐죠."

그러나 앤트렐 극장 주인들은 더 이상 수익이 나지 않는다고 말했다. ¹⁷²그래서 래글런 씨는 그들이 요구하는 저렴한 가격에 극장을 매입한 뒤 직장을 그만두고 갤트우드 시의회 보조금을 지원 받아 복원에 착수했다.

¹⁷⁵복원 작업은 원래 디자인의 아름다움을 드러내는 쪽으로 복제하는 데 중점을 두었다고 그는 설명한다. <u>작업반원들은 극장의 옛 사진들을 참고했으나</u>, 동시에 휠체어 접근성 향상 같은 일부 현대식 개선도 이루어졌다.

¹⁷⁴래글런 씨는 마녀와 거인들이 사는 환상의 나라를 여행하는 친구들의 이야기인 〈꿈꾸는 듯한 1년〉을 극장 첫 공연작품으로 선택했는데, 이는 "모든 연령대가 즐길 수 있는 작품"이기 때문이라고 한다. 그는 출연진이나 제작진 일원이 되고자 하는 사람들은 www.antrelltheater.com을 방문해 더 자세한 정보를 얻으라고 권한다.

> 어휘 restore 복원하다 performance 공연 draw 끌어오다, 당기다 beloved 소중한, 애정하는 inspire 감동하게 만들다, 영감을 주다 profitable 수익이 나는 reveal 드러내다, 보여주다 replicate 복제하다, 모사하다 accessibility 접근성 production 작품

172 사실 관계 확인

번역 기사에서 래글런 씨에 관해 언급한 것은?
(A) 이전 극장 주인들의 친구다.
(B) 20년 동안 전문 배우였다.
(C) 갤트우드 시에서 자금을 받았다.
(D) 처음 참관한 연극은 〈유리 깃발〉이었다.

해설 네 번째 단락에서 래글런 씨가 저렴한 가격에 극장을 매입한 뒤 갤트우드 시의회 보조금을 지원받아 복원에 착수했다(Mr. Raglan bought it for the low price ~ and set about restoring it with the help of a grant from the Galtwood city council)고 했으므로, (C)가 정답이다.

어휘 decade 10년

> ▸▸ Paraphrasing 지문의 a grant from the Galtwood city council → 정답의 funding from the city of Galtwood

173 세부 사항

번역 래글런 씨는 젊은 시절 어디에 살았는가?
(A) 로켓 가
(B) 4번가
(C) 니콜스 대로
(D) 카든 길

해설 세 번째 단락에서 과거를 회상하며 '카든 길에 있는 우리 집에서 극장까지 걸어오곤 했다(We used to walk over from our house on Carden Lane)'라고 했으므로, 레글런 씨가 카든 길에 살았음을 알 수 있다. 따라서 (D)가 정답이다.

174 사실 관계 확인

번역 〈꿈꾸는 듯한 1년〉에 관해 언급된 것은?
(A) 줄거리에 신비한 요소가 포함되어 있다.
(B) 인기 영화가 원작이다.
(C) 등장인물 일부는 어린이들이다.
(D) 래글런 씨는 배경을 현대로 바꿀 것이다.

해설 마지막 단락에서 〈꿈꾸는 듯한 1년〉(A Faraway Year)을 '마녀와 거인들이 사는 환상의 나라를 여행하는 친구들의 이야기(the story of a group of friends' journey through a fantastical land of witches and giants)'라고 소개했으므로, (A)가 정답이다.

> ▸▸ Paraphrasing 지문의 story → 정답의 plot
> 지문의 a fantastical land of witches and giants → 정답의 magical elements

175 문장 삽입

번역 [1], [2], [3], [4]로 표시된 곳 중에서 다음 문장이 가장 적합한 곳은?
"작업반원들은 극장의 옛 사진들을 참고했다."
(A) [1]
(B) [2]
(C) [3]
(D) [4]

해설 주어진 문장에서 작업반원들이 극장의 옛 사진들을 참고했다(Work crews used old photographs of the theater for reference)고 했으므로, 앞에서 먼저 해당 사진들을 참고해야 하는 이유 또는 상황이 언급되어야 한다. [3] 앞에서 극장 복원 작업이 원래 디자인의 아름다움을 드러내는 쪽으로 복제하는 데 중점을 두었다(The work ~ has focused on revealing and replicating the beauty of its original design)며 그 이유를 밝혔으므로, (C)가 정답이다.

176-180 이메일 + 보도자료

> 발신: 로돌포 에스코르자 〈r.escorza@oqui-mail.com〉
> 수신: 마르셀라 페리 〈anb-recruiting.com〉
> 제목: 회신: 오스본 렌터카에서의 기회
> 날짜: 8월 7일
> 첨부: 이력서
>
> 페리 씨께,
>
> 연락 주셔서 감사합니다. 저는 오스본 렌터카에 대해 잘 알고 있고 이번 공석에 관심이 있습니다. 첨부된 이력서를 봐주십시오. ¹⁷⁶이그젝-링크에 있는 제 프로필 페이지에서 보신 것보다 제 경력을 더 자세히 아시게 될 겁니다.
>
> 하지만 전 파넬라에서 만족하고 있으며 아주 좋은 기회가 아니면 그만둘 생각이 없다는 점을 먼저 솔직하게 말씀 드립니다. 글로벌 경영진의 지원과 미국 시장에서 최선의 결정을 내릴 수 있는 자율권이 모두 제게 있는 상황이어야 합니다. 만약 오스본이 이 조건들을 흔쾌히 ¹⁷⁷맞춰 주신다면, 기꺼이 이 자리에 대해 더 논의하겠습니다.
>
> 만약 저를 계속 후보자로 고려하시게 된다면, 다음 단계는 무엇인지 알려주십시오. ¹⁷⁸앞으로 며칠간 출장 때문에 애틀랜타를 떠나겠지만, 서신 연락은 계속 하겠습니다.
>
> 로돌포 에스코르자
> 운영 담당 수석 부사장
> 파넬라 항공

어휘 opening 공석 understanding 이해, 파악 career 경력 up front 미리, (먼저) 솔직하게 content 만족하는, 행복한 autonomy 자율권 position 자리, 직위 candidacy 입후보 correspondence 서신 operation 운영, 영업

오스본 렌터카, 미국 신임 임원 임명

(10월 22일)—오스본 렌터카는 로돌포 에스코르자를 미국 내 운영 이사로 채용했다. 에스코르자 씨는 은퇴하는 자넷 허프 씨를 대신할 예정이다.

에스코르자 씨는 23년 동안 여행과 항공업계의 다양한 분야에서 일했다. 소비자 여행상품 온라인 판매업체인 글로배스틱의 수석 상품 담당관으로서, 그는 인기 높은 렌터카 예약 서비스를 신설하는 일을 감독했다. 가장 최근에 그는 파넬라 항공의 운영 담당 수석 부사장을 역임했다. ¹⁷⁹이 자리에 있을 때 그는 운영비를 늘리지 않고 항공사의 안전 등급을 높였다.

오스본 렌터카는 불과 4년 전 미국 시장에 진출한 영국 기업이다. 현재 플로리다 주와 조지아 주에 18개소 지점과 500대 이상의 차량을 보유하고 있다. ^{178/180}에스코르자 씨는 애틀랜타에 있는 미국 본사에서 근무하며, 오스본 렌터카가 미국 남동부 등지에서 계속 성장할 수 있도록 이끌어 주리라 기대된다.

어휘 replace 대체하다, 후임이 되다 sector 부문 oversee 감독하다 build up 강화하다, 높이다 safety rating 안전 등급 operational cost 운영 비용 headquarters 본사 continued 지속적인, 계속된

---

176 추론 / 암시 [고난도]

번역 에스코르자 씨는 페리 씨가 자신을 어떻게 알게 되었다고 암시하는가?
(A) 웹사이트를 통해
(B) 잡지 기사를 통해
(C) 서로가 아는 지인을 통해
(D) 회의를 통해

해설 이메일의 첫 번째 단락을 보면, 에스코르자 씨는 페리 씨가 이그젝-링크에 있는 자신의 프로필을 봤을 것(what you saw on my profile page on Exec-Link)으로 추측하고 있으므로, (A)가 정답이다.

어휘 mutual 서로의 acquaintance 지인

▶▶ Paraphrasing 지문의 on my profile page on Exec-Link → 정답의 Through a Web site

---

177 동의어 찾기

번역 이메일에서 2번째 단락 4행의 "meet"와 의미상 가장 가까운 것은?
(A) 모이다
(B) 수행하다
(C) 인접하다
(D) 충족시키다

해설 'meet'이 포함된 부분은 '만약 오스본이 이 조건들을 흔쾌히 맞춰 준다면(If Osborne is willing to meet these conditions)'이라는 의미로 해석되는데, 여기서 meet는 '맞추다, 충족시키다'라는 뜻으로 쓰였다. 따라서 '충족시키다, 이행하다'라는 의미의 (D) fulfill이 정답이다.

---

178 연계 [고난도]

번역 에스코르자 씨에 관해 암시된 것은?
(A) 오스본 렌터카는 그의 급여를 인상하는 데 동의했다.
(B) 채용 과정이 두 달도 채 걸리지 않았다.
(C) 페리 씨와 통화했다.
(D) 이사할 필요가 없을 것이다.

해설 이메일의 세 번째 단락에서 에스코르자 씨는 자신이 며칠간 출장 때문에 애틀랜타를 떠나 있는다(I will be away from Atlanta on a business trip)고 했는데, 보도자료의 마지막 단락을 보면 에스코르자 씨가 애틀랜타에 있는 오스본 렌터카의 미국 본사에서 근무할 예정(From its national headquarters in Atlanta, Mr. Escorza is expected to lead its continued growth)임을 알 수 있다. 에스코르자 씨가 이미 애틀랜타에서 살고 있기 때문에 회사를 옮기더라도 이사할 필요는 없을 것이므로, (D)가 정답이다.

---

179 세부 사항 [고난도]

번역 보도자료에 따르면 에스코르자 씨가 파넬라 항공에서 성취한 것은?
(A) 지출 감소
(B) 안전 개선
(C) 새로운 서비스 실시
(D) 승객 만족도 제고

해설 보도자료의 두 번째 단락에서 에스코르자 씨가 파넬라 항공에서 근무할 때 운영비를 늘리지 않고 항공사의 안전 등급을 높였다(he built up the airline's safety ratings without increasing its operational costs)고 했으므로, (B)가 정답이다.

▶▶ Paraphrasing 지문의 built up the airline's safety ratings → 정답의 Improvements in safety

---

180 사실 관계 확인

번역 오스본 렌터카에 관해 언급된 것은?
(A) 여러 나라에 지부를 두고 있다.
(B) 확장을 시도하고 있다.
(C) 설립자가 퇴사한다.
(D) 다른 회사에 인수되었다.

해설 보도자료의 마지막 단락에서 에스코르자 씨가 오스본 렌터카의 지속적인 성장을 이끌 것이라 기대된다(Mr. Escorza is expected to lead its continued growth throughout the southeastern United States and beyond)고 했으므로, 오스본 렌터카가 사업을 확장할 계획임을 알 수 있다. 따라서 (B)가 정답이다.

어휘 attempt 시도하다, 노력하다 expand 확장하다 acquire 인수하다

▶▶ Paraphrasing 지문의 continued growth throughout the southeastern United States and beyond → 정답의 expand

---

181-185 웹페이지 + 이메일

www.nationalbaseballfederation.com/llions/tickets/groups

단일 경기 단체 및 기업 이용권

랜치너 라이온즈 경기 참관은 가족, 친구와 함께 행사를 축하하거나, 고객을 접

Test 5

대하거나, 직원들에 감사를 표시하는 즐거운 방법입니다. [182(B)]랜치너 필드는 단체와 기업의 수요에 맞는 다수의 편의시설을 자랑하며, 모든 옵션에는 경기장 주차 할인 혜택이 포함됩니다.

덕아웃 섹션	라이온즈 파티오
– 일반 실외 좌석 – 랜치너 필드 상점에서 쓸 수 있는 '라이온즈 벅스' 15달러 – 티켓별 요금제: 10~200명 단체 이용 가능	[182(D)]시야가 넓어 잘 보이는 실외 테이블 좌석 – [182(A)]입장부터 7회까지 야구장 음식(핫도그, 팝콘 등) 무제한 제공 – 티켓별 요금제: 2~6인 단체에 가장 적합
패스트볼 데크	[185]다이아몬드 라운지
– 실내, 트인 좌석 – 입장부터 마지막 회까지 야구장 음식 무제한 제공 – 티켓별 요금제: 2~10인 단체에 가장 적합	– [185]실내, 막힌 좌석 – '클래식' 음식 패키지 – [185]티켓 25장
홈런 스위트	
– 실내, 막힌 좌석, 홈 플레이트 뒤쪽 가장 좋은 위치 2곳 중 하나 – '프리미엄' 음식 패키지 – 티켓 50장	

[181]더 자세한 정보를 원하면 (708) 555-0186번 고객응대부로 전화하거나 또는 여기를 클릭해 실시간 채팅 서비스에 접속하세요.

어휘 attend 참석[참관]하다 celebrate 축하하다, 기념하다 appreciation 감사 an array of 다수의 amenity 편의시설 fare 음식 admission 입장 catering 음식 공급 (서비스), 제공되는 음식 hospitality 응대

발신: 안드레 델가도
수신: 키스 홀트
제목: 요청
날짜: 7월 15일

키스,

[184]8월 4일 저녁 라이온즈 야구 경기 입장권 구입을 알아봐 주셨으면 합니다. 그 주에 우리를 방문하는 리오소 일렉트로닉스 단체의 대표인 윌시 씨와 조금 전 이야기를 나누었는데, 그 스포츠를 좋아한다고 하시더군요. [183]그들의 태블릿 컴퓨터를 마케팅하기 위해 우리가 준비하고 있는 제안서에 자신이 있긴 하지만, 이와 별개로 대표단이 랜치너에서 즐거운 시간을 보낼 수 있도록 해야 합니다.

[185]좌석 종류는 여름 더위를 피할 수 있게 냉방이 되는 옵션을 선택하세요. 그리고 물론 단체에는 우리 직원들도 포함되므로 15명에서 20명 정도 수용해야 해요.

선택사항을 검토해 추천하는 옵션을 보내 주세요.

고마워요.

안드레

어휘 mention 언급하다 confident 자신 있는 delegation 대표단 climate-controlled 냉난방이 되는 accommodate 수용하다 recommendation 추천(하는 것)

---

181 사실 관계 확인

번역 랜치너 라이온즈 고객응대부에 관해 알 수 있는 것은?
(A) 사무실에서 랜치너 필드가 내려다보인다.
(B) 온라인 채팅 플랫폼을 운영한다.
(C) 다국어로 서비스를 제공한다.
(D) 신입사원을 모집하고 있다.

해설 웹페이지 하단을 보면, 더 자세한 정보를 원할 경우 고객응대부에 전화하거나 링크를 클릭해 실시간 채팅 서비스에 접속할 것(For more information, call the hospitality department ~ or click <u>here</u> to access its live chat service)을 권하고 있다. 따라서 랜치너 라이온즈 고객응대부가 온라인 채팅 플랫폼을 운영한다는 것을 알 수 있으므로, (B)가 정답이다.

▶▶ Paraphrasing 　지문의 its live chat service
→ 정답의 an online messaging platform

---

182 사실 관계 확인

번역 라이온즈 파티오의 혜택이 아닌 것은?
(A) 무료 음식
(B) 더 저렴한 주차요금
(C) 경기장 조기 입장
(D) 뚜렷한 경기 시야

해설 웹페이지의 표를 보면, 라이온즈 파티오 이용 시 시야가 넓어 잘 보이는 테이블 좌석(Outdoor seating at tables with excellent sight lines)에서 경기를 관람하고 입장부터 7회까지 야구장 음식을 무제한으로(Unlimited ballpark fare ~ from admission through the 7th inning) 제공받는다고 했으므로, (D)와 (A)를 확인할 수 있다. 또한 첫 번째 단락에서 모든 옵션에는 경기장 주차 할인 혜택이 포함된다(all options include discounts on stadium parking)고 했으므로, (B)도 혜택에 해당된다. 따라서 언급되지 않은 (C)가 정답이다.

어휘 complimentary 무료의

▶▶ Paraphrasing 　지문의 Unlimited ballpark fare
→ 보기 (A)의 Complimentary food
지문의 discounts on stadium parking
→ 보기 (B)의 A lower parking fee
지문의 excellent sight lines
→ 보기 (D)의 A clear view

---

183 추론 / 암시

번역 델가도 씨는 어디에서 근무하겠는가?
(A) 스포츠 텔레비전 방송국
(B) 공업 기기 공급회사
(C) 전자제품 제조업체
(D) 광고 대행사

해설 이메일의 첫 번째 단락에서 델가도 씨가 리오소 일렉트로닉스의 태블릿 컴퓨터를 마케팅하기 위해 준비하고 있는 제안서에 자신 있다(I feel confident about the proposal we're putting together for marketing their tablet computers)고 했으므로, 델가도 씨가 광고 대행사에 근무한다고 추론할 수 있다. 따라서 (D)가 정답이다.

184 사실 관계 확인

번역 월시 씨에 관해 알 수 있는 것은?
(A) 야구 팬이다.
(B) 발표를 주도할 것이다.
(C) 예전에 랜치너에서 살았다.
(D) 생일이 8월 4일이다.

해설 이메일의 첫 번째 단락에서 델가도 씨는 홀트 씨에게 라이온즈 야구 경기 입장권 구입을 알아봐 달라(I'd like you to look into purchasing tickets for the Lions baseball game)고 요청한 후, 월시 씨가 그 스포츠를 좋아한다고 했다(she mentioned that she loves the sport)며 그 이유를 밝혔다. 따라서 월시 씨가 야구 팬이라는 것을 알 수 있으므로, (A)가 정답이다.

185 연계

번역 홀트 씨는 어떤 옵션을 추천하겠는가?
(A) 덕아웃 섹션
(B) 패스트볼 데크
(C) 다이아몬드 라운지
(D) 홈런 스위트

해설 이메일의 두 번째 단락에서 델가도 씨는 홀트 씨에게 냉방이 되며(As for the type of seats, please choose a climate-controlled option) 15명에서 20명 정도 수용 가능한(it will need to accommodate between 15 and 20 people) 옵션을 찾아보라고 했다. 웹페이지의 표를 보면, 이 조건을 충족시키는 옵션은 실내 좌석(Indoor, private seating) 티켓이 25장 제공되는 다이아몬드 라운지(Diamond Lounges)이므로, (C)가 정답이다.

186-190 웹페이지 + 작업 일정 + 고객 후기

http://www.jackfogelphotography.com

잭 포겔 포토그래피

☞ 잭 포겔 포토그래피는 카운티 최고의 부동산 사진 회사입니다. 고객님이 부동산 중개인이든, 부동산을 빨리 팔고 싶은 개인 주택 주인이든, 당사는 가능한 한 최고 품질의 사진을 제공합니다. 지역 내 다른 부동산 사진 회사들과 달리 당사는 아래와 같은 서비스를 제공합니다.

- **186(A)다음 날 처리 보장** – 다음 날까지 이미지를 얻지 못하면 무료*
  (**189***토요일 방문 시 처리 기간 2일)

- **186(B)간편한 결제 옵션** – 사진 촬영 당일 신용카드 또는 회사 수표로 결제

- **186(D)부동산 규모에 관계없이 고정 가격 책정** – 자세한 내용은 <u>요금 페이지</u>를 참조하세요.

창립자인 잭 포겔은 여전히 수많은 사진 촬영을 직접 진행하고 있으며, 당사와 협업하는 사진작가는 모두 최소 10년 이상의 경력을 갖고 있습니다. 그들은 최선의 각도와 조명을 선택해 고객님이 부동산을 더 빨리 매도할 수 있도록 도울 것입니다. 당사 서비스에 대한 후기를 보려면 <u>추천 글 페이지</u>를 방문하세요.

어휘 county 자치주 real estate 부동산 property 부동산, 집 turnaround 작업에 걸리는 기간 regardless of ~에 관계없이 testimonial 추천 글

오늘의 촬영 시간					**190**날짜: 8월 23일
사진작가	시간	주소	사진 수	결제	비고
187잭 포겔	오전 11시	던 가 177번지	25	신용카드	외장 플래시 필요
187잭 포겔	오후 2시	레예스 가 865번지	15	신용카드	
190브래드 멀	오후 3시	퍼 가 262번지	10	수표	
엘런 사토	오후 1시	모이 로 190번지	35	신용카드	단골 고객

어휘 external 외부[외장]의

http://www.jackfogelphotography.com/testimonials

가장 최근의 고객 후기

"부동산 중개인으로서, 이 회사를 적극 추천해요. 몇 주 전에 **188**촉박하게 사진 촬영을 예약했는데, 사진작가가 사토 씨가 일찍 도착해 열심히 일해줬어요. **189**단 이틀 만에 고화질 이미지를 받았고, 회사 수표로 결제할 수 있었어요."
　　　　　　　　　　　　　　　—리사 토바이어스, 8월 26일 수요일

"프로답지만 가격이 적당해요. 전 원래 사진 10장 패키지를 예약했는데, 마지막에 15장 찍기로 결정했어요. 잘한 결정이었어요. **190**사진작가인 멀 씨는 훌륭했어요. **189/190**촬영 이틀 후인 오늘 막 사진을 받았는데 멋져요."
　　　　　　　　　　　　　　　— **190**래리 호지스, 8월 25일 월요일

어휘 with little notice 촉박하게 affordable 가격이 적당한

186 사실 관계 확인

번역 포겔 씨 회사의 독특한 특징으로 열거되지 않은 것은?
(A) 인도 시간 보장
(B) 수용하는 결제 방식
(C) 정교한 장비 사용
(D) 서비스의 가격 구조

해설 웹페이지의 두 번째 단락에서 잭 포겔 포토그래피는 다른 부동산 사진 회사들과 다르다며 언급한 특징 중, '다음 날 처리 보장(Guaranteed next-day turnaround)'에서 (A)를, '간편한 결제 옵션(Easy payment options)'에서 (B)를, '부동산 규모에 관계없이 고정 가격 책정(Fixed pricing, regardless of the property's size)'에서 (D)를 확인할 수 있다. 따라서 언급되지 않은 (C)가 정답이다.

어휘 sophisticated 정교한

▶▶ **Paraphrasing** 　지문의 **next-day turnaround**
　　　　　　　　　→ 보기 (A)의 **guaranteed delivery times**
　　　　　　　　　지문의 **payment options**
　　　　　　　　　→ 보기 (B)의 **payment methods**
　　　　　　　　　지문의 **Fixed pricing**
　　　　　　　　　→ 보기 (D)의 **The price structure**

Test 5

187 추론 / 암시

번역 작업 일정에서 오전 11시 촬영에 관해 암시된 것은?
(A) 하루 중 가장 긴 시간이 걸린다.
(B) 주로 실내에서 진행된다.
(C) 단골 고객을 위한 것이다.
(D) 3시간이 걸리지 않는다.

해설 작업 일정 표를 보면, 포겔 씨가 오전 11시와 오후 2시에 각각 다른 사진 촬영을 진행할 예정이라고 되어 있다. 따라서 그의 오전 11시 작업은 3시간 이내로 끝날 것이라고 추론할 수 있으므로, (D)가 정답이다.

어휘 regular client 단골 고객

188 동의어 찾기

번역 고객 후기에서 1번째 단락 2행의 "notice"와 의미상 가장 가까운 것은?
(A) 예고
(B) 주의
(C) 사퇴 발표
(D) 공개 게시

해설 'notice'가 포함된 부분은 '촉박하게 사진 촬영을 예약했다(I booked a photo shoot with little notice)'라는 의미로 해석되는데, 여기서 notice(예고, 통지)는 with little과 함께 '충분한 예고 없이, 촉박하게'라는 표현으로 쓰인다. 따라서 '예고, 통지'라는 의미의 (A) warning이 정답이다.

189 연계 [고난도]

번역 최근 후기를 올린 고객들의 공통점은?
(A) 사진에 특별한 편집이 필요했다.
(B) 촬영이 토요일에 있었다.
(C) 부동산 중개업소에서 일한다.
(D) 미리 착수금을 냈다.

해설 고객 후기에서 토바이어스 씨와 호지스 씨 모두 촬영 이틀 후에 사진을 받았다(I got the high-quality images back in only two days/I just received my photos today, two days after the shoot)고 했는데, 웹페이지의 두 번째 단락을 보면 토요일 방문 시 처리 기간이 이틀 걸린다(two day turnaround for Saturday visits)고 되어 있다. 따라서 두 고객 모두 토요일에 촬영을 했다고 추론할 수 있으므로, (B)가 정답이다.

어휘 deposit 착수금, 예치금

190 연계

번역 호지스 씨가 촬영을 맡긴 부동산은?
(A) 던 가 177번지
(B) 레예스 가 865번지
(C) 퍼 가 262번지
(D) 모이 로 190번지

해설 호지스 씨가 8월 25일 월요일(Monday, August 25)에 쓴 후기에서 사진작가인 멀 씨가 훌륭했다(Mr. Mull, the photographer, was excellent)고 한 후, 촬영 이틀 후인 오늘 막 사진을 받았다(I just received my photos today, two days after the shoot)고 했으므로, 호지스 씨의 부동산 촬영이 작업 일정표에 적힌 날짜(Date: August 23)에 진행되었음을 알 수 있다. 작업 일정표를 보면, 멀 씨가 촬영을 진행한 장소는 퍼 가 262번지(262 Fir Drive)이므로, (C)가 정답이다.

191-195 설명서 + 이메일 + 이메일

> 텔지스 호텔
>
> **모닝썬 4잔 커피메이커**
> **사용 설명서**
>
> 1. 포트를 열판에서 꺼낸다.
> 2. 포트 뚜껑을 열고 포트의 표시선을 이용, 원하는 양만큼 물을 채운다. 포트를 닫는다.
> 3. 포트의 물을 커피메이커 상단의 물통에 붓는다.
> 4. 포트를 열판에 도로 놓는다.
> ¹⁹²5. 커피메이커 상단의 필터 바구니에 종이 필터를 넣는다.
> 6. 분쇄 커피를 원하는 양만큼 필터에 넣는다. 한 컵에 분쇄 커피 1~1.5큰술을 권장한다.
> 7. 커피메이커 뚜껑을 꽉 닫는다.
> 8. '온' 버튼을 눌러 내리기 시작한다. 전원 표시등이 꺼질 때까지 열판에서 포트를 꺼내지는 않는다.
>
> ¹⁹¹사용하고 나면 다시 사용하기 전에 반드시 청소해야 하지만, 직접 시도하지는 마십시오. 청소담당 직원이 매일 객실 방문 시 하겠습니다.

어휘 instructions (제품 사용) 설명서 indicator 지표, 표시 reservoir 저장소 securely 꽉, 안전하게 brew (커피·차 등을) 내리다, 우리다 attempt 시도하다

> 발신: 비키 슈미트
> 수신: 트래비스 피터스
> 제목: 커피메이커 문제
> 날짜: 1월 11일
>
> 안녕하세요 트래비스,
>
> ¹⁹⁴우리가 브루긴스 사를 통해 구입한 리웬 '모닝썬' 커피메이커와 관련하여 사소한 고객 불만이 접수됐어요. ¹⁹²고객들은 커피메이커에서 먼저 필터 바구니를 꺼내지 않으면 사실상 필터를 넣을 수 없다고 하네요. ¹⁹²/¹⁹⁴그런데 우리가 제공한 설명서에는 그런 내용이 명시되어 있지 않고, 필터도 좀 제거하기 어려워서 그렇게 하는 게 맞는 건지 잘 모르겠다고 해요.
>
> ¹⁹³비즈니스 스위트룸에 있는 자레스 홈 커피메이커와 조식실에 있는 퀄케도의 설명서를 확인했는데 결과가 엇갈렸어요. 퀄케도 모델은 바구니를 꺼내라고 하고 자레스는 그렇지 않아요. 하지만 자레스에 대해 불만이 접수된 적은 없어요.
>
> 이 문제를 조사해 주시겠어요?
>
> 고마워요.
>
> 비키

어휘 actually 사실상, 실제로   specify 명시하다

발신: 트래비스 피터스

수신: 비키 슈미트

제목: 회신: 커피메이커 문제

날짜: 1월 12일

안녕하세요 비키,

¹⁹⁴제조사에 전화했더니 설명서에 해당 추가 단계를 명시해야 한다고 확인해 줬어요. 제조사에서 아주 미안해 하면서 제품 설명서를 수정할 계획이라고 했어요. 그래서 제가 현재 객실에 있는 설명서를 수정된 것으로 바꾸려고 해요.

¹⁹⁵이런 일이 일어난 건 제가 설명서에 있는 지침을 실제로 해보지도 않고 그대로 옮겼기 때문이에요. 다른 기계들은 괜찮았었거든요. 그런데 이제 와서 보니 무모한 행동이었네요. ¹⁹⁵죄송해요. 다시는 이런 실수 안 할게요.

트래비스

어휘 manufacturer 제조사 apologetic 미안해 하는 revise 수정하다 replace 바꾸다 current 현재의

191 추론 / 암시　[고난도]

번역 설명서에서 모닝썬 커피메이커에 관해 암시된 것은?
　(A) 사용자가 내리는 시간을 조정할 수 있다.
　(B) 텔지스 호텔에서 이 커피메이커 용으로 특별한 물을 공급한다.
　(C) 청소해야 한다는 것을 표시하기 위해 표시등에 불이 들어온다.
　(D) 텔지스 호텔은 하루 한 번만 필요할 것으로 예상한다.

해설 설명서 하단에서 커피 메이커를 사용하고 나면 다시 사용하기 전에 반드시 청소해야 한다(The machine must be cleaned between uses)고 했지만, 투숙객에게 직접 하지는 말라고 당부했다. 이어 청소담당 직원이 매일 객실 방문 시 한다(The cleaning staff will do it during their daily visit to your room)며 하루에 한 번만 청소할 것임을 드러냈으므로, 텔지스 호텔은 모닝썬 커피메이커가 하루에 한 번만 이용될 것으로 예상한다고 볼 수 있다. 따라서 (D)가 정답이다.

▸▸ Paraphrasing　지문의 daily → 정답의 once per day

192 연계

번역 슈미트 씨는 사용자가 어떤 단계에 확신이 없다고 하는가?
　(A) 2단계
　(B) 3단계
　(C) 5단계
　(D) 6단계

해설 첫 번째 이메일의 첫 단락을 보면, 커피메이커에서 먼저 필터 바구니를 꺼내지 않으면 사실상 필터를 넣을 수 없고(you can't actually put the filter into the filter basket without taking it out of the coffee maker first) 필터도 제거하기 어려워서 그렇게 하는 게 맞는 건지 모르겠다(the filter is a little hard to remove, so people aren't sure if it's the right thing to do or not)는 고객들의 불만이 적혀 있다. 이는 설명서의 5번째 단계인 '커피메이커 상단의 필터 바구니에 종이 필터를 넣는다(5. Insert a paper filter into the filter basket in the top of the coffee maker)'와 관련이 있으므로, (C)가 정답이다.

193 세부 사항

번역 첫 번째 이메일에 따르면 텔지스 호텔에 있는 것은?
　(A) 세탁 서비스
　(B) 조식 전용 공간
　(C) 고객 불만을 분석하는 전산 시스템
　(D) 출장자를 위한 우수고객 보상 프로그램

해설 첫 번째 이메일의 두 번째 단락에서 피터스 씨가 조식실에 있는 퀄케도의 설명서를 확인했다(I checked the instructions for ~ the Qualcedo in the breakfast room)고 했으므로, 텔지스 호텔에 조식을 위한 전용 공간이 있음을 알 수 있다. 따라서 (B)가 정답이다.

어휘 dedicated 전용의

▸▸ Paraphrasing　지문의 the breakfast room
→ 정답의 A dedicated place for morning meals

194 연계

번역 피터스 씨는 어떤 회사에 연락했겠는가?
　(A) 리웬
　(B) 브루긴스 사
　(C) 자레스 홈
　(D) 퀄케도

해설 두 번째 이메일의 첫 단락에서 피터스 씨는 제조사에 연락했더니 설명서에 누락된 부분이 있었음을 확인해 주었다(I called the manufacturer, and they confirmed that the instructions should have specified that extra step)고 했는데, 첫 번째 이메일의 첫 단락을 보면 고객들이 리웬의 '모닝썬' 커피메이커 설명서에 필터 관련 안내가 명시되어 있지 않은 것(the instructions ~ don't specify that)에 대해서 불만을 제기했다(We've received some minor guest complaints about the Lywen "Morning Sun" coffee makers)고 되어 있다. 따라서 피터스 씨가 '모닝썬' 커피메이커의 제조사인 리웬에 연락했을 것으로 추론할 수 있으므로, (A)가 정답이다.

195 세부 사항

번역 피터스 씨는 무엇에 대해 사과하는가?
　(A) 설명서대로 직접 해보지 않은 것
　(B) 설명서의 내용을 잘못 옮긴 것
　(C) 대신 다른 커피 머신을 사지 않은 것
　(D) 동료의 걱정을 묵살한 것

해설 두 번째 이메일의 두 번째 단락에서 피터스 씨는 자신이 설명서에 있는 지침을 실제로 해보지도 않고 그대로 옮겼기 때문에 문제가 발생했다(this happened because I just copied the instructions in the manual without actually trying them out)고 한 후 이에 대해 사과했다. 따라서 (A)가 정답이다.

어휘 dismiss 묵살하다

▸▸ Paraphrasing　지문의 without actually trying them out
→ 정답의 Not testing instructions himself

196-200 웹페이지 + 양식 + 이메일

---

http://www.cityofrowder.gov/business/signs

간판 규정

로우더 기획개발부(DPDS)는 간판의 상업적 이용과 관련된 시 규정의 시행을 감독합니다. [196]부서 직원들은 업체들에게 우호적인 분위기를 조성하는 동시에, 시민들을 위해 쾌적한 생활공간을 유지하고자 노력하고 있습니다.

시의 간판 관련 조례 전체가 여기에 나열되어 있지만, 여러분의 편의를 위해 가장 보편적인 형태의 임시 상업용 간판에 대한 정보를 아래에 간략한 형태로 제공합니다.

개업 간판: DPDS의 승인이 있으면 신규 업체는 최대 30일 동안 개업 광고 간판을 전시할 수 있다. 이는 단독 옥외 입간판이 허용되는 유일한 경우이다.

휴일 판촉 간판: 업체들은 DPDS의 승인 없이 크리스마스, 새해 연휴 관련 판촉 간판을 최대 15일간 전시할 수 있고, 기타 명시된 여섯 개의 공휴일과 관련된 안내표지판을 최대 5일간 전시할 수 있다.

기타 대형 판촉용 현수막: [197]표면적 20제곱피트가 넘는 기타 모든 홍보 현수막은 DPDS의 승인이 필요하다. 이런 현수막은 한 번에 최대 14일, 연간 3회까지 전시할 수 있다.

[200(C)]DPDS의 결정에 반대하십니까? 시의회에 재심사를 청구하는 방법을 알아보려면 여기를 클릭하십시오.

어휘 regulation 규정 oversee 감독하다 enforcement 시행 favorable 우호적인 atmosphere 분위기 comprehensive 전체의, 포괄적인 ordinance 조례 temporary 임시의 commercial 상업적인 simplified 간략한, 간소화된 circumstance 상황, 경우 approval 승인 free-standing 단독으로 서 있는 permit 허용하다 promotional 홍보(용)의 file an appeal 재심사를 청구하다

로우더 시
기획개발부

상업용 간판 허가 신청서

신청자: 게일 브록
주소: 엘리스 가 922번지, 로우더, 미시간 48097
전화: (810) 555-0124   이메일: gail.brock@ubi-mail.com
업체: 빛나는 보석 미용실
주소: 메인 가 640번지, 로우더, 미시간 48097   장소 ID: 0943-886

프로젝트 설명: [197]24제곱피트 크기의 현수막을 걸어 미용실 개업 5주년 기념일 및 관련 할인 행사를 홍보하려고 합니다. [198]현수막에는 "빛나는 보석 미용실, 5년 영업 기념" 문구가 크게 표시되고 "6월 6~8일 모든 서비스 15퍼센트 할인"이 작은 글자로 표시됩니다. 분홍색 배경에 검정색 글씨입니다. 디자인 시안 이미지는 첨부 파일을 참조하십시오. 할인이 끝나는 6월 8일까지 허용되는 최장 기간 동안 미용실 창문 위쪽에 걸려고 합니다.

어휘 description 설명 anniversary 기념일 mock-up (실물 크기의) 모형, 시안

발신: 레이먼드 모건 〈ray.morgan@cityofrowder.gov〉
수신: 게일 브록 〈gail.brock@ubi-mail.com〉
제목: 신청서 답변
날짜: 5월 8일

브록 씨께,

[199]유감스럽지만, 기획개발부(DPDS)는 최근에 접수하신 임시 상업 간판 허가 신청을 승인할 수 없습니다. 도심 상권에 적용되는 시의 외관 기준법상 간판에 밝은 색상을 사용할 수 없습니다(로우더 시 자치법 9조 34항 130호). [200(B)]이 문제를 해결한 디자인과 함께 신청서를 다시 제출해 주십시오.

[200(A)]이 결정에 궁금한 점이 있으면 555-0186번으로 전화하시면 됩니다.

레이먼드 모건
부국장
기획개발부

어휘 appearance 외관 standard 기준, 표준 (규범) municipal 지방 자치제의 address 해결하다

---

196 사실 관계 확인

번역 웹사이트에서 DPDS에 관해 언급된 것은?
(A) 직원들 실력이 쟁쟁하다.
(B) 부서 간 합병의 결과다.
(C) 두 집단의 요구에 부응하고자 한다.
(D) 최근 새로운 간판 관련 조례를 제정했다.

해설 웹페이지의 첫 번째 단락에서 DPDS 부서 직원들은 업체들에게 우호적인 분위기를 조성하는 동시에 시민들을 위해 쾌적한 생활공간을 유지하고자 노력하고 있다(Its staff is committed to providing a favorable atmosphere for businesses while also maintaining a pleasant living space for citizens)고 했다. 따라서 DPDS가 두 집단의 요구에 부응하고자 노력하고 있음을 알 수 있으므로, (C)가 정답이다.

어휘 merger 합병

197 연계

번역 브록 씨가 간판을 전시할 수 있는 기간은?
(A) 최대 5일
(B) 최대 14일
(C) 최대 15일
(D) 최대 30일

해설 양식의 프로젝트 설명(Project description)란에서 브록 씨는 24제곱피트 크기의 현수막을 걸어 미용실 개업 5주년 기념 행사를 홍보하고 싶다(I would like to hang a 24-square-foot banner to advertise the fifth anniversary ~ related sales event)고 했는데, 웹페이지를 보면 표면적 20제곱피트가 넘는 대형 판촉용 현수막(promotional banners over 20 square feet in surface area)은 한 번에 최대 14일, 연간 3회까지 전시할 수 있다(These banners may be displayed for up to 14 days at a time, three times per year)고 명시되어 있다. 따라서 (B)가 정답이다.

198 추론 / 암시

번역 브록 씨가 자신의 업체에 관해 암시하는 것은?
(A) 양식에 첨부된 사진에 등장한다.
(B) 교차로에 위치한다.
(C) 예전에는 주인이 다른 사람이었다.
(D) 고객에게 임시 할인을 제공할 예정이다.

해설 양식의 프로젝트 설명(Project description)란에서 브록 씨는 현수막에 "6월 6~8일 모든 서비스 15퍼센트 할인"이라는 문구를 작은 글자로 표시할 것(The banner would display ~ "15% Off All Services June 6-8" in smaller text)이라고 했으므로, 브록 씨가 임시 할인을 제공할 예정이라고 추론할 수 있다. 따라서 (D)가 정답이다.

▶▶ **Paraphrasing**   지문의 **15% Off All Services June 6-8**
→ 정답의 **a temporary discount**

199 세부 사항

번역 모건 씨가 브록 씨의 신청을 기각한 이유는?
(A) 디자인에 필요한 글자가 누락되었다.
(B) 간판 색상이 규정에 부합하지 않는다.
(C) 시 행정구에서 특정 광고 방식을 허용하지 않는다.
(D) 간판의 위치가 안전 기준에 맞지 않는다.

해설 이메일의 첫 번째 단락에서 기획개발부(DPDS)는 브록 씨의 간판 허가 신청을 승인할 수 없다(DPDS cannot approve your recent application)고 한 후, 도심 상권에 적용되는 시의 외관 기준법상 간판에 밝은 색상을 사용할 수 없다(The city's appearance standards for the downtown business district do not allow the use of bright colors in signs)며 그 이유를 밝혔으므로, (B)가 정답이다.

어휘 conform to ~에 부합하다

▶▶ **Paraphrasing**   지문의 **cannot approve**
→ 질문의 **reject**
지문의 **The city's appearance standards**
→ 정답의 **a regulation**

200 연계   고난도

번역 브록 씨가 취할 수 있는 행동으로 언급되지 않은 것은?
(A) 모건 씨에게 연락
(B) 간판 계획 변경
(C) 시의회에 결정 재검토 요청
(D) 다른 허가증을 위한 신청서 제출

해설 이메일에서 모건 씨가 브록 씨에게 색상 문제를 해결한 디자인과 함께 신청서를 다시 제출하라(Please resubmit your application with a design that addresses this issue)고 한 후, 신청 기각 결정에 대해 궁금한 점이 있으면 자신에게 전화를 하라(Should you have any questions about this decision, you may call me)고 덧붙인 부분에서 (A)와 (B)를 확인할 수 있다. 또한 웹페이지의 마지막 단락에서 DPDS의 결정에 반대하는 경우(Do you disagree with a DPDS decision?) 링크를 클릭해 시의회에 재심사를 청구하는 방법을 알아보라(Click here to find out how to file an appeal with the city council)고 했으므로, (C)도 브록 씨가 취할 수 있는 행동이다. 따라서 언급되지 않은 (D)가 정답이다.

어휘 alter 변경하다

▶▶ **Paraphrasing**   지문의 **call me**
→ 보기 (A)의 Contacting Mr. Morgan
지문의 **a design that addresses this issue**
→ 보기 (B)의 Altering the plan for the sign
지문의 **file an appeal with the city council**
→ 보기 (C)의 Asking the city council to review a decision

TEST 6

101 (C)	102 (B)	103 (B)	104 (D)	105 (A)
106 (D)	107 (D)	108 (A)	109 (D)	110 (D)
111 (A)	112 (C)	113 (B)	114 (C)	115 (C)
116 (A)	117 (A)	118 (B)	119 (D)	120 (B)
121 (B)	122 (C)	123 (A)	124 (C)	125 (B)
126 (D)	127 (C)	128 (A)	129 (D)	130 (B)
131 (A)	132 (C)	133 (D)	134 (D)	135 (D)
136 (B)	137 (A)	138 (D)	139 (C)	140 (A)
141 (B)	142 (C)	143 (B)	144 (C)	145 (C)
146 (B)	147 (A)	148 (B)	149 (D)	150 (A)
151 (C)	152 (B)	153 (B)	154 (C)	155 (B)
156 (D)	157 (D)	158 (D)	159 (D)	160 (C)
161 (A)	162 (C)	163 (C)	164 (D)	165 (D)
166 (C)	167 (D)	168 (A)	169 (D)	170 (B)
171 (D)	172 (D)	173 (A)	174 (C)	175 (D)
176 (B)	177 (A)	178 (D)	179 (B)	180 (A)
181 (D)	182 (C)	183 (B)	184 (B)	185 (B)
186 (A)	187 (B)	188 (C)	189 (D)	190 (A)
191 (C)	192 (C)	193 (A)	194 (D)	195 (D)
196 (D)	197 (A)	198 (B)	199 (A)	200 (C)

PART 5

101 인칭대명사의 격 _ 주격

해설 목적격 관계대명사(that/which)가 생략된 관계사절에서 동사 created의 주어 역할을 하는 자리이다. 의미상 선행사 artwork가 created의 목적 어가 되므로, 빈칸에는 창작의 주체를 가리키는 대명사가 들어가야 한다. 따라서 Penelope Styles를 대신하는 주격 인칭대명사 (C) she가 정답 이다.

번역 페넬로페 스타일스는 앤드루스 플라자 빌딩 로비를 위해 본인이 만들었던 예 술작품을 자랑스럽게 여긴다.

어휘 artwork 예술 작품 create 만들다, 창조하다

102 명사 자리 _ to부정사의 목적어 _ 어휘

해설 빈칸은 to schedule의 목적어 역할을 하는 명사 자리로, 전치사구 with one of our experienced attorneys의 수식을 받는다. 따라서 변호사 와 함께 하는 일정을 나타내는 명사가 들어가야 자연스러우므로, '상담' 이라는 의미의 (B) consultation이 정답이다. (A) consultant는 '상담 가'라는 의미로 문맥상 적절하지 않고, (C) consulted는 동사/과거분사, (D) consults는 동사로 품사상 빈칸에 들어갈 수 없다.

번역 오늘 클린터 어소시에이츠에 전화하셔서 당사의 노련한 변호사 중 한 분과 첫 상담 일정을 잡으세요.

어휘 initial 처음의 experienced 노련한 attorney 변호사 consult 상담하다

103 명사 어휘

해설 건물의 월별 에너지 비용(monthly energy expenses)과 관련된

정보를 나타내는 가산명사가 들어가야 하므로, '견적'이라는 의미의 (B) estimate가 정답이다.

번역 펠처 부동산의 웹사이트는 매물로 나온 각 부동산의 월별 에너지 비용 견적을 제공한다.

어휘 real estate 부동산 (사무실) expense 비용 list (팔 물건으로) 내놓다, 나와 있다 property 부동산 advice 조언 evidence 증거 advantage 이점

104 전치사 어휘 〔고난도〕

해설 빈칸 앞에 있는 up 22%가 특정 시점이나 기준점으로부터 22% 증가했다 는 뜻을 나타내므로, '~부터, ~이래'라는 의미의 (D) from이 정답이다. 참고로, (A) than은 비교급 표현과 쓰여야 하므로 빈칸에 들어갈 수 없다.

번역 새로운 텔레비전 광고 덕분에, 목공 강좌 등록이 지난 학기 이래 22퍼센트가 늘었다.

어휘 commercial 광고 enrollment 등록 carpentry 목공 semester 학기

105 동사 어휘

해설 문맥상 빈칸의 목적어인 직원 생산성(employee productivity)을 측 정 혹은 평가의 대상으로 보는 것이 자연스러우므로, '평가하다'라는 의 미의 (A) assessing이 정답이다. 참고로, productivity는 assess나 measure뿐만 아니라 증감 동사(improve, increase, reduce 등)와도 자주 쓰인다.

번역 리나 오크스는 디어모드 코스메틱 메인 창고에서의 이번 달 직원 생산성을 평 가할 것이다.

어휘 productivity 생산성 warehouse 창고 present 제시하다 discipline 훈련하다 resume 다시 시작하다

106 부사 어휘

해설 boost profits를 적절히 수식하는 부사를 선택해야 한다. 웹사이트를 재 설계하면(Redesigning our Web site) 더 많은 고객을 유치하게 되어 결국 수익을 늘리는 데 도움이 될 것이라는 내용이므로, '결과적으로'라는 의미의 (D) consequently가 정답이다.

번역 우리 웹사이트를 재설계하면 더 넓은 고객층을 확보하여 결과적으로 수익을 증대하는 데 도움이 될 것이다.

어휘 attract 유치하다, 끌어들이다 a broad range of 다양한, 넓은 범위의 boost 증대하다 profit 수익 closely 긴밀히 rarely 드물게 typically 일반적으로

107 대명사 어휘

해설 빈칸은 「정관사(the)+형용사(only)」의 수식을 받는 명사 자리로, 주어 The emergency exit row seats의 주격 보어 역할을 한다. 주격 보 어가 명사일 경우 주어와 동일한 대상을 나타내므로, seats를 대신하 며 the only의 수식을 받을 수 있는 (D) ones가 정답이다. (A) some, (B) these, (C) whose는 the only의 수식을 받을 수 없다.

번역 비상구 좌석열은 팔걸이 속에 접이식 테이블이 장착된 유일한 좌석이다.

어휘 emergency exit 비상구   equipped with ~이 장착된
armrest 팔걸이

108 상관접속사

해설 직원 사규에 복장과 신발에 대한(on acceptable apparel and footwear) 지침은 있지만 헤어스타일에 관한 지침은 없다(not on hairstyles)는 내용이 되어야 자연스럽다. 따라서 not과 함께 '하지만 ~는 아니다'라는 의미를 완성하는 (A) but이 정답이다. 참고로, 상관접속사 'B but not A'는 'not A but B'와 동일한 뜻으로 쓰인다.

번역 직원 사규에 용인되는 복장과 신발에 대한 지침은 있지만 헤어스타일에 관한 지침은 없다.

어휘 employee handbook 직원 사규   acceptable 용인되는
apparel 복장

109 동사 어휘

해설 전국에서 가장 깨끗한 천연 샘물(the cleanest natural spring water in the country)은 셸웨이 계곡이 내세울 만한 특징이므로, '자랑하다, 자랑할 만한 ~을 가지고 있다'라는 의미의 (D) boasts가 정답이다.

번역 에메랄드 산 기슭에 위치한 셸웨이 계곡은 전국에서 가장 깨끗한 천연 샘물을 자랑한다.

어휘 situated ~에 위치한   excel 뛰어나다, 능가하다   emphasize
강조하다   distinguish 구별하다

110 부사 어휘

해설 빈칸에는 비교급 형용사 lower를 강조하여 지출(expenses)이 줄어든 정도를 적절히 묘사하는 부사가 들어가야 자연스럽다. 따라서 '눈에 띄게, 현저히'라는 의미의 (D) noticeably가 정답이다. 참고로, (A) highly(매우)는 low와 어울려 쓰이지 않으며 원급 형용사를 수식하므로 빈칸에 들어갈 수 없다.

번역 그 은행에서 전자결제로 시스템을 전환하자 문구류 지출이 눈에 띄게 줄었다.

어휘 electronic billing 전자결제   stationery 문구류   heavily 무겁게
considerately 사려 깊게, 신중하게

111 동사 어형 _ 태 _ 시제   고난도

해설 주어인 the item이 폐기되는 대상이므로, 빈칸에는 수동태 동사가 들어가야 한다. 따라서 (A) is discarded와 (B) has been discarded 중 하나를 선택해야 하는데, 분실물의 일반적인 처리 관행(2개월 보관 후 폐기된다)을 설명하고 있으므로, 현재시제인 (A) is discarded가 정답이 된다.

번역 분실물은 최대 2개월 동안 헬스장 접수창구에 보관되며 이후 해당 물품은 폐기된다.

어휘 lost property 분실물   discard 폐기하다

112 동사 어형 _ 현재분사   고난도

해설 All employees ------- for any reason이 주어, must submit이 동

사인 문장으로, 빈칸부터 reason까지가 employees를 수식하는 역할을 한다. 따라서 형용사 역할을 할 수 있는 (B) resigned와 (C) resigning 중 하나를 선택해야 하는데, 직원들(employees)은 사임을 하는 주체이므로, 능동의 의미를 내포한 (C) resigning이 정답이 된다. 참고로, resign은 타동사 및 자동사로 모두 쓰일 수 있는데, 타동사로 쓰일 경우 사임하는 직책이나 자리가 목적어로 오게 된다.

번역 어떤 이유로든 사임하는 모든 직원은 기록 보존용으로 공식 서한을 인사부에 제출해야 한다.

어휘 submit 제출하다   recordkeeping 기록[문서] 보존   purpose
목적, 용도   resign 사임하다, 스스로 물러나다

113 부사 자리

해설 빈칸 없이도 완전한 문장으로, '10건의 민원이 있다'라는 내용을 수식하는 부사가 들어가야 자연스럽다. 따라서 '이미, 벌써'라는 의미의 (B) already가 정답이다. (A) all이 들어갈 경우 '모든 10건의 민원이 있다'라는 내용이 되어 어색하고, (C) other than은 '~외에, ~를 제외하고'라는 뜻으로 앞에 대조되는 대상이 나와야 하므로 빈칸에 적절하지 않다. (D) as many는 '(앞에 언급된 수)와 같은 만큼의'라는 의미로 바로 뒤에 숫자가 올 수 없으므로 빈칸에 들어갈 수 없다.

번역 호텔 지배인은 수영장 주변 개보수 작업에서 나는 소음 때문에 이미 10건의 민원이 들어왔다고 말한다.

어휘 complaint 민원   renovation 개보수

114 형용사 자리 _ 명사 수식   고난도

해설 빈칸이 부정관사 a와 「형용사(educational)+명사(proposal)」 사이에 있으므로, educational을 수식하는 부사 또는 proposal을 수식하는 형용사가 들어갈 수 있다. 문맥상 '논란적으로 교육적인 제안'보다 '논란이 많은 교육안'이라는 내용이 되어야 자연스러우므로, 형용사인 (C) controversial(논란이 많은)이 정답이 된다.

번역 교육청은 지역 역사 교육법을 바꾸자는 논란 많은 교육안을 논의할 것이다.

어휘 school board 교육청, 교육 위원회   debate 논의하다
educational 교육의, 교육적인   controversy 논란
controversially 논쟁적으로

115 명사 어휘

해설 스즈키 박사의 이름을 따서 병동을 명명한 것(The new ward was named after Dr. Suzuki)은 그의 공헌(contributions)을 인정했기 때문이라고 볼 수 있다. 따라서 in 및 of와 함께 '~를 인정하여'라는 의미를 완성하는 (C) recognition이 정답이다. 참고로, in association with, under an obligation to부정사, in recognition of, on the occasion of 등의 표현은 암기해 두는 것이 좋다.

번역 새 병동은 스즈키 박사가 병원에 기여한 귀중한 공헌을 인정해 박사의 이름을 따서 명명되었다.

어휘 ward 병동   name after ~의 이름을 따서 명명하다   association
제휴   obligation 의무   occasion 경우

116 명사 자리 _ 동명사의 목적어 _ 어휘

해설 동명사 choosing의 목적어 역할을 하는 명사 자리이므로, 빈칸에는 선택/선정의 대상이 될 수 있는 명사가 들어가야 한다. 따라서 '후임자'라는 의미의 (A) successor가 정답이다. (D) success는 '성공'이라는 뜻으로 문맥상 어색하며, (B) succeeds는 동사, (C) succeeding은 동명사/현재분사로 품사상 빈칸에 들어갈 수 없다.

번역 그래디 씨는 7월에 하던 가구 CFO에서 물러나기 전에 후임자 선정에 적극적인 역할을 할 것이다.

어휘 step down 물러나다   succeed 뒤를 잇다, 계승하다

117 형용사 어휘

해설 animated movies를 수식하는 자리로, 전치사구 for children as young as three와 어울리는 형용사가 들어가야 한다. 어린이들의 나이에 맞는 애니메이션 영화를 상영할 것이라는 내용이므로, '적합한, 적절한'이라는 의미의 (A) appropriate가 정답이다. 참고로, (A) appropriate는 전치사 for 외에도 to와 쓰일 수 있고, (B) equivalent to, (C) cautious는 about과 어울려 쓰인다.

번역 여름이면 콜팩스 공공도서관은 3살 어린이들에게 적합한 애니메이션 영화를 상영할 예정이다.

어휘 equivalent 동등한   cautious 조심하는   tentative 잠정적인

118 전치사 어휘   고난도

해설 빈칸은 Royes Travel Agency를 목적어로 취하는 전치사 자리로, 문맥상 로예스 여행사를 통해 휴가를 예약하라는 내용이 되어야 자연스럽다. 따라서 '~와 함께, ~의 서비스를 이용하여'라는 의미의 (B) with가 정답이다.

번역 즐겁고 수월한 여행을 하고 싶으시다면, 로예스 여행사를 통해 여름 휴가를 예약하십시오.

어휘 ensure 반드시 ~하게 하다, 보장하다   effortless 노력을 들이지 않는, 수월한

119 동사 어휘

해설 strict safety policies를 목적어로 취하는 동사 자리로, 이유/목적을 나타내는 to부정사구(to prevent accidents in its factories)의 수식을 받는다. 따라서 사고 예방을 위해 하는 행위를 나타내는 동사가 필요하므로 '(정책을) 시행하다, 집행하다'라는 의미의 (D) enforces가 정답이다.

번역 카로바 매뉴팩처링은 공장의 사고를 방지하기 위해 엄격한 안전 정책을 시행한다.

어휘 manufacturing 제조   strict 엄격한   prevent 막다, 방지하다   entail 수반하다   produce 생산하다   presume 추정하다, 간주하다

120 동사 어형 _ 태 _ 시제

해설 주어 a large amount of merchandise의 동사 자리이다. 상품(merchandise)은 파손되는 대상으로, 수동태가 쓰여야 한다. 또한 '~했을 무렵'이라는 뜻의 「By the time+주어+과거시제」 표현이 주절을 수식하고 있으므로, 빈칸에는 과거 이전부터 과거까지의 상황을 나타내는 동사가 들어가야 한다. 따라서 수동태 과거완료 동사인 (B) had been damaged가 정답이다.

번역 작업자들이 매장 지붕을 수리하기 위해 도착했을 때는 많은 상품이 파손되어 있었다.

어휘 repair 수리하다   a large amount of 다량의   merchandise 상품

121 부사절 접속사 _ 어휘

해설 빈칸 뒤 완전한 절(the new prehistoric fossil exhibits are being set up)을 이끄는 접속사 자리로, 보기에서 (B) as와 (C) so that 중 하나를 선택해야 한다. 전시물 설치는 방문객의 출입을 금지하고 있는(is temporarily off-limits to visitors) 이유이므로, '~때문에'라는 뜻으로 쓰일 수 있는 (B) as가 정답이다. (C) so that(~하도록)은 목적을 나타내므로 현재 진행시제(are being set up)와는 어울리지 않는다. (A) touring은 동명사/현재분사로 절을 이끌 수 없고, (D) who는 명사절/관계사절 접속사로 뒤에 불완전한 절이 나와야 한다.

번역 새로운 선사 시대 화석 전시물들이 설치되고 있기 때문에 박물관 남쪽 건물은 일시적으로 방문객 출입이 금지된다.

어휘 temporarily 일시적으로   off-limits 출입금지의   prehistoric 선사 시대의   fossil 화석   exhibit 전시(물)

122 동사 어형 _ to부정사

해설 The first customer부터 stickers까지가 주어, will receive가 동사인 문장이다. 빈칸은 the café's reward book을 목적어로 취하면서 주어 The first customer를 수식하는 역할을 하므로, 능동태 준동사가 들어갈 수 있다. 따라서 (C) to fill이 정답이다.

번역 카페의 쿠폰북에 스티커 100개를 채우는 첫 번째 고객은 1년치 무료 커피를 받는다.

어휘 reward book (고객 보상 제도용) 쿠폰북   supply 공급(품)

123 부사 자리 _ 동명사 수식

해설 동명사구(training new hires in customer service etiquette)를 수식하는 부사 자리이므로, '몸소, 직접'이라는 의미의 (A) personally가 정답이다. (B) more personal과 (C) personal은 형용사, (D) personalizes는 동사로 품사상 빈칸에 들어갈 수 없다.

번역 슐라이먼 씨는 신입사원이 입사하면 몸소 고객 서비스 예절을 가르치는 쪽을 선호한다.

어휘 new hire 신입사원   personalize 개인의 필요에 맞추다

124 전치사 자리 _ 어휘   고난도

해설 빈칸은 50 meters of a body of water를 목적어로 취해 littering을 수식하는 전치사 자리이다. 수역 50미터는 특정 범위를 나타내므로, '~이내에, ~ 안에'라는 의미의 전치사 (C) within이 정답이다. (B) during은 '(특정 기간) 동안'이란 뜻의 전치사로 문맥상 어색하고, (A) nearby(인근의; 근처에는)는 형용사/부사, (D) anywhere(어디든지)는 부사로 빈칸에 들어갈 수 없다.

번역 수역 50미터 이내에서 쓰레기를 버리다 적발되는 사람은 250달러의 벌금이 부과된다.

어휘 individual 개인, 사람 litter (쓰레기를) 버리다; 쓰레기 body of water (호수, 강 등) 수역 be subject to ~의 대상이다 fine 벌금

125 형용사 자리 _ 목적격 보어 `고난도`

해설 빈칸은 「make + 목적어(the CEO's annual sales target) + 목적격 보어」 구조에서 목적격 보어에 해당하는 자리이다. 사업 확장(expansion)이 연간 매출 목표를 달성 가능한 상태로 만들 수 있을지 회의적이라는 내용이므로, 빈칸에는 형용사가 들어가야 자연스럽다. 따라서 '달성할 수 있는'이라는 의미의 (B) attainable이 정답이다. (A) attain은 '달성하다'라는 뜻의 타동사로 구조상 빈칸에 들어갈 수 없다. 또한 make는 특별한 경우(eg. make oneself understood)를 제외하고는 과거 분사를 목적격 보어로 취하지 않으므로, (C) attained도 정답이 될 수 없다. 명사인 (D) attainment(성취, 달성)의 경우, 목적어와 동일한 대상을 가리키지 않으므로 빈칸에는 적절하지 않다.

번역 멘젤 씨는 사업 확장을 통해 CEO의 연간 매출 목표를 연말까지 정말로 달성할 수 있을지 회의적이다.

어휘 expansion (사업) 확장 annual 연간의

126 부사 어휘

해설 동사 avoid를 적절히 수식하는 부사를 선택하는 문제이다. 연락처 제공을 회피하는 것(avoid providing a contact phone number)은 문의량을 줄이기 위해 의도적으로 하는 행동이라고 볼 수 있으므로, '의도적으로, 고의로'라는 의미의 (D) intentionally가 정답이다.

번역 일부 관공서는 일반인의 문의량을 줄이기 위해 의도적으로 연락처 제공을 회피한다.

어휘 avoid -ing ~하기를 회피하다 in an effort to ~하기 위해 cut down 줄이다 inquiry 문의 adequately 적절히 formerly 이전에 proficiently 능숙하게

127 명사 어휘 `고난도`

해설 in response to의 목적어 역할을 하는 명사 자리로, 전치사구 in demand for vegan-friendly products의 수식을 받는다. 패스트푸드점의 메뉴 변경은 채식주의자 친화적인 제품의 수요 증가에 따른 대응책으로 볼 수 있다. 따라서 '급증, 급등'이라는 의미의 (C) surge가 정답이다.

번역 채식주의자 친화적인 제품에 대한 수요가 급증하자 많은 패스트푸드점들이 이에 대응해 메뉴를 대폭 변경했다.

어휘 significantly 대폭 in response to ~에 대응하여 demand 수요 vegan (완전) 채식주의자 pace 속도 flow 흐름 phase 단계

128 전치사 어휘

해설 목표를 명확히 정하는 행위(clearly determine our objectives)는 협상 개시(the commencement of negotiations) 전에 이뤄져야 하므로, '~ 전에'라는 의미의 (A) before가 정답이다.

번역 만약 협상 개시 전에 우리의 목표를 명확히 정하지 않으면, 효과적으로 협상할 수 없을 것이다.

어휘 determine 정하다 objective 목표 commencement 개시 negotiation 협상 bargain 협상하다 effectively 효과적으로 on behalf of ~을 대신하여 according to ~에 따라 against ~에 반하여

129 명사 자리 _ to부정사의 목적어 _ 복합명사 `고난도`

해설 pollution과 함께 복합명사를 이루어 to carry out의 목적어 역할을 하는 명사 자리로, 수행해야 하는 일을 나타내는 명사가 들어가야 한다. 따라서 pollution과 함께 '오염 감시'라는 의미를 완성하는 (D) monitoring이 정답이다.

번역 오웬버그 공기 청정 협회는 도시 곳곳에 설치된 센서를 이용해 실시간으로 오염 감시 작업을 실시한다.

어휘 sensor 감지기 place 배치하다, 설치하다 carry out 수행하다, 실시하다 monitor 감시하다; 모니터

130 동사 어휘

해설 빈칸에는 축제 기간에 시의회가 주차요금(the charges for parking)에 대해 취할 수 있는 조치를 나타내는 동사가 들어가야 자연스럽다. 따라서 '면제하다, (권리를) 포기하다'라는 의미의 (B) waive가 정답이다.

번역 시의회는 음악축제가 열리는 주말에 메인 가 주차요금을 면제할 예정이다.

어휘 charge 요금 contend 주장하다 delegate 위임하다 redeem (빚을) 상환하다, 상품[현금]으로 바꾸다

PART 6

131-134 공지

페어팩스 공공도서관 회원님들께 알립니다:

도서관의 예약 시스템 이용 시, 해당 품목은 24시간 동안만 대출대에 보관된다는 점을 유념하십시오. **131**만약 그 기간 내에 보관 품목을 찾아가지 않으면, 다시 대출 가능 대상으로 전환됩니다.

132도서관 품목을 예약해 두는 방법은 여러 가지입니다. 첫째, 대출대에서 직원에게 이야기하면 됩니다. 원하는 품목이 이용 가능하게 되면, 따로 보관됩니다. 또한 도서관 곳곳에 **133**설치된 데이터베이스 터미널 또는 웹사이트를 이용해 품목 예약 요청을 할 수 있습니다.

품목을 **134**예약할 때는 상기 시간 제한을 염두에 두십시오. 이는 회원들이 다양한 책, 잡지, 멀티미디어 자료를 즐길 수 있게 하려는 저희의 목표를 뒷받침하는 정책 중 하나입니다.

어휘 hold system (도서관 등에서 시행하는) 예약 시스템 bear in mind 유념하다 circulation desk 대출대 circulation 순환, 유통 set aside 따로 보관하다 policy 정책 support 지탱하다 ensure 반드시 ~하게 하다, 보장하다 a wide selection of 다양한

131 가정법 _ 도치

해설 해당 절의 동사 fail을 현재시제로 볼 경우 빈칸에는 완전한 절을 이끄는 접속사가 들어갈 수 있고, 동사원형으로 볼 경우에는 If가 생략된 후 도치된 가정법 구문의 조동사 Should가 들어갈 수 있다. 내용을 살펴보면, 빈칸이 포함된 절(you fail to collect an on-hold item within that timeframe)은 조건을 가정하고, 주절(it will be put back into circulation)은 그 결과를 설명하고 있다. 따라서 조건을 나타내는 가정법 구문에 쓰이는 (A) Should가 정답이다. 참고로, 원래 구조는 「If + 주어(you) + should + 동사원형(fail)」이다. 다른 접속사는 의미상 어색하며, (C) Yet(그렇지만)의 경우 구조상으로도 빈칸에 들어갈 수 없다.

132 문맥에 맞는 문장 고르기

번역 (A) 회원가입 신청이 이보다 쉬울 수는 없습니다.
(B) 소장 품목을 직접 둘러보거나 온라인으로 검색할 수 있습니다.
(C) 도서관 품목을 예약해 두는 방법은 여러 가지입니다.
(D) 민원을 제기하시려면 다음 단계를 따르세요.

해설 빈칸 앞에서는 도서관 예약 시스템 이용 시 주의해야 할 사항을 명시했고, 뒤에서는 품목을 예약하는 방법을 첫 번째(First)부터 나열하고 있다. 따라서 예약 방법이 여러 가지 있다고 소개한 (C)가 빈칸에 들어가야 가장 자연스럽다.

어휘 file a complaint 민원을 제기하다

133 동사 어형 _ 과거분사 고난도

해설 빈칸은 전치사구 throughout the library와 함께 the database terminals를 수식하는 역할을 한다. 따라서 형용사 역할을 할 수 있는 to부정사 또는 분사가 들어갈 수 있다. 데이터베이스 터미널(database terminals)은 도서관에 설치된 것이므로, 수동의 의미를 내포한 과거분사 (D) installed가 정답이다.

어휘 install 설치하다

134 동사 어휘 고난도

해설 첫 번째 단락에서 예약한 품목은 24시간 동안만 대출대에 보관된다는 점을 유념하라(please bear in mind that items are only held at the circulation desk for 24 hours)고 권고했는데, 빈칸을 포함한 문장에서 한 번 더 상기 시간 제한(the above time limit)을 강조하고 있다. 따라서 해당 부분은 '예약 시, 예약할 때'라는 내용이 되어야 자연스러우므로, (B) reserving이 정답이다.

어휘 purchase 구입하다 reserve 예약하다 return 반납하다

135-138 이메일

발신: 미나 왕
수신: 전 직원
제목: 고객 서비스 워크숍
날짜: 1월 21일

직원 여러분께,

2월 5일에 열릴 제1차 긍정적 고객 소통(PCI) 워크숍에 대해 다시 한 번 알려드리고자 메일을 드립니다. 워크숍은 유명한 동기부여 강사이자 〈고객 만족을 위

한 핵심 요소들〉의 저자인 팀 엘리슨 씨에 의해 135진행될 예정입니다.

우리는 엘리슨 씨에게 고객 유치, 만족 및 유지에 가장 136중요한 태도와 관행에 대해 논의해 달라고 요청했습니다. 시리즈의 첫 번째 세션인 만큼, 하워드 보팅 회장님의 소개 말씀이 137먼저 있겠습니다. 회장님께서는 워크숍의 전반적인 목표에 대해 말씀하실 예정입니다. 공간상 각 워크숍은 100명 이내로만 참석 가능하며, 접수는 선착순입니다. 138참석할 의향이 있다면 인사과를 방문하세요.

미나 왕

인사부장

어휘 remind 상기시키다 positive 긍정적인 renowned 유명한 motivational 동기를 부여하는 author 저자 customer satisfaction 고객 만족 practice 관행 attract 유치하다, 끌어들이다 retain 유지하다 introductory 소개의, 서론의 aim 목표 registration 접수 first-come, first-served basis 선착순

135 동사 어형 _ 태 _ 시제

해설 주어 It(=our first Positive Customer Interaction workshop)은 엘리슨 씨에 의해 진행되는 행사를 가리키므로, 수동태 동사가 쓰여야 한다. 또한 이 행사는 이메일 작성일인 1월 21일을 기준으로 미래(February 5)에 열릴 예정이므로, 수동태 미래시제 동사인 (D) will be led가 정답이다.

136 형용사 자리 _ 주격 보어 고난도

해설 that이 이끄는 주격 관계대명사절에서 선행사 the attitudes and practices를 보충 설명하는 주격 보어 자리로, most와 함께 최상급을 이룬다. 따라서 '~에 중요한'이라는 의미로 전치사 to와 함께 쓰이는 형용사 (B) critical이 정답이다. 참고로, critical은 '비판적인, 비평하는'이라는 뜻으로도 쓰인다. 명사인 (A) critics(비평가)와 (D) criticisms(비판)도 보어 역할을 할 수 있지만, 선행사와 같은 대상을 가리키지 않으며 문맥상 most의 수식을 받기에도 어색하므로 빈칸에 들어갈 수 없다.

어휘 critically 비판적으로, 결정적으로

137 동사 어휘 _ 과거분사

해설 회장의 소개말(an introductory talk by our president)은 워크숍 세션과 연관된 일정이므로, 빈칸에는 진행 순서를 나타내는 동사가 들어가야 자연스럽다. 따라서 '앞서다, 선행하다'라는 뜻을 가진 precede의 과거분사형 (A) preceded가 정답이다. 여기서 precede는 수동태로 쓰였으므로, by 뒤에 오는 것이 시간 순서상 먼저 일어나는 일이다.

어휘 officiate 공무를 수행하다 combine 결합하다 record 기록하다

138 문맥에 맞는 문장 고르기 고난도

번역 (A) 이 회비는 귀하의 경험을 개선하는 데 사용될 예정이니 믿으셔도 됩니다.
(B) 취소된 세미나를 보충하는 세션이 추후 개최될 예정입니다.
(C) 전액 환불 요청은 전화나 이메일로 할 수 있습니다.
(D) 참석할 의향이 있다면 인사과를 방문하세요.

해설 앞 문장에서 접수는 선착순(registrations will be accepted on a first-come, first-served basis)이라고 했으므로, 빈칸에도 접수와 관련된 내용이 들어가야 문맥상 자연스럽다. 따라서 접수처(personnel office)를 언급한 (D)가 정답이다.

어휘 rest assured 믿어도 된다 enhance (가치를) 높이다 makeup 보충(물)

139-142 편지

> 5월 22일
> 가브리엘라 헤론
> 데이턴 가 4827번지
> 베이커스필드, 캘리포니아 93311
>
> 헤론 씨께,
>
> 헤라클레스 피트니스 센터에서 확장을 위한 보수 작업이 예정되어 있다는 점을 알려드립니다. **139**이에 따라 6월 3일부터 9일까지는 휴업합니다. 최근 랜털로 어패럴이 떠나면서 비우게 된 인근 상업 공간을 인수하여, 이를 사양이 다양한 피트니스 스튜디오로 구성된 추가 공간으로 전환할 예정입니다. **140**이렇게 하면 더 다양한 운동 강좌를 제공할 수 있게 됩니다. 현재 이용 가능한 센터 내 구역은 6월 10일 오전 7시 평소와 같이 영업이 재개되고, 새로 생긴 공간은 다음 달부터 **141**사용될 예정입니다.
>
> 이번 임시 **142**휴업에 대해 사과 드리며 양해해 주시면 감사하겠습니다. 또한, 6월 15일부터 프런트 데스크와 온라인 www.herc-fitness.com/schedule에서 확인할 수 있는 7월 일정표에서 새로 제공되는 강좌를 살펴보시기 바랍니다.
>
> 게리 샐린저
> 헤라클레스 피트니스 센터

어휘 Please be advised that ~를 알아두세요 undergo 겪다 renovation 개선, 보수 expand 확장하다 acquire 인수하다 adjacent 인접한 vacate 비우다, 떠나다 convert 전환하다 contain 포함하다 specification 사양 temporary 임시의 appreciate 감사해 하다 offering 제공하는 것, 강좌

139 접속부사

해설 빈칸 앞 문장에서 헤라클레스 피트니스 센터의 보수 작업이 예정되어 있다(Hercules Fitness Center is scheduled to undergo renovations)고 했고, 뒤에서는 휴업을 한다(we will be shut down)고 했다. 따라서 빈칸에는 앞 내용에 따른 결과를 소개할 때 쓰이는 접속부사가 들어가야 자연스러우므로, '이에 따라, 그래서'라는 의미의 (C) Accordingly가 정답이다.

어휘 occasionally 가끔

140 문맥에 맞는 문장 고르기

번역 (A) 이렇게 하면 더 다양한 운동 강좌를 제공할 수 있게 됩니다.
(B) 점점 더 많은 사람들이 더 건강한 생활습관으로 바꾸고 있습니다.
(C) 기존 주차장에는 더 이상 공간이 충분하지 않습니다.
(D) 저희 시설은 지역 출판물에서 높은 평가를 받았습니다.

해설 빈칸 앞 문장에서 최근에 인근 상업 공간을 인수했으며, 이를 사양이 다양한 피트니스 스튜디오로 구성된 추가 공간으로 전환할 예정(We have acquired the adjacent commercial ~ and will be converting it into an additional space mainly containing fitness studios of various specifications)이라고 했다. 따라서 빈칸에도 확장과 관련된 내용이 들어가야 문맥상 자연스러우므로, 예상되는 효과를 언급한 (A)가 정

답이다. 참고로, (A)의 This는 앞 문장 전체를 대신한다.

어휘 sufficient 충분한 existing 기존의 publication 출판(물)

141 명사 자리 _ 전치사의 목적어 _ 어휘 [고난도]

해설 전치사 into의 목적어 역할을 하는 명사 자리로, 보기에서 (B) use와 (D) users 중 하나를 선택해야 한다. bring A into B가 'A를 특정 상황(B)에 처하게 하다'라는 뜻이므로, 해당 부분은 새로운 공간(the new space)이 사용 가능하게 된다는 내용이 되어야 자연스럽다. 따라서 '사용'이라는 뜻의 (B) use가 정답이다.

142 명사 어휘

해설 this temporary의 수식을 받는 명사 자리로, 빈칸에는 사과하는 (apologize for) 이유를 나타내는 명사가 들어가야 한다. 첫 번째 단락에서 6월 3일부터 9일까지 피트니스 센터가 휴업한다(we will be shut down from June 3 to June 9)고 했으므로, 이에 대해 사과하고 있음을 알 수 있다. 따라서 '폐쇄, 휴업'이라는 의미의 (D) closure가 정답이다.

어휘 relocation 이전 negligence 태만 congestion 혼잡, 밀집

143-146 기사

> **미들런즈 바이오사이언스, 신임 R&D 이사 임명**
>
> 미들런즈 바이오사이언스는 R&D 부서의 클리포드 맥스웰을 회사의 신임 연구 개발 이사로 **143**선정했다. 이 바이오 연료 제조업체는 어제 웹사이트에 올린 게시물을 통해 맥스웰 씨의 **144**임명을 발표했다. 미들런즈의 CEO 엘렌 스턴은 이렇게 말했다고 한다. "맥스웰 씨를 이사진으로 맞이하게 되어 기쁩니다. 그의 전문지식으로 우리는 연구 목표를 **145**달성하는 데 성공할 수 있을 겁니다."
>
> 웹 게시물에 따르면 맥스웰 씨는 생명공학 박사학위를 취득한 직후 미들런즈에 입사했다. **146**그는 하급 연구원으로 시작했지만 그 자리에 오래 머물지는 않았다. 그는 근면함과 혁신적인 아이디어 덕분에 회사에서 꾸준히 승진했다. 12월 10일 맡게 될 새로운 역할에서 맥스웰 씨는 미들런즈의 연구 개발 목표를 결정하고 실행하게 된다.

어휘 bioscience 생명과학 biofuel 바이오 연료 quote 전하다, 인용하다 expertise 전문지식 earn 취득하다 doctoral degree 박사학위 steadily 꾸준히 diligence 근면함 assume (책임이나 역할을) 맡다 implement 실행하다 objective 목표

143 동사 어형 _ 태 _ 시제

해설 주어 Midlands Biosciences의 동사 자리로, Clifford Maxwell을 목적어로 취하는 능동태 동사가 필요하다. 주어가 회사명일 경우 단수 동사와 복수 동사를 모두 사용할 수 있는데, 뒤에 오는 내용을 살펴보면 이사 임명은 이미 완료된 상태이므로, (B) has chosen이 정답이 된다.

144 명사 어휘

해설 앞 문장에서 미들런즈 바이오사이언스가 맥스웰 씨를 회사의 신임 연구 개발 이사(to be the company's new research and development director)로 선정했다고 했으므로, 빈칸에는 맥스웰 씨의 직급 변경

과 관련된 명사가 들어가야 자연스럽다. 따라서 '임명'이라는 의미의
(D) appointment가 정답이다.

어휘 retirement 은퇴 candidacy 출마, 입후보 initiative 계획

145 동사 어형 _ 전치사 + 동명사 [고난도]

해설 빈칸에는 명사구 our research goals를 목적어로 취하면서 자동사
succeed를 수식할 수 있는 형태가 들어가야 한다. 따라서 succeed
와 어울려 쓰이는 전치사 in과 동명사 reaching으로 이루어진 (C) in
reaching이 정답이다. 「주격 관계대명사+동사」인 (A) that reaches와
「과거분사+전치사」인 (B) reached by는 앞에 수식하는 대상이 없으므
로 빈칸에 들어갈 수 없다. 또한 succeed는 타동사로 쓰일 경우 '~의 뒤
를 잇다, 대체하다'라는 뜻을 나타내기 때문에 (D) the reaching of는 문
맥상 적절하지 않다.

146 문맥에 맞는 문장 고르기 [고난도]

번역 (A) 이번 조치는 능률을 높이겠다는 회사의 목표를 반영하고 있다.
(B) 그는 하급 연구원으로 시작했지만 그 자리에 오래 머물지는 않았다.
(C) 이사회는 그의 후임자를 찾기 위해 광범위하게 조사하고 있다.
(D) 그의 최근 연구 프로젝트는 업계 내에서 많은 관심을 받았다.

해설 빈칸 앞 문장에서 맥스웰 씨의 입사(Mr. Maxwell joined Midlands)를,
뒤에서는 회사에서의 승진(He rose steadily through the company's
ranks)을 언급했으므로, 맥스웰 씨의 회사 내 직급과 관련된 내용이 빈칸
에 들어가야 자연스럽다. 따라서 (B)가 정답이다.

어휘 reflect 반영하다 streamlined 능률적인, 간소화된 extensive
광범위한 replacement 후임자

PART 7

147-148 초대장

이곳 솔즈베리 요리학교에 초대하오니 오셔서 회원전용 요리 시연을 즐기세요!

초빙 객원 셰프:
구스타프 페롯
뉴욕 시에 있는 5성급 레스토랑 패트리지 비스트로의 주인

페롯 셰프가 6월 14일 오전 9시 15분부터 11시 45분까지 강습용
3번 주방에서 다양한 지중해 요리를 능숙하게 준비하는 방법을 시연합니다.
147이번 시연은 현재 요리학교의 고급 요리 강좌에 등록된 사람들을 위해 특별히
마련된 것입니다. 148공간은 250명으로 제한되어 있으며, 6월 8일 이전에 행정
실 이브라힘 씨와 얘기해서 참석 의사를 확정해 주셔야 합니다.

어휘 exclusive 전용의 demonstration 시연 culinary
요리(법)의 expertly 능숙하게, 전문적으로 Mediterranean 지중해의
specifically 특별히, 구체적으로 enroll 등록하다 advanced
고급의, 상급의 confirm 확인하다, 확정하다 intention 의사, 의도
administration 행정

147 추론 / 암시

번역 누구에게 보내는 초대장이겠는가?
(A) 요리 강사
(B) 음식 평론가
(C) 요리사 지망생
(D) 식당 손님

해설 마지막 단락에서 이번 시연은 현재 요리학교의 고급 요리 강좌에 등록된 사
람들을 위해 특별히 마련된 것(This demonstration has been specifically arranged for those currently enrolled in the institute's
advanced cooking courses)이라고 했으므로, 요리사 지망생에게 보내
는 초대장이라고 추론할 수 있다. 따라서 (C)가 정답이다.

어휘 aspiring 장차 ~가 되고 싶은

▶▶ **Paraphrasing** 지문의 those currently enrolled in the
institute's advanced cooking courses
→ 정답의 Aspiring cooks

148 사실 관계 확인

번역 행사에 관해 알 수 있는 것은?
(A) 매년 개최된다.
(B) 참석자들이 활동에 참여할 것이다.
(C) 오후에 끝난다.
(D) 입장이 제한된다.

해설 마지막 단락에서 공간이 250명으로 제한되어 있다(Space is limited to
250 people)고 했으므로, (D)가 정답이다.

어휘 restricted 제한된

▶▶ **Paraphrasing** 지문의 limited → 정답의 restricted

149-150 쿠폰

리알토 펫마트

리알토 펫마트는 10주년 기념행사의 일환으로 단골 고객님들께 보답하고자
합니다. 1503월 1일부터 3월 14일까지, 이 쿠폰을 계산원에게 건네면 50달러
이상 구매 시 15달러를 할인 받을 수 있습니다. 149이 쿠폰은 현금으로 교환할
수 없고 자동 계산대에서는 사용할 수 없으며, 3월 14일 오후 9시에 만료됩니다.
전체 약관을 보시려면 www.rialtopetmart.ca/voucher을 방문하세요.

어휘 reward 보답하다 anniversary celebration 기념행사
checkout operator 계산원 purchase 구매(품) expire (기한이)
만료되다 terms and conditions 약관

149 사실 관계 확인

번역 리알토 펫마트에 관해 언급된 것은?
(A) 최근 신규 지점을 개점했다.
(B) 현재 계산원을 모집하고 있다.
(C) 회원제 보상 프로그램을 운영한다.
(D) 셀프 계산대가 있다.

해설 중반부에서 쿠폰은 자동 계산대에서는 사용할 수 없다(This voucher ~ cannot be used at our automated checkout kiosks)고 했으므로, 리알토 펫마트에 셀프 계산대가 있다는 것을 알 수 있다. 따라서 (D)가 정답이다.

▶▶ **Paraphrasing** 지문의 **automated checkout kiosks**
→ 정답의 **self-checkout machines**

150 세부 사항

번역 쿠폰을 사용하기 위해 쇼핑객들이 해야 하는 것은?
(A) 최소한의 금액 쓰기
(B) 매장 2회 방문
(C) 매장 관리자에게 쿠폰 제시
(D) 웹페이지에서 쿠폰 활성화

해설 초반부에서 쿠폰을 계산원에게 건네면 50달러 이상 구매 시 15달러를 할인 받을 수 있다(you may ~ receive $15 off any purchase valued at $50 or more)고 했으므로, (A)가 정답이다.

▶▶ **Paraphrasing** 지문의 **any purchase valued at $50 or more** → 정답의 **Spend a minimum amount**

151-152 문자 메시지

수지 레비	(오후 2시 4분)
히데오, 아직 3층이에요?	
히데오 후지타	(오후 2시 5분)
예, 회의가 방금 끝났어요. 뭐 필요한 거 있어요?	
수지 레비	(오후 2시 6분)
151컴퓨터에 새 그래픽 디자인 프로그램 세트를 설치하려고 하는데 문제가 생겼어요. 이걸 제게 추천해준 사람을 찾아줬으면 해서요.	
히데오 후지타	(오후 2시 7분)
우리 회사 사람이에요?	
수지 레비	(오후 2시 8분)
예, 152웹 디자인팀에 있는 키 큰 남자예요.	
히데오 후지타	(오후 2시 10분)
우리 웹 디자인팀은 규모가 꽤 커요.	
수지 레비	(오후 2시 11분)
152아, 미안해요. 짧은 금발 머리를 한 사람이에요. 아마 신입일 거예요.	
히데오 후지타	(오후 2시 13분)
누구를 말하는지 알 것 같아요. 이름이 크리스 맞죠?	
수지 레비	(오후 2시 14분)
그래요, 맞는 것 같아요! 시간 날 때 아무 때나 제 사무실에 들르라고 전해주세요. 고마워요, 히데오.	

어휘 suite (제품) 세트 recommend 추천하다 blond(e) 금발의

151 세부 사항

번역 레비 씨의 문제는?
(A) 회의에 늦었다.
(B) 전자기기가 켜지지 않는다.
(C) 소프트웨어를 설치할 수 없다.
(D) 일부 그래픽이 혼란스럽다.

해설 레비 씨가 오후 2시 6분 메시지에서 컴퓨터에 새 그래픽 디자인 프로그램 세트를 설치하려고 하는데 문제가 생겼다(I'm trying to set up that new graphic design suite on my computer, but I'm having problems)고 했으므로, (C)가 정답이다.

▶▶ **Paraphrasing** 지문의 **set up that new graphic design suite**
→ 정답의 **install some software**

152 의도 파악

번역 오후 2시 10분, 후지타 씨가 "우리 웹 디자인팀은 규모가 꽤 커요"라고 쓴 의도는?
(A) 신입사원을 채용할 필요가 없다.
(B) 좀 더 자세한 설명이 필요하다.
(C) 공간의 규모가 걱정된다.
(D) 팀원 중 누군가가 특정 기술을 가지고 있을 것이다.

해설 레비 씨가 오후 2시 8분 메시지에서 웹 디자인팀에 있는 키 큰 남자(the tall guy on the Web design team)를 찾아달라고 하자 후지타 씨가 '우리 웹 디자인팀은 규모가 꽤 커요(Our Web design team is rather large)'라고 응답한 것이다. 이에 레비 씨는 사과를 한 후 남자에 대한 구체적인 설명(He's the one who has short blonde hair ~ might be new)을 덧붙였다. 따라서 후지타 씨가 좀 더 자세한 설명이 필요하다는 의도로 쓴 메시지라고 추론할 수 있으므로, (B)가 정답이다.

어휘 description 설명

153-154 광고

글로우 세차
킹스맨 가 3476번지, 랜싱 48213
새로운 디럭스 세차 및 프리미엄 세부 세차 서비스를 이용해 보세요!

디럭스 세차
차량당 25달러, 약 15분 소요
– 애벌 세척, 차대 세척, 외부 세척
– 기계 공기 건조 + 부드러운 수건으로 수동 건조

프리미엄 세부 세차
차량당 35달러, 약 45분 소요
– 전체 실내 청소 (X-프레스 에어 기술로 모든 틈과 균열에서 먼지와 오물 제거)
– 좌석 덮개 전체를 유연제로 세척, 카펫이 깔린 부분을 세제로 세척
– 154도장 보호 및 광채를 극대화하기 위해 손으로 "X폴리머" 왁스 도포

153요청 시 디럭스 세차 및 프리미엄 세부 통합 세차 서비스가 단돈 50달러에 가능!

153 사실 관계 확인

번역 글로우 세차에 대해 알 수 있는 것은?
(A) 디럭스 세차는 30분 이상 걸린다.
(B) 통합 서비스는 할인해 준다.
(C) 특정 종류의 자동차를 전문으로 한다.
(D) 청소용품을 판매한다.

해설 광고 하단에서 25달러인 디럭스 세차 서비스와 35달러인 프리미엄 세부 세차 서비스를 함께 이용할 시 단돈 50달러에 가능하다(Deluxe Wash + Premium Detailing Package Deal available on request for only $50)고 했으므로, (B)가 정답이다.

▶▶ Paraphrasing 지문의 Deluxe Wash + Premium Detailing Package Deal
→ 정답의 combined services

154 세부 사항

번역 X-폴리머 제품의 용도는?
(A) 차량 내부를 유연제 세척
(B) 차량 창문에서 물기 제거
(C) 차량 도장 작업 보호
(D) 차량 외부 먼지 제거

해설 프리미엄 세부 세차 서비스를 설명한 부분에서 X폴리머 제품을 도장 보호 및 광택을 위해 사용하는 왁스(wax for supreme paint protection and shine)라고 했으므로, (C)가 정답이다.

▶▶ Paraphrasing 지문의 wax for supreme paint protection
→ 정답의 Protecting a vehicle's paint job

155-157 공지

마르티노 헬스푸드 고객님께,

사업주인 디노 마르티노를 비롯한 마르티노 헬스푸드 팀은 지난 5년 동안 해리슨 가에 있는 매장에서 즐거운 마음으로 여러분들께 서비스를 제공해 왔지만, 이제 변화가 필요한 시점입니다. 156유기농 식료품까지 포함하도록 재고품 범위를 넓힌 이후로, 수요를 따라잡기 위해 고군분투해 오고 있습니다. 계산대 줄이 계속 길어진다는 점을 알아차리셨을 겁니다. 현재 저희는 하루에 받는 시내 주문 건수를 간신히 감당하고 있습니다.

155따라서 재고량을 늘리고 고객님들께 더욱 효율적인 서비스를 제공할 수 있도록 7월 1일 도심에 있는 더 큰 건물로 이전하고자 합니다. 새롭게 개선된 마르티노 헬스푸드는 스러시 가 411번지에 위치할 예정입니다.

모든 고객 회원권과 보상은 유효하며 변경되지 않으므로 안심하십시오. 이전에 관한 자세한 내용은 월간 소식지를 통해 제공됩니다. 157아직 소식지를 받고 계시지 않는다면 고객 서비스 데스크를 방문해 구독하세요.

155 주제 / 목적

번역 공지의 주된 목적은?
(A) 새로운 유형의 상품 홍보
(B) 매장 이전 알림
(C) 새 사업주 소개
(D) 향후 보수에 관한 세부정보 제공

해설 첫 번째 단락에서 현재 겪고 있는 문제점을 언급한 후, 두 번째 단락에서 문제점을 개선하기 위해 7월 1일에 더 큰 건물로 이전하고자 한다(we will move to a larger building in the downtown core on July 1)고 했으므로, 매장 이전을 알리기 위한 공지임을 알 수 있다. 따라서 (B)가 정답이다.

▶▶ Paraphrasing 지문의 move to a larger building
→ 정답의 the store's relocation

156 추론 / 암시 [고난도]

번역 마르티노 헬스푸드에 관해 가장 사실에 가까운 것은?
(A) 직원들의 의견을 구한다.
(B) 가족 경영 사업체이다.
(C) 재정난을 겪고 있다.
(D) 점점 인기를 얻고 있다.

해설 첫 번째 단락에서 늘어나는 수요를 따라잡기 위해 고군분투하고 있다(we have been struggling to keep up with demand)고 한 후, 계산대 줄이 계속 길어진다(checkout lines continue to get longer)고 했으므로, 마르티노 헬스푸드가 점점 인기를 얻고 있다고 추론할 수 있다. 따라서 (D)가 정답이다.

어휘 solicit 구하다 financial 재정의

157 세부 사항

번역 공지를 읽는 일부 사람들에게 권장하는 일은?
(A) 정기 우편물 신청
(B) 친구에게 회원 가입 추천
(C) 개장 행사 참석
(D) 보상 포인트 빨리 사용

해설 세 번째 단락에서 아직 소식지를 받고 있지 않는다면 고객 서비스 데스크를 방문해 구독할 것(If you do not already receive the newsletter, please visit the customer service desk to subscribe)을 권하고 있으므로, (A)가 정답이다.

▶▶ Paraphrasing 지문의 subscribe → 정답의 sign up
지문의 the newsletter → 정답의 a regular mailing

158-160 보도자료

어휘 **workmanship** 기술 **understandably** 당연히, 이해할 만하게 **inferior** 낮은, 열등한 **circulate** 돌다 **noticeable** 눈에 띄는 **adhere to** ~을 지키다 **unequivocally** 분명히, 모호하지 않게 **assemble** 조립하다 **durable** 내구성이 뛰어난 **committed to** ~에 전념하는

158 주제 / 목적

번역 보도자료의 목적은?
(A) 장난감 신제품 출시
(B) 제품 회수 공표
(C) 환불 받는 방법 설명
(D) 고객 우려 해소

해설 첫 번째 단락에서 플레이스마트는 자사의 장난감이 저품질로 제작되었다는 소문으로 인해 많은 고객들이 관련 내용을 문의하고 일부 경우 환불을 요구하기도 했다(many customers contacting us to ask whether the toys are truly of inferior quality, and in some cases, demanding a refund)고 한 후, 보도자료 전반에서 고객들의 우려를 해소하기 위한 설명을 이어 가고 있다. 따라서 (D)가 정답이다.

어휘 **obtain** 받다

159 사실 관계 확인 고난도

번역 갤럭시 해적 장난감에 관해 언급되지 않은 것은?
(A) 다른 나라에서 제조된다.
(B) 단종되었다.
(C) 온라인에서 광고되었다.
(D) 오락 매체에 기반을 두고 있다.

해설 두 번째 단락의 '장난감이 해외 공장에서 생산된 것은 사실이다(it is true that the toys are produced at a plant overseas)'에서 (A)를, 첫 번째 단락의 '몇몇 웹사이트들은 심지어 그 세트에 해당하는 당사 광고까지 삭제했다(several Web sites have even removed our advertise-

ments for the range)'에서 (C)를, '애니메이션 텔레비전 쇼에 등장하는 액션 피규어와 차량들이 포함되어 있다(Galaxy Pirate toy line, which includes action figures and vehicles from the animated television show)'에서 (D)를 확인할 수 있다. 따라서 언급되지 않은 (B)가 정답이다.

어휘 **discontinue** 단종하다

▶▶ **Paraphrasing** 지문의 produced ~ overseas → 보기 (A)의 manufactured in a different country
지문의 Web sites → 보기 (C)의 online
지문의 the animated television show → 보기 (D)의 some entertainment media

160 문장 삽입 고난도

번역 [1], [2], [3], [4]로 표시된 곳 중에서 다음 문장이 가장 적합한 곳은?
"실제로 당사는 매주 조립 공정에 대한 품질보증 점검을 실시하고 있다."
(A) [1]
(B) [2]
(C) [3]
(D) [4]

해설 제시문이 앞 내용에 대한 설명을 덧붙일 때 쓰는 In fact로 시작하므로, 이전에 품질보증 점검(weekly quality assurance checks on the assembly line)과 관련된 회사의 조치가 먼저 언급되어야 한다. [3] 앞에서 플레이스마트가 공장 운영자들과 긴밀한 협력을 통해 제품에 고급 소재가 사용되는지, 적절한 제조 단계가 지켜지고 있는지 확인하고 있다(Playsmart works ~ to ensure that high-grade materials are being used and proper manufacturing steps are being adhered to)고 했으므로, 이 뒤에 주어진 문장이 들어가야 자연스럽다. 따라서 (C)가 정답이다.

161-163 이메일

발신: 치넨예 우메
수신: 전 직원
제목: 직원 추천 상여금
날짜: 6월 29일

안녕하세요 여러분.

¹⁶¹립딘스 그룹에서 자금 지원을 받는 조건으로 이제 빨리 인력을 확충해야 하므로, 직원 추천 상여금 제도에 대해 여러분 모두에게 다시 한번 알리기 적합한 때가 된 것 같네요. 공석에 추천한 사람이 채용되면 그 사람을 추천한 직원은 500달러의 보너스를 받을 수 있습니다. 참여에 관심이 있으시면 당사 웹사이트의 "일자리" 페이지를 정기적으로 확인하세요.

¹⁶²해당 직책에 필요한 자격요건을 모두 갖춘 후보만을 추천하는 것이 매우 중요하다는 점 유의하세요. 도움이 안 되는 추천을 줄이기 위해 올해 초에 새로운 단계별 지급 제도를 도입했습니다. 기억하시겠지만, 이렇게 하면 각 단계에 맞는 상여금을 추천자에게 지급하게 됩니다.

- ¹⁶³추천 받은 사람이 대면 면접 대상자로 선정될 시 1차로 20퍼센트 지급
- ¹⁶³후보자 채용 시 30퍼센트 추가
- 신입사원이 90일 경과 후에도 여전히 직원으로 근무할 시 나머지 50퍼센트

추천서 제출 방법에 관한 지침을 포함하여, 해당 제도 관련 상세 내용을 확인하고 싶다면 직원 사규 28페이지를 참조하세요. 직원 사규에서 다루지 않은 문제는 제게 전화(내선 233번)하거나 이메일을 보내세요.

감사합니다.

치녠예 우메
인사부장
파톤도 테크놀로지

어휘 expand 확장하다 referral 추천 entitle (받을) 자격을 부여하다 candidate 후보자 qualification 자격요건 institute 도입하다 tiered 단계로 된 entail 수반하다

---

161 사실 관계 확인 　　　　　고난도

번역 파톤도 테크놀로지에 관해 알 수 있는 것은?
(A) 최근 외부 투자를 유치했다.
(B) 웹사이트에 새로운 페이지가 추가되었다.
(C) 직원 사규가 전자문서로 배포된다.
(D) 올해 처음으로 추천 상여금을 시행했다.

해설 첫 번째 단락에서 립딘스 그룹에서 자금 지원을 받는 조건으로 빨리 인력을 확충해야 한다(we have to quickly expand our workforce as a condition of the funding we received from Ribdins Group)고 했으므로, 외부로부터 투자를 받고 있음을 알 수 있다. 따라서 (A)가 정답이다.

어휘 distribute 배포하다 implement 시행하다

▶▶ Paraphrasing 지문의 the funding we received from Ribdins Group
→ 정답의 outside investment

---

162 추론 / 암시 　　　　　고난도

번역 우메 씨는 과거 이 제도에 어떤 문제가 있었다고 암시하는가?
(A) 잘못된 경로를 통한 추천서 제출
(B) 추천된 사람들의 다양성 결여
(C) 부적합 후보자 추천
(D) 상여금 연체

해설 두 번째 단락에서 자격을 모두 갖춘 후보를 추천하는 게 중요하다며 도움이 안 되는 추천을 줄이기 위해(to cut down on the number of unhelpful recommendations) 올해 초에 새로운 단계별 지급 제도를 도입했다고 했다. 따라서 과거에 부적합 후보자를 추천한 사례가 있었다는 것을 추론할 수 있으므로, (C)가 정답이다.

어휘 diversity 다양성 endorsement 지지, 추천 unsuitable 부적합한

---

163 세부 사항 　　　　　고난도

번역 추천자가 정확히 상여금 절반을 받게 되는 시점은?
(A) 신청 완료 후
(B) 대면 면접 제안 후
(C) 채용 제안이 수락된 후
(D) 수습기간 경과 후

해설 두 번째 단락의 상여금 지급 단계를 보면, 추천된 사람이 면접 대상자로 선정될 경우 20퍼센트(First 20% when the referred person is chosen for an in-person interview)를 받고, 해당 후보자가 채용되면 30퍼센트를 추가로 받는다(Additional 30% when the candidate is hired)고 되어 있다. 즉, 상여금의 절반인 50%를 받게 되는 시점은 추천한 후보자가 채용된 시점이므로, (C)가 정답이다.

어휘 probationary 수습 중인

▶▶ Paraphrasing 지문의 the candidate is hired
→ 정답의 a job offer has been accepted

164-167 온라인 채팅

리아 영 [오후 1시 4분] 웨이드, 어슬러, 잠깐 시간 돼요? [164]방금 경영진이 다음에 발간될 유럽 탐험가 여행 책자에서 다룰 목적지 두 곳을 새로 선택해서 제게 얘기해 줬어요. 국가 한 곳과 도시 한 곳이에요.
웨이드 코빈 [오후 1시 8분] 좋아요! 어디예요?
리아 영 [오후 1시 10분] [165]경영진에서 룩셈부르크에 대한 자세하고 광범위한 안내서와 베네치아에 관한 포켓 크기의 도시 안내서를 원하네요.
어슬러 에릭손 [오후 1시 11분] 아, 제가 룩셈부르크에서 오래 지내 봤는데, 멋진 곳이에요.
리아 영 [오후 1시 14분] 정말 그렇죠. [166]그래서 5월 1일부터 6월 29일까지 룩셈부르크에 현장 조사원 2명을 파견하고, 6월 1일부터 6월 30일까지 베네치아에 1명을 파견할 예정이에요. 7월 첫째 주에 이들의 기록을 전부 받으면, 예정된 출판일과 출시일 전에 정보를 편집하는 데 한 달 정도 여유가 있을 거예요.
어슬러 에릭손 [오후 1시 16분] 그 정도면 시간이 충분하네요. [167]그러면 편집 단계를 위해 만반의 준비를 할 수 있도록 제가 이번 주에 출판물 별로 레이아웃 디자인을 시작하면 되겠네요.
웨이드 코빈 [오후 1시 22분] 그게 현명한지 잘 모르겠어요, 어슬러. 불가리아 책 기억나요?
어슬러 에릭손 [오후 1시 23분] [167]좋은 지적이에요, 웨이드. 이번에는 경영진이 포함시키고 싶은 내용이 정확히 뭔지 알게 될 때까지 기다릴게요.
리아 영 [오후 1시 25분] 그럼 되겠네요. 좋아요, 내일 경영진과 회의 후에 더 자세한 정보를 드릴게요.

어휘 destination 목적지 extensive 광범위한 approximately 대략 publication 출판(물)

---

164 주제 / 목적

번역 영 씨가 동료에게 첫 번째 메시지를 보낸 이유는?
(A) 우열을 가리기 힘든 제안들에 대해 의견을 묻기 위해
(B) 출판물 일부를 수정하자고 권고하기 위해
(C) 프로젝트를 위한 그들의 노고에 감사하기 위해
(D) 앞으로 있을 과업을 알려주기 위해

해설 영 씨가 오후 1시 4분 메시지에서 경영진이 다음에 발간될 유럽 탐험
가 여행 책자에서 다룰 목적지 두 곳을 새로 선택해서 자신에게 얘기했다
(Management just told me about two new destinations they
have chosen for us to cover in our next European Explorer
travel books)고 한 후, 해당 프로젝트에 관련된 이야기를 이어 가고 있
다. 따라서 앞으로 해야 하는 업무를 알려주기 위해 보낸 메시지임을 알 수
있으므로, (D)가 정답이다.

어휘 competing 경합하는 assignment 과제, 과업

165 추론 / 암시

번역 베네치아 책에 관해 암시된 것은?
(A) 7월에 출판될 예정이다.
(B) 소형일 것이다.
(C) 개정판이다.
(D) 코빈 씨의 책임이다.

해설 영 씨가 오후 1시 10분 메시지에서 경영진이 베네치아에 관한 포켓 크기
의 도시 안내서를 원한다(They want ~ a pocket-sized city guide
for Venice)고 했으므로, 베네치아 책은 소형으로 제작될 것임을 추론할
수 있다. 따라서 (B)가 정답이다.

어휘 revised 수정된, 개정된 responsibility 책임

▶▶ Paraphrasing 지문의 pocket-sized
→ 정답의 compact

166 세부 사항

번역 영 씨가 제공하는 정보는?
(A) 조사원의 자격요건
(B) 글의 최대 길이
(C) 여행 기간
(D) 편집 이유

해설 영 씨가 오후 1시 14분 메시지에서 5월 1일부터 6월 29일까지 룩셈부르
크에 현장 조사원 2명을 파견하고 6월 1일부터 6월 30일까지 베네치아
에 한 명을 파견할 예정(we'll be sending two field researchers to
Luxembourg from May 1 to June 29, and one to Venice from
June 1 to June 30)이라며 현장 조사원의 수와 출장 기간에 대한 정보
를 제공하고 있다. 따라서 (C)가 정답이다.

167 의도 파악

번역 오후 1시 22분에 코빈 씨가 "불가리아 책 기억나요?"라고 적은 의도는?
(A) 에릭슨 씨는 곧 끝내야 할 다른 과제가 있다.
(B) 새 책이 성공하리라는 에릭슨 씨의 기대가 너무 높다.
(C) 에릭슨 씨는 참고용으로 기존 레이아웃 견본을 사용할 수 있다.
(D) 에릭슨 씨가 특정 절차를 너무 일찍 시작해서는 안 된다.

해설 에릭슨 씨가 오후 1시 16분 메시지에서 이번 주에 출판물 별로 레이아
웃 디자인을 시작하면 되겠다(I can start designing the layout for
each publication this week)고 했는데, 이에 대해 코빈 씨가 '불가리
아 책 기억나요?(Remember the Bulgaria book?)'라고 반문하자,
에릭슨 씨는 좋은 지적(Good point)이라고 한 후 이번에는 경영진이 포
함시키고 싶은 내용이 정확히 뭔지 알게 될 때까지 기다리겠다(I'll wait
to see exactly what Management wants to be included this
time)고 했다. 따라서 에릭슨 씨에게 서두르지 말라고 조언하려는 의도로

쓴 메시지라고 추론할 수 있으므로, (D)가 정답이다.

어휘 expectation 기대 existing 기존의 template 견본
reference 참조

168-171 기사

올해의 '영국 건축상' 수상자 발표

런던 (12월 15일)—약 250개의 최종 후보 중에서 선정된 50개의 특이한 구조
물들이 올해 영국 건축가나 영국에 사무소를 둔 외국 건축가들이 만든 가장 혁
신적인 건축물로 선정되어 권위 있는 '영국 건축상'을 받았다. [168]이제 22번째를
맞는 '영국 건축상'은 런던 건축 디자인 박물관과 영국 도시계획 예술센터가 공동
으로 수여한다. 이들은 초고층 건물, 기업 본사, 교량, 공원 정자, 병원, 개인 주
거지, 학술 기관 등 매우 다양한 방식으로 우리 삶을 형성하는 특출한 현대 건축
물을 설계한 건축가의 공로를 표창한다.

올해의 대표적 수상자 중에는 [171]사이먼 소프 (768대의 차량을 수용할 수 있으
며 다양한 친환경적 특징을 지닌 근사한 9층짜리 주차장으로, 센트럴 맨체스터
에 있는 '메이틀랜드 가 주차장' 설계), [169]마커스 프라이어 (숨이 멎는 듯한 195
미터짜리 보행자용 다리로, 독특하게 음악에 맞춰 깜빡이는 별 모양 LED 전구
4,500개가 달린 '수평선 다리' 설계), [170]이소벨 맥더프 (옥상에 온수 수영장이
딸린 28층짜리 고급 아파트로, 에딘버러의 번화한 쇼핑지역 인근에 위치한 '스파
이어' 설계) 등이 있다.

[170]예년과 마찬가지로, 수상자 수가 굉장히 많아서 12월 12일 금요일부터 12월
14일 일요일까지 사흘 밤 동안 시상식이 진행되었다. 개막일 밤에는 기업 및 상
업 부문, 토요일에는 주거 및 도시계획 부문, 그리고 마지막 날 밤에는 기관 부문
상을 수여했다. [171]'메이틀랜드 가 주차장'은 도시계획 부문 상과 더불어 최고 영
예인 '올해의 가장 혁신적인 디자인 상'을 건축가에게 안겨줌으로써, 같은 해에 2
개의 상을 수상한 최초의 건축물이 되어 새로운 역사를 썼다.

어휘 extraordinary 특출한 structure 구조물, 건물
shortlisted 최종 후보에 오른 prestigious 권위 있는 innovative
혁신적인 architecture 건축물 architect 건축가 present
수여하다 recognize 표창하다, 공로를 인정하다 contemporary
현대의 skyscraper 초고층 건물 corporate 기업의 pavilion
(공원 등의) 정자, 별관 residence 주거지 institution 기관
stunning 근사한, 멋진 eco-friendly 친환경적인 breathtaking
숨막히는 pedestrian 보행자, 보행자용의 uniquely 독특하게
synchronize 동시에 움직이게[발생하게]하다 sheer (대규모 크기, 수
등을 강조하여) 굉장히 ceremony (행사 등의) 식

168 사실 관계 확인 [고난도]

번역 영국 건축상에 관해 언급된 것은?
(A) 두 기관이 협업해 수여한다.
(B) 다양한 액수의 상금이 따라온다.
(C) 최근 부문 목록이 증가했다.
(D) 영국 시민만 상을 받을 자격이 있다.

해설 첫 번째 단락에서 런던 건축 디자인 박물관과 영국 도시계획 예술센터가
공동으로 영국 건축상을 수여한다(the British Architecture Awards
are jointly presented by the London Museum of Architecture
& Design and the British Centre for Urban Planning & Art)고
했으므로, (A)가 정답이다.

어휘 collaborate 협업하다 eligible 자격이 되는

Test 6

>> **Paraphrasing** 지문의 jointly presented by the London Museum of Architecture & Design and the British Centre for Urban Planning & Art → 정답의 Two organizations collaborate to issue

169 세부 사항

번역 기사에 따르면 프라이어 씨의 디자인에서 특별한 점은?
(A) 상업지역과의 융화
(B) 친환경적 특징
(C) 빛과 소리의 조합
(D) 인상적인 높이

해설 두 번째 단락에서 프라이어 씨가 설계한 '수평선 다리(Horizon Bridge)'에 독특하게도 음악에 맞춰 깜빡이는 별 모양 LED 전구 4,500개가 달려 있다(uniquely equipped with 4,500 blinking LED stars synchronized with music)고 했으므로, (C)가 정답이다.

어휘 integration 통합, 융화 environmentally-friendly 친환경적인 combination 조합 impressive 인상적인

>> **Paraphrasing** 지문의 4,500 blinking LED stars synchronized with music → 정답의 combination of light and sound

170 추론 / 암시 고난도

번역 맥더프 씨는 언제 수상하겠는가?
(A) 12월 12일
(B) 12월 13일
(C) 12월 14일
(D) 12월 15일

해설 두 번째 단락에서 수상자 중 한 명인 맥더프 씨가 설계한 '스파이어(The Spire)'가 품격 있는 28층짜리 아파트 건물(an elegant 28-floor apartment building)이라고 했는데, 세 번째 단락을 보면 12월 12일 금요일부터 12월 14일 일요일까지 사흘 밤 동안 시상식이 진행되었으며(the awards were given out over the course of three evenings and three ceremonies from Friday, 12 December to Sunday, 14 December) 토요일에 주거 및 도시계획 부문 상이 수여되었다(Saturday's awards were for the Residential and Urban Planning categories)고 나와 있다. 따라서 아파트를 설계한 맥더프 씨가 12월 13일에 수상을 했다고 추론할 수 있으므로, (B)가 정답이다.

171 추론 / 암시

번역 소프 씨에 관해 암시된 것은?
(A) 과거에 상을 받은 적이 있다.
(B) 토요일에 상을 수여했다.
(C) 공로상을 받았다.
(D) 올해 두 개의 상을 받았다.

해설 두 번째 단락에서 소프 씨가 메이틀랜드 가 주차장을 설계했다(Simon Thorpe for Maitland Street Car Park)고 했는데, 마지막 단락에서 메이틀랜드 가 주차장이 건축가에게 같은 해에 두 개의 상을 안겨준 최초의 건축물이 되었다(Maitland Street Car Park ~ being the first structure to win its architect two awards in the same year)고

118

했으므로, 그가 올해 두 개의 상을 받았음을 알 수 있다. 따라서 (D)가 정답이다.

>> **Paraphrasing** 지문의 win its architect two awards in the same year → 정답의 He received two awards this year

172-175 이메일

수신: 렌 골드만 (lgoldman@whizzomail.net)
발신: 최미경 (mkchoi@summitsc.com)
제목: 스파크라이트 화덕
날짜: 9월 6일

골드만 씨께,

귀하의 최신 특허 발명품 관련 정보 꾸러미를 받고 아주 기뻤습니다. 스파크라이트 화덕은 굉장한 제품으로 보이며, 저희 서밋 스포츠 & 캠핑 매장에 들여놓았으면 합니다. **172(A)/(B)휴대성과 태양열 충전 옵션이 굉장히 마음에 듭니다.** 하지만 설계 방식에 관해 몇 가지 질문이 있습니다. **175먼저, 공기분사기가 장작불에 산소를 공급하는 방식을 이해하기 쉽게 설명해 주시겠어요? 저희는 이러한 방식이 안전한지 조금 우려하고 있습니다.** **172(C)또 정보 꾸러미에는 스마트폰 앱을 통해 불길 세기를 조절할 수 있는 방법도 정리돼 있습니다.** 이 앱은 어떤 운영 체제와 호환되나요?

빠른 시일 내에 이 간단한 질문들에 대답해 주셨으면 좋겠고, 또한 화덕 하나를 가지고 당사 본사에 직접 방문해 주셨으면 합니다. 아시다시피, 당사 임원들은 새로운 제품을 구매하고 판매하는 계약을 승인하기 전에 사용되는 모습을 직접 보고 싶어합니다. **1739월 13일 오후 2시에 열리는 회의에 참석하셔서 할당된 1시간 동안 기기의 기능 및 성능을 소개해주시면 감사하겠습니다.**

174지금도 가장 잘 팔리는 제품으로 손꼽히는 귀하의 캠핑용 난로와 다기능 냉각기의 인기는 말할 것도 없고, 보내신 제품 사양과 사진을 토대로 볼 때 스파크라이트 화덕을 구비하는 쪽으로 결정하리라 확신합니다. 답신 기다리겠습니다.

최미경
구매부장
서밋 스포츠 & 캠핑

어휘 patented 특허를 받은 portability 휴대성 charging 충전 clarify 이해하기 쉽게 설명하다 air jet 공기 분사기 pump (물·공기 등을) 퍼내다, 내보내다 intensity 세기 operating system 운영 체제 compatible with ~와 호환되는 at one's earliest convenience 가급적 빨리, 형편 닿는 대로 executive 임원 firsthand 직접 allot 할당하다 function 기능 capability 성능, 활용성 specification 사양 multifunctional 다기능의

172 사실 관계 확인 고난도

번역 스파크라이트 화덕에 관해 사실이 아닌 것은?
(A) 재생 에너지를 사용할 수 있다.
(B) 운반이 쉽다.
(C) 모바일 기기와 연결된다.
(D) 특허 확정을 기다리고 있다.

해설 첫 번째 단락의 '휴대성과 태양열 충전 옵션이 마음에 든다(We love its portability and solar charging option)'에서 (A)와 (B)를, '정보 꾸

러미에는 스마트폰 앱을 통해 불길 세기를 조절할 수 있는 방법도 정리
돼 있다(the information pack outlines how the fire intensity
can be controlled via smartphone app)'에서 (C)를 확인할 수 있
다. 첫 문장에서 스파크라이트가 최근에 특허를 받은 제품(latest patent
invention)임을 알 수 있으므로, 틀린 정보를 언급한 (D)가 정답이다.

어휘 renewable 재생 가능한

▶▶ **Paraphrasing** 지문의 **solar charging**
→ 보기 (A)의 **renewable energy**
지문의 **portability**
→ 보기 (B)의 **easy to transport**
지문의 **be controlled via smartphone app**
→ 보기 (C)의 **connects to mobile devices**

173 세부 사항 ··· 고난도

번역 최 씨가 골드만 씨에게 요청한 일은?
(A) 실황 시연
(B) 시제품 전달
(C) 계약조건 제안
(D) 제조 현장 방문

해설 두 번째 단락에서 골드만 씨에게 회의에 참석해 기기의 기능과 성능을 소
개해주면 감사하겠다(We would be grateful if you could attend a
meeting ~ to showcase the device's functions and capabilities)고 했으므로, (A)가 정답이다.

어휘 demonstration 시연 prototype 시제품

▶▶ **Paraphrasing** 지문의 **showcase the device's functions
and capabilities**
→ 정답의 **Give a live demonstration**

174 추론 / 암시

번역 서밋 스포츠 & 캠핑에 관해 유추할 수 있는 것은?
(A) 더 많은 스포츠웨어를 구비할 계획이다.
(B) 골드만 씨의 전 고용주다.
(C) 골드만 씨가 만든 다른 상품들을 구비하고 있다.
(D) 스파크라이트 화덕을 처음 주문했다.

해설 세 번째 단락에서 골드만 씨의 캠핑용 난로와 다기능 냉각기가 인기 있다
는 점(the popularity of your camping stove and multifunctional
cooler, which are still among our top sellers)을 언급했으므로,
서밋 스포츠 & 캠핑이 골드만 씨가 만든 다른 상품을 구비하고 있음을 추
론할 수 있다. 따라서 (C)가 정답이다.

▶▶ **Paraphrasing** 지문의 **are ~ among our top sellers**
→ 정답의 **stocks**
지문의 **your camping stove and
multifunctional cooler** → 정답의 **other
products created by Mr. Goldman**

175 문장 삽입

번역 [1], [2], [3], [4]로 표시된 곳 중에서 다음 문장이 가장 적합한 곳은?
"저희는 이러한 방식이 안전한지 조금 우려하고 있습니다."
(A) [1]
(B) [2]
(C) [3]
(D) [4]

해설 주어진 문장 앞에서 안전이 우려되는 '이러한 방식(such a mechanism)'
이 먼저 언급되어야 한다. [2] 앞에서 공기분사기가 장작불에 산소를 공
급하는 방식을 이해하기 쉽게 설명해달라(would you mind clarifying
how the air jets pump oxygen into the wood fire?)고 했으므로,
이 뒤에 주어진 문장이 들어가야 자연스럽다. 따라서 (B)가 정답이다.

176-180 광고 + 등록 양식

신생기업을 위한 성장전략

새로운 회사를 성장시키고 개선하고 싶지만 어디서부터 시작해야 할지 확신이
없으시다고요? 바로 풀브리지 그로스 스트레티지스가 여러분을 위한 곳입니다.
저희는 초보 사업주들에게 유용한 다채로운 주제의 세미나를 제공합니다. [176]수
십 년간의 전문적인 실무를 통해 얻은 지혜와 최신 경영기법 및 추세에 대한 최첨
단 지식을 결합해 각 과목을 가르칩니다. 아래는 올 가을에 제공하는 세미나 샘
플입니다.

함께하기 (세미나 코드 #1809) – 비용: 48달러
[177(B)]이 세미나는 직원들이 효과적으로 함께 일하도록 격려하는 다양한 전략을
제공합니다.
*9월 3일 수요일 오전 10시 – 오후 12시: 본관, 204호실

[179]**내일의 시장** (세미나 코드 #3487) – 비용: 95달러
이 세미나는 제품이나 서비스에 더 많은 고객을 유치하는 방법에 대한 조언을
제공합니다.
*9월 24일 수요일 오전 10시 – 오후 3시: 연수원, 3호실

시야 넓히기 (세미나 코드 #2276) – 비용: 149달러
[177(C)]이 세미나는 사업주들에게 신규 지점 개설 계획 시 고려해야 하는 사항들
에 대한 핵심 조언을 제공합니다.
*10월 15일 수요일 오전 10시 – 오후 4시: 본관, 206호실

속도 유지하기 (세미나 코드 #3785) – 비용: 109달러
[177(D)]이 세미나는 [178]탄력 근무제 등 인기 있는 직원 특전을 소개하고 시행 방
식을 설명합니다.
*11월 5일 수요일 오전 10시 – 오후 4시: 연수원, 4호실

자세한 내용은 www.fulbridge-gs.com을 참조하세요.

어휘 strategy 전략 unsure 확신이 없는 an array of 다양한
novice 초보자 hands-on 하는, 실천하는 cutting-edge
최첨단의 understanding 지식, 이해 encourage 독려[격려]하다
effectively 효율적으로 flexible working hours 탄력 근무제
implement 시행하다

풀브리지 그로스 스트래티지스 – 세미나 등록	
이름:	로빈 부키
주소:	밸럭 가 84번지, 시애틀, 워싱턴 98121
전화:	555-0139
이메일:	r.booky@globenet.com
세미나 코드:	179#3487
결제 방법:	은행 이체
의견:	9월에 연수원에서 열리는 풀브리지 세미나에 처음 참석하는데, 정말 기대하고 있어요. 179요청하신 대로 귀사 계좌로 등록비 59달러를 보냈습니다. 딱 한 가지 걱정되는 점은 제가 아주 멀리 살고 있어서 오전 10시까지 연수원에 도착하지 못할 수도 있다는 거예요. 180이 점이 크게 문제가 될지 이메일로 알려주시면 감사하겠습니다. 고맙습니다.

어휘 registration 등록　concern 걱정, 우려 사항　appreciate 감사해 하다

176 추론 / 암시　　고난도

번역 풀브리지 그로스 스트래티지스에 관해 암시된 것은?
　(A) 홈페이지에서 샘플 교재를 제공하고 있다.
　(B) 강사들에게 실무 경험이 있다.
　(C) 요청 시 맞춤화된 수업 제공이 가능하다.
　(D) 매 시즌 같은 세미나를 개최한다.

해설 광고의 첫 번째 단락에서 수십 년간의 전문적인 실무를 통해 얻은 지혜와 최신 경영기법 및 추세에 대한 최첨단 지식을 결합해 각 과목을 가르친다(Each one is taught with a combination of wisdom earned through decades of hands-on professional work and cutting-edge understanding of the latest management techniques and trends)고 했으므로, 강사들에게 실무 경험이 있다고 추론할 수 있다. 따라서 (B)가 정답이다.

▶▶ **Paraphrasing**　지문의 hands-on professional work
　→ 정답의 practical business experience

177 사실 관계 확인　　고난도

번역 열거된 세미나에서 다루지 않는 주제는?
　(A) 구매 결정 관련해 고객에게 조언하기
　(B) 직원 간 팀워크 강화하기
　(C) 기업에 신규 사업장 추가하기
　(D) 직원에게 특정 혜택 부여하기

해설 직원들이 효과적으로 함께 일하도록 격려하는 다양한 전략(a variety of strategies for encouraging your employees to work together effectively)을 제공하는 '함께하기(Coming Together)' 세미나에서 (B)가, 신규 지점 개설 계획 입안 시 고려해야 하는 사안들에 대한 필수적인 조언(essential tips on what to consider when planning to open a new branch)을 해주는 '시야 넓히기(Broaden Your Horizons)' 세미나에서 (C)가, 탄력근무제 등 인기 있는 직원 특전을 소개하고 시행 방식을 설명하는(introduces popular employee perks, such as flexible working hours, and explains how to implement them) '속도 유지하기(Keeping the Pace)' 세미나에서 (D)가 다뤄진다는 것을

확인할 수 있다. 따라서 언급되지 않은 (A)가 정답이다.

▶▶ **Paraphrasing**　지문의 encouraging your employees to work together
　→ 보기 (B)의 Fostering teamwork between employees
　지문의 to open a new branch
　→ 보기 (C)의 Adding new work sites
　지문의 popular employee perks
　→ 보기 (D)의 certain benefits to staff

178 동의어 찾기

번역 광고에서 5번째 단락 2행의 "flexible"과 의미상 가장 가까운 것은?
　(A) 점진적인
　(B) 순종적인
　(C) 구부릴 수 있는
　(D) 변경 가능한

해설 'flexible'을 포함한 부분은 '탄력 근무제(flexible working hours)'라는 의미로 해석되는데, 여기서 flexible은 '탄력적인, 융통성 있는'이라는 뜻으로 쓰였다. 따라서 '변경 가능한'이라는 의미의 (D) variable이 정답이다.

179 연계

번역 부키 씨가 잘못 읽은 것 같은 정보는?
　(A) 세미나 장소
　(B) 세미나 비용
　(C) 세미나가 개최되는 달
　(D) 세미나 시작 시간

해설 부키 씨가 작성한 등록 양식의 세미나 코드(Seminar Code: #3487)에 해당하는 세미나는 '내일의 시장(Tomorrow's Market)'이다. 비용이 95달러라고 나와 있는데, 등록 양식의 의견(Comments)란을 보면 부키 씨가 등록비 59달러를 보냈다(I have sent the $59 registration fee to your corporate account)고 했으므로, 세미나 비용을 잘못 읽었다고 추론할 수 있다. 따라서 (B)가 정답이다.

180 세부 사항　　고난도

번역 부키 씨가 풀브리지 그로스 스트래티지스에 요청한 것은?
　(A) 위험 요소가 얼마나 심각한지 판단하기
　(B) 정책에 예외 두기
　(C) 대체안 모아서 정리하기
　(D) 특정 상황에 대한 새로운 소식을 정기적으로 알려주기

해설 등록 양식의 의견(Comments)란에서 지각이 크게 문제가 될지 이메일로 알려주면 감사하겠다(I would appreciate it if someone could let me know via e-mail whether this would be a major problem)고 했으므로, (A)가 정답이다.

어휘 determine 판단하다, 결정하다　seriousness 심각성　exception 예외　compile 모아서 정리하다　alternative 대안의

▶▶ **Paraphrasing**　지문의 whether this would be a major problem
　→ 정답의 the seriousness of a risk

181-185 소책자 정보 + 고객 후기

카스텔렌테 물품 보관 회사
주거용 물품 보관소

카스텔렌테의 주거용 물품 보관소는 다양한 크기로 제공되며, 최소 2주 또는 그 이상 원하는 기간 동안 대여할 수 있습니다. [181](C)짐 포장과 해체가 쉽도록 보관소는 모두 1층에 설치되어 있으며, 자체 보안 경보기와 카메라를 갖추고 있습니다. [181](B)언제든, 어느 요일이든 본인의 물품에 접근할 수 있도록 고객이 자물쇠 열쇠를 보관합니다. [181](A)게다가 내장형 냉난방 시스템은 보관소가 위험할 정도로 뜨겁거나 차가워지지 않도록 해줍니다.

보관소 유형	크기	주/월 비용*	적합한 짐:
A	13.6m²	52파운드 / 208파운드	방 세 개짜리 집의 내용물
B	6.7m²	32파운드 / 128파운드	방 하나짜리 아파트의 내용물
[183]C	3.4m²	18파운드 / 72파운드	몇 가지 가구 품목
D	1.6m²	10파운드 / 40파운드	상자 몇 개

*[182]보증금 50파운드도 필요합니다. 카스텔렌테 물품 보관 회사는 대여 기간 종료 시 보관소가 더럽거나 손상되어 있을 경우, 보증금의 전부 또는 일부를 반환하지 않을 수 있습니다.

어휘 residential 주거용(의) a variety of 다양한 ground floor 1층 security 보안 access 접근하다, 이용하다 belongings 물건, 소지품 built-in 내장된 ensure ~하게 하다 deposit 보증금

---

http://www.birminghamsmartreviews.com/storage/0421

카스텔렌테 물품 보관 회사 후기

[184]저는 6개월 연구 프로그램을 위해 독일로 이사를 가야 했을 때 물건을 보관하려고 카스텔렌테에서 보관소를 빌렸습니다. 이용해 보니 더할 나위 없이 좋았습니다. [185]우선 제가 공간이 얼마나 필요한지 잘 모르자 직원이 부담을 주지 않고 친절하게 옵션을 설명해 줬습니다. 그녀는 또한 계약하기 전에 제가 임대 계약조건을 확실히 이해하도록 해줬습니다. [183/185]그리고 제 물건, 그러니까 침대, 서랍장, 작은 가전제품들을 가지고 왔을 때, 당직 근무자가 짐을 내리고 효율적으로 정리할 수 있도록 도와주었습니다. 6개월 후, 모든 것이 제가 둔 그대로 안전하게, 습기 없는 상태로 있었습니다. 카스텔렌테는 훌륭한 셀프 보관 시설입니다.

키에라 리츠, 12월 2일

어휘 representative (담당) 직원 pressure 부담을 주다 terms 조건 appliance 가전제품 unload 짐을 내리다 organise (organize) 정리하다 efficiently 효율적으로

---

181 사실 관계 확인

번역 각 보관소의 특징으로 언급되지 않은 것은?
(A) 온도 조절
(B) 24시간 접근성
(C) 보안 시스템
(D) 전기 콘센트

해설 소책자 첫 번째 단락의 '내장형 냉난방 시스템은 보관소가 위험할 정도로 뜨겁거나 차가워지지 않도록 해준다(our built-in heating and

---

cooling systems ~ in your unit)'에서 (A)를, '언제든, 어느 요일이든 물건에 접근할 수 있도록 임대자가 자물쇠 열쇠를 보관한다(You ~ can access your belongings at any time, on any day of the week)'에서 (B)를, '자체 보안 경보기와 카메라를 갖추고 있다(Each one ~ has its own security alarm and camera)'에서 (C)를 확인할 수 있다. 따라서 언급되지 않은 (D)가 정답이다.

▶▶ Paraphrasing 지문의 heating and cooling systems
→ 보기 (A)의 Temperature control

지문의 you can access your belongings at any time, on any day of the week
→ 보기 (B)의 24-hour accessibility

지문의 security alarm and camera
→ 보기 (C)의 security system

---

182 세부 사항

번역 정보에 따르면, 추가 요금이 있는 것은?
(A) 2주 미만의 임대 기간 선택
(B) 1층 보관소 대여
(C) 불량 상태로 보관소 방치
(D) 보관소 열쇠 교체

해설 소책자 하단에서 보증금이 필요하다고 한 후, 대여 기간 종료 시 보관소가 더럽거나 손상되어 있을 경우 보증금의 전부 또는 일부를 반환하지 않을 수 있다(Castellente Storage Company may keep all or part of this if the rental unit is found to be dirty or damaged)고 했다. 따라서 창고를 불량한 상태로 방치할 시 추가로 비용을 지불해야 한다는 것을 알 수 있으므로, (C)가 정답이다.

▶▶ Paraphrasing 지문의 if the rental unit is found to be dirty or damaged
→ 정답의 Leaving a unit in poor condition

---

183 연계

번역 리츠 씨는 어떤 보관소를 임대했겠는가?
(A) A형
(B) B형
(C) C형
(D) D형

해설 고객 후기 중반부에서 리츠 씨는 침대, 서랍장, 작은 가전제품들을 보관소에 가지고 왔다(I brought over my stuff—a bed, a dresser, some small appliances)고 했는데, 이는 소책자 표에 명시된 '몇 가지 가구 품목(Several items of furniture)'에 해당한다고 볼 수 있다. 따라서 리츠 씨가 C형 보관소를 임대했을 것으로 추론할 수 있으므로, (C)가 정답이다.

---

184 세부 사항

번역 리츠 씨가 몇 가지 물건을 보관해야 했던 이유는?
(A) 잠시 외국에 가서 살았다.
(B) 더 작은 집으로 이사했다.
(C) 거주지를 개조하고 있었다.
(D) 새로운 취미를 위한 용품을 샀다.

해설   고객 후기 초반부에서 6개월 연구 프로그램을 위해 독일로 이사를 가야 했을 때 물건을 보관하려고 카스텔렌테에서 보관소를 빌렸다(I rented a unit ~ to store my belongings in when I had to move to Germany for a six-month study program)고 했으므로, (A)가 정답 이다.

어휘   temporarily 잠시   relocate 이사하다

▶▶ Paraphrasing 지문의 **store my belongings**
                → 질문의 **store some items**
            지문의 **move to Germany for a six-month study program**
                → 정답의 **went to live abroad temporarily**

185 사실 관계 확인

번역   리츠 씨가 카스텔렌테 물품 보관 회사에 관해 명시한 것은?
    (A) 시설이 넓다.
    (B) 직원들이 잘 도와준다.
    (C) 평판이 훌륭하다.
    (D) 계약서가 이해하기 쉽다.

해설   고객 후기 초반부에서 직원이 부담을 주지 않고 친절하게 옵션을 설명해 줬다(their representative kindly explained the options without pressuring me)고 했고, 중반부에서도 당직 근무자가 짐을 내리고 효율 적으로 정리할 수 있도록 도와주었다(the worker on duty offered to help me unload it and organise it all efficiently)며 직원들이 도와 준 사례를 구체적으로 언급했다. 따라서 (B)가 정답이다.

어휘   reputation 평판

▶▶ Paraphrasing 지문의 **representative / worker**
                → 정답의 **staff**

186-190 웹페이지 + 웹페이지 + 이메일

http://www.rosensteinconcerthall.com/events

소개	행사	표	위치	연락처

로젠슈타인 콘서트홀
다가오는 행사

자세한 내용을 확인하고 티켓을 구매하시려면 행사 제목을 클릭하세요. 아니면 여기를 클릭해 '로젠슈타인 가족(모든 연령의 음악 애호가들을 위한 쇼)'과 '위대 한 연주자들(전 세계 악기 연주자들을 위한 쇼케이스)' 같은 테마 시리즈를 둘러 보세요.

186/188 11월 15일, 토요일	186 11월 22-23일, 토요일-일요일
오후 7:30-9:30	오후 7:30-10:00
셀리아 무디를 기리는 공연	재즈 연주**
188 버지스 오케스트라가 이 유명 작 곡가의 작품에서 선별해 연주한다.	XO 재즈 4인조가 현대 팝 히트곡을 재즈로 재해석한 곡을 선보인다.
186 11월 29일, 토요일	186 12월 7일, 일요일
오후 7:00-8:30.	오후 7:00-9:00
기억에 남을 만한 밤	〈초록 계곡〉의 노래*
테너 안토니오 비안치가 자신의 대표 곡 몇 곡을 부른다.	버지스 오케스트라가 고전 영화 음악 을 연주한다.

---

*190 별표(*)가 하나인 행사는 정기회원만 이용할 수 있습니다. 로젠슈타인 콘서 트홀 정기회원이 되면 누릴 수 있는 혜택 전체를 보시려면 여기를 클릭하세요.
**별표가 두 개인 행사는 회원권에 포함되지 않으며 별도로 비용을 지불해야 합 니다.

어휘   alternatively 또는, 그렇지 않으면   explore 둘러보다, 알아보다 instrumentalist 악기 연주자   celebration 기념   composer 작곡가   rendition 연주   present 선보이다   spin 재해석, 재해석한 것 score 음악, 악보   asterisk 별표   subscriber 정기회원, 구독자

---

http://www.rosensteinconcerthall.com/tickets/payment/18780

소개	행사	표	위치	연락처

로젠슈타인 콘서트홀
구매해 주셔서 감사합니다!

표는 아래 주소로 배송됩니다. 187 그러나 표가 도착하기 전에 교환 또는 취소해 야 할 경우에 대비해 이 페이지를 캡쳐하거나 출력해 두세요.

예약 확인 번호:	59289289		
이름:	웨인 저지	이메일:	wjudge@solomail.com
주소:	레드우드 파크 114번지 버지스, 텍사스 77014	전화:	555-0103

188 행사 날짜:	11월 15일		
매수:	2장	좌석 구역:	C
가격:	100달러	결제 방법:	요우자페이 온라인
구입 날짜:	10월 20일		

예약 세부사항을 꼼꼼하게 확인하세요. 오류를 발견하면 inquiries@ rosenstein.com으로 이메일을 보내 도움을 요청하세요.

수신: 〈support@rosenstein.com〉
발신: 〈wjudge@solomail.com〉
제목: 콘서트
날짜: 12월 18일

안녕하세요.

190 얼마 전 공연에서 아주 멋진 경험을 하고 콘서트홀 정기회원권을 구매했어요. 지금 다가오는 공연 표를 구매하려고 하는데, 이게 정기회원 서비스에 포함되 지 않은 공연이더라고요. 189 그런데 10퍼센트를 할인 받으려고 해당 칸에 회원 번호를 입력하면 "유효하지 않은 회원 번호"라는 빨간색 문자가 표시되고 할인이 적용되지 않네요. 정확한 번호로 하고 있는 건 확실해요. 이 문제를 확인해보고 다시 연락해주시겠어요? 감사합니다.

웨인 저지

어휘   invalid 유효하지 않은   look into 살펴보다, 조사하다

186 세부 사항

번역 첫 번째 웹페이지에 올라온 행사의 공통점은?
(A) 주말에 열린다.
(B) 행사 지속 시간이 같다.
(C) 단체 공연자가 포함된다.
(D) 모두 하루씩만 제공된다.

해설 첫 번째 웹페이지의 표를 보면 '셀리아 무디를 기리는 공연(A Celebration of Celia Moody)'과 '기억에 남을 만한 밤(A Night to Remember)'은 토요일에, '재즈 연주(Renditions in Jazz)'는 토요일과 일요일에, '초록 계곡의 노래(Songs of *Green Valley*)'는 일요일에 진행된다고 나와 있다. 따라서 모든 행사가 주말에 열린다는 것을 알 수 있으므로, (A)가 정답이다.

187 세부 사항

번역 두 번째 웹페이지에서 저지 씨에게 지시하는 행위는?
(A) 이메일 받은 편지함 확인
(B) 예약 정보 저장
(C) 집에서 표 출력
(D) 취소 기한 확인

해설 두 번째 웹페이지의 첫 단락에서 표가 도착하기 전에 교환 또는 취소해야 할 경우에 대비해 이 페이지를 캡처하거나 출력해 둘 것을 권장한다(we recommend that you print or take a screenshot of this page in case you need to exchange or cancel your tickets)고 했으므로, (B)가 정답이다.

▶▶ **Paraphrasing** 지문의 **print or take a screenshot of this page**
→ 정답의 **Save his booking information**

188 연계 [고난도]

번역 저지 씨가 참석한 콘서트에서 들은 것은?
(A) 가수의 노래 공연
(B) 영화 음악
(C) 다른 장르로 바뀐 노래
(D) 한 사람이 작곡한 곡들

해설 두 번째 웹페이지의 행사 날짜(Date of Event)에서 저지 씨가 11월 15일 콘서트에 참석했다는 것을 확인할 수 있다. 첫 번째 웹페이지의 표를 보면, 11월 15일은 버지스 오케스트라가 유명 작곡가의 작품을 선별해 공연한(The Burgess Orchestra performs selected works of the famous composer) 날이므로, (D)가 정답이다.

▶▶ **Paraphrasing** 지문의 **selected works of the famous composer**
→ 정답의 **Musical pieces written by one person**

189 주제 / 목적

번역 저지 씨가 이메일을 쓴 이유는?
(A) 서비스에 대한 감사 표시
(B) 기술적 문제 보고
(C) 구매 확인 요청
(D) 약관 문의

해설 이메일의 중반부에서 저지 씨는 할인을 받고자 칸에 회원 번호를 입력하면 "유효하지 않은 회원 번호"라는 빨간색 문자가 표시되고 할인이 적용되지 않는다(when I enter my subscriber number in the box provided ~ I see red text saying "Invalid subscriber number", and the discount isn't applied)고 했다. 이후 이 문제를 처리해달라고 요청하고 있으므로, (B)가 정답이다.

어휘 terms of an agreement (이용) 약관

190 연계 [고난도]

번역 저지 씨에 관해 가장 사실에 가까운 것은?
(A) 회원 전용 공연에 참석할 수 있는 자격이 있다.
(B) 정기 간행물을 받기 시작할 것이다.
(C) 특별한 지위의 특혜를 오해했다.
(D) 아동 친화적인 오락물에 관심이 있다.

해설 이메일의 초반부에서 저지 씨는 자신이 콘서트홀 정기회원권을 구매했다(I just purchased a subscription to your concert hall)고 했는데, 첫 번째 웹페이지의 하단을 보면 별표(*)가 하나 있는 행사는 정기회원만 이용할 수 있다(Events with an asterisk (*) are only available to subscribers)고 되어 있다. 따라서 저지 씨가 회원 전용 공연에 참석할 자격이 있음을 알 수 있으므로, (A)가 정답이다.

어휘 exclusive 회원 전용의 publication 출판(물)

▶▶ **Paraphrasing** 지문의 **only available**
→ 정답의 **exclusive**

191-195 공지 + 기사 + 이메일

찰스턴 중앙박물관

오는 3월에 진행될 과학 전시회 '보이지 않는 세계: 미생물' 개막을 [192]**기념해** 2월 26일 축하연을 개최할 예정입니다. [191]**지난 수년간 후한 기부금으로 저희 기관을 후원해주셨으니, 여러분도 이 즐거운 행사를 축하하는 자리에 저희와 함께 해주셨으면 합니다.**

축하연 상세 정보:
2월 26일 토요일 오후 6시–9시 30분
찰스턴 중앙박물관 동관
실버 스타 출장요리 회사에서 제공하는 뷔페

[194]**'보이지 않는 세계: 미생물'은 3월 3일부터 5월 31일까지 진행되며, 가장 작은 생명체의 경이로움을 묘사한 전시물 250여 점을 선보입니다.**

어휘 host 개최하다 reception 축하연, 환영회 exhibition 전시(회) invisible 눈에 보이지 않는 microorganism 미생물 institution 기관 generous 후한 donation 기부(금) celebrate 기념하다, 축하하다 depict 묘사하다

미드웨스턴 가제트

찰스턴 중앙박물관, 권위 있는 상 수상하다

글: 질 브래드퍼드

메리트 (4월 20일)—[193]찰스턴 중앙박물관이 4월 18일에 사상 최초로 열린 중서부 예술과학상 시상식에서 '학술문헌상'을 받았다. 중서부 지식재단이 준비한 이 행사는 예술계 및 과학계 회원들 6,000여명이 참석한 가운데 워싱턴 컨벤션 홀에서 열렸다.

찰스턴 중앙박물관은 '보이지 않는 세계: 미생물' 전시회를 보완하는 상세하고 재미있는 정보 꾸러미로 상을 받았다. 수석 디자이너 유이 타카하시는 상을 받은 후 정보 꾸러미의 삽화를 다수 제공한 그래픽 디자이너 레이먼드 슐럽에게 감사를 표현했다. 그녀는 또한 현재 개편 작업 중인 박물관 웹사이트에서 이 꾸러미를 대중에게 공개할 것이라고 약속했다.

[195]'보이지 않는 세계: 미생물'은 과학자 토마스 엘슨이 구상했으며, 그는 건축가 피오나 왓슨의 지식 및 전문기술의 힘을 빌려 전시물을 제작했다. 이 전시회 표의 판매고가 이전의 모든 전시회를 뛰어넘으면서 박물관은 엄청난 성공을 거두었다. [194]이곳에서 전시가 끝나면 인접해 있는 조지타운으로 운송되어 약 두 달 동안 조지타운 과학연구소에 전시될 예정이다.

어휘 prestigious 권위 있는 put on (행사 등을) 준비하다, 상연하다 audience 관중 supplement 보완하다 illustration 삽화 publically 공개적으로 under construction 구축 중인, 작업 중인 conceptualize 개념화하다, 구상하다 enlist (협력, 참여를) 요청하여 얻다 expertise 전문기술[지식] tremendous 거대한, 엄청난 top 뛰어넘다, 1위를 하다 transport 운송하다 neighboring 인접한, 인근의 approximately 대략

수신: 〈jillbradford@midwestern.com〉
발신: 〈kevinshaw@gomail.net〉
날짜: 4월 22일
제목: 최근 기사

브래드퍼드 씨께,

최근 찰스턴 중앙박물관이 중서부 예술과학상을 수상한 것에 관해 보도해주셔서 처음엔 기뻤습니다. [195]그런데 제 이름이 나오는 부분을 기다리며 들떠서 기사를 읽던 도중, 제가 했던 작업이 피오나 왓슨의 공으로 잘못 돌려진 것을 발견했습니다. 피오나 왓슨은 그 과정에서 단지 조언자 역할을 했을 뿐입니다. 매우 실망스러웠습니다. 앞으로는 기사를 쓰실 때 좀 더 철저한 조사를 해주셨으면 합니다.

케빈 쇼

어휘 coverage 보도 attribute ~ 덕분으로 여기다, ~의 공으로 돌리다 merely 단지 disappointing 실망스러운 encourage 권하다 carry out 수행하다 thorough 철저한

191 세부 사항

번역 공지의 대상은?
(A) 박물관 직원
(B) 잠재 전시자
(C) 재정 기부자
(D) 대학생

해설 공지의 첫 번째 단락에서 지난 수년간 후한 기부금으로 후원해준 사람들(As someone who has supported our institution with generous donations over the years)을 축하 행사에 초대하고 있으므로, (C)가 정답이다.

▶▶ Paraphrasing 지문의 someone who has supported our institution with generous donations → 정답의 Financial donors

192 동의어 찾기 고난도

번역 공지에서 1번째 단락 1행의 "mark"와 의미상 가장 가까운 것은?
(A) 규정하다
(B) 평가하다
(C) 기리다
(D) 낙인 찍다

해설 'mark'가 포함된 부분은 '과학전시회의 개막을 기념하기 위해(to mark the opening of the science exhibition)'라는 의미로 해석되는데, 여기서 mark는 '(중요 사건을) 기념하다, 기리다'라는 뜻으로 쓰였다. 따라서 '(중요성, 우수성을) 인정하다, 기리다'라는 의미의 (C) acknowledge가 정답이다.

193 사실 관계 확인

번역 중서부 예술과학상 시상식에 관해 알 수 있는 것은?
(A) 이전에는 개최되지 않았다.
(B) 찰스턴 중앙박물관에서 열렸다.
(C) 타카하시 씨가 주최했다.
(D) 생방송으로 진행되었다.

해설 기사의 첫 번째 단락에서 찰스턴 중앙박물관이 사상 최초로 열린 중서부 예술과학상 시상식(the first-ever Midwestern Arts & Science Awards ceremony)에서 학술문헌상을 받았다고 했으므로, 시상식이 이전에 개최된 적이 없다는 것을 알 수 있다. 따라서 (A)가 정답이다.

어휘 previously 이전에

▶▶ Paraphrasing 지문의 first-ever → 정답의 not been held previously

194 연계 고난도

번역 6월 1일에 무슨 일이 있겠는가?
(A) 수상 후보 지명 기간이 시작된다.
(B) 온라인에서 일부 교육 자료가 공개된다.
(C) 강연회가 모금단체의 후원을 받을 것이다.
(D) 전시회가 다른 도시로 옮겨갈 것이다.

해설 공지의 마지막 단락에서 '보이지 않는 세계: 미생물' 전시회가 3월 3일부터 5월 31일까지 진행된다("The Invisible World: Microorganisms" will run from March 3 to May 31)고 했는데, 기사의 마지막 단락을 보면 박물관에서 전시가 끝난 후 인접해 있는 조지타운으로 운송되어(After its run there comes to an end, it will be transported to neighboring Georgetown) 약 두 달 동안 조지타운 과학연구소에 전시될 예정이라고 되어 있다. 따라서 (D)가 정답이다.

어휘 nomination (후보 등의) 지명 release 공개하다

▶▶ **Paraphrasing** 지문의 it will be transported to neighboring Georgetown → 정답의 An exhibition will move to a different town

195 연계　　　　　　　　　　　　　　[고난도]

번역　쇼 씨는 무엇을 했겠는가?
(A) 정보 꾸러미를 위한 삽화를 제공했다.
(B) 기관을 대표해 수상했다.
(C) 전시회의 기본 아이디어를 구상했다.
(D) 박물관 전시물을 만들었다.

해설　이메일의 중반부에서 쇼 씨는 기사를 읽던 도중 자신이 한 작업이 피오나 왓슨의 공으로 잘못 돌려진 것을 발견했다(as I read through the article ~ I found that my work had been mistakenly attributed to Fiona Watson)며 문제점을 제기했다. 기사의 마지막 단락을 보면, 건축가 피오나 왓슨의 지식 및 전문기술의 힘을 빌려 전시물이 제작되었다(who enlisted the knowledge and expertise of architect Fiona Watson to construct the exhibits)고 했으므로, 이 작업이 쇼 씨가 한 것이라고 추론할 수 있다. 따라서 (D)가 정답이다.

어휘　on behalf of ~을 대표하여　display 전시(품)

▶▶ **Paraphrasing** 지문의 construct the exhibits → Constructed some museum displays

196-200 신청 양식 + 이메일 + 첨부물

소토릭 시
임시 음식 시설 신청서

특별 행사 기간 중 소토릭 시내에서 임시 식음 시설을 운영할 수 있는 허가를 받으려면 이 양식을 제출해 주십시오.

신청자: 린 맥킨리　　　　　행사명: 세계 공예 축제
업체: 린즈 타코스　　　　　주최: 소토릭 관광청
주소: 웨스트 로 32번지, 소토릭, 뉴욕 47372　날짜: 5월 8~10일
전화: 555-0153　　　　　위치: 소토릭 대공원

첨부 자료 (달리 명시하지 않는 한 필수 제출):
(a) 식품/음료 준비 및 제공을 위해 현장에서 사용될 모든 시설 및 장비의 사진
(b) 판매될 모든 식품/음료 품목 목록 및 사전 포장되지 않은 모든 품목의 성분
(c) ¹⁹⁶소토릭 시청 앞으로 보내는 50달러 수표, 신청서가 행사 10일 전 이내에 제출되는 경우에는 100달러
(d) ¹⁹⁸소토릭 보건국의 검사 증명서 (시설에서 가스로 작동하는 기구를 사용하고자 하는 판매자에 한하여 필요)

지원자 서명: 린 맥킨리
날짜: 4월 19일

어휘　temporary 임시의　facility 시설　ingredient 성분　non-prepackaged 사전에 포장되지 않은　payable to (수표 등이) ~를 수취인으로 하는　certificate 증명서　inspection 검사, 조사　vendor 판매업자　intend 계획하다, 의도하다

수신: 에인절 뮤노즈 외 3명
발신: 린 맥킨리
날짜: 5월 3일
제목: 세계 공예 축제 부스
첨부: 일정, 축제 지도

모두 안녕하세요,

이번 주말 세계 공예 축제에서 린즈 타코스의 일원으로 참석하는 데 동의해줘서 고마워요. ¹⁹⁹첨부된 일정표에 나온 지침을 ¹⁹⁷따르는 것 외에도, 시에서 발행한 식품안전 점검표를 오전 근무조가 작성해야 한다는 점 알아두세요. 그리고 금요일과 토요일 오후 근무조는 식품을 주의 깊게 보관하고 부스를 잠가야 한다는 점도 유념하시기 바래요. 실제 식품 판매 시간은 교대 시간보다 30분 늦게 시작해 30분 일찍 끝나므로 이 업무를 하기에 시간이 충분할 거예요.

¹⁹⁸저녁 손님이 몰리기 전에 물량이 떨어지기 시작하거나, 가스 그릴이 작동을 멈추거나(전에도 있었던 일), 다른 문제가 발생하면 주말 내내 식당을 관리하고 있을 저나 그레디에게 연락하세요.

고마워요.

린

어휘　represent ~를 대표하다, ~의 일원으로 참석하다　in addition to ~ 외에도　instruction 지침　shift (교대) 근무조, 근무시간　fill out 작성하다　plenty of 많은　run low 떨어지다, 부족하게 되다

린즈 타코스

세계 공예 축제 일정

	금요일	토요일	일요일
¹⁹⁹오전 근무조 ²⁰⁰(오전 9시30분 - 오후 2시)	린 광선	린 ¹⁹⁹론	댈러스 광선
오후 근무조 (오후 2시-6시)	에인절 댈러스	에인절 켄	댈러스 린

• 4번가의 판매자 전용 주차장 및 출입구를 사용하세요.
• 신분증을 지참하세요. (판매자 명단과 대조하여 이름 확인 예정)
• ²⁰⁰부스에 도착할 시간이 있도록 최소한 15분 일찍 도착하세요.

196 세부 사항

번역　맥킨리 씨가 양식과 함께 제공하도록 요구 받은 것은?
(A) 직원 명단
(B) 임시 시설의 청사진
(C) 사업자등록증 사본
(D) 관공서 지불금

해설　신청 양식의 첨부 자료 목록에서 소토릭 시청 앞으로 보내는 수표를 함께 제출해달라(A check payable to Sotorik City Hall for $50 OR ~ $100)고 했으므로, (D)가 정답이다. 다른 보기는 목록에 명시되어 있지 않다.

▶▶ **Paraphrasing** 지문의 A check payable to Sotorik City Hall → 정답의 A payment to a government office

197 동의어 찾기

번역 이메일에서 1번째 단락 2행의 "following"과 의미상 가장 가까운 것은?
(A) ~을 준수하는
(B) 이해하는
(C) 동반하는
(D) 차후의

해설 'following'을 포함한 부분은 '첨부된 일정의 지침을 따르는 것 외에 (In addition to following the instructions on the attached schedule)'라는 의미로 해석된다. 따라서 '준수하는, 따르는'이라는 의미의 (A) complying with가 정답이다.

198 연계 〔고난도〕

번역 맥킨리 씨에 관해 암시된 것은?
(A) 신청이 급히 처리되어야 했다.
(B) 장비가 검사를 통과했다.
(C) 음식 촬영 전문 사진작가를 고용했다.
(D) 요리기구를 대여하기로 했다.

해설 이메일의 두 번째 단락에서 맥킨리 씨는 축제에서 가스 그릴이 작동을 멈추면 자신이나 그래디에게 연락하라(if the gas grill stops working ~ please contact me or Grady)고 했는데, 신청 양식의 첨부 자료 목록을 보면 가스로 작동하는 기구를 사용하고자 하는 판매자(vendors intending to use gas-powered appliances in their facility)는 소토릭 보건국의 검사 증명서(A certificate of inspection from the Sotorik Department of Health)를 제출해야 한다고 되어 있다. 따라서 맥킨리 씨가 축제에서 사용할 가스 그릴이 장비 검사를 통과했을 것으로 추론할 수 있으므로, (B)가 정답이다.

어휘 expedite 급히[신속히] 처리하다

199 연계 〔고난도〕

번역 론은 직장 동료와 무엇을 하겠는가?
(A) 서류 작성하기
(B) 축제 현장까지 승용차 같이 타기
(C) 회사 자산 지키기
(D) 비품 들고 오기

해설 첨부된 일정표에서 론이 오전 근무조(Early Shift)에 속해 있음을 확인할 수 있다. 이메일의 첫 단락을 보면, 오전 근무조가 시에서 발행한 식품안전 점검표를 작성해야 한다(there will be a city-issued food safety checklist that the early shift workers must fill out)고 쓰여 있으므로, 그가 동료와 함께 점검표를 작성할 거라고 추론할 수 있다. 따라서 (A)가 정답이다.

▶▶ **Paraphrasing** 지문의 **fill out**
→ 정답의 **complete**
지문의 **a city-issued food safety checklist**
→ 정답의 **some paperwork**

200 추론 / 암시

번역 첨부파일에서 세계 공예 축제의 판매자들에 관해 암시된 것은?
(A) 상품 종류별로 분류된다.
(B) 신분증을 받는다.
(C) 매일 오전 9시 30분 이전에 입장할 수 있다.
(D) 월요일에 부스를 해체할 수 있다.

해설 맥킨리 씨가 직원들에게 전달한 일정표 하단을 보면 부스에 도착할 시간이 있도록 최소한 15분 일찍 도착하라(Arrive at least 15 minutes early so that you have time to get to the booth)고 되어 있다. 일정표에 따르면 오전 근무조(Early Shift)가 오전 9시 30분에 시작하므로, 판매자들은 그 이전에 입장이 가능할 것으로 추론할 수 있다. 따라서 (C)가 정답이다.

어휘 merchandise 상품   disassemble 해체하다

TEST 7

101 (B)	102 (D)	103 (A)	104 (C)	105 (B)
106 (C)	107 (C)	108 (D)	109 (D)	110 (B)
111 (C)	112 (A)	113 (A)	114 (B)	115 (B)
116 (A)	117 (C)	118 (D)	119 (B)	120 (C)
121 (D)	122 (D)	123 (A)	124 (A)	125 (C)
126 (D)	127 (B)	128 (A)	129 (C)	130 (B)
131 (D)	132 (B)	133 (D)	134 (D)	135 (B)
136 (A)	137 (C)	138 (A)	139 (C)	140 (D)
141 (C)	142 (B)	143 (A)	144 (A)	145 (D)
146 (B)	147 (C)	148 (A)	149 (B)	150 (D)
151 (D)	152 (C)	153 (C)	154 (B)	155 (A)
156 (B)	157 (C)	158 (B)	159 (D)	160 (A)
161 (A)	162 (A)	163 (B)	164 (D)	165 (B)
166 (C)	167 (D)	168 (B)	169 (C)	170 (A)
171 (B)	172 (C)	173 (D)	174 (A)	175 (C)
176 (A)	177 (A)	178 (B)	179 (D)	180 (C)
181 (D)	182 (C)	183 (D)	184 (C)	185 (B)
186 (D)	187 (D)	188 (C)	189 (D)	190 (B)
191 (A)	192 (C)	193 (D)	194 (C)	195 (A)
196 (C)	197 (A)	198 (B)	199 (B)	200 (D)

PART 5

101 소유대명사 _ 전치사의 목적어 　고난도

해설 전치사 in의 목적어 역할을 하는 자리로, 빈칸을 포함한 전치사구는 동사원형 park를 수식한다. 따라서 빈칸에는 주차 장소를 가리키는 대명사가 들어가야 하므로, Mr. Ezra's parking space를 대신하는 소유대명사 (B) his가 정답이다.

번역 로이 씨의 주차공간이 입구에서 멀리 떨어져 있어, 에즈라 씨는 친절하게도 부상이 나을 때까지 로이 씨가 자신의 주차공간에 주차하는 데 동의했다.

어휘 entrance 입구　injury 부상　heal 낫다

102 명사 자리 _ 동사의 주어

해설 형용사 powerful과 분사구 provided by the Yarov-A coat's fabric의 수식을 받는 명사 자리로, will make sure의 주어 역할을 한다. 따라서 '보호'라는 의미의 명사인 (D) protection이 정답이다. (A) protected는 동사/과거분사, (B) protects는 동사, (C) protectively는 부사로 품사상 빈칸에 들어갈 수 없다.

번역 야로브-A 코트 원단은 보온성이 강력해 세계에서 가장 추운 곳에서도 따뜻하게 지낼 수 있게 해준다.

어휘 fabric 직물, 원단　protect 보호하다

103 명사 어휘 　고난도

해설 빈칸을 포함한 분사구문(Designed ~ as possible)이 로린 컨벤션 센터가 다양한 행사를 열기에 이상적인 장소(an ideal venue for a wide variety of events)가 되는 근거를 제시하고 있다. 따라서 해당 부분은 다양한 요구에 부합하는 센터의 특성을 나타내야 하므로, '융통성, 유연성'이

라는 의미의 (A) flexibility가 정답이다.

번역 융통성을 최대한 발휘하도록 설계된 로린 컨벤션 센터는 다양한 행사를 열기에 이상적인 장소다.

어휘 ideal 이상적인　venue (행사) 장소　a wide variety of 다양한　enthusiasm 열정　financing 자금 조달　accuracy 정확도

104 전치사 어휘

해설 명사 years와 결합해 동사 has been providing을 수식하는 전치사 자리이다. 따라서 현재완료와 어울려 쓰여 '~동안'이라는 의미를 나타내는 (C) for가 정답이다. 참고로, (A) in도 years와 함께 '수년간, 오랫동안'이라는 의미로 쓰일 수 있지만, not이나 최상급이 포함된 문장에서만 가능하다. (D) during 뒤에는 특정 기간을 나타내는 명사(구)가 온다.

번역 패티슨 은행은 오랫동안 갓 대학을 졸업한 사람들에게 신입으로 일할 기회를 제공해 왔다.

어휘 opportunity 기회　recent 최근의　university graduate 대졸자

105 부사 어휘

해설 동사 face를 적절히 수식하는 부사를 선택해야 한다. 경쟁이 치열한 사업 환경(competitive business environment)에서 새로운 문제들에 직면하는 상황을 묘사한 문장이므로, '끊임없이, 빈번히'라는 의미의 (B) constantly가 빈칸에 들어가야 자연스럽다. 참고로, '다양한 문제들에 직면한다(face diverse challenges)'라고 할 수는 있지만 diversely가 face를 수식해 '문제들에 다양하게 직면한다'라고 하는 것은 어색하다.

번역 특히 경쟁이 치열한 오늘날 사업 환경에서 식당 주인들은 끊임없이 새로운 문제들에 직면한다.

어휘 competitive 경쟁이 치열한　environment 환경　heavily 심하게, 무겁게　diversely 다양하게　variably 일정하지 않게, 변하기 쉽게

106 명사 어휘

해설 동사 affect의 목적어 역할을 하는 명사 자리로, 전치사구 of your computer의 수식을 받는다. 따라서 빈칸에는 소프트웨어 업데이트 시 영향을 받는 대상이 들어가야 하므로, '성능'이라는 의미의 (C) performance가 정답이다.

번역 바이러스 백신 소프트웨어는 업데이트 실행 시 일시적으로 컴퓨터의 성능에 영향을 줄 수 있다.

어휘 temporarily 잠시　affect 영향을 주다　innovation 혁신　measurement 측정　representation 묘사, 대의권

107 부사 자리 _ 동사 수식 _ 비교급

해설 소셜 미디어 마케팅과 텔레비전 광고를 비교하는 문장으로, 빈칸에는 동사 reaches를 수식하는 비교급 부사가 들어가야 한다. 따라서 than과 함께 '~보다 더 효과적으로'라는 의미를 나타내는 (C) more effectively가 정답이다. (A) effective는 형용사, (B) effectively는 원급 부사, (D) effectiveness는 명사로 빈칸에 들어갈 수 없다.

번역 시장 보고서는 소셜 미디어 마케팅이 텔레비전 광고보다 젊은 소비자들에게 더 효과적으로 다가간다는 점을 시사했다.

어휘 indicate 나타내다, 시사하다 consumer 소비자 effective
효과적인 effectiveness 유효(성)

108 동사 어휘

해설 주방 제품 회사가 자사의 목표를 설명하는 문장이므로, '최고 품질의 주방
기구를 생산/제공하고자 한다'라는 내용이 되어야 자연스럽다. 따라서 '생
산하다'라는 의미의 (D) produce가 정답이다. 참고로, (C) remain은 자
동사/연결동사로 목적어를 취할 수 없다.

번역 클레바라틱스 서플라이는 전문 요리사를 위한 최고 품질의 주방기구 생산을
목표로 한다.

어휘 supply 공급(품) aim 목표로 하다 equipment 기구 commit
전념하다, 맡기다 earn 얻다 remain 남다, 여전히 ~이다

109 접속사 / 전치사 어휘

해설 learning을 동명사로 볼 경우 전치사가, 현재분사로 볼 경우 부사절에
서 축약된 분사구문을 이끄는 부사절 접속사가 들어갈 수 있다. 내용을
살펴보면 기타를 배우는 것과 관련된 일반적인 조언을 하고 있으므로,
'~할 때'라는 뜻의 (D) When이 빈칸에 들어가야 자연스럽다. 참고로,
(A) Whether는 분사구문으로 축약된 부사절을 이끌 수 없다.

번역 기타를 배울 때는 프란마우어-5처럼 내구성이 좋은 모델로 연습하세요.

어휘 durable 내구성이 좋은, 튼튼한

110 명사 어휘

해설 빈칸이 포함된 to부정사구는 동일한 고객번호가 두 번 이상 입력될 시
(if the same client number is entered) 알림이 뜨게 하는 목
적을 나타낸다. 따라서 '중복을 방지하기 위해'라는 의미를 완성하는
(B) duplication(중복, 복제)이 정답이다.

번역 기록 중복을 방지하기 위해 데이터베이스에 동일한 고객번호가 두 번 이상 입
력되면 알림이 뜬다.

어휘 prevent 방지하다, 예방하다 notification 알림 transportation
전송 organization 조직 differentiation 차별

111 부사 자리 _ to부정사 수식 〔고난도〕

해설 to부정사의 to 뒤에서 decline을 수식하는 부사 자리이므로, '꾸준히, 끊
임없이'라는 의미의 (C) steadily가 정답이다. 참고로, (A) steady는 형용
사/동사 외에 부사(흔들리지 않게, 안정되게)로도 쓰일 수 있지만, 이 경우
동사의 뒤에 위치해야 한다.

번역 온라인으로 옮겨 가는 업체가 늘면서 간판과 현수막 판매량이 계속해서 꾸준
히 감소하고 있다.

어휘 continue to 계속 ~하다 decline 감소하다 steady 꾸준한;
진정시키다, 안정되다; 안정되게

112 전치사 어휘

해설 '바닥을 미끄럼 방지 마감(non-slip finish)으로 처리하라고 권고했다'라
는 내용이므로, 수단/도구를 나타내는 전치사 (A) with(~로, ~를 가지
고)가 정답이다. 참고로, 여기서 treat는 '(~를 사용하여) 처리하다'라는

뜻으로 「treat A with B」 구조로 쓰였다.

번역 안전 컨설턴트는 업무현장 사고를 예방하기 위해 바닥에 미끄럼 방지 마감 처
리를 하라고 권고했다.

어휘 flooring 바닥재 non-slip finish 미끄럼 방지 마감

113 형용사 어휘 _ 과거분사 〔고난도〕

해설 community center를 적절히 수식하는 과거분사를 선택하는 문제이
다. 건설 공사에 대해 경과 보고(a progress report on the construction)를 한다는 것은 주민센터가 곧 지어질 예정임을 의미하므로, '계획된,
예정된'이라는 뜻의 (A) planned가 정답이다.

번역 다음 시청 회의에서는 관계자들이 예정된 주민센터 건립에 대한 경과 보고를
할 예정이다.

어휘 official 관계자, 공무원 nominated 후보로 지명된 acquainted
안면이 있는 relieved 안도하는

114 명사 자리 _ 동사의 목적어

해설 「동사(help)+목적어(young children)+목적격 보어(gain ~
concepts)」의 구조에서 gain의 목적어 역할을 하는 명사 자리이다. 따
라서 '익숙함, (특정 주제에) 정통함'이라는 의미의 (B) familiarity가 정
답이다. (A) familiarly는 부사, (C) familiarized는 동사/과거분사,
(D) more familiar는 비교급 형용사로 품사상 빈칸에 들어갈 수 없다.

번역 스마트-텍 사는 어린 아이들이 과학적 개념에 익숙해지도록 돕는 교육용 장
난감을 만든다.

어휘 gain 얻다 familiarly 친근하게 familiarized 익숙해진, 정통한
familiar 익숙한

115 부사 어휘 〔고난도〕

해설 콤마 뒤 주절에서는 부지 밖 창고를 활용하는 것이 경제적인 해결책(a
very affordable solution)이라고 주장하고 있는데, 빈칸이 포함된 절은
Though(비록 ~일지라도)로 시작하여 양보·대조의 의미를 나타내고 있
다. 따라서 일부 관리자들은 해당 주장과 다른 생각을 가지고 있을지도 모
른다는 내용이 되어야 자연스러우므로, '달리'라는 뜻의 (B) otherwise가
정답이다. 참고로, otherwise는 say, think, decide와 같은 동사 뒤에
붙어 '다르게[다른 방식으로] ~하다'라는 표현으로 쓰인다. (A) particularly, (C) moreover, (D) formerly의 경우 문장(절) 끝에 쓰이지 않기
때문에 구조상으로도 빈칸에 들어갈 수 없다.

번역 일부 관리자들은 생각이 다를 수도 있겠지만, 오래된 종이 문서를 보관하기
위해 부지 밖 창고를 활용하는 것은 굉장히 경제적인 해결책이다.

어휘 off-site 부지 밖의 storage 창고, 저장 affordable (가격이)
경제적인, 적당한 solution 해결책 particularly 특히
moreover 게다가 formerly 이전에

116 전치사 자리 _ 어휘

해설 명사 experience를 목적어로 취하는 전치사 자리로, (A) regardless
of, (B) instead of, (D) as much as 중 하나를 선택해야 한다. 많은 기
업가들(Many entrepreneurs) 저지른다고 한 것으로 보아 경험의 유무
와는 상관없는 실수임을 알 수 있다. 따라서 '~와 상관없이'라는 의미의
(A) regardless of가 정답이 된다.

번역 많은 기업가들이 경험과 상관없이 사업을 너무 빨리 확장하는 실수를 저지르기도 한다.

어휘 entrepreneur 기업가 expand 확장하다 instead of ~ 대신 nevertheless 그렇지만

117 동사 어형_조동사 + 동사원형_태

해설 조동사 can 뒤의 동사원형 자리로, 보기에서 (B) raise와 (C) be raised 중 하나를 선택해야 한다. 관계사절의 동사는 선행사(chairs and desks)와 수·태가 일치해야 하는데, 의자와 책상은 높이가 조정될 수 있는 대상이므로, 수동태 동사어형인 (C) be raised가 정답이다.

번역 다음에 사무용 가구를 구매할 때는 다양한 높이로 올릴 수 있는 의자와 책상으로 골랐으면 합니다.

어휘 propose 제안하다 a variety of 다양한 height 높이

118 동사 어휘

해설 명사구 all of its produce를 목적어로 취하는 동사 자리로, 전치사구 from local organic farms의 수식을 받는다. 지역 유기 농장은 농산물을 구해오는 곳이라고 볼 수 있으므로, '얻다, 입수하다'라는 의미의 (D) obtains가 정답이다.

번역 수나라 식품시장은 모든 농산물을 지역 유기 농장에서 구해온다.

어휘 produce 농산물 succeed 뒤를 잇다, 성공하다 proceed 진행하다 intend 의도하다

119 목적격 보어 자리_과거분사 [고난도]

해설 「동명사(Keeping)+목적어(your customers)+목적격 보어」 구조에서 customers를 보충 설명하는 목적격 보어 자리로, 부사 fully의 수식을 받는다. 따라서 형용사 역할을 하는 (B) satisfied와 (C) satisfying 중 하나를 선택해야 한다. 고객들은 만족을 느끼게 되는 대상이므로, 수동의 의미를 내포한 과거분사 (B) satisfied가 정답이 된다.

번역 고객들이 전적으로 만족감을 느끼도록 유지하는 일은 대체로 능숙하게 불만사항을 해결하는 역량에 좌우된다.

어휘 depend on ~에 좌우되다 resolve 해결하다 professional 능숙한, 전문적인 satisfy 만족시키다

120 재귀대명사 어휘 [고난도]

해설 that이 이끄는 관계사절에서 can teach의 목적어 역할을 하는 재귀대명사를 선택해야 한다. 주격 관계대명사 that이 3인칭 단수명사 robot를 대신하므로, 이를 되가리키는 (C) itself가 정답이다.

번역 노바레이크 테크 사 연구원들은 기초적인 새 과업을 스스로 학습할 수 있는 로봇을 개발해 오고 있다.

어휘 researcher 연구원

121 동사 자리

해설 주어인 Digital videos의 동사 자리로, larger amounts of data를 목적어로 취한다. 따라서 동사 자리에 들어갈 수 있는 (D) require이 정답이다. 동명사/현재분사 (A) requiring과 (C) having required, to부정사 (B) to require은 모두 준동사로 문장의 동사 자리에 들어갈 수 없다.

번역 디지털 동영상은 특히 고화질로 볼 때 대다수 다른 애플리케이션보다 더 많은 데이터가 필요하다.

어휘 amount 양 especially 특히 high definition 고화질 require 요구하다

122 전치사 어휘

해설 '(기간이) 연장되다'라는 뜻의 동사 extend와 시점을 나타내는 June을 적절히 연결해 주는 전치사가 들어가야 한다. 따라서 '~을 넘겨, ~을 지나'라는 의미의 (D) past가 정답이다.

번역 도로 개선 사업은 몇 차례 지연되었는데, 소식통에 따르면 공사가 6월을 지나서까지 연장될 수도 있다고 한다.

어휘 improvement 개선 sources 소식통, 정보원

123 형용사 자리_목적격 보어_어휘

해설 「동사(has made)+목적어(importing goods from the United States)+목적격 보어(more ~ us)」 구조에서 more의 수식을 받으며 목적격 보어 역할을 하는 형용사 자리이다. 문맥상 달러화 가치의 하락(drop in the value of the dollar)으로 미국 제품 수입이 더 많은 이윤을 내게 되었다는 내용이 되어야 자연스럽다. 따라서 more 및 for와 함께 '~에게 더 이익이 되는, ~를 위해 더 이윤을 내는'이라는 의미를 완성하는 형용사 (A) profitable이 정답이다. (C) profiting을 자동사(이익을 얻다)에서 파생된 현재분사로 보더라도, 문맥상 어색하며 전치사 by/from과 쓰여야 하기 때문에 빈칸에는 들어갈 수 없다.

번역 최근 달러화 가치가 하락하면서 미국에서 상품을 수입하는 것이 우리에게 더 이득이 되었다.

어휘 recent 최근의 import 수입하다 profitable 이익이 되는 profitability 수익성 profit 이익[소득]을 주다[얻다]; 이점, 이익

124 접속사 자리_어휘

해설 빈칸이 두 개의 완전한 절 사이에 있으므로, 접속사인 (A) once와 (C) whereas 중 하나를 선택해야 한다. 사용적합성 테스트가 완료 되어야(complete usability testing) 새 웹사이트가 출시될 수 있으므로, '일단 ~하면, ~하자마자'라는 의미의 (A) once가 정답이 된다. (B) ever는 부사, (D) upon은 전치사로 절을 이끌 수 없다.

번역 새로운 웹사이트는 개발자들이 사용적합성 테스트를 완료하자마자 출시될 예정이다.

어휘 be expected to ~할 예정이다 usability test 사용적합성 테스트 whereas ~이지만

125 부사 어휘

해설 동사 will work를 적절히 수식하는 부사를 선택하는 문제로, 박물관 직원들(museum's staff)과 IT 전문가들 팀(team of IT experts)이 일하는 방식을 묘사하는 부사가 들어가야 자연스럽다. 따라서 '협업하여, 협력적으로'라는 의미의 (C) collaboratively가 정답이다.

번역 박물관 직원들과 IT 전문가들로 구성된 팀이 협업해 가상현실 전시회를 기획할 것이다.

어휘 expert 전문가 virtual reality 가상현실 exhibit 전시회
relatively 비교적[상대적]으로 unusually 대단히, 특이하게
absently 멍하니

126 형용사 어휘 고난도

해설 주어인 company negotiators를 보충 설명하는 형용사 자리이다. 합
병 논의가 더디게 진행되고 있는 불리한 상황이지만(Although the
merger discussions have progressed slowly) 회사의 교섭자들은
협상이 타결되리라 생각한다는 내용이므로, 빈칸에는 이들의 긍정적인 태
도를 나타내는 단어가 들어가야 자연스럽다. 따라서 '낙관적인'이라는 의미
의 (D) optimistic이 정답이다.

번역 합병 논의는 더디게 진행되어 왔지만 회사 교섭자들은 협상이 타결되리라 낙
관하고 있다.

어휘 merger 합병 negotiator 교섭자 deal 협상 ongoing 진행되는
probable 가능한, 개연성 있는 dedicated 헌신하는

127 부사절 접속사

해설 빈칸 뒤 완전한 절(regular deadlines are met)을 이끄는 접속사 자리
이므로, '~을 전제로, ~라면'이라는 의미의 부사절 접속사 (B) provided
that이 정답이다. 참고로, 여기서 that은 생략될 수 있다. (A) as for,
(C) concerning, (D) in case of는 모두 전치사로 절을 이끌 수 없다.

번역 새로운 정책에 따르면 일부 선정된 직원들은 정기 마감일을 맞춘다는 것을 전
제로 재택근무를 할 수 있다.

어휘 meet a deadline 마감일을 맞추다 as for ~에 관해 말하면
concerning ~에 관한 in case of ~의 경우

128 동사 어휘

해설 빈칸을 포함한 부사절이 로즈마리가 이탈리아 요리에서 가장 흔하게 사
용되는 허브(the most commonly used herbs)인 이유를 설명하
고 있다. 로즈마리(the plant)가 이탈리아 지역의 따뜻하고 건조한 기후
(the region's warm, dry climate)에서 잘 자라고 많이 생산되기 때
문이라는 내용이 되어야 자연스러우므로, '잘 자라다, 번성하다'라는 의미
의 (A) thrives가 정답이다. 참고로, (B) flatters, (C) characterizes,
(D) absorbs는 모두 타동사로 구조상으로도 빈칸에 들어갈 수 없다.

번역 로즈마리는 이탈리아 요리에서 가장 흔하게 사용되는 허브 중 하나인데, 왜냐
하면 그 지역의 따뜻하고 건조한 기후에서 잘 자라기 때문이다.

어휘 commonly 흔히 flatter 아첨하다 characterize 특징짓다
absorb 흡수하다

129 부사절의 축약 _ 분사구문 고난도

해설 빈칸이 부사절 접속사 If와 부사 incorrectly 사이에 있으므로, 빈
칸에는 절에서 축약된 분사구문이 들어갈 수 있다. 따라서 과거분
사 (C) installed가 정답이다. 참고로, 원래 구조는 If it is installed
incorrectly이다.

번역 소프트웨어 프로그램이 잘못 설치될 경우, 시작 메뉴에 오류 메시지가 표시된다.

어휘 incorrectly 잘못되게, 부정확하게 install 설치하다 display
표시하다

130 명사절 접속사 고난도

해설 주어가 없는 절(was discussed in the last department meeting)
을 이끄는 접속사 자리로, 빈칸이 이끄는 절이 전치사 of의 목적어 역할을
한다. 따라서 불완전한 절을 이끄는 명사절 접속사가 빈칸에 들어가야 하
므로, (B) what(~한 것)이 정답이다. (A) that은 명사절 접속사로 쓰일
경우 완전한 절을 이끌고, (C) everything과 (D) it은 대명사로 절을 이끌
수 없다.

번역 조 씨는 지난 부서회의에서 논의된 내용을 상세히 기록했다.

어휘 transcript 필기록

PART 6

131-134 이메일

수신: 돈 첸 〈don-chen@mail.org〉
발신: 브룬디 스토리지 〈brundy-storage@mail.com〉
날짜: 1월 30일
제목: 스페이스 1032 새 소식

첸 씨께,

브룬디 스토리지는 귀하가 저희와 계속해서 거래해 주시는 것에 대해 감사 드리
고 싶습니다.

최근 이 일대에서 보관 공간에 대한 **131**수요가 크게 늘면서 임대료가 올랐습니
다. 이런 시장 상황에 따라 3월 1일 일요일부터 스페이스 1032 월 임대료가
208달러로 변경될 **132**예정입니다.

이번 **133**조정에 따른 귀하의 임대료 인상분은 2%도 안 됩니다. **134**이 가격에도
여전히 충분한 값어치를 누리시는 것이니 안심하세요. 새 요금은 동일한 크기의
보관소를 처음 임대하는 고객이 현재 내는 요금보다 여전히 낮은 가격입니다.

다시 한 번, 브룬디 스토리지의 오랜 고객으로 거래해 주시는 점 감사드립니다.

브룬디 스토리지 경영진

어휘 appreciate 감사해 하다 loyalty 충성, 충실 rental rate
임대료 increase 오르다 due to ~ 때문에 condition 상황, 조건
represent 나타내다, 해당하다 current 현재의 grateful 감사해
하는

131 명사 어휘

해설 빈칸을 포함한 전치사구가 임대료 상승(rental rates have increased)
의 이유를 설명하고 있으므로, '더 늘어난 수요'라는 의미를 완성하는
(C) demand(수요, 요구)가 정답이다.

어휘 range 범위 sales 매출(량) renovation 수리

132 동사 어형 _ 시제

해설 주어 the new monthly rent의 동사 자리로, 시간 표현 starting on
Sunday, March 1의 수식을 받는다. 이메일을 쓴 날짜(Date: January
30)를 기준으로 새로운 월 임대료가 적용되는 시점(March 1)은 미래이
므로, (B) will be가 정답이다.

133 명사 자리 _ 동사의 주어 _ 어휘

해설 빈칸은 동사 represents의 주어 역할을 하는 명사 자리로, 지시형용사 This의 한정 수식을 받는다. 따라서 보기에서 명사인 (B) adjuster와 (D) adjustment 중 하나를 선택해야 한다. 2프로 미만의 임대료 인상분(less than a 2% increase in your rental rate)에 해당하는 (represent) 대상이 주어가 되어야 하므로, 앞서 언급된 월 임대료 인상을 가리키는 (D) adjustment(조정, 수정)가 정답이 된다. (B) adjuster는 '조정자'라는 뜻으로 문맥상 적절하지 않고, (A) adjusts는 동사, (C) adjustable은 형용사로 품사상 빈칸에 들어갈 수 없다.

어휘 adjust 조정하다 adjustable 조정할 수 있는

134 문맥에 맞는 문장 고르기 고난도

번역 (A) 이 문제에 관해 의견을 주신 모든 고객님들께 감사 드립니다.
(B) 임차인이 줄면서 당사가 지금 규모를 축소하고 있다는 점 강조하고 싶습니다.
(C) 임대차계약서의 약관은 크게 다를 수 있으므로 유의하세요.
(D) 이 가격에도 여전히 충분한 값어치를 누리시는 것이니 안심하세요.

해설 빈칸 앞 문장에서 임대료 인상이 미미함(less than a 2% increase in your rental rate)을 강조했고, 뒤에서는 새 요금이 처음 임대하는 고객이 내는 현 요금보다 여전히 싼 가격(Your new rate is still lower than the current rate for first-time customers renting a storage unit)이라고 했다. 따라서 빈칸에도 임대료 인상에 대해 첸 씨를 안심시키는 내용이 들어가야 자연스러우므로, (D)가 정답이다.

어휘 emphasize 강조하다 tenant 임차인 downsize (규모 등을) 축소하다 terms and conditions 약관 vary 다르다 rest assured 안심해도 된다 receive a good value 충분히 값어치 있는 것을 받다

135-138 웹페이지

페트랄라 퍼블리싱은 선두적인 출판사로, 손으로 직접 하는 미술 및 공예 취미를 가진 독자들의 135구미에 맞춘 교본을 발행하고 있습니다. 새로운 인재와 참신한 아이디어를 지원하는 일은 저희 사업에서 가장 중요한 부분을 차지합니다. 136그러한 이유로 당사는 이 분야의 서적에 추가로 유용한 기여를 하고 싶은 사람들에게 도서를 제안해 달라고 적극적으로 요청합니다. 137당사 편집팀은 책으로 나오면 좋을 만한 구상을 현실화할 수 있습니다. 수많은 당사 작가들에게 책을 쓰는 일은 언젠가 이루어지기 바랐던 138먼 꿈일 뿐이었습니다. 당사의 격려와 지도로 그들은 계속해서 멋진 신작을 만들어 출판했습니다. 제출 지침을 보시려면 여기를 클릭하세요.

어휘 publisher 출판사 instructional 교육의, 지도하는 hands-on 손으로 직접 해보는 actively 적극적으로 seek 구하다, 얻다 addition 추가 body ~의 모음, 많은 양 encouragement 격려 guidance 지도 submission 제출

135 동사 어형 _ 현재분사

해설 Petralla Publishing이 주어, is가 동사, a leading publisher of instructional books가 보어인 문장으로, 빈칸 이하가 instructional books를 수식하고 있다. 따라서 형용사 역할을 할 수 있는 준동사가 빈칸에 들어가야 하므로, 현재분사인 (B) catering이 정답이다. 문장에 이미 동사(is)가 있고 빈칸 앞에 접속사가 없으므로, 나머지 보기는 빈칸에 들어갈 수 없다.

어휘 cater to 구미에 맞추다, ~의 요구에 부응하다

136 접속부사

해설 빈칸 앞 문장에서 새로운 인재와 참신한 아이디어를 지원하는 일이 사업에서 가장 중요한 부분을 차지한다(Supporting fresh talent and ideas is a key part of our business)고 했고, 뒤에서는 사람들에게 도서를 제안해 달라고 적극적으로 요청한다(we actively seek book proposals from people)고 했다. 따라서 빈칸에는 기업의 특정 목표/과제와 그에 따른 행동을 자연스럽게 연결해주는 접속 부사가 들어가야 하므로, '그러한 이유로'라는 의미의 (A) For that reason이 정답이다.

어휘 by comparison 그에 비해 afterward 그후 alternatively 대신에

137 문맥에 맞는 문장 고르기 고난도

번역 (A) 어느 날 교육자들이 검토용으로 최근 서적들을 요청할 수 있습니다.
(B) 전화 약속을 잡아 이 문제에 대해 더 자세히 이야기하겠습니다.
(C) 당사 편집팀은 책으로 나오면 좋을 만한 구상을 현실화할 수 있습니다.
(D) 연구에 따르면 동화는 여전히 어린 독자들에게 더 인기가 있습니다.

해설 빈칸 앞 문장에서 사람들에게 도서를 제안해달라고 적극적으로 요청한다(we actively seek book proposals from people)고 했는데, 뒤에서는 수많은 작가들에게 책을 쓰는 일은 언젠가 이루어지기를 바랐던 꿈(For many of our authors, writing a book was only ~ something they had hoped to do someday)일 뿐이었지만 회사의 격려와 지도(With our encouragement and guidance)를 통해 그들이 이 꿈을 이뤘다고 덧붙였다. 따라서 빈칸에는 사람들의 제안을 실현하는 데 회사가 하는 역할과 관련된 내용이 들어가야 자연스러우므로, (C)가 정답이다.

어휘 title 서적 appointment 약속 editor 편집자 promising 성공할 것 같은, 유망한 fairy tale 동화 appeal 관심을 끌다, 매력적이다

138 형용사 어휘 고난도

해설 빈칸의 수식을 받는 dream이 something they had hoped to do someday와 동격 관계를 이루므로, 빈칸에는 그저 바라기만 했던 꿈의 특징을 묘사하는 형용사가 들어가야 문맥상 자연스럽다. 따라서 '먼, 동떨어진'이라는 의미의 (A) distant가 정답이다.

어휘 vacant 비어 있는, 멍한 subtle 미묘한, 교묘한 deep 깊은, 심오한

139-142 기사

도르트룬드 (3월 19일)—지난 토요일과 일요일에 열린 제25회 연례 도르트룬드 민속음악축제에 6,000명이 넘는 기록적인 군중이 모였다. 주최측에 따르면, 이렇게 엄청난 139참석자 수는 올해 행사의 새로운 특색 덕분이라고 한다. 140예를 들어, 더욱 다양한 음악 스타일이 선보였다. 사상 처음으로 공연 출연진에 인기 포크 그룹뿐만 아니라 쿠바 맘보밴드, 폴란드 무용단, 141심지어 재즈 독주자까지 포함되었다. 다양한 전통악기 연주 기법을 보여주기 위해 142기획된 실습 워크숍에 참석자들이 참여할 수 있는 기회도 있었다. 주최측은 인기가 많았던 이 두 가지 변동 사항 모두 내년 축제까지 이어질 것이라고 말한다.

어휘 annual 연례의 draw 끌어들이다 organizer 주최자

impressive 인상적인　credit ~의 공으로 돌리다　feature 특징,
특색　lineup 출연진　ensemble 합주단, 무용단　attendee 참석자
various 다양한　instrument 악기　carry over 계속하다

139　명사 어휘　고난도

해설　this impressive의 수식을 받는 명사 자리로, 문장의 주어 역할을 한다.
이 주어가 앞 문장에서 언급한 '6,000명이 넘는 기록적인 군중(a record
crowd of over 6,000 people)'을 가리키므로, 빈칸에는 참석자의 규
모를 나타내는 명사가 들어가야 한다. 따라서 '참석자 수'라는 의미의
(C) turnout이 정답이다.

어휘　prize 상　funding 기금　rating 등급

140　문맥에 맞는 문장 고르기

번역　(A) 그들은 전통 문화가 앞으로도 계속 바뀔 수 있다고 말했다.
　　(B) 자원봉사자 모두 무료 식사와 특별 제작된 축제 티셔츠를 받았다.
　　(C) 사실, 음악에 대한 배경 지식이 있다고 해서 반드시 감상을 더 잘할 수 있
　　　　는 건 아니다.
　　(D) 예를 들어, 더욱 다양한 음악 스타일이 선보였다.

해설　빈칸 앞에서 참석자 수가 많아진 것은 올해 행사의 새로운 특색 덕분
이라고 했고(credited to the new features of this year's event)이라고 했고,
뒤에서 축제에 참여한 다양한 장르의 공연 출연진을 나열했다. 따라서 새
로운 특색의 예시로 다양해진 음악 스타일을 언급한 (D)가 빈칸에 들어가
야 자연스럽다.

어휘　background 배경 지식　appreciation 감상　diverse 다양한
represent 제시하다, 보여주다

141　부사 _ 명사구 강조

해설　빈칸에는 명사구 jazz soloists를 수식하는 한정사/형용사나 명사구를
강조하는 일부 부사가 들어갈 수 있다. 재즈 독주자가 쿠바 맘보밴드, 폴란
드 무용단과 함께 이례적으로 민속음악축제에 참가한 상황을 강조해야 자
연스러우므로, '심지어'라는 의미의 부사인 (C) even이 정답이다. 「not
only A but also B」에서 B에 해당하는 참가자들을 나열한 부분으로
(A) yet(그런데도, 더더구나)이 들어가기에는 어색하다. (B) very는 명사
를 수식할 경우 「한정사+very+명사」 구조로 쓰이며, (D) much는 불가
산명사와 쓰이므로 빈칸에 들어갈 수 없다.

142　동사 어형 _ 과거분사

해설　빈칸 앞에 완전한 절이, 뒤에 to부정사가 있으므로, 빈칸 이하가 명사
workshops를 수식하고 있음을 알 수 있다. 따라서 빈칸에는 형용사 역
할을 할 수 있는 준동사가 들어갈 수 있는데, 워크숍은 기획되는 대상이므
로, 수동의 의미를 내포한 과거분사 (B) designed가 정답이 된다.

143-146　정보문

텍사스 댈러스에서 열리는 HGA 연례 생활용품 무역박람회 – 참석해야 하는
이유

60여 년 동안, 생활용품협회(HGA)는 세계 유수의 제조업체들이 만든 생활용
품을 선보이는 업계 최대 규모의 무역박람회를 ¹⁴³개최해 왔습니다. 소매점 구

매담당자들은 도매 납품업체와 만나 사업 제휴를 맺을 기회를 잡기 위해 해마다
참석합니다. 귀사를 경쟁업체와 차별화하고 시장에서 우위를 확보하게 해줄 독
창적인 제품을 찾고 싶으십니까? ¹⁴⁴그저 박람회장을 걸어 다니면서 전시품을 둘러
보기만 하세요. 분명 혁신적이고 새로운 생활용품을 ¹⁴⁵발견하실 겁니다. ¹⁴⁶이
밖에도 업계 현안에 대한 담화와 워크숍도 있습니다. HGA 무역박람회에 참석하
시면 생활용품의 최신 동향에 대한 정보를 반드시 파악하실 수 있습니다.

어휘　household goods 생활용품　trade show 무역박람회
manufacturer 제조업체　purchase 구매하다　retail store
소매점　wholesale supplier 도매 납품업체　seize (기회 등을)
잡다　original 독창적인　merchandise 상품　distinguish
구별하다, 차별화하다　competitor 경쟁업체　gain 얻다　market
advantage 시장에서의 우위　explore 둘러보다, 탐사하다
innovative 혁신적인　attend 참석하다　assured 보장 받는　stay
up to date 최신 정보를 알다

143　동사 어형 _ 태 _ 시제

해설　주어 the Household Goods Association (HGA)의 동사 자리로, 명사
구 the industry's largest trade show를 목적어로 취한다. 따라서 능
동태 동사 중 하나를 선택해야 하는데, 과거부터 현재까지의 기간을 나타
내는 For more than 60 years의 수식을 받고 있으므로, 현재완료시제
인 (A) has hosted가 정답이 된다.

144　부사 어휘

해설　빈칸을 포함한 명령문은 앞 질문(Are you looking for original
merchandise to distinguish your business from competitors
and gain a market advantage?)에 대한 해결책을 제시하고 있다. 따
라서 이 방안이 얼마나 간단하고 쉬운지를 강조하는 부사가 들어가야 자연
스러우므로, '그저, 간단히'라는 의미의 (A) Simply가 정답이다.

어휘　lately 최근에　closely 면밀히, 밀접하게　shortly 곧

145　동사 어휘　고난도

해설　명사구 innovative new household products를 목적어로 취하
는 동사 자리이다. 앞 문장에서 독창적인 상품을 찾고 있다면(Are you
looking for original merchandise ~?) 박람회장에서 전시품을 둘러
보라고 권했으므로, 해당 부분은 그렇게 할 경우 반드시 혁신적인 제품을
찾게 될 거라는 내용이 되어야 자연스럽다. 따라서 '발견하다'라는 의미의
(D) discover가 정답이다.

어휘　utilize 이용하다　navigate 길을 찾다　demonstrate 시연하다

146　문맥에 맞는 문장 고르기　고난도

번역　(A) 집을 관리하는 기타 몇 가지 중요한 방법들이 있습니다.
　　(B) 이 밖에도 업계 현안에 대한 담화와 워크숍도 있습니다.
　　(C) 전시된 빈티지 아이템 중 몇 개는 50년이 넘었습니다.
　　(D) 용무를 다 보시면 저희가 제공하는 무료 점심 뷔페를 즐기세요.

해설　빈칸 앞 문장에서 박람회를 돌아보면 혁신적이고 새로운 생활용품을 발견
하게 될 것(discover innovative new household products)이라고
했고, 뒤에서는 생활용품의 최신 동향에 대한 정보를 파악할 수 있다(By
attending the HGA trade show, you are assured of staying up

to date on the latest trends in household goods)고 했다. 따라서 빈칸에도 생활용품 관련 정보를 얻을 수 있는 박람회에 대한 설명이 들어가야 자연스러우므로, (B)가 정답이다.

어휘 in addition 이 밖에도 complimentary 무료인

PART 7

147-148 공지

회의실 규정

지역사회 단체는 다음 조건 하에 클리어리 시 공공도서관 회의실을 무료로 이용할 수 있습니다. 회의실에서 개최되는 모든 지역사회 회의는 무료여야 하며 대중에게 공개되어야 합니다. 회의실은 도서관 정규 개관 시간에만 이용할 수 있습니다. 회의실 예약 요청은 도서관 온라인 예약 시스템을 통해 해야 합니다. 단체는 당월 또는 다음 달에 이용할 회의실을 예약할 수 있습니다. 어떤 경우에도 14일 기간 내에 회의실을 두 차례 이상 예약할 수 없습니다. **148예약은 선착순으로 접수됩니다.**

147모든 회의실에는 의자와 회의용 탁자가 구비되어 있다는 점 알아두세요. 회의실 신청 시 도서관 소유의 시청각 장비를 요청할 수 있으며, 반드시 도서관 카드로 대여해야 합니다.

어휘 available 이용 가능한 at no charge 무료로 (= free of charge) condition 조건 normal 정규의 request 요청 reserve 예약하다 via ~을 통해 reservation 예약 under no circumstances 어떠한 경우에도 ~ 않다 on a first-come, first-served basis 선착순으로 equipped with ~이 구비된 audiovisual equipment 시청각 장비 application 신청 check out (도서관 등에서) 대여하다

147 추론 / 암시

번역 도서관 회의실에 관해 암시된 것은?
(A) 이용객이 좌석을 재배치할 수 있다.
(B) 최대 수용인원이 서로 다를 수 있다.
(C) 시청각 장비가 없다.
(D) 도서관 정규시간 이외에도 사용할 수 있다.

해설 마지막 단락에서 모든 회의실에 의자와 회의용 탁자가 구비되어 있다(all rooms are equipped with chairs and conference tables)고 했지만, 회의실 신청 시 도서관 소유의 시청각 장비를 요청할 수 있다(Library-owned audiovisual equipment may be requested)고 했다. 즉 회의실에 시청각 장비는 구비되어 있지 않아 별도로 요청해야함을 추론할 수 있으므로, (C)가 정답이다.

어휘 rearrange 재배치하다 patron 이용객 capacity 수용인원

148 사실 관계 확인

번역 공지에 따르면 회의실 예약에 대한 설명으로 옳은 것은?
(A) 접수된 순서대로 받는다.
(B) 일정 시점 이후 취소 시 위약금이 있다.
(C) 직접 방문해 요청해야 한다.
(D) 한 달 전에 미리 해야 한다.

해설 첫 번째 단락에서 예약은 선착순으로 접수한다(Reservations are accepted on a first-come, first-served basis)고 했으므로, (A)가 정답이다. 예약 요청은 도서관 온라인 예약 시스템을 통해(via the library's online reservation system) 해야 하고, 당월 또는 다음 달에(for the current month or the following month) 이용할 회의실을 예약할 수 있다고 했으므로, (C)와 (D)는 잘못된 내용이다.

어휘 order 순서 penalty 위약금, 불이익 in advance 미리

▶▶ Paraphrasing 지문의 **accepted on a first-come, first-served basis**
→ 정답의 **taken in the order they are received**

149-150 구인 광고

구인: 그래픽디자이너 (디지털미디어)

회사/위치: 스트로벨스 사 본사, 해밀턴, 온타리오

스트로벨스에서 디지털 마케팅 활동에 필요한 그래픽을 디자인할 창의적인 인재를 찾고 있습니다. 여기에는 회사 웹사이트, 온라인 광고, 소셜 미디어, 휴대전화 앱 등이 포함됩니다. 합격자는 또한 회사를 대표해 업계 무역박람회에 참석하고 사내 교육을 통해 디지털 통신 동향에 대한 최신 정보를 습득하게 됩니다. **149자격 요건에는 최소 2년간 광고대행사에서 그래픽 디자이너로 일한 경력과 디지털 디자인 소프트웨어를 능숙하게 다루는 능력이 포함됩니다.**

스트로벨스 사는 가족 소유의 편의점 체인으로, 바쁜 고객들에게 간식과 간단한 식사를 제공합니다. 당사는 언론으로부터 주에서 직원이 일하기 좋은 5대 기업으로 인정받았습니다. 당사는 또한 지점이 위치한 지역사회에 열렬히 헌신하는 것으로 유명합니다. **150회사는 해마다 몇몇 자선 단체를 위한 모금 활동을 후원합니다.**

어휘 creative 창의적인 individual 개인, 사람 initiative 계획(안), 활동 on one's behalf ~을 대표[대신]하여 acquire 습득하다 in-house 사내의 current 최신 정보에 정통한 qualification 자격 (요건) proficiency 능숙하게 다룸 on the go 바쁜, 끊임없이 활동하는 earn 얻다 recognition 인정, 표창 commitment 헌신 fundraising 모금 charitable organization 자선 단체

149 사실 관계 확인

번역 일자리의 요건으로 언급된 것은?
(A) 컴퓨터 프로그래밍 분야의 학력
(B) 광고대행사에 고용된 과거 이력
(C) 사내 교육과정을 기획할 수 있는 검증된 능력
(D) 무역박람회 준비 경험

해설 첫 번째 단락을 보면, 최소 2년간 광고대행사에서 그래픽 디자이너로 일한 경력이 있어야 한다(Qualifications include a minimum of 2 years' experience as a graphic designer in an advertising agency)고 했으므로, (B)가 정답이다.

어휘 educational background 학력 proven 검증된 organize 준비하다

▶▶ Paraphrasing 지문의 **Qualifications**
→ 질문의 **a requirement for the job**

150 사실 관계 확인

번역 스트로벨스 사에 관해 알 수 있는 것은?
(A) 다양한 직원 표창 프로그램이 있다.
(B) 최근에 본사를 이전했다.
(C) 배달 서비스를 운영한다.
(D) 지역 자선 단체를 지원한다.

해설 두 번째 단락에서 회사가 몇몇 자선 단체를 위한 모금 활동을 후원한
다(the company sponsors fundraising activities for several
charitable organizations)고 했으므로, (D)가 정답이다.

어휘 recognition 표창 relocate 이전하다 charity 자선 단체

▶▶ Paraphrasing   지문의 **sponsors ~ several charitable**
organizations
→ 정답의 **supports local charities**

151-152 표

도시철도 표 쿠폰 01 중 01   여행 시 소지

승객 이름: 스티븐 릭비   예약 번호: 834253   3월 19일
발행처: 도버   발행: 대면
152좌석 등급: 비즈니스 클래스   열차 번호: 192
출발지: 도버   목적지: 버논 하이츠
출발 시각: 오후 1시 45분   도착 시각: 오후 3시 44분

151탑승 시 사진이 있는 신분증 필요   총 요금: 53달러*
*환불/교환 위약금 적용   * 변경 수수료 적용
→152단골 승객 프로그램에 가입해 할인된 가격에 일반석을 프리미엄 좌석으로
업그레이드하세요. 자세한 내용은 www.city-railways.com을 참조하세요.

어휘 retain 소지하다 issue 발행; 발행하다 coach 보통석
penalty 위약금 frequent rider (열차 등을) 자주 이용하는 승객

151 추론 / 암시

번역 릭비 씨에 관해 암시된 것은?
(A) 승차 중 식사를 할 예정이다.
(B) 도시철도를 자주 탄다.
(C) 무료로 여행 일정을 변경했다.
(D) 여행 중에 신분증을 제시해야 한다.

해설 탑승권 하단을 보면 탑승 시 사진이 있는 신분증이 필요(Photo ID
required on board)하다고 했으므로, 릭비 씨가 여행 중 신분증을 제시
해야 함을 알 수 있다. 따라서 (D)가 정답이다.

어휘 itinerary 여행 일정

▶▶ Paraphrasing   지문의 **on board**
→ 정답의 **during his trip**

152 추론 / 암시

번역 도시철도에 관해 암시된 것은?
(A) 전화로 예약을 받는다.
(B) 웹사이트가 최근에 개선되었다.
(C) 열차에는 여러 등급의 좌석이 있다.
(D) 온라인으로 예매한 표는 할인해준다.

해설 릭비 씨의 좌석 등급(Class of Seating: Business Class)과 하단
에 나온 좌석 업그레이드 관련 문구(get discounted upgrades from
Coach to Premium Class seating)에서 열차에 여러 등급의 좌석이
있음을 추론할 수 있다. 따라서 (C)가 정답이다.

153-154 문자 메시지

토드 밀레 (오후 1시 23분)
안녕하세요, 마리사. 오늘 오후에 아래층 회의실 쓸 수 있나요?
마리사 코즐로우스키 (오후 1시 24분)
예, 열려 있어요. 오늘 거래처 고객과 회의가 있나요?
토드 밀레 (오후 1시 24분)
153아뇨, 조경회의에서 할 발표 연습만 하면 돼요. 제 최신 정원설계 프로젝트를 보여주는 슬라이드를 추가했거든요.
마리사 코즐로우스키 (오후 1시 25분)
잘하셨어요. 154아, 그 회의실에 있는 영사기는 다른 리모컨을 써요. 참고 캐비닛에 있는데 제가 갖다 드릴게요.
토드 밀레 (오후 1시 26분)
괜찮아요. 154어차피 사무실에서 다른 자료들을 가져와야 해서요.
마리사 코즐로우스키 (오후 1시 27분)
알겠어요. 예행연습 잘 하세요.

어휘 landscape architecture 조경 material 자료

153 추론 / 암시

번역 밀레 씨는 누구이겠는가?
(A) 건물 관리인
(B) 회의 주최자
(C) 조경가
(D) 정보기술 전문가

해설 밀레 씨가 오후 1시 24분 메시지에서 조경회의에서 할 발표 연습만 하
면 된다(I just need to practice the presentation I'll give at the
landscape architecture conference)고 한 후, 자신의 최신 정원설계
프로젝트를 보여주는 슬라이드를 추가했다(I added a slide showing
my latest garden design project)고 했으므로, 밀레 씨가 조경 설계
와 관련된 일을 한다고 추론할 수 있다. 따라서 (C)가 정답이다.

어휘 superintendent 관리자 organizer 주최자 expert 전문가

154 의도 파악

번역 오후 1시 26분에 밀레 씨가 "괜찮아요"라고 쓴 의미는 무엇인가?
(A) 발표에 능하다.
(B) 더 이상 도움은 필요 없다.
(C) 적당한 수납공간이 있다.
(D) 거래처와 업무관계가 돈독하다.

해설 코즐로우스키 씨가 오후 1시 25분 메시지에서 회의실용 리모컨을 갖다 주겠다(I can bring it down for you)고 제안했는데, 이에 대해 밀레 씨가 '괜찮아요(I'm good)'라고 응답한 후, 어차피 사무실에서 자료들을 가져와야 한다(I have to get some other materials from the office)며 자신이 직접 할 수 있다는 의사를 내비쳤다. 따라서 코즐로우스키 씨의 도움을 거절하려고 한 말임을 알 수 있으므로, (B)가 정답이다.

155-157 온라인 기사

http://www.keys-to-success.com/articles/023421

전문가가 공유하는 몇 가지 공통된 조언

155집을 잘 보여주려면 준비가 필요합니다. 고객들은 여러분이 지역 동네와 매물로 나온 부동산을 훤히 꿰뚫고 있다고 확신하고 싶어합니다. 156집을 보여주려고 예비 구매자를 태우고 갈 때는 반드시 미리 길을 외워 두세요. 보여주기 전날 그 집까지 운전하는 연습을 해도 좋습니다. 부동산으로 가는 도중에 길을 잃는다면 그 지역에 대한 지식이 부족하다는 인상을 주게 됩니다. 157예비 구매자에게 집을 구경시켜 줄 때는 주택과 주변 지역에 대한 정보가 담긴 구매자용 꾸러미를 몇 개 가져가는 것이 좋습니다. 받는 사람은 누구나 고마워할 것이고, 여러분은 필요 시 질문에 답하며 해당 자료를 참고할 수 있을 것입니다. 심지어 해당 지역의 종이 지도 역시 도움이 될 수 있습니다. 또한 집에 들어가는 열쇠가 맞는지도 확인하세요. 엉뚱한 열쇠를 갖고 있거나 열쇠가 없으면 좋은 인상을 주지 못합니다.

어휘 expert 전문가 preparation 준비 expertise 전문 지식 property 부동산, 건물 prospective 예비의, 장래의 memorize 외우다 suggest 시사하다 en route to ~로 가는 도중에 lack 부족 surrounding 주변의 district 구역, 지역 confirm 확인하다 access 접근하다, 들어가다 impression 인상

155 추론 / 암시

번역 누구를 위한 기사이겠는가?
(A) 부동산 영업사원
(B) 주택 수리 전문가
(C) 자원봉사 관광가이드
(D) 최초 주택구입자

해설 초반부에서 집을 잘 보여주려면 준비가 필요하다(Showing homes well requires preparation)고 한 후, 해당 지역 및 매물로 나온 부동산에 대한 전문 지식(your expertise in local neighborhoods and properties for sale)이 있다는 것을 고객들에게 보여주어야 한다며 이에 관련된 조언을 이어 갔다. 따라서 부동산 영업사원을 대상으로 한 글임을 추론할 수 있으므로, (A)가 정답이다.

156 세부 사항

번역 기사를 쓴 이가 제안하는 일은?
(A) 문 열쇠 추가 세트 제작
(B) 미리 이동 경로 숙지
(C) 경치 좋은 지점에서 잠깐 멈추기
(D) 지역 봉사 기회 조사

해설 초반부에서 예비 구매자를 태우고 갈 때는 반드시 미리 길을 외워두라(When you drive a prospective buyer ~ be sure you have memorized the directions ahead of time)고 한 후, 보여주기 전

날 그 집까지 운전하는 연습을 해도 좋다(You may even want to practice driving to the home the day before the showing)고 조언했다. 따라서 (B)가 정답이다.

어휘 scenic 경치가 좋은

▶▶ **Paraphrasing** 지문의 memorized the directions ahead of time → 정답의 Mastering travel routes in advance

157 문장 삽입

번역 [1], [2], [3], [4]로 표시된 곳 중에 다음 문장이 가장 적합한 곳은?
"받는 사람은 누구나 고마워할 것이고, 여러분은 필요 시 질문에 답하며 해당 자료를 참고할 수 있을 것입니다."
(A) [1]
(B) [2]
(C) [3]
(D) [4]

해설 받는 사람도 고마워하고 부동산 영업사원에게도 도움이 될만한 자료(the material)가 앞에서 먼저 언급되어야 한다. [3] 앞에서 주택과 주변 지역에 대한 정보가 담긴 구매자용 꾸러미를 몇 개 가져가라(bring several copies of a buyers' packet with information about the home and the surrounding district)고 조언했으므로, 이 뒤에 주어진 문장이 들어가야 자연스럽다. 따라서 (C)가 정답이다. 참고로, it과 the material은 a buyers' packet을 가리킨다.

158-160 편지

이본 클라크
베이츠 가 803번지
보웬시, 일리노이 60419

클라크 씨께,

보웬 시의 유소년 축구 연맹 코치 중 한 분이시니, 곧 있을 보웬 시 공원 여가 위원회의 특별 회의에 대해서 알고 계시면 좋을 것 같습니다. 회의는 2월 4일 화요일 오후 6시 30분 시청 5호실에서 열립니다.

158의제는 공원과 예산 중 일부를 호반 공원의 여가 편의시설을 개선하는 데 배정하자는 피오렐로 사우로 공원과장의 제안입니다. 159구체적으로 명시하자면, 유소년 축구경기장 장비보관소 건물을 촬영한 사진에 튀어나온 못, 판자벽에 뚫린 구멍, 금간 창문 등이 보이는데, 이 문제들이 반드시 처리되어야 한다는 겁니다.

사우로 과장은 경기장 점수판에 현대식 전기조명을 설치하는 안에 대해서도 논의할 예정입니다. 160그는 세이퍼트 전기사로부터 이러한 작업에 드는 총비용 견적을 받아냈습니다. 회의에서 위원회는 이 계획에 대한 대중의 의견을 구할 예정입니다.

유소년 축구 연맹에서는, 해당 프로젝트의 영향을 받으실 수 있는 당사자 중 한 분으로서 귀하께서도 회의에 참석하셔서 귀중한 의견을 공유해 주시기를 적극 권고 드리는 바입니다.

캘빈 워터스
보웬 시 유소년 축구 연맹 이사회장

158 추론 / 암시

번역 곧 있을 회의의 목적은 무엇이겠는가?
(A) 최신 공원 행사 일정 제공
(B) 공원 개선을 위한 자금조달 논의
(C) 공모 결과 발표
(D) 새로 임명된 공원 관계자 소개

해설 두 번째 단락에서 회의 의제가 호만 공원의 여가 편의시설을 개선하는 데 공원과 예산 중 일부를 배정하자는 제안(The topic will be ~ proposal to allocate a portion of the Parks Department's budget to upgrade Hohman Park's recreational amenities)이라고 했으므로, (B)가 정답이다.

어휘 financing 자금조달 improvement 개선(점) appoint 임명하다

▶▶ Paraphrasing 지문의 to allocate a portion of the Parks Department's budget
→ 정답의 financing
지문의 to upgrade Hohman Park's recreational amenities
→ 정답의 for park improvements

159 추론 / 암시

번역 경기장 보관소 건물에 관해 암시된 것은?
(A) 추가적인 용도로 쓰일 수 있다.
(B) 새로운 위치로 옮겨질 것이다.
(C) 유료로 대여할 수 있다.
(D) 수리가 필요하다.

해설 두 번째 단락에서 유소년 축구경기장 장비보관소 건물을 촬영한 사진에 보이는 튀어나온 못, 판자벽에 뚫린 구멍, 금 간 창문 등이 수리되어야 한다(photos ~ show exposed nails, holes in the siding, and cracked windows that must be taken care of)고 했으므로, (D)가 정답이다.

어휘 function 기능, 용도

▶▶ Paraphrasing 지문의 must be taken care of
→ 정답의 in need of repair

160 세부 사항

번역 편지에 따르면 사우로 씨가 최근에 한 일은?
(A) 견적서 수령
(B) 다른 도시공원 사진 촬영
(C) 지역 스포츠 행사 참석
(D) 공원 안내책자 개정

해설 세 번째 단락에서 사우로 씨가 공원시설 개선 작업에 필요한 총 비용 견적을 확보했다(He has secured an estimate ~ of the overall cost of these endeavors)고 했으므로, (A)가 정답이다.

어휘 revise 개정하다, 수정하다

▶▶ Paraphrasing 지문의 has secured an estimate of the overall cost
→ 정답의 Received a cost estimate

161-163 온라인 후기

[161]Book-bargains.com "신뢰도가 가장 높은 웹 기반 중고서적 판매처"

고객 후기: 〈로고 디자인 영감〉 (소프트커버, 148쪽)
[161]후기 번호: Book-bargains.com에서 구매한 품목 7개 중 1개
(다른 후기를 보려면 여기를 클릭)
후기 날짜: 5월 26일
고객명: 제프 스탁스   V 구매 확인
전체 평가 등급: 우수
의견: 휴대하기 쉬운 이 소책자에는 매우 효과적인 유명 로고 디자인 55가지의 샘플이 있어요. 모든 로고는 흰색 바탕에 컬러로 되어 있으며, 관련 글에는 로고들의 창작 내력이 설명되어 있고 디자인 요소가 분석되어 있습니다. [162]본문 외에, 출판사는 사려 깊게 메모용으로 빈 페이지 10쪽을 제공했는데, 이게 좋은 점 같아요. 로고는 소프트웨어 개발사부터 택배 배송 서비스 업체까지 다양한 기업에서 선정되었어요. 후자는 제게 가장 흥미로운 챕터였던 "움직임을 나타내는 패턴"에서 다루어졌어요. [163]이 섹션에는 또한 제가 가장 좋아하는 디자인도 포함되어 있었는데요, 바로 혁신으로 유명한 운동기계 제조업체인 즐라타리악스의 역동적인 로고입니다. 이 책은 어느 상업 디자이너에게나 귀중한 자료입니다.

어휘 secondhand 중고의 inspiration 영감 verify 확인하다
compact 소형의 present 보여주다, 제시하다 effective
효과적인 accompanying 동반하는, 관련이 있는 analyze 분석하다
element 요소 thoughtfully 사려 깊게 feature 특징; (특별히)
포함하다 commercial 상업의

161 추론 / 암시

번역 스탁스 씨에 관해 가장 사실에 가까운 것은?
(A) 온라인으로 중고 책을 여러 권 구입했다.
(B) 서점 소속의 전문 구매자다.
(C) 최근 독서토론 모임에 가입했다.
(D) 다양한 회사의 로고를 만들었다.

해설 후기 번호(Review number)를 보면 스탁스 씨가 Book-bargains.com에서 구매한 품목이 총 7개인 것(1 of 7 for items purchased from Book-bargains.com)을 알 수 있는데, 상단 문구에서 Book-bargains.com을 '신뢰도가 가장 높은 웹 기반 중고서적 판매처(The most trusted Web-based seller of secondhand books)'로 소개하고 있으므로, 그가 온라인으로 중고책 여러 권을 구매했음을 알 수 있다. 따라서 (A)가 정답이다.

162 사실 관계 확인

번역 〈로고 디자인 영감〉에 관해 언급된 것은?
(A) 빈 페이지가 들어간 부분이 있다.
(B) 전자책으로도 이용할 수 있다.
(C) 스탁스 씨의 친구가 이 책을 위해 조사했다.
(D) 현재 절판되었다.

해설 의견(Comments) 중반부에서 출판사가 사려 깊게도 메모용으로 빈 페이지 10쪽을 제공했다(the publisher has thoughtfully provided about ten empty pages for taking notes)고 했으므로, (A)가 정답이다.

▶▶ Paraphrasing 지문의 ten empty pages
→ 정답의 a section of blank pages

163 세부 사항

번역 즐라타리악스는 어떤 회사인가?
(A) 컴퓨터 소프트웨어 개발업체
(B) 피트니스 장비 제조업체
(C) 택배 배송 서비스 업체
(D) 그래픽 디자인 회사

해설 의견(Comments) 후반부에서 즐라타리악스를 '운동기계 제조업체(a maker of exercise machines)'라고 소개하므로, (B)가 정답이다.

▶▶ Paraphrasing 지문의 a maker of exercise machines
→ 정답의 A fitness equipment manufacturer

164-167 웹페이지 발표문

www.curiosom.com/news/0111

1월 11일 – 큐리오섬닷컴 결제 처리사 변경에 관한 공식 발표 – 가입자들에게 의미하는 것

164약 15년 전 창립된 이래로, 큐리오섬닷컴은 사진작가들이 지구촌과 사진을 공유할 수 있는 최고의 장소로 성장했습니다. 166당사가 무제한 사진 업로드 특권이 있는 유료 서비스 이용권을 제공하기 시작했을 때, 경영진은 이용료 청구를 처리하는 데 브레이너드-플러스 결제 처리 서비스를 선택했습니다. 이 결정은 브레이너드-플러스가 당사의 1년 및 2년 약정 요금제를 자동 갱신할 수 있다는 사실에 입각한 것이었습니다.

165/166하지만 지난 6월 당사가 파나맛닷컴의 자회사가 되면서, 청구 시스템을 통합하기 위해 파나맛닷컴의 결제 처리사인 디지텍스-D로 전환하는 과정에 착수했습니다. 166아쉽게도, 디지텍스-D는 당사의 이전 결제 처리사에서 시작된 큐리오섬닷컴 이용권을 갱신할 수 없다고 통보했습니다. 이는 지난해 6월 30일 또는 그 이전에 서비스 이용을 시작한 큐리오섬닷컴 회원 모두에게 영향을 미칩니다. 이 문제를 해결하기 위해, 당사는 해당 회원에게 이용권을 조기 갱신해 20퍼센트 할인 혜택을 받으시라고 권하고 있습니다. 이렇게 하면 이용권이 종료일까지 중단 없이 계속되며 자동으로 갱신됩니다. 167아무런 조치도 취하지 않을 경우, 현재 이용권이 끝날 때 가입자 프로필과 청구 정보를 업데이트해야 합니다. 그러면 선택한 약정 요금제에 대해 정규 요금이 부과됩니다. 그러므로 영향을 받는 모든 가입자들에게 조기 갱신을 강력히 권하는 바입니다.

어휘 regarding ~에 관한 processor 처리사 subscriber 가입자, 구독자 inception 창립 premier 최고의, 제1의 venue 장소 subscription (서비스) 이용(권), 구독 privilege 특권 renew 갱신하다 subsidiary 자회사 unify 통합하다 unfortunately 아쉽게도 originate 시작되다, 유래하다 affect 영향을 미치다 take advantage of ~을 이용하다, 혜택을 받다 uninterrupted 중단 없이

164 추론 / 암시

번역 큐리오섬닷컴은 어떤 종류의 업체이겠는가?
(A) 시각 예술가를 위한 디지털 잡지
(B) 광고분석 서비스
(C) 온라인 회계 앱
(D) 사진 공유 플랫폼

해설 첫 번째 단락에서 큐리오섬닷컴은 사진작가들이 지구촌과 사진을 공유할 수 있는 최고의 장소(the premier venue for photographers to share their pictures with the entire global community)라고 했으므로, 사진 공유 플랫폼임을 알 수 있다. 따라서 (D)가 정답이다.

▶▶ Paraphrasing 지문의 venue for photographers to share their pictures
→ 정답의 photo sharing platform

165 세부 사항 [고난도]

번역 발표문에 따르면, 지난해에 있었던 일은?
(A) 기념일 축하행사
(B) 기업 인수
(C) 신제품 출시
(D) 서비스 이용료 인상

해설 발표문이 1월에 게시되었는데, 두 번째 단락의 초반부에서 지난 6월 큐리오섬닷컴이 파나맛닷컴의 자회사가 되었다(we became a subsidiary of Panamat.com last June)고 했으므로, (B)가 정답이다.

▶▶ Paraphrasing 지문의 we became a subsidiary of Panamat.com
→ 정답의 A business acquisition

166 세부 사항 [고난도]

번역 현재 할인 대상자는?
(A) 최근 일주일 이내에 서비스를 시작한 가입자
(B) 3년 이상의 갱신기간을 선택한 가입자
(C) 원래 브레이너드-플러스에서 청구서를 받았던 가입자
(D) 파나맛닷컴의 회원이기도 한 가입자

해설 첫 번째 단락에서 큐리오섬닷컴이 원래는 브레이너드-플러스 결제 처리 서비스(the Brainard-Plus payment processing service to handle our billing for subscriptions)를 이용했다는 것을 알 수 있고, 두 번째 단락에서 지난 6월 파나맛닷컴의 자회사가 되며 결제 처리사를 디지텍스-D로 전환(switching to their payment processing firm, Digitexx-D)하게 되었음을 알 수 있다. 그런데 디지텍스-D가 이전의 결제 처리사, 즉 브레이너드-플러스에서 시작된 큐리오섬닷컴 이용권을 갱신할 수 없다(they cannot renew any Curiosom.com subscriptions that originated on our prior payment processor)고 통보하자, 이를 해결하기 위해 작년 6월 30일 이전에 서비스 이용을 시작했던 회원들(all Curiosom.com members who began their subscription on or before June 30 of last year)에게 이용권을 조기 갱신하고 20퍼센트 할인 혜택을 받으라(we are encouraging these members to take advantage of a 20% discount)고 권하고 있다. 따라서 현재 할인 대상자는 작년 6월 30일 이전에 큐리오섬닷컴에서 서비스를 이용하기 시작해 브레이너드-플러스에서 청구서를 받았던 가입자이므로, (C)가 정답이다.

167 문장 삽입 고난도

번역 [1], [2], [3], [4]로 표시된 곳 중에서 다음 문장이 가장 적합한 곳은?

"그러면 선택한 약정 요금제에 대해 정규 요금이 부과됩니다."

(A) [1]
(B) [2]
(C) [3]
(D) [4]

해설 주어진 문장 앞에서 정규 요금이 부과되는 상황이 언급되어야 한다. [4] 앞 내용을 보면 이용권을 조기 갱신할 시 20프로 할인을 받게 되며(take advantage of a 20% discount on early subscription renewals) 그 뒤로 중단 없이 서비스 이용이 가능하다고 했고, 이렇게 하지 않으면 현재 이용권이 만료될 때 가입자 프로필과 청구 정보를 업데이트해야 한다(If you take no action, you will have to update your subscriber profile and billing information at the end of your current subscription)고 했다. 후자의 경우 할인 요금이 아닌 정규 요금이 부과된다는 내용이 되어야 자연스러우므로, (D)가 정답이다.

168-171 온라인 채팅

오렐리아 라모스 [오후 2시 4분]
모두 안녕하세요. 그냥 확인하는 건데요. 고객 포럼 페이지를 위한 브레인스토밍은 어떻게 돼가요? 기사 아이디어 좀 얻었나요?
피터 시우 [오후 2시 5분]
예. 창고에 조명을 제대로 설치하는 법에 관해서 안내문을 쓰려고요.
오렐리아 라모스 [오후 2시 6분]
좋아요. 168우리 회사에서 조명용품을 구매하는 기업 고객들도 많으니까, 포럼 내용이 그들의 요구를 반영해야죠. 다른 아이디어 있나요?
린다 멜로 [오후 2시 7분]
169개인 소비자 고객을 위해서, 놀이방에 가장 적합한 조명 기기를 고르는 법에 관한 팁을 써볼까 생각하고 있었어요. 선택지가 너무 많거든요.
오렐리아 라모스 [오후 2시 7분]
그렇죠.
린다 멜로 [오후 2시 8분]
170또 모이셰 비에츠에 대해 소개하는 글을 써볼까 해요. 그는 재활용된 산업용 파이프로 벽 전등을 만드는 공예가예요.
오렐리아 라모스 [오후 2시 9분]
좋은데요. 전에 170그 사람하고 같이 일했죠?
린다 멜로 [오후 2시 10분]
170예, 제가 견습생이었어요.
피터 시우 [오후 2시 11분]
그러니까 생각나네요. 저한테 다른 생각이 있어요. 171흔히 쓰이는 일부 기술용어들을 명확하게 설명하는 게시물을 만들어서 이해하기 더 쉽도록 해야 해요.
오렐리아 라모스 [오후 2시 12분]
171아주 유용하겠네요. 그렇게 해주시겠어요?
피터 시우 [오후 2시 13분]
171물론이죠.
오렐리아 라모스 [오후 2시 14분]
좋아요. 두 분 모두 의견 고마워요. 이번 주 후반에 진행 상황을 확인할게요.

어휘 brainstorming 브레인스토밍, 자유로운 아이디어 회의 properly 제대로 commercial client 상업 활동을 하는 고객, 기업 고객 purchase 구입하다 supplies 용품 reflect 반영하다 consumer client 개인 소비자 고객 lighting fixture 조명 기기 artisan 공예가, 장인 apprentice 견습생 clarify 명확하게 설명하다 input 의견, 생각 progress 진행 상황

168 추론 / 암시

번역 참가자들은 어떤 회사에서 일하겠는가?

(A) 원예도구 제작업체
(B) 조명용품 판매업체
(C) 보관 시설 체인점
(D) 전기기사들을 위한 업계 간행물

해설 라모스 씨가 오후 2시 6분 메시지에서 자신들의 회사에서 조명용품을 구매하는 기업 고객들이 많다(We do have many commercial clients that purchase lighting supplies from us)고 했으므로, 참가자들이 조명용품 판매업체에서 일한다고 추론할 수 있다. 따라서 (B)가 정답이다.

어휘 trade (특정 유형의) 사업, 업계 publication 간행(물)

169 의도 파악

번역 오후 2시 7분, 멜로 씨가 "선택지가 너무 많거든요"라고 쓴 의미는?

(A) 동료가 결정하는 데 시간이 더 필요할 수 있다.
(B) 그녀는 글을 어떻게 시작해야 할지 잘 모른다.
(C) 선택지가 너무 많아 고객이 어쩔 줄 몰라 할 수 있다.
(D) 그녀는 여러 건의 제안이 인상 깊었다.

해설 멜로 씨가 오후 2시 7분 메시지에서 개인 소비자 고객을 위해 놀이방에 가장 적합한 조명 기기를 고르는 법에 관한 팁을 써볼까 생각하고 있었다(For our consumer clients, I was thinking of writing tips on how to select the best lighting fixtures)고 한 후, 선택지가 너무 많다며 해당 주제를 고려한 이유를 덧붙였다. 따라서 고객이 선택에 어려움을 겪을지도 모른다고 생각하고 있음을 알 수 있으므로, (C)가 정답이다.

어휘 overwhelmed 어쩔 줄 모르는, 압도된

170 사실 관계 확인

번역 멜로 씨에 관해 알 수 있는 것은?

(A) 비에츠 씨의 지도 아래 일했다.
(B) 재활용 계획안을 짠다.
(C) 현재 집을 개조하고 있다.
(D) 한때 잡지 기자였다.

해설 멜로 씨가 오후 2시 8분 메시지에서 모이셰 비에츠에 대해 소개하는 글을 쓸까 한다(I could also write a profile on Moishe Wietz)고 했는데, 이에 대해 라모스 씨가 같이 일한 적이 있지 않냐며 확인하자(You used to work with him, right?) 멜로 씨가 그렇다고 한 후, 그의 견습생이었다(I was his apprentice)고 덧붙였다. 따라서 (A)가 정답이다.

어휘 initiative 계획(안), 활동

▶▶ Paraphrasing 지문의 I was his apprentice
→ 정답의 She worked under Mr. Wietz's guidance

171 세부 사항

번역 시우 씨가 하기로 한 일은?
(A) 고객 만족도를 측정하기 위한 자료 수집
(B) 일부 표현을 설명하는 콘텐츠 개발
(C) 알림 메모를 공유 일정에 게시
(D) 신규 인턴십 프로그램 감독

해설 시우 씨가 오후 2시 11분 메시지에서 흔히 쓰이는 일부 기술용어들을 명확하게 설명하는 게시물을 만들어야 한다(We should create a post that clarifies some common technical terms)고 제안했는데, 라모스 씨가 유용하겠다며 시우 씨에게 해당 작업을 해달라(Could you do that?)고 요청했다. 시우 씨가 이 요청을 수락(Sure thing)한 것이므로, (B)가 정답이다.

어휘 measure 측정하다 customer satisfaction 고객 만족도 reminder 알리는 것 supervise 감독하다

▶▶ **Paraphrasing** 지문의 **create a post that clarifies some common technical terms**
→ 정답의 **Develop content that explains some expressions**

172-175 기사

기업가 뉴스-타임스   4월 23일

172카페 주인이 알아야 할 사항

글 카일라 리치

▶ ¹⁷²개인 카페를 운영하는 사람들은 제품에 얼마를 청구해야 할지에 대한 결정이 수익에 지대한 영향을 미친다는 사실을 머지않아 알게 된다. 카페 간 경쟁이 치열하기 때문에 제품 및 서비스의 최적 가격을 결정하는 것이 중요하다.

▶ ¹⁷³거의 10년 전 카페 커넥티브를 처음 열었을 때, 필자는 더 우수한 서비스를 제공하면서 주요 커피 전문 체인점과 동일한 가격을 청구하는 것이 목표였다. 이 전략으로 고객 유치에는 성공했지만, 괜찮은 수입을 올리지는 못했다. 사업 첫해 이후 시장조사 연구를 의뢰해 보니 대다수 고객은 개인 커피숍이 더 수준 높은 서비스와 제품 품질을 제공한다는 것을 이미 인지하고 있었다. 나는 이 점을 염두에 두고 품질이 더 뛰어나고 비싼 고급 커피 제품을 내놓기 시작했다.

▶ ¹⁷⁴타사보다 높은 가격의 타당성을 입증하기 위해, 한층 더 나아가 필자는 카페를 동네 모임 장소로 만들어 틈새 시장을 개척하기 위해 노력해왔다. 매달 고객을 위해 커피 내리기 워크숍이나 커피 시음회 등 재미있는 특별 행사를 진행하고 있다. 이러한 모임들이 점포 이미지에 긍정적인 영향을 끼치고 있다.

▶ 물론 경쟁업체보다 가격을 낮출 수도 있지만, 그렇다고 해서 수익성을 보장할 정도로 추가 매출이 충분하게 나온다는 보장은 없다. 어쨌든 개인 카페 주인들은 장비와 제품에 ¹⁷⁵상당히 큰돈을 투자했으므로 최대한 수익을 올려야 한다.

¹⁷³저자 소개: 디 시티 출신인 리치 씨는 그곳에서 성황리에 카페를 영업하고 있으며, 바로 지난주부터 전 세계 카페 및 찻집 주인들을 위한 온라인 자료 사이트인 www.cafe-owners.com을 운영하고 있다.

어휘 independent 자영의, 개인의 offering 제공물, 제품 effect 영향 profit 수익 competition 경쟁, 경쟁 상대 determine 결정하다 optimal 최적의 aim 목표로 하다 superior 우수한 strategy 전략 attract 유치하다 decent 괜찮은, 상당한

---

earnings 수입 commission 의뢰하다 perceive 인지하다 justify 타당성을 입증하다 carve out a niche 틈새 시장을 개척하다 impact 영향 establishment 영업소, 점포 profitability 수익성 inventory 재고, 제품 returns 수익 operational 운영 중인

172 주제 / 목적

번역 기사가 작성된 이유는 무엇이겠는가?
(A) 많은 카페들이 수익을 내지 못하는 이유 설명
(B) 카페 직원 관리 팁 제공
(C) 카페 주인에게 가격 책정에 관해 조언
(D) 카페 산업의 최근 동향 약술

해설 기사 제목(What Café Owners Should Know...)을 보면 카페 주인을 대상으로 하는 글임을 알 수 있다. 첫 번째 단락에서 제품 및 서비스의 최적 가격을 결정하는 것이 중요하다(it is important to determine the optimal prices for products and services)고 한 후, 개인 카페 운영자에게 가격 책정과 관련된 조언을 이어 가고 있다. 따라서 (C)가 정답이다.

▶▶ **Paraphrasing** 지문의 **how much to charge**
→ 정답의 **pricing**

173 사실 관계 확인 [고난도]

번역 카페 커넥티브에 관해 알 수 있는 것은?
(A) 10년 넘게 영업하고 있다.
(B) 격주로 특별 행사를 연다.
(C) 마케팅 책에 소개됐다.
(D) 리치 씨의 고향에 있다.

해설 두 번째 단락에서 리치 씨는 자신이 거의 10년 전 카페 커넥티브를 처음 열었다(I first opened Café Connective nearly 10 years ago)고 했는데, 하단의 저자 소개(About the author)를 보면 디 시티 출신인 리치 씨가 그곳에서 카페를 영업하고 있다(A native of Dee City, Ms. Leitch runs a successful café there)고 했으므로, 카페 커넥티브가 리치 씨의 고향인 디 시티에 있음을 알 수 있다. 따라서 (D)가 정답이다. 거의 10년 전(nearly 10 years ago)에 열었다고 했으며, 매달 고객을 위해 재미있는 특별 행사를 진행하고 있다(Every month, I hold fun special events)고 했으므로, (A)와 (B)는 정답이 될 수 없다.

174 세부 사항 [고난도]

번역 카페 커넥티브에서 변경사항이 시행된 한 가지 이유는?
(A) 경쟁업체와 차별화하기 위해
(B) 고객 대기 시간을 단축하기 위해
(C) 환경에 미치는 영향을 줄이기 위해
(D) 더 즐겁게 일할 수 있는 곳으로 만들기 위해

해설 세 번째 단락에서 리치 씨는 타사보다 높은 가격의 타당성을 입증하기 위해 자신의 카페를 동네 모임 장소로 만들어 틈새 시장을 개척하기 위해 노력해왔다(To further justify my higher prices, I have made efforts to carve out a niche for my café as a neighborhood meeting place)고 했다. 이는 경쟁업체와 차별화하기 위한 전략이라고 볼 수 있으므로, (A)가 정답이다.

어휘 differentiate 차별화하다

175 동의어 찾기 [고난도]

번역 4번째 단락 3행의 "good"과 의미상 가장 가까운 것은?
(A) 만족스러운
(B) 신뢰할 수 있는
(C) 상당한
(D) 유용한

해설 'good'을 포함한 부분은 '장비와 제품에 상당히 큰돈을 투자했다
(have invested a good amount of money in equipment and
inventory)'라는 의미로 해석되는데, 여기서 good은 '상당한, 꽤 많은'이
라는 뜻으로 쓰였다. 따라서 '상당한'이라는 의미의 (C) substantial이 정
답이다.

176-180 기사 + 웹페이지 공지

콜웨이 시 연극단 〈케이건 스트리트〉 공연

콜웨이 시(6월 3일)—178콜웨이 시 연극단(CCTG)이 6월 10일 금요일부터 6
월 26일 일요일까지 유쾌하게 웃기는 도나 메이슨의 연극 〈케이건 스트리트〉로
여름 시즌을 시작한다. 금요일, 토요일 공연은 오후 7시, 일요일 공연은 오후 2
시에 시작한다.

176/180연극은 젊은 부부 브래드와 메리가 새로 이사온 이웃인 켄과 재니스를 바
비큐 저녁식사에 초대하여 함께 시간을 보낸 날을 중심으로 펼쳐진다. 야외에서
요리하며 식사하는 동안, 두 커플은 몇 주 차이로 같은 여행사를 통해 아프리카를
횡단하는 육로 여행을 갔다는 사실을 알게 된다. 등장인물들이 해외여행에서 있
었던 재미있고 대담하며 감동적인 일화를 나누면서, 연극은 관객을 경이로움으로
177이끈다.

웨스트 타운의 에릭 그리피, 힐사이드 시티의 에이미 윤, 이스트 밸리의 케빈 브
래독, 웨스트 타운의 벳시 말리키 등이 출연한다. 1786월 10일 공연이 끝나면
관객들은 공연자들을 만나서 함께 사진을 찍을 수 있다. 또한 조지 멀웨이 감독이
참석해 관객들의 질문에 직접 답할 예정이다.

CCTG에 대해 더 자세한 내용을 알고 싶다면 www.colway-theater.org을
방문하면 된다. 표는 웹사이트나 매표소에서 구입할 수 있다.

어휘 kick off 시작하다 delightfully 유쾌하게 center around
~를 중심으로 이루어지다 overland 육로의 anecdote 일화
inspirational 감동을 주는 aspect 측면 audience 관객 be on
hand 참석하다, (필요시) 가까이에 있다

---

http://www.colway-theater.org/home

콜웨이 시 연극단(CCTG)

6월 6일 새 소식: 179CCTG 경영진은 여름 시즌의 첫 번째 연극 〈케이건 스트
리트〉를 매주 토요일 오후 2시에 추가로 상연할 예정임을 발표하게 되어 기쁩니
다. 금요일과 토요일 저녁 공연은 오후 7시, 일요일 낮 공연은 오후 2시입니다.

180콜웨이 시 출신인 조지 멀웨이가 연출하는 이 연극에서, 재능 있는 케빈 브래
독이 주연으로 브래드 역을 맡아 연극단과 함께 무대에 데뷔합니다. 메리 역의 에
이미 윤, 켄 역의 에릭 그리피, 재니스 역의 벳시 말리키가 합류합니다.

어휘 management 경영진 matinee 낮 공연 direct 연출하다
feature (배우를) 주연시키다 talented 재능 있는

---

176 세부 사항

번역 〈케이건 스트리트〉는 주로 무엇에 관한 내용인가?
(A) 공통된 경험을 가진 이웃들
(B) 한 가족의 익살스러운 요리 실수
(C) 새로운 문화에 적응하는 이민자들
(D) 이사를 자주 하면 어려운 점

해설 기사의 두 번째 단락에서 연극은 젊은 부부 브래드와 메리가 새로 이사온
이웃인 켄과 재니스를 바비큐 저녁식사에 초대하여 함께 시간을 보낸 날
을 중심으로 펼쳐진다(The play centers around a day in the life of
Brad and Mary, a young married couple who invite their new
neighbors)고 한 후, 두 커플이 몇 주 차이로 같은 여행사를 통해 아프리
카를 횡단하는 육로 여행을 갔다는 사실을 알게 되며(that they went on
the same tour company's overland journey across Africa just
a few weeks apart) 여행에서 있었던 일화를 나눈다(the characters
share anecdotes ~ of international travel)고 했다. 따라서 공통된
경험을 가진 이웃들의 이야기임을 알 수 있으므로, (A)가 정답이다.

어휘 immigrant 이민자 adapt to ~에 적응하다 challenge 어려운 점
frequently 자주

177 동의어 찾기 [고난도]

번역 기사에서 2번째 단락 11행의 "carries"와 의미상 가장 가까운 것은?
(A) 나아가게 하다
(B) 유지하다
(C) 소통하다
(D) 포착하다

해설 'carries'를 포함한 부분은 '연극은 관객을 경이로움으로 이끈다(the play
carries audiences toward a sense of wonder)'라는 의미로 해석되
는데, 여기서 carries는 '이끈다, 나르다'라는 뜻으로 쓰였다. 따라서 '나아
가게 하다, 몰고 가다'라는 의미의 (A) propel이 정답이다.

178 세부 사항 [고난도]

번역 〈케이건 스트리트〉 초연 관객들이 받게 될 것은?
(A) 앞으로 나올 CCTG 작품 시사회
(B) 출연자들과 교류할 수 있는 기회
(C) 극장 투어 경품 추첨 참가
(D) 연극 주제와 관련된 작은 선물

해설 기사의 첫 번째 단락에서 콜웨이 시 연극단(CCTG)이 6월 10일 금요일
에 연극 〈케이건 스트리트〉로 여름 시즌을 시작한다(The Colway City
Theater Group (CCTG) will kick off its summer season with ~
play Cagen Street, running from Friday, June 10)고 했으므로,
초연이 6월 10일에 열린다는 것을 알 수 있다. 기사의 세 번째 단락에서 6
월 10일에 공연이 끝나면 관객들은 공연자들을 만나서 함께 사진을 찍을 수
있다(After the performance on June 10, audience members
can meet and take photos with the performers)고 했으므로, (B)
가 정답이다.

어휘 preview 시사회 drawing 추첨 (행사)

▶▶ Paraphrasing 지문의 meet and take photos with the
performers
→ 정답의 interact with the cast

179 주제 / 목적

번역 공지의 주요 목적은 무엇일 것 같은가?
(A) 표 조기 구매 장려하기
(B) 연극 연출자에게 경의 표하기
(C) 배우의 은퇴 알리기
(D) 확장된 공연 일정 알리기

해설 웹페이지 공지의 첫 번째 단락에서 〈케이건 스트리트〉를 매주 토요일 오후 2시에 추가로 상연할 예정임을 발표하게 되어 기쁘다(The management of the CCTG is happy to announce that we will offer extra performances, at 2:00 P.M. each Saturday, for *Cagen Street*)고 했으므로, 추가된 공연 일정을 알리기 위한 공지라고 볼 수 있다. 따라서 (D)가 정답이다.

어휘 retirement 은퇴 publicize 알리다, 홍보하다 expand 확장하다

▶▶ **Paraphrasing** 지문의 **extra** → 정답의 **expanded**

180 연계   고난도

번역 브래독 씨에 관해 암시된 것은?
(A) CCTG 웹사이트 동영상에 등장한다.
(B) 6월 26일 오후 7시에 공연한다.
(C) 윤 씨가 맡은 캐릭터의 남편 역을 맡을 예정이다.
(D) 멀웨이 씨와 같은 도시 출신이다.

해설 웹페이지 공지의 두 번째 단락에서 케빈 브래독이 주연으로 브래드 역을 맡는다(The play ~ will feature the talented Kevin Braddock, making his stage debut with our group, in the role of Brad)고 한 후, 각 역할을 맡은 배우들(Amy Yoon, as Mary; Eric Griffey, as Ken; and Betsy Maliki, as Janice)을 나열했다. 여기서 윤 씨가 메리 역인 것을 확인할 수 있는데, 기사의 두 번째 단락을 보면 극중 브래드와 메리가 결혼한 부부(Brad and Mary, a young married couple)임을 알 수 있으므로, 브래독 씨는 윤 씨가 맡은 캐릭터의 남편 역할임을 알 수 있다. 따라서 (C)가 정답이다.

181-185 보고서 개요 + 이메일

골마크 리서치

밀크셰이크 음료 4종에 대한 시장조사 요약

고객사명: 몬트로이 스팟

설명: 골마크 리서치는 대형 패밀리 레스토랑 체인인 몬트로이 스팟으로부터 밀크셰이크 음료 4종에 대한 소비자 반응을 평가해 달라는 의뢰를 받았다. **181(A)**이번 조사는 8월 중순에서 9월 중순 사이에 오하이오 주 클리블랜드와 펜실베이니아 주 피츠버그에 있는 이 회사의 레스토랑에서 이루어졌다. 참가자들은 자신이 사는 지역에 있는 식당에 가도록 안내 받았고, 그곳에서 무작위로 배정된 밀크셰이크 음료 4가지 맛 중 하나를 시음했다. **181(B)/(C)**그런 다음 휴대폰으로 링크에 접속해 객관식 질문과 주관식 질문으로 구성된 설문조사에 응했다.

전반적인 결과:

1번 샘플: *바나나와 체리 맛*
응답자 중 "아주 맛있다"로 응답한 비율 – 79%
182가장 많이 나온 의견: "바나나 맛이 너무 많이 난다", "체리 맛이 별로 나지 않는다"

2번 샘플: *파인애플과 망고 맛*
응답자 중 "아주 맛있다"로 응답한 비율 – 82%
182가장 많이 나온 의견: "상쾌한 맛", "파인애플 맛이 부족하다"

1843번 샘플: *솔티드 캐러멜 맛*
184응답자 중 "아주 맛있다"로 응답한 비율 – 84%
가장 많이 나온 의견: "진한 맛", "끌리는 색감"

4번 샘플: *코코넛과 바닐라 맛*
응답자 중 "아주 맛있다"로 응답한 비율 – 87%
가장 많이 나온 의견: "걸쭉한 식감", "단맛이 딱 적당하다"

어휘 casual dining restaurant (편안한 분위기의) 패밀리 레스토랑 assess 평가하다 location 지점 participant 참가자 instruct 안내하다 assign 배정하다 sample 시음[시식]하다 access 접속하다 consist of 구성되어 있다 overall 전반적인 finding 결과 respondent 응답자 indicate 나타내다, 표시하다 refreshing 상쾌한 texture 식감, 질감

수신: 바바라 밀리건 〈b.milligan@goalmarkkresearch.com〉
발신: 칼 펠라 〈c.pella@goalmarkkresearch.com〉
날짜: 10월 2일
제목: 몬트로이 스팟 조사연구 결과
첨부파일: 그래프와 표

안녕하세요, 바바라,

요청하신 대로 몬트로이 스팟 보고서용 그래프와 표를 첨부했어요. **185**당신이 고안한 전자 설문지는 의견을 끌어내는 데 상당히 효과적이었어요. 특히 우리 회사가 이전에 온라인 양식을 사용한 적이 없다는 점을 고려하면, 조사 과정이 매우 순조롭게 진행되어 다행이에요.

183이 고객사를 위해 실시했던 이전 연구 결과를 토대로 보니, 대부분의 결과는 제 예상과 일치했어요. 그런데 한 가지 결과가 두드러졌어요. **184**가장 인기 없으리라 생각했던 맛이 두 번째로 인기가 있었네요. 이건 정말 예상하지 못했어요.

고객사에게 제공할 권고안을 뒷받침할 정보가 더 필요하면 알려주세요.

고마워요.

칼

어휘 questionnaire 설문지 effective 효과적인 elicit 끌어내다 consistent with ~와 일치하는 project 예상하다 stand out 두드러지다 end up 결국 ~하다 anticipate 예상하다
---

181 사실 관계 확인   고난도

번역 시장조사 연구에 관해 언급되지 않은 것은?
(A) 두 도시에서 실시되었다.
(B) 모바일 기기를 사용해야 했다.
(C) 설문에는 객관식 질문이 있었다.
(D) 참가자마다 4개의 음료를 시음했다.

해설 시장조사에 대해 설명(Description)한 부분을 보면, 조사가 오하이오 주 클리블랜드와 펜실베이니아 주 피츠버그에 있는 레스토랑에서 이루어졌다(The study took place ~ at the company's restaurant locations in Cleveland, Ohio and Pittsburgh, Pennsylvania)는 것과 참가자들이 휴대폰으로 링크에 접속해 객관식 질문과 주관식 질문에 답했다(They ~ had to access a link via their mobile phone and take a survey consisting of multiple-choice and open-ended questions)는 것을 확인할 수 있다. 하지만 참가자들이 무작위로 배정된 4가지 맛 중 하나를 시음했다(They were randomly assigned one of the four flavors)고 했으므로, 잘못된 정보를 언급한 (D)가 정답이다.

182 세부 사항 고난도

번역 음료 샘플 2종이 공통으로 받았던 의견은?
(A) 식감이 너무 걸쭉하다.
(B) 맛이 상쾌했다.
(C) 맛의 배합이 고르지 않았다.
(D) 색채가 끌린다.

해설 전반적인 결과(Overall findings) 부분에서 음료별로 가장 많이 나온 의견(Most frequent comments)을 보면, 1번 샘플("too much banana flavor", "couldn't taste much cherry")과 2번 샘플("not enough pineapple taste")에서 과일 맛의 배합이 고르지 않다는 공통 의견을 확인할 수 있다. 따라서 (C)가 정답이다.

어휘 uneven 고르지 않은

183 추론 / 암시

번역 몬트로이 스팟에 관해 사실인 것은?
(A) 다른 지역으로 확장할 계획이다.
(B) 피츠버그에 본사를 두고 있다.
(C) 다양한 병 음료를 제공한다.
(D) 과거에 골마크 리서치 사의 자문을 구한 적이 있다.

해설 이메일의 두 번째 단락에서 펠라 씨는 몬트로이 스팟을 위해 실시했던 이전 연구 결과를 토대로 보니(Based on our previous studies for this client) 대부분의 결과가 자신의 예상과 일치했다고 했다. 따라서 몬트로이 스팟이 이전에도 골마크 리서치 사에 조사를 의뢰한 적이 있다고 추론할 수 있으므로, (D)가 정답이다.

184 연계

번역 펠라 씨가 예상했던 것보다 더 긍정적인 의견을 받은 샘플은?
(A) 1번 샘플
(B) 2번 샘플
(C) 3번 샘플
(D) 4번 샘플

해설 이메일의 두 번째 단락에서 펠라 씨는 자신이 가장 인기 없으리라 생각했던 맛이 두 번째로 인기가 있었다(What I had thought would be the least popular flavor ended up being the second most popular)고 했는데, 보고서 개요의 결과 부분을 보면 두 번째로 인기 있는 맛은 '아주 맛있다'라는 응답 비율이 84%에 달했던 3번 샘플임을 확인할 수 있다. 따라서 (C)가 정답이다.

185 사실 관계 확인

번역 밀리건 씨에 관해 알 수 있는 것은?
(A) 한때 식품 제조업체에서 일했다.
(B) 회사에서 처음으로 전자 설문지를 만들었다.
(C) 10월에 고객과 만날 예정이다.
(D) 시장 보고서를 위해 그래프를 수정했다.

해설 이메일의 첫 번째 단락에서 펠라 씨는 밀리건 씨에게 그녀가 고안한 전자 설문지가 상당히 효과적이었다(The electronic questionnaire you designed was quite effective)고 한 후, 회사가 이전에 온라인 양식을 사용한 적이 없다는 점(our firm had never used the online format before)을 언급했다. 따라서 밀리건 씨가 회사에서 처음으로 전자 설문지를 만들었음을 알 수 있으므로, (B)가 정답이다.

어휘 manufacturer 제조업체 revise 수정하다

▶▶ Paraphrasing 지문의 The electronic questionnaire you designed → 정답의 She created a ~ electronic survey
지문의 our firm had never used the online format before → a firm's first electronic survey

186-190 소식지 기사 + 전단지 + 이메일

알타 프로퍼티즈 소식지   8월호

시카고—알타 프로퍼티즈는 입주민의 안락함과 편리함을 중요하게 여깁니다. [186]그래서 당사는 런드리 플래쉬라는 주문형 서비스와 제휴를 맺었다는 사실을 알리게 되어 기쁩니다. 이 서비스는 입주민의 세탁물을 수거한 후, 세탁한 의류를 이용이 편리한 보관함에 다시 배달합니다.

우리 아파트 두 동 모두 이 서비스를 이용할 수 있게 됩니다. 보관함은 8월 20일 멘워스 빌딩의 입주민 휴게실, 8월 27일 코트웨이 빌딩 헬스장 맞은편에 설치됩니다. 모든 입주민은 각자에게 배정된 사물함 열쇠를 건물 관리자로부터 받게 됩니다. [187]각 건물 로비에 있는 프런트 데스크 안내인이 런드리 플래쉬 직원이 서명하고 출입할 수 있도록 관리하는 일을 맡을 예정입니다.

[189(C)]세탁물 수거는 회사 웹사이트 www.laundry-flash.com을 통해 쉽게 예약할 수 있습니다. [189(A)]서비스 소요시간은 이틀이며, 당일 특급 서비스 옵션도 이용할 수 있습니다. [189(B)]세탁비는 셔츠 한 벌에 3달러, 바지 한 벌에 5달러, 정장이나 드레스 한 벌에 15달러입니다. [189(D)]로비에서 구하실 수 있는 회사 전단지에 할인 쿠폰이 제공됩니다.

어휘 property 부동산, 건물 comfort 편안함 convenience 편리함 on-demand service 주문형 서비스 tenant 입주민, 세입자 garment 의류 installation 설치 assigned 배정된 attendant 안내인 entrust 위임하다, 맡기다 turnaround time 소요시간; 회송 시간 flyer 전단지

런드리 플래쉬

세탁물을 수거하고, 세탁하고, 이틀 후에 다시 배달해 드릴 것을 보장합니다!

알타 프로퍼티즈 빌딩 입주민 여러분께 알립니다. 당사는 여러분께 서비스를 제공해 드릴 만반의 [188]준비가 되어 있습니다!

[189(D)]특별 쿠폰 (코드번호 166) – 멘워스 빌딩과 코트웨이 빌딩 입주민들에 한해, 총 20달러 이상의 서비스 이용 시 10퍼센트를 할인해 드립니다.

서비스 요청 방법 – [189(C)]당사 웹사이트 www.laundry-flash.com을 방문해 온라인 예약 섹션으로 가세요. 555-0129번으로 전화하셔도 됩니다.

수거 일정

190북부 구역 (에이버리 가 5320번지 멘워스 빌딩 포함) – 월요일, 수요일, 금요일.

남부 구역 (딕슨 가 1811번지 코트웨이 빌딩 포함) – 화요일, 목요일, 토요일

가격 (이틀이 걸리는 기본 서비스, 수거 및 배달 포함 비용) – **189(B)셔츠 3달러, 바지 5달러, 드레스 8달러, 정장 15달러, 세탁 후 개는 서비스 파운드 당 1.6달러, 189(A)당일 특급 서비스 추가 요금 10달러**

세탁물 가방 – 모든 고객은 첫 번째 배달 시 무료로 세탁물 가방을 하나씩 받게 되며, 향후 서비스 요청 시 사용할 수 있도록 보관하십시오. 세탁물 가방은 각 14달러에 추가로 구입할 수 있습니다.

어휘 mention 언급하다, 기재하다 surcharge 추가 요금
complimentary 무료인 additional 추가의 purchase 구입하다

수신: 제이콥 그리츠 (j-gritz@mail.com)
발신: 〈orders@laundry-flash.com〉
제목: 런드리 플래쉬 확인
날짜: 9월 1일

서비스를 신청해 주셔서 감사합니다—확인 번호 22176158.

190고객 성명: 제이콥 그리츠   보관함 번호: 12
190주소: 에이버리 가 5320번지   세탁물 수거 날짜: 9월 2일 월요일

품목	가격	품목 합계
셔츠 (세탁)	3달러 X 4	12달러
바지 (세탁)	5달러 X 4	20달러
세탁 가방	0달러	
	– 3.2달러 10퍼센트 쿠폰 코드 166	
	총 28.8달러	

결제 수단: 1362로 끝나는 신용카드

어휘 confirmation 확인

---

186 주제 / 목적

번역 소식지 기사의 주된 목적은?
(A) 독자에게 의견 구하기
(B) 입주민의 꾸준한 이용에 감사하기
(C) 수리 진행 상황 보고
(D) 신규 서비스 관련 세부 정보 제공

해설 소식지 기사의 첫 번째 단락에서 런드리 플래쉬라는 주문형 서비스와 제휴를 맺었다는 사실을 알리게 되어 기쁘다(we are pleased to announce that we have formed a partnership with Laundry Flash, an on-demand service)고 한 후, 해당 서비스에 대한 설명을 이어 가고 있다. 따라서 (D)가 정답이다.

187 세부 사항

번역 소식지 기사에 따르면 멘워스 빌딩과 코트웨이 빌딩의 공통점은?
(A) 입주민을 위한 운동시설을 갖추고 있다.
(B) 같은 날 사물함이 설치될 예정이다.
(C) 임대 매물의 개수가 같다.
(D) 안내인이 있는 프런트 데스크가 있다.

해설 소식지 기사의 두 번째 단락에서 각 건물 로비에 있는 프런트 데스크 안내인이 런드리 플래쉬 직원이 서명하고 출입할 수 있도록 관리하는 일을 맡을 예정(The front desk attendant in each building's lobby will be entrusted with signing in the Laundry Flash personnel)이라고 했으므로, 두 빌딩 모두 안내인이 있는 프런트 데스크가 있음을 알 수 있다. 따라서 (D)가 정답이다.

▶▶ Paraphrasing 지문의 each building
→ 질문의 the Menworth and the Courtway buildings
지문의 The front desk attendant
→ 정답의 attended front desks

188 동의어 찾기

번역 전단지에서 1번째 단락 2행의 "set"과 의미상 가장 가까운 것은?
(A) 추정된
(B) 복원된
(C) 준비된
(D) 고정된

해설 'set'을 포함한 부분은 '당사는 여러분께 서비스를 제공해 드릴 만반의 준비가 되어 있습니다(we're all set to do business with you)'라는 의미로 해석되는데, 여기서 set은 '준비가 된'이라는 뜻으로 쓰였다. 따라서 (C) ready가 정답이다.

189 연계

번역 기사에서 정확하지 않을 수 있는 정보는?
(A) 신속 처리 옵션
(B) 의류 세탁비
(C) 웹 주소
(D) 쿠폰 사용 가능 여부

해설 소식지 기사의 마지막 단락에서 세탁비가 셔츠 한 벌에 3달러, 바지 한 벌에 5달러, 정장이나 드레스 한 벌에 15달러(Cleaning fees are $3 per shirt, $5 per pair of pants, and $15 per suit or dress)라고 했지만, 전단지에 나온 가격(Pricing) 정보에는 셔츠 3달러, 바지 5달러, 드레스 8달러, 정장 15달러(Shirt $3, Pair of Pants $5, Dress $8, Suit $15)라고 되어 있다. 따라서 기사의 드레스 세탁비가 정확하지 않다고 볼 수 있으므로, (B)가 정답이다. 참고로, 기사와 전단지에 나온 (A), (C), (D) 관련 정보는 서로 일치한다.

어휘 expedite 신속하게 처리하다

190 연계

번역 그리츠 씨에 관해 가장 사실에 가까운 것은?
(A) 세탁물 가방을 추가로 요청했다.
(B) 멘워스 빌딩에 산다.
(C) 화요일에 옷을 돌려받을 것이다.
(D) 신용카드 사용으로 할인을 받을 것이다.

해설 이메일에 적힌 그리츠 씨의 주소(Address: 5320 Avery Street)와 전단지의 수거 일정(Pickup Schedule)에 나온 멘워스 빌딩의 주소(the Menworth Building at 5320 Avery Street)가 같다. 따라서 그리츠 씨가 멘워스 빌딩에 산다고 추론할 수 있으므로, (B)가 정답이다.

191-195 웹페이지 + 이메일 + 온라인 후기

www.jerroldssupply.com/about

제럴드 서플라이

회사 소개

당사는 식품 서비스 업체들을 대상으로 하는 지역 최대의 회원제 창고형 할인점입니다.

자격 있는* 업체라면 누구나 무료로 회원이 될 수 있습니다. 다음과 같은 굉장한 혜택을 누리세요:

- **원스톱 쇼핑** – 모든 주요 브랜드의 식음료와 주방 장비, 심지어 요리사 복장까지 구비하고 있습니다. 단 한 번 방문으로 필요한 물품을 모두 사 가세요.
- **최소 구매 요건 없음** – 193(B)/(C)당사는 일반인도 이용이 가능한 바스코 클럽 및 기타 창고형 할인점들과 가장 중요한 면에서 차별성을 보여줍니다. 제럴드 서플라이에서는 물품을 대량으로 구입할 필요가 전혀 없습니다.
- **특별 행사 광고** – 회원들에게 매달 이메일을 보내 특별 할인 행사 소식을 알려 드립니다.

*주의: 당사는 도매 시장으로 일반인에게 개방되지 않습니다. 회원증은 식당을 소유하거나 운영하는 사람에게만 발급됩니다. 191/192처음 매장을 방문할 때 식품 서비스 업체로 허가 받았음을 증명하는 유효 서류를 제시해야 합니다. 그러면 카드를 발급 받게 되는데, 이는 양도가 불가능합니다. 하지만 달마다 쇼핑객 한 명을 데려오실 수 있습니다. 단, 해당자는 입장할 때 사진이 있는 신분증을 제시해야 합니다.

어휘 supply 용품, 공급(품) warehouse store 창고형 할인점 operator 사업자, 사업체 qualified 자격 있는 benefit 혜택 stock 구비해 두다, 갖추고 있다 equipment 장비 apparel 의류 in bulk 대량으로 special 특별한 것, 특별가; 특별한 wholesale 도매 valid 유효한 transferable 양도할 수 있는 present 제시하다, 보여주다

수신: 스텔라 애들슨
발신: 티나 롤리
날짜: 10월 9일
제목: 내일 볼일 – 관심 있나요?

안녕하세요, 스텔라,

194내일 아침에 제럴드 서플라이에 가서 식당에서 사용할 냅킨과 포장 용기를 구비해 놓아야 해요. 당신이 저번에 그 창고형 할인점에 가보고 싶다고 하길래, 이번에 혹시 같이 갈 의향이 있는지 궁금해요. 오전 9시 정각에 당신이 사는 아파트 앞으로 데리러 갈 수 있어요. 문자 하거나 이메일로 회신해서 갈 수 있는지 알려줘요.

방문할 때는 꼭 신분증을 지참하고 편안한 신발을 신으세요. 매장 면적이 넓어서 많이 걸어야 하거든요. 195또 냉동 코너를 둘러보고 싶으면 겉옷을 챙겨 오세요. 꽤 추워요.

내일 만났으면 좋겠어요.

티나

어휘 errand 볼일, 심부름 stock up 구비해 두다, 비축해 두다 carry-out 포장해서 사 가는 음식 container 용기 express 표현하다 outerwear 겉옷

후기 게시자: 스텔라 애들슨　　　　　**후기 게시일: 10월 11일**

어제 제럴드 서플라이에 처음 가봤어요. 198(A)바스코 클럽과 마찬가지로 굉장히 저렴한 가격에 상품을 판매하는 창고형 할인점이죠. 그런데 그 매장과 달리 평면 TV나 컴퓨터 장비는 팔지 않아요. 대신 식당을 계속 운영하는 데 필요한 모든 것을 제공해요. 6,000개 들이 종이 냅킨도 봤어요! 더욱 놀라운 것은 다양한 냉동 해산물을 구비하고 있었어요. 195전 생각했던 것보다 그 코너에 훨씬 오래 있었는데 스웨터를 가져왔으면 좋겠다 싶었어요. 매장이 붐비고 계산대 줄이 길지만, 줄이 빨리 빠져요. 전 운 좋게도 회원권 있는 사람을 알아서 그녀가 비품을 살 때 손님으로 갈 수 있었어요.

어휘 impressively 인상적으로, 굉장히 flat-screen 평면 화면 up and running 운영 중인, 영업 중인 vast 방대한 intend 계획하다, 의도하다

---

191 사실 관계 확인

번역 웹페이지에서 제럴드 서플라이에 관해 명시된 것은?
(A) 회원권은 양도할 수 없다.
(B) 일주일 내내 문을 연다.
(C) 요리사를 위한 요리교실을 연다.
(D) 자동 계산대를 갖추고 있다.

해설 웹페이지의 마지막 단락에서 회원 카드는 양도가 불가능하다(a card that is not transferable)고 했으므로, (A)가 정답이다.

▶ **Paraphrasing** 지문의 not transferable
→ 정답의 may not be transferred

---

192 세부 사항

번역 제럴드 서플라이의 회원 카드를 받는 데 필요한 것은?
(A) 이메일 초대장
(B) 최소 월 구매액
(C) 유효한 사업자 등록증
(D) 사진이 있는 신분증 두 종류

해설 웹페이지의 마지막 단락에서 식품 서비스 업체로 허가 받았음을 증명하는 유효 서류를 제시해야(you must present a valid document showing you are licensed as a food service business) 회원 카드가 발급된다고 했으므로, (C)가 정답이다.

▶ **Paraphrasing** 지문의 a valid document showing you are licensed as a food service business
→ 정답의 A valid business license

---

193 연계　　　　　[고난도]

번역 바스코 클럽에 관해 암시되지 않은 것은?
(A) 가전제품을 판매한다.
(B) 일반인이 쇼핑할 수 있다.
(C) 상품은 대량으로만 구입할 수 있다.
(D) 모회사가 제럴드 서플라이와 같다.

해설　온라인 후기의 초반부에서 제럴드 서플라이는 바스코 클럽과 달리 평면 TV나 컴퓨터 장비는 팔지 않는다(unlike that store(=Bascor Club), it does not sell flat-screen TVs or computer equipment)고 했으므로, 바스코 클럽에서는 가전제품을 판매한다고 추론할 수 있다. 또한 웹페이지의 두 번째 혜택에서 일반인도 이용이 가능한(open-to-the-public) 바스코 클럽 및 기타 창고형 매장들과 달리 제럴드 서플라이에서는 물품을 대량으로 구입할 필요가 전혀 없다(you never have to buy items in bulk at Jerrold's Food Supply)고 했으므로, 바스코 클럽에서는 일반인도 쇼핑할 수 있지만 상품은 대량으로만 구입할 수 있음을 추론할 수 있다. 따라서 근거를 찾을 수 없는 (D)가 정답이다.

194 사실 관계 확인

번역　이메일에서 롤리 씨가 구매하겠다고 언급한 한 가지는?
(A) 요리 도구
(B) 식기류
(C) 식품 포장재
(D) 원재료

해설　이메일의 첫 번째 단락에서 롤리 씨는 식당에서 사용할 냅킨과 포장 용기를 구비해 놓아야 한다(I have to ~ stock up on napkins and carry-out containers for the restaurant)고 했으므로, (C)가 정답이다.

▶▶ Paraphrasing　지문의 carry-out containers for the restaurant → 정답의 Food packaging

195 연계　[고난도]

번역　애들슨 씨에 관해 가장 사실에 가까운 것은?
(A) 롤리 씨의 충고를 따르지 않았다.
(B) 제럴드 서플라이로 가는 일정이 연기되었다.
(C) 결국 롤리 씨와 함께 가지 못했다.
(D) 유난히 붐비는 날 제럴드 서플라이에 갔다.

해설　이메일의 두 번째 단락에서 롤리 씨는 애들슨 씨에게 냉동 코너를 둘러보고 싶으면 겉옷을 챙겨오라(if you'd like to look around the freezer section, bring some kind of outerwear)고 조언했는데, 애들슨 씨가 쓴 온라인 후기의 중반부를 보면 스웨터를 가져가지 않아서 후회했다(it made me wish I'd brought a sweater)고 되어 있다. 따라서 그녀가 롤리 씨의 충고를 따르지 않았다고 추론할 수 있으므로, (A)가 정답이다. 참고로, 매장이 붐볐지만 계산대 줄이 빨리 빠졌다고 했기 때문에 (D)를 사실로 보기 어렵다.

196-200 발표 유인물+안건+문자 메시지

귀사 웹사이트 개선법

발표자: 그렉 우, 웹사이트 컨설턴트

대상: 브렉스비 사이클 사　　　　날짜: 5월 2일

회사 웹사이트의 장점:
- 196(B)멋진 색채 조합—사이트를 탐색할 때 보기 편안함
- 196(A)모든 제품군의 사진이 매력적임—크기 및 공간배치가 적절함
- 196(D)"왜 사이클링을 시작하는가?"라는 제목의 코너는 사이클링의 건강상 이점을 설득력 있게 설명

회사 웹사이트의 단점:
- 각 페이지에 글과 정보가 너무 많음—혼란스러울 수 있음
- 로딩에 시간이 너무 많이 소요됨—일부 고객은 이것 때문에 사이트에서 나갈 수 있음
- 구매 시 복잡한 결제 절차—작성할 양식이 너무 많음

실행 계획 – 회사의 승인을 받아 다음 방식으로 웹사이트를 개선하고자 함:
- 198사이트를 열면 재생되는 디지털 동영상을 제거해 로딩에 필요한 시간 대폭 단축
- 결제 절차를 간소화하는 동시에, 결제 옵션(예: 신용카드, 상품권, 전자 상거래 계정 등)을 더 눈에 잘 띄는 그래픽으로 제시
- 사이트에 회사의 최신 전기 자전거 제품군에 대한 별도 코너를 만들고 자전거 충전 방법에 대한 간략한 설명을 포함

어휘　color scheme 색채 조합　comfortable 편안한　appealing 매력적인, 눈길을 끄는　spacing 공간배치　appropriate 적절한　persuasively 설득력 있게　confusing 혼란스러운　complicated 복잡한　checkout process 결제 절차, 대여 절차　approval 승인　improve 개선하다　streamline 간소화하다　prominent 두드러진, 눈에 잘 띄는　separate 분리된, 별도의　explanation 설명　charge 충전하다

브렉스비 사이클 사

5월 30일 전략회의* 제안 안건

오후 2시	**논제 개요** – 진행 중인 회사 웹사이트 개선 작업
오후 2시 15분	**의제 1** – 198컨설턴트의 제안 중 실행된 사항(더 빨라진 로딩 시간, 더 잘 보이는 결제 옵션, 최신 제품 코너 추가) 및 기각된 사항(더 간결해진 결제 절차)에 대한 자세한 설명과 함께 현재 웹사이트 시연
오후 3시	**의제 2** – 디지털 마케팅 담당 이사 트로이 바든이 컨설턴트 방문 시 제안되었던 소소한 사이트 추가 수정 사항 발표
오후 4시	**의제 3** – 197온라인 채팅 지원 서비스 제공 시 장단점 논의. 사내 웹 개발자인 프레드 캘러웨이가 진행
오후 4시 30분	200**의제 4** – 사이트에 적용해볼 만한 쌍방향 기능에 관해 집단 자유토론
오후 5시	**폐회**

* 영업부장 앨리슨 혈이 진행: 참석자는 노트북 컴퓨터를 가져올 것

어휘　ongoing 진행 중인　effort (특정 목적을 이루려는) 활동, 작업, 노력　walk-through (주로 직접 보여 주는) 단계적인 설명, 시연　implement 실행하다　reject 기각하다　modification 수정(사항)　pros and cons 장단점　in-house 사내의　potential 잠재적인, 가능한　interactive 상호의, 쌍방형의　feature 기능, 특징　adjournment 폐회

발신: 프레드 캘러웨이 [5월 30일 오전 10시 17분]

안녕하세요, 앨리스. 방금 경쟁사 웹사이트를 조사했는데 흥미로운 게 있네요. 한 코너에서 컴퓨터 마우스나 터치 스크린을 199조작해 '주문 제작'할 수 있는 자전거의 디지털 이미지를 제공해요. 회의 참석자 모두에게 이걸 보여주려고 해요. 200그러니 사이트에 적용해볼 만한 쌍방향 기능에 관한 토론 시간에 15분을 더 할당했으면 해요. 고마워요.

Test 7

> 어휘 competitor 경쟁사 customize 주문 제작하다
> manipulate 조작하다 allot 할당하다

196 사실 관계 확인

번역 브렉스비 사이클 사 웹사이트의 장점으로 언급되지 않은 것은?
(A) 제품 이미지
(B) 색상 선택
(C) 글자의 크기
(D) 자전거 타기와 건강 관련 내용

해설 유인물에 나열된 회사 웹사이트의 장점(Strengths of company's Web site) 중 '모든 제품군의 사진이 매력적임(Appealing photos of all product lines)'에서 (A)를, '멋진 색채 조합(Attractive color schemes)'에서 (B)를, '사이클링의 건강상 이점을 설득력 있게 설명(Section ~ persuasively outlines health benefits of cycling)'에서 (D)를 확인할 수 있다. 따라서 언급되지 않은 (C)가 정답이다.

> ▶▶ Paraphrasing 지문의 photos of all product lines
> → 보기 (A)의 image of merchandise
> 지문의 color schemes
> → 보기 (B)의 choice of color
> 지문의 Section ~ outlines health benefits of cycling → 보기 (D)의 content on cycling and health

197 추론 / 암시   고난도

번역 5월 30일 회의 참석자들이 할 것 같은 일은?
(A) 제안의 장점 토론
(B) 대여받은 노트북 컴퓨터 사용
(C) 컨설턴트의 발표 듣기
(D) 프로젝트 마감일 결정

해설 안건의 세 번째 의제에서 온라인 채팅 지원 서비스 제공 시의 장단점을 논의(Discussion of pros and cons of offering online chat support)할 예정이라고 되어 있으므로, (A)가 정답이다. 참고로, 노트북 컴퓨터는 참석자가 가져와서 사용하는 것이기 때문에 (B)는 정답이 될 수 없다.

> ▶▶ Paraphrasing 지문의 Discussion of pros ~ of offering online chat support
> → 정답의 Debate the merits of a proposal

198 연계   고난도

번역 최근 브렉스비 사이클 사 웹사이트에 생겼을 것 같은 변화는?
(A) 설명 페이지가 단축되었다.
(B) 디지털 동영상이 제거되었다.
(C) 결제 절차가 간소화되었다.
(D) 제품 범주가 변경되었다.

해설 유인물에 적힌 웹사이트 개선 실행 계획(Action plan)에서 사이트를 열면 재생되는 디지털 동영상을 제거해 로딩에 필요한 시간을 대폭 단축하겠다(Removing a digital video that plays when the site is launched, which will greatly reduce the time needed for loading)고 했는데, 안건의 첫 번째 의제를 보면 컨설턴트의 제안에 따라 실행된 사항(implemented ~ suggestions from consultant) 중 하나로 '더 빨라진 로딩 시간(faster loading time)'이 언급되었다. 따라서 디지털 동영상이 제거되었다고 추론할 수 있으므로, (B)가 정답이다

어휘 eliminate 제거하다

> ▶▶ Paraphrasing 지문의 Removing a digital video
> → 정답의 A digital video was eliminated

199 동의어 찾기

번역 문자 메시지에서 4행의 "manipulating"과 의미상 가장 가까운 것은?
(A) 속이기
(B) 작동하기
(C) 변경하기
(D) 설치하기

해설 'manipulating'을 포함한 부분은 '컴퓨터 마우스나 터치 스크린을 조작하여(by manipulating a computer mouse or touch screen)'라는 의미로 해석된다. 따라서 '작동하기, 조작하기'라는 의미의 (B) operating이 정답이다.

200 연계

번역 캘러웨이 씨가 시간을 더 많이 잡고 싶은 의제는?
(A) 의제 1
(B) 의제 2
(C) 의제 3
(D) 의제 4

해설 문자 메시지의 후반부에서 캘러웨이 씨는 사이트에 적용해볼 만한 쌍방형 기능에 관한 토론 시간에 15분을 더 할당하고 싶다(I'd like to allot 15 more minutes to our discussion on potential interactive features)고 했는데, 이 토론은 안건에서 4번째 의제(Brainstorming of potential interactive features for site)에 해당된다. 따라서 (D)가 정답이다.

> ▶▶ Paraphrasing 지문의 would like to allot 15 more minutes
> → 질문의 want to schedule more time

TEST 8

101 (C)	**102** (A)	**103** (D)	**104** (B)	**105** (B)
106 (D)	**107** (C)	**108** (C)	**109** (B)	**110** (A)
111 (C)	**112** (C)	**113** (A)	**114** (D)	**115** (D)
116 (A)	**117** (B)	**118** (B)	**119** (D)	**120** (D)
121 (C)	**122** (D)	**123** (A)	**124** (B)	**125** (B)
126 (D)	**127** (C)	**128** (A)	**129** (C)	**130** (A)
131 (B)	**132** (C)	**133** (D)	**134** (A)	**135** (C)
136 (C)	**137** (B)	**138** (D)	**139** (C)	**140** (D)
141 (D)	**142** (A)	**143** (B)	**144** (D)	**145** (D)
146 (B)	**147** (A)	**148** (C)	**149** (D)	**150** (A)
151 (C)	**152** (D)	**153** (D)	**154** (C)	**155** (C)
156 (A)	**157** (D)	**158** (C)	**159** (C)	**160** (B)
161 (C)	**162** (C)	**163** (A)	**164** (C)	**165** (B)
166 (A)	**167** (B)	**168** (B)	**169** (D)	**170** (B)
171 (D)	**172** (D)	**173** (B)	**174** (C)	**175** (A)
176 (B)	**177** (A)	**178** (D)	**179** (B)	**180** (D)
181 (D)	**182** (B)	**183** (C)	**184** (D)	**185** (A)
186 (B)	**187** (B)	**188** (C)	**189** (A)	**190** (D)
191 (B)	**192** (D)	**193** (C)	**194** (B)	**195** (A)
196 (D)	**197** (B)	**198** (A)	**199** (C)	**200** (C)

PART 5

101 소유대명사 _ 주격 보어 `고난도`

해설 주격 관계대명사 that이 이끄는 절의 주격 보어 자리로, to keep의 수식을 받으며 선행사 a souvenir photo와 동격 관계를 이룬다. 따라서 빈칸에는 참가자들이 간직할 기념사진을 가리키는 대명사가 들어가야 하므로, participants' souvenir photo를 대신하는 소유대명사 (C) theirs가 정답이다.

번역 단체관광이 끝날 때마다 참가자들은 보관용으로 기념사진을 하나 받을 것이다.

어휘 participant 참가자 souvenir photo 기념사진

102 명사 자리 _ 주격 보어

해설 주어 The key의 주격 보어 자리로, key와 동격 관계를 이루는 명사 또는 key를 보충 설명하는 형용사가 들어갈 수 있다. 성공의 열쇠가 무엇인지 정의하는 문장이므로, 주어와 보어가 동격 관계를 이루어야 자연스럽다. 따라서 '진짜임, 진정성'이라는 의미의 명사인 (A) authenticity가 정답이다. (B) authentic은 '진짜인, 정확한'이라는 의미로 문맥상 어색하고, (C) authenticate는 동사, (D) authentically는 부사로 품사상 빈칸에 들어갈 수 없다.

번역 토속음식점 운영 시 성공의 열쇠는 진짜 전통음식을 내는 것이다.

어휘 ethnic 민족적인, 토속적인 authenticate 진짜임을 증명하다 authentically 진정으로

103 동사 어휘

해설 how가 이끄는 명사절을 목적어로 취하는 타동사 자리이다. 프로젝트에 얼마나 더 많은 나무가 포함될지는 아직 정해지지 않은 사항으로, 조경사들이 판단해야 할 일이라고 볼 수 있다. 따라서 '판정하다, 판단하다'라는 의미의 (D) determine이 정답이다.

번역 시의 조경사들은 스펜서 운하사업에 얼마나 더 많은 나무가 포함될지를 판단하기 위해 노력하고 있다.

어휘 landscape architect 조경사 canal 운하 reflect 반영하다 encourage 독려하다 strengthen 강화하다

104 전치사 어휘

해설 명사 request를 목적어로 취하는 전치사 자리로, 빈칸을 포함한 전치사구는 동사구 can be mailed를 수식한다. 요청 시 카탈로그 발송이 가능하다는 내용이 되어야 자연스러우므로, request와 함께 '요청 시, 요청하면'이라는 의미를 완성하는 (B) on이 정답이다. 참고로, on 대신 upon이나 by를 쓸 수도 있으며, 고정 표현이니 암기해 두는 것이 좋다.

번역 요청 시 당사 제품에 대한 설명과 이미지가 담긴 인쇄 카탈로그를 고객님들께 우편으로 발송해 드립니다.

어휘 description 설명

105 부사 어휘

해설 빈칸을 포함한 to부정사구(to perform ~ conditions)는 어떤 목적을 위해 기계가 설계되었는지를 설명하고 있다. 따라서 작동 기능을 긍정적으로 묘사하는 부사가 빈칸에 들어가야 자연스러우므로, '확실하게, 안정적으로'라는 의미의 (B) reliably가 정답이다.

번역 산드락스 사의 채굴 기계는 아무리 열악한 조건에서도 안정적으로 작동하도록 설계되었다.

어휘 mining 채굴 perform 작동하다 harsh 혹독한 successively 연속해서 spaciously 넓게 thoughtfully 사려 깊게

106 명사 어휘

해설 전치사 at의 목적어 역할을 하는 명사 자리로, 빈칸을 포함한 전치사구가 동사 walk를 수식하고 있다. 느긋하다(relaxed)는 것은 걸음의 빠르기를 묘사하는 표현이므로, '속도'라는 의미의 (D) pace가 빈칸에 들어가야 자연스럽다. 참고로, pace는 전치사 at과 어울려 쓰인다.

번역 초보 등산객은 느긋한 속도로 걷고 너무 빨리 가지 않는 것이 좋다. 특히 가파른 길에서는 말이다.

어휘 recommend 권고하다 novice 초보 avoid -ing ~하는 것을 피하다 steep 가파른 stretch 뻗기 approach 접근

107 부사 자리 _ 동사 수식

해설 빈칸을 포함한 원급 표현 as ~ as possible이 동사 is operating을 수식하고 있으므로, 빈칸에는 부사가 들어가야 한다. 따라서 '효율적으로'라는 의미의 (C) efficiently가 정답이다.

번역 가정의 난방 시스템이 최대한 효율적으로 작동하도록 하려면 6개월마다 점검 해야 한다.

어휘 ensure 확실히 ~하게 하다, 보장하다 operate 작동하다 efficiency 효율 efficient 효율적인

108 부사 어휘

해설 be동사와 to부정사 사이에 들어갈 수 있는 형용사나 부사를 선택하는 문제이다. 앞절이 긍정문이고 뒷절이 but으로 시작하기 때문에, '계획은 있지만 정확한 위치는 결정되지 않았다'라는 내용이 되어야 자연스럽다. 따라서 be동사와 to부정사 사이에 들어가 '아직 ~하지 않고 있다'라는 의미를 완성하는 (C) yet이 정답이다. 「be yet to부정사」, 「have yet to부정사」 구문은 암기해 두는 것이 좋다.

번역 이스트 힐스 시티에 연구개발 센터를 신축한다는 계획은 있지만 정확한 위치는 아직 결정되지 않았다.

어휘 exact 정확한

109 동사 어휘 고난도

해설 damage를 목적어로 취하는 동사 자리로, 빈칸이 포함된 절은 「so+형용사+that+완전한 절(너무 ~해서 ~하다)」 구문에서 결과 부분에 해당한다. 내구성이 뛰어나서(so durable) 떨어져도 손상을 입지 않는다는 내용이 되어야 자연스러우므로, '(상처, 피해 등을) 입다, 당하다'라는 의미의 (B) sustain이 정답이다.

번역 엑스텔리아 X10 휴대전화는 내구성이 뛰어나서 단단한 표면에 떨어져도 손상을 입지 않을 것이다.

어휘 durable 내구성이 좋은 surface 표면 terminate 끝내다 diminish 감소하다 commit 전념하다, 맡기다

110 형용사 자리 _ 명사 수식

해설 빈칸에는 personal을 수식하는 부사, 또는 Web sites를 수식하는 형용사가 들어갈 수 있다. 문맥상 개발 대상인 웹사이트를 수식하는 형용사가 들어가야 자연스러우므로, '멋들어진, 인상적인'이라는 의미의 (A) impressive가 정답이다. '인상적으로 개인적인'이라는 내용이 되면 어색하므로, (C) impressively는 정답이 될 수 없다.

번역 락스미테크 사는 합리적인 가격에 멋들어진 개인용 및 업체용 웹사이트를 개발한다.

어휘 affordable (가격이) 합리적인, 알맞은

111 부사절 접속사 고난도

해설 빈칸 뒤 완전한 절(supplies last)을 이끄는 접속사 자리이므로, '~하는 동안, ~하는 한'이라는 의미의 부사절 접속사 (C) while이 정답이다. (A) toward, (B) during, (D) within은 모두 전치사로 완전한 절을 이끌 수 없다.

번역 페어뷰 시의 새로운 재활용 통은 주민들에게 무료이며 재고가 떨어지지 않는 한 이용 가능하다.

어휘 supply 공급[비축]량, 물자 last 지속되다

112 전치사 어휘

해설 명사구 its mission statement를 목적어로 취하는 전치사 자리이다. 회사의 비전과 목표(The company's vision and objectives)는 회사 강령에 요약될 만한 내용이므로, '~안에'라는 의미의 (C) in이 정답이다.

번역 회사의 비전과 목표는 회사 강령에 간략히 요약되어 있다.

어휘 objective 목표 summarize 요약하다 briefly 간략히 mission statement 강령

113 형용사 어휘

해설 전치사 for와 어울려 쓰이는 형용사를 선택하는 문제이다. 공간을 거의 차지하지 않는 점(it occupies very little space)을 근거로 들어 특정 자전거가 소형 아파트에 적합하다고 주장하고 있으므로, '(~에) 이상적인, 안성맞춤인'이라는 뜻의 (A) ideal이 정답이다. 참고로, (D) capable은 전치사 of와 어울려 쓰인다.

번역 VT-5 실내운동용 자전거는 공간을 거의 차지하지 않기 때문에 소형 아파트에 안성맞춤이다.

어휘 exercise bike 실내운동용 자전거 occupy 차지하다 deliberate 신중한, 고의의 convincing 설득력 있는 capable 할 수 있는

114 부사 어휘 고난도

해설 과거분사 labeled를 적절히 수식하는 부사를 선택해야 한다. 힘들이지 않고(with minimum effort) 조립할 수 있게끔 라벨이 붙여진 방식을 묘사하는 부사가 빈칸에 들어가야 자연스럽다. 따라서 '명확하게, 뚜렷하게'라는 의미의 (D) explicitly가 정답이다.

번역 레나크 사의 모형 만들기 세트는 별로 힘들이지 않고 조립할 수 있도록 라벨이 명확하게 부착된 점이 특징이다.

어휘 kit (조립용) 세트 assemble 조립하다 minimum 최소한의 effort 힘, 노력 extremely 극도로 remotely 멀리서 promptly 지체 없이

115 명사 자리 _ 동사의 목적어

해설 that이 생략된 절에서 동사 finds의 목적어 역할을 하는 명사 자리이므로, '영감'이라는 의미의 (D) inspiration이 정답이다. 참고로, finds 바로 뒤에 목적격 보어 역할을 하는 to부정사나 형용사가 오려면, 앞에 목적격 관계대명사 혹은 선행사가 있어야 한다(eg. which he finds to be~).

번역 사진 공모전 우승자인 마크 머도는 공허한 사막 풍경에서 영감을 얻는다고 말한다.

어휘 empty 공허한 scenery 풍경 inspire 영감을 주다

116 동사 어형 _ 태

해설 조동사 can 뒤에 오는 동사원형 자리이다. 빈칸 뒤에 목적어가 없으므로, 주어인 mobile phones가 도구로 사용되는 대상임을 알 수 있다. 따라서 수동태 동사원형인 (A) be used가 정답이다.

번역 새로운 교육용 애플리케이션 덕분에 휴대전화가 교실에서 학습 도구로 이용될 수 있다.

117 전치사 어휘

해설 공원의 자체 관광버스(its own tour buses)는 통행이 가능하지만 일반 차량은 불가능하다는 내용이 되어야 자연스럽다. 즉, 자체 관광버스는 예외에 해당되므로, '~을 제외하고'라는 의미의 (B) except for가 정답이다.

번역 그린벨드 공원은 바이오 연료로 운행되는 자체 관광버스를 제외하고는 경치 좋은 공원 도로에서의 차량통행을 일체 허용하지 않는다.

어휘 vehicle 차량 scenic 경치 좋은 bio-fuel (재생 가능한) 바이오 연료 throughout ~ 내내 regardless of ~에 상관없이

118 형용사 자리 _ 분사

해설 빈칸은 interior designer를 꾸며주는 형용사 자리로, 부사 highly(매우)의 수식을 받는다. 따라서 보기에서 형용사 역할을 할 수 있는 분사 (A) accomplishing과 (B) accomplished 중 하나를 선택해야 하는데, '매우 뛰어난(=이미 업적을 이룬) 디자이너'라는 의미가 되어야 자연스러우므로, 과거분사형 형용사 (B) accomplished(유능한, 뛰어난)가 정답이 된다.

번역 매우 유능한 인테리어 디자이너인 알폰소 그리에코는 아주 다양한 고객들에게 디자인 해법을 제공한다.

어휘 a wide variety of 아주 다양한 accomplish 성취하다 accomplishment 성취

119 대명사 자리 _ 전치사의 목적어 _ 수 일치

해설 전치사 to의 목적어 역할을 하는 명사 자리로, 주격 관계대명사 who가 이끄는 절의 수식을 받는다. 빈칸은 선행사로서 관계사절의 동사 is와 수가 일치해야 하므로, 단수 대명사인 (D) anyone이 정답이 된다. 한정사인 (A) every는 명사 역할을 할 수 없고, (B) all 및 (C) those는 is와 수가 일치하지 않으므로 빈칸에 들어갈 수 없다. 참고로, all은 단수 동사와 쓰일 수도 있지만, who와 함께 사용되면 '~하는 모든 사람들'이라는 뜻을 나타내므로 복수 동사와 쓰여야 한다.

번역 맨징 취업박람회는 현재 고용 상태와 무관하게 새 일자리를 찾는 사람이면 누구나 참여할 수 있다.

어휘 career fair 취업박람회 without regard to ~에 상관없이 employment status 고용 상태

120 명사 어휘

해설 과거분사 limited의 수식을 받는 명사 자리로, 전치사 on과 어울려 쓰이는 단어가 들어가야 한다. 소셜 미디어 게시물(social media posts)과 사람들의 구매 결정(people's buying decisions) 간의 관계를 나타내는 문장이므로, '영향, 효과'라는 의미의 (D) impact가 정답이다. 참고로, '제휴, 관계'라는 뜻의 (C) association은 전치사 with와 함께 쓰인다.

번역 최근 연구에 따르면 소셜 미디어 게시물이 사람들의 구매 결정에 거의 영향을 미치지 않는다고 한다.

어휘 decision 결정 limited 아주 많지는 않은, 한정된 value 가치 function 기능

121 동사 어휘

해설 빈칸이 포함된 to부정사구(to ------- their meal options)는 고객

이 자신의 취향에 맞게(to suit their exact tastes) 이용할 수 있는 서비스를 나타낸다. 따라서 '주문 제작하다, 맞춤 주문하다'라는 의미의 (C) customize가 정답이다.

번역 제네빅 케이터링 사는 고객이 자신의 취향에 딱 맞게 식사 옵션을 맞춤 주문할 수 있도록 허용한다.

어휘 catering 음식조달업 suit 맞추다 taste 취향 fasten 매다 monitor 관찰하다, 감시하다 patronize 애용하다

122 형용사 자리 _ 명사 수식 [고난도]

해설 빈칸에는 professional을 수식하는 부사 또는 references를 수식하는 형용사가 들어갈 수 있다. 문맥상 제출하는 추천서의 특징을 묘사하는 단어가 들어가야 자연스러우므로, '긍정적인, 호의적인'이라는 뜻의 (D) positive가 정답이 된다. '긍정적으로 전문적인'이라는 내용이 되면 어색하므로 (C) positively는 정답이 될 수 없다.

번역 지원자들은 긍정적인 내용의 직장 추천서를 제공할 수 있는 3명의 이름을 요구 받을 것이다.

어휘 candidate 지원자 professional reference (전 직장 상사, 동료 등이 써주는) 추천서

123 명사 자리 _ to부정사의 목적어 [고난도]

해설 to attract의 목적어 역할을 하는 명사 자리로, 전치사구 for our brand의 수식을 받는다. 따라서 '(언론의) 관심, 홍보'라는 의미의 (A) publicity가 정답이다. 참고로, (D) public은 동사의 목적어로 쓰일 경우 the나 소유격과 같은 한정사와 쓰여 '대중, 사람들'이라는 의미를 나타내므로, 빈칸에는 적합하지 않다.

번역 마케팅 팀원들은 온라인 언론매체에 기사를 기고해 당사 브랜드를 홍보하고 있다.

어휘 contribute 기고하다 news outlet 언론매체 attract 끌어내다 publically 공공연하게, 공적으로 (= publicly) publicize 알리다, 홍보하다 public 대중의; 대중

124 부사절 접속사

해설 완전한 두 절을 이어주는 접속사 자리이므로, '~하자마자, ~하는 대로'라는 의미의 부사절 접속사인 (B) as soon as가 정답이다. (A) beginning from, (C) no earlier, (D) up to는 완전한 절을 이끌 수 없다.

번역 부스 씨는 후임자가 적절히 교육 받는 대로 해외사무소로 옮길 계획이다.

어휘 transfer 옮기다 replacement 후임자 properly 적절히, 제대로 up to 최대 ~까지; ~에 달려 있는

125 부사 자리 _ 동사 수식

해설 「주어(the company)+동사(rewards)+목적어(them)」 구조의 완전한 절 뒤에서 rewards를 수식하는 부사 자리이므로, '재정적으로'라는 의미의 (B) financially가 정답이다. (A) financial은 형용사, (C) finances는 명사/동사, (D) financed는 동사/과거분사로 품사상 빈칸에 들어갈 수 없다.

번역 영업사원들이 분기 매출 목표를 초과 달성하면 회사는 상여금 형태로 재정적으로 보상한다.

Test 8

어휘 exceed 초과하다 quarterly 분기의 reward 보상하다
financial 재정적인 finance 재정; 자금을 대다

어휘 earn 받다 ample 충분한 recognition 인정 manufacturer
제조업체 certification 인증(서), 증명(서)

126 가정법 과거완료 _ 태 　　고난도

해설 주어인 the shipping company의 동사 자리이다. If가 이끄는 절의 동사가 had been lost이므로, 과거 사실의 반대 상황을 가정하는 가정법 과거완료(「If+주어+had+p.p. ~, 주어+조동사 과거형+have+p.p.~」) 구문임을 알 수 있다. 따라서 (A) would have been offered와 (D) would have offered 중 하나를 선택해야 하는데, 운송회사는 보상을 제공하는(to compensate) 주체이므로, 능동태 동사인 (D) would have offered가 정답이 된다. 「offer+to부정사」는 '기꺼이 ~하겠다고 하다, 자청하다'라는 뜻으로 암기해 두면 좋다.

번역 운송 중에 소포가 분실되었던 거라면, 운송회사에서 기꺼이 손실을 보상하겠다고 제의했을 것이다.

어휘 transit 운송 compensate 보상하다

127 부사절 접속사 　　고난도

해설 빈칸 뒤 완전한 절(you are traveling for leisure or business)을 이끄는 접속사 자리이므로, or와 짝을 이루어 부사절 접속사로 쓰일 수 있는 (C) Whether가 정답이다. (A) Notwithstanding도 (주로 that과 함께) 접속사로 쓰일 수 있지만 '~일지라도'라는 뜻으로 문맥상 어색하다. (B) Either의 경우 or와 함께 상관접속사로 쓰일 수 있지만, 부사절과 주절을 이어줄 수는 없으므로 빈칸에 들어갈 수 없다. (D) No matter는 뒤에 how와 같은 의문사가 와야 부사절을 이끌 수 있다.

번역 여가를 위해 여행하든, 업무를 위해 여행하든, 위치가 편리한 호텔을 선택하는 것이 중요하다.

어휘 convenient 편리한 notwithstanding ~에도 불구하고; ~일지라도

128 형용사 어휘 　　고난도

해설 명사구 wording of the contract를 적절히 수식하는 형용사를 선택하는 문제이다. 계약서의 표현이 여러 가지 해석(multiple interpretations)을 초래한 원인은 명료하지 않았기 때문이라고 볼 수 있다. 따라서 '애매모호한'이라는 의미의 (A) ambiguous가 정답이다.

번역 안타깝게도 계약서의 모호한 표현 때문에 의미에 대해 여러 해석이 나왔다.

어휘 unfortunately 안타깝게도 contract 계약(서) interpretation 해석 forceful 강력한 widespread 널리 퍼진 skeptical 회의적인

129 동사 어형 _ 동명사

해설 분사형 전치사인 including의 목적어 역할을 하는 동시에 명사구 the first local manufacturer를 주격 보어로 취하는 자리이다. 따라서 동명사인 (C) being이 정답이다. (A) that is는 명사절이 아닌 관계사절(주격 관계대명사+be동사)이므로, including의 목적어 역할을 할 수 없다.

번역 FNR 금속은 지역 제조업체 최초로 '친환경 공장' 인증서를 받는 등 충분히 인정 받고 있다.

130 명사절 접속사 　　고난도

해설 명사구 shape and size를 한정 수식하는 동시에 절(shape and size may be required)을 이끄는 접속사 자리이다. 빈칸이 이끄는 절이 전치사 in의 목적어 역할을 하므로, 명사절 접속사가 들어가야 한다. 따라서 (A) whatever(어떤 ~이든)가 정답이다. (D) any는 한정사, (B) particular와 (C) contrast는 명사로, 모두 절을 이끌 수 없으므로 빈칸에 들어갈 수 없다.

번역 앨라랙스 그래픽스는 어떤 모양과 크기가 필요하든 모든 종류의 간판을 인쇄할 수 있다.

어휘 in particular 특히 in contrast ~에 반해

PART 6

131-134 이메일

수신: 현재 고객님들
발신: 새플러 운송회사
제목: 최신 정보
날짜: 11월 30일

전자상거래 업체를 위한 **최신 정보** – 반송 라벨을 만드는 솔루션

온라인 매매 거래가 지속적으로 증가하면서 전자상거래 업체들은 최근 구입했으나 **131원치 않게 된** 상품을 반품하려는 고객들의 요청을 더 많이 처리해야 하는 상황에 놓였습니다. 출고되는 소포마다 반품 라벨을 포함하면 고객이 물품을 **132더 쉽게** 반송할 수 있습니다. 반송 라벨은 상품이 구매**133된** 회사의 주소를 적은 스티커입니다. **134거기에는** 반품 중인 소포를 추적하기 위한 바코드도 내장돼 있습니다. 새플러 운송의 라벨 솔루션 소프트웨어는 명료하고 실용적인 반송 라벨을 만듭니다. 소프트웨어를 사용해 몇 분 만에 샘플 라벨을 만들어 보려면 여기를 클릭하세요. 그런 다음 업체용 소프트웨어를 구입할지 여부를 선택할 수 있습니다.

어휘 e-commerce 전자상거래 ongoing 지속되는 rise 증가 transaction 거래 mean 의미하다, ~하게 되다 outbound 나가는, 출고되는 elegant 세련된, 명료한 functional 기능적인, 실용적인

131 형용사 어휘 _ 과거분사

해설 return의 목적어 역할을 하는 명사 merchandise를 수식하는 형용사 자리로, 상품이 반품되는 사유를 나타내는 단어가 들어가야 자연스럽다. 따라서 '원치 않는'이라는 의미의 (B) unwanted가 정답이다.

어휘 canceled 취소된 unintended 뜻밖의 expired 만료된

132 형용사 자리 _ 목적격 보어 _ 어휘 　　고난도

해설 빈칸은 「makes+목적어(the process of sending items back)+목적격 보어」 구조에서 목적격 보어에 해당하는 자리이다. 직역하면 '물품 반

송 과정을 더 쉽게 만든다'라는 내용으로, 빈칸이 목적어의 특징에 대해 설명하고 있다. 따라서 형용사가 들어가야 자연스러우므로, '더 쉬운'이라는 의미의 (C) easier이 정답이다. (A) ease는 동사로서 '(통증 등이) 가벼워지다, 천천히 움직이다', 명사로서 '안락함, 용이함'이라는 뜻으로 쓰이므로, 문맥상 적절하지 않다. 부사는 make의 목적격 보어가 될 수 없고, 과거분사도 특별한 경우(eg. make oneself heard)를 제외하고는 불가능하므로, (B) easily와 (D) eased는 빈칸에 들어갈 수 없다.

133 관계부사

해설 완전한 절(the goods were purchased)을 이끌어 장소 명사 company를 수식하는 자리이므로, 관계부사 (A) where이 정답이다. 참고로, (B) whose는 소유격이기 때문에 뒤에 정관사 the 없이 바로 명사가 와야 하고, (C) that이나 (D) which는 관계대명사로 쓰일 경우 주어나 목적어가 없는 불완전한 절을 이끈다.

134 문맥에 맞는 문장 고르기　[고난도]

번역 (A) 거기에는 반품 중인 소포를 추적하기 위한 바코드도 내장돼 있습니다.
(B) 완전히 만족하지 못하는 상품은 교환할 수 있습니다.
(C) 더 나은 결과를 얻으려면 고객들은 그것을 나중에 배송하는 게 좋습니다.
(D) 온라인 업체로서 가정에서 편안히 물건을 팔 수 있습니다.

해설 빈칸 앞에서 반송 라벨은 회사의 주소를 적은 스티커(A return label is a sticker stating the address of the company)라고 소개했고, 뒤에서 새플러 운송의 라벨 솔루션 소프트웨어는 명료하고 실용적인 반송 라벨을 만든다(Saffler Shipping's label solution software makes elegant and functional return shipping labels)고 했다. 따라서 빈칸에도 반송 라벨과 관련된 설명이 들어가야 자연스러우므로, (A)가 정답이다. 참고로, 대명사 It은 A return label을 대신한다.

어휘 track 추적하다　comfort 편안함

135-138 웹페이지

롱몬트 부동산 회사 - 가상 홈 투어

현대 디지털 기술 덕분에, 주택 매수자들은 이제 가상 홈 투어를 통해 거주지를 떠나지 135않고도 부동산을 볼 수 있습니다. 롱몬트 부동산은 대다수 매물에 이러한 투어를 제공함으로써, 업계 혁명에 앞장서고 있습니다.

136당사의 모든 가상 투어에는 각 부동산의 사진과 쌍방형 동영상이 포함되어 있습니다. 투어는 각 가정의 모든 공간을 3차원 이미지로 제공하는 카메라를 이용해 137제작됩니다. 이 이미지를 통해 시청자는 직접 보는 것과 동일한 방식으로 디지털로 집을 '돌아다닐' 수 있습니다.

일단 가상 투어가 당사 사이트에 업로드되면, 고객들은 컴퓨터나 모바일 기기를 이용해 138거의 모든 곳에서 가상 투어를 볼 수 있습니다. 이 기술은 예비 주택 매수자들의 이동 시간과 수십 달러의 휘발유 값을 절약해 줄 겁니다.

가상 투어를 제공하는 현재 부동산 매물을 보시려면 <u>여기</u>를 클릭하세요.

어휘 virtual 가상의　property 부동산, 건물　at the forefront 선두에 있는, 앞서 있는　industry 업계, 산업　revolution 혁명　dimensional 차원의　manner 방식　in person 직접 guarantee 보장하다, 반드시 ~하게 하다　prospective 예비의

135 전치사 어휘

해설 동사구 look at properties와 동명사구 leaving their own residence를 적절히 연결해 주는 전치사를 선택하는 문제이다. 가상 홈 투어(virtual tours of homes)를 통해 주택 매수자들이 자신의 거주지에서 부동산을 살펴보는 것이 가능하다는 내용이므로, '거주지를 떠나지 않고'라는 의미를 완성하는 (C) without이 정답이다.

136 문맥에 맞는 문장 고르기

번역 (A) 일부 지역에서는 집값이 오르고 있지만 다른 지역에서는 그대로 유지되고 있습니다.
(B) 설문에 응답한 매수자들은 또한 직접 집을 방문하는 쪽을 선호한다고 밝혔습니다.
(C) 당사의 모든 가상 투어에는 각 부동산의 사진과 쌍방형 동영상이 포함되어 있습니다.
(D) 이 거주지에 대해 궁금한 점이 있으시면 저희 전문가 한 명이 도와드리겠습니다.

해설 빈칸 앞 문장에서 롱몬트 부동산은 대다수 매물에 가상 홈 투어를 제공한다(providing such tours for most of our properties)고 했고, 뒤에서는 가상 홈 투어의 제작 방식(using a camera that provides three-dimensional images of all the spaces in each home)을 설명했다. 따라서 빈칸에도 가상 홈 투어와 관련된 내용이 들어가야 자연스러우므로, (C)가 정답이다.

어휘 increase 오르다, 상승하다　region 지역　stay steady (가격 등이) 유지되다, 보합세를 보이다　interactive 쌍방형의

137 동사 어형 _ 시제　[고난도]

해설 주어인 The tours의 동사 자리이다. 해당 문장이 현재 제공 중인 홈 투어가 제작되는 방식을 설명하고 있으므로, 빈칸에는 일반적인 사실을 설명할 때 쓰이는 단순 현재시제 동사가 들어가야 자연스럽다. 따라서 (B) are created가 정답이다.

138 부사 어휘

해설 anywhere를 적절히 수식하는 부사를 선택하는 문제이다. 컴퓨터나 모바일 기기를 사용하여 가상 투어를 본다면 장소의 제약이 거의 없다고 할 수 있다. 따라서 anywhere와 함께 '거의 모든 곳'이라는 의미를 완성하는 (D) almost가 정답이다. 참고로, almost, nearly 등 측정/계산과 관련된 일부 부사는 명사를 수식할 수 있다.

139-142 전단지

플로럼 시의 자연 둘레길을 둘러보세요 – 편의시설 새 단장!

플로럼 공원여가과는 6개월에 걸친 둘레길 개선사업이 여름에 맞춰 완료되었음을 발표하게 되어 뿌듯합니다. 139둘레길 전체가 다시 한 번 방문객에게 개방됩니다. 공사 중에 인내심을 갖고 기다려 주셔서 감사합니다.

개선된 사항은 다음과 같습니다. 플로럼 공원 연못을 가로지르는 새 판자길을 설치해 습지 지역에 140안전하게 접근할 수 있도록 하였습니다. 141게다가, 지역 주민과 외지 방문객 모두가 좋아해 통행량이 많은 블루 트레일이 더 많은 등산객을 수용할 수 있도록 넓어졌습니다. 다른 산책길에도 소소한 개선이 많이

이루어졌습니다.

가파른 언덕길을 오르는 힘겨운 등산부터 평평한 초원을 따라 느긋하게 걷는 산책까지, 개선된 자연 둘레길에서는 모두가 자신의 **142역량**에 맞춰 도보여행을 즐길 수 있습니다. www.florham-trails.org를 방문하시면 쌍방형 둘레길 지도를 보실 수 있습니다.

어휘 trail 오솔길, 둘레길 amenity 편의시설 improvement 개선 (사항) patience 인내심 construction 공사 process 과정 extend (길 등이) 뻗다, 이어지다 wetland 습지 well-traveled 통행량이 많은 accommodate 수용하다 challenging 어려운, 힘든 leisurely 느긋한, 여유로운 steep 가파른 flat 평평한 meadow 초원

139 문맥에 맞는 문장 고르기 〔고난도〕

번역 (A) 공원과 직원들은 자원봉사자들과 긴밀하게 협력합니다.
(B) 조직적인 등산 동호회가 점점 더 인기를 끌고 있습니다.
(C) 둘레길 전체가 다시 한 번 방문객에게 개방됩니다.
(D) 도시의 공원 제도는 길고 흥미로운 역사를 가지고 있습니다.

해설 빈칸 앞 문장에서 6개월에 걸친 둘레길 개선사업이 완료되었다(its six-month trail improvement project has been completed in time for summer)는 소식을 알렸고, 뒤에서는 인내심을 갖고 기다려 준 것에 대해 감사(We thank you for your patience during the construction process)를 전했다. 따라서 빈칸에도 둘레길의 재개방과 관련된 내용이 들어가야 문맥상 자연스러우므로, (C)가 정답이다.

어휘 organized 조직적인 entire 전체의

140 부사 자리 _ 현재분사 수식

해설 현재분사 providing을 수식하는 부사 자리이므로, '안전하게'라는 의미의 (D) safely가 정답이다. (A) safe와 (C) safest는 형용사, (B) safety는 명사로 품사상 빈칸에 들어갈 수 없다. 참고로, safe는 비격식체에서 부사 역할을 하기도 하지만, 이 경우 동사 뒤에 오게 된다.

141 접속부사

해설 빈칸 앞 문장에서 개선 사항 중 하나로 새 판자길(a new boardwalk)이 설치된 것을 언급했고, 뒤에서는 블루 트레일이 더 넓어졌다(Blue Trail ~ has been widened)며 또 다른 개선 사항을 설명했다. 따라서 추가적인 사항을 덧붙일 때 쓰이는 (D) In addition(게다가, 또한)이 정답이다.

142 명사 어휘

해설 of all과 함께 전치사구를 이루어 people을 수식하는 명사 자리이다. 둘레길에서 힘겨운 등산부터 느긋하게 걷는 산책(From challenging climbs ~ to leisurely walks)까지 다양한 난이도의 코스를 즐길 수 있다는 내용이므로, '역량, 능력'을 의미하는 (A) abilities가 빈칸에 들어가야 가장 자연스럽다.

어휘 holiday 휴일 landscape 풍경 benefit 혜택

143-146 정보문

지역 재배 식품 – 간략한 개요

지역 재배 식품에 대한 구체적인 정의는 없다. 그러나 대체로 판매 **143지점**에 비교적 가까운 곳에서 재배되는 식품으로 알려져 있다. 지역 재배 식품을 구입하면 더 많은 돈이 식량 재배업자들에게 직접 돌아간다**144는 점에서** 지역 경제에 도움이 될 수 있다. 지역 농부들은 제품을 시장에 내놓으려고 외부 유통업체의 서비스를 이용할 필요가 거의 없다. **145따라서 이들의 수입이 지역 내에 머물 가능성이 높다.** 거의 일년 내내, 농산물 직판장이나 야외 농장 가판대에서 지역 재배 식품을 **146구할 수 있다.** 농산물은 제철에만 판매되므로 신선하고 풍미가 넘친다. 지역 재배 식품을 사는 것이 개별 소비자에게도 이득이 된다는 의미이다.

어휘 specific 구체적인 definition 정의 generally 일반적으로 relatively 비교적, 상대적으로 purchase 구입하다 regional 지역의 distributor 유통업체 get A to market A를 시장에 내놓다 farmers' market 농산물 직판장 produce 농산품 advantage 장점, 이득 individual 개개인의, 개별의

143 명사 어휘

해설 지역 재배 식품(It=locally grown food)에 대해 간략히 정의하는 문장으로, 위치나 장소와 관련된 단어가 들어가야 자연스럽다. 따라서 of sale과 함께 '판매 지점'이라는 의미를 완성하는 (B) point가 정답이다.

어휘 volume 양, 부피 manner 방식

144 접속사 자리 _ 어휘 〔고난도〕

해설 완전한 두 절을 이어주는 접속사 자리이다. 뒷절(더 많은 돈이 식량 재배업자들에게 직접 돌아간다)의 내용을 앞절(지역 재배 식품을 구입하면 지역 경제에 도움이 될 수 있다)에 나온 판단의 근거로 보는 것이 가장 자연스럽다. 따라서 '~라는 점에서, ~이므로'라는 의미의 (A) in that이 정답이다. (B) based on 역시 근거를 나타내는 표현이지만 접속사가 아니므로 답이 될 수 없다. (D) in case도 접속사 역할을 할 수 있지만, 해당 절이 앞으로 일어날 일을 가정하는 상황은 아니므로, 빈칸에는 적절하지 않다.

어휘 based on ~을 토대로 owing to ~ 덕분에 in case ~인 경우에는

145 문맥에 맞는 문장 고르기 〔고난도〕

번역 (A) 게다가 농부들은 방문객에게 텃밭 가꾸기 비결을 알려줄 수도 있다.
(B) 사실 가공식품을 많이 먹으면 건강에 안 좋을 수도 있다.
(C) 그러므로 식품 운송 산업은 계속 성장하고 있다.
(D) 따라서 이들의 수입이 지역 내에 머물 가능성이 높다.

해설 보기 네 개 모두 접속 부사로 시작하므로, 빈칸 앞 문장의 내용을 집중적으로 살펴보아야 한다. 지역에서 농산물을 재배해 가까운 곳에서 판매할 경우, 농부들이 외부 유통업체의 서비스를 이용할 필요가 거의 없다(Local farmers almost never require the services of an outside distributor)고 했으므로, 이와 관련된 내용이 빈칸에 들어가야 한다. 따라서 불필요한 지출이 줄어든 결과를 예측한 (D)가 정답이다.

어휘 processed food 가공식품 transportation 운송 earning 수입, 소득 be more likely to ~할 가능성이 높다

146 동사 어형 _ 시제

해설 주어인 locally grown food 뒤에 오는 본동사 자리이므로, (B) is available과 (C) had been available 중 하나를 선택해야 한다. 지문 전반에서 현재시제를 사용하여 지역 재배 식품과 관련된 일반적인 정보를 제공하고 있고 해당 절이 During much of the year의 수식을 받고 있으므로, 빈칸에도 현재시제 동사가 들어가야 자연스럽다. 따라서 (B) is available이 정답이다.

PART 7

147-148 영수증

```
            아얄리 슈퍼마켓
        147(C)노스 위버 시 지점
           데번 로 12번지
         매장 전화: 555-0163
                        5월 3일   오후 2시 28분

블루베리 머핀(5개들이)        3.7달러
병에 든 생수(12개들이)        4.9달러
채소 수프(작은 캔)           2.2달러
말린 과일 스낵(큰 봉지)       5.8달러
            *** 총   16.6달러
                현금   20달러
                잔돈   3.4달러
```

147(C)노스 위버 시 지점에서 구매해 주셔서 감사합니다!

점장: 데이브 소토

147(D)계산원: 3번 셀프 계산대

147(B)고객 서비스 데스크에서 우대 회원 카드를 신청해 비용을 절감해 보세요!

저희의 서비스는 어떤가요? 148www.ayali-survey.com을 방문해 의견을 주시고 500달러를 받을 수 있는 기회도 잡으세요.* PIN 번호 334 05081을 사용해 로그인하고 설문 조사를 완료하세요.

*경품 추첨에 대한 자세한 내용은 고객 서비스 카운터에 문의하세요.

어휘 preferred 우선되는, 선호되는 complete 완료하다, 작성하다 inquire 문의하다 prize drawing 경품 추첨

147 추론 / 암시   고난도

번역 아얄리 슈퍼마켓에 관해 암시되지 않은 것은?
(A) 제과제빵류는 구내에서 만든다.
(B) 일부 쇼핑객에게 고객 우대 카드를 발급한다.
(C) 매장 지점이 둘 이상이다.
(D) 고객이 직접 자신의 구매품을 계산 처리할 수 있다.

해설 '우대 회원 카드를 신청하세요(Sign up ~ for a preferred shopper card)'에서 (B)를, '노스 위버 시 지점에서 구매해 주셔서 감사합니다 (Thank you for shopping at our North Weaver City location)'에서 (C)를, '셀프 계산대(SELF-CHECKOUT)'에서 (D)를 추론할 수 있다. 하지만 매장에서 판매되는 제과제빵류가 현장에서 만들어지는 지 추론할 근거는 없으므로, (A)가 정답이다.

어휘 on the premises 구내에서 loyalty card 고객 우대 카드

▶▶ Paraphrasing 지문의 a preferred shopper card
→ 보기 (B)의 loyalty card
지문의 our North Weaver City Branch/location → 보기 (C)의 It has more than one store location
지문의 SELF-CHECKOUT → 보기 (D)의 Its customers can process their own purchases

148 세부 사항

번역 고객들은 어떻게 설문조사에 참여하라고 지시 받는가?
(A) 서비스 카운터에서 양식을 얻어서
(B) 현재 전화번호를 제공해서
(C) 지정된 웹사이트에 접속해서
(D) 경영진에게 직접 이야기해서

해설 하단에서 www.ayali-survey.com을 방문해 의견을 달라고 한 후, 로그인해서 설문 조사를 완료하라(Use PIN number ~ to log in and complete the survey)고 권하고 있다. 따라서 (C)가 정답이다.

어휘 obtain 얻다 access 이용하다, 접속하다 designated 지정된 management 경영진

▶▶ Paraphrasing 지문의 complete the survey
→ 질문의 participate in a survey
지문의 Visit www.ayali-survey.com
→ 정답의 accessing a designated Web site

149-150 웹페이지

```
덴워드 사 고객 후기

최근 게시물: 6월 9일

게시자: 제프 앤더슨, 지부장, 스탠더드 페이퍼 사

덴워드 사는 뛰어난 서비스를 제공합니다. 149최근 회사가 확장하는 바람에 새로 고용된 생산직 및 창고 관리직 직원들을 위해 추가로 유니폼을 촉박하게 주문해야 했습니다. 덴워드 사는 우리에게 필요한 것을 제공했고, 배송기사 스탠 씨는 시간을 엄수했고 공손했습니다. 옷의 품질은 우수하며, 회사 로고도 쉽게 추가해 줍니다. 그들은 항상 고객의 요구에 즉각 대응합니다.

회사 답변: 감사합니다, 앤더슨 씨! 고객 만족은 항상 덴워드 사가 가장 중시하는 부분입니다. 150당사는 우리 지역에서 최초로, 비즈니스 소프트웨어 개발자 협회에서 상을 받은 주문 관리 프로그램인 ACPS(선진 고객 처리 시스템)를 채택한 회사입니다. 이 최첨단 솔루션을 통해 더 빠르고 정확하게 주문을 추적하고 분류할 수 있어, 정시 배송률이 99.6퍼센트에 이릅니다.
```

어휘 owing to ~ 때문에 expansion (사업) 확장 on short notice 촉박하게 punctual 시간을 정확하게 지키는 courteous 공손한 responsive 즉각 대응하는, 호응하는 utmost 최고의, 극도의 employ 이용하다, 채택하다 cutting-edge 최첨단의 sort 정리하다, 분류하다 accurately 정확하게

149 추론 / 암시

번역 덴워드 사는 어떤 업체일 것 같은가?
(A) 음식 배달 서비스업체
(B) 종이 제품 제조업체
(C) 건물 관리업체
(D) 작업복 공급업체

해설 첫 번째 단락에서 앤더슨 씨가 새로 고용된 생산직 및 창고 관리직 직원들을 위해 유니폼을 추가로 주문해야 했다(I had to order extra uniforms for our newly hired production and warehouse staff)고 한 후, 덴워드 사가 필요한 것을 제공했다(Dennward Co. provided us with what we needed)고 했다. 따라서 덴워드 사가 유니폼 공급업체라고 추론할 수 있으므로 (D)가 정답이다.

▶▶ **Paraphrasing** 지문의 **uniforms for our newly hired production and warehouse staff**
→ 정답의 **work apparel**

150 사실 관계 확인

번역 ACPS에 관해 알 수 있는 것은?
(A) 업계의 인정을 받았다.
(B) 앤더슨 씨의 요구에 맞게 맞춤 제작되었다.
(C) 몇 가지 버전으로 출시되었다.
(D) 사용하기 쉽다는 평가를 받는다.

해설 두 번째 단락에서 ACPS를 비즈니스 소프트웨어 개발자 협회에서 상을 받은 주문 관리 프로그램(ACPS ~ an order management program that has won awards from the Business Software Developers Association)이라고 소개하고 있으므로, (A)가 정답이다.

어휘 achieve 달성하다, 성취하다 recognition 인정, 표창 tailor 맞춤 제작하다 suit 맞추다 release 출시하다

▶▶ **Paraphrasing** 지문의 **has won awards from the Business Software Developers Association**
→ 정답의 **has achieved industry recognition**

151-152 문자 메시지

브래드 이크발 [오전 10시 40분]
151마리아, 새 소프트웨어를 설치하러 방금 컴퓨터실로 왔어요. 냉방 시스템이 또 이상하게 작동하는 거 알고 있었어요? 여기 안이 꽤 덥네요.

마리아 디 [오전 10시 41분]
네, 문제가 있다는 건 알고 있어요. 방금 HVAC 회사에 전화해서 수리 기사를 보내달라고 했어요.

브래드 이크발 [오전 10시 42분]
그래요? 152그럼 그 사람이 고칠 때까지 기다렸다가 그 후에 이 일을 끝내야겠어요. 여기 온도가 기분을 불쾌하게 하네요.

마리아 디 [오전 10시 43분]
정말요? 내일 오는데요.

브래드 이크발 [오전 10시 44분]
아, 그렇군요. 152더워도 일하는 수밖에 없겠네요.

어휘 HVAC (Heating, Ventilating, and Air Conditioning) 냉난방 및 환기, 공기 조화 기술 assignment 과업, 과제 temperature 온도 uncomfortable 불쾌한, 불편한

151 추론 / 암시

번역 이크발 씨는 누구이겠는가?
(A) 에어컨 수리공
(B) 사무용 가구 설치 담당자
(C) 컴퓨터 기술자
(D) 건물 관리인

해설 이크발 씨가 오전 10시 40분 메시지에서 새 소프트웨어를 설치하러 컴퓨터실에 왔다(I just came down here to the computer room to install the new software)고 했으므로, 컴퓨터 기술자라고 추론할 수 있다. 따라서 (C)가 정답이다.

152 의도 파악

번역 오전 10시 43분에 디 씨가 "내일 오는데요"라고 말한 의도는?
(A) 그녀에게 아직 정보가 없다.
(B) 그녀는 도와 줄 수 없을 것이다.
(C) 이크발 씨는 일을 서둘러 끝내야 한다.
(D) 이크발 씨가 예상했던 것보다 더 오래 지연될 수도 있다.

해설 이크발 씨가 오전 10시 42분 메시지에서 수리 기사가 냉방 시스템을 고칠 때까지 기다렸다가 그 후에 일을 끝내야겠다(I'll wait to finish this assignment until after they've fixed it)고 했는데, 이에 대해 디 씨가 수리 기사는 내일 온다고 하자 이크발 씨가 기다리지 않고 그냥 진행하겠다고 했다. 따라서 수리 작업이 이크발 씨의 예상보다 더 오래 지연될 수 있음을 알리려는 의도라고 볼 수 있으므로, (D)가 정답이다.

153-154 이메일

수신: 콘스탄스 베일러 〈constance-baylor@mail.com〉
발신: 〈greenbrandtbooks@green-brandt.com〉
제목: 구매
날짜: 8월 1일

베일러 씨께,

구매해 주셔서 감사합니다. 153저희 우편물 처리기가 예기치 못하게 고장이 나서, 고객님께서 주문하신 〈초보자를 위한 목공술〉이 처리 도중 파손되었음을 알려드립니다. 하지만 동일한 책으로 중고품이 있는데, 뒷면 표지가 살짝 색이 바랬고 아래쪽 가장자리에 습기로 생긴 얼룩이 조금 있습니다. 페이지들은 접거나 표시한 흔적 없이 깨끗합니다.

만약 이 대체 도서를 주문하고 싶으시다면, 새 책과의 가격 차이를 반영해 고객님 계좌에 7달러를 입금하겠습니다.

154이 이메일에 월요일에(8월 4일)까지 회신해 어떻게 진행하고 싶으신지 알려주세요. 그렇지 않으면 주문을 자동으로 취소하고, 구매가격 전액을 돌려드리겠습니다.

양해해 주시면 감사하겠습니다.

그린브란트 북스 직원 일동

어휘 carpentry 목공(술) novice 초보자 process 처리하다
unexpected 예기치 못한 malfunction 고장 mailing
machine 우편물 처리기 faded 색이 바랜 moisture 수분, 습기
stain 얼룩 replacement 대체(품) credit 입금하다; 적립금, 포인트
reflect 반영하다 proceed 진행하다

153 주제 / 목적

번역 이메일을 쓴 이유는 무엇이겠는가?
(A) 새로운 할인 프로그램에 대한 정보 제공하기
(B) 베일러 씨의 주문에 문제가 있다는 것을 알리기
(C) 가격 인상에 대한 설명 제공하기
(D) 수집용 도서 구매 관련 지침을 명확히 설명하기

해설 첫 번째 단락에서 베일러 씨가 주문한 책이 처리 도중 파손되었음을 알린다(We would like to inform you that the book you ordered ~ was damaged during processing)고 한 후 사후 처리 방식을 제시하고 있다. 따라서 (B)가 정답이다.

어휘 clarify 명확히 설명하다 collectible 수집할 가치가 있는

154 추론 / 암시

번역 베일러 씨가 월요일까지 이메일에 회신하지 않으면 어떤 일이 일어나겠는가?
(A) 보너스 포인트를 받지 못할 것이다.
(B) 대체 품목을 받을 것이다.
(C) 전액을 환불 받을 것이다.
(D) 계정을 업그레이드할 기회가 사라질 것이다.

해설 세 번째 단락에서 이메일에 월요일까지 회신해달라(Please reply to this e-mail by Monday)고 요청한 후, 그렇지 않으면 주문을 자동으로 취소하고 구매가격 전액을 돌려주겠다(Otherwise, we will ~ return the full amount of the purchase price to you)고 했다. 따라서 (C)가 정답이다.

어휘 substitute 대체품

▶▶ Paraphrasing 지문의 reply to → 질문의 respond to
지문의 Otherwise
→ 질문의 not respond to the e-mail by Monday
지문의 return the full amount of the purchase price → 정답의 a full refund

155-157 보도자료

스토리무어 극단, 온라인 방송 프로 데뷔

즉시 보도용(6월 22일)—스토리무어 극단(STC)은 극찬을 받은 코미디극 〈대가족의 재회〉를 성황리에 공연하며 지난 시즌을 마무리했다. 155극단 역사상 최다 관객을 동원한 이번 작품에는 연극의 주제, 즉 가족 모임의 즐거운 측면들에 관해 공연 후 진행된 패널 토론이 포함됐다. 156STC 홍보 담당 이사인 글로리아 채텀 씨는 이 열띤 대화를 보고, 회사 직원들이 극장에서 일어나는 창작 과정에 대해 이야기하는 오디오 팟캐스트를 제작해 보자는 아이디어를 냈다. '디자인이 왜 중요한가'라는 제목의 첫 회는 6월 19일에 게시되었다. 여기에는 〈대가족의 재회〉 담당 의상 디자이너 할 브레디와 연극 무대 디자이너 미셸 린들리의 흥미진진

한 대화가 담겨 있다. 두 번째 에피소드는 6월 26일에 올라올 예정으로, 연출 감독과의 대화가 포함될 예정이다. 157채텀 씨는 30분짜리 에피소드를 매주, 혹은 일주일에 두 번 정도 지속적으로 올릴 계획이다. 그러나 그녀는 30분짜리 프로그램 하나를 제작하는 데 며칠이 걸리기도 한다고 말했다. 팟캐스트는 www.stc-theater.org/podcast에서 무료로 들을 수 있다.

어휘 programming 방송 프로 (편성) conclude 마무리하다
highly-praised 극찬을 받은 lively 활기를 띤, 생생한 public
relations 대외 홍보 come up with 떠올리다, 제안하다
engaging 관심을 사로잡는, 흥미진진한

155 사실 관계 확인

번역 〈대가족의 재회〉에 관해 알 수 있는 것은?
(A) 출연진에는 글로리아 채텀이 포함되었다.
(B) 감독이 두 명이었다.
(C) 관객수 기록을 세웠다.
(D) 제작비가 많이 들었다.

해설 초반부에서 〈대가족의 재회〉가 극단 역사상 최다 관객을 동원했다(which brought in the biggest crowds in the company's history)고 했으므로, (C)가 정답이다.

어휘 attendance 참석자수, 참석률

▶▶ Paraphrasing 지문의 brought in the biggest crowds in the company's history
→ 정답의 set an attendance record

156 사실 관계 확인

번역 STC 팟캐스트에 관해 언급된 것은?
(A) 패널 토론에서 영감을 얻었다.
(B) 관객 기부로 재원을 마련할 것이다.
(C) 청취자에게 유료 구독을 요구한다.
(D) 특히 기자들을 위해 제작되었다.

해설 중반부에서 STC 홍보 담당 이사가 공연 후에 있었던 패널 토론(post-performance panel discussions)의 열띤 대화를 보고 오디오 팟캐스트를 제작해보자는 아이디어를 냈다(These lively conversations led the STC's public relations director ~ to come up with the idea of developing an audio podcast)고 했으므로, (A)가 정답이다.

어휘 inspire 영감을 수다 fund 재원을 마련하다, 자금을 조달하다
donation 기부 paid subscription 유료 구독

▶▶ Paraphrasing 지문의 led ~ to come up with the idea
→ 정답의 inspired

157 문장 삽입

번역 [1], [2], [3], [4]로 표시된 곳 중에서 다음 문장이 가장 적합한 곳은?
"그러나 그녀는 30분짜리 프로그램 하나를 제작하는 데 며칠이 걸리기도 한다고 말했다."
(A) [1]
(B) [2]
(C) [3]
(D) [4]

해설 주어진 문장 앞에서 먼저 she가 가리키는 대상과, 30분짜리 프로그램과 관련된 내용이 언급되어야 한다. [4] 앞에서 채텀 씨가 30분짜리 팟캐스트 에피소드를 매주, 혹은 일주일에 두 번 정도 지속적으로 올릴 계획(Chatham plans to continue posting 30-minute episodes each week, or perhaps twice a week)이라고 했으므로, 이 뒤에 제시문이 들어가야 자연스럽다. 따라서 (D)가 정답이다.

158-160 온라인 목록

¹⁵⁸나이지리아 소식통—서아프리카에서 신뢰도가 가장 높은 경제지 온라인 판

나이지리아 최고의 광고 대행사 둘러보기

게시: 하루 전, ¹⁵⁸마달리나 이칸데 조회수1242

최근 몇 달 동안, 많은 구독자분들이 나이지리아 최고의 광고 대행사 목록을 발표해 달라고 제안했습니다. ¹⁵⁸아래에 열거된 대행사들은 제가 이 출간지를 위해 과거에 인터뷰 했던 기업가들이 강력 추천한 곳입니다.

마케팅 리치—20년 전에 설립된 마케팅 리치는 나이지리아 최대의 광고 대행사 중 하나로, 라고스 시와 아부자 시에 지사를 두고 있다. ¹⁵⁹주요 거래처인 단구미 식품제조사의 요구를 충족하기 위해 최근 세네갈에 현장사무소를 개설해 시장 조사연구를 실시했다.

퓨전텍—운영한 지 4년 만에, 라고스 시와 아부자 시에 사무실을 두고 있는 이 국내 광고 대행사는 디지털 마케팅 캠페인으로 높이 평가 받게 되었다. ¹⁵⁹지난해에는 라면 제조업체인 선머루 브랜드를 고객사로 추가했다. 이 대행사는 온라인 광고 시리즈를 제작해 수상한 바 있는데, 바로 이 회사를 위한 광고였다.

올루와 솔루션—10년 된 전문 대행사로 나이지리아, 가나, 케냐에 사무실을 두고 있다. 다수의 기타 대행사들과 달리, 이 업체는 고객사가 새로운 브랜드를 개발하고 선보일 수 있도록 돕는 데 주안점을 두고 있다. ¹⁵⁹최근 BCC 산업이 포장 과자 제품군을 성공적으로 출시하도록 하는 임무를 맡은 바 있다. ¹⁶⁰또한 이 대행사는 프로스펙타 테크와 제휴하여, 기업들이 브랜드 이미지를 개선하기 위한 온라인 고객 설문조사를 만들 수 있는 소프트웨어 프로그램인 인포매트-플러스를 개발한 것으로 유명하다.

어휘 subscriber 구독자 suggest 제안하다 publish 발표하다, 출간하다 advertising agency 광고 대행사 recommend 추천하다 enthusiastically 열렬히, 강력하게 publication 출간지, 출판물 conduct 실시하다, 수행하다 operation 운영, 영업 domestic 국내의 highly respected 평판이 좋은, 높이 평가 받는 client base 고객층 award-winning 상을 받은 decade 10년 specialty 전문 ensure 보장하다, ~하게 하다 packaged 포장된 enable ~할 수 있게 하다 improve 개선하다

158 추론 / 암시

번역 이칸데 씨는 누구이겠는가?
(A) 광고 대행사 소유주
(B) 서점 관리자
(C) 소프트웨어 개발자
(D) 경제 기자

해설 상단에서 〈나이지리아 소식통〉을 서아프리카에서 신뢰도가 가장 높은 경제지(West Africa's most trusted business journal)라고 소개했고, 글을 게시한(Posted: ~ by Madalina Ikande) 이칸데 씨가 자신이 과

거에 기업가들을 인터뷰했다(the business leaders I've interviewed in the past for this publication)고 했으므로, 그녀가 경제 기자임을 추론할 수 있다. 따라서 (D)가 정답이다.

159 세부 사항 [고난도]

번역 목록에 기재된 광고 대행사의 공통점은?
(A) 두 개 이상 국가에 사무소를 두고 있다.
(B) 5년 이상 영업해왔다.
(C) 식품업계 고객들과 일한다.
(D) 같은 도시에 본사를 두고 있다.

해설 마케팅 리치(Marketing Reach)의 주요 고객사(a major client)가 단구미 식품제조사라고 되어 있고, 퓨전텍(Fusiontekk)은 지난해 라면 제조업체인 선머루 브랜드를 고객사로 추가(it added ~ a maker of instant noodle products, to its client base)했다고 했으며, 올루와 솔루션(Olouwaa Solutions)이 BCC 산업의 포장 과자 제품군 출시를 도왔다(it was tasked with ensuring a successful launch for BCC Industries' line of packaged snacks)고 했다. 따라서 모두 식품업계 고객들과 일한다는 것을 알 수 있으므로, (C)가 정답이다.

어휘 industry 업계, 산업 be headquartered in ~에 본사[본부]를 두다

160 추론 / 암시 [고난도]

번역 인포매트-플러스는 무엇에 사용되겠는가?
(A) 브랜드 공개 언급 추적
(B) 고객 의견 수렴
(C) 시장조사 자료 분석
(D) 소셜 미디어 계정 관리

해설 마지막 단락에서 인포매트-플러스(Infomatt-Plus)를 기업에서 온라인 고객 설문조사를 만들 수 있는 소프트웨어 프로그램(a software program that enables businesses to create online customer surveys in service of improving their brand image)으로 소개하고 있으므로, (B)가 정답이다.

어휘 mention 언급(된 내용) analyze 분석하다

▶▶ Paraphrasing 지문의 customer surveys
→ 정답의 customer feedback

161-163 정보문

로나트 부동산 회사

¹⁶¹임대 임박 → 스나이더 가 2번지에 위치한 편의시설이 많은 임대 복합 건물, 던마워 빌딩

던마워 빌딩은 블록 하나를 거의 전부 차지하고 있으며, 안락한 아파트 생활에 다수의 편의시설을 더했습니다. 편의시설에는 실내 수영장이 딸린 1층 피트니스 센터가 포함됩니다. 넓은 로비는 입주민들의 개방형 사무실 역할을 하며, 건물은 인근 가게와 식당에 굉장히 가깝습니다. ¹⁶²원래 의류 생산 시설로 지어졌던 던마워 빌딩은 고풍스러운 외관에 세부적인 건축 장식이 아름답게 보존되어 있습니다. 건물에 있는 38가구는 구조가 다양한 원룸과 투룸 아파트로 구성되어 있습니다.

입주는 7월 1일부터 가능합니다. **163**6월 5일 이전에 신청하면 로나트 부동산 회사에서 신규 신청을 처리하는 데 드는 고정 수수료 50달러를 면제해 드립니다.

> **어휘** Properties 부동산 회사 an abundance of 많은 amenity 편의시설 complex 복합 건물, 단지 spacious 넓은 co-working space 개방형 사무실 garment 의류 facility 공장, 시설 preserved 보존된 architectural 건축의 consist of 구성되어 있다 occupancy 입주 waive (비용 등을) 면제해 주다, 권리를 포기하다 customary fee (특정 서비스에 대한) 고정 수수료, 고정요율에 따른 수수료 application 신청(서)

161 주제 / 목적

번역 주로 무엇에 관한 정보인가?
(A) 개회식
(B) 도시 지역
(C) 주택 공실
(D) 사업 기회

해설 복합 건물 던마워 빌딩(The Dunmawr Building, an amenity-rich rental complex at 2 Snyder Street)의 임대가 임박했다(RENTING SOON)고 한 후, 지문 전반에서 임대 부동산인 아파트에 대해 설명하고 있다. 따라서 (C)가 정답이다.

어휘 vacancy 비어 있음

162 사실 관계 확인

번역 던마워 빌딩에 관해 알 수 있는 것은?
(A) 거리 두 곳에 출입구가 있다.
(B) 야외 레크리에이션 시설을 갖추고 있다.
(C) 이전에는 공장이었다.
(D) 유서 깊은 지역에 있다.

해설 두 번째 단락에서 던마워 빌딩이 원래 의류 생산 시설로 지어졌다(Built originally as a garment production facility, the Dunmawr Building)고 했으므로, (C)가 정답이다.

> ▶▶ **Paraphrasing** 지문의 Built originally as a garment production facility
> → 정답의 previously a factory

163 추론 / 암시   고난도

번역 로나트 부동산 회사에 관해 암시된 것은?
(A) 보통 임대 신청인에게 수수료를 부과한다.
(B) 상업용 부동산을 전문으로 한다.
(C) 임대인에게 단기 임대를 제공한다.
(D) 직원을 추가로 채용할 계획이다.

해설 마지막 단락에서 6월 5일 이전에 입주 신청을 하면 고정 수수료 50달러를 면제해 준다(Apply before June 5 and Rohnart Properties will waive its customary $50 fee)고 했으므로, 평상시에는 임대 신청인에게 수수료를 부과한다고 추론할 수 있다. 따라서 (A)가 정답이다.

164-167 이메일

> 발신: 영양 소식지 〈healthnutrition-newsletter@maynard.edu〉
> 수신: 재닛 리 〈j.lee@mail.com〉
> 제목: MU 영양 소식지
> 날짜: 3월 1일
>
> **메이너드 대학교 영양 소식지**
>
> 리 씨께,
>
> 요즘에는 건강한 식습관에 대한 정보가 지나치게 많이 쏟아지고 있습니다. TV 쇼에서 온라인 요리 포럼에 이르기까지, 수많은 출처들이 모순을 보이며 과학적 권위에 의심을 품게 만드는 영양학적 조언을 제공하고 있죠. **164**그래서 매달 메이너드 대학 영양 소식지에서 읽는 모든 정보가 믿을 만 하다는 주요 근거를 말씀드려야겠다고 결심하게 되었습니다.
>
> **167**모든 기사는 편집진 및 메이너드 대학교 영양과학대학 소속의 유수한 영양 전문가들이 조사하여 작성하고 있으며, 쉽게 따를 수 있고 과학에 근거한 건강 관련 조언을 제공합니다. 소식지는 항상 일상어로 작성되며, 복잡한 의학용어가 많지 않습니다. **165**게다가 저희는 소식지에 광고를 싣지 않아 식품업계의 기업 광고주들의 구미를 맞출 의무가 없으므로, 인기 있는 음식의 영양 품질에 대해 자유롭게 논의할 수 있습니다.
>
> 예를 들어, 현재 소식지에는 가장 건강에 좋은 파스타 종류에 관한 공정한 안내 글이 실려 있습니다. www.mu-health.com을 방문해 'A12' 코드를 입력해서 해당 호의 온라인 판 전체를 시험 삼아 읽어 보시기를 권해 드립니다. **164**저희가 발간하는 특별한 출판물을 구독하고 싶어 지시기를 바라는 마음에서 이렇게 권유 드립니다. 신규 가입 할인 혜택으로 1년간 인쇄판이나 디지털만을 정규 요금에서 35퍼센트 할인된 32달러에 구독하실 수 있습니다.
>
> **166**저희 기록에 따르면 현재 대학교 동문회 웹사이트에서 무료로 "건강 관련 최신 정보" 이메일을 받고 계신 것으로 확인되어 이렇게 연락 드립니다. 매월 발행되는 저희 소식지는 훨씬 더 상세한 건강 지침을 제공하므로, 이번 특가를 이용하시기를 강력히 추천 드립니다.
>
> 데이비드 아흐메드
> 편집국장, 메이너드 대학 영양 소식지

> **어휘** nutrition 영양 overload 지나치게 많이 주다 vast 방대한 dispense 나눠주다, 제공하다 conflicting 모순되는, 상반되는 questionable 미심쩍은, 의심스러운 authority 권위 lead ~하게 하다, 유도하다 bring up (화두를) 꺼내다 primary 주요한 research 조사[연구]하다 editorial 편집의 leading 선도적인, 유수의 expert 전문가, 권위자 obligation 의무 corporate 기업의 advertiser 광고주 impartial 공정한 entirety 전체, 완전한 형태 subscribe to ~을 구독하다 extraordinary 특별한, 비범한 publication 출판(물) introductory 초기의, 신규의 reach out to ~에게 연락하다 indicate 나타내다 alumni 동문회 guidance 지침 urge 강력히 추천하다, 촉구하다 take advantage of ~를 이용하다

164 주제 / 목적

번역 이메일의 주요 목적은?
(A) 소식지의 새로운 편집 방침에 대한 최신 정보 제공
(B) 건강에 관한 다양한 전문가들의 권고사항 비교
(C) 구독 기반 출판물의 장점 설명
(D) 일련의 기사에 대한 협업 제안

해설 첫 번째 단락에서 메이너드 대학 영양 소식지에서 읽는 모든 정보는 믿을 수 있다는 주요 근거를 알리고자 한다(This leads me to bring up the primary reason you can trust everything you read in each monthly Maynard University Nutrition Newsletter)고 한 후, 이메일 전반에서 메이너드 대학 영양 소식지의 장점 및 혜택을 설명하고 있다. 세 번째 단락을 보면 소식지가 구독 기반 서비스(subscribe to our extraordinary publication)임을 알 수 있으므로, (C)가 정답이다.

어휘 policy 정책 compare 비교하다 recommendation 권고 various 다양한 outline (간략히) 설명하다 benefit 장점 collaboration 협업

165 사실 관계 확인

번역 소식지에 관해 가장 사실에 가까운 것은?
(A) 더 이상 인쇄판으로 판매되지 않는다.
(B) 광고가 없다.
(C) 주로 과학자를 대상으로 한다.
(D) 텔레비전 쇼와 관련이 있다.

해설 두 번째 단락에서 소식지에 광고를 싣지 않는다(the newsletter carries no advertising)고 했으므로, (B)가 정답이다.

어휘 aim ~를 대상으로 하다, 목표로 하다 associated 연관된, 관련된

▶▶ Paraphrasing 지문의 the newsletter carries no advertising
→ 정답의 It does not have advertisements

166 추론 / 암시

번역 리 씨에 관해 암시된 것은?
(A) 메이너드 대학을 졸업했다.
(B) 온라인 요리 교실을 가르친다.
(C) 한때 아흐메드 씨와 함께 일했다.
(D) 무료 서비스를 취소하려고 했다.

해설 리 씨는 이메일의 수신인이다. 네 번째 단락을 보면, 리 씨가 현재 대학교 동문회 웹사이트에서 무료로 "건강 관련 최신 정보" 이메일을 받고 있는 것으로 확인되어(our records indicate you currently receive free "health update" e-mails from our university's alumni Web site) 연락한다고 했으므로, 그녀가 메이너드 대학 졸업생임을 추론할 수 있다. 따라서 (A)가 정답이다.

▶▶ Paraphrasing 지문의 our university's alumni
→ 정답의 graduated from Maynard University

167 문장 삽입 [고난도]

번역 [1], [2], [3], [4]로 표시된 곳 중에서 다음 문장이 가장 적합한 곳은?
"소식지는 항상 일상어로 작성되며, 복잡한 의학용어가 많지 않습니다."
(A) [1]
(B) [2]
(C) [3]
(D) [4]

해설 주어진 문장에서 소식지의 언어적 특징을 설명하며 내용이 어렵지 않다는 점을 드러내고 있으므로, 앞서 이와 관련된 언급이 있어야 한다. [2] 앞에서 소식지의 모든 기사는 쉽게 따를 수 있고 과학에 근거한 건강 관련 조언을 제공한다(Each article ~ gives science-based health advice that is easy to follow)고 했으므로, 이 뒤에 주어진 문장이 들어가야 자연스럽다. 따라서 (B)가 정답이다.

168-171 온라인 채팅

실시간 채팅	
아미르 나자리 (오전 9시 22분)	모두들 안녕하세요. [168]전 지금 회의실에서 팀 발표를 연습하고 있어요. 방금 기존 로고와 새 로고를 나란히 비교한 슬라이드를 검토했어요. 우리가 변경한 내용에 대한 설명과 함께요. 좋아 보이네요.
나디아 곤 (오전 9시 23분)	[169]우리가 그래픽을 선택한 이유를 보여주는 제 슬라이드 추가하셨나요?
아미르 나자리 (오전 9시 24분)	[169]네. 아주 유용했어요.
나디아 곤 (오전 9시 25분)	동영상은 화면상으로 어떻게 보이던가요?
아미르 나자리 (오전 9시 26분)	그게 문제예요. 재생이 안 돼요.
린다 웨이드 (오전 9시 27분)	[170]포맷을 바꿔보세요.
아미르 나자리 (오전 9시 28분)	알았어요. 잠깐만요.
나디아 곤 (오전 9시 37분)	돼요?
아미르 나자리 (오전 9시 38분)	됐어요. 이제 되네요.
린다 웨이드 (오전 9시 39분)	[170]제안이 도움이 됐나요?
아미르 나자리 (오전 9시 40분)	언제나처럼요.
데일 강 (오전 9시 41분)	[171]리모컨으로 동영상을 일시 정지할 수 있다는 것도 기억하세요. 몇 차례 해보는 것도 좋겠어요. 버튼 조작이 어려울 수 있거든요.
아미르 나자리 (오전 9시 42분)	좋은 생각이에요. 고마워요.

어휘 comparison 비교 original 원래의 description 설명 tricky 다루기 힘든

168 추론 / 암시

번역 팀 발표 주제는 무엇이겠는가?
(A) 로고 디자인 수정
(B) 현재 및 미래 매출 전망
(C) 경쟁 브랜드 개요
(D) 제품의 특징을 설명하는 방법

해설 나자리 씨가 오전 9시 22분 메시지에서 팀 발표를 연습하고 있다(I'm here ~ practicing the presentation for our team)고 한 후, 기존 로고와 새 로고를 나란히 비교한 슬라이드를 검토했다(I just reviewed the slides with side-by-side comparisons of the original and new logos)고 했다. 따라서 로고 디자인 수정에 관한 팀 발표라고 추론할 수 있으므로, (A)가 정답이다.

어휘 revision 수정 forecast 전망 compete 경쟁하다

169 추론 / 암시 고난도

번역 나자리 씨에 관해 암시된 것은?
(A) 아직 홍보영상을 보지 못했다.
(B) 발표 전략에 관한 워크숍을 진행한다.
(C) 작업팀의 그래픽 디자이너들을 모두 고용했다.
(D) 곤 씨의 내용을 발표에 포함했다.

해설 곤 씨가 오전 9시 23분 메시지에서 그래픽을 선택한 이유를 보여주는 자신의 슬라이드 추가했는지(Did you add my slides showing the reasons for our selection of graphics?) 물었는데, 이에 대해 나자리 씨가 그렇다고 한 후, 아주 유용했다(they were very useful)며 의견을 덧붙였다. 따라서 (D)가 정답이다.

어휘 incorporate 포함하다

▶▶ Paraphrasing 지문의 **add my slides**
→ 정답의 **incorporated Ms. Ghosn's content**

170 의도 파악 고난도

번역 오전 9시 40분에 나자리 씨가 "언제나처럼요"라고 쓴 의미는 무엇인가?
(A) 팀은 종종 촉박하게 변경 사항을 반영해야 한다.
(B) 동료가 신뢰할만한 문제 해결책을 조언한다.
(C) 컴퓨터에서 문제가 거듭 발생한다.
(D) 종종 비디오 포맷 변환하는 일을 돕는다.

해설 웨이드 씨가 오전 9시 27분 메시지에서 문제를 겪고 있는 나자리 씨에게 동영상 포맷을 바꿔보라(Try changing its format)고 조언한 후, 오전 9시 39분 메시지에서 자신의 제안이 도움이 됐는지(Did the suggestion help?) 확인했는데, 이에 대해 나자리 씨가 언제나처럼 그렇다고 응답한 것이다. 따라서 웨이드 씨가 늘 신뢰할만한 해결책을 조언해 준다는 의도로 쓴 메시지라고 볼 수 있으므로, (B)가 정답이다.

어휘 dependable 신뢰할 수 있는 troubleshooting 문제 해결

171 세부 사항

번역 강 씨가 나자리 씨에게 제안하는 것은?
(A) 도입부 외우기
(B) 예상되는 청중의 질문 생각해 두기
(C) 섹션 사이에 휴식 시간 잡기
(D) 부속품 사용 연습하기

해설 강 씨가 오전 9시 41분 메시지에서 나자리 씨에게 리모컨으로 동영상을 일시 정지할 수 있다(you can pause the video with the remote control unit)고 알려준 후, 몇 차례 해보는 것도 좋을 것 같다(You may want to try it out a few times)고 제안했다. 따라서 (D)가 정답이다.

▶▶ Paraphrasing 지문의 **try it out**
→ 정답의 **Practice using an accessory**
지문의 **the remote control unit**
→ 정답의 **an accessory**

172-175 기사

고난도 *(Test 8 tab)*

문화유산 박물관에서 일상생활 기념물 전시한다

헤즐럿 뷰—어마어마한 옛 보물 소장품들을 둘러본 방문객들은 킬러 문화유산 박물관을 "숨은 보석"이라고 부른다. ^{172(B)}이 박물관에는 3만 점 이상의 소장품이 있는데, 이들은 농장 단지의 용도를 변경한 후 그 위에 지은 거대한 건물 네 동에 전시되어 있다. ¹⁷⁴전시품들은 헤즐럿 뷰에서 평생을 살아온 마빈 킬러의 개인 소장품으로, 그가 어린 시절부터 모은 지역 기념물들이다. ^{172(A)}요즘 킬러가 박물관의 정원 정자에서 쉬고 있는 모습을 자주 볼 수 있는데, 이 정자에서 방문객들은 전시 중인 옛 농기구들을 직접 조작해 볼 수 있다. "박물관 설립은 킬러 씨의 꿈이었습니다." 현재 소규모 단체 투어를 이끌고 있는 시설 관리자 줄리아 할스테드는 말했다.

박물관 전시물과 역사 연대표는 이 지역의 다양한 일상생활사를 ¹⁷³다루고 있다. ^{172(C)}박물관 일부에는 킬러 씨가 은퇴할 때까지 소유하고 운영했던 센트럴리아 다이너의 온전한 칸막이 좌석 및 카운터를 포함해, 지역 산업 기념물이 전시되어 있다. 골동품 인쇄기에서 오래된 교복에 이르기까지, 기타 유서 깊은 물건들도 다양하게 전시 중이다. 박물관을 둘러보면서 많은 방문객들이 전시물을 보고 옛 추억을 떠올린다.

¹⁷⁴박물관은 소도시인 헤즐럿 뷰 바로 외곽에 있는 리지 로 1100번지에 위치해 있다. 주 7일 오전 8시부터 오후 5시까지 개관한다. 입장료는 성인 8달러, 학생 5달러다. ¹⁷⁵느긋하게 박물관의 소장품을 모두 보려면 3시간 이상 잡아 두어야 한다. 박물관은 또한 다양한 특별 행사에 참가할 수 있는 회원제 프로그램을 제공한다. 박물관에 대한 자세한 정보는 www.keeler-mus.org을 방문하면 된다.

어휘 heritage (문화) 유산 memorabilia 기념물, 수집품 explore 둘러보다, 탐사하다 massive 거대한 repurpose 용도를 변경하다 complex 단지 represent 보여주다, 나타내다 gather (up) 모으다 pavilion 정자 operate 조작하다, 작동하다, 운영하다 equipment 기구, 장비 facility 시설 exhibit 전시(회), 전시품 a variety of 다양한 aspect 측면, 모습 industry 산업 intact 온전한 retirement 은퇴 a wide range of 다양한 printing press 인쇄기 set aside 확보하다, 챙겨두다 in a leisurely manner 느긋하게

172 사실 관계 확인 고난도

번역 박물관 소장품에 대해 언급되지 않은 것은?
(A) 양방향 전시물이 있다.
(B) 여러 건물에 보관되어 있다.
(C) 킬러 씨가 예전에 하던 업체 일부분을 전시한다.
(D) 과거 방문객들이 기증한 물품들이 포함된다.

해설 첫 번째 단락에서 방문객들이 전시 중인 옛 농기구들을 직접 조작해 볼 수 있다(visitors can try their hand at operating the antique farm equipment on display)는 것과 소장품이 건물 네 동에 보관되어 있다(The museum is home to more than 30,000 items, displayed in four massive buildings)는 것을 확인할 수 있다. 또한 두 번째 단락을 통해 킬러 씨가 운영했던 식당의 칸막이 좌석 및 카운터가 전시되어 있다(Part of the museum shows off ~ an intact seating booth and service counter from Centralia Diner, which Mr. Keeler owned and operated until his retirement)는 것도 알 수 있다. 따라서 언급되지 않은 (D)가 정답이다.

어휘 feature 포함하다 interactive 양방향의, 상호적인 donate 기증하다

> ▶▶ Paraphrasing 지문의 try their hand at operating the antique farm equipment → 보기 (A)의 interactive exhibits
> 지문의 displayed in four massive buildings → 보기 (B)의 housed in multiple buildings
> 지문의 an intact seating booth and service counter from Centralia Diner, which Mr. Keeler owned → 보기 (C)의 sections of Mr. Keeler's former business

173 동의어 찾기

`고난도`

번역 2번째 단락 2행의 "cover"와 의미상 가장 가까운 것은?
(A) ~을 대신하다
(B) ~와 관련되다
(C) 동봉하다
(D) 보증하다

해설 'cover'를 포함한 문장은 '박물관 전시물과 역사 연대표는 이 지역의 다양한 일상생활사를 다루고 있다(The museum's exhibits and historical timelines cover a variety of aspects of daily life in the region)'라는 의미로 해석되는데, 여기서 cover는 '~를 다루다, 포함하다'라는 뜻으로 쓰였다. 따라서 '~와 관련되다, ~에 대해 언급하다'라는 의미의 (B) relate to가 정답이다.

174 추론 / 암시

번역 킬러 씨에 관해 암시된 것은?
(A) 지역 보석가게도 운영한다.
(B) 할스테드 씨에게 농장을 구입했다.
(C) 자신의 박물관 부지 근처에서 자랐다.
(D) 취미로 정원 가꾸기를 시작했다.

해설 첫 번째 단락에서 킬러 씨가 헤즐럿 뷰에서 평생 거주해 왔다(Marvin Keeler, a lifelong resident of Hazlett View)고 했는데, 마지막 단락을 보면 박물관이 헤즐럿 뷰 바로 외곽에 있음(The museum is located ~ just outside the small town of Hazlett View)을 알 수 있다. 따라서 킬러 씨가 박물관 부지 근처에서 자랐다고 추론할 수 있으므로, (C)가 정답이다.

> ▶▶ Paraphrasing 지문의 just outside → 정답의 near

175 세부 사항

번역 기사를 쓴 이가 추천하는 것은?
(A) 몇 시간 잡고 시설 둘러보기
(B) 웹사이트를 통해 1회 방문권 구매
(C) 새 멤버십 프로그램 등록
(D) 특별 단체관광 참여

해설 마지막 단락에서 느긋하게 박물관의 소장품을 모두 보려면 3시간 이상 잡아 두어야 한다(Visitors should set aside three or more hours to view all of the museum's objects)고 했으므로, (A)가 정답이다.

> ▶▶ Paraphrasing 지문의 set aside three or more hours to view all of the museum's objects → 정답의 Allowing several hours to look around a facility

176-180 온라인 후기 + 답변

리뷰 플러스   --지역 최고의 온라인 후기 사이트

알레로 비스트로 후기   작성자: 맷 브로우스키
맷 브로우스키 프로필   → 리뷰 플러스 회원 기간: 5년 7개월
          총 후기 게시물: 32개   게시 사진: 11장

알레로 비스트로는 음식의 질은 좋지만, 청구되는 가격을 고려하면 품질이 더 좋아야 한다고 생각해요. ¹⁷⁹전 두부 버거(13달러), 버섯 수프(7달러), 크로스컷 감자튀김(8달러)과 "농장 특선" 샐러드 요리(9달러)를 주문했습니다. 모두 꽤 맛있었어요. 건강에 좋은 샐러드 옵션이 몇 가지 있지만, 어떤 이유인지 타코 샐러드는 메뉴에서 없어졌더군요. ¹⁷⁷전에 여기서 먹어 본 적이 있는데, 다시 메뉴에 추가되었으면 해요. ¹⁷⁶일반적으로 여기 음식은 장인이 화려하게 준비한 요리에는 그다지 관심이 없고 건강에 신경 쓰는 사람들 마음에 들 거예요. 방문했을 때 가장 긍정적인 부분은 직원들의 응대였어요. 제가 방문했을 때 식당이 작아 붐비긴 했지만, 1분도 되지 않아 웨이터가 제 테이블에 왔어요.

어휘 reasonably 꽤, 상당히 appeal to ~의 마음에 들다 health-conscious 건강에 신경 쓰는 be concerned with ~에 관심이 있다 artisanal 장인의 responsiveness 응대, 대응성

답변: 리사 트라파니, 알레로 비스트로 총지배인

안녕하세요 맷,

의견 감사합니다. 저희는 친절한 응대, 그리고 무엇보다도 까다로운 기준으로 식재료를 공수한다는 점에 자부심을 느낍니다. ¹⁷⁹특히 감자튀김은 모두 유기농으로 재배된 감자로 만듭니다. 올 시즌 물량이 ¹⁷⁸빠듯해 최근에는 다른 재배 농가의 감자를 공급받아야 했습니다. ¹⁷⁹따라서 이 메뉴에 해당하는 비용은 청구서에 적용되지 않았습니다. 고객님께서 이러한 조치를 아셨으면 합니다; 만약 모르셨다면, 영수증을 보시면 확인하실 수 있습니다.

가장 최근에 겪으신 것보다 더 나은 경험을 제공해 드릴 수 있다고 확신하므로, 고객님을 저희 식당으로 다시 초대하고 싶습니다. ¹⁸⁰이 사이트상에서 메시지로 제게 이메일 주소를 보내주시겠습니까? 저희 고객 서비스 관리자가 고객님의 방문 경험에 대해 자세히 알고자 합니다.

다시 한 번 감사 드리며,

리사 트라파니, www.alerro-bistro.com

어휘 hospitality 친절한 응대 source 공급받다, 얻다 organically 유기농으로 in particular 특히 accordingly 따라서 charge 요금, 비용 notice 알아차리다 supervisor 관리자

176 추론 / 암시　　　　　　　　　　　　[고난도]

번역　브로우스키 씨가 알레로 비스트로의 음식에 관해 암시하는 것은?
(A) 양이 많다.
(B) 간단한 방식으로 준비된다.
(C) 가격이 놀랄 만큼 싸다.
(D) 식당 장식과 어울리지 않는다.

해설　온라인 후기의 후반부에서 알레로 비스트로의 음식은 장인이 화려하게 준비한 요리에는 그다지 관심이 없고 건강에 신경 쓰는 사람들 마음에 들 것 (the food here would appeal to health-conscious diners who are not concerned with fancy artisanal food preparation)이라고 했으므로, 음식이 간단한 방식으로 준비된다고 추론할 수 있다. 따라서 (B)가 정답이다.

어휘　portion (음식의) 1인분　décor 장식

177 사실 관계 확인

번역　브로우스키 씨에 관해 가장 사실인 것은?
(A) 전에 알레로 비스트로에서 식사한 적이 있다.
(B) 동네 건강식품점 직원이다.
(C) 온라인 후기를 쓸 때마다 사진을 올린다.
(D) 평일에 알레로 비스트로에 갔다.

해설　온라인 후기의 중반부에서 브로우스키 씨가 이전에 알레로 비스트로에서 타코 샐러드를 먹어 본 적이 있다(I've had it here before)고 했으므로, (A)가 정답이다.

▶▶ Paraphrasing　지문의 had it here before
→ 정답의 eaten at Alerro's Bistro previously

178 동의어 찾기

번역　답변에서 1번째 단락 3행의 'tight'와 의미상 가장 가까운 것은?
(A) 엄격한
(B) 부족한
(C) 꽉 찬
(D) 튼튼하게 고정된

해설　'tight'를 포함한 부분은 '올 시즌 물량이 빠듯해서(As supplies have been tight this season)'라는 의미로 해석되는데, 여기서 tight는 '빠듯한, 부족한'이라는 뜻으로 쓰였다. 따라서 (B) lacking이 정답이다.

179 연계

번역　브로우스키 씨의 청구서에서 얼마가 제외됐겠는가?
(A) 7달러
(B) 8달러
(C) 9달러
(D) 13달러

해설　답변의 첫 번째 단락에서 원래 감자튀김은 유기농으로 재배된 감자로 만들지만 올 시즌 물량이 빠듯해 최근에 다른 재배 농가의 감자를 조달해야 했다고 한 후, 이에 따라 해당 메뉴 비용을 청구하지 않았다(the charge for that dish was not applied to your bill)고 했다. 온라인 후기의 초반부에 브로우스키 씨가 주문한 음식을 나열한 부분에서 크로스컷 감자튀김(cross-cut fries)이 8달러임을 확인할 수 있으므로, (B)가 정답이다.

180 추론 / 암시

번역　브로우스키 씨가 답신하면 트라파니 씨는 어떻게 하겠다고 하는가?
(A) 식사비 전액 환불
(B) 사업주에게 불만 사항 알리기
(C) 전자 쿠폰 보내기
(D) 연락처 전달

해설　답변의 두 번째 단락에서 브로우스키 씨에게 이메일 주소를 메시지로 보내달라(Could you send me a message through this site and provide your e-mail address?)고 요청한 후, 고객 서비스 관리자가 브로우스키 씨의 방문 경험에 대해 자세히 알고자 한다(Our customer service supervisor would like to know more about your visit)고 덧붙였다. 따라서 트라파니 씨가 고객 서비스 관리자에게 브로우스키 씨의 이메일 주소를 전달할 거라고 추론할 수 있으므로, (D)가 정답이다.

181-185 웹페이지 + 이메일

> **브라이트레인 퍼블리싱에 오신 것을 환영합니다!**
>
> 브라이트레인 퍼블리싱은 마케팅 전략 관련 최첨단 안내서를 발행하는 출판사입니다. 약 15년 전 창립한 이후, 당사는 유용한 인기 도서 수백 권을 내놓았습니다. 최근 발매된 책들을 소개합니다:
>
> 〈제품 설명서 잘 쓰는 법〉 삽화가 딸린 이 책에서는, 저명한 광고 카피라이터 잭 쇼펠이 매출을 창출하는 제품 설명서 작성에 대한 실용적인 조언을 드립니다. **181(A)**이는 쇼펠 씨의 데뷔작이며 저희는 이 책이 해당 분야의 고전이 되리라 확신합니다. 페이퍼백 – 27달러 + **181(B)**5달러 배송비 **181(C)**전자책 13달러
>
> 〈호텔 창업〉 **182**영감을 주는 이 책은 기업가 정신에 초점을 맞추고 있어, 저희가 이전에 출간했던 책과는 다릅니다. 서비스업 전문가 휴 창가라스가 쓴 글에는 관광업 기반이 탄탄하지 않은 지역에서도 호텔 사업을 시작할 수 있는 핵심 원칙들이 생생하게 담겨 있습니다. 페이퍼백 – 22달러 + **181(B)**4달러 배송비
>
> 〈전자상거래 매출 증대〉 이 책의 저자인 루이스 마자는 수익성 있는 온라인 사업체를 설립하는 데 있어 기술 관련 전문지식보다 마케팅 기술이 훨씬 더 중요하다는 견해를 **183**갖고 있습니다. 그녀는 온라인 매출을 올리는 팁을 제공하고, 유수한 전자상거래 컨설턴트들의 연락처 목록도 제공합니다. 페이퍼백 – 29달러 + **181(B)**6달러 배송비 **181(C)**전자책 14달러
>
> 〈소셜 미디어를 통한 판매〉 **184**〈온라인 시대〉지 편집장 에이미 강이 쓴 종합서로, 소셜 미디어 사이트를 통해 효과적으로 판매하는 법에 관해 상세한 방향을 제시하며, 매출을 상승시키는 것으로 입증된 단어들을 정리한 24쪽짜리 보너스 포켓북이 포함되어 있습니다. 하드커버 – 37달러 + **181(B)**7달러 배송비

어휘　cutting-edge 최첨단의　founding 창립, 설립　release 발매품　description 설명(서)　illustrated 삽화가 있는　volume 책　noted 저명한　practical 실용적인　generate 창출하다　confident 확신하는　classic 고전　inspiring 영감을 주는　entrepreneurship 기업가 정신　hospitality 접객, 환대　expert 전문가　lay down (규칙 등을) 제시하다, 명시하다　get ~ off the ground ~을 시작하다, 실행에 옮기다　region 지역　expertise 전문지식　profitable 이윤을 내는　supply 제공하다　list 목록을 제시하다, 정리하다　comprehensive 종합적인, 포괄적인　effective 효과적인　proven 입증된

발신: 에릭 류 〈eric-liu@mail.com〉

수신: 엘런 트레몬트 〈ellen-tremont@mail.com〉

날짜: 10월 18일

제목: 유용한 것

안녕하세요 엘런,

184브라이트레인 퍼블리싱에서 직원 연수 워크숍에 쓰려고 주문한 책이 방금 도착했어요. 아주 훌륭해 보이고, 부록으로 함께 온 소책자에 '상품을 더 많이 파는 힘 있는 말'이 가득하네요. 다 보면 둘 다 보내드릴게요.

185그리고 교육 모듈 개발 건은 어떻게 돼 가는지 계속 알려주세요. 아직 할 일이 많겠지만, 시간은 충분해요.

고마워요.

에릭

어휘   merchandise 상품   come along (작업 등이) 되어 가다
training module 교육 모듈 (교육에 필요한 프로그램, 자료 등의 집합체)

181   사실 관계 확인   고난도

번역   브라이트레인 퍼블리싱에 관해 가장 사실과 거리가 먼 것은?
(A) 신인 작가의 작품을 출판했다.
(B) 배송비는 별도 부과한다.
(C) 일부 책은 디지털판을 제공한다.
(D) 잡지 에디터에 의해 설립되었다.

해설   〈제품 설명서 잘 쓰는 법〉이 쇼펠 씨의 데뷔작(This is Mr. Schoeffel's debut book)이라고 한 것에서 (A)를 확인할 수 있고, 각 도서의 설명 끝에 배송비가 나와 있으므로 (B) 역시 사실임을 알 수 있다. 또한 〈제품 설명서 잘 쓰는 법〉과 〈전자상거래 매출 증대〉 관련 설명의 마지막 부분에 전자책(Electronic edition) 가격이 나온 것으로 보아 (C)도 확인이 가능하다. 따라서 언급되지 않은 (D)가 정답이다.

어휘   impose 부과하다   separate 별도의

▶▶ Paraphrasing   지문의 Mr. Schoeffel's debut book
→ 보기 (A)의 a work by a first-time author
지문의 shipping → 보기 (B)의 a separate charge for delivery
지문의 Electronic edition
→ 보기 (C)의 digital editions

182   추론 / 암시

번역   〈호텔 창업〉에 관해 암시된 것은?
(A) 일부 지역은 발송이 안 된다.
(B) 출판사에서 해당 유형으로는 처음 낸 책이다.
(C) 관광업계 전문가들이 추천한다.
(D) 다른 신간보다 집필하는 데 시간이 더 걸렸다.

해설   〈호텔 창업〉 관련 설명을 보면, 해당 책이 기업가 정신에 초점을 맞추고 있다는 점에서 이전에 출간했던 책들과 다르다(making it different from any of our previous releases)고 했으므로, (B)가 정답이다.

▶▶ Paraphrasing   지문의 different from any of our previous releases
→ 정답의 the first book of its type

183   동의어 찾기   고난도

번역   웹페이지에서 4번째 단락 1행의 "holds"와 의미상 가장 가까운 것은?
(A) 포함하다
(B) 확보하다
(C) 견지하다
(D) 중단하다

해설   'holds'를 포함한 부분은 '(특정) 견해를 갖고 있다(holds the view that ~)'는 의미로 해석되는데, 여기서 holds는 '(의견 등을) 가지고 있다, 지니다'라는 뜻으로 쓰였다. 따라서 '(주장 등을) 고수하다, ~을 견지하다'라는 의미의 (C) adheres to가 정답이다.

184   연계

번역   류 씨가 최근에 구입한 책은 무엇이겠는가?
(A) 〈제품 설명서 잘 쓰는 법〉
(B) 〈호텔 창업〉
(C) 〈전자상거래 매출 증대〉
(D) 〈소셜 미디어를 통한 판매〉

해설   이메일의 첫 번째 단락에서 류 씨가 브라이트레인 출판사에서 주문한 책이 방금 도착했다(The book I ordered from Brightlane Publishing ~ just arrived)고 한 후, 부록으로 함께 온 소책자에 '상품을 더 많이 파는 힘 있는 말'이 가득하다(the booklet that came with it is full of "power words that sell more merchandise")고 덧붙였다. 웹페이지를 보면, 〈소셜 미디어를 통한 판매〉 관련 설명에서 매출을 상승시키는 것으로 입증된 단어들을 정리한 24쪽짜리 보너스 포켓북이 포함되어 있다(this comprehensive volume ~ includes a bonus 24-page pocket book listing words that are proven to increase sales)고 했으므로, 류 씨가 〈소셜 미디어를 통한 판매〉를 구입했을 것으로 추론할 수 있다. 따라서 (D)가 정답이다.

185   세부 사항

번역   류 씨가 트레몬트 씨에게 부탁하는 일은?
(A) 프로젝트 진행 상황 보고하기
(B) 교육 세션을 이끌 후임 진행자 찾기
(C) 직원 발표 내용 교정하기
(D) 업무 경비 상환하기

해설   이메일의 두 번째 단락에서 교육 모듈 개발 건이 어떻게 돼 가는지 계속 알려줄 것(please keep me posted on how you are coming along with developing your training module)을 요청했으므로, (A)가 정답이다.

어휘   replacement 후임자   proofread 교정하다   reimburse 상환하다

▶▶ Paraphrasing   지문의 keep me posted on how you are coming along with developing your training module
→ 정답의 Provide him with a progress report on a project

186-190 웹페이지 + 회의 요약본 + 온라인 등록 양식

http://www.cityofstenley.gov/services/recycling-waste

스텐리 시 〉〉 주민을 위한 재활용 및 폐기물 수거 서비스

➤ 스텐리 시는 그루비 산업(GIC)과 계약을 체결해 시 전역에서 폐기물을 수거합니다. 재활용되지 않는 폐기물은 우선 시 북쪽에 있는 스텐리 시 이송시설(SCTF)로 옮겨진 뒤 매립지로 운반됩니다. **186재활용 가능한 모든 소재는 GIC가 관리하는 재활용 시설로 보내져 현장에서 처리됩니다.** 재활용 쓰레기는 매주 지정된 재활용 수거일 오전 6시 이전에 도로 경계석 옆에 두어야 합니다. **187시는 모든 가정과 업체에 재활용 쓰레기통을 각 유형마다 1개씩 제공합니다.**

➤ 파란색 - 캔, 병 등 가정 재활용품용
➤ **187빨간색 - 잡초, 잎 등 퇴비성 정원 폐기물용 ***
➤ **187초록색 - 크고 작은 나뭇가지 등 기타 모든 정원 폐기물용**
➤ **190노란색 - 컴퓨터 및 주변기기, 휴대전화, 전기 부속품 등 전자 폐기물용**

             * 3월 중순부터 12월 중순까지 수거 가능

어휘 contract 계약을 하다 transfer 운송, 이송 transport 운반하다, 옮기다 landfill 매립지 curb 도로 경계석, 연석 designated 지정된 compostable 퇴비성의 limb 큰 나뭇가지 peripheral 주변기기; 주변의

1884월 28일 화요일 스텐리 시 정례 주간 회의 요약

참석: 레이 콘리 시장, 드류 모로 폐기물관리국장, 예산위원 전원, GIC 직원 유니스 우

신규 모바일 애플리케이션: 모로 씨는 GIC(그루비 산업)가 특별히 시민들을 위해 개발한 휴대전화 앱인 '재활용 알림이'가 5월 1일 금요일에 출시된다고 발표했다. **188이 앱의 선임 개발자인 우 씨는 기능 조작법을 시연했다.** **189모로 씨는** 주간 재활용 수거 일정이 구역에 따라 다음과 같이 나뉠 거라고 확인해 주었다: 1구역(주소가 "북부"로 등록된 주거지) - 매주 화요일; 2구역(주소가 "북부"로 등록된 업체) - 매주 수요일; 3구역(주소가 "남부"로 등록된 주거지) - 매주 목요일; 4구역(주소가 "남부"로 등록된 업체) - 매주 금요일. **189이 달의 첫 번째 수거일은 5월 5일, 6일, 7일, 8일로, 각각 1, 2, 3, 4구역에 해당한다.**

어휘 go live 실행되다, 이용 가능해지다 demonstration 시연 navigate 조작하다, 둘러보다 feature 기능 confirm 확인하다 divide 나누다 sector 구역 residence 주거지 respectively 각각

재활용 알림이
등록 화면

알림 등록을 하려면 아래 영역을 작성한 후 "제출"을 누르세요.

오늘 날짜: 5월 1일
거주자 이름: 데비 과리니   이메일: Debbie@mail.com
189주소: 북부 브레들리 가 1736번지
부동산 유형: ☑주거용   ☐ 상업용
(선택) 재활용 도우미에게 문의하세요.
190어떻게 컴퓨터 키보드 및 스피커, 전력 케이블을 버려야 하나요?

[제출]

189매주 수거일 하루 전에 미리 알림 문자를 받게 됩니다. 재활용 도우미가 어떤 통을 사용해야 하는지 알려드릴 수 있습니다.

어휘 registration 등록 field 영역, 칸 property 부동산 dispose 버리다

---

186 사실 관계 확인

번역 GIC에 관해 언급된 것은?
(A) 정보기술 부서를 확충하고 있다.
(B) 자체 재활용 설비를 운영한다.
(C) 재활용 용기를 제조한다.
(D) SCTF 옆에 위치해 있다.

해설 웹페이지 안내문의 초반부에서 재활용 가능한 모든 소재는 GIC가 관리하는 재활용 시설로 보내진다(All recyclable material is sent to the GIC-managed recycling facility)고 했으므로, (B)가 정답이다.

▶▶ **Paraphrasing** 지문의 the GIC-managed recycling facility
→ 정답의 its own recycling facility

---

187 추론 / 암시   고난도

번역 스텐리 시에 관해 가장 사실에 가까운 것은?
(A) 다수의 주거용 부동산에 마당이 있다.
(B) 재활용되지 않는 폐기물은 해외로 운송된다.
(C) 11월에는 일부 재활용품을 수거하지 않는다.
(D) 유리를 금속과 분리해 폐기하도록 시민에게 요구한다.

해설 웹페이지 안내문의 중반부에서 스텐리 시가 모든 가정과 업체에게 재활용 쓰레기통을 각 유형마다 1개씩 제공한다(The city provides every home and business with one (1) of each type of bin for recyclables)고 되어 있는데, 나열된 쓰레기통의 유형을 보면 정원 폐기물용 쓰레기통이 2종(Red, Green)이나 된다. 따라 다수의 가정에 마당이 있다고 볼 수 있으므로, (A)가 정답이다.

▶▶ **Paraphrasing** 지문의 every home
→ 정답의 its residential properties
지문의 yard
→ 정답의 outdoor land

---

188 사실 관계 확인

번역 우 씨에 관해 언급된 것은?
(A) 금융위원회 위원이다.
(B) 현재 스텐리 시에 거주하고 있다.
(C) 4월 28일에 모바일 앱 사용법을 설명했다.
(D) 한때 콘리 씨의 사무실에서 일했다.

해설 회의 요약본을 보면 4월 28일에 열린 회의에서 선임 개발자인 우 씨가 앱 기능 조작법을 시연했다(Ms. Woo, the lead developer of the app, gave a demonstration on navigating its features)고 되어 있다. 따라서 (C)가 정답이다.

어휘 illustrate 예를 들어(실제로 보여주며) 설명하다

▶▶ **Paraphrasing** 지문의 gave a demonstration
→ 정답의 illustrated how to use

Test 8

189 연계

번역 과라니 씨는 언제 알림 메시지를 받겠는가?
(A) 5월 4일
(B) 5월 5일
(C) 5월 6일
(D) 5월 7일

해설 온라인 등록 양식에서 과라니 씨가 북부 지역(Address: 1736 Bradley Street North)에 거주하고(Type of property: (V) residential) 있음을 확인할 수 있는데, 회의 요약본에서 신규 앱에 관해 정리한 부분을 보면, 주소가 북부로 등록된 주거지(residences with "North" addresses)는 1구역(Zone 1)에 해당하며 해당 구역의 첫 번째 수거일이 5월 5일(The first pick-up dates for the month will be May 5 ~ for Zones 1)이라고 되어 있다. 온라인 등록 양식 하단에서 지정된 수거일 하루 전에 알림 문자를 받게 된다(You will receive a reminder text message one day before your pick-up day each week)고 했으므로, 과라니 씨가 5월 4일에 알림 문자를 받을 것으로 추론할 수 있다. 따라서 (A)가 정답이다.

190 연계

번역 과라니 씨가 문의한 폐기물은 어떤 통을 사용해야 하는가?
(A) 파란색 쓰레기통
(B) 빨간색 쓰레기통
(C) 초록색 쓰레기통
(D) 노란색 쓰레기통

해설 온라인 등록 양식에서 과라니 씨가 컴퓨터 키보드 및 스피커, 전력 케이블을 어떻게 버려야 하는지(How do I dispose of Computer keyboards and speakers, power cables?) 문의했는데, 웹페이지 하단을 보면 전자제품은 노란색(Yellow – for electronic waste, including computers and peripherals, mobile phones, and electrical accessories) 쓰레기통에 버려야 한다고 되어 있으므로, (D)가 정답이다.

191-195 발표문 + 참가 신청서 + 이메일

〈바베이도스 라이프〉지 사진 공모전에 참가하세요!

[191]수상 사진은 바베이도스 및 해외에 살고 있는 7만 명 이상의 잡지 독자들이 볼 수 있습니다. [193(B)]당사 사진 공모전은 모든 아마추어 사진작가, 즉 사진작가로 수입을 버는 사람이 아니라면 누구나 참가할 수 있습니다. [193(D)]모든 참가자는 바베이도스 거주자여야 합니다. [193(A)]각 참가자는 한 부문에 최대 10개의 이미지를 제출할 수 있습니다.

참가 양식(www.magazine-contest.com에서 다운로드 가능)과 사진을 반드시 2월 15일까지 온라인으로 제출하세요.

상위 3개의 사진은 6월 특집호인 "바베이도스의 백미"에 실리며, 선외가작상 수상자들은 이름이 언급될 예정입니다. 편집자들은 향후 월간지에 포함시킬 선외가작상 수상 사진들도 검토할 것입니다. 만약 당사가 잡지에 사진을 [192]게재하고 싶어지면, 연락을 드려 1회성으로 사용할 수 있도록 준비하겠습니다.

각 부문별 상:

1위 – 현금 300달러	3위 – 〈바베이도스 라이프〉 2년 구독권
2위 – 현금 150달러	선외가작상 – 〈바베이도스 라이프〉 티셔츠 1장

궁금한 점은 editor@barbados-mag.com으로 이메일을 보내세요.

어휘 internationally 국제적으로, 해외에 contest 대회 earn 벌다 entrant (경기 등의) 참가자 ensure 반드시 ~하게 하다 electronically 전자 기기로, 온라인으로 appear 등장하다, 실리다 Honorable Mention 선외가작상 (입선은 되지 않았으나 꽤 잘된 작품에 주는 상) inclusion 포함 subscription 구독(권)

바베이도스 라이프 사진 공모전
참가 양식

사진 부문: _____ 축제 (행사에서 촬영)
　　　　　 　V 　 야생 생물 (동물, 곤충 또는 식물)
　　　　　 _____ 풍경 (전망과 경치)

이름: *아이다 세라노*　　이메일 주소: *serrano@mail.com*

각 사진에 제목과 설명을 첨부하고 촬영 장소와 시기를 구체적으로 밝히세요. [194]아래 공간에 사진을 둘러싼 특별한 상황이 있으면 설명하세요:

저는 자원봉사 안내인으로 투어를 이끌면서 이 사진들을 찍었습니다.

서명: *Ida Serrano*

어휘 scenery 풍경 vista (아름다운) 경치 description 설명 specify 구체적으로 밝히다, 명시하다 circumstance 상황

발신: 제임스 말린 <marlin@barbados-mag.com>
수신: 아이다 세라노 <serrano@mail.com>
날짜: 4월 17일
제목: 축하합니다!

세라노 씨께,

[194]축하합니다—〈바베이도스 라이프〉지는 1월 24일 열대나비 정원에서 찍은 귀하의 사진 중 하나(나비 #2)를 선외가작상에 선정했습니다. [193(A)/(B)/(D)]저희는 귀하가 참가 요건을 모두 충족했음을 확인했습니다. 상을 받으시려면 5일 이내에 제게 이메일로 회신하세요. [195]이메일 주실 때, 귀하의 이름을 특별호에 포함해도 괜찮은지 확인해 주세요.

궁금한 점이 있으시면 이메일을 주시기 바랍니다.

제임스 말린, 사진 편집자

어휘 recognize (상으로) 인정하다, 표창하다 claim 받아 내다, 청구하다

191 사실 관계 확인

번역 발표문에서 〈바베이도스 라이프〉지에 관해 명시하는 것은?
(A) 격월로 나온다.
(B) 바베이도스 외부에 독자가 있다.
(C) 매 호마다 사진 공모전이 있다.
(D) 바베이도스 축제를 후원한다.

해설 발표문의 첫 번째 단락에서 수상 사진은 바베이도스 및 해외에 살고 있는 잡지 독자들이 볼 수 있다(Your winning photograph could be seen by our magazine's ~ readers living in Barbados and internationally)고 했으므로, 바베이도스 외부에도 독자가 있음을 알 수 있다. 따라서 (B)가 정답이다.

▶▶ **Paraphrasing** 지문의 readers living in Barbados and internationally
→ 정답의 readers outside of Barbados

192 동의어 찾기

번역 발표문에서 3번째 단락 3행의 "run"과 의미상 가장 가까운 것은?
(A) 편집하다
(B) 감독하다
(C) 평가하다
(D) 게재하다

해설 'run'을 포함한 부분은 '만약 당사가 잡지에 사진을 게재하고 싶다면(If we wish to run your photo in the magazine)'이라는 의미로 해석되는데, 여기서 run은 '싣다, 게재하다'라는 뜻으로 쓰였다. 따라서 '(인쇄 매체에) 싣다, 게재하다'라는 의미의 (D)가 정답이다.

193 연계   고난도

번역 아이다 세라노에 관해 사실이 아닌 것은?
(A) 10개 이하의 이미지를 제출했다.
(B) 사진으로 수입을 올리지 않는다.
(C) 참가작이 2월 15일 이후에 접수되었다.
(D) 현재 바베이도스 거주자다.

해설 이메일의 중반부에서 세라노 씨가 사진 공모전 참가 요건을 모두 충족했다(We have confirmed that you have met all entry requirements)고 했는데, 이 참가 요건은 발표문에서 확인할 수 있다. 발표문의 첫 번째 단락에서 각 참가자가 한 부문에 최대 10개의 이미지를 제출할 수 있다(Each entrant may submit up to 10 images in any one category)고 했고, 사진작가로 수입을 버는 사람이 아니라면 누구나 참가할 수 있으며(Our photo contest is open to ~ anyone who does not earn any income as a photographer), 모든 참가자는 바베이도스 거주자여야 한다(All entrants must be residents of Barbados)고 했다. 따라서 세라노 씨가 (A), (B), (D)에 해당하는 조건을 충족했다고 볼 수 있다. 하지만 두 번째 단락에서 사진은 반드시 2월 15일까지 제출되어야 한다(your photos are submitted electronically no later than February 15)고 했으므로, 사실이 아닌 (C)가 정답이다.

▶▶ **Paraphrasing** 지문의 up to 10 images
→ 보기 (A)의 10 or fewer images
지문의 does not earn any income as a photographer
→ 보기 (B)의 income does not come from photography

194 연계

번역 세라노 씨의 사진 중 하나에 관해 암시된 것은?
(A) 티셔츠 디자인에 선보일 예정이다.
(B) 정원을 돌아보면서 찍은 사진이다.
(C) 두 개의 다른 부문에 제출되었다.
(D) 부상으로 현금이 나올 것이다.

해설 참가 신청서 하단에서 세라노 씨는 자신이 투어를 이끌면서 사진을 찍었다(I captured these images while I was leading tours)고 적었는데,

이메일의 첫 번째 단락에서 〈바베이도스 라이프〉지가 열대나비 정원에서 찍은 세라노 씨의 사진 중 하나를 선외가작상으로 선정했다(Barbados Life magazine has recognized one of your photographs ~ taken at the Tropical Butterfly Garden)고 했다. 따라서 세라노 씨가 열대나비 정원 투어 도중에 찍은 사진이라고 추론할 수 있으므로, (B)가 정답이다.

195 세부 사항

번역 말린 씨가 세라노 씨에게 부탁하는 일은?
(A) 세라노 씨의 이름이 실리도록 허락하기
(B) 대체품으로 적합한 다른 부상 목록 작성하기
(C) 향후 문의는 다른 부서로 직접 하기
(D) 우편물 발송을 위해 집 주소 확인해 주기

해설 이메일의 후반부에서 말린 씨가 특별호에 세라노 씨의 이름을 포함해도 괜찮은지 확인해달라(please confirm that it is OK for us to include your name in our special issue)고 요청했으므로, (A)가 정답이다.

어휘 permission 허락 suitable 적합한 substitute 대체품

▶▶ **Paraphrasing** 지문의 confirm that it is OK
→ 정답의 Give permission
지문의 to include your name in our special issue → 정답의 for her name to be published

196-200 기사 + 칼럼 + 웹페이지

벨리 시 뉴스   3월 20일

새 지배인이 벨리 호텔을 위한 새로운 마케팅 계획을 세우다

글: 경제 기자 사라 코지

달만 카운티와 헨리 카운티를 가르는 프런티지 로에 위치한 200년 역사의 벨리 호텔은 녹음이 우거진 정원으로 둘러싸여 있어 투숙객에게 편안한 숙박을 제공한다.

196/198필자가 머무는 동안, 시설 관리인인 모니카 후는 지역 기업가 댄 크로스비 씨가 소유하고 있는 이 호텔을 홍보할 야심 찬 마케팅 계획이 있다고 말했다. 크로스비 씨는 3년째 성장 중인 카페 사업에 더 집중하고자 지난해 말 그녀를 고용했다.

이야기를 나누면서 필자는 호텔 웹사이트가 호화로운 편의시설을 제대로 보여주지 않았다고 말했다. **197**그녀는 웃으면서 태블릿 기기를 집어 들더니 새로 디자인한 사이트의 한 페이지를 가리켰는데, 바로 여기서 아름답게 꾸며진 각 객실의 이미지를 보여주고 있었다. 그런 다음 그녀는 이 호텔을 헨리 카운티 탐방의 출발점으로 홍보하고자 하는 자신의 계획에 대해 설명했다. 헨리 카운티는 많은 볼거리를 자랑하지만 달만 카운티보다 방문객이 훨씬 적다. 그녀는 호텔의 새 안내책자가 방문객들에게 '헨리 카운티를 경험하도록' 독려한다고 말한다.

후 씨는 벨리 호텔의 저녁 메뉴도 '모든 예산에 맞출 수 있는' 옵션이 포함되도록 다시 짤 계획이라고 말했다. **196**현재 호텔의 선물가게는 크로스비 씨가 장인의 솜씨로 만든 허브와 향신료를 판매하고 있다.

Test 8

어휘 **separate** 분리하다, 가르다 **surround** 둘러싸다 **shaded** 녹음이 우거진, 그늘진 **ambitious** 야심찬 **entrepreneur** 기업가 **represent** 보여주다, 나타내다 **amenity** 편의시설 **effort** (특정 성과를 거두려는) 계획적 활동, 노력 **launch point** 시작점, 발사점 **attraction** 볼거리, 명소 **budget** 예산 **artisanal** 장인의 **spice** 향신료

벌리 시 뉴스   3월 24일

헨리 카운티 탐방

글: 198**여행 칼럼니스트 짐 스칸다르**

벌리 시-최근에 필자는 벌리 호텔에 묵으면서 헨리 카운티의 매력적인 명소들을 탐방했다. 198**호텔 지배인은 헨리 카운티 관광협회(HCTA)의 브라이언 쿠조 회장과 필자를 만나게 해줬고**, 그는 하루 동안 카운티 관광을 안내했다. 관광은 호텔 근처에 위치한 고급 레스토랑 중 하나인 라이트 비스트로에서의 맛있는 아침식사로 시작됐다. 그런 다음 우리는 예술로 유명한 지역인 그레일리 타운에 들르고 팩스턴 공원 역사마을을 둘러보았다. 199**여행의 하이라이트는 오픈된 바지선을 타고 가이드의 설명을 들으며 팩스턴 운하를 따라 내려가는 유람선 코스였다.** 쿠조 씨는 이 지역에 대단한 열정을 보여주었다. 필자는 이곳에서 많은 명소를 구경하라고 강력히 추천한다.

어휘 **explore** 탐방하다, 답사하다 **association** 협회 **highly-rated** 고급의, 일류의 **narrated cruise** 가이드의 설명을 들으며 하는 유람선 여행 **barge** 바지선 **enthusiasm** 열정 **sight** 명소, 관광지

---

www.birleyhotel.com/home

벌리 호텔에서 묵으면서 헨리 카운티를 경험해 보세요.

휴식 서비스 알아보기	197**숙박** **객실 보기**
식사 식사 메뉴 보기	탐방 근처 명소를 둘러보기

*벌리 호텔은 단체 행사를 환영합니다. 프로젝터와 스피커 시스템을 갖춘 대형 회의실 대여가 가능합니다. 200**호텔에는 전기자전거 및 전기차 충전소가 마련되어 있으며 투숙객은 무료로 이용할 수 있고, 투숙객이 아닌 경우 15달러가 부과됩니다.**

어휘 **feature** 포함하다 **charging station** 충전소

---

196 추론 / 암시   고난도

번역 벌리 호텔에 관해 가장 사실에 가까운 것은?
(A) 최근 객실 점유율이 높아졌다.
(B) 고풍스러운 가구로 장식되어 있다.
(C) 칼럼니스트에게 할인 숙박을 제공했다.
(D) 업주가 만든 식품 관련 제품을 판매한다.

해설 기사의 두 번째 단락에서 벌리 호텔은 지역 기업가 댄 크로스비 씨의 소유(the hotel, which is owned by local entrepreneur Dan Crosby)라고 했는데, 마지막 단락을 보면 호텔 선물가게에서 크로스비 씨가 장인의 솜씨로 만든 허브와 향신료를 판매하고 있다(its gift shop sells artisanal herbs and spices created by Mr. Crosby)고 되어 있다. 따라서 (D)가 정답이다.

어휘 **occupancy** 점유

▶▶ **Paraphrasing** 지문의 **sells artisanal herbs and spices created by Mr. Crosby**
→ 정답의 **sells food-related products made by its owner**

---

197 연계

번역 후 씨가 코지 씨에게 보여준 웹사이트 코너는?
(A) 휴식
(B) 숙박
(C) 식사
(D) 탐방

해설 기사의 세 번째 단락에서 후 씨가 코지 씨에게 아름답게 꾸며진 객실의 이미지가 있는 페이지를 보여주었다(she ~ pointed out a page on the newly-redesigned site showcasing images of each beautifully-decorated guest room)고 했는데, 웹페이지를 보면 객실을 볼 수 있는 코너는 '숙박(Stay, View our rooms)'임을 확인할 수 있다. 따라서 (B)가 정답이다.

---

198 연계   고난도

번역 쿠조 씨에 관해 암시된 것은?
(A) 후 씨로부터 칼럼니스트를 소개 받았다.
(B) 크로스비 씨의 카페 중 한 곳에서 식사를 대접했다.
(C) 관광 여행 중에 코지 씨와 이야기를 나누었다.
(D) 벌리 호텔 안내책자를 디자인했다.

해설 여행 칼럼니스트(Travel Columnist)인 스칸다르 씨가 쓴 칼럼의 초반부를 보면, 호텔 지배인이 헨리 카운티 관광협회의 브라이언 쿠조 회장과 자신을 만나게 해줬다(The hotel's manager put me in contact with Brian Kuzo, president of the Henley County Tourist Association)고 했는데, 기사의 두 번째 단락에서 호텔 지배인이 후 씨(facility manager Monica Hu)임을 알 수 있다. 따라서 쿠조 씨가 후 씨로부터 칼럼니스트인 스칸다르 씨를 소개받았다고 추론할 수 있으므로, (A)가 정답이다.

어휘 **refer A to B** A를 B에게 소개하다

▶▶ **Paraphrasing** 지문의 **put ~ in contact with**
→ 정답의 **was referred ~ to**

199 사실 관계 확인

번역 헨리 카운티에 관해 알 수 있는 것은?
(A) 달만 카운티보다 관광객을 더 많이 받는다.
(B) 달만 카운티보다 먼저 사람들이 정착해 살았다.
(C) 방문객들은 보트 투어를 할 수 있다.
(D) 최근에 공원이 확장되었다.

해설 칼럼의 후반부에서 스칸다르 씨는 헨리 카운티 여행의 하이라이트가 오픈된 바지선을 타고 가이드의 설명을 들으며 팩스턴 운하를 따라 내려가는 유람선 코스였다(The highlight of the trip was a ~ cruise down Paxton Canal in an open-air barge)고 했다. 따라서 헨리 카운티 방문객들이 보트 투어를 할 수 있다고 볼 수 있으므로, (C)가 정답이다.

어휘 settle 정착시키다, 이주하여 개발하다   expand 확장하다

> ▶▶ **Paraphrasing**   지문의 **cruise down Paxton Canal in an open-air barge** → 정답의 **boat tours**

200 세부 사항

번역 호텔이 손님들에게 무료로 제공하는 것은?
(A) 시청각 장비 사용
(B) 식물 관리 기법에 관한 워크숍
(C) 전기차 충전시설
(D) 일부 의류 세탁

해설 웹페이지 하단에서 호텔에 전기자전거 및 전기차 충전소가 마련되어 있으며 투숙객은 무료로 이용할 수 있다(The hotel ~ features charging stations for electric bikes and cars, which are free to guests)고 했다. 따라서 (C)가 정답이다.

> ▶▶ **Paraphrasing**   지문의 **free** → 질문의 **at no charge**
> 지문의 **charging stations for electric bikes and cars** → 정답의 **Charging facilities for electric vehicles**

101 (B)	**102** (C)	**103** (B)	**104** (D)	**105** (B)
106 (A)	**107** (C)	**108** (C)	**109** (B)	**110** (C)
111 (D)	**112** (A)	**113** (C)	**114** (D)	**115** (D)
116 (B)	**117** (A)	**118** (B)	**119** (C)	**120** (A)
121 (D)	**122** (C)	**123** (A)	**124** (B)	**125** (D)
126 (D)	**127** (B)	**128** (A)	**129** (C)	**130** (A)
131 (A)	**132** (C)	**133** (D)	**134** (B)	**135** (B)
136 (C)	**137** (B)	**138** (D)	**139** (C)	**140** (D)
141 (D)	**142** (A)	**143** (A)	**144** (B)	**145** (C)
146 (C)	**147** (B)	**148** (D)	**149** (D)	**150** (C)
151 (A)	**152** (C)	**153** (C)	**154** (B)	**155** (A)
156 (B)	**157** (D)	**158** (B)	**159** (D)	**160** (B)
161 (D)	**162** (C)	**163** (C)	**164** (A)	**165** (D)
166 (A)	**167** (C)	**168** (A)	**169** (D)	**170** (B)
171 (B)	**172** (C)	**173** (A)	**174** (D)	**175** (A)
176 (D)	**177** (C)	**178** (B)	**179** (D)	**180** (A)
181 (A)	**182** (C)	**183** (D)	**184** (A)	**185** (B)
186 (A)	**187** (B)	**188** (C)	**189** (D)	**190** (D)
191 (C)	**192** (D)	**193** (D)	**194** (B)	**195** (A)
196 (B)	**197** (D)	**198** (C)	**199** (C)	**200** (A)

PART 5

101 형용사 자리 _ 주격 보어

해설 주어인 Providing excellent support to customers를 보충 설명하는 주격 보어 자리이다. 온라인 채팅 플랫폼이 있으면(with Woshett's online chat platform) 고객 지원 서비스 제공이 수월해진다는 내용으로, '간단한'이라는 뜻의 형용사 (B) simple이 정답이다. 참고로, simplify는 타동사로서 목적어를 취해야 하므로, 현재분사형인 (D) simplifying은 빈칸에 들어갈 수 없다.

번역 워셋의 온라인 채팅 플랫폼이 있으면 고객에게 탁월한 지원 서비스를 제공하는 일이 간단해진다.

어휘 support 지원 simplify 간소화하다

102 형용사 어휘

해설 적당한 가격과 단순한 디자인(With its affordability and straightforward design)의 재봉틀은 재봉을 취미로 즐기는 사람들에게 적합하므로, 빈칸에는 이들(sewers)의 성향을 적절히 묘사하는 형용사가 들어가야 한다. 따라서 '가벼운, 격식을 차리지 않는'이라는 의미의 (C) casual이 정답이다.

번역 적당한 가격과 단순한 디자인의 크루저 10 재봉틀은 가볍게 재봉을 즐기는 사람들에게 안성맞춤이다.

어휘 affordability 적당한 가격 straightforward 단순한 sewing machine 재봉틀 sewer 재봉하는 사람 durable 튼튼한 wealthy 부유한

103 동사 어형 _ 태 _ 시제

해설 부사절 접속사 when이 이끄는 절의 동사 자리로, their prices를 목적어로 취한다. 따라서 능동태 보기 중 미래 시간 표현인 next month와 어울리는 동사를 선택해야 하는데, 시간의 부사절에서는 현재시제 동사가 미래를 나타내므로, (B) lowers가 정답이 된다.

번역 미즈 사는 다음 달에 모발관리 제품의 가격을 낮추면 매출이 늘어날 것이라 예상하고 있다.

어휘 improve 증진되다, 개선되다 lower 낮추다

104 동사 어휘　　　고난도

해설 that절의 동사 caused의 목적격 보어 역할을 하는 to부정사에 해당하는 자리이다. 잦은 해외출장 가능성(the prospect of frequent international travel)이 후보자(him=the candidate)로 하여금 승진(the promotion to manager)과 관련해 어떤 결정을 내리게 했는지 나타내는 동사가 들어가야 한다. 따라서 '거절하다, 사양하다'라는 의미의 (D) decline이 정답이다. 참고로, decline은 자동사로 쓰일 경우 '감소하다'라는 뜻을 나타낸다. (B) withhold는 '~를 주지 않다, (제공을) 보류하다'라는 의미로 '승낙(consent, approval), 지불(payment)' 등의 명사와는 어울려 쓰이지만, '승진을 주지 않고 보류한다'고 할 수는 없기 때문에 빈칸에는 적절하지 않다.

번역 그 후보자는 부장 승진을 사양한 것이 잦은 해외출장 가능성 때문이라고 말했다.

어휘 candidate 후보자 prospect 가능성 frequent 잦은 promotion 승진 retreat 물러서다 enroll 등록하다

105 부사 어휘

해설 빈칸 뒤 to부정사구(to qualify her for national competition)와 결합해 형용사 high를 수식하는 부사 자리이다. 폴크 씨의 점수가 전국대회 출전 자격을 얻을 만큼 높지는 않았다는 내용이므로, '(~할 만큼) 충분히'라는 의미의 (B) enough가 정답이다. enough는 형용사나 부사를 뒤에서 수식하여 '~하기에 충분히 ~한'이라는 뜻을 나타낸다. 참고로, (C) much는 형용사를 뒤에서 수식해 줄 수 없다.

번역 폴크 씨의 점수는 개인 최고 기록이긴 했지만 전국대회 출전 자격을 얻을 만큼 충분히 높지는 않았다.

어휘 personal record 개인 최고 기록 qualify 자격을 얻다 competition 대회

106 전치사 어휘

해설 모든 강좌가 당초 일정대로(as initially scheduled) 진행된다고 한 반면에, 빈칸의 목적어 역할을 하는 "Ethics in Nursing"은 시간이 옮겨졌다(has been moved to Tuesday evenings)고 했다. 즉, '간호 윤리학'은 예외 사항에 해당하므로, '~을 제외하고'라는 의미의 (A) except가 빈칸에 들어가야 자연스럽다.

번역 학과의 가을 강좌는 화요일 저녁으로 옮긴 '간호 윤리학'을 제외하고 모두 당초 일정대로 진행된다.

어휘 initially 당초 ethics 윤리학

107 재귀대명사 고난도

해설 전치사 for의 목적어 역할을 하는 명사 자리이므로, 재귀대명사 (C) himself와 소유대명사 (D) his 중 하나를 선택해야 한다. 웰링턴 씨 자신 및 동료가 머물 호텔을 요청한 것이므로, 주어인 Mr. Wellington을 대신하는 재귀대명사 (C) himself가 정답이 된다. 참고로, 해당 구조에서 (B) his own이 빈칸에 들어갈 경우 뒤에 바로 명사가 와야 한다.

번역 웰링턴 씨는 자신과 동료 두 명을 위해 회의장과 가까운 호텔을 요청했다.

어휘 adjacent to ~에 가까운

108 형용사 자리 _ 명사 수식 _ 어휘

해설 to hold의 목적어인 복합명사 phone conversations를 수식하는 형용사 자리로, 문맥상 통화의 성격을 묘사하는 단어가 들어가야 자연스럽다. 따라서 '사적인'이라는 의미의 (C) private가 정답이다. 과거분사 (D) privatized도 형용사 역할을 할 수 있지만, '민영화된'이라는 뜻으로 빈칸에는 적절하지 않다.

번역 사무실은 칸막이 없이 트인 공간이므로 직원들은 사적인 통화를 할 때 비어 있는 회의실을 사용해야 한다.

어휘 open floor plan 칸막이나 벽이 없이 트인 공간 unoccupied 비어 있는 privately 은밀히 privacy 사생활 privatize 민영화하다

109 부사 어휘

해설 동사 recommends의 목적어인 동명사구 rubbing coconut oil into its surface를 수식하는 부사 자리이다. 힐지 홈에서 권장하는 가구 관리 방식, 즉 오일을 바르는 행위를 적절히 수식하는 단어가 필요하므로, '가끔, 이따금씩'이라는 의미의 (B) occasionally가 정답이다.

번역 힐지 홈에서는 목재가구 관리를 위해 가끔 코코넛 오일을 가구 표면에 문지를 것을 권장합니다.

어휘 maintain 유지하다 rub 문지르다 surface 표면 carelessly 부주의하게 unexpectedly 예상외로 recently 최근에

110 관계대명사 _ 주격

해설 불완전한 절(is better known for his television work)을 이끄는 동시에, 해당 절에서는 주어 역할을 하는 접속사 자리이다. 빈칸이 이끄는 절이 Mel Frazier에 대해 부연 설명을 하고 있으므로, Mel Frazier를 가리키는 주격 관계대명사 (C) who가 정답이 된다. (A) someone은 대명사로 절을 이끌 수 없고, (B) whoever는 부사절 접속사로 쓰일 수 있지만 '누가 ~이[하]든'이라는 뜻으로 특정 대상(Mel Frazier)에 대해 부연 설명을 하기에는 적절하지 않다. (D) that은 관계대명사일 때 「선행사＋콤마」 뒤에 올 수 없다.

번역 영화사는 감독이 텔레비전 작품으로 더 유명한 멜 프레지어를 영화 주연으로 캐스팅하도록 마지못해 허락했다.

어휘 studio 영화사 reluctantly 마지못해 star 주연

111 명사 어휘 고난도

해설 동사 have의 목적어 역할을 하는 명사 자리로, to부정사구 to assign tasks to employees의 수식을 받는다. '직원들에게 업무를 할당하는 것'은 회사 규정에 나올 법한 감독관의 직권이므로, '권한'이라는 의미의 (D) authority가 정답이다.

번역 회사 규정에는 교대조 감독관이 직원들에게 업무를 할당할 권한이 있다고 명시되어 있다.

어휘 regulation 규정 state 명시하다 supervisor 감독관 assign 할당하다 amenity 편의시설 adjustment 조정 intention 의도

112 부사 자리 _ to부정사 수식

해설 to부정사의 동사원형 enter를 수식하는 부사 자리이므로, '반복해서, 여러 차례'라는 의미의 (A) repeatedly가 정답이다. (B) repetition은 명사, (C) repetitive는 형용사, (D) repeat은 동사로 품사상 빈칸에 들어갈 수 없다.

번역 형편없이 설계된 애폰틀 모바일 앱은 사용자가 앱을 열 때마다 반복해서 로그인 정보를 입력하게 한다.

어휘 poorly 형편없이 repetition 반복 repetitive 반복적인 repeat 반복하다

113 전치사 어휘 고난도

해설 설문에 참여한 소비자들이 name-brand products와 generic ones(=products) 중 전자를 선호했다(preferred)는 내용의 문장이다. 따라서 「prefer A over B」의 형태로 'B보다 A를 선호하다'라는 의미를 완성하는 (C) over이 정답이다. 참고로, over 대신 to를 쓸 수도 있다.

번역 도시 소비자들을 대상으로 한 피트먼 그룹의 설문조사에서 많은 참여자들이 브랜드가 없는 일반 제품보다 유명 브랜드 제품을 선호했다.

어휘 participant 참여자 urban 도시의 prefer 선호하다 generic 일반적인, 상표 등록이 되어 있지 않은

114 동사 어형 _ 동명사 _ 전치사의 목적어

해설 명사구 unnecessary expenses를 목적어로 취하면서 전치사 to의 목적어 역할을 하는 동명사 자리이므로, (D) avoiding이 정답이다. '~에 익숙하다'라는 의미의 'be(come) accustomed to'와 같이 to가 전치사로 쓰이는 표현은 to부정사의 to와 구별하여 기억해야 한다.

번역 몇 년 동안 제한된 예산으로 운영하다 보니 우리는 불필요한 지출을 피하는 데 익숙해졌다.

어휘 restricted 제한된 budget 예산 unnecessary 불필요한 expense 지출 avoid 피하다

115 형용사 어휘

해설 주어인 passengers를 보충 설명하는 주격 보어 자리로, to부정사(to use the metro system's payment card)와 어울려 쓰이는 형용사를 선택해야 한다. 보안상 문제(security issues)가 결제카드를 이용하는 승객에게 미친 부정적인 영향을 나타내는 단어가 들어가야 문맥상 자연스러우므로, '(~하기) 주저하는, 망설이는'이라는 의미의 (D) hesitant가 정답이다. 참고로, (A) critical과 (B) sensitive는 전치사 to와 함께 쓰인다.

번역 보안상 문제가 있다는 소문 때문에 승객들은 지하철 결제카드 사용하기를 망설이고 있다.

어휘 critical 결정적인 sensitive 민감한 unsuitable 부적합한

116 명사 자리 _ 동사의 직접 목적어

해설 「offers + 간접 목적어(readers interested in real estate investment) + 직접 목적어(practical ------)」 구조에서 직접 목적어에 해당하는 명사 자리이다. 형용사 practical 앞에 한정사가 없으므로 빈칸에는 불가산명사가 들어가야 한다. 따라서 '지침, 안내'라는 뜻의 (B) guidance가 정답이다. (A) guide는 명사로 쓰일 경우 '안내(서), 안내원'이라는 뜻의 가산 명사가 되므로 빈칸에는 적절하지 않다.

번역 베일리 씨의 최근 책은 부동산 투자에 관심 있는 독자들에게 해당 분야에 입문하는 실용적인 지침을 제공한다.

어휘 real estate 부동산 guide 안내서, 안내원; 안내하다 guidable 인도할 수 있는, 가르치기 쉬운

117 부사 어휘

해설 경영진이 기업 정책(Corporate policies)을 시행(enforce)할 때 취해야 하는 입장 또는 태도를 나타내는 부사가 들어가야 자연스러우므로, '일관성 있게, 한결같이'라는 의미의 (A) consistently가 정답이다.

번역 기업 정책은 직원들이 이해하기 쉬워야 하며 경영진에 의해 일관성 있게 시행되어야 한다.

어휘 management 경영진 relatively 비교적 shortly 곧 supposedly 아마

118 접속사 자리

해설 빈칸 뒤 완전한 절(her session drew almost 30 people)을 이끄는 접속사 자리이므로, '~에도 불구하고, ~이긴 하지만'이라는 의미의 부사절 접속사 (B) Although가 정답이다. (A) Nevertheless는 접속부사, (C) Prior to와 (D) Apart from은 전치사로 완전한 절을 이끌 수 없다.

번역 세션에 30명 가까이 모였지만, 사토 씨는 적어도 한 번은 개인별로 대화를 나누려고 노력했다.

어휘 endeavor 노력하다 individually 개인별로 nevertheless 그럼에도 불구하고 prior to ~ 전에 apart from ~을 제외하고

119 명사 어휘 [고난도]

해설 자전거 주차시설을 많이 짓는 것(Building ample bike parking facilities)은 자전거 타기를 장려(to promote cycling among the public)하기 위해 스톤빌에서 취한 대책 중 하나라고 볼 수 있다. 따라서 동사 take와 어울려 쓰이며 '조치, 대책'이라는 의미를 나타내는 (C) measures가 정답이다. 참고로, '목표'라는 뜻의 (B) objectives는 주로 have, meet, achieve 등의 동사와 쓰인다.

번역 자전거 주차시설을 많이 짓는 것은 스톤빌이 대중의 자전거 타기를 장려하기 위해 취한 조치들 중 하나일 뿐이다.

어휘 ample 많은 promote 장려하다 indicator 지표 objective 목표 term 용어

120 형용사 자리 _ 명사 수식

해설 동사 receive의 목적어 역할을 하는 불가산명사 access를 수식하는 형용사 자리이다. 따라서 '전용의, 독점적인'이라는 의미의 (A) exclusive가 정답이다. (B) excludes와 (C) exclude는 동사, (D) exclusively는 부사로 품사상 빈칸에 들어갈 수 없다.

번역 오즈번 오페라 서포터즈 클럽 회원들은 티켓 및 상품 할인 혜택에 대한 전용 이용권을 받는다.

어휘 access 이용(권) merchandise 상품 exclude 제외하다 exclusively 독점적으로, 전용으로

121 동사 어형 _ 시제

해설 Ever since(~한 이래로)가 이끄는 부사절의 동사가 began이므로, 주절에는 광고를 시작한 과거 시점부터 현재까지의 방문자수 동향을 설명하는 현재완료 시제가 쓰여야 자연스럽다. 따라서 현재완료 진행형인 (D) have been visiting이 정답이다.

번역 〈엔터프라이징 나우〉에 광고를 시작한 뒤부터 출장자들이 우리 호텔을 대거 찾고 있다.

어휘 business traveler 출장차 방문하는 여행객

122 전치사 어휘 [고난도]

해설 팀과 문화적 차이(their cultural differences)가 있었지만 끈끈한 관계를 형성했다(has built a strong relationship with her team)는 내용이므로, '~에도 불구하고'라는 의미의 (C) notwithstanding이 빈칸에 들어가야 가장 자연스럽다.

번역 필립스 씨는 문화적 차이에도 불구하고 베이징 지사에서 팀과 끈끈한 관계를 형성했다.

어휘 difference 차이 on behalf of ~을 대표[대신]하여 in addition to ~에 더하여 in exchange for ~ 대신에

123 명사 자리 _ 동사의 주어 [고난도]

해설 정관사 The와 전치사구 of workshops 사이에서, will enable의 주어 역할을 하는 명사 자리이다. 더 많은 정보를 다룰 수 있게 하는(to cover ~ more information) 방법은 워크숍 시간을 연장하는 것이므로, '늘리기, 연장'이라는 뜻의 (A) lengthening이 정답이 된다. 여기서 workshops는 "의미상" lengthening의 목적어 역할을 하며, 빈칸 앞에 정관사 the가 있으므로 반드시 of와 함께 쓰여야 한다. 최상급 형용사인 (B) lengthiest의 경우, 뒤에 명사 workshop이 생략되었다고 가정하더라도 의미상 어색하며 to a full day와 연결되지 않으므로 빈칸에는 적절하지 않고, (D) length 역시 '길이'라는 뜻으로 부적절하다.

번역 워크숍 기간을 꼬박 하루로 늘리면 각 워크숍에서 훨씬 더 많은 정보를 다룰 수 있을 것이다.

어휘 enable 가능하게 하다 significantly 훨씬 lengthen 늘리다

124 동사 어휘 [고난도]

해설 결혼식 기획을 전문으로 하기로 선택한 것(Choosing to specialize in wedding planning)과 최선의 결정 중 하나(one of the best decisions)가 의미상 동격 관계를 이루고 있다. 따라서 to be와 함께 이

러한 관계를 완성시키는 동사가 빈칸에 들어가야 하므로, '~임이 입증되다, 판명되다'라는 의미의 (B) prove가 정답이다. 참고로, 이때 prove는 연결동사(linking verb)와 같은 역할을 한다.

번역 결혼식 기획을 전문으로 하기로 선택한 일은 또한 이벤트가 내린 최선의 결정 중 하나로 판명될 수도 있다.

어휘 decision 결정 unite 결합하다 envision 상상하다 strive 노력하다

125 부사절 접속사 자리 _ 어휘

해설 빈칸 뒤 완전한 절(Zinte Apparel decides not to have us run its marketing campaign)을 이끄는 접속사 자리로, (B) As soon as, (C) In order that, (D) Even if 중 하나를 선택해야 한다. 진트 어패럴로 부터 마케팅 캠페인을 의뢰 받지 못하더라도 가장 성공적인 분기가 될 것이라는 내용이므로, 빈칸에는 양보·대조의 접속사가 들어가야 자연스럽다. 따라서 '~ 일지라도'라는 의미의 (D) Even if가 정답이 된다.

번역 비록 진트 어패럴이 우리에게 마케팅 캠페인을 의뢰하지 않겠다고 결정하더라도, 이번 분기는 여전히 순조롭게 나아가 역사상 가장 성공적인 분기가 될 것이다.

어휘 quarter 분기 on track 순조롭게 나아가는, 제대로 진행되고 있는

126 부사 자리 _ 과거분사 수식 _ 비교급 고난도

해설 과거분사 traveled를 수식하는 부사 자리로, 보기에서 (C) most frequently와 (D) more frequently 중 하나를 선택해야 한다. 문맥을 살펴보면 폭포로 가는 두 경로 Summers Road와 Highway 24를 서로 비교하고 있으므로, 비교급인 (D) more frequently가 빈칸에 들어가야 가장 자연스럽다.

번역 차량 통행이 더 많은 24번 고속도로보다 서머스 로드로 캐스웰 폭포에 가는 것이 사실상 더 쉽다.

어휘 waterfall 폭포 frequently traveled 차량 통행이 많은

127 형용사 어휘 고난도

해설 주어인 Patrons를 보충 설명하는 주격 보어 자리로, to부정사(to connect to our wireless Internet service)와 어울려 쓰이는 형용사가 들어가야 한다. 카페 고객은 무선 인터넷 서비스를 이용해도 된다고 허가하는 내용이므로, '~해도 좋은'이라는 의미의 (B) welcome이 정답이다. 참고로, (A) possible은 주격 보어로 쓰일 경우 사람 주어와 어울려 쓰이지 않는다. (C) suggested는 전치사 for와, (D) beneficial은 전치사 to/for와 함께 쓰인다.

번역 메이슨 카페 고객은 영수증에 있는 비밀번호를 이용해 자유롭게 무선 인터넷 서비스에 접속해도 됩니다.

어휘 patron 고객 receipt 영수증 beneficial 이로운

128 동사 어형 _ (should) + 동사원형 고난도

해설 that절의 주어 the store's loyalty program의 동사 자리로, 프로그램은 재설계되는 대상이므로 수동태가 쓰여야 한다. 본동사로 '제안하다, 권고하다'라는 의미의 have recommended가 쓰였기 때문에 that절의 동사는 '~해야 한다'는 의미를 나타내는 「(should)+동사원형」이 되어야 한

다. 따라서 조동사 should가 생략된 형태인 (A) be redesigned가 정답이다.

번역 컨설턴트들은 매장의 고객 우대 제도가 더 즉각적이고 가시적인 보상을 제공하게끔 재설계되어야 한다고 권고했다.

어휘 loyalty program 고객 우대 제도, 멤버십 프로그램 immediate 즉각적인 tangible 가시적인, 실체적인

129 to부정사 관용 표현

해설 빈칸이 when절의 동사 are와 동사원형 reach 사이에 있으므로, reach를 준동사로 만들 수 있는 보기를 선택해야 한다. 따라서 '막 ~하려고 하는'이라는 의미의 (C) about to가 정답이다. (B) close to(~에 가까운, ~에 다다른)의 to는 전치사로, 뒤에 동명사가 와야 한다. (A) nearly는 부사, (D) within은 전치사로 are와 reach 사이에 들어갈 수 없다.

번역 직원이 주당 최대 근로시간 허용치에 도달하려고 하면, 전자 시간 기록 시스템이 감독관에게 통보한다.

어휘 notify 통보하다 supervisor 감독관 limit 제한, (범위 내의) 최대 허용치

130 명사 어휘 고난도

해설 냉장 트럭(refrigerated trucks) 덕분에 배송 식품이 위험한 문제를 겪지 않는다는 내용이므로, 빈칸에는 온도(temperature)와 관련된 위험 요소를 나타내는 단어가 들어가야 한다. 따라서 '변동, 동요'라는 의미로 전치사 in과 자주 쓰이는 (A) fluctuations가 정답이다.

번역 프리기고의 냉장 트럭은 식품이 배송 중에 위험한 온도 변화에 노출되지 않도록 한다.

어휘 refrigerated 냉장한 undergo (문제 등을) 겪다 boundary 경계 sensation 감각 standard 기준

PART 6

131-134 이메일

발신: ⟨accounts@final-tally.com⟩
수신: 토냐 벨
제목: 무료 체험판 종료
날짜: 2월 7일

벨 씨께,

파이널 탤리 무료 체험판이 2월 10일에 종료될 **131예정입니다.** 이는 클라우드 기반의 종합 회계 솔루션을 사용할 시간이 사흘밖에 남지 않았다는 의미입니다. 파이널 탤리가 귀하의 소규모 업체에서 그날그날의 재정을 관리하는 일뿐만 아니라 **132전반적인** 재정 상황을 파악하는 데에도 도움이 되었기를 바랍니다. 계속 파이널 탤리를 사용하시려면 계정에 로그인해 유료 가입자가 되십시오.

이용권을 구매하지 않으면, 파이널 탤리에 저장 중인 자료를 회수할 수 있는 시간은 60일입니다. **133이후에는** 계정과 관련된 모든 데이터가 삭제됩니다. 또한 가입하지 않기로 결정하게 된 특별한 이유가 있다면 알려주십시오. **134저희는 언제나 개선 방안을 찾고 있습니다.**

감사합니다.

파이널 탤리 팀

어휘 trial 체험판, 시험 사용 tally (총계 등의) 기록 comprehensive 종합적인, 포괄적인 organize 관리하다, 정리하다 finance 재정, 재무 paid subscriber 유료 가입자 subscription 가입, 이용(권) retrieve 회수하다 associated 관련된

131 동사 어형 _ 태 _ 시제

해설 주어인 Your free trial(무료 체험판)은 종료일이 정해지는 대상이므로, 보기에서 수동태 동사 중 하나를 선택해야 한다. 이메일 작성일(Date: February 7)을 기준으로 체험판 종료일(on February 10)은 미래이므로, '~할 예정이다'라는 의미의 (A) is scheduled가 정답이 된다.

132 형용사 어휘

해설 상관접속사 'not just A but also B(A뿐만 아니라 B도)'가 organize your small business's day-to-day finances와 understand its ------ financial situation을 연결하고 있다. 따라서 day-to-day(그날 그날의)처럼 기간이나 범위를 묘사하는 형용사가 빈칸에 들어가야 자연스러우므로, '전반적인'이라는 의미의 (C) overall이 정답이다.

어휘 preliminary 예비의 assorted 갖가지의 foremost 가장 중요한

133 접속부사

해설 빈칸 앞 문장에서 저장 중인 자료를 회수할 수 있는 시간은 60일(you will have 60 days to retrieve any materials you are storing)이라고 했는데, 뒤에서는 계정과 관련된 모든 데이터가 삭제된다(all data associated with your account will be deleted)며 주어진 기간 이후에 발생할 법한 일을 안내했다. 따라서 전후 상황을 연결하는 접속부사가 빈칸에 들어가야 자연스러우므로, '이후, 그 뒤에'라는 의미의 (D) Afterward가 정답이다.

134 문맥에 맞는 문장 고르기 `고난도`

번역 (A) 저희는 고객님의 답장을 간절히 기다리고 있습니다.
(B) 저희는 언제나 개선 방안을 찾고 있습니다.
(C) 적합할 만한 몇 가지 옵션이 저희에게 있습니다.
(D) 저희는 나머지 팀원들에게도 칭찬을 돌리고 싶습니다.

해설 앞 문장에서 가입하지 않기로 결정하게 된 특별한 이유가 있다면 알려달라(if there is a particular reason you end up deciding not to subscribe, please let us know)고 요청했으므로, 빈칸에는 요청의 이유 또는 목적이 들어가야 문맥상 자연스럽다. 따라서 (B)가 정답이다.

어휘 eagerly 간절히 appropriate 적합한, ~에 맞는

135-138 설명서

지문 채취 설명서

귀하가 장기 비자를 받을 자격이 있는지 확인하려면 엄지손가락과 나머지 손가락이 선명하게 찍힌 지장이 필요합니다. 지문을 ¹³⁵**찍으려면** 검정 인주가 필요

할 겁니다. 손가락 하나를 인주에 대고 굴려 손가락에 인주가 고루 묻도록 합니다. 신원확인 양식에서 그 손가락에 ¹³⁶**해당하는** 칸을 찾으세요. 칸에 손가락 한쪽을 누른 후 일정한 입력을 유지하며 손가락 반대쪽으로 굴리세요. 다른 손가락도 모두 이 과정을 반복하세요. 흐릿하게 찍힌 지문은 해당 칸에 충분한 공간이 ¹³⁷**남아 있는** 경우에만 다시 찍을 수 있습니다. ¹³⁸**그렇지 않으면 새 양식으로 이 과정을 다시 시작하세요.**

어휘 fingerprinting 지문 채취 impression (도장 등을) 찍기, 자국 eligible for ~을 받을 자격이 되는, ~의 대상인 evenly 고르게 background check 신원확인 maintain 유지하다 pressure 압력 procedure 과정 attempt 시도하다 sufficient 충분한

135 동사 어형 _ to부정사

해설 빈칸은 명사구 your own fingerprints를 목적어로 취해 콤마 뒤 절을 수식하는 역할을 하므로, to부정사나 분사가 들어갈 수 있다. 검정 잉크가 필요한 것은 지문을 찍기 위해서라고 볼 수 있으므로, '~하기 위해'라는 의미의 (B) To take가 정답이 된다.

136 동사 어휘

해설 주격 관계대명사 that이 이끄는 절의 동사 자리로, 보기에서 전치사 to와 어울려 쓰이는 자동사를 선택해야 한다. 빈칸의 주어 역할을 하는 that이 the box (on the background check form)를 대신하고 있으므로, 빈칸 이하는 양식에서 지문을 찍는 칸에 대한 설명이 되어야 한다. 따라서 '그 손가락에 해당하는 칸'이라는 의미를 완성하는 (C) corresponds(해당하다, 상응하다)가 정답이다. 참고로, (D) consents도 to와 함께 쓰이는 자동사이지만 '~에 동의하다'라는 뜻이므로 빈칸에는 적합하지 않다.

어휘 devote 헌신하다 designate 지정하다

137 동사 어형 _ 현재분사

해설 빈칸 앞에 완전한 절이 왔으므로, 빈칸에는 전치사구 in the appropriate box와 결합해 명사 space를 수식할 수 있는 준동사가 들어가야 한다. remain은 자동사/연결동사로서 '남아 있다'라는 뜻을 나타내므로, 현재분사인 (B) remaining이 정답이 된다. 참고로, 자동사의 과거분사는 완료의 의미를 내포하는 일부 경우(eg. fallen leaves)를 제외하고는 단독으로 명사를 꾸밀 수 없다.

138 문맥에 맞는 문장 고르기 `고난도`

번역 (A) 그렇게 하면 지문에 심각한 결점이 생길 수 있습니다.
(B) 그 날짜 직전까지 다시 지문이 채취될 필요가 없습니다.
(C) 마지막으로 참가자가 손을 깨끗이 닦을 수 있도록 합니다.
(D) 그렇지 않으면 새 양식으로 이 과정을 다시 시작하세요.

해설 빈칸 앞 문장에서 지문이 흐릿하게 찍힌 경우 해당 칸에 충분한 공간이 있으면 다시 찍을 수 있다(You may attempt to retake unclear impressions only if there is sufficient space)고 했으므로, 빈칸에도 이와 관련된 내용이 들어가야 자연스럽다. 따라서 공간이 없는 반대(Otherwise)의 경우에 취해야 할 조치를 안내한 (D)가 정답이다.

어휘 imperfection 결함 thoroughly 깨끗하게 wipe off 닦다

139-142 회람

발신: 제리 무어

수신: 전 직원

주제: 회계부 구역

안녕하세요 여러분,

최근 건물 개조 후 많은 직원들이 출입구에서 휴게실로 가거나 그 반대로 갈 때 회계사들이 있는 구역을 통과하고 있습니다. 이렇게 가는 방법이 139 **가장 편리하다**는 건 알지만, 이 관행이 계속되도록 놔둘 수는 없습니다. 회계사들이 이로 인해 주의가 굉장히 산만해진다고 보고했습니다. 140 **더 중요한 것은 그들이 자유롭게 기밀자료를 다룰 수 있어야 한다는 겁니다.** 제 조언에 따라 회계사들은 문을 잠가보기도 하고 지나가는 직원들에게 직접 그러지 말라고 요구하기도 했지만 141 **어떤** 노력을 통하지 141 **않았습니다.** 따라서 건물 관리팀이 회계 구역과 휴게실 사이의 문을 무거운 가구로 막아둘 수 있게 허가했습니다. 이 회람은 내일부터는 그 문을 절대 사용할 수 없다는 것을 여러분 모두에게 알리기 위한 것입니다. 이에 맞춰 142 **경로**를 조정하십시오.

제리 무어

인사부장

어휘 accounting 회계 following ~후에 pass through ~를 관통하다 practice 관행 distracting 주의를 산만하게 만드는 maintenance 관리, 정비 permission 허가 intend to ~하고자 하다 notify 통지하다, 알리다 absolutely 절대 unusable 사용할 수 없는 adjust 조정하다 accordingly 이에 맞춰

139 형용사 자리 _ 주격 보어

해설 빈칸은 주어 this way를 보충 설명하는 주격 보어 자리로, the의 한정 수식을 받는 명사나 형용사의 최상급이 들어갈 수 있다. 문맥상 편리한 정도를 묘사하는 형용사가 들어가야 자연스러우므로, (C) most convenient 가 정답이다. '이렇게 가는 방법은 편리함이다'라는 동격 관계를 이루지 않으므로 (B) convenience는 정답이 될 수 없다.

140 문맥에 맞는 문장 고르기

번역 (A) 만약 비슷한 문제를 겪고 있다면, 우리는 함께 경영진에게 이야기할 수 있습니다.

(B) 휴게실은 어쨌든 그런 대화를 나누기에 더 좋은 장소가 될 것입니다.

(C) 먼저 노크해 접근하고 있다고 미리 알리십시오.

(D) 더 중요한 것은 그들이 자유롭게 기밀자료를 다룰 수 있어야 한다는 겁니다.

해설 빈칸 앞 문장에서 회계사들이 자신들의 근무 구역을 통해 휴게실에 출입하는 사람들 때문에 주의가 산만해진다며 보고했다(The accountants have reported that they find it very distracting)고 했고, 뒤에서는 회계사들이 취한 조치(On my advice, they have tried locking the door and directly asking the employees who do this to stop)를 나열했다. 따라서 회계사들이 이러한 조치를 취한 이유 또는 명분이 빈칸에 들어가야 자연스러우므로, (D)가 정답이다.

어휘 confidential 기밀의

141 한정사 어휘 고난도

해설 앞절에서 문제를 해결하기 위해 시도한 두 가지 노력(they have tried

locking the door and directly asking the employees who do this to stop)을 나열했는데 이 뒤에 but이 왔으므로, 해당 절은 이 두 가지 노력이 성공하지 못했다는 내용이 되어야 자연스럽다. 따라서 '어느 ~도 아닌'이라는 의미의 (D) neither가 정답이다.

142 명사 어휘

해설 빈칸에는 앞서 언급된 내용에 따라(accordingly) 조정해야(adjust) 하는 대상이 들어가야 한다. 앞 문장에서 내일부터 회계부 구역과 휴게실을 통하는 문을 절대 사용할 수 없다(from tomorrow, the door will be absolutely unusable)고 했으므로, 이 문을 통과하는 이동 경로가 조정 대상임을 알 수 있다. 따라서 '경로, 길'이라는 의미의 (A) routes가 정답이다.

어휘 priority 우선순위 estimate 견적(서) greeting 인사(말)

143-146 기사

〈사건 수사〉 르위츠 에피소드 방송 예정

르위츠 (10월 2일)— 텔레비전 드라마 〈사건 수사〉 중 143 **주로** 르위츠에서 촬영된 에피소드가 오늘 밤 9시 NBO 채널에서 방송된다.

드라마의 주연인 패리다 아바우드와 헨리 브라이언트가 전국을 돌아다니며 범죄를 해결하는 형사로 출연한다. 오늘 밤 에피소드에서 그들은 실종 사건을 조사하기 위해 144 **가상의** 도시인 마른데일에 찾아간다.

법원, 켈리 공원, 버틀러 잡화점 등 르위츠 시내 여러 곳이 촬영지로 선정되어 스태프가 상상한 장소를 구현했다. 145 **이 장면들은 8월에 일주일 동안 촬영되었다.** 하지만 여느 때처럼 에피소드의 시작과 끝은 드로머리 시에 있는 세트장에서 촬영되었다.

시 관계자인 알버트 청은 이 방송이 다른 제작사들의 146 **관심**을 끌었으면 한다고 말했다. "더 많은 영화 및 텔레비전 프로젝트를 환영합니다."

어휘 shoot 촬영하다 detective 형사 investigate 조사하다 disappearance 실종 location 촬영지 embody 구현하다 official 관계자, 공무원 attract ~를 끌다, 유치하다

143 부사 어휘 고난도

해설 was shot in Lewitts를 적절히 수식하는 부사를 선택해야 한다. 세 번째 단락에서 해당 에피소드의 시작과 끝은 드로머리 시에 있는 세트장에서 촬영되었다(the beginning and end of the episode were shot on sets in Dromery City)고 했으므로, 이를 제외한 스토리의 주요 부분이 르위츠 시에서 촬영되었음을 알 수 있다. 따라서 '주로'라는 의미의 (A) primarily가 정답이다.

어휘 highly 매우 overly 지나치게 exclusively 독점으로

144 형용사 어휘

해설 town (of Marndale)을 적절히 수식하는 형용사를 선택해야 한다. 주인공인 형사들(they=detectives)이 방문하는 마른데일은 드라마 에피소드 속의 도시이다. 따라서 '가상의, 허구의'라는 의미의 (B) fictional이 정답이다. (C) adjacent는 '인접한, 인근의'라는 뜻으로, 에피소드 내에서 어디와 가까운 도시인지 알 수 없으므로 빈칸에는 부적절하다.

어휘 authentic 진짜인 diverse 다양한

145 문맥에 맞는 문장 고르기

번역 (A) 다른 장소는 모두 르위츠 정부의 허가가 필요하다.
(B) 주민들은 이들 지역의 교통 체증을 예상해야 한다.
(C) 이 장면들은 8월에 일주일 동안 촬영되었다.
(D) 지금까지 이 에피소드는 평론가와 시청자의 호평을 받았다.

해설 빈칸 앞 문장에서 르위츠 시내 여러 곳이 촬영지로 선정되었다고(Several locations around Lewitts ~ were chosen)고 했지만, 뒤에서는 여느 때처럼 에피소드의 시작과 끝은 드로머리 시에 있는 세트장에서 촬영되었다고(As usual ~ the beginning and end of the episode were shot on sets in Dromery City)고 했다. 따라서 빈칸에는 앞서 언급된 르위츠 시내에서의 촬영과 관련된 내용이 들어가야 자연스러우므로, 촬영 시기 및 기간을 언급한 (C)가 정답이다.

어휘 permit 허가 traffic disruption 교통 체증 well-received 호평 받는 critic 비평가 viewer 시청자

146 명사 자리 _ 동사의 목적어   `고난도`

해설 동사 attracts의 목적어 역할을 하는 명사 자리로, 전치사구 of other productions의 수식을 받는다. 따라서 보기에서 (A) attendant(안내원, 종업원)와 (C) attention(관심, 이목) 중 하나를 선택해야 하는데, '제작사의 관심을 끌다'라는 내용이 되어야 자연스러우므로, (C) attention이 정답이다. 참고로, attention은 attract, catch, draw 등의 동사와 자주 쓰인다.

어휘 attentive 주의 깊은 attend 참석하다 attending 주치의로 근무하는

PART 7

147-148 웹페이지

www.leampter.com/order
리앰프터 사

주문 요약

주문을 완료하기 전에 검토하세요.

148(A)
배송지: 보모스 대학교
관리부
데릭 맥과이어 귀하
유니버시티 가 1660번지
보모스, 미시시피 38637

148(C)
결제방법: 0455로 끝나는 신용카드
청구주소: 배송주소와 동일
148(B)
선호하는 배송방식: 표준 육로 배송

제품	수량	단가	총액
중간 강도 쓰레기봉지 (200개 들이 상자)	5	25달러	125달러
13와트 형광등 전구 (12개 들이 상자)	1	4.2달러	4.2달러

147 12볼트 무선 드릴	1	129달러	129달러
내화학 고무장갑 (10개 들이 상자)	2	10.4달러	20.8달러
		배송비	24.99달러
		총액	303.99달러

판촉 코드: _____

주문하기

어휘 maintenance 관리, 정비 c/o ~ 귀하 preference 선호 fluorescent 형광의 cordless 코드가 없는, 무선의 chemical-resistant 화학약품에 잘 견디는

147 추론 / 암시

번역 리앰프터 사는 어떤 업체이겠는가?
(A) 가구점
(B) 철물 소매업체
(C) 사무용품 유통업체
(D) 자동차 부품 제조업체

해설 제품(Product) 목록에 12볼트 무선 드릴(12-volt cordless drill)이 포함된 것으로 보아, 리앰프터 사가 철물 소매업체임을 추론할 수 있다. 따라서 (B)가 정답이다.

148 사실 관계 확인

번역 맥과이어 씨가 제공하지 않은 정보는?
(A) 주문품 배송 장소
(B) 물품 배송 방법
(C) 결제 시 사용할 것
(D) 할인 대상인 이유

해설 맥과이어 씨는 배송지(Ship to:), 선호하는 배송방식(Shipping preference:), 결제방법(Payment method:) 항목을 모두 작성했지만 할인 코드를 입력하는 부분은 빈칸으로 두었다. 따라서 확인되지 않는 (D)가 정답이다.

어휘 eligible for ~의 대상인

▶▶ **Paraphrasing** 지문의 Ship to → 보기 (A)의 Where the order should be sent
지문의 Shipping preference → 보기 (B)의 How the goods should be shipped
지문의 Payment method → 보기 (C)의 What he will use to make a payment

149-150 온라인 채팅

주디 클라인 (오후 2시 14분)
에릭, 마침 온라인 상태라니 잘 됐네요. 150오늘 아침에 당신의 출장비 환급 요청을 처리하다가 문제가 생겼어요.

에릭 홀랜드 (오후 2시 15분)
안녕하세요, 주디. 무슨 문제였나요?

174

주디 클라인 (오후 2시 16분)

미안하지만, 잠깐만 기다려주세요. [149]양식을 바로 여기에 둔 줄 알았는데, 그 이후로 몇 가지 다른 서류들을 작업해서요.

에릭 홀랜드 (오후 2시 16분)

알았어요.

주디 클라인 (오후 2시 19분)

[149]아, 여기 있네요. [150]'기타' 항목에 5월 25일 24.38달러의 금액을 기재했잖아요. 근데 당신이 설명란에 써 놓은 걸 읽을 수가 없네요. 거기에 뭐라고 썼는지 기억하세요? "h"로 시작하는 것 같아요.

에릭 홀랜드 (오후 2시 20분)

흠. 제가 당신 책상으로 갈게요.

주디 클라인 (오후 2시 21분)

오, 그럼 좋죠. 곧 봐요.

어휘 process 처리하다 reimbursement 환급
miscellaneous 기타 description 설명

149 추론 / 암시

번역 클라인 씨에 관해 암시된 것은?

(A) 종종 동료들의 질문 때문에 방해를 받는다.
(B) 가끔 소프트웨어 프로그램을 여는 데 어려움을 겪는다.
(C) 채팅하기 전에 프린터에서 몇 페이지를 가져왔다.
(D) 채팅 중에 서류를 찾고 있다.

해설 클라인 씨는 오후 2시 16분 메시지에서 자신이 홀랜드 씨의 양식을 바로 앞에 둔 줄 알았지만 그렇지 않다(I thought I had the form right here, but ~)는 것을 드러냈다. 이후 오후 2시 19분 메시지에서 '여기 있다(here we are)'고 했으므로, 그녀가 채팅 중에 서류를 찾고 있었음을 추론할 수 있다. 따라서 (D)가 정답이다.

어휘 retrieve 가져오다

▶▶ Paraphrasing 지문의 the form
→ 정답의 some paperwork

150 의도 파악

번역 오후 2시 20분에 홀랜드 씨가 "제가 당신 책상으로 갈게요"라고 쓴 의도는?

(A) 요청이 빨리 처리돼야 한다.
(B) 실물 양식을 제출하고 싶다.
(C) 자금을 어디에 썼는지 기억하지 못한다.
(D) 절차를 시연하겠다고 제안하고 있다.

해설 클라인 씨가 오후 2시 14분 메시지에서 홀랜드 씨의 출장비 환급 요청을 처리하다가 문제가 생겼다(I ran into a problem processing your travel reimbursement request)고 했고, 오후 2시 19분 메시지에서 홀랜드 씨가 기타 항목에 기재한 비용의 설명란을 읽을 수 없다며 쓴 내용이 기억이 나는지(Do you remember what you wrote there?) 물었다. 이에 대해 홀랜드 씨가 클라인 씨의 책상으로 가서 자신이 직접 보겠다고 한 말이므로, 그가 해당 비용을 어디에 썼는지 기억하지 못한다고 추론할 수 있다. 따라서 (C)가 정답이다.

어휘 physical 실물의 recall 기억하다 demonstrate 시연하다
procedure 절차

151-152 기사

뉴스 소식을 받는 새로운 방법

(10월 15일)-〈볼드윈 타임즈〉는 70년 넘게 볼드윈 시민들이 선호하는 일일 뉴스 소식통이었습니다. 하지만 요즘 사람들은 사건 사고를 하루에 한 번이 아니라 일어나는 즉시 알고 싶어합니다. [151]이러한 이유로 오늘 아침 당사는 웹사이트보다 훨씬 더 편리한 대안이 될 수 있는 〈볼드윈 타임즈〉 앱을 출시했습니다.

[152]이 앱으로, 독자 여러분은 인쇄판과 온라인판에서처럼 심도 있는 현지 보도는 물론 지역 및 전국 뉴스에 대한 통찰력 있는 분석을 얻을 수 있습니다. 그러나 앱을 통해서는 맞춤 설정이 가능한 푸시알림 기능을 사용해 관심 있는 분야의 뉴스 속보가 있다는 알림도 받을 수 있습니다. 앱 콘텐츠는 첫 달 무료이며, 이후에는 매달 4.99달러만 지불하면 됩니다. 지금 주요 앱 스토어를 방문해 다운로드하십시오.

어휘 preferred 선호하는 release 출시하다 convenient
편리한 alternative 대안 in-depth 심도 있는 coverage
보도 insightful 통찰력 있는 analysis (analyses) 분석
customizable 맞춤으로 할 수 있는 notification 통보 alert 알림
breaking news 속보

151 주제 / 목적

번역 기사의 목적은?

(A) 디지털 제품 광고
(B) 지역 동향에 대한 정보 제공
(C) 회사 이력 요약
(D) 새 칼럼 출범 알리기

해설 첫 번째 단락에서 뉴스 웹사이트보다 훨씬 더 편리한 대안이 될 수 있는 〈볼드윈 타임즈〉 앱을 출시했다(we released the Boldwin Times app ~ as an even more convenient alternative to our Web site)고 한 후, 앱과 관련된 설명을 하며 다운로드하라고 권하고 있다. 따라서 앱 광고가 목적임을 알 수 있으므로, (A)가 정답이다.

▶▶ Paraphrasing 지문의 the Boldwin Times app
→ 정답의 a digital product

152 사실 관계 확인   고난도

번역 〈볼드윈 타임즈〉에 관해 알 수 있는 것은?

(A) 한때 지역에서 가장 인기 있는 간행물이었다.
(B) 경제 뉴스 보도로 유명하다.
(C) 콘텐츠를 접할 수 있는 방법이 두 가지 이상이다.
(D) 많은 독자들이 볼드윈 외곽에 살고 있다.

해설 두 번째 단락에서 새로 출시된 앱으로 인쇄판과 온라인판에서처럼 심도 있는 현지 보도는 물론 지역 및 전국 뉴스에 대한 통찰력 있는 분석을 얻을 수 있다(With our app, readers can get the same ~ analyses of regional and national news that they have come to expect from our print and online editions)고 했으므로, 〈볼드윈 타임즈〉의 콘텐츠를 접할 수 있는 방법이 세 가지임을 알 수 있다. 따라서 (C)가 정답이다.

어휘 publication 간행(물)

153-155 광고

헤이즐리 시네마에서 저녁과 영화 "모두" 즐기세요!

헤이즐리 시네마에 식사하면서 영화를 볼 수 있는 펀페어 홀이 영업을 개시합니다! 153(B)/155모든 상영관 입장권 소지자들은 팝콘뿐만 아니라 영화관 전통과는 약간 거리가 있는 햄버거, 피자 같은 음식도 즐길 수 있습니다. 그리고 이 모든 것은 버튼만 누르면 이용할 수 있습니다—영화가 상영되는 도중에도 말이죠! 153(D)종업원이 주문을 받고 좌석으로 음식을 가져다 드리며, 이 좌석은 일반 좌석보다 넓고, 집어넣을 수 있는 간이 탁자를 갖췄습니다. 펀페어 홀에서 식사하면서 영화를 감상하는 독특한 경험은, 〈빌레건트 헤럴드〉가 이미 "빌레건트 영화 애호가를 위한 최고의 선택"이라고 칭했던 영화관에 추가된 흥미진진한 요소입니다.

3월 헤이즐리 시네마 특별 행사:

감독 초대 상영 〈서더랜드〉: 153(A)3월 19일 펀페어 홀에 오셔서, 스토리가 탄탄한 이 새 드라마 영화가 전국에 개봉되기 전에 먼저 보세요. 상영 후 타네샤 롭슨 감독이 영화에 대해 토론하고 관객의 질문을 받을 예정입니다.

키즈 화요일: 154영화 매주 화요일 아침, 부모는 6세 미만의 자녀를 데려와 아동용 영화를 볼 수 있습니다. 성인은 1인당 5달러, 어린이는 1인당 2달러만 내면 됩니다.

어휘 screening 상영 extra-wide (기존/일반 제품보다는) 더 넓은 equipped with ~을 갖춘 retractable 집어넣을 수 있는 unique 독특한 addition 추가(된 것) enthusiast 애호가 thoughtful 잘 짜여진, 스토리가 탄탄한 wide release 전국 개봉[상영]

---

153 사실 관계 확인   [고난도]

번역 펀페어 홀에 관해 언급되지 않은 것은?
(A) 곧 있을 시사회 상영 장소이다.
(B) 고객들은 다양한 음식을 주문할 수 있다.
(C) 신문에 평이 실렸다.
(D) 좌석이 넓다.

해설 특별 행사에 대한 설명 중 영화가 전국에서 개봉하기 전에 펀페어 홀에서 먼저 보라고(Come to Funfare Hall on March 19 to see the ~ new drama before its wide release)고 한 부분에서 (A)를, 첫 번째 단락 중 상영관 입장권 소지자들은 팝콘뿐만 아니라 다른 음식도 즐길 수 있다(Ticketholders ~ can enjoy not just popcorn but also less traditional movie fare)고 한 부분에서 (B)를, 좌석이 일반 좌석보다 넓다(your seat, which is extra-wide)고 한 부분에서 (D)를 확인할 수 있다. 따라서 언급되지 않은 (C)가 정답이다. 참고로, 〈빌레건트 헤럴드〉가 "빌레건트 영화 애호가를 위한 최고의 선택"이라고 칭했던 것은 영화관(the cinema that the *Billegant Herald* has already called "the top choice for film enthusiasts in Billegant")이며, 펀페어 홀은 이제 막 영업을 시작하는 단계이므로, (C)는 사실이 아니다.

▶▶ Paraphrasing 지문의 to see the ~ new drama before its wide release
→ 보기 (A)의 preview screening
지문의 enjoy not just popcorn but also less traditional movie fare
→ 보기 (B)의 order a variety of foods
지문의 extra-wide
→ 보기 (D)의 spacious

---

154 사실 관계 확인

번역 3월 주간 행사에 관해 알 수 있는 것은?
(A) 초등학생 단체를 대상으로 한다.
(B) 일부 관객은 티켓 가격이 더 저렴하다.
(C) 일정에는 대화형 토론이 포함되어 있다.
(D) 오래된 영화를 볼 수 있는 기회를 제공한다.

해설 마지막 단락에서 3월 매주 화요일 아침 부모는 6세 미만의 자녀를 데려와 아동용 영화를 볼 수 있으며 성인은 1인당 5달러, 어린이는 1인당 2달러만 내면 된다(Every Tuesday morning in March, parents can bring kids under six years old to screenings ~ for just $5 per adult and $2 per child)고 했다. 따라서 어린이들의 티켓 가격이 더 저렴한 것을 알 수 있으므로, (B)가 정답이다.

▶▶ Paraphrasing 지문의 Every Tuesday → 질문의 weekly
지문의 for just $5 per adult and $2 per child → 정답의 ticket prices are lower for some viewers

---

155 문장 삽입

번역 [1], [2], [3], [4]로 표시된 곳 중에서 다음 문장이 가장 적합한 곳은?
"그리고 이 모든 것은 버튼만 누르면 이용할 수 있습니다—영화가 상영되는 도중에도 말이죠!"
(A) [1]
(B) [2]
(C) [3]
(D) [4]

해설 주어진 문장 앞에서 먼저 '버튼만 누르면 이용할 수 있는 이 모든 것(all of this)'이 가리키는 대상이 언급되어야 한다. [1] 앞에서 상영관 입장권 소지자들은 팝콘뿐만 아니라 햄버거, 피자 같은 음식도 즐길 수 있다(Ticketholders to all screenings in the hall can enjoy not just popcorn but also less traditional movie fare)며 이용 가능한 대상을 명시했으므로, (A)가 정답이다.

156-158 고객 후기

www.tradespeoplereview.com

홈 〉〉 도시 〉〉 오마하 〉 배관공 〉〉 풀턴 배관

후기 작성자: 하퍼 퀸테로   게시: 3월 22일

친구가 채드 풀턴 팀에 욕실 개조 작업을 맡긴 적이 있었고, 저에게 그 업체를 추천했어요. 156전 주방 수도꼭지가 꽉 잠겨 있는데도 물이 뚝뚝 떨어지는 걸 발견하고, 문제를 해결하기 위해 풀턴 배관 측에 연락했어요. 제가 통화한 직원이 전화로 견적을 제공했는데 적당한 가격이었어요. 157/158하지만 제가 강조하고 싶은 건 직원들이 얼마나 빨리 도착했는지예요. 전화를 한 지 불과 20분 만에 도착했답니다! 158이게 확실히 서비스에서 가장 좋은 점이에요. 물론 저 같은 경우 수해를 입을 만한 문제는 아니었기 때문에 그럴 필요까진 없었지만 말이에요. 하지만 긴급한 상황에 처한 사람이라면 이게 얼마나 고마운지 알 거예요. 어쨌든 풀턴 씨 및 함께 동행한 직원은 신속하고 능숙하게 작업했어요. 전 풀턴 배관을 적극 추천합니다.

어휘 renovation 개조, 수리 faucet 수도꼭지 resolve 해결하다 representative 직원 estimate 견적 affordable

(가격이) 적당한 emphasize 강조하다 definitely 분명히,
확실히 emergency 응급 appreciate 고마워하다, 환영하다
accompany 동행하다 professionally 능숙하게 certainly
확실히, 정말로

156 세부 사항

번역 퀸테로 씨가 풀턴 배관을 고용한 이유는?
(A) 집 수압을 높이려고
(B) 결함이 있는 수도꼭지를 수리하려고
(C) 욕실을 수리하려고
(D) 주방기기를 연결하려고

해설 초반부에서 퀸테로 씨가 주방 수도꼭지에서 물이 떨어지는 걸 발견하고
문제를 해결하기 위해 풀턴 배관 측에 연락했다(When I discovered
that water was dripping from my kitchen faucet ~ I contacted
Fulton Plumbing to resolve the issue)고 했으므로, (B)가 정답이다.

어휘 improve 높이다, 개선하다 water pressure 수압 faulty 결함이
있는 tap 수도꼭지 hook up 연결시키다 appliance 기기, 가전제품

▶▶ Paraphrasing 지문의 water was dripping from my
kitchen faucet
→ 정답의 a faulty tap
지문의 resolve the issue
→ 정답의 have ~ repaired

157 세부 사항

번역 퀸테로 씨는 풀턴 배관의 어떤 측면을 가장 자세히 설명했는가?
(A) 다양한 서비스 옵션
(B) 직원들의 태도
(C) 작업비
(D) 대응 시간

해설 중반부에서 퀸테로 씨가 강조하고 싶은 건 직원들이 얼마나 빨리 도착
했는지(what I want to emphasize is how quickly the workers
arrived)라고 한 후, 전화를 한 지 불과 20분 만에 도착했다(just twenty
minutes after I made the call)며 구체적인 설명을 덧붙였다. 또한 이
서비스를 칭찬하며 후기를 이어 갔으므로, (D)가 정답이다.

158 추론 / 암시

번역 풀턴 배관이 제공했던 서비스에 관해 암시된 것은?
(A) 회사의 전문 분야다.
(B) 퀸테로 씨는 급하게 필요한 일로 여기지 않았다.
(C) 퀸테로 씨는 이전에 다른 업체에서 동일한 서비스를 받은 적이 있다.
(D) 상담 방문도 포함했다.

해설 중반부에서 퀸테로 씨는 풀턴 배관에 전화를 한 지 불과 20분 만에 직원
이 도착했다고 한 후, 자신과 같은 경우 수해를 입을 만한 문제는 아니었기
때문에 그럴 필요까진 없었다(it wasn't really necessary in my case
because my issue was unlikely to cause water damage)고 덧
붙였다. 따라서 (B)가 정답이다.

어휘 specialty 전문 분야 urgently 급하게 obtain 받다
consultation 상담

159-160 광고

도나: 화초의 대가

사무실에서 식물을 활용해 활기찬 근무 환경을 조성하고 있습니까? 아니면 접
수원 책상 발치에 양치식물 화분만 있고 나머지 장식은 지루한 그림들로만 구성
되어 있나요?

159안타깝게도 대다수 사무실은 식물을 살려두는 것이 쉽지 않다는 걱정에, 생
기 넘치는 갖가지 식물들을 보는 즐거움을 놓치고 있습니다. 하지만 굉장히 튼
튼해 고급 토양도, 물을 자주 줄 필요도 없는 식물 종이 많다는 것을 아시나요?

160원하는 효과를 극대화하려면 어떤 식물을 사서 어떻게 배열할지 도나가 권해
드리겠습니다. 관리가 거의 필요 없는 식물들을 사려 깊게 선택해 사무실을 다시
꾸며 드리면, 직원들의 사기 및 생산성을 개선하는 효과를 보게 되어 놀라실 겁
니다. 지금 (990) 555-0107번으로 도나에게 전화해 시작해 보십시오.

어휘 greenery 초목 create 조성하다 nurturing 성장하는
분위기의, 활기찬 work environment 근무 환경 fern 양치식물
receptionist 안내원, 접수원 be composed of ~로 구성되어 있다
vibrant 생기 넘치는 assortment (갖가지) 모음 resilient 튼튼한
frequent 빈번한 recommend 추천하다, 권하다 arrange
배치하다 maximize 극대화하다 desired 원하는 require 필요로
하다 upkeep 유지 resulting 결과로 보이는 improvement
개선 morale 사기 productivity 생산성

159 세부 사항

번역 광고에 따르면, 많은 사무실이 식물을 많이 두지 않는 편을 선택하는 이유는?
(A) 구매하기에 비싸다.
(B) 강한 냄새를 풍긴다.
(C) 활력이 떨어지는 분위기를 조성한다.
(D) 제대로 돌보기 어려워 보인다.

해설 두 번째 단락에서 대다수 사무실이 식물을 계속 살려 두는 것이 쉽지 않
다는 걱정에 식물들을 보는 즐거움을 놓치고 있다(most offices miss
out on the joys of a ~ assortment of flora because they are
concerned that it will not be easy to keep the plants alive)고
했으므로, (D)가 정답이다.

어휘 properly 제대로

▶▶ Paraphrasing 지문의 miss out on the joys of ~ flora
→ 질문의 not to have many plants
지문의 not ~ easy to keep the plants alive
→ 정답의 difficult to care for properly

160 세부 사항

번역 어떤 서비스가 광고되고 있는가?
(A) 정기적인 현장 방문 식물 관리
(B) 식물을 활용한 장식방법 관련 조언
(C) 식물 재배 방법에 관한 교육
(D) 원하지 않는 식물 처분

해설 세 번째 단락에서 사무실에 어떤 식물을 사서 어떻게 배열할지 도나가 권
해 주겠다(Let Donna recommend which plants to buy and how
to arrange them)고 했으므로, (B)가 정답이다.

어휘 tending 관리 disposal 처분

▶▶ **Paraphrasing** 지문의 recommend ~ how to arrange them(=plants) → 정답의 Advice on decorating with plants

161-164 이메일

발신: 더글러스 맥코이
수신: 이츠미 와키모토
제목: 시범 시행 결과
날짜: 1월 28일
첨부: 보고서

안녕하세요 와키모토 씨,

161방금 새 안전 조치 시범 시행에 대한 보고서를 받았는데, 결과가 명확합니다. 공사 시작 전에 작업위험분석(JHA)을 실시하는 것이 프로젝트를 순조롭게 진행하고 비용을 절감하는 데 긍정적인 효과를 줍니다. 보고서 전문이 첨부되어 있지만, 여기에 요점을 요약하겠습니다.

162로빈슨 타워, 스파크 아파트, 브라이언트 마켓 등 3개 프로젝트에 대해 지난 2년간 이 조치를 시행했으며, 브로슬리 컨설팅에 의뢰해 같은 기간 진행된 다른 프로젝트들과 비교분석해 보았습니다. 163JHA로 부상을 비롯한 여러 문제들을 예방했기 때문에, 로빈슨 타워와 브라이언트 마켓은 비슷한 프로젝트보다 각각 8퍼센트, 11퍼센트 더 빠르게 완공되었고 비용도 6퍼센트, 10퍼센트 적게 들었습니다. 스파크 아파트는 두 범주 모두 평균치에 불과했지만, 계절에 맞지 않은 지역 날씨로 큰 문제에 직면했다는 점을 고려하면 우수하다고 할 수 있습니다. 비교해 보자면, 유사한 문제들에 부딪힌 휴버트 빌딩은 예정보다 15퍼센트나 늦었고 비용도 평균보다 13퍼센트 많이 들었습니다.

JHA 시행에 사용된 초기 시간과 비용은 "이미" 이 데이터에 반영되어 있다는 점 기억하십시오. 제가 보기엔 가능한 한 빨리 모든 프로젝트에 이 과정을 시행해야 합니다. 164준비가 되면 만나서 이 아이디어를 다른 부서들에게 어떻게 제시할지 얘기해 보는 게 어떨까요? 알려주세요.

더그

어휘 trial 시범 시행 measure 조치 conduct 실시하다, 수행하다 hazard 위험 analysis 분석 construction 공사 keep A on track A를 순조롭게 진행하다 reduce 줄이다 attach 첨부하다 summarize 요약하다 implement 시행하다 injury 부상 prevent 예방하다 complete 완성[완공]하다 respectively 각각 merely 단지 ~에 불과한 average 평균(치) considering that ~하다는 것을 고려하면 face 직면하다 unseasonable 계절에 맞지 않은 regional 지역의 run into 부딪히다 factor A into B A를 B에 반영하다 present 제시하다

161 추론 / 암시

번역 시범 시행에서 어떤 조치를 시험했겠는가?
(A) 부상 사고 즉시 조사
(B) 작업자에게 일어날 수 있는 위험 상황 미리 연구
(C) 작업자에게 안전 개선안 제의 독려
(D) 특정 직급에 대해 추가 자격 요구

해설 첫 번째 단락에서 새 안전 조치 시범 시행에 대한 보고서를 받았다고 한 후, 공사 시작 전에 작업위험분석(JHA)을 실시하는 것이 긍정적인 효과가

있다(conducting a job hazard analysis (JHA) before construction begins has a positive effect)고 했다. 따라서 시범 시행에서 잠재적 위험을 미리 연구했을 것으로 추론할 수 있으므로, (B)가 정답이다.

어휘 immediately 즉시 investigate 조사하다 incident 사고 potential 잠재적인, 일어날 수 있는 qualification 자격

▶▶ **Paraphrasing** 지문의 conducting a job hazard analysis (JHA) before construction → 정답의 Studying potential dangers ~ ahead of time

162 사실 관계 확인

번역 시범 시행에 관해 알 수 있는 것은?
(A) 당초 계획보다 오래 지속되었다.
(B) 외부 기업이 관여했다.
(C) 결과가 예상 밖이었다.
(D) 해당 자료가 일반 대중에게 공개될 예정이다.

해설 두 번째 단락에서 브로슬리 컨설팅에 의뢰해 안전 조치가 시범 시행된 프로젝트와 다른 프로젝트들을 비교분석했다(We ~ had Broseley Consulting analyze and compare those projects to our other projects that took place in the same period)고 했으므로, (B)가 정답이다.

어휘 external 외부의 unexpected 예상 밖의 release 공개하다

▶▶ **Paraphrasing** 지문의 had Broseley Consulting analyze and compare → 정답의 involved an external company

163 세부 사항

번역 가장 성공적으로 완료된 프로젝트는?
(A) 로빈슨 타워
(B) 스파크 아파트
(C) 브라이언트 마켓
(D) 휴버트 빌딩

해설 두 번째 단락에서 로빈슨 타워와 브라이언트 마켓은 비슷한 프로젝트보다 각각 8퍼센트, 11퍼센트 더 빠르게 완공되었고 비용도 6퍼센트, 10퍼센트 적게 들었다(Robinson Tower and Bryant Market were completed 8% and 11% faster and cost 6% and 10% less than similar projects, respectively)고 했고, 스파크 아파트는 두 범주 모두 평균치에 불과했다(Sparks Apartments was merely average in both categories)고 했다. 따라서 완공 속도와 비용 절감 면에서 가장 큰 차이를 보였던 브라이언트 마켓을 가장 성공적인 프로젝트라고 볼 수 있으므로, (C)가 정답이다.

164 세부 사항

번역 맥코이 씨가 제안한 일은?
(A) 홍보 전략 수립
(B) 서비스 제공업체 조사
(C) 일부 계산 재확인
(D) 시행 과정 간소화

해설 세 번째 단락에서 맥코이 씨는 와키모토 씨에게 함께 만나 이 아이디어를

다른 부서들에 어떻게 제시할지 논의하자(why don't we meet to talk about how to present this idea to the other departments?)고 제안했다. 따라서 (A)가 정답이다.

어휘 promotional 선전하는, 홍보하는 calculation 계산
streamline 간소화하다

▶▶ Paraphrasing 지문의 **why don't we**
→ 질문의 **suggest**
지문의 **how to present this idea to the other departments**
→ 정답의 **a promotional strategy**

165-167 회람

수신: 젬 패션 이사진
발신: 래리 메이, 공급 및 관리 부장
날짜: 10월 2일
주제: 운영 관련 새 소식

아시다시피, 젬 패션 운영 부서에 속한 저희로선 바쁜 한 해였습니다. ¹⁶⁵새 제조 시설 다섯 곳의 개설을 감독했고, 현재 다섯 곳 모두 온전히 가동 중임을 알려 드리게 되어 기쁩니다. 상품은 지난해에 설정한 목표에 맞추어 빠른 속도로 생산되고 있습니다.

하지만 사업에서 한 가지 특정 분야가 걱정됩니다. ¹⁶⁶고객 서비스 팀과 연락해 보니, 상품이 고객에게 약속한 기한 내에 배달되지 않고 있다는 점이 분명해 졌습니다. 제가 개인적으로 이 건에 대해 조사해 보았더니 현재 이용 중인 배송회사가 우리 회사의 요구를 충족하기에 충분한 차량을 보유하고 있지 않았습니다. 따라서 주문이 밀리고 고객 불만이 많아졌습니다.

¹⁶⁷그러므로 배송회사 대표와 만나 계약 조건에 대해 논의할 것을 제안합니다. 그들에게 이 문제에 대한 책임을 묻고 필요에 따라 서류 수정을 요구할 필요가 있습니다. 이 조치를 취하는 것에 대해 우려나 제안사항이 있으시면 내선번호 553으로 전화하거나 larry.may@jem-fashion.com으로 이메일을 보내주십시오.

래리

어휘 operational 운영(상)의 oversee 감독하다
manufacturing hub 제조 시설 particular 특정한 liaise 연락을 취하다 investigation 조사 insufficient 불충분한 backlog 밀린 일 terms (계약) 조건 hold A accountable A에게 책임을 묻다, 책임지게 하다

165 사실 관계 확인

번역 젬 패션에 관해 언급된 것은?
(A) 지난해에 최고 수익을 달성했다.
(B) 부서를 개편했다.
(C) 신제품 라인을 출시했다.
(D) 최근에 확장했다.

해설 첫 번째 단락에서 새 제조 시설 다섯 곳이 개설되었음(We have overseen the opening of five new manufacturing hubs)을 알 수 있으므로, (D)가 정답이다.

어휘 undergo 겪다, 받다 expansion 확장

▶▶ Paraphrasing 지문의 **the opening of five new manufacturing hubs**
→ 정답의 **an expansion**

166 사실 관계 확인

번역 메이 씨가 언급한 문제는?
(A) 주문 처리가 제때 완료되지 않고 있다.
(B) 제조 시설이 아직 가동되지 않는다.
(C) 상품에 결함이 있는 것으로 판명되었다.
(D) 택배 차량이 자주 고장 나고 있다.

해설 두 번째 단락에서 상품이 고객에게 약속한 기한 내에 배달되지 않고 있다(our goods are not being delivered within the timeframe promised to our customers)는 문제점을 언급했으므로, (A)가 정답이다.

어휘 defective 결함이 있는

▶▶ Paraphrasing 지문의 **our goods are not being delivered within the timeframe promised**
→ 정답의 **Orders are not being completed on time**

167 세부 사항

번역 메이 씨는 젬 패션에서 어떻게 하자고 제안하는가?
(A) 고객 관리자 교체
(B) 불만처리 절차 개정
(C) 계약 재협상
(D) 공개 사과

해설 세 번째 단락에서 메이 씨는 배송회사 대표와 만나 계약 조건에 대해 논의할 것(I propose meeting with the head of the delivery firm to discuss the terms of our contract)을 제안한 후, 필요에 따라 서류 수정을 요구할 필요가 있다(We need to ~ demand changes to the document as necessary)고 주장했다. 따라서 (C)가 정답이다.

어휘 replace 교체하다 account 고객(사) revise 개정하다
procedure 절차 renegotiate 재협상하다 apology 사과

▶▶ Paraphrasing 지문의 **discuss the terms of our contract, demand changes to the document**
→ 정답의 **Renegotiate an agreement**

168-171 편지

굿윈 플레이스 콘도미니엄 협회
브래들리 가 9070번지
아벤텔, 온타리오 N0G 1Y0

8월 18일

홀리오 살라자르
503호

살라자르 씨께,

굿윈 플레이스 콘도미니엄 협회에서 안부 전합니다. 콘도 규약에 추가되는 항목

을 공식적으로 알려드리고자 편지를 씁니다. ¹⁶⁸9월 1일부터 집 주인들은 더 이상 집 일부를 단기 임대(6개월 미만)할 수 없게 됩니다. 이러한 관행이 "Owillo.com 이용"을 통해 이루어지고 있음을 알고 계시리라 봅니다. 하지만 이 금지는 어떤 경로를 통해서든, 심지어 오프라인에서 설정된 단기 임대에도 적용됩니다.

아시다시피, 이번 추가 항목은 몇 달간의 논의 끝에 실시한 협회 회원들의 공식 투표 결과입니다. ¹⁷¹따라서 모든 회원에 대해 법적 구속력이 있고, 단 한 번이라도 규정을 어기면 상당한 과태료가 부과됩니다. 여러 번 위반하면 협회에서 법적 조치를 취할 예정입니다. ¹⁶⁹자세한 내용은 동봉된 규칙 전문(제3조 B항 12호)을 참조하십시오.

¹⁷⁰여러분 중 단기 임대 금지에 반대표를 던진 분들도, 단기 임대를 불허하는 것이 상당히 유익하다는 점을 명심해 두시기 바랍니다. 첫째, 우리 부지에 오고 가는 비거주자들이 끊임없이 유입됨으로써 야기되는 보안 문제가 없어질 것입니다. 더욱이, 화기애애한 이웃 공동체로서 굿윈 플레이스의 정신이 지켜질 것입니다.

이 변경사항을 이해하였음을 확인하는 의미에서, 동봉된 양식에 서명해 8월 31일까지 협회 사무소로 반송하십시오. 서명을 거부한다고 해서 규칙에서 면제되는 것은 아니라는 점에 유의하십시오.

코트니 그레이엄
회장
굿윈 플레이스 콘도미니엄 협회
동봉.

어휘 condominium 아파트 bylaw 규약, 내규 practice 관행 legally binding 법적 구속력이 있는 violate 위반하다 substantial 상당한 fine 과태료 enclose 동봉하다 considerable 상당한 benefit 이득 eliminate 없애다 constant 끊임없는 stream 유입, 흐름 preserve 보존하다 confirm 확인하다, 확인해 주다 refusal 거부 exempt 면제하다

---

168 추론 / 암시

번역 사람들이 Owillo.com을 이용해 무엇을 할 수 있겠는가?
(A) 자신의 부동산에 유료 숙박 유치하기
(B) 이웃과 소통하기
(C) 공유 공간의 문제점 보고하기
(D) 지역의 주택가격 추정치 보기

해설 첫 번째 단락에서 콘도(아파트) 주인들은 더 이상 집 일부를 단기 임대할 수 없게 된다(unit owners will no longer be allowed to let any part of their unit for short-term rental)고 한 후, 이러한 관행이 "Owillo.com 이용"을 통해 이루어지고 있음(You may be familiar with this practice as "using Owillo.com")을 드러냈다. 따라서 Owillo.com을 이용해 사람들이 자신의 콘도를 임대할 수 있었다고 추론할 수 있으므로, (A)가 정답이다.

▶▶ Paraphrasing 지문의 let any part of their unit for ~ rental → 정답의 Arrange paid stays on their property

169 세부 사항

번역 편지에 딸린 것은?
(A) 투표용지
(B) 정비 작업 시간표
(C) 통계 자료 모음
(D) 규정 발췌

해설 두 번째 단락에서 단기 임대 금지 관련 자세한 내용은 동봉된 규칙 전문(제 9조 B항 12호)을 참조하라(see the full text of the rule (Article 9, Section B, Clause 12), which is enclosed)고 했으므로, 해당 규칙의 발췌문이 편지에 첨부되었음을 알 수 있다. 따라서 (D)가 정답이다.

▶▶ Paraphrasing 지문의 is enclosed → 질문의 come with
지문의 the full text of the rule → 정답의 An excerpt from a set of regulations

어휘 statistics 통계 (자료) excerpt 발췌(본)

170 추론 / 암시 고난도

번역 굿윈 플레이스 일부 거주민들에 관해 암시된 것은?
(A) 안전점검을 의뢰했다.
(B) 제안에 반대 의사를 표명했다.
(C) 벌금을 물게 되었다.
(D) 집을 개조하고자 한다.

해설 세 번째 단락에서 거주민들 중 단기 임대 금지에 반대표를 던진 사람들(those among you who voted against the ban)이 있었음을 암시했으므로, (B)가 정답이다.

어휘 opposition 반대 incur (비용을) 물게 되다, 발생시키다 alteration 개조

▶▶ Paraphrasing 지문의 those among you → 질문의 some residents
지문의 voted against the ban → 정답의 expressed opposition

171 문장 삽입 고난도

번역 [1], [2], [3], [4]로 표시된 곳 중 다음 문장이 가장 적합한 곳은?
"여러 번 위반하면 협회에서 법적 조치를 취할 예정입니다."
(A) [1]
(B) [2]
(C) [3]
(D) [4]

해설 주어진 문장에서 여러 번 위반하면 협회에서 법적 조치를 취할 예정이라고 했으므로, 이 앞에서 먼저 위반 행위와 관련된 내용이 언급되어야 한다. [2] 앞에서 단 한 번이라도 단기 임대 금지 규정을 어기면 상당한 과태료가 부과된다(violating the rule even a single time will result in a substantial fine)고 했으므로, 이 뒤에 주어진 문장이 이어져야 자연스럽다. 따라서 (B)가 정답이다.

어휘 provoke 유발하다 legal action 법적 조치

172-175 온라인 채팅

브래더 공공도서관 직원 채팅
클리프턴 샌더스 (오전 10시 19분) 안녕하세요, 아만다, 제프리. ¹⁷²지난주에 북 클럽 참가자들한테 받은 의견 카드를 살펴보고 있는데, 여러분이 알아야 할 문제가 있어요.
아만다 토마스 (오전 10시 20분) 뭔데요, 클리프턴?
클리프턴 샌더스 (오전 10시 22분) 고전서 클럽 참가자의 절반 이상이 "리더가 토론 중재 업무를 잘 못하고 있다"는 글을 썼어요. 그룹 리더인 사브리나가, 참가자 한 명이 이야기를 너무 많이 하는데도 놔둔 것 같아요.
아만다 토마스 (오전 10시 23분) ¹⁷⁵아, 맞아요, 도일이 올해 들어간 그룹이에요. 도서관 북 클럽에 자주 참가하는 사람인데, 리더가 단호하지 않으면 대화를 독점하는 경향이 있어요.
제프리 심 (오전 10시 24분) 오, 도일! ¹⁷³처음으로 클럽 리더가 됐는데 그 사람을 상대해야 되다니, 사브리나도 참 안됐어요.
클리프턴 샌더스 (오전 10시 25분) 평소처럼 사브리나에게 이런 의견이 있었다고 요약해줘야 할까요, 아니면 특별한 대응이 필요할까요?
아만다 토마스 (오전 10시 26분) 뭔가 조치를 취해야 해요. 제가 그녀와 자리를 마련해서 참가자들이 전보다 더 골고루 토론에 기여하게끔 하는 방법을 조언할게요. ¹⁷⁴하지만 지금 당장은 회의에 가야 해요. 다른 건 없나요, 클리프턴?
제프리 심 (오전 10시 27분) ¹⁷⁵전 사브리나와 사이도 꽤 좋고, 전에 도일이 있는 그룹을 이끌어야 했던 경험이 있어요. 어쩌면 제가 그녀와 얘기해야 하겠군요.
아만다 토마스 (오전 10시 28분) 그래요, 제프리. 좋은 생각이에요.
클리프턴 샌더스 (오전 10시 29분) 고마워요, 제프리. 좋아요, 두 분 다 나중에 얘기해요.

어휘 **participant** 참가자 **moderate** 중재하다, (토론) 사회를 보다 **dominate** 독점하다, 지배하다 **assertive** 단호한 **balance** 균형을 맞추다 **contribution** 기여

172 주제 / 목적

번역 메시지 작성자들이 논의하고 있는 것은?
(A) 다가오는 행사 광고
(B) 북 클럽 책 선정
(C) 도서관 프로그램 평가
(D) 자동화 과정의 비효율성

해설 샌더스 씨가 오전 10시 19분 메시지에서 도서관 북 클럽 참가자들한테 받은 의견 카드를 살펴보다가 문제를 발견했다(I'm going through the comment cards that we got from book club participants ~ and there's an issue I think you should know about)며 토마스 씨 및 심 씨에게 말했고, 이후 참가자들이 준 의견을 토대로 논의를 이어가고 있다. 따라서 (C)가 정답이다.

어휘 **evaluation** 평가 **inefficiency** 비효율성

▶▶ **Paraphrasing** 지문의 **the comment cards**
→ 정답의 **Evaluations**

173 사실 관계 확인 고난도

번역 사브리나에 관해 알 수 있는 것은?
(A) 역할을 처음 맡았다.
(B) 작가 지망생이다.
(C) 무보수 자원봉사자다.
(D) 자유롭게 임무를 떠맡을 수 있다.

해설 심 씨가 오전 10시 24분 메시지에서 사브리나가 처음으로 북 클럽 리더가 됐는데 토론에서 대화를 독점하는 사람을 상대하게 되다니 안됐다(It's too bad that Sabrina has to deal with him her first time leading a club)고 했으므로, (A)가 정답이다.

어휘 **aspiring** 지망하는 **take on an assignment** 임무를 떠맡다

▶▶ **Paraphrasing** 지문의 **her first time leading a club**
→ 정답의 **new to a role**

174 의도 파악

번역 오전 10시 26분에 토마스 씨가 "다른 건 없나요, 클리프턴?"이라고 쓸 때 의미하는 것은?
(A) 문제를 해결할 수 있는 다른 대안이 있었으면 한다.
(B) 결정을 내릴 충분한 정보가 없다.
(C) 일을 깜박해서 걱정하고 있다.
(D) 대화를 끝내도 괜찮은지 알고 싶다.

해설 토마스 씨가 오전 10시 26분 메시지에서 사브리나를 도와주고 싶지만 지금 당장은 회의에 가야 한다(But I need to run to a meeting right now)며 대화를 전환한 후 덧붙인 말이므로, 자신이 대화를 끝내도 괜찮은지 샌더스 씨에게 양해를 구하는 의도라고 볼 수 있다. 따라서 (D)가 정답이다.

어휘 **alternative** 대체하는 **resolve** 해결하다 **acceptable** 괜찮은

175 세부 사항

번역 심 씨는 자신에게 어떤 경험이 있다고 말하는가?
(A) 까다로운 이용객 상대하기
(B) 기술에 대해 교육하기
(C) 건물 견학 인솔하기
(D) 특정 유형의 글 편집하기

해설 토마스 씨가 오전 10시 23분 메시지에서 사브리나가 담당하는 그룹에 대화를 독점하여 사회자를 힘들게 하는 도일이 있다고 했는데, 심 씨가 오전 10시 27분 메시지에서 도일이 있는 그룹을 이끌어야 했던 경험이 있다(I've had to lead a group with Doyle in it before)며 사브리나를 도와주겠다고 했다. 따라서 (A)가 정답이다.

▶▶ **Paraphrasing** 지문의 **lead a group with Doyle**
→ 정답의 **Handling a difficult patron**

176-180 정보문 + 이메일

몬타라 캠핑장
캠핑시설 정보

몬타라 캠핑장은 몬타라 국립공원을 찾는 방문객을 위한 훌륭한 숙박 옵션입니다. **180경비대원들이 언제든 하이킹 코스, 낚시터, 그리고 재미있는 활동을 추천해 드리며, 심지어 본인들의 상징인 납작모자에 대한 질문에도 대답해 드립니다!** 캠핑장 화장실과 샤워시설은 모든 야영객이 **176공유하며,** 아래와 같은 캠핑장이 대여 가능합니다 (모든 곳에 화덕 포함):

- 개척자 (1박 15달러): 텐트 1동 및 차량 1대 공간
- 모험가 (1박 20달러): 텐트 1동 및 차량 1대 공간 (피크닉 테이블 포함)
- 탐험가 (1박 18달러): 캠핑카 1대 공간
- **179선도자 (1박 26달러): 캠핑카 1대 공간 (수도 및 전기 포함)**

177공원이 시즌 처음으로 개장하는 3월 초와 공휴일에는 수요가 많아 사전예약을 강력히 권고하니 유의하시기 바랍니다.

몬타라 캠핑장에 예약하려면 www.campingmontara.gov를 방문하세요.

어휘 lodging 숙박 ranger 경비대원 activity 활동 iconic 상징적인 facility 시설 motor home 캠핑카 demand 수요 advance booking 사전 예약

수신: ⟨info@campingmontara.gov⟩
발신: ⟨s.kohl@kellipsco.com⟩
날짜: 6월 29일
제목: 몬타라 캠핑장

담당자께:

저는 최근 몬타라 캠핑장에서 일주일 동안 머물렀습니다. 장소 자체는 훌륭했지만, 캠핑카용 편의시설에 실망했습니다. **179체류 이틀째부터 그 주 주말까지 캠핑장에 전기가 들어오지 않았습니다. 178따라서 전 수도 및 전기가 없는 캠핑카 공간 요금만 내면 된다고 생각하며, 차액을 돌려주셨으면 합니다. 180당직인 공원 경비대원 쳇 라인하트 씨는 매우 친절했고, 제게 도움 줄 사람과 연락할 수 있도록 이 이메일 주소를 알려줬습니다.** 이 이메일로 회신하면 제게 연락할 수 있습니다.

감사합니다.

새넌 콜

어휘 disappointed with ~에 실망한 amenity 편의시설

---

176 동의어 찾기

번역 정보문에서 1번째 단락 4행의 "shared"와 의미상 가장 가까운 것은?
(A) 분할된
(B) 논의된
(C) 알려진
(D) 공동으로 사용되는

해설 'shared'를 포함한 부분은 '캠핑장 화장실과 샤워시설은 모든 야영객이 공유한다(Restroom and shower facilities at the campground are shared among all campers)'라는 의미로 해석되므로, '공동으로 사용되는'이라는 의미의 (D) used in common이 정답이다.

---

177 추론 / 암시 　　　　고난도

번역 몬타라 국립공원에 관해 암시된 것은?
(A) 습한 기후 지역에 있다.
(B) 다른 어떤 국립 공원보다 방문객이 더 많다.
(C) 일년 중 일부 기간에 문을 닫는다.
(D) 최근 공원 경비대원을 더 고용했다.

해설 정보문의 하단에서 공원이 시즌 처음으로 개장하는 3월 초와 공휴일에는 수요가 많다(demand is high in early March, when the park first opens for the season)고 했으므로, 몬타라 국립공원이 시즌제로 운영됨을 알 수 있다. 따라서 (C)가 정답이다.

---

178 주제 / 목적

번역 콜 씨가 이메일을 쓴 이유는?
(A) 설명서 수정을 제안하려고
(B) 부분 환불을 요청하려고
(C) 부정적인 후기를 쓴 이유를 설명하려고
(D) 불만사항 처리현황을 확인하려고

해설 이메일의 중반부에서 며칠 간 캠핑장에 전기가 들어오지 않았으니 수도 및 전기가 없는 캠핑카 공간 요금만 내면 된다(we should only be charged the rate for motor home sites without water and electricity)고 생각한다며 차액을 돌려줄 것(I'd like the difference to be sent back to me)을 요청했다. 따라서 (B)가 정답이다.

어휘 revise 수정하다 description 설명(서) partial 부분적인 status 현황

> ▶▶ Paraphrasing 지문의 would like the difference to be sent back
> → 정답의 request a partial refund

---

179 연계

번역 콜 씨는 어떤 캠핑장을 예약했겠는가?
(A) 개척자
(B) 모험가
(C) 탐험가
(D) 선도자

해설 이메일의 초반부에서 콜 씨는 자신의 캠핑장에 전기가 들어오지 않았다(the electricity for our campsite didn't work)는 문제점을 언급했는데, 정보문에 나열된 캠핑장을 보면 전기가 포함된(electricity included) 캠핑장은 '선도자(Pathfinder)'뿐이다. 따라서 (D)가 정답이다.

---

180 연계 　　　　고난도

번역 라인하트 씨에 관해 알 수 있는 것은?
(A) 근무 시 특별한 형태의 모자를 착용한다.
(B) 다른 캠핑장으로 옮기라고 권했다.
(C) 임시로 화덕에 접근할 수 있었다.
(D) 유명한 산에서 도보여행을 인솔한다.

해설 이메일의 후반부에서 라인하트 씨가 공원 경비대원(The park ranger on duty, Chet Rinehart)이라고 했는데, 정보문의 첫 번째 단락을 보면 경비대원들이 본인들의 상징인 납작모자에 대한 질문에도 대답해 준다(Its team of rangers ~ even answer questions about their iconic flat hats)고 되어 있다. 따라서 공원 경비대원인 라인하트 씨가 근무 시

특별한 형태의 모자를 착용한다고 볼 수 있으므로, (A)가 정답이다.

> ▶▶ **Paraphrasing** 지문의 **their iconic flat hats**
> → 정답의 **a special type of headgear**
> 지문의 **on duty** → 정답의 **at work**

181-185 회의 일정 + 공지

<table>
<tr><td colspan="3" align="center">소매 약국 관리자 협회(ARPM) 제11차 연례 회의</td></tr>
<tr><td colspan="3">181일정: 2일차 – 12월 4일</td></tr>
<tr><td>오전 8:00 – 9:00</td><td>지정 호텔의 셔틀 서비스</td><td></td></tr>
<tr><td>오전 9:15 – 9:30</td><td>아니타 모리슨, ARPM 부사장 발언</td><td>대강당</td></tr>
<tr><td>오전 9:30 – 10:45</td><td>아침 세션 1
"영업 및 마케팅 전략 재정비"
드루 에스피노, 카루소 제약 솔루션 컨설턴트</td><td>대강당</td></tr>
<tr><td>오전 11:00 –
오후 12:15</td><td>아침 세션 2
"판매 정보 관리 시스템 기술을 개선할 때인가?"
켈리 파월, 〈오늘날의 소매 약국〉 웹사이트 편집자</td><td>대강당</td></tr>
<tr><td>오후 12:30 – 2:00</td><td>점심 뷔페</td><td>남관</td></tr>
<tr><td>183오후 2:00 – 3:15</td><td>**오후 세션 1**
"환자 관리에 관한 효과적인 직원 교육"
마샬 할로웨이, 얼스워스 약국 매니저</td><td>**대강당**</td></tr>
<tr><td>오후 3:30 – 4:45</td><td>오후 세션 2
"대비하라: 소매 약국의 미래 동향"
라드카 비엘릭, 팩스 약학대학교 교수</td><td>대강당</td></tr>
<tr><td>오후 5:00 – 8:00</td><td>181폐막연회</td><td>대연회장</td></tr>
</table>

• 각 강연자와 해당 세션 정보는 www.arpm-conf.com을 참조하세요.
• 182각 세션의 마지막 30분은 청중 질의응답 시간으로 잡혀 있습니다.
• 오전 및 오후 휴식시간에 강당 밖에서 다과가 제공될 예정입니다.

어휘 designated 지정된 remark 발언 refine 재정비하다, 다듬다 point of sale 판매 시점 정보 관리 시스템, 판매 지점 effective 효과적인 banquet 연회 reserve 따로 잡아 두다 refreshments 다과

공지

183개인적인 사유로 마샬 할로웨이 씨가 오늘 예정된 "환자 관리에 관한 효과적인 직원 교육" 세션에 함께 할 수 없게 되었습니다. 184대기 강연자로 ARPM의 최고 운영 책임자인 사라 휴즈 씨가 대체 세션을 진행할 예정입니다. "비효율을 찾아 없애는 방법"이라는 제목의 발표에서 그녀는 약국의 시간과 돈을 낭비하는 문제를 파악하고 해결하는 5단계 시스템을 설명하겠습니다. 183이러한 변동 사항 때문에 큰 불편을 겪어 휴즈 씨의 발표에 참석하는 것보다 금전적 보상을 원하는 참석자는 세션이 시작되기 전에 등록 창구에서 요청해야 합니다.

185또한, 회의센터 경영진은 어젯밤 남관의 출장 요리 냉장고가 고장 나 오늘 점심에 제공되기로 했던 음식의 상당량이 상했다고 통보했습니다. 대신 첨부된 쿠폰을 사용해 가까운 식당에서 점심을 사 드십시오. 오늘밤 저녁 행사는 계획대로 진행됩니다.

이처럼 불편을 끼쳐 드려 깊이 사과 드리며, 양해를 구합니다.

– ARPM 제11차 연례 회의 주최측

어휘 personal 개인적인, 사적인 standby 대기[대용]의 replacement 대체 entitled 제목이 붙여진 describe 설명하다 eliminate 제거하다 inefficiency 비효율(성) identify 파악하다 address 해결하다 attendee 참석자 inconvenienced 불편을 겪는, 불편함을 느끼는 compensation 보상 catering 음식 공급 attached 첨부된 apologize 사과하다

181 추론 / 암시 [고난도]

번역 회의에 관해 가장 사실에 가까운 것은?
(A) 이틀에 걸쳐서 열린다.
(B) 행사장 안에 숙소가 있다.
(C) 녹화해 온라인으로 방송할 것이다.
(D) 주로 학자들이 참석한다.

해설 회의 일정표 상단에서 2일차 일정(Schedule for: Day 2)이라고 했는데, 마지막 일정을 보면 폐막연회(Closing Banquet)가 예정되어 있으므로, 이틀에 걸쳐 열린 회의라고 추론할 수 있다. 따라서 (A)가 정답이다.

어휘 venue 장소, 행사장 accommodation 숙소 academic 학자

182 세부 사항

번역 회의 일정에 따르면 회의 참석자들이 할 수 있는 것은?
(A) 특정 음료를 강당에 가지고 오기
(B) 새로운 유형의 소매 장비 시험하기
(C) 각 세션이 끝날 무렵에 질문하기
(D) 회의 내용에 대한 반응 온라인으로 공개하기

해설 회의 일정표 하단에서 각 세션의 마지막 30분은 청중 질의응답 시간으로 잡혀 있다(The last half hour of each session will be reserved for audience Q&A)고 했으므로, (C)가 정답이다.

어휘 beverage 음료 equipment 장비 reveal 공개하다 electronically 전자 기기로, 온라인으로

> ▶▶ **Paraphrasing** 지문의 **audience**
> → 질문의 **conference attendees**
> 지문의 **be reserved for ~ Q&A**
> → 정답의 **Ask questions**

183 연계

번역 참석자들은 몇 시까지 불편에 대한 배상을 요구해야 하는가?
(A) 오전 9시 30분
(B) 오전 11시
(C) 오후 12시 30분
(D) 오후 2시

해설 공지의 첫 번째 단락에서 마샬 할로웨이 씨가 예정된 세션을 진행할 수 없다고 한 후, 변동 사항 때문에 큰 불편을 겪어 금전적 보상을 원하는 참석자는 세션이 시작되기 전에 등록 창구에서 요청해야 한다(Attendees who feel strongly inconvenienced by this change and would prefer financial compensation ~ must make this request at the registration desk before the session begins)고 했다. 회의 일정표를 보면, 할로웨이 씨의 세션이 오후 2시에 시작하므로, (D)가 정답이다.

Test 9

▶▶ **Paraphrasing** 지문의 would prefer financial compensation
→ 질문의 ask to be reimbursed

지문의 feel strongly inconvenienced
→ 질문의 for an inconvenience

184 추론 / 암시　　고난도

번역　휴즈 씨에 관해 암시된 것은?
(A) 비상사태에 대비해 강연을 준비했다.
(B) 다른 강연자의 자료를 사용할 것이다.
(C) 예정보다 늦게 끝낼 것이다.
(D) 이전 ARPM 회의에서 강연했다.

해설　공지의 첫 번째 단락에서 마샬 할로웨이 씨의 부재로 대기 강연자인 사라 휴즈 씨가 대체 세션을 이끌 예정(Sarah Hughes, our standby speaker ~, will lead a replacement session)이라고 했으므로, 그녀가 비상사태에 대비해 강연을 준비했다고 추론할 수 있다. 따라서 (A)가 정답이다.

어휘　in case of an emergency 비상사태에 대비해

185 사실 관계 확인

번역　공지에 언급된 두 번째 문제의 원인은 무엇인가?
(A) 음식 주문 실수
(B) 고장 난 기기
(C) ARPM 회원들의 잘못된 처신
(D) 계획에 없던 인근 도로의 공사

해설　공지에 언급된 두 번째 문제(In addition)는 남관의 출장요리 냉장고가 고장 나 행사일 점심에 제공되기로 했던 음식의 상당량이 상했다(the South Hall's catering fridge failed ~, spoiling much of the food that would have been served at lunch)는 것이다. 따라서 (B)가 정답이다.

어휘　malfunction 고장 나다　behavior 처신

▶▶ **Paraphrasing** 지문의 the South Hall's catering fridge failed → 정답의 A malfunctioning appliance

186-190 이메일 + 광고 + 이메일

발신: 사울 스트릭랜드
수신: 달린 깁슨
제목: 딕슨 에듀테크
날짜: 7월 6일

안녕하세요 달린,

우리 고객사 중 유망한 신생 기업인 딕슨 에듀테크와 관련해 메일 드립니다. 혹시 잘 모르실 수도 있어 말씀드리자면, 주 제품은 게임 같은 기능을 활용해 재미있게 학습할 수 있도록 만든 직원 교육 플랫폼이에요. **186/189최근 우리 회사가 제공하는 마케팅 서비스 외에 홍보 전담 회사가 필요할 정도로 성장해, 그**

쪽 커뮤니케이션 매니저인 빅터 보스웰이 우리에게 적합한 곳을 추천해 줄 수 있는지 물었어요. **187특히 그들은 기술업계와 연계되어 있고 합리적인 비용에 홍보 서비스를 제공해 줄 업체를 원해요. 186당신이 정보기술 쪽 책임자시니 이 분야에 특별한 혜안이 있지 않을까 해서요.**

어떤 아이디어라도 주시면 정말 감사하겠어요.

고마워요.

사울 스트릭랜드
마케팅 전문가
포샌트 마케팅

어휘　in regards to ~에 관해　promising 유망한　start-up 신생의　familiar with ~을 잘 아는　recently 최근　dedicated 전담하는, 헌신하는　public relations 홍보　suitable 적합한　recommendation 추천　affordable (가격 등이) 적당한, 합리적인　insight 혜안

룬데이 파트너즈
홍보 서비스

룬데이 파트너즈는 귀사가 이제 막 시작하는 회사든, 자리를 잡은 회사든 간에, 스마트한 최첨단 서비스를 제공할 준비가 되어 있습니다. 시간을 들여 귀사의 브랜드, 난제, 목표를 이해해 귀사를 위한 독특하고 효과적인 홍보 전략을 짜겠습니다.

다음은 룬데이 파트너즈를 선택해야 하는 몇 가지 이유입니다:
■ 광고문안 작성부터 행사 지원까지 다양한 서비스를 제공합니다.
■ 당사는 선진 디지털 도구를 사용해 귀사의 브랜드 인식에 관한 귀중한 데이터를 제공합니다.
■ **187부동산, 기술, 금융 등 여러 분야에 특별한 단골 거래처들이 있습니다.**

188www.luneday.com을 방문해 만족도가 높은 다수의 고객들이 쓴 추천 글을 확인하세요.

어휘　established 자리를 잡은, 인정 받는　cutting-edge (최)첨단의　craft 공들여 만들다　effective 효과적인　a wide range of 다양한　advanced 선진의, 고급의　perceive 인식하다　connection 단골 거래처, 연줄　testimonial 추천하는 글

발신: 신디 파딜라 〈c.padilla@luneday.com〉
수신: 빅터 보스웰 〈v.boswell@dixon-edutech.com〉
제목: 회의 후속 작업
189날짜: 8월 2일

보스웰 씨께,

189어제 사무실에서 이야기 나눠서 즐거웠어요. 190그때 말했듯이, 저는 이제 귀사의 상황과 목표에 대해 얻은 정보를 바탕으로 적절한 전문가들로 구성된 팀을 모아 위탁하신 업무를 처리하겠습니다. 그런 다음 2~3주 후에 다시 회의를 잡아 저희의 전략을 제시하고 귀사의 승인을 받겠습니다. 필요시, 제안하신 대로 포샌트 마케팅 사에 있는 귀사의 담당 관리자와 조율하겠습니다.

이 과정에 관해 궁금한 점이 있으시면 전화나 이메일로 연락하십시오. 그리고 귀사의 홍보 작업을 위해 룬데이 파트너즈를 선택해 주셔서 다시 한 번 감사드립니다.

신디 파딜라
광고주 담당자
룬데이 파트너즈

어휘 follow-up 후속 조치[작업] assemble 모으다 appropriate
적절한 specialist 전문가 account (광고) 위탁한 일, 위탁 광고주,
거래처 approval 승인 coordinate 조율[조정]하다 process 절차,
과정

186 주제 / 목적

번역 첫 번째 이메일의 목적은?
(A) 고객 문의 관련 도움 요청
(B) 직원 교육 자료 소개
(C) 도급업체 관련 어려움 보고
(D) 활동 범위에 대한 우려 표명

해설 첫 번째 이메일의 첫 단락에서 고객사의 커뮤니케이션 매니저인 빅터 보
스웰이 적합한 홍보 전담 회사를 추천해줄 수 있는지(Victor Boswell,
their communications manager, has asked if we can make a
suitable recommendation) 문의했다고 한 후, 깁슨 씨에게 이 분야
에 특별한 혜안이 있지 않을까 싶어 연락한다(I wondered if you might
have some special insight in this area)고 했다. 따라서 고객 문의
관련 도움을 요청하기 위한 이메일이라고 볼 수 있으므로, (A)가 정답이다.

어휘 contractor 도급[하청]업체 endeavor (조직적인) 활동, 프로젝트,
노력

187 연계 고난도

번역 깁슨 씨가 스트릭랜드 씨에게 룬데이 파트너즈를 추천할 것 같은 이유는 무엇
이겠는가?
(A) 가격대
(B) 기술 도구
(C) 타 업계와의 연계
(D) 라이브 행사 서비스

해설 첫 번째 이메일의 첫 단락에서 스트릭랜드 씨는 깁슨 씨에게 고객사
가 기술업계와 연계되어 있고 합리적인 비용에 홍보 서비스를 제공
해 줄 업체를 원한다(they'd like an affordable PR provider with
ties to the tech industry)고 했는데, 광고의 두 번째 단락을 보면 룬
데이 파트너즈가 기술 분야에 특별한 단골 거래처들이 있음(We have
special connections in several fields, including real estate,
technology, and finance)을 알 수 있다. 따라서 (C)가 정답이다.

▶▶ Paraphrasing 지문의 ties to the tech industry / special
connections in several fields
→ 정답의 connections in another industry

188 세부 사항

번역 광고에 따르면 룬데이 파트너즈 웹사이트에서 이용할 수 있는 것은?
(A) 예약 양식
(B) 해당 분야의 현재 동향 자료
(C) 작업에 대한 긍정적인 피드백
(D) 최고 경영진의 프로필

해설 광고의 마지막 단락에서 웹사이트를 방문해 만족도가 높은 고객들의 추천
글을 확인할 것(Visit us at www.luneday.com to see testimonials
from our many satisfied clients)을 권고했으므로, (C)가 정답이다.

어휘 executive 경영진, 간부

▶▶ Paraphrasing 지문의 at www.luneday.com
→ 질문의 on Luneday Partners' Web site
지문의 testimonials from our many
satisfied clients → 정답의 Positive
feedback about its work

189 연계

번역 파딜라 씨는 8월 1일에 누구를 만났는가?
(A) 딕슨 에듀테크 영업사원
(B) 딕슨 에듀테크의 커뮤니케이션 매니저
(C) 포산트 마케팅의 정보기술 책임자
(D) 포산트 마케팅의 마케팅 전문가

해설 두 번째 이메일의 첫 단락에서 파딜라 씨가 보스웰 씨에게 어제 이야기 나
눠서 즐거웠다(It was a pleasure to speak with you ~ yesterday)
고 했는데, 이메일의 날짜(Date: August 2)로 보아 8월 1일에 보스웰
씨를 만났다고 추론할 수 있다. 첫 번째 이메일을 보면 보스웰 씨가 딕슨
에듀테크의 커뮤니케이션 매니저(Victor Boswell, their communications manager)임을 알 수 있으므로, (B)가 정답이다.

190 사실 관계 확인

번역 파딜라 씨는 다음에 무엇을 할 것이라고 하는가?
(A) 발표회 일정 잡기
(B) 전략 제안서 업데이트
(C) 사업예산 책정
(D) 광고주를 위한 팀 구성

해설 두 번째 이메일의 첫 단락에서 파딜라 씨가 이제 적절한 전문가들로 구성
된 팀을 모아 보스웰 씨의 회사가 위탁한 업무를 처리하겠다(I will now
assemble a crew of appropriate specialists ~ to handle your
account)고 했으므로, (D)가 정답이다.

▶▶ Paraphrasing 지문의 assemble a crew of appropriate
specialists
→ 정답의 Form an account team

191-195 기사 + 소책자 페이지 + 이메일

렐스데일의 예술
글 세인 웰러

렐스데일 (9월 10일)—어린이 여름 수업이 끝난 지 불과 몇 주 만에 렐스데일
주민센터는 또 다른 흥미진진한 활동을 계획하기 시작했다. [194]제32회 연례 렐
스데일 지역 아트쇼가 10월 22~28일 주간에 주민센터 강당에서 열린다.

이 행사는 32년 전 지역 수채화 화가인 그랜트 린지 씨가 친구들을 초대해 작은 쇼에서 그림을 함께 전시하면서 시작되었다. 이후 렐스데일의 전문 시각 예술가 및 아마추어 시각 예술가 모두가 재능을 발휘할 수 있는 기회로 성장했다.

194현 체제에서는, 주민센터장인 티나 조던 씨가 이끌고 말커 대학 미술사학자 아드난 칼리프 등이 포함된 위원회가 심사하는 공모전이 아트쇼의 주를 이룬다. 또한 쇼에 나오는 예술작품 대다수는 판매용이다. 192판매 수익의 25퍼센트는 센터 건물과 부지 유지비를 지원하는 데 쓰인다.

191센터의 레크리에이션 담당 부국장 겸 이 쇼의 기획자인 경혜란 씨는 모든 연령, 배경, 예술 분야의 시민들에게 전시를 고려해 보라고 적극 권장한다. 관심 있는 사람들은 www.rellsdaleart.com을 방문해 설명을 보면 된다.

어휘 activity 활동 auditorium 강당 exhibit 전시하다; 전시 display 전시하다 feature ~를 주특징으로 하다, 특별히 포함하다 committee 위원회 proceed 수익 upkeep 유지(비) organizer 기획자 discipline 분야, 학과

제32회 렐스데일 지역 아트쇼

렐스데일 지역 아트쇼에 오신 것을 환영합니다! 렐스데일 주민센터는 우리 지역의 예술적 재능을 찬양하는 자리에 여러분이 함께해 주셔서 기쁩니다.

야간 개회식 환영회 일정
오후 5시 – 개관
오후 6시 – 렐스데일 슈퍼마켓에서 기부한 다과 제공
오후 7시 – 194심사위원장의 환영사 및 공모전 결과 발표
오후 9시 – 폐관

기타 유용한 정보:
✦ 193/195특정 작품을 찾으려면 3, 4페이지에서 예술가 이름을 알파벳 순으로 정렬한 전체 작품 목록을 참고하세요.
✦ 작품 구입에 대해 문의하시려면 직원과 즉시 상담하세요. 판매는 선착순이라는 점 명심하세요!

1951페이지

어휘 celebrate 기념하다, 찬양하다 gift 재능 provision 제공 refreshments 다과 donate 기증하다 purchase 구입하다; 구입품 promptly 즉시 first come, first served 선착순

발신: 새뮤얼 메이휴
수신: 유레일리아 프로서
제목: 문의
날짜: 11월 4일

프로서 씨께,

안녕하세요. 195제 친구 앤 왓슨이 렐스데일 지역 아트쇼에 전시된 당신의 목재 조각품을 샀어요. 멋진 것 같아서 제 사무실에도 하나 두었으면 해요. 앤이 구입한 작품에 딸려 온 명함에서 당신의 이메일 주소를 얻었어요. 제게 답장을 보내 판매할 만한 다른 작품이 있으신지 알려주시겠어요? 고마워요.

새뮤얼 메이휴

어휘 sculpture 조각품 gorgeous 멋진, 훌륭한 purchase 구매품

---

191 주제 / 목적

번역 기사의 한 가지 목적은?
(A) 모금활동의 성공 사례 설명하기
(B) 지역 예술가들의 업적을 널리 알리기
(C) 사람들에게 지역 행사에 참여하라고 요청하기
(D) 주민센터에서 새롭게 제공하는 수업 알리기

해설 기사 전반에서 전시회를 설명한 후, 마지막 단락에서 전시회 기획자가 모든 연령, 배경, 예술 분야의 시민들에게 전시를 고려해 보라고 적극 권장한다(the center's vice director of recreation and the show's organizer, urges citizens of all ages, backgrounds, and artistic disciplines to consider exhibiting)며 마무리했다. 따라서 지역 행사 참여를 독려하려는 목적으로 쓰인 기사라고 볼 수 있으므로, (C)가 정답이다.

어휘 publicize 홍보하다 accomplishment 업적 offering 제공하는 것, 강좌

> ▶▶ Paraphrasing 지문의 urges citizens of all ages, backgrounds, and artistic disciplines to consider exhibiting
> → 정답의 invite people to participate in a community event

192 세부 사항

번역 모인 자금 일부는 어떻게 사용될 것인가?
(A) 시설 유지관리
(B) 청소년을 위한 수업 개설
(C) 역사책 발간
(D) 공모전 수상자 포상

해설 기사의 세 번째 단락에서 판매 수익의 25퍼센트가 센터 건물과 부지 유지비를 지원하는 데 쓰인다(Twenty-five percent of the proceeds of each sale goes toward funding the upkeep of the center's buildings and grounds)고 했으므로, (A)가 정답이다.

> ▶▶ Paraphrasing 지문의 Twenty-five percent of the proceeds of each sale
> → 질문의 some collected funds
> 지문의 funding the upkeep of the center's buildings and grounds
> → 정답의 To maintain a facility

193 세부 사항

번역 소책자 페이지에 따르면, 미술품 목록은 어떻게 구성되어 있는가?
(A) 예술 분야별로
(B) 작품 제목별로
(C) 작품 위치별로
(D) 창작자 이름별로

해설 소책자 페이지의 '기타 유용한 정보(Other helpful information)'에서 미술품을 구매하려면 예술가 이름을 알파벳 순으로 정렬한 전체 작품 목록을 참고하라(see the full list of entries ordered alphabetically by artist)고 했으므로, (D)가 정답이다.

194 연계   고난도

번역 10월 22일 공식 석상에서 발언한 사람은 누구인가?
(A) 린지 씨
(B) 조던 씨
(C) 칼리프 씨
(D) 경 씨

해설 기사의 첫 번째 단락에서 제32회 연례 렐스데일 지역 아트쇼가 10월 22일~28일 주간에 열린다고 했으므로, 10월 22일이 행사 개회식 날임을 알 수 있다. 소책자 페이지의 야간 개회식 환영회 일정(Schedule of the Opening Night Reception)을 보면 심사위원장의 환영사 및 공모전 결과 발표(Welcoming remarks and announcement of contest results by the head of the judging committee)가 있다고 되어 있는데, 기사의 세 번째 단락에서 티나 조던 씨가 심사 위원회를 이끈다(the art show features a contest judged by a committee led by Tina Jordan)고 나와 있다. 따라서 심사위원장인 조던 씨가 10월 22일에 공식 석상에서 발언할 것이라 추론할 수 있으므로, (B)가 정답이다.

195 연계   고난도

번역 프로서 씨에 관해 가장 사실에 가까운 것은?
(A) 소책자의 다른 페이지에 언급되었다.
(B) 모임에 다과를 기부했다.
(C) 왓슨 씨에게 이메일을 받았다.
(D) 렐스데일에 사는 아마추어 시각 예술가다.

해설 이메일의 초반부에서 메이휴 씨는 자신의 친구가 렐스데일 지역 아트쇼에 전시된 프로서 씨의 목재 조각품을 샀다(My friend ~ bought the wooden sculpture you exhibited in the Rellsdale Community Arts Show)고 했는데, 소책자 1페이지(Page 1)에 있는 '기타 유용한 정보(Other helpful information)'를 보면 3, 4페이지에 예술가 이름이 알파벳 순으로 정렬된 전체 작품 목록(To locate a certain work of art, see the full list of entries ordered alphabetically by artist on pages 3 and 4)이 있음을 알 수 있다. 따라서 전시회에 출품한 프로서 씨가 소책자의 3 또는 4 페이지에 언급되었을 것이라 추론할 수 있으므로, (A)가 정답이다.

196-200 구인 광고 + 회의록 + 블로그 글

여름 법무 인턴

길비 지역에서 상법 분야에 점차 입지를 다지고 있는 후안 어소시에이츠가 6월 1일부터 7월 31일까지 법무 인턴십을 제공합니다. 인턴은 법률조사 및 분석, 각종 법률문서 초안 작성, 의뢰인 회의 참석, 특별 프로젝트 완료 등을 수행하게 되며, 이 모든 활동에서 노련한 변호사의 지도와 피드백을 받는 혜택을 누립니다.

요건
• 법학전문대학원을 최소 1년 이상 수료한 법학전문대학원 재학생
• 워터프런트 지구 내에 있는 법률사무소 사무실에서 주 30시간 근무 가능한 자

우대 자격
• 지역, 주, 연방 상법 관련 지식
• [197]롤렌토와 같은 법률조사 플랫폼 사용 능력

[196](A)/(C)/(D)지원하려면 다음 서류들을 3월 31일까지 이메일 marlon.terry @huanelegal.com으로 보내세요: 1페이지 분량의 자기소개서, 이력서, 로스쿨 성적증명서, 그리고 3~5페이지 정도의 작문 견본.

어휘 presence 입지 commercial 상업의 legal research 법률조사 analysis 분석 draft 초안을 작성하다 attend 참석하다 benefit 혜택 direction 지도, 지시 seasoned 노련한 attorney 변호사 familiarity 지식, 숙지 proficiency 숙달, 사용 능력 transcript 성적증명서

인턴십 기록 - 격주 회의록

날짜: 7월 8일 수요일
인턴: 르네 월터스
관리자: 말론 테리

이전 프로젝트/경험에 대한 성찰
• 온라인 소매업체 세법 분석: 말론이 "요약" 섹션을 개선하기 위한 전반적인 의견과 제안을 내놓았다.
• 소보 슈즈와 회의: 르네의 질문에 답하며, 말론이 의뢰인의 예기치 않은 요청을 처리할 수 있는 방안들에 대해 논의했다.

진행 중인 프로젝트 업데이트
• 비공개 계약 이력에 대한 블로그 게시물: [197]르네가 롤렌토를 사용해 일하는 데 어려움을 겪고 있다고 보고했다. 말론이 7월 10일 오후 1시로 교육 일정을 잡았다.
• 마르키타 카페 고용계약서 초안 작성: 르네가 지니 윌커슨과 필요한 회의 일정을 잡지 못하고 있다. 말론은 이 건과 관련해 지니에게 연락할 예정이다.

새 업무
• [199]블레어–로그, LLC의 운영 약정서 초안 작성: 잠정적으로 7월 15일 마감; 르네는 내부 네트워크의 "운영 약정서" 파일에 있는 자료를 참조해야 한다.

어휘 reflection (과거 행위의) 기록, 성찰 retailer 소매업체 general 일반적인 improve 개선하다 disclosure 공개 employement contract 고용 계약서 operating agreement 운영 약정서 LLC (Limited Liability Company) 유한책임회사 tentatively 잠정적으로 due 마감인 refer to ~을 참조하다 resource 자료 internal 내부의

---

http://www.huanelegal.com/blog

후안 어소시에이츠의 첫 인턴과 작별

글 아키라 치넨
[199]7월 28일 화요일 게시

우리 사무소에서 일하는 르네 월터스의 인턴십이 이번 주 말에 끝납니다. 월터스 씨는 지난 두 달 동안 말론 테리 변호사의 지도 [198]아래 다양한 업무를 해왔습니다. 여러분은 아마 월터스 씨가 테리 씨와 회의에 참석하는 것을 보거나, 비공개 계약에 관한 블로그 게시물을 읽었을 것입니다.

[199]월터스 씨는 어제 운영 약정서 초안을 완성하면서, 여기서 얻은 실무 경험이

매우 귀중했다고 제게 말했습니다. 그녀는 또한 테리 씨의 사려 깊은 멘토링에 특히 감사하다고 말했습니다.

테리 씨는 "이 짧은 시간에도 월터스 씨가 훌쩍 성장하는 것을 보았기 때문에 월터스 씨를 지도하는 일이 정말 즐거웠다"고 말했습니다. 200그는 인턴십 프로그램이 훨씬 더 많은 학생 참여자들과 함께 내년 여름에도 다시 시행되기를 희망한다고 했습니다.

사무소 전 직원은 금요일 오후 4시 A 회의실에서 열리는 월터스 씨의 송별회에 오시기 바랍니다.

어휘 supervision 감독 associate (법률 사무소에서 지분을 보유하지 않은) 변호사 practical 실무의, 실질적인 thoughtful 사려 깊은 express 표현하다

---

196 사실 관계 확인

번역 구인 광고에서 지원자들에게 제출하라고 요구하지 않은 것은?
(A) 학교 성적 기록
(B) 직장 관련 추천서
(C) 경력 목록
(D) 작문 역량을 보여주는 증거

해설 구인 광고의 마지막 단락에서 지원하려면(To apply, e-mail the following documents) 자기소개서(a one-page cover letter), 이력서(your résumé), 로스쿨 성적증명서(your law school transcript), 작문 견본(a writing sample of between three and five pages)을 제출하라고 되어 있다. 따라서 언급되지 않은 (B)가 정답이다.

어휘 professional reference (전 직장 상사, 동료 등이 써주는) 직장 관련 추천서

▶▶ Paraphrasing 지문의 law school transcript → 보기 (A)의 A record of school performance
지문의 résumé → 보기 (C)의 A list of career experiences
지문의 a writing sample → 보기 (D)의 Evidence of writing skills

---

197 연계

번역 회의록에 따르면 월터스 씨는 어떤 문제를 겪었는가?
(A) 임원 회의 준비하기
(B) 글로 된 피드백 이해하기
(C) 특정 지역으로 통근하기
(D) 전자 조사 도구 사용하기

해설 회의록의 '진행 중인 프로젝트 업데이트(Updates on ongoing projects)'에서 월터스 씨가 롤렌토를 사용해 일하는 데 어려움을 겪고 있다고 보고했다(Renée reported difficulty working with Rolento)고 했는데, 구인 광고의 '우대 자격(Preferred qualifications)'을 보면, 롤렌토가 법률조사 플랫폼(legal research platforms such as Rolento)임을 알 수 있다. 즉, 월터스 씨가 컴퓨터 소프트웨어 사용에 문제를 겪은 것이므로, (D)가 정답이다.

▶▶ Paraphrasing 지문의 reported difficulty → 질문의 had trouble
지문의 research platform → 정답의 electronic research tool

---

198 동의어 찾기

번역 블로그 글에서 1번째 단락 2행의 "under"와 의미상 가장 가까운 것은?
(A) 그녀 자신의 직함인
(B) ~에 의해 감춰진
(C) ~의 권한 아래 있는
(D) ~보다 적은

해설 'under'를 포함한 부분은 '변호사의 지도 아래(under the supervision of associate)'라는 의미로 해석되는데, 여기서 under는 '~ 아래, ~ 하에'라는 뜻으로 쓰였다. 따라서 '~의 권한 아래 있는'이라는 의미의 (C) subject to가 정답이다.

---

199 연계 　고난도

번역 월터스 씨에 관해 암시된 것은?
(A) 문서를 네트워크 폴더에 올렸다.
(B) 의뢰인 응대에 관한 테리 씨의 조언을 수용했다.
(C) 프로젝트 하나가 마감일이 연기되었다.
(D) 그녀를 위한 특별교육은 진행되지 않았다.

해설 블로그 글의 두 번째 단락에서 월터스 씨가 어제 운영 약정서 초안을 완성했다(she finished up a draft of an operating agreement yesterday)고 했는데, 글이 게시된 날짜(Posted Tuesday, July 28)로 보아 운영 약정서 초안이 7월 27일에 완성되었음을 알 수 있다. 회의록의 '새 업무(New assignments)' 항목을 보면, 운영 약정서 초안 작성(Drafting of operating agreement) 마감일이 잠정적으로 7월 15일(Tentatively due July 15)이라고 했으므로, 해당 업무 마감일이 연기되었다고 추론할 수 있다. 따라서 (C)가 정답이다.

어휘 postpone 연기하다

---

200 세부 사항 　고난도

번역 블로그 글에 따르면, 테리 씨는 인턴십 프로그램을 어떻게 바꾸고 싶어하는가?
(A) 자리 수 늘리기
(B) 지속 기간 연장하기
(C) 더 많은 직원 참여시키기
(D) 참가자에게 더 많은 책임 부여하기

해설 블로그 글의 세 번째 단락에서 테리 씨가 인턴십 프로그램이 훨씬 더 많은 학생 참여자들과 함께 다시 시행되기를 희망한다(He expressed hopes that the internship program would take place again ~ with even more student participants)고 했으므로, (A)가 정답이다.

어휘 extend 연장하다 duration 지속 기간 responsibility 책임

▶▶ Paraphrasing 지문의 with even more student participants → 정답의 By increasing the number of positions

TEST 10

101 (D)	**102** (C)	**103** (C)	**104** (C)	**105** (A)
106 (B)	**107** (D)	**108** (A)	**109** (B)	**110** (B)
111 (D)	**112** (A)	**113** (D)	**114** (B)	**115** (C)
116 (A)	**117** (C)	**118** (A)	**119** (D)	**120** (B)
121 (B)	**122** (A)	**123** (A)	**124** (D)	**125** (C)
126 (C)	**127** (D)	**128** (B)	**129** (A)	**130** (B)
131 (A)	**132** (B)	**133** (B)	**134** (C)	**135** (A)
136 (C)	**137** (B)	**138** (C)	**139** (D)	**140** (C)
141 (B)	**142** (D)	**143** (C)	**144** (D)	**145** (D)
146 (A)	**147** (A)	**148** (D)	**149** (D)	**150** (D)
151 (D)	**152** (A)	**153** (B)	**154** (C)	**155** (B)
156 (B)	**157** (A)	**158** (C)	**159** (A)	**160** (B)
161 (C)	**162** (D)	**163** (D)	**164** (C)	**165** (B)
166 (C)	**167** (B)	**168** (C)	**169** (D)	**170** (C)
171 (D)	**172** (B)	**173** (D)	**174** (A)	**175** (C)
176 (D)	**177** (A)	**178** (B)	**179** (D)	**180** (D)
181 (A)	**182** (B)	**183** (B)	**184** (C)	**185** (C)
186 (B)	**187** (B)	**188** (A)	**189** (D)	**190** (D)
191 (B)	**192** (C)	**193** (D)	**194** (C)	**195** (B)
196 (A)	**197** (C)	**198** (A)	**199** (D)	**200** (B)

PART 5

101 명사 어휘 <고난도>

해설 to serve의 목적어를 선택하는 문제이다. 요청 시 출장요리업자들(caterers)이 추가적으로 제공할 만한 것은 디저트의 양이라고 볼 수 있으므로, '몫, 분량'이라는 의미의 (D) portions가 정답이다.

번역 출장요리업자들은 요청 시에만 디저트 분량을 추가로 제공하라는 지시를 받았다.

어휘 caterer 출장요리업자[업체] be instructed to ~하라고 지시 받다 additional 추가의 upon request 요청 시 recipe 조리법

102 인칭대명사의 격 _ 「소유격 + own」

해설 빈칸이 to prepare의 목적어 역할을 하는 복합명사 income tax report 앞에 있으므로, 명사를 한정 수식할 수 있는 인칭대명사가 들어가야 한다. 따라서 소유격 인칭대명사를 포함한 (C) his own이 정답이다.

번역 헤이즈 씨는 수년 동안 세금 소프트웨어를 이용해 자신의 소득세 신고서를 작성해왔다.

어휘 prepare 준비하다, (보고서 등을) 작성하다 income tax 소득세

103 전치사 어휘

해설 시간 표현 February 11를 목적어로 취하는 전치사 자리로, on처럼 특정 시점과 쓰일 수 있는 전치사가 들어가야 한다. 제출 기한(must be ~ submitted)을 설명하는 문장이므로, '~ 전에'라는 의미의 (C) before가 빈칸에 들어가야 가장 자연스럽다. 참고로, (A) within은 '~ 이내로'라는 뜻으로 뒤에 기간을 나타내는 표현이 온다. (B) until(~까지)은 특정 시점까지 동작 및 상태가 지속된다는 것을 의미하고, (D) from(~부터)은 시

작 시점을 나타내므로, 문맥상 빈칸에 적절하지 않다.

번역 모든 출품작은 2월 11일 이전에 서명 및 제출되어야 고려 대상이 된다.

어휘 entry 출품작 submit 제출하다

104 부사절 접속사 자리 _ 어휘

해설 빈칸 뒤 완전한 절(more graduates would apply for its specialist positions)을 이끄는 접속사 자리이므로, 보기에서 (A) If, (C) So that, (D) As soon as 중 하나를 선택해야 한다. 더 많은 졸업생들이 전문직에 지원하게끔 현장학습을 주최(to host field trips)하는 거라고 볼 수 있으므로, 목적을 나타내는 (C) So that(~하도록, ~할 수 있게)이 정답이다.

번역 클럽 팜스는 더 많은 졸업생이 자사의 전문직에 지원할 수 있도록 대학 농학 수업을 위한 현장학습을 주최하는 데 동의했다.

어휘 graduate 졸업생 host 주최하다 agricultural 농학의, 농업의

105 동사 어형 _ 과거분사

해설 that이 이끄는 동격절(that grocery chains ~ delivery service)에서 목적어에 해당하는 명사구 the environmental problems를 수식하는 자리이다. 따라서 보기에서 형용사 역할을 할 수 있는 과거분사 (A) associated와 현재분사 (C) associating 중 하나를 선택해야 하는데, '배달 서비스와 관련된 환경 문제'라는 의미가 되어야 하므로 (A) associated(~와 연관된, 관련된)가 정답이 된다. associate가 자동사로서 with와 쓰일 경우 '~와 어울려 지내다'라는 뜻을 나타내므로, (C) associating은 적절하지 않다.

번역 식품 체인점들이 배달 서비스와 관련된 환경 문제를 해결하는 한 가지 방법은 재활용 가능한 포장재를 사용하는 것이다.

어휘 address 해결(하려)하다 environmental 환경의 reusable 재활용 가능한

106 부사 어휘

해설 '너무 ~해서 ~할 수 있다/없다'라는 의미의 「so + 형용사 + that + 완전한 절」 구문에서 결과를 나타내는 that절에 해당하는 부분이다. 공사 소음이 너무 커서(The construction noise ~ was so loud) 동료들이 하는 말을 들을 수 없었다는 내용이 되어야 자연스러우므로, 빈칸에는 부정의 뜻을 지닌 부사가 들어가서 could hear를 수식해야 한다. 따라서 '거의 ~ 아니다'라는 의미의 (B) hardly가 정답이다.

번역 옆 건물에서 나는 공사 소음이 너무 커서 우리는 동료들이 하는 말을 좀체 들을 수 없었다.

어휘 construction 공사 coworker 동료

107 명사 자리 _ 동사의 주어 _ 어휘 <고난도>

해설 문장의 주어 역할을 하는 명사 자리로, 보기에서 (A) receipt, (C) recipient, (D) reception 중 하나를 선택해야 한다. 주격 보어인 a surprise to critics와 의미상 동격 관계를 이루어야 하므로, 평론가들을 놀라게 한 요인을 나타내는 명사가 들어가야 한다. 따라서 '청중의(by audiences) 반응, 환영'이라는 의미를 완성하는 (D) reception이 정답이다.

Test 10

번역 그 밴드의 새 앨범에 대한 청중의 열렬한 반응에 평론가들은 놀랐다.

어휘 enthusiastic 열렬한 audience 청중 critic 평론가 receipt 영수증, 수령 receive 받다 recipient 받는 사람 reception 반응, 환영(회)

108 부정대명사 `고난도`

해설 관계사절에서 동사 impressed의 주어 역할을 하는 (대)명사 자리로, 전치사구 of whom(=of several candidates)의 수식을 받는다. 따라서 '여러 지원자 중 누구도 ~않다'라는 의미를 완성하는 (A) none이 정답이다. 참고로, (B) nobody 다음에는 of가 올 수 없다. (C) those 뒤에 of가 올 경우 'the ones'와 같은 의미를 나타내며 앞서 언급된 명사의 반복을 피하기 위해 사용되는데, 이 문장에서는 whom이 이미 Several candidates를 대신하고 있기 때문에 빈칸에 들어갈 수 없다. (D) both는 '둘 다'라는 뜻으로 Several과 수가 일치하지 않으므로 정답이 될 수 없다.

번역 여러 지원자가 접수 담당자 직 면접을 봤지만, 그중 어느 누구도 채용 위원회에 좋은 인상을 남기지 못했다.

어휘 candidate 후보자, 지원자 interview 면접을 보다, 면접하다 receptionist 접수 담당자 impress 인상을 남기다 hiring committee 채용 위원회

109 동사 어휘 `고난도`

해설 프로젝트 팀장(The project leader)의 책임(responsible for)을 설명하는 동명사를 선택해야 한다. 계획에 새로운 소식이 있다면(updates to the plan) 팀원들(the members of the team)에게 알려야 하므로, '통지하기, 알리기'라는 의미의 (B) notifying이 정답이다. 참고로, notify는 「notify A of B」의 구조로 쓰여 'A에게 B를 알리다'라는 뜻을 나타낸다. 이러한 동사의 구조적 특징은 암기해 두는 것이 좋다. 다른 보기는 구조적으로도 빈칸에 맞지 않는다.

번역 프로젝트 팀장은 계획에 새로운 소식이 있으면 무엇이든 팀원들에게 통지할 책임이 있다.

어휘 be responsible for ~에 책임이 있다 coordinate 조정하다 recruit 모집하다 credit (공을) 돌리다

110 형용사 어휘

해설 대출(loan)을 받으려는 소규모 사업주(small business owners)의 특징을 적절히 묘사하는 형용사를 선택해야 한다. 따라서 '장차 ~가 되려는'이라는 의미의 (B) aspiring이 정답이다.

번역 아름은행은 소규모 사업주가 되려는 사람들에게 매력적인 금리로 대출을 제공한다.

어휘 attractive 매력적인 interest rate 금리 relative 상대적인 unprecedented 전례가 없는 customary 관습상의

111 동사 어형 _ 태 _ 시제

해설 주어인 the air conditioning units는 사람에 의해 설치되는 대상이므로, 수동태 동사 중 하나를 선택해야 한다. 주절의 동사가 should be assigned로 에어컨 설치 후 해야 될 일을 나타내고 있으므로, Once가

이끄는 부사절에는 현재 시제가 들어가야 자연스럽다. 따라서 수동태 현재 동사인 (D) are installed가 정답이다. 참고로, 시간/조건의 부사절 접속사에서는 현재 시제가 미래를 대신한다.

번역 에어컨 장치가 설치되면, 각 층마다 직원 한 명을 배정해 에어컨 사용을 감독하게끔 해야 한다.

어휘 assign 배정하다 install 설치하다

112 부사 어휘 `고난도`

해설 현재완료 동사를 이루는 has와 been sterilized 사이에 들어갈 부사를 선택하는 문제이다. 과거에 오염되었을지도 모른다(may have been contaminated)는 추정 후에 소독을 완료한 것이므로, '이후, 그 후로'라는 의미의 (A) since가 정답이다. 참고로, since가 have와 p.p. 사이에 들어가면 '특정 시점 이후에'라는 뜻을 나타낸다. (B) so가 '그래서'라는 뜻의 접속사로 쓰이려면 has 앞에 들어가야 하고, (C) yet의 경우 빈칸 위치에 들어가려면 앞에 부정어가(eg. No + 주어 + has + yet + been) 있어야 한다. (D) enough는 부사로 쓰일 때 동사/형용사/부사 뒤에 와야 한다.

번역 위험한 화학물질에 오염되었을 수도 있으므로 이후 실험실은 소독되었다.

어휘 laboratory 실험실 contaminate 오염시키다 hazardous 위험한 chemical substance 화학물질 sterilize 소독하다

113 부사 자리 _ 동명사 수식

해설 전치사 for의 목적어인 동명사 maneuvering을 수식하는 부사 자리이다. 따라서 '능숙하게, 솜씨 있게'라는 의미의 (D) skillfully가 정답이다. maneuvering을 현재분사로 볼 경우 구조적으로는 명사 (A) skills도 빈칸에 들어갈 수 있지만, 토론을 중재하고 진행하는 주체는 기술이 아닌 사회자이므로, 문맥상 적절치 않다. (B) skilled는 동사/과거분사, (C) skillful은 형용사로 품사상 빈칸에 들어갈 수 없다.

번역 패널 사회자는 몇 가지 어려운 주제를 다루면서 토론을 능숙하게 이끌어 높이 평가 받았다.

어휘 moderator 사회자 praise for ~으로 높이 평가 받다 maneuver (교묘히, 잘) 조정하다, 처리하다

114 전치사 어휘 `고난도`

해설 $100을 목적어로 취하는 전치사 자리인데, 문맥을 살펴보면 고정 성과급(a flat commission)이 $100에 해당한다는 내용이다. 따라서 동격 관계를 나타낼 수 있는 (B) of가 정답이다.

번역 비고르 커뮤니케이션즈 영업사원들은 판매된 케이블 패키지당 100달러의 고정 성과급을 받는다.

어휘 representative 직원 flat 고정의, 균일한 commission 성과급, 수수료

115 명사 자리 _ 동사의 주어

해설 Travel과 함께 복합명사를 이루어, 등위접속사 and가 연결하는 두 동사 will ~ be processed와 are의 주어 역할을 하는 자리이다. 따라서 are와 수가 일치하는 복수명사가 들어가야 하므로, (C) reimbursements가 정답이다.

번역   출장비 상황은 여행에서 돌아온 뒤에만 처리되며 경영진의 승인 여부에 달려 있다.

어휘   process 처리하다   contingent ~에 달려 있는
managerial 경영진의   approval 승인   reimburse 상환하다
reimbursement 상환

116 전치사 어휘

해설   '가스턴 테크와의 오랜 관계(our longstanding relationship with Garston Tech)'는 가스턴 테크가 앱 개발에 중요한 역할을 하게 될 것이라는 판단의 근거가 된다. 따라서 '~을 고려하면, 감안하면'이라는 의미의 (A) Given이 정답이다.

번역   가스턴 테크와의 오랜 관계를 감안하면, 새로운 애플리케이션을 개발하는 데 가스턴 테크가 중요한 역할을 하게 된다는 건 놀라운 일이 아니다.

어휘   longstanding 오래 지속된   it is no surprise 놀라운 일이 아니다, 당연하다   notwithstanding ~에도 불구하고   beyond ~를 넘어서
in place of ~ 대신에

117 부사절 접속사 _ 어휘

해설   빈칸 앞절에서는 고객에게 프런트 데스크로 전화를 하라고 권하고 있고, 뒷절에서는 전화를 해야 하는 경우를 언급하고 있다. 따라서 접속사 whenever처럼 쓰여 '~할 때면 언제든지, 언제나'라는 의미를 나타내는 (C) anytime이 정답이다. 참고로, anytime은 부사이지만 'at any time'을 뜻하며 의미상 명사를 포함하고 있기 때문에 뒤에 관계부사 when이 생략된 형태로 쓰인다고 볼 수 있다.

번역   부노드 호텔 고객들은 서비스가 필요할 때면 언제든지 프런트 데스크에 전화해도 된다.

어휘   patron 고객   be encouraged to ~하도록 권유 받다, ~하는 것이 좋다   as though 마치 ~인 것처럼

118 형용사 자리 _ 주격 보어 [고난도]

해설   명사 symptoms를 수식하는 주격 관계사절에서 연결 동사 prove와 함께 쓰여 주격 보어 역할을 하는 자리이다. 따라서 특정 증상(symptoms)이 다른 약물에(to other medications) 보이는 반응을 묘사하는 형용사가 들어가야 하므로, '내성이 있는, ~에 잘 견디는'이라는 의미의 (A) resistant가 정답이다. (D) resistible은 '(힘·유혹 등이) 저항할 수 있을 만한'이라는 뜻으로 문맥상 어색하다.

번역   임상시험 결과에 따르면, 이 약은 다른 약물에는 내성이 있는 증상을 치료할 수 있다.

어휘   clinical trial 임상시험   symptom 증상   medication 약물
resist 견디다

119 동사 어휘 [고난도]

해설   목적어 considerable influence와 어울리는 동사를 선택하는 문제이다. 장 씨의 디자인 스타일이 후대 건축가들에게(over later generations of architects) 상당한 영향력을 끼쳤다는 내용이 자연스러우므로, '가하다, (영향력 등을) 행사하다'라는 의미의 (D) exerted가 정답이다.

번역   비록 생전에는 인기가 없었지만, 장 씨의 독특한 디자인 스타일은 후대 건축가들에게 상당한 영향을 끼쳤다.

어휘   considerable 상당한   influence 영향   architect 건축가
invest 투자하다   confer (자격을) 부여하다   dominate 지배하다

120 동사 어형 _ 분사 구문 _ 태 [고난도]

해설   빈칸이 부사절 접속사 when 뒤에 있으므로, 절에서 축약된 형태인 분사가 들어갈 수 있다. 부사절에서 생략된 주어 they(=customers)는 너무 많은 옵션(too many options)을 제공받는 대상이므로, 수동의 의미를 내포한 과거분사 (B) offered가 정답이 된다.

번역   대체로 고객들은 선택할 수 있는 옵션이 너무 많으면 결정하는 데 어려움을 겪는다.

어휘   in general 대체로   struggle with ~하는 데 어려움을 겪다

121 부사절 접속사 자리 _ 어휘

해설   두 개의 완전한 절을 연결하는 접속사 자리로, 보기에서 (A) as much as, (B) after, (D) in case 중 하나를 선택해야 한다. 해당 절이 라텍스 페인트를 사용할 수 있는 조건을 나타내고 있으므로, '표면에 초벌 페인트가 한 겹 도포된 후에만'이라는 내용이 되어야 자연스럽다. 따라서 only와 결합해 '~한 후에만' 이라는 뜻을 나타내는 (B) after가 정답이다. 참고로, only after가 문장 앞에 올 경우, 뒤따르는 절의 주어와 동사는 도치된다.

번역   아무것도 없는 표면에 소건 브랜드의 초벌 페인트가 한 겹 도포된 후에만 소건 라텍스 페인트를 사용할 수 있다.

어휘   primer 초벌 도료   apply 도포하다   bare 아무것도 없는, 맨

122 명사 어휘

해설   작지만 잘 정돈된 공간에서 선보이는 건강 관련 제품들(wellness products)의 가짓수가 만족스럽다(satisfying)는 내용의 문장이다. 따라서 「an array of 명사」의 형태로 '다수의, 일련의'라는 의미를 나타내는 (A) array(모음, 무리)가 정답이다.

번역   스페셜티 헬스 앤 코스메틱 마트는 작지만 잘 정돈된 공간에서 만족스러운 건강 관련 제품 다수를 선보인다.

어휘   wellness 건강   well-organized 잘 정돈된   substitute 대용물
expectation 예상   outcome 결과

123 형용사 어휘 [고난도]

해설   도치된 주어 its effectiveness at keeping data secure의 주격 보어 역할을 하는 형용사를 선택하는 문제이다. 소프트웨어를 구매한 여러 가지 이유 중(among the reasons) '데이터 보안 유지에 효과적인 것'이 가장 큰 비중을 차지했다는 내용이 되어야 자연스럽다. 따라서 '주된, 주요한'이라는 의미의 (A) Primary가 정답이다. 참고로, 「among the + 복수명사」 앞에는 primary, chief와 같이 돋보이는 대상을 묘사하는 형용사가 자주 온다.

번역   프랭클린 서점이 이 소프트웨어를 구매한 주된 이유는 데이터 보안 유지에 효과적이기 때문이었다.

어휘   informative 유익한   productive 생산적인   selective 선별하는

124 부사 자리

해설 Ms. Nakano가 주어, is가 동사, the hardest-working executive가 주격 보어인 완전한 문장이다. 따라서 빈칸에는 문장 구성에 영향을 미치지 않는 부사가 들어가야 하므로, '세평에 의하면, 평판에 따르면'이라는 의미의 (D) reputedly가 정답이다.

번역 나카노 씨는 시바타 엔지니어링에서 가장 열심히 일하는 임원으로 통한다.

어휘 executive 임원　reputation 평판　reputable 평판이 좋은　repute 평하다; 평판

125 형용사 어휘

해설 주어 it(=the outdoor summer exhibition "Rock Art")을 보충 설명하는 형용사를 선택하는 문제이다. 1회성 전시회의 인기(popularity)가 가져온 결과(has led)를 나타내는 문장이므로, 공원과에서 해당 전시회를 상설화 할 수 있는지 검토하고 있다는 내용이 되어야 자연스럽다. 따라서 '상설의, 영구적인'이라는 의미의 (C) permanent가 정답이다.

번역 야외 여름 전시회 '록 아트'가 인기를 얻자 공원과에서는 상설화가 가능한지 검토하고 있다.

어휘 exhibition 전시(회)　feasible 실현 가능한　mandatory 의무의　abundant 풍부한

126 가정법 과거완료 _ 태 [고난도]

해설 주어인 Techmart의 동사 자리이다. If가 이끄는 절의 동사가 had received이므로, 과거 사실의 반대 상황을 가정하는 가정법 과거완료 구문(「If+주어+had+p.p. ~, 주어+조동사의 과거+have+p.p. ~」)임을 알 수 있다. 따라서 보기에서 (C) would have decided와 (D) would have been decided 중 하나를 선택해야 하는데, 테크마트는 계약을 결정하는 주체이므로, 능동태 동사인 (C) would have decided가 정답이 된다.

번역 만약 우리의 최신 V2 커피 메이커 시제품이 제품 체험단에게 높은 점수를 받았더라면, 테크마트는 우리와 장기 계약을 맺기로 결정했을 것이다.

어휘 prototype 시제품　long-term 장기적인　contract 계약

127 전치사 자리 _ 어휘

해설 명사 the self-check-in kiosks를 목적어로 취하는 전치사 자리로, (B) together with와 (D) thanks to 중 하나를 선택해야 한다. 무인 탑승 수속대는 서비스 카운터 대기 시간을 줄인(Wait times ~ have been cut in half) 요인이라고 볼 수 있으므로, '~ 덕분에'라는 의미의 (D) thanks to가 정답이 된다. 참고로, kiosks와 it 사이에는 목적격 관계대명사(which/that)가 생략되어 있다.

번역 최근 도입한 무인 탑승 수속대 덕분에 스카이스피어 항공의 서비스 카운터 대기 시간이 절반으로 줄었다.

어휘 self-check-in kiosk 무인 탑승 수속대　recently 최근　introduce 도입하다

128 부사 어휘 [고난도]

해설 빈칸을 포함한 that절이 회의 참가자들의 불만(displeased)을 유발한 원인을 설명하고 있다. 워크숍 진행 일정(scheduled ~ to take place)과 관련하여 불만을 표현할만한 상황은 두 개 뿐인 워크숍이 같은 시간대에 열려서 참가 기회가 제한되는 것이다. 따라서 '동시에'라는 의미의 (B) simultaneously가 정답이다.

번역 일부 회의 참석자들은 주최측이 두 개 뿐인 통계 관련 워크숍을 동시에 열리도록 잡은 것에 불만이었다.

어휘 participant 참석자　organizer 주최측　statistics 통계(학)　identically 동일하게　intentionally 고의로　adversely 불리하게, 반대로

129 접속사 자리 _ 도치 [고난도]

해설 완전한 두 절을 연결하는 접속사 자리인데, 빈칸 뒤에 오는 절이 「조동사(do)+주어(they)+동사원형(receive)」의 구조로 도치되어 있다. 따라서 빈칸에는 부정의 의미를 내포한 접속사가 들어가야 하므로, (A) nor가 정답이다.

번역 그 블로그에서 사용되는 사진의 작가는 이름이 밝혀지지 않으며, 기고에 대한 보상도 받지 않는다.

어휘 compensation 보상　contribution 기여, 기고(물)

130 동사 어휘 [고난도]

해설 명사 the system을 목적어로 취하는 동사 자리로, 빈칸을 포함한 to부정사구는 주격 보어로서 임시직 회계사에게 배정된 임무(The next task assigned to the interim accountant)를 설명하고 있다. 회계사가 자금 지원 시스템을 대상으로 할 법한 일을 나타내야 하므로, '점검하다, 정비하다'라는 의미의 (B) overhaul이 정답이다.

번역 임시직 회계사에게 배정된 다음 과제는 연구 프로젝트에 자금을 지원하는 시스템을 점검하는 것이다.

어휘 assign 배정하다　interim 임시의, 잠정적인　accountant 회계사　fund 자금을 대다　grant 주다, 승인하다　deduct 공제하다　experiment 실험하다

PART 6

131-134 이메일

발신: 테레사 예이츠
수신: 어마 심즈
제목: 그리엘 완구 프로젝트 팀
날짜: 9월 2일

안녕하세요 어마,

요청하신 대로, 제가 은퇴하면 수석 엔지니어들 중 누가 그리엘 완구 팀장으로 저를 대신해야 할지 생각해 봤어요. 필요하다면 카렌이 그 일을 할 수도 있겠지만, 저는 트레버를 추천해요. 공학에 대한 이해도는 카렌이 **131 더 우수할 지도** 모르지만, 언제나 명확하게 의사소통이 되는 건 아니에요. 의사소통은 관리하는 데 있어서 매우 중요하죠. 반면에 트레버는 상당한 공학 노하우를 가지고 있는데, 뛰어난 대인관계 기술로 이를 **132 넓히고 있어요**. 제 생각에는 훌륭한 프로젝트 팀장이 **133 될 것 같아요.**

결정을 내리기 위해 더 많은 정보가 필요하거나, 제 추천에 대해 직접 만나서 상의하고 싶으면 알려주세요. **134**전 업무를 마무리하느라 일주일 내내 사무실에 있을 거예요.

– 테레사

어휘 request 요청하다 replace 대신하다 retire 은퇴하다 probably 아마도 recommendation 추천 grasp 이해 decent 괜찮은, 상당한 outstanding 뛰어난 interpersonal 대인관계의 in person 직접[몸소]

131 형용사 어휘

해설 주어인 Karen's grasp of engineering을 보충 설명하는 형용사 자리이다. 앞 문장에서 카렌과 트레버를 비교 대상으로 제시했고, but 뒤에 오는 절에서 카렌의 부족한 점(she doesn't always communicate clearly)을 언급했다. 따라서 해당 절은 카렌의 이해도가 트레버보다 낮다는 내용이 되어야 자연스러우므로, '더 우수한, 우위의'라는 의미의 (A) superior이 정답이다.

어휘 urgent 긴급한 maximum 최대의 eager 갈망하는

132 동사 어휘 고난도

해설 주어 Trevor의 동사 자리로, 그의 뛰어난 대인관계 기술(outstanding interpersonal skills)이 공학 노하우(engineering know-how)에 미치는 긍정적인 영향을 나타내야 자연스럽다. 따라서 '증폭시키다, 넓히다'라는 의미의 (B) amplifies가 정답이다.

어휘 prioritize 우선시하다 assess 평가하다 designate 지정하다

133 동사 어형 _ 시제

해설 주어 he 뒤에 오는 동사 자리이다. 예이츠 씨가 자신의 후임자로 트레버를 추천하며 그가 좋은 프로젝트 팀장이 될 것이라고 예측하는 내용이므로, 미래 상황을 상상/예측할 때 쓰이는 (B) would be가 정답이다.

134 문맥에 맞는 문장 고르기 고난도

번역 (A) 그리고 이 흥미진진한 기회에 다시 한 번 감사 드려요.
(B) 전 특별히 선호하는 사람은 없으니 당신 마음에 드는 사람으로 고르세요.
(C) 전 업무를 마무리하느라 일주일 내내 사무실에 있을 거예요.
(D) 다루어야 할 소소한 사항이 몇 가지 더 있을 뿐이에요.

해설 앞 문장에서 예이츠 씨가 자신이 추천한 사람에 대해 직접 만나 상의하고 싶으면 알려달라(Please let me know ~ if you would like to discuss my recommendation in person)고 했으므로, 빈칸에도 이와 관련된 내용이 들어가야 자연스럽다. 따라서 자신의 일정을 언급하며 이번 주 내내 언제든 사무실에서 만날 수 있음을 암시한 (C)가 정답이다. 참고로, 첫 번째 단락에서 예이츠 씨가 트레버를 추천한다(Trevor is my recommendation)고 했으므로, 특별히 선호하는 사람이 없다(I have no particular preference)고 한 (B)는 적절하지 않다.

어휘 preference 선호, 선호하는 사람[것] wrap up 마무리하다 assignment 업무, 과업

135-138 보도자료

멜라핀 교향악단
언론 홍보국

5월부터 멜라핀 교향악단은 "음악 공유하기" 프로그램에서 매달 특별 콘서트를 연주하고 인터넷으로 실시간 중계할 예정이다.

이 프로그램은 음악에 대한 접근성을 높이는 데 헌신하는 단체인 오카포 재단의 보조금으로 가능해졌다. **135**그 밖의 활동으로는 장애아들을 위한 음악 캠프 등이 있다. 음악 공유하기는 주로 거동에 문제가 있는 사람들을 위한 것이지만, 일반 대중에게도 공개될 예정이다.

이 콘서트가 열리는 **136**동안 실시간으로 교향악단 웹사이트 www.melapin-symphony.com 페이지를 통해 무료로 볼 수 있다. **137**단, 해당 페이지에 접속하려면 방문자는 회원 계정을 만들고 로그인해야 할 것이다.

교향악단 단원들과 관계자들은 오카포 재단과 협력하게 되어 기쁘게 생각한다. 다이키 사노 감독은 이렇게 말했다. "우리 음악을 더 많은 사람들과 공유할 수 있는 기회는 **138**영광이죠. 정말 감사합니다."

어휘 livestream 실시간으로 방송하다[시청하다] grant 보조금 organization 단체, 조직 dedicated to ~에 헌신하는, 전념하는 access 접근성; 접근[접속]하다 mobility 이동, 거동 viewable 시청할 수 있는 be required to ~해야 한다 collaborate 협업하다 grateful 감사해 하는

135 문맥에 맞는 문장 고르기 고난도

번역 (A) 그 밖의 활동으로는 장애아들을 위한 음악 캠프 등이 있다.
(B) 기금으로 심지어 인터넷을 통해 콘서트를 생중계할 수 있게 된다.
(C) 나중에는 멜라핀 심포니 홀에 휠체어 공간도 추가되었다.
(D) 이전에는 공연 도중 관객이 무대 뒤에 갈 수 없었다.

해설 빈칸 앞에서 '음악 공유하기' 프로그램이 음악에 대한 접근성을 높이는 데 (increasing access to music) 헌신하는 오카포 재단의 보조금으로 가능해졌다고 했고, 뒤에서 이 프로그램이 주로 거동에 문제가 있는 사람들 (people with mobility issues)을 위한 것이라고 했으므로, 해당 프로그램이나 오카포 재단에 관한 내용이 빈칸에 들어가야 한다. (A)와 (B) 중에서 하나를 선택해야 하는데, 보조금의 주 용도가 콘서트의 생중계이므로 이 자금으로 '심지어' 생중계까지 가능해진다고 한 (B)는 적절치 않다. 따라서 취지가 유사한 재단의 활동을 언급한 (A)가 정답이다.

어휘 disability 장애 patron 관객, 고객

136 부사절 접속사 _ 어휘

해설 완전한 절(they take place)을 이끄는 접속사 자리로, (B) unless와 (C) as 중 하나를 선택해야 한다. 문맥상 콘서트가 진행되는 동안 실시간으로 웹사이트에서 보는 것이 가능하다(will be viewable ~ on the symphony's Web site)는 내용이 되어야 자연스러우므로, '~할 때, ~하는 동안에'라는 의미의 (C) as가 정답이다.

137 접속부사 고난도

해설 앞 문장에서 콘서트는 교향악단 웹사이트의 페이지를 통해 무료로 볼 수 있다(The concerts will be viewable for free through a page on the symphony's Web site)고 했는데, 빈칸 뒤에서는 해당 페이지

에 접속하려면 회원 계정을 만들고 로그인해야 할 것(visitors may be required to create and log in through a member account in order to access the page)이라며 제약 사항을 언급했다. 따라서 '다만, 하지만'이라는 의미의 (B) However가 정답이다.

어휘   namely 즉, 다시 말해   likewise 또한, 게다가

138 명사 자리 _ 주격 보어   고난도

해설   주어 The opportunity to share our music with more people의 주격 보어 자리로, '음악을 더 많은 사람들과 공유할 수 있는 기회'와 동격 관계를 이루는 명사가 들어가야 자연스럽다. 따라서 '영예, 영광'을 뜻하는 (C) an honor가 정답이다. 참고로, honor가 '예우하다, 영예를 주다'라는 뜻의 타동사로 쓰일 경우 목적어를 취해야 하므로, (B) to honor와 (D) honoring은 빈칸에 들어갈 수 없다. 과거분사인 (A) honored는 '영광으로 생각하는, 영예를 느끼는'이라는 의미로, 사람 명사가 주어로 온다.

139-142 편지

5월 11일

샤히나 싱
보우필드 가 83번지
베닝엄, 영국
BN4 7DA

싱 씨께,

최근에 귀하가 도로 포장의 열악한 상태와 울퉁불퉁한 평판 ¹³⁹**때문에** 타이어가 펑크 난 일을 설명하신 편지를 받았습니다. 편지에서 지적하셨듯이, 댁 인근 지역의 도로와 포장 상태는 꽤 오랫동안 보수가 절실히 필요했습니다. ¹⁴⁰**제가 이 상황을 바로잡는 데 전력을 기울이고 있다는 점 알아주십시오.**

5월 18일부터 작업반원들이 보우필드 가 및 지역 내 다른 거리 몇 군데에 있는 평판을 모두 제거하고 다시 설치할 예정입니다. 이들은 또한 지난 3월 주민회의에서 많은 운전자들이 불평했던 도로에 파인 구멍 역시 고칠 것입니다. 이 소식이 해당 지역에 ¹⁴¹**살고 있는** 귀하와 인근 주민들에게 좋은 소식으로 다가오기를 바랍니다.

차 사고 건에 대해 사과 드리니 받아주시기 바랍니다. 계획된 작업이 앞으로 유사한 ¹⁴²**사고가** 발생하지 않도록 예방하리라 확신합니다.

마이크 듀크
시의회 의원

어휘   describe 설명하다   pavement 포장(한 구역)   flat tyre 펑크 난 타이어   uneven 울퉁불퉁한, 고르지 못한   paving slab (도로 포장용) 평판   desperate 절실한   pothole (도로) 움푹 팬 곳   motorist 운전자   fellow 같은 처지의, 주변의   constituent 주민, 유권자   prevent 예방하다   occur 발생하다

139 전치사 어휘   고난도

해설   명사구 the uneven paving slabs를 목적어로 취하는 전치사 자리이다. '울퉁불퉁한 평판'은 타이어 펑크(the flat tyre)의 원인이므로, '~ 때문에'라는 의미의 (D) due to가 정답이다. 참고로, 'suffered by' 형태로 쓰이려면 suffered 앞에는 문제, by 뒤에는 문제를 겪는 주체가 와야 한다. 따라서 (A) by는 정답이 될 수 없다. (B) following은 시간의 전후 순서,

---

(C) during은 기간을 나타내므로 빈칸에 적절하지 않다.

140 문맥에 맞는 문장 고르기   고난도

번역   (A) 작업이 마침내 완료되었다고 발표하게 되어 뿌듯합니다.
(B) 안타깝게도 도로 수리는 올해 예산에 없습니다.
(C) 제가 이 상황을 바로잡는 데 전력을 기울이고 있다는 점 알아주십시오.
(D) 귀하의 제안을 고려하고 해결책을 찾도록 노력하겠습니다.

해설   빈칸 앞 문장에서 도로 보수가 절실히 필요했다(the roads and pavements in your neighbourhood have been in desperate need of repair for quite some time)고 했고, 뒤에 오는 단락에서는 예정된(Beginning on 18 May) 보수 작업과 관련된 설명을 이어가고 있다. 따라서 문제 해결에 대한 의지를 보여주는 (C)가 빈칸에 들어가야 가장 자연스럽다. 빈칸 뒤에서 예정된 보수 작업을 설명하고 있으므로, (A), (B), (D)는 모두 적절하지 않다.

어휘   unfortunately 안타깝게도   rectify 바로잡다

141 현재분사

해설   전치사 to의 목적어 역할을 하는 명사구 your fellow constituents를 수식하는 자리다. 따라서 보기에서 현재분사 (B) residing(살고 있는)과 형용사 (D) residential(거주의, 주거용의) 중 하나를 선택해야 한다. 싱 씨와 인근 주민들은 현재 지역에 살고 있는 사람들이므로, (B) residing이 정답이다. 참고로, (D) residential은 주로 명사 앞에 온다.

어휘   reside 살다

142 명사 어휘

해설   재발 방지(prevent ~ from occurring in the future)의 대상을 나타내는 명사를 선택해야 한다. 앞 문장에서 싱 씨의 차에 발생한 사고(the incident with your car)를 언급했으므로, 빈칸에도 이와 유사한 의미의 단어가 들어가야 자연스럽다. 따라서 '사고'라는 뜻의 (D) accidents가 정답이다.

어휘   inaccuracy 부정확   misunderstanding 오해   cancelation 취소

143-146 광고

다이아몬드 재봉
로렌스 3번 가 308번지, 555-0184
www.diamondsewing.com

다이아몬드 재봉은 로렌스 주민들의 옷 입은 모습이 ¹⁴³**멋있게** 보이도록 10년 넘게 도와드리고 있습니다. 고객님의 사이즈가 바뀌었든, 새로운 구매품이 딱 맞지 않든, 당사의 재봉 전문가들은 언제나 여러분에게 필요한 수선 서비스를 제공할 준비가 되어 있습니다. ¹⁴⁴**당사는 바지를 줄일 수 있고, 셔츠에 다트를 넣는 등 많은 작업을 할 수 있습니다.**

당사는 ¹⁴⁵**특히** 웨딩드레스, 턱시도, 기타 정장을 전문으로 합니다. 수많은 신부와 신랑이 다이아몬드 재봉이 수선한 옷을 입고 식장을 걸었습니다.

해지고 닳거나 찢어진 옷이 있나요? 당사는 전문 ¹⁴⁶**수선** 서비스도 제공합니다!

아끼는 청바지나 빈티지 재킷을 버리기 전에 무료 상담을 받으러 오세요. 월요일부터 금요일은 오전 9시부터 오후 5시까지, 그리고 토요일은 오전 9시부터 오후 12시까지 문을 엽니다.

어휘 sewing 재봉 purchase 구매(품) fit 맞다 alteration 수선 specialize in ~를 전문으로 하다 formalwear 정장 frayed 해진 worn 낡은 rip 찢다 expert 전문적인 consultation 상담

143 형용사 자리 _ 주격 보어 _ 현재분사

해설 「helping+목적어(the people of Lawrence)+목적격 보어(look ~)」의 구조에서 look의 주체인 the people of Lawrence를 보충 설명하는 형용사 자리이다. 따라서 보기에서 (B) stunned(깜짝 놀란)와 (C) stunning(멋진) 중 하나를 선택해야 하는데, '주민들이 멋지게 보이도록'이라는 내용이 되어야 자연스러우므로, (C) stunning이 정답이다.

144 문맥에 맞는 문장 고르기

번역 (A) 오늘날 비즈니스 전문가에게는 딱 맞는 정장이 필수입니다.
(B) 주문은 당사 웹사이트를 통해서 온라인만으로도 가능합니다.
(C) 저희가 보유한 디자인 견본 컬렉션 중에서 선택하기만 하세요.
(D) 당사는 바지를 줄일 수 있고, 셔츠에 다트를 넣는 등 많은 작업을 할 수 있습니다.

해설 빈칸 앞 문장에서 재봉 전문가들이 언제나 고객에게 필요한 수선 서비스를 제공할 준비가 되어 있다(our sewing specialists are always ready to make the alterations you need)고 했고, 뒤에서는 수선 전문 분야를 나열했다. 따라서 빈칸에도 수선 서비스와 관련된 내용이 들어가야 자연스러우므로, (D)가 정답이다.

어휘 entirely 온전히 template 모형 dart 다트 (몸에 붙도록 솔기를 좁히는 재봉 기법)

145 부사 어휘

해설 다이아몬드 재봉에서 제공하는 수선 서비스 중 전문으로 하는 분야들 (specialize in wedding gowns, tuxedoes, and other formalwear)을 나열한 문장이다. 따라서 '특히'라는 의미의 (D) particularly가 빈칸에 들어가야 자연스럽다.

어휘 ideally 이상적으로 recently 최근 exceedingly 대단히

146 명사 어휘 [고난도]

해설 다이아몬드 재봉에서 제공하는 전문적인 서비스를 나타내는 명사를 선택해야 한다. 다음 문장에서 아끼는 청바지나 빈티지 재킷을 버리기 전에 무료 상담을 받으러 오라(Come see us ~ before you throw away that beloved pair of jeans or vintage jacket)고 권했으므로, 낡은 의류(frayed, worn or ripped)를 수선하는 서비스도 제공한다는 것을 알 수 있다. 따라서 '수선'이라는 의미의 (A) mending이 정답이다.

어휘 manufacturing 제조(업) laundering 세탁 styling 스타일링, 매만지기

PART 7

147-148 공지

> **공지**
>
> [147]이 실내용 자전거에 달린 모니터가 아령을 손에 든 채 사용한 사람에 의해 산산조각이 난 것으로 보입니다. 보안 카메라를 보면 그 일을 했음직한 사람은 회원이 우리 센터에 들어올 때 따라 들어온 비회원이었다는 것 정도만 알 수 있으므로, 확신할 수는 없습니다. [148]제발 다른 사람이 함께 건물에 들어오지 못하게 하십시오. 누군가 카드를 분실했거나 가져오는 것을 잊어버렸다고 주장하며 같이 들어가자고 하면, 밖에서 기다리라고 하고 프런트에 알려 주십시오. 감사합니다.
> —하운슬러 피트니스 센터 경영진

어휘 stationary bicycle (고정된) 실내용 자전거 shatter 산산조각 내다 hand weight 아령 security camera 보안 카메라 claim 주장하다

147 추론 / 암시 [고난도]

번역 공지는 어디에서 보이겠는가?
(A) 손상된 기계 위
(B) 건물 출입구 외부
(C) 훈련용 웨이트 옆
(D) 접수 구역 뒤

해설 초반부에서 '이 실내용 자전거에 달린 모니터가 산산조각이 났다(the monitor on this stationary bicycle was shattered)'고 하며 지시형용사 this를 사용했으므로, 공지가 손상된 운동기구 위에 있을 것으로 추론할 수 있다. 따라서 (A)가 정답이다.

▶▶ Paraphrasing 지문의 shattered → 정답의 damaged
지문의 stationary bicycle
→ 정답의 machinery

148 세부 사항

번역 공지를 읽은 사람들이 요청 받은 일은?
(A) 보안 카메라 가로막지 않기
(B) 한 번에 한 가지 유형의 장비 사용
(C) 카드 분실 즉시 신고
(D) 시설 내 타인 출입 허용하지 않기

해설 중반부에서 센터 출입 시 다른 사람이 함께 건물에 들어오지 못하게 할 것 (Please do not allow other people to enter the building with you)을 요청했으므로, (D)가 정답이다.

어휘 refrain from ~하는 것을 삼가다

▶▶ Paraphrasing 지문의 do not allow other people to enter the building → 정답의 Refrain from letting others into a facility

149-150 문자 메시지

알렉스 화이트, 오후 3시 9분

149브라티슬라바, 쉬는 날 귀찮게 해서 미안한데요, 잠깐 물어볼 게 있어요. 장갑이 거의 다 떨어졌어요. 지난주에 주문하지 않았나요?

브라티슬라바 코박, 오후 3시 11분

예, 어제 들어왔는데 포장을 풀 기회가 없었어요. 제 책상 위에 있는 상자 안에 있어요.

알렉스 화이트, 오후 3시 13분

네, 보이네요. 고마워요! 오늘 예약 없이 방문한 환자가 몇 명 있어서 예상보다 빨리 장갑이 떨어졌어요.

브라티슬라바 코박, 오후 3시 14분

그렇군요. 얼마나 많이 가져갔는지, 누구를 위한 것인지 기록이 필요해요.

알렉스 화이트, 오후 3시 16분

150아, 그냥 월요일에 얘기해도 될까요? 이미 접수 창구에 돌아왔어요.

브라티슬라바 코박, 오후 3시 17분

미안하지만 그러기엔 너무 멀어요. 150그냥 접착식 메모지에 써서 제 방문에 붙여주실래요? 우리 둘 다 잊어버릴 위험은 감수하지 않는 게 좋겠어요.

알렉스 화이트, 오후 3시 18분

그럼요, 그렇게 할게요. 다시 한 번 고마워요, 브라티슬라바.

어휘 unpack 포장을 풀다 walk-in 예약 없이 방문하는 patient 환자 sticky note 접착식 메모지 risk 위험을 감수하다 either (부정문에서) 둘 다

---

149 추론 / 암시

번역 코박 씨에 대한 설명 중 가장 사실에 가까운 것은?
(A) 일부 물품을 다 써버렸다.
(B) 개인 사무실이 없다.
(C) 볼일을 보러 나갔다.
(D) 현재 근무 중이 아니다.

해설 화이트 씨가 오후 3시 9분 메시지에서 코박 씨에게 쉬는 날 귀찮게 해서 미안하다(I'm sorry to bother you on your day off)고 했으므로, 코박 씨가 현재 근무 중이 아님을 추론할 수 있다. 따라서 (D)가 정답이다.

어휘 use up 다 쓰다 go on an errand 볼일을 보러 가다

> ▶▶ Paraphrasing 지문의 on your day off
> → 정답의 not currently on duty

150 의도 파악

번역 오후 3시 17분에 코박 씨가 "그러기엔 너무 멀어요"라고 쓴 의도는?
(A) 수치가 잘못 계산되었다고 주장하고 있다.
(B) 문서의 수정 사항을 비판하고 있다.
(C) 장소 찾기를 거부하고 있다.
(D) 일을 미루자는 제안에 반대하고 있다.

해설 화이트 씨가 오후 3시 16분 메시지에서 장갑 사용 기록을 월요일에 말해줘도 되는지(can I just tell you on Monday?) 물었는데, 이에 대해 코박 씨가 그건 너무 멀었으니 문에 메모를 남겨달라고 요청하며 둘 다 잊어

버릴 위험은 감수하지 않는 게 좋겠다(I'd rather not risk either of us forgetting)고 덧붙였다. 즉, 잊어버리기 전에 미루지 말고 처리하자는 의도로 한 말이므로, (D)가 정답이다.

어휘 figure 수치 miscalculate 잘못 계산하다 modification 수정 refuse 거부하다 oppose 반대하다

151-153 동의서

티카드 사

시장조사 참여 동의서 양식

18세부터 34세까지 남성을 대상으로 한 이번 연구에 참여하기로 동의해 주셔서 감사합니다. 151두 가지 버전의 얼굴용 면도기 텔레비전 광고를 보시고 각각에 대한 의견을 말해달라는 요청을 받으실 겁니다. 전 과정은 약 30분 정도 소요됩니다.

아래 항목을 읽고, 옆에 있는 상자에 성함의 첫 글자를 쓰셔서 동의한다는 것을 명시해 주십시오.

• 152연구 중 응답이 녹음되는 것과 개인 식별 정보가 제거된 녹음 □ 파일이 티카드 내부에서 사용되는 것에 동의합니다.

• 연구에 참여하는 것을 그만두고 싶다면 연구진에게 알려 언제든 □ 지 그만둘 수 있음을 이해합니다.

• 153이후 이 연구의 내용에 대해 이야기하거나 실물 또는 디지털 □ 자료를 만들지 않겠습니다.

• 이 연구에 대해 갖고 있는 의문은 모두 연구원들에게 물어보았 □ 습니다.

참가자명: _____   서명 _____

날짜: _____

어휘 consent 동의, 허락; 동의[허락]하다 participate in ~에 참여하다 facial razor 얼굴용 면도기 entire 전체의 process 과정 approximately 약 adjacent 옆에 있는, 가까운 indicate 나타내다, 명시하다 response 응답 identifying information (개인) 식별 정보 internally 내부적으로 physical 실물의 material 자료

---

151 세부 사항

번역 참가자들은 연구를 위해 무엇을 할 것인가?
(A) 시험적으로 제품사용
(B) 두 가지 디자인 비교
(C) 습관에 대해 설명
(D) 동영상 시청

해설 첫 번째 단락에서 참가자들이 두 가지 버전의 얼굴용 면도기 텔레비전 광고를 보고(You will be shown two versions of a television advertisement) 의견을 말해야 된다고 했으므로, (D)가 정답이다.

어휘 compare 비교하다

> ▶▶ Paraphrasing 지문의 be shown two versions of a television advertisement
> → 정답의 Watch some video clips

152 세부 사항

번역 양식에 따르면 연구 후에 어떤 일이 있는가?
(A) 데이터는 익명으로 처리된다.
(B) 일부 녹음은 파기한다.
(C) 후속 질문이 발송된다.
(D) 연구진이 참가자들의 질문에 답할 것이다.

해설 세 번째 단락의 첫 번째 항목에서 개인 식별 정보가 제거된 녹음 파일이 티카드 내부에서 사용되는 것에(the use of these recordings, with my identifying information removed, internally by Ticard) 동의를 구하고 있으므로, 데이터가 익명으로 처리될 것임을 알 수 있다. 따라서 (A)가 정답이다.

어휘 anonymize 익명으로 하다

▶▶ **Paraphrasing** 지문의 with my identifying information removed → 정답의 The data will be anonymized

153 세부 사항

번역 참가자는 무엇을 하기로 동의해야 하는가?
(A) 정직하게 의견 말하기
(B) 연구 관련 정보 기밀로 유지하기
(C) 이전 연구 참여 여부 공개하기
(D) 일정 기간 양식 사본 보관하기

해설 참가자는 연구 내용에 대해 이야기하거나 실물 또는 디지털 자료를 만들지 않겠다(I will not speak about or create any physical or digital materials about the contents of this study)는 세 번째 항목에 동의해야 한다. 따라서 (B)가 정답이다.

어휘 confidential 기밀의 disclose 공개하다 retain 가지다, 보유하다

▶▶ **Paraphrasing** 지문의 not speak about or create any physical or digital materials about the contents of this study → 정답의 Keep information about the study confidential

154-155 이메일

발신: 코디 맥네어
수신: 사만다 넬슨
제목: 회신: 느린 인터넷 속도
날짜: 3월 29일

안녕하세요 사만다,

154지난주에 받으신 회사 제공 노트북의 인터넷 속도가 느리다니 유감이에요. 자택 인터넷 서비스가 문제가 아니라고 하신 말씀 믿어요. 회사 노트북에서 연결 속도가 느리다고 보고한 게 당신이 처음이 아니데다가, 상황을 살펴본 결과, 문제는 우리가 사용 중인 가상 사설망(VPN)이라는 점이 분명해졌거든요. VPN은 회사가 아닌 다른 장소에서 우리 네트워크에 보안 연결을 제공하는 중요한 역할을 하고 있어 제거되면 안돼요. 현재 속도 문제가 적을 것 같은 다른 VPN을 알아보고 있어요. 제공자를 바꾸기로 결정하면 당연히 알려드릴 겁니다.

아쉽지만 지금 우리가 해줄 수 있는 건 이 설명뿐이에요. 155언급하신 생산성 문제와 관련해서, 얼마든지 이 이메일을 상관에게 전달하셔도 됩니다. 그리고 혹시

더 궁금한 게 있으면 알려주세요.

코디 맥네어
정보 기술부

어휘 company-provided 회사에서 제공한 claim 주장하다 virtual 가상의 provider 제공자[업체] explanation 설명 supervisor 상관, 관리자 in reference to ~와 관련하여 productivity 생산성 concern 문제, 우려사항

154 추론 / 암시 　 고난도

번역 넬슨 씨에 관한 설명 중 가장 사실에 가까운 것은?
(A) 네트워크 일부에 접근할 수 있는 권한이 없다.
(B) 어떤 장비를 교체해 달라고 요청했다.
(C) 사용 설명서를 읽지 않았다.
(D) 현재 원격으로 일하고 있다.

해설 첫 번째 단락에서 넬슨 씨에게 회사 제공 노트북의 인터넷 속도가 느린 점(you're experiencing slow Internet speeds with the company-provided laptop)에 대해 유감을 표한 후, 자택 인터넷 서비스가 문제가 아니라는(the problem is not your home Internet service) 넬슨 씨의 주장을 믿는다고 했다. 따라서 그녀가 현재 재택근무를 하고 있다고 추론할 수 있으므로, (D)가 정답이다.

어휘 authorize 권한을 부여하다 replace 교체하다 remotely 원격으로

155 세부 사항

번역 맥네어 씨가 넬슨 씨에게 허락한 일은?
(A) 노트북에서 프로그램 제거
(B) 다른 사람과 메시지 공유
(C) 문제가 재발하면 집으로 연락
(D) 승인된 공급업체 대신 대체 업체 이용

해설 두 번째 단락에서 멕네어 씨는 자신이 쓴 이메일을 얼마든지 상관에게 전달해도 된다(Feel free to forward this e-mail to your supervisor)고 했으므로, (B)가 정답이다.

어휘 uninstall 제거하다 reoccur 재발하다 alternative 대체하는 것

▶▶ **Paraphrasing** 지문의 forward this e-mail to your supervisor → 정답의 Share his message with another person

156-157 공고문

블리자드 하키
기자회견

블리자드 경영진은 새로운 홈구장에서 팀을 승리로 이끌 임무를 맡은 분을 소개해 드릴 수 있게 되어 기쁩니다. 156블리자드 구단주인 돌로레스 이케다 씨가 팀의 신임 단장을 소개하는 기자회견을 진행할 예정입니다. 기자회견은 이케다 씨의 연설, 신임 단장의 연설, 질의응답 시간, 사진 촬영 시간으로 구성됩니다.

장소: 샬라드 경기장 기자실 (1층, 북쪽 입구 근처)
157공간이 제한되어 있으므로 입장권을 확보하려면 기자 신분증을 지참하십시오.

시간:　6월 8일 수요일 오전 11시
　　　10시 45분까지 출석해 착석하십시오.

연락처: 렉스 웰치, 블리자드 언론 홍보 담당자
　　　rex.welch@blizzard-hockey.com

어휘　**management** 경영진　**task** 과업을 맡기다　**general manager** (스포츠 구단) 단장　**press credential** 기자 신분증, 기자 출입증　**ensure** 보장하다, 확보하다　**entry** 입장(권)

156 세부 사항

번역　기자회견에서 무엇이 발표될 예정인가?
　　(A) 하키팀 이전
　　(B) 스포츠 임원 선임
　　(C) 프로 선수와의 계약
　　(D) 새로운 시합 공간 건설 계획

해설　첫 번째 단락에서 블리자드 구단주가 팀의 신임 단장을 소개하는 기자회견을 진행할 예정(owner of the Blizzard, is hosting a press conference to introduce the team's new general manager)이라고 했으므로, (B)가 정답이다.

어휘　**relocation** 이전　**appointment** 선임, 임명

▶▶ **Paraphrasing**　지문의 **to introduce the team's new general manager** → 정답의 **The appointment of a sports executive**

157 추론 / 암시　　고난도

번역　기자회견에 관해 암시된 것은?
　　(A) 기자들에게 우선 입장권을 준다.
　　(B) 시설을 둘러볼 기회가 있을 것이다.
　　(C) 웰치 씨가 이케다 씨 뒤에 발언할 것이다.
　　(D) 홍보용 선물을 나누어 줄 것이다.

해설　기자회견이 열리는 장소(Where)에 관한 설명에서 공간이 제한되어 있으니 입장권을 확보하려면 기자 신분증을 지참하라(Space will be limited, so bring press credentials to ensure entry)고 했으므로, 기자들에게 우선 입장권을 준다고 추론할 수 있다. 따라서 (A)가 정답이다.

어휘　**priority** 우선

▶▶ **Paraphrasing**　지문의 **to ensure entry** → 정답의 **Priority admissioin**

158-160 편지

12월 7일

딕스넷 호텔
선셋 가 1520번지
밴쿠버, 브리티시 컬럼비아 V54 1R9

담당자님께,

[159] 12월 2~4일에 밴쿠버를 방문했을 때 귀사의 호텔에 머물렀는데, 기억에 남는 경험을 나누고 싶어요.

[159] 체류 마지막 날, 공항까지 렌터카를 몰고 가려는데 렌터카 배터리가 방전되었더군요. [160] 렌터카 업체에 연락했는데 직원이 2시간 이내로는 지원을 보낼 수 없다고 했어요. 그러면 비행기를 놓칠 수도 있었어요. [159] 로비에서 휴대전화로 이런 대화를 나눴는데, 다행히 프런트 데스크 직원인 델레이 스콧이 우연히 들었어요. 그는 자신의 차량과 케이블을 이용해 제 렌터카에 시동을 걸어주겠다고 제안했어요. 저는 감사한 마음으로 승낙했고, 그가 흔쾌히 빠른 속도로 작업을 해줘서 제시간에 공항에 도착할 수 있었어요.

여러 가지 측면에서 호텔에 만족했지만, 가장 인상 깊었던 것은 바로 이런 친절한 행동이었어요. [158] 스콧 씨는 도움이 필요한 손님을 돕기 위해 기꺼이 추가로 귀중한 역량을 발휘한 것에 대해 보상을 받을 자격이 있어요. 호텔에 이를 위한 정책이 마련돼 있기를 바라요.

트래비스 퀸

어휘　**memorable** 기억에 남는　**overhear** 우연히 듣다　**jump-start** 다른 차 배터리에 연결해 시동을 걸다　**cheerful** 흔쾌히 하는, 마음에서 우러난　**efficient** 효율적인　**establishment** (호텔·가게 등의) 시설　**impressive** 인상 깊은　**deserve** 자격이 있다　**reward** 보상하다　**supplementary** 추가적인, 보완하는　**in place** ~를 위한 준비가 되어 있는, 마련이 되어 있는

158 주제 / 목적

번역　편지의 주요 목적은?
　　(A) 추가 서비스 제안
　　(B) 시설에 대한 불만 제기
　　(C) 직원 칭찬
　　(D) 정책 세부사항 질문

해설　퀸 씨는 두 번째 단락에서 호텔 직원인 스콧 씨에게 도움을 받았던 상황을 설명한 후, 세 번째 단락에서 그가 보상을 받을 자격이 있다(Mr. Scott deserves to be rewarded for being willing to use his valuable supplementary abilities to help out a guest in need)고 했다. 따라서 직원을 칭찬하기 위한 이메일이라고 볼 수 있으므로, (C)가 정답이다.

어휘　**convey** 주다, 전하다　**praise** 칭찬

159 추론 / 암시　　고난도

번역　스콧 씨는 12월 4일에 무엇을 했겠는가?
　　(A) 배정된 근무 장소에서 잠시 자리를 비웠다.
　　(B) 개인 구역에서 모바일 기기를 충전했다.
　　(C) 투숙객에게 주차된 차량을 옮기라고 요청했다.
　　(D) 공항 웹사이트에서 정보를 검색했다.

해설　첫 번째 단락을 보면 12월 4일은 퀸 씨가 호텔에 머문 마지막 날(I stayed at your hotel ~ on December 2-4)임을 알 수 있다. 두 번째 단락에서 퀸 씨는 이날 렌터카 배터리가 방전되어 어려움을 겪고 있을 때 프런트 데스크 직원인 스콧 씨가 본인의 차량과 케이블을 이용해 렌터카에 시동을 걸어주었고, 덕분에 제시간에 공항에 도착할 수 있었다(his cheerful and efficient work allowed me to arrive at the airport on time)고 했다. 따라서 스콧 씨가 퀸 씨를 돕기 위해 자신의 근무 장소인 프런트 데스크를 잠시 떠났을 것으로 추론할 수 있으므로, (A)가 정답이다.

160 문장 삽입

번역 [1], [2], [3], [4]로 표시된 곳 중에서 다음 문장이 가장 적합한 곳은?
"그러면 비행기를 놓칠 수도 있었어요."
(A) [1]
(B) [2]
(C) [3]
(D) [4]

해설 주어진 문장 앞에서 비행기를 놓칠 만한 상황(This)이 언급되어야 한다. [2] 앞에서 렌터카 회사에 연락했지만 2시간 이내로는 지원을 받을 수 없다는 말을 들었다(their representative said that they would not be able to send assistance for two hours)고 했으므로, 이 뒤에 주어진 문장이 들어가야 자연스럽다. 따라서 (B)가 정답이다.

161-163 구인 공고

직책: 지역 영업사원(파트타임)	**회사명:** 로터노즈 사
근무지: 캘리포니아 주 스톡턴 지역	**공고 게시일:** 10일 전

세부사항: 로터노즈는 가족 소유 식품 제조사로 건강에 신경 쓰는 소비자를 겨냥한 간식을 전문으로 합니다. ^{161(A)}당사 제품은 모두 천연 원료를 80퍼센트 이상 사용해 만듭니다. ^{161(D)}당사는 1,100명이 넘는 직원들이 건강하고 즐겁게 일할 수 있는 회사가 되기 위해 전력을 다하고 있습니다. ^{161(B)}지난해 로터노즈 사는 스톡턴기업협회(SBA)로부터 '웰빙 직장' 상을 받았습니다.

지역 영업사원은 특정 지역의 식료품점에 로터노즈 제품을 납품하는 일을 담당합니다. 그 밖에 필수 업무로는 재고를 점검하고, 매장 선반에 회사 제품이 제대로 갖추어져 있는지 확인하는 것입니다. 로터노즈 제품을 최적의 조합으로 제공하려면 점장들과 정기적으로 소통해야 하므로 훌륭한 소통 능력이 필수입니다.

채용 합격자는 지정된 경로를 따라 22피트짜리 배송 트럭을 운전하게 됩니다. ¹⁶²근무 중에는 태블릿 컴퓨터를 이용해 재고 데이터도 입력합니다. 배정된 근무 시간은 목요일에서 일요일 오후 4시부터 10시까지(주 24시간)입니다.

이 직책에 지원하려면 www.rotunnos.com/jobs를 방문해 설명에 따라 이력서를 업로드하세요. ¹⁶³면접 자격을 얻으려면 지원자는 20분 정도 걸리는 기본 컴퓨터 능력시험에서 일정한 점수를 받아야 합니다.

어휘 route salesperson 지정된 도로 인근 지역 담당의 영업사원 health-conscious 건강에 신경 쓰는, 건강을 염려하는 ingredient 재료 committed to ~에 전념하는 present 수여하다, 주다 specific 특정한 essential 필수의 conduct 수행하다 inventory 재고 stock 재고를 갖추다 interaction 의사 소통 suitable 적절한 successful candidate 합격자 assigned 지정된, 배정된 instruction 설명, 지시 qualify for ~의 자격을 얻다 achieve 달성하다 proficiency 능력

161 사실 관계 확인

고난도

번역 로터노즈 사에 관해 언급되지 않은 것은?
(A) 제품들은 대부분 천연 재료로 제조된다.
(B) 기업 단체에서 인정 받았다.
(C) 정기적으로 다수의 구인 공고를 게시한다.
(D) 1,100명 이상을 고용하고 있다.

해설 첫 번째 단락의 '로터노즈 사의 제품은 모두 천연 원료를 80퍼센트 이상 사용해 만든다(All of our products are made from at least 80% natural ingredients)'에서 (A)를, '로터노즈 사가 스톡턴기업협회로부터 '웰빙 직장' 상을 받았다(Rotunno's, Inc. was presented with a "Workplace Well-being" award from the Stockton Business Association)'에서 (B)를, '1,100명이 넘는 직원들이 건강하고 즐겁게 일할 수 있는 회사가 되기 위해 전력을 다하고 있다(We are committed to making our business a healthy and enjoyable place to work for our more than 1,100 employees)'에서 (D)를 확인할 수 있다. 따라서 언급되지 않은 (C)가 정답이다.

어휘 recognize (상, 표창 등으로) 인정하다

▶▶ **Paraphrasing** 지문의 at least 80% → 보기 (A)의 mostly
지문의 was presented with a "Workplace Well-being" award from the Stockton Business Association → 보기 (B)의 has been recognized by a business group
지문의 more than 1,100 employees → 보기 (D)의 over 1,100 people

162 사실 관계 확인

번역 광고된 직책의 업무로 언급된 것은?
(A) 신규 거래 고객 확보
(B) 무역 박람회에서 전시 준비
(C) 휴대용 장치에 데이터 입력
(D) 상사에게 업데이트 사항 보고

해설 세 번째 단락에서 근무 중 태블릿 컴퓨터를 이용해 재고 데이터를 입력한다(While on duty, the employee will also use a tablet computer to input inventory data)고 했으므로, (C)가 정답이다.

어휘 acquire 확보하다 supervisor 상사, 관리자

▶▶ **Paraphrasing** 지문의 to input inventory data → 정답의 Entering data
지문의 a tablet computer → 정답의 a portable device

163 세부 사항

번역 구직자들이 해야 하는 일은?
(A) 기밀 정보 보호 약속
(B) 전문자격증 사본 제출
(C) 전화 면접 잘하기
(D) 기술력 입증

해설 마지막 단락에서 지원자는 기본 컴퓨터 능력시험에서 일정한 점수를 얻어야 한다(candidates must achieve a certain score in a basic computer proficiency test)고 했으므로, (D)가 정답이다.

▶▶ **Paraphrasing** 지문의 achieve a certain score in a basic computer proficiency test → 정답의 Demonstrate technical skills

Test 10

164-167 광고

해리스&권 그룹

해리스&권 그룹은 고품질의 영어 및 한국어 어학 서비스를 합리적인 가격에 제공하고 있습니다. 서울 중심부에 위치한 당사는 모든 규모의 국내외 및 국제 기업을 도와 소통의 격차를 해소해 왔습니다.

164(B)/(C)당사의 서비스로는 인쇄물과 디지털 자료 번역, 비디오 및 오디오 클립을 전사하는 작업, 대면 회의와 대규모 행사를 위한 통역 등이 있습니다. 164(A)최대 300명의 참가자에게 원활한 통역 음성을 전송할 수 있는 오디오 시스템도 대여합니다.

자동 통번역 소프트웨어는 여전히 오류가 잦아 심각한 혼란을 야기할 수 있으며, 해당 분야에 학위가 있는 사람일지라도 전문 번역가/통역사의 전문성을 신뢰할 수 없는 경우가 많습니다. 165이런 이유로 해리스&권 그룹은 영어와 한국어 모두 모국어 수준으로 유창하게 구사하며 성장한 어학 전문가만 고용합니다. 당사가 생산한 결과물은 오류가 없을 뿐만 아니라, 문화적 뉘앙스를 포착하고 세심하게 전달할 것이라 보장합니다.

당사 웹사이트 www.hkgroup.co.kr을 방문해 절차에 대해 자세히 알아보고, 만족한 고객들의 추천 글을 읽어 보세요. 그러고 나서 해리스&권 그룹에 프로젝트 의뢰를 논의하고 싶으시면 "연락" 코너에 있는 편리한 양식을 이용하세요. 167신뢰할 만한 서비스 비용 견적을 기꺼이 미리 제공하겠습니다. 166또한 공공의 이익을 위해 봉사하는 기관을 대표해 문의하시는 거라면, 비영리 단체를 위한 특별 요금에 대해 문의하세요.

어휘 reasonable 합리적인, 비싸지 않은 assist 돕다 domestic 국내의 translation 번역 transcription 전사, 글로 옮기는 작업 interpretation 통역(된 음성) ensure ~하게 하다, 보장하다 transmission 전송 confusion 혼란 expertise 전문성 unreliable 신뢰할 수 없는 degree 학위 guarantee 보장하다 capture 포착하다 sensitively 세심하게, 민감하게 convey 전달하다 testimonial 추천 글 quote 견적(서) up front 미리 public good 공공의 이익 nonprofit 비영리 단체

164 사실 관계 확인

번역 해리스&권 그룹이 제공하는 서비스로 나열되지 않은 것은?
(A) 전문 장비 대여
(B) 텍스트 언어 변환
(C) 오디오 자료의 서면 원고 제작
(D) 사업에서 문화적 차이에 대한 조언

해설 두 번째 단락의 '원활한 통역 음성을 전송하는 오디오 시스템도 대여한다(We also rent out audio systems that can ensure the smooth transmission of interpretations)'에서 (A)를, '서비스로는 인쇄물과 디지털 자료 번역, 비디오 및 오디오 클립을 전사하는 작업 등이 있다(Our services include translation of printed and digital materials, transcription of video and audio clips)'에서 (B)와 (C)를 확인할 수 있다. 따라서 언급되지 않은 (D)가 정답이다.

어휘 conversion 변환

▶▶ Paraphrasing 지문의 rent out audio systems that can ensure the smooth transmission of interpretations → 보기 (A)의 Lending of specialized equipment

지문의 translation of printed and digital materials → 보기 (B)의 Conversion of the language of a text
지문의 transcription of ~ audio clips → 보기 (C)의 Making a written copy of audio materials

165 사실 관계 확인

번역 해리스&권 그룹 직원들의 특징으로 언급된 것은?
(A) 상당한 경력
(B) 자라면서 2개 국어를 완벽하게 익힐 수 있는 성장 환경
(C) 학과목에 대한 진지한 학문적 연구
(D) 기술에 대한 광범위한 교육

해설 세 번째 단락에서 해리스&권 그룹은 영어와 한국어 모두 외국어 수준으로 유창하게 구사하며 성장한 어학 전문가만 고용한다(Harris & Kwon Group only employs language specialists who grew up using both English and Korean with native fluency)고 했으므로, (B)가 정답이다.

어휘 substantial 상당한 upbringing 자라면서 받은 교육 extensive 광범위한

▶▶ Paraphrasing 지문의 grew up using both English and Korean with native fluency → 정답의 A completely bilingual upbringing

166 추론 / 암시

번역 해리스&권 그룹에 관해 암시된 것은?
(A) 2개국 이상에 지부를 두고 있다.
(B) 특정 분야 기업에 전문으로 서비스를 제공한다.
(C) 사회에 이로운 사업을 하는 고객은 할인해 준다.
(D) 최근 직원 수를 늘렸다.

해설 마지막 단락에서 공공의 이익을 위해 봉사하는 기관을 대표해 문의할 경우, 비영리 단체를 위한 특별 요금에 대해 문의하라(if you are inquiring on behalf of an organization that serves the public good, ask about our special rates for nonprofits)고 했으므로, 이들을 위해 할인을 제공한다고 추론할 수 있다. 따라서 (C)가 정답이다.

어휘 benefit 이롭게 하다

▶▶ Paraphrasing 지문의 our special rates for nonprofits → 정답의 a discount
지문의 an organization that serves the public good → 정답의 clients whose work benefits society

167 세부 사항

번역 광고에 따르면 해리스&권 그룹이 신규 고객을 위해 할 수 있는 일은?
(A) 가격 견적서 미리 제공
(B) 해당 산업의 용어 조사
(C) 임원진이 직접 쓴 추천서 제공
(D) 맞춤형 작업 절차 생성

해설 마지막 단락에서 신뢰할 만한 서비스 비용 견적을 기꺼이 미리 제공하겠다 (We are happy to provide a reliable quote for the cost of our services up front)고 했으므로, (A)가 정답이다.

어휘 estimate 견적서 terminology 용어 reference 추천서 executive 임원 customized 맞춤형의

▶▶ Paraphrasing 지문의 **provide a reliable quote for the cost ~ up front** → 정답의 **Supply a price estimate in advance**

168-171 온라인 채팅

가이 월리스, 오전 11시 24분
모두들 안녕하세요? 귀찮게 해서 미안하지만, 웹사이트에 올릴 이미지를 어디서 구해야 할지 궁금해서요. 우리 블로그에 올릴 최신 게시물을 위해 몇 장 필요해요.

제리 그랜트, 오전 11시 25분
미안해요, 모르겠어요.

사니아 나자르, 오전 11시 26분
마크는 스톡 사진을 다운받을 때 포토필드를 사용했던 것 같아요. ¹⁶⁸마크가 그 사이트 로그인 정보를 주지 않았나요?

가이 월리스, 오전 11시 26분
확인해 볼게요.

가이 월리스, 오전 11시 28분
¹⁶⁸아, 그렇네요, 여기 보여요! 고마워요, 사니아.

피터 첸, 오전 11시 29분
¹⁶⁹잠시 마크 업무를 대신해 보니까 어때요, 가이?

가이 월리스, 오전 11시 30분
힘들어요. 이런 경우가 많이 있었어요. 일을 하는 데 필요한 정보를 구할 수 없거나 분류가 명확하지 않은 거죠.

피터 첸, 오전 11시 31분
지난해 제가 로빈의 직책을 인계 받았을 때도 같은 문제가 있었어요. ¹⁷⁰정말 업무 절차를 좀 더 명확하게 문서화해야 해요. 무엇보다도, 사규집에 그렇게 나와 있잖아요.

가이 월리스, 오전 11시 32분
오 정말요? 몰랐어요.

피터 첸, 오전 11시 33분
대다수 직원이 모르고 있어요. 모두가 시간을 별도로 들여 문서를 만드는 것을 독려하자고 에이미에게 이야기하려고 해요.

제리 그랜트, 오전 11시 34분
좋은 생각이에요. ¹⁷¹그리고 주저하지 말고 우리에게 질문하세요, 가이. 넘겨짚다가 실수하는 것보다는 나으니까요.

가이 월리스, 오전 11시 35분
¹⁷¹고마워요. 정말 감사합니다.

어휘 stock photo 사용권이 대여/판매되는 사진 fill in for 잠시 ~대신 일을 봐주다, ~를 대신하다 available 이용 가능한 label 분류하다, 라벨을 붙이다 document 문서화하다 company handbook 사규집 after all 어쨌든 be aware of 알다, 인지하다 encourage 독려하다 hesitant 망설이는 appreciate 감사하다, 환영하다

168 세부 사항

번역 오전 11시 28분에 월리스 씨가 찾았다고 보고한 것은?
(A) 디지털 이미지 파일
(B) 온라인 기사 초안
(C) 사용자 이름과 암호
(D) 블로그 게시물에 달린 댓글

해설 나자르 씨가 오전 11시 26분 메시지에서 마크가 사이트 로그인 정보를 주지 않았나(Didn't he give you the log-in information for that site?)고 물었고, 이에 대해 월리스 씨가 오전 11시 28분 메시지에서 '여기 보인다(I see it)'며 찾았음을 알렸다. 따라서 (C)가 정답이다.

어휘 draft 초안

▶▶ Paraphrasing 지문의 **the log-in information** → 정답의 **A user name and password**

169 추론 / 암시

번역 월리스 씨에 관해 암시된 것은?
(A) 일시적으로 동료의 업무를 처리하고 있다.
(B) 최근에 채용된 사원이다.
(C) 최근에 휴가에서 돌아왔다.
(D) 이전에는 내부 웹사이트를 알지 못했다.

해설 첸 씨가 오전 11시 29분 메시지에서 월리스 씨에게 잠시 마크 대신 일하는 게 어떤지(How are you finding it filling in for Mark, Guy?) 물었으므로, 월리스 씨가 일시적으로 그의 업무를 처리하고 있다고 추론할 수 있다. 따라서 (A)가 정답이다.

어휘 temporarily 일시적으로 leave of absence 휴가

▶▶ Paraphrasing 지문의 **filling in for Mark** → 정답의 **temporarily handling a colleague's duties**

170 의도 파악 [고난도]

번역 오전 11시 31분에 첸 씨가 "무엇보다도, 사규집에 그렇게 나와 있잖아요"라고 쓴 의도는?
(A) 월리스 씨에게 정보를 알아보라고 지시하고 있다.
(B) 월리스 씨의 업무를 도울 수 없는 이유를 설명하고 있다.
(C) 업무 책임의 중요성을 강조하고 있다.
(D) 회사 정책이 시대에 뒤떨어졌다고 넌지시 암시하고 있다.

해설 첸 씨가 오전 11시 31분 메시지에서 업무 절차를 좀 더 명확하게 문서화해야 한다(We really should be documenting our job processes more clearly)고 한 후, 이렇게 하라고 사규집에 나와 있다는 것을 알리기 위해 덧붙인 말이다. 따라서 업무 절차를 문서화하는 작업의 중요성을 강조하려는 의도로 쓴 메시지라고 추론할 수 있으므로, (C)가 정답이다.

어휘 instruct 지시하다 outdated 시대에 뒤떨어진

171 세부 사항 [고난도]

번역 윌리스 씨는 그랜트 씨에게 무엇에 대해 감사하는가?
(A) 지시가 정확한지 확인해 준 것
(B) 문서 위치를 공유한 것
(C) 과제를 잘못 이해한 일을 양해해 준 것
(D) 불편함을 야기할 수도 있는 것에 대해 안심시킨 것

해설 그랜트 씨는 오전 11시 34분 메시지에서 윌리스 씨에게 주저하지 말고 질문하라(please don't feel hesitant to ask us questions, Guy)고 한 후, 그 편이 넘겨짚다가 실수하는 것보다는 낫다(It's better than guessing and making a mistake)고 덧붙였다. 그랜트 씨가 자신이 불편해 질지도 모르는 상황을 감수하고 언제든 질문해도 괜찮다고 안심시키자 윌리스 씨가 감사하다(I appreciate that)고 했으므로, (D)가 정답이다.

어휘 assignment 과제 reassure 안심시키다

▶▶ **Paraphrasing** 지문의 **to ask us questions** → 정답의 **potentially causing inconvenience**

172-175 기사

〈지역 뉴스 트리뷴〉   10월 22일

바인 하이츠 지구에 있는 3개의 업소, 바크스데일 베이커리, 트리올로 그릴, 레일리 빨래방이 최근 문을 닫았다. [174]발보아 쇼핑몰에도 입점해 있는 지역 체인점인 바크스데일 베이커리는 10월 9일 바인 하이츠 지점을 폐업했다. [172](A)회사 대변인인 브렌다 치우 씨는 다수의 인근 커피전문점들이 제빵류까지 판매 품목을 넓히고 있어 이 지역에서 "경쟁하기가 어려워졌다"고 말했다.

[173]멕시코—일본 퓨전 레스토랑인 트리올로 그릴은 2주째 문이 닫힌 채로 있었으며, 이제 문에는 '임대 가능'이라는 팻말이 걸려 있다. 인기가 많았던 이 식당은 듀 가 56번지에서 영업해 오고 있었다. [173]식당 주인 안토니오 크루즈 씨는 앨빈 파크 근처에 있는 더 넓은 공간에서 식당을 다시 연다고 말했다.

레일리 빨래방은 지난주에 문을 닫았다. 이곳은 고객에게 셀프로 하는 동전 세탁기를 제공했으며, 세탁비누 자판기도 갖추고 있었다. [172](C)주인인 돌로레스 레일리는 "최근 이런저런 개발로 동네가 변하고 있다"고 말했다. "델토네 같은 신축 아파트 건물에는 내부에 세탁기와 건조기가 구비되어 있어요. 따라서 우리 서비스에 대한 수요가 줄어들고 있어요." [175]그녀는 최근 몇몇 지역 빨래방이 식당으로 바뀌고 있는 추세라고 덧붙였다. 실제로, 그녀의 업소가 나간 자리에 이탈리아 식당이 곧 들어올 예정이다.

레일리 씨는 업소를 버틀러 가 17번지로 옮겼는데, 이곳에서는 대량 세탁 서비스도 제공하기 시작했다. 바인 하이츠 지구에 아직 남아 있는 셀프 빨래방은 런드리 브리즈 한 곳뿐이다.

[172](D)또한 이 지구에서 멕시코 음식을 제공하는 곳은 탐피코 브리토 한 곳만 남아 있고, 푸드트럭 아이비 퀵 바이츠가 유일하게 일본 음식을 제공한다.

어휘 district (특정) 지구, 구역 laundromat 동전 빨래방 regional 지역의 spokesperson 대변인 compete 경쟁하다 neighborhood 이웃(의), 인근(의) expand 확대하다 offering 제공품 eatery 식당 establishment (호텔, 식당 등의) 시설, 업체 coin-operated 동전으로 작동하는 vending machine 자판기 development 개발 be equipped with ~가 구비되어 있다 demand 수요 decrease 감소하다 convert 바꾸다, 전환하다

commercial laundry service (주로 업체를 대상으로 하는) 대량 세탁 / 관리 서비스

172 추론 / 암시 [고난도]

번역 바인 하이츠 지구에 관해 암시되지 않은 것은?
(A) 제과점에겐 경쟁이 심한 시장이다.
(B) 현재 동전 세탁소가 다수 있다.
(C) 새로 지은 주택이 있다.
(D) 이동식 식품 시설에서 음식을 제공한다.

해설 첫 번째 단락의 '다수의 인근 커피전문점들이 제빵류까지 판매 품목을 넓히고 있어 이 지역에서 경쟁하기가 어려워졌다(it "had become difficult to compete" in the area, as a number of neighborhood coffee shops have been expanding their offerings of baked goods)'는 회사 대변인의 말이 인용된 부분에서 (A)를, 세 번째 단락에서 레일리 빨래방 주인이 최근 이런저런 개발(With all the recent development)로 델토네 같은 신축 아파트가 생겼다(The new apartment buildings, such as the Deltonne)고 언급한 부분에서 (C)를, 마지막 단락의 '푸드트럭 아이비 퀵 바이츠가 일본 음식을 제공한다(a food truck, Ivy's Quick Bites, offers its only Japanese food)'에서 (D)를 확인할 수 있다. 네 번째 단락에서 바인 하이츠 지구에 셀프 빨래방 업체는 하나만 남았다고 했으므로, 동전 세탁소가 다수 있다고 볼 수는 없다. 따라서 (B)가 정답이다.

어휘 competitive 경쟁이 심한

▶▶ **Paraphrasing** 지문의 **difficult to compete**
→ 보기 (A)의 **competitive**
지문의 **The new apartment buildings**
→ 보기 (C)의 **newly-built housing**
지문의 **a food truck ~ offers** → 보기 (D)의 **is served by mobile food facilities**

173 사실 관계 확인

번역 트리올로 그릴에 관해 알 수 있는 것은?
(A) 최근에 주인이 바뀌었다.
(B) 커피 음료로 유명했다.
(C) 완전히 폐업한 것은 아니다.
(D) 지역에 처음 생긴 퓨전 식당이었다.

해설 두 번째 단락에서 트리올로 그릴이 2주째 문이 닫혀 있었고 이제 '임대 가능'이라는 팻말이 걸려 있다(Triollo Grill ~ has been closed for two weeks and a "space available" sign now hangs on its door)고 했는데, 뒤 문장에서는 트리올로의 주인이 더 넓은 공간에서 식당을 다시 연다(Its owner ~ will reopen his establishment in a larger space)고 했다. 따라서 완전히 폐업한 것이 아님을 알 수 있으므로, (C)가 정답이다.

174 세부 사항

번역 바인 하이츠 지구 밖에 있는 건물은?
(A) 발보아 쇼핑몰
(B) 델토네
(C) 런드리 브리즈
(D) 탐피코 브리토

해설 첫 번째 단락에서 발보아 쇼핑몰에도 입점해 있는 지역 체인점이 바인 하이츠 지점을 폐업했다(a regional chain that also has a location in Balboa Shopping Mall, closed its Vine Heights location)고 했으므로, 발보아 쇼핑몰은 바인 하이츠 지구 밖에 있음을 알 수 있다. 따라서 (A)가 정답이다. 참고로 (B)는 세 번째 단락에서, (C)는 네 번째 단락에서, (D)는 마지막 단락에서 바인 하이츠 지구 안에 있음을 확인할 수 있다.

175 문장 삽입 고난도

번역 [1], [2], [3], [4]로 표시된 곳 중에서 다음 문장이 가장 적합한 곳은?
"실제로 그녀의 업소가 나간 자리에 이탈리아 식당이 곧 들어올 예정이다."
(A) [1]
(B) [2]
(C) [3]
(D) [4]

해설 주어진 문장은 앞에서 언급한 내용을 보충 설명(Indeed)하는 역할을 하며, 업소가 나간 자리에 식당이 들어오는 예를 제시하고 있다. [3] 앞에서 빨래방 주인인 돌로레스 레일리가 최근 몇몇 지역 빨래방이 식당으로 바뀌고 있는 추세라고 덧붙였다(as part of a trend, several local laundromats are being converted into restaurants)고 했으므로, 이 뒤에 주어진 문장이 예시로 들어가야 자연스럽다. 따라서 (C)가 정답이다.

176-180 정보문 + 이메일

아르테시아 학원의 가을 강좌

강좌는 9월 25일 주에 시작합니다. 178각 수업은 매주 같은 날, 8회 모입니다. 수업에는 필요한 재료비가 모두 포함되어 있습니다. 176가을학기 내 두 번째/세 번째/네 번째 강좌 수강생에게는 수업료의 80퍼센트만 청구됩니다.

강좌/가격	설명	세션별 요일/시간
실내 생물 소묘 (285달러)	177중급 화가에게 추천되는 수업으로, 매주 다른 살아 있는 모델이 등장합니다.	화요일/오후 6:30 - 7:30 수요일/오후 7:00 - 8:00 목요일/오후 6:30 - 7:30
178도자기 (300달러)	수강생들은 물레성형 기법을 배워 그릇, 꽃병 등을 만들게 됩니다. 177모든 레벨 환영.	178월요일/오후 6:30 - 8:30 목요일/오후 6:30 - 8:30
수채화 (260달러)	초보자 대상 수업으로 풍경화를 중심으로 기초 수채화 기법을 가르칩니다.	월요일/오후 6:00 - 7:00 수요일/오후 6:00 - 7:00 목요일/오후 7:00 - 8:00
스크린 인쇄 (280달러)	스크린 인쇄 과정을 배워 자신만의 티셔츠를 만들어 보세요. 초보자를 위해 고안된 수업으로 이전에는 제공된 적이 없습니다.	화요일/오후 6:30 - 8:00

강의에 등록하거나 자세한 내용을 보려면 www.artesiainst.com/autumn을 방문하세요. 등록 마감일은 9월 12일입니다. 빨리 등록하시기를 적극 권합니다.

어휘 institute 학원, 기관 material 재료 charge 부과하다, 청구하다 term 학기 intermediate 중급의 wheel-throwing (도자기) 물레성형 intend ~를 목적[대상]으로 하다 landscape 풍경화 register 등록하다

수신: 신시아 로페즈 〈c.lopez@artesiainst.com〉
발신: 박태우 〈t.park@artesiainst.com〉
날짜: 11월 22일
제목: 의견 설문조사

신시아에게,

수업 마지막 날 수강생들에게 배포한 의견 설문조사의 응답을 정리하는 일을 마쳤어요. 당신의 수업은 압도적으로 긍정적인 평가를 받았고, 모든 수강생이 다른 사람에게 추천하겠다고 말했어요. 178수업이 인기가 좋아서 학기당 2교시로는 부족하다고 생각해요. 179가능하면 겨울 학기에 추가 수업을 하셨으면 하는데, 이 문제는 이번 주 금요일 직원 만찬에서 더 논의해 보면 될 것 같아요. 만찬은 학원에서 걸어갈 만한 장소에서 열릴 예정인데, 일정은 잠정적으로 오후 7시에 잡혀 있어요. 180파블로가 준비하고 있으니, 혼자 참석하실지 아니면 배우자와 함께 참석하실지 그에게 알려주세요.

노고에 감사드립니다!

태우

어휘 compile 정리하다 distribute 배포하다 overwhelmingly 압도적으로 popularity 인기 additional 추가의 within walking distance 걸어갈 수 있는 거리에 tentatively 잠정적으로 arrangement 준비, 마련 attend 참석하다 spouse 배우자

176 세부 사항

번역 수강생이 할인 받을 수 있는 방법은?
(A) 학원을 친구들에게 추천
(B) 수강료 전액을 선납
(C) 조기 등록기한을 준수
(D) 두 개 이상의 강좌에 등록

해설 정보문의 상단에서 가을학기 내 두 번째/세 번째/네 번째 강좌 수강생에게는 수업료의 80퍼센트만 청구된다(Students are charged 80% of the class fee for second/third/fourth classes within the autumn term)고 했으므로, (D)가 정답이다.

▶▶ Paraphrasing 지문의 are charged 80% of the class fee
→ 질문의 get a discount
지문의 for second/third/fourth classes
→ 정답의 By enrolling in more than one class

177 사실 관계 확인 고난도

번역 가을 수업에 대한 설명으로 옳은 것은?
(A) 두 개는 중급 실력을 가진 학생에게 적합하다.
(B) 두 개는 처음으로 열리고 있다.
(C) 하나는 매주 다른 강사에게 배운다.
(D) 하나는 나머지 다른 수업들보다 하루 세션이 짧다.

해설 정보문의 표를 보면, 수채화 및 스크린 인쇄 수업은 초보자 대상인 반면, 실내 생물 소묘 수업은 중급 화가에게 추천한다(Recommended for intermediate artists)고 했고, 도자기 수업은 모든 레벨을 환영한다(All levels welcome)고 되어 있다. 따라서 중급 실력을 가진 학생에게 적합한 수업이 두 개임을 확인할 수 있으므로, (A)가 정답이다. 처음으로 열리

는 수업은 스크린 인쇄뿐이며, 실내 생물 소묘 및 수채화 수업이 1시간, 도자기는 2시간, 스크린 인쇄는 1시간 반 동안 진행되므로 (B), (D)는 틀린 내용이다.

178 연계

번역 로페즈 씨는 어떤 수업을 가르치겠는가?
(A) 실내 생물 소묘
(B) 도자기
(C) 수채화
(D) 스크린 인쇄

해설 이메일의 첫 번째 단락에서 로페즈 씨의 수업이 인기가 좋아서 학기당 2교시로는 부족하다고 생각한다(Because of the popularity of your teaching, I don't think two classes per term is enough)고 했는데, 정보문의 상단을 보면 각 수업은 매주 같은 날 모인다(Each class will meet on the same day each week)고 되어 있고, 표에 따르면 매주 2회 진행된 수업(Mondays/6:30 P.M.–8:30 P.M. / Thursdays/6:30 P.M.–8:30 P.M.)은 도자기(Pottery) 뿐이다. 따라서 (B)가 정답이다.

179 세부 사항

번역 박 씨는 로페즈 씨가 어떻게 하기를 바라는가?
(A) 신규 채용된 강사 교육
(B) 설문조사 결과 검토
(C) 근무시간 확대
(D) 다음 학기 물품 요청

해설 이메일의 첫 번째 단락에서 로페즈 씨에게 겨울 학기에 추가 수업을 했으면 한다(I'd like you to teach an additional class for the winter term)고 했으므로, (C)가 정답이다.

▶▶ Paraphrasing 지문의 teach an additional class
→ 정답의 Increase her working hours

180 세부 사항

번역 만찬과 관련하여 파블로는 어떤 정보가 필요한가?
(A) 참석자의 식품 알레르기 여부
(B) 어떤 시간이 가장 편리한가
(C) 어떤 식당을 선호하는가
(D) 손님을 데려올지 여부

해설 이메일의 끝부분에서 파블로가 직원 만찬 준비를 하고 있으니 그에게 혼자 참석할지 아니면 배우자와 함께 참석할지 알려주라(Pablo is making the arrangements, so please let him know if you will attend alone or with your spouse)고 했다. 따라서 (D)가 정답이다.

▶▶ Paraphrasing 지문의 if you will attend alone or with your spouse
→ 정답의 Whether a guest will be brought

181-185 모바일 기기 캡쳐 화면 + 온라인 기사

아이챗
모바일 버전 3.0
상위 사용자 후기

케리 루카스 ★★★★☆ (별 4.5개)
아이챗은 어디서든 가족, 친구와 연락할 수 있어서 정말 좋아요. 알리반타에서 이용할 수 있는 화상 채팅 앱을 몇 가지 시도해 봤는데, 이게 제일 좋네요. 184(A)메뉴를 맞춤으로 설정하거나 숨길 수 있게 해줬으면 좋겠어요—색깔 때문에 눈이 아파요.

도미닉 프레이저 ★★★★☆ (별 4개)
183아이챗이 "보이지 않기" 상태 설정을 다시 제공하는 게 기쁘긴 하지만, 182아직도 이모티콘 종류가 굉장히 한정되어 있어요. 182/184(B)스팽글러처럼, 다른 회사에서 이모티콘을 만들어 플랫폼에 제공할 수 있게 해야 합니다.

치엔 응우옌 ★☆☆☆☆ (별 1개)
181/184(C)무스를 사용해 계정에 돈을 충전하는 기능이 안 되네요. 그 편이 신용카드 정보를 넘겨주는 것보다 훨씬 안전한데도 말이에요. 삭제할래요.

욜란다 카스티요 ★★★★☆ (별 4개)
이 앱이 자동으로 실행되지 않도록 사용자가 막을 수 있게 해주세요! 제가 쓰는 타이터스 폰은 배터리 수명이 그다지 길지 않은데 아이챗 때문에 배터리가 더 빨리 닳아요. 그것만 빼면 아무런 불만이 없습니다. 비디오와 음질이 안정적이에요.

어휘 keep in touch with ~와 연락하다 customize 맞춤으로 설정하다 limited 한정적인 allow ~하게 하다 account 계정 hand over 넘겨주다, 전달하다 uninstall (설치한 앱, 프로그램 등을) 삭제하다 automatically 자동적으로 run out 닳다, 소모되다 complaint 불만 reliable 안정적인, 믿을만한

플랫포뮬라 모바일용 아이챗 버전 3.1 출시
글 아드리아나 러셀, 4월 8일 오전 10시 35분

이번 주 초, 플랫포뮬라는 화상 채팅 앱인 아이챗의 최신 모바일 버전을 출시했다. 184(A)버전 3.1은 영상을 위한 공간을 더 확보하도록 숨길 수 있는 간단한 메뉴가 특징이다. 184(C)또한 사용자들이 무스를 통해 계정에 충전하고 스타메일에서 연락처를 불러올 수 있는 등 더 많은 통합 기능을 지원한다. 184(B)플랫포뮬라의 업데이트 공지에는 사용자들이 아이챗에서 제3자 개발사로부터 이모티콘을 구매할 수 있게 됐다고 자랑한다. 하지만 아직 앱 상에서는 확인이 되지 않는다. 게다가 아이챗의 데스크톱 버전에서 인기 있는 기능인 화면 공유 기능이 마침내 모바일 버전에서 이용 가능하게 되었다.

185플랫포뮬라는 3년 전 아이챗 개발업체를 창업자인 거스 다니엘슨으로부터 인수했다. 183이 회사가 주도한 첫 업데이트 버전인 2.0은 사용자들에게 거센 비난을 받았다. 사용자 상태를 "보이지 않기"로 설정하는 기능 등, 기존에 있다가 해당 버전에서 제거된 몇 가지 기능이 3.0에서 복원되기도 했다.

지금까지 버전 3.1의 온라인 후기는 긍정적이다. 플랫포뮬라가 다음에는 아이챗 비즈니스의 모바일 버전을 업데이트하리라 예상된다.

어휘 launch 출시하다 feature ~가 특징이다, ~를 특별히 포함하다; 기능 simplified 간소화된 support 지원하다 integration 통합(기능) import (데이터를) 불러오다 founder 창업자 spearhead 주도하다 criticism 비난 preexisting 기존에 있었던 status 상태 invisible 보이지 않는 restore 복구하다

181 사실 관계 확인

번역 응우옌 씨는 무엇을 염려하고 있다고 말하는가?
(A) 금융 정보의 보안
(B) 온라인 활동의 해로움
(C) 채팅 서비스의 비용 증가
(D) 모바일 앱 삭제의 어려움

해설 캡처 화면의 세 번째 후기에서 응우옌 씨는 아이챗에서 무스를 사용해 계정에 돈을 충전하는 기능이 안 된다(It doesn't let you use Mooth to add money to your account)며, 이 방법이 신용카드 정보를 넘겨주는 것보다 훨씬 안전하다(that's much safer than handing over your credit card information)고 덧붙였다. 이 기능이 없어서 앱을 삭제한다고 했으므로, (A)가 정답이다.

▶▶ **Paraphrasing** 지문의 **credit card information**
→ 정답의 **financial information**

182 사실 관계 확인

번역 아이챗의 경쟁 상대로 언급된 것은?
(A) 알리반타
(B) 스팽글러
(C) 무스
(D) 타이터스

해설 캡처 화면의 두 번째 후기에서 아이챗의 이모티콘 종류가 굉장히 한정되어 있다(the range of emoticons is still really limited)고 한 후, 스팽글러처럼 다른 회사에서 이모티콘을 만들어 플랫폼에 제공할 수 있게 해야 한다(It should allow other companies to make emoticons for its platform, like Spangler does)고 했으므로, 스팽글러가 아이챗의 경쟁 상대임을 알 수 있다. 따라서 (B)가 정답이다.

183 연계 [고난도]

번역 프레이저 씨에 관해 암시된 것은?
(A) 그가 쓴 후기의 일부는 데스크톱 버전에 관한 것이다.
(B) 2.0 버전의 아이챗을 사용해 봤다.
(C) 아이챗을 사용하는 주된 이유는 업무 때문이다.
(D) 아이챗을 다운로드하기 위해 돈을 지불했다.

해설 캡처 화면의 두 번째 후기를 작성한 프레이저 씨는 아이챗이 "보이지 않기" 상태 설정을 다시 제공해서 기쁘다(I'm glad that Eyechat is offering "invisible" status again)고 했는데, 기사의 두 번째 단락을 보면 해당 기능이 2.0버전에서 제거되었다가 3.0버전에서 다시 복원되었다(Several of the preexisting features that were removed from that version, such as the ability to set the user status to "invisible", were restored in 3.0)고 쓰여 있다. 따라서 프레이저 씨가 2.0 버전도 사용한 경험이 있다고 추론할 수 있으므로, (B)가 정답이다.

184 연계 [고난도]

번역 아이챗 업데이트 버전에서 누구의 제안이 채택되지 않았는가?
(A) 루카스 씨
(B) 프레이저 씨
(C) 응우옌 씨
(D) 카스티요 씨

해설 온라인 기사 첫 번째 단락의 '버전 3.1은 숨길 수 있는 간단 메뉴가 특징이다(Version 3.1 features a simplified menu that can be hidden)'에서 루카스 씨의 바람이, '아이챗에서 제3자 개발자로부터 이모티콘을 구매할 수 있게 되었다(Eyechat now allows users to buy emoticons from third-party developers)'에서 프레이저 씨의 제안이, '사용자들이 무스를 통해 계정에 충전을 할 수 있다(allowing users to charge their account through Mooth)'에서 응우옌 씨의 의견이 반영되었음을 확인할 수 있다. 하지만 앱이 자동으로 실행되지 않도록 사용자가 막을 수 있게 해달라(Please let users stop this app from starting automatically)는 카스티요 씨의 제안에 대한 언급은 없으므로, (D)가 정답이다.

185 사실 관계 확인 [고난도]

번역 플랫포뮬라에 관해 언급된 것은?
(A) 3년 전에 설립되었다.
(B) 한때 다니엘슨 씨가 대표를 맡았다.
(C) 아이챗의 최초 제작사가 아니다.
(D) 일부 개발 업무를 외주에 맡겼다.

해설 온라인 기사의 두 번째 단락에서 플랫포뮬라가 3년 전 아이챗 개발업체를 창업자로부터 인수했다(Platformula bought EyeChat's developer from its founder ~ three years ago)고 했으므로, 플랫포뮬라는 아이챗의 최초 개발사가 아님을 알 수 있다. 따라서 (C)가 정답이다.

어휘 outsource 외주에 맡기다

186-190 이메일 + 부동산 매물 목록 + 이메일

> 발신: 에두아르도 웨스트
> 수신: 수잔 바커
> 제목: 목록
> 날짜: 1월 16일
>
> 안녕하세요 수잔,
>
> 일전에 회의를 마친 뒤, 제가 머워리 빌딩 매물에 썼던 설명을 검토해봐 주실 용의가 있다고 하셨었죠. 여기 있어요:
>
> 머워리 빌딩의 전문 사무실 공간 임대 가능. 모퉁이에 위치. **187(A)탁 트인 중앙 구역에 방 3개(하나는 싱크대 구비)**, 1인용 화장실 2개 및 **187(C)수납장**. 전용 냉난방 시스템, 얼룩 방지 카펫 구비. 엘리베이터 이용 가능. **187(D)하루 종일 자연광 받음!**
>
> 그리고 머워리 빌딩에 관해 평상시에 쓰는 단락을 추가할게요. 어떻게 생각하세요? **186선배 중개사로서 조언해 주시면 감사하겠습니다.**
>
> 감사합니다.
>
> 에두아르도

어휘 look over 검토하다 description 설명 listing (부동산) 매물 single-stall (화장실·샤워실 등이) 1인용의 storage closet 수납장 dedicated 전용의 stain-resistant 얼룩이 잘 지지 않는 access 이용(권) appreciate 감사하다

www.property-finder.com/commercial/9320

플로이드 가 416번지 (머워리 빌딩), 2층

사진
평면도
지도

★

휴리스크

규모: 1,512제곱피트　　층: 2층　　기간: 3년
190임대료: 연간 27,972달러 (연간 18.5달러/제곱피트)

설명: 멋진 머워리 빌딩의 전문 사무실 공간 임대 가능. 187(D)하루 종일 자연광을 받는 아주 좋은 모퉁이 위치. 187(A)탁 트인 넉넉한 중앙구역에 사무실/회의실용 방 2개, 주방/휴게실용 방 1개, 1인용 화장실 2개, 187(C)보안 장치가 있는 수납장. 연비 좋은 전용 냉난방 시스템 구비. 편리한 엘리베이터 이용 가능.

위치: 머워리 빌딩은 휴리스크 시내에서 북쪽으로 3마일 떨어진 320번 고속도로의 붐비는 파레데스 단지에 위치한다. 불과 5년 전에 건축되었고 지상 주차 공간이 넉넉하다. 188임대료에는 건물 유지 보수비와 로비 보안요원의 인건비가 포함되지만 공공요금은 포함되지 않는다.

연락처: 에두아르도 웨스트, 랩니 부동산

어휘　generous 넉넉한　secure 보안 장치가 있는, 안전한
energy-efficient 연비가 좋은　surface 표면의, 지상의　lease 임대
building maintenance 건물 유지　personnel 직원　utility
(수도, 전기 같은) 공공사업

발신: 달린 불러드
수신: 아미르 람다니
제목: 쓸 만한 사무 공간
날짜: 1월 19일

안녕하세요 아미르,

189월요일에 보여드린 길바르도 가 사무실이 마음에 드셨다는 건 알지만, 방금 고객님 업체에 훨씬 더 어울릴 만한 새로운 공간에 대해 알게 됐어요. 머워리 빌딩의 2층 모퉁이 공간으로, 빛이 많이 들어와요. 190길바르도 가 사무실보다 크지만 제곱피트당 비용은 같아요. 길바르도 가 사무실이 시내와 조금 더 가깝지만, 머워리 빌딩이 고속도로 바로 옆에 있어서 편의상 큰 차이는 없을 거예요. 그리고 머워리 사무 임대 기간이 더 짧아서, 마음에 들지 않으면 오래 머물지 않아도 돼요.

고객님께서 이 새로운 공간을 꼭 봐야 한다고 생각해요. 관심 있으시면 알려주세요. 그러면 제가 둘러볼 일정을 잡을게요.

달린

어휘　fit 잘 맞는 것　viewing (부동산 등) 둘러보기

---

186 추론 / 암시

번역　바커 씨에 관해 암시된 것은?
(A) 현재 웨스트 씨의 상사이다.
(B) 웨스트 씨보다 업무 경험이 더 많다.
(C) 사무실 건물에 대한 설명을 썼다.
(D) 회의에서 과제를 주었다.

해설　첫 번째 이메일의 세 번째 단락에서 웨스트 씨가 바커 씨에게 선배 중개사로서 조언해 주면 감사하겠다(I'd appreciate any advice you can give as a senior agent)고 했으므로, 바커 씨가 웨스트 씨보다 업무 경험이 더 많다고 추론할 수 있다. 따라서 (B)가 정답이다.

▶▶ Paraphrasing　지문의 as a senior agent
　　→ 정답의 has more work experience

---

187 연계　　　고난도

번역　초안에는 언급되었지만, 공간에 관한 공식 설명에는 언급되지 않은 사항은?
(A) 세 번째 밀폐 공간
(B) 바닥재의 종류
(C) 보안 시스템
(D) 빛 노출

해설　첫 번째 이메일에 있는 초안과 부동산 매물의 공식 설명을 대조해 보아야 한다. 우선, 초안에는 '탁 트인 중앙구역에 방 3개(open central area plus three rooms)', 공식 설명에는 '탁 트인 넉넉한 중앙구역에 사무실/회의실용 방 2개, 주방/휴게실용 방 1개(Generous open central area plus two offices/conference rooms and one kitchen/break room)라고 되어 있으므로, (A)를 확인할 수 있다. 또한 초안의 '수납장(storage closet)'이 공식 설명에는 '보안 장치가 있는 수납장(secure storage closet)'이라고 된 것에서 (C)를, '하루 종일 자연광 받음(Receives natural light throughout the day)'이 '하루 종일 자연광을 받는 아주 좋은 모퉁이 위치(Excellent corner location that receives natural light throughout the day)'라고 된 것에서 (D)를 확인할 수 있다. 하지만 초안에 있던 '얼룩 방지 카펫(stain-resistant carpeting)'이 공식 설명에는 언급되지 않았으므로, (B)가 정답이다.

어휘　enclosed 밀폐된　exposure 노출

---

188 추론 / 암시

번역　머워리 빌딩 세입자가 추가 비용을 지불해야 하는 것은?
(A) 수도 기반시설 사용
(B) 온도 조절 시스템 수리
(C) 옥외 주차구역 출입
(D) 건물 출입구 보안서비스

해설　부동산 매물 설명의 두 번째 단락에서 임대료에 공공요금은 포함되지 않는다(The lease rate includes fees ~ but not utilities)고 했으므로, 세입자가 수도 시설 사용료는 따로 지불해야 한다는 것을 알 수 있다. 따라서 (A)가 정답이다. 지상 주차장이 제공되고 임대료에 건물 유지 보수비와 보안 요원의 인건비가 포함되므로, (B), (C), (D)는 추가 비용을 지불할 필요가 없다.

어휘　infrastructure 기반시설

▶▶ Paraphrasing　지문의 utilities
　　→ 정답의 Usage of water infrastructure

---

189 추론 / 암시

번역 불러드 씨는 누구이겠는가?
(A) 람다니 씨의 사업 파트너
(B) 람다니 씨의 법률 고문
(C) 람다니 씨의 부동산 중개업자
(D) 람다니 씨의 보좌관

해설 두 번째 이메일의 첫 단락에서 불러드 씨는 자신이 람다니 씨에게 월요일에 보여준 길바르도 가 사무실(the Gilbardo Street office that I showed you on Monday) 외에 새로운 공간에 대해 알게 됐다(I've just learned about a new space that might be an even better fit for your business)고 한 후, 그에게 머워리 빌딩의 사무실을 추천했다. 따라서 불러드 씨가 람다니 씨의 부동산 중개업자라고 추론할 수 있으므로, (C)가 정답이다.

190 연계 고난도

번역 길바르도 가 사무실에 관해 판단할 수 있는 것은?
(A) 1,500제곱피트가 넘는 공간이 있다.
(B) 휴리스크 중심지에서 3마일 이상 떨어져 있다.
(C) 5년 이상의 임대기간을 요구한다.
(D) 임대료가 연간 28,000달러가 안 된다.

해설 두 번째 이메일의 첫 단락에서 머워리 빌딩의 2층에 있는 사무실이 길바르도 가 사무실보다 크지만 제곱피트당 가격은 같다(It's larger than the Gilbardo Street office, but the price per square foot is the same)고 했는데, 부동산 매물 설명을 보면 머워리 빌딩의 2층에 있는 사무실의 임대료가 28,000달러 미만(Rate: $27,972/year)이라는 것을 확인할 수 있다. 따라서 (D)가 정답이다. 참고로, 길바르도 가 사무실이 머워리 빌딩의 사무실(1,512제곱피트)보다 작다고만 나와 있으므로, 정확한 크기를 판단할 수 있는 근거는 없다. 마찬가지로, 머워리 빌딩 사무실의 임대 기간(3년)이 더 짧다고만 언급되었으므로, 길바르도 가 사무실의 최소 임대 기간을 확인할 수 있는 근거도 없다. 머워리 빌딩이 휴리스트 시내에서 3마일 떨어진 곳에 있다고 했는데, 길바르도 가 사무실은 이보다 가깝다고 했으므로, (B)는 틀린 내용이다.

191-195 안내책자 + 이메일 + 공지

콜링데일 역사박물관

주요 전시회

목재, 강철과 콘크리트	콜린스 씨의 서재
작은 주택 및 상가부터 공장과 초고층 빌딩에 이르기까지 콜링데일의 건물 뒤에 숨겨진 재미있는 이야기들을 알아보세요.	¹⁹¹콜링데일 출신이자 〈키에라 스미스〉 시리즈의 작가인 디애나 콜린스의 삶을 들여다보는 이 전시는 작가의 팬들 중 성인이 되어버린 이들도 분명 즐거워할 것입니다.
털복숭이와 함께한 50년	**산맥 너머**
최근 콜링데일 동물원 50주년을 맞아 조성된 이 전시회는 동물원의 역사와 놀라운 동물들의 발자취를 추적합니다.	니콜라스 비카리오에 대해 들어본 적이 없을지라도, 인근의 트루하드 산맥을 그린 그의 아름다운 그림들을 보고나면 결코 그의 이름을 잊지 못할 것입니다.

유의사항

–¹⁹²단체 방문객을 환영합니다만, 8명이 넘는 인원을 데려오실 계획이라면 24시간 전에 미리 예약하세요. www.corlingdalehistory.com 온라인 예약 시

스템에서 예약할 수 있습니다.

–가이드 투어는 영어로만 제공되지만, 셀프 가이드 오디오 투어는 기타 다양한 언어로도 제공됩니다.

어휘 exhibition 전시(회) fascinating 매력적인 range (from A to B) 범위가 ~에 이르다 storefront 가게 앞, 상가 skyscraper 고층 건물 delight 기쁘게 하다 fur 털, 부드러운 털이 있는 동물 anniversary 기념일, 주년 trace (발자취 등을) 추적하다 facility 기관, 시설 creature 생물, 동물 in advance 미리

발신: 〈verag@corlingdalehistory.com〉
수신: 〈chiranjeevi.somchai@ben-mail.net〉
제목: 회신: 오늘 방문?
날짜: 7월 15일

송차이 씨께,

오늘 오후에 방문하신다는 것을 알려주셔서 감사합니다. ¹⁹²보통 고객님 같은 단체는 적어도 도착 하루 전에 통지해야 하지만, 다행히 이번에는 수용해 드릴 수 있게 되었습니다.

¹⁹⁴보통 3층에서 열리는 〈산맥 너머〉 전시회를 언급하셨길래 미리 말씀드리면, 해당 전시회는 현재 영국의 미한 박물관에 대여 중입니다. ¹⁹³1층 선물가게에 관련 상품들이 있긴 합니다만, 만약 이 전시회가 고객님 단체의 주요 볼거리라면, 전시회가 이곳에서 다시 열리는 8월로 방문 일정을 조정하는 것을 고려해 보시기 바랍니다.

그래도 오기로 결정하신다면, 오늘 오후에 만나 뵙기를 바랍니다.

베라 고든
운영 관리자
콜링데일 역사박물관

어휘 require 요구하다 accommodate 수용하다, 맞추다 warn 미리 말하다 currently 현재 related merchandise 관련 상품 attraction 볼거리, (관광) 명소 reschedule 일정을 조정하다

죄송합니다!

¹⁹⁴보통 이 공간에 자리하는 전시회가 현재 런던의 미한 박물관에 대여 중입니다. 전시회는 8월 1일에 이곳에서 다시 열릴 예정입니다. 만약 그때 전시회를 다시 보러 오고 싶으시면, 안내 데스크에 귀하의 ¹⁹⁵일행이 무료 입장할 수 있는 방법을 물어보십시오. 불편을 끼쳐드려 죄송합니다.

– 콜링데일 역사박물관 직원

어휘 house 보관[소장]하다, 자리를 내어주다 admission 입장 apologize 사과하다 inconvenience 불편

191 세부 사항

번역 안내책자에 따르면, 다음 중 주요 전시회의 주제에 해당하는 것은?
(A) 섬유 제조
(B) 아동 도서 작가
(C) 도시의 그림
(D) 지역 야생동물

해설 주요 전시회(Major Exhibitions) 목록을 보면, '콜린스 씨의 서재(Ms. Collins's Library)'가 〈키에라 스미스〉 시리즈 작가인 디애나 콜린스의 삶을 들여다보는 전시회로, 성인이 되어버린 팬들도 즐거워할 것(This look into the life of ~ writer of the *Kiera Smith* series, is sure to delight her fans—even the ones who have grown up)이라고 되어 있다. 따라서 콜린스 씨가 아동 도서 작가임을 추론할 수 있으므로, 이 전시회 주제를 바르게 설명한 (B)가 정답이다. 나머지 보기에 해당하는 전시회는 책자에서 찾을 수 없다.

192 연계

번역 솜차이 씨의 단체에 관해 맞는 설명은?
(A) 8명이 넘는 인원으로 구성되어 있다.
(B) 일부 회원들은 화가의 친척이다.
(C) 일부 회원들은 영어를 못한다.
(D) 개인 가이드 투어를 받을 것이다.

해설 이메일의 첫 번째 단락에서 솜차이 씨의 규모와 같은 단체는 보통 도착하기 적어도 하루 전에 통지해야 한다(we do usually require groups like yours to give us at least one day's notice before arrival)고 했는데, 안내책자에 적힌 유의사항(Notes)을 보면, 8명이 넘는 인원을 데려올 계획이라면 24시간 전에 미리 예약하라(please make a reservation 24 hours in advance if you plan to bring more than eight people)고 되어 있다. 따라서 솜차이 씨의 단체도 8명이 넘는 인원으로 구성되어 있다고 추론할 수 있으므로, (A)가 정답이다.

▶▶ Paraphrasing 지문의 bring more than eight people → 정답의 consists of more than eight individuals

193 세부 사항

번역 고든 씨가 솜차이 씨에게 추천한 것은?
(A) 공연 예약
(B) 한정판 상품 구매
(C) 해외 단체 연락
(D) 나중에 박물관 견학

해설 이메일의 두 번째 단락을 보면, 고든 씨는 솜차이 씨가 언급했던 전시회가 대여 중이라고 알린 후, 만약 이 전시회가 단체의 주요 볼거리라면 8월로 방문 일정을 조정하는 것을 고려해보라(if the exhibition is the main attraction for your group, you should consider rescheduling your visit for August)고 권했다. 따라서 (D)가 정답이다.

▶▶ Paraphrasing 지문의 rescheduling your visit for August → 정답의 Touring the museum on a later date

194 연계

번역 공지는 콜링데일 역사박물관 몇 층에 게시되어 있겠는가?
(A) 1층
(B) 2층
(C) 3층
(D) 4층

해설 공지의 초반부를 보면 '보통 이 공간에 자리하던 전시회가 현재 런던의 미한 박물관에 대여 중(The exhibition normally housed in this space is currently on loan to London's Meehan Museum)'이라고 되어 있는데, 이메일의 두 번째 단락에 3층에 전시되는 〈산맥 너머〉 전시회가 현재 영국의 미한 박물관에 대여 중(Since you mentioned the ~ exhibition that is normally located on our third floor, I have to warn you it is currently on loan to the Meehan Museum)이라고 했다. 따라서 이 공지가 3층에 게시되어 있을 것으로 추론할 수 있으므로, (C)가 정답이다.

195 동의어 찾기

번역 공지에서 1번째 단락 4행의 "party"와 의미상 가장 가까운 것은?
(A) 축하
(B) 사람의 집합
(C) 참가
(D) 휴식

해설 'party'를 포함한 부분은 '귀하의 일행이 무료 입장할 수 있는 방법(how your party can get free admission)'이라는 의미로 해석되는데, 여기서 party는 '일행, 단체'라는 뜻으로 쓰였다. 따라서 '사람의 집합'이라는 뜻의 (B) collection of people이 정답이다.

196-200 웹페이지 + 이메일 + 기사

http://www.shalkon.gov/council/foster

아를린 포스터
4구역 하원의원 (구역 지도)

비록 시의회에서는 첫 임기지만, 아를린은 공익 사업 분야에서 모든 경력을 쌓아 왔다. 196그녀는 쟌트리에서 자라 그곳에 있는 대학에 다녔다. 정치학 학위를 받고 졸업한 후, 부담없는 가격의 주택 건설을 장려하는 벤킨스 기반의 비영리 단체에서 처음 일했다. 그 후 살론으로 이사해 전직 시의원 미첼 블레어의 보좌진이 되었다. 이 역할에서 주거용 및 상업용 부동산을 친환경적으로 개선하기 위한 세제 혜택인 SETIP 패키지와 같은 프로젝트를 도왔다.

아를린은 의회에 입성한 후, 영 애비뉴의 확장을 계획하는 등 살콘 전역의 교통 체증 문제를 개선하는 데 주력해 왔다. 197그녀는 유권자들과 열린 소통의 장을 유지하는 데 전력을 다하고 있으며, 화요일 오전과 목요일 오후를 따로 비워 두고 오로지 대중과 만나는 일에 쓰고 있다.

소속 위원회: 교통   연락처 정보
          예산 검토

어휘 representative 하원의원, 대표 public service 공익 사업 attend (대학교 등을) 다니다 nonprofit 비영리의 affordable (가격이) 부담없는 assist 돕다 tax incentive 세제 혜택 environmentally-friendly 환경친화적인 improvement 개선 (작업) residential 주거용의 commercial 상업용의 property 부동산 traffic congestion 교통체증 constituent 유권자, 주민 reserve (시간 등을) 따로 비워 두다 exclusively 오로지

발신: 올리버 코르테즈
수신: 아를린 포스터
제목: 회신: 전달: 웹스터 로드 표지판
날짜: 9월 2일

의원님께,

197저희 팀이 시내 도로 표지판을 담당하고 있어서 뷰캐넌 국장님이 의원님의 문의를 저에게 198전달했습니다.

가장 중요한 질문에 대답하면—그렇습니다. 표지판 설계에는 제약이 있습니다. 199일반 교통 표지판 양식(녹색 바탕에 흰색 문자) 또는 샬콘 시 안내 표지판 양식(연한 금색 바탕에 흰색 문자와 시 로고) 중 하나여야 합니다. 또한 후자 옵션은 도로 한쪽에 서 있는 표지판에만 사용할 수 있다는 점 유의하십시오.

이번 주에 만나뵙고 이 옵션들에 대해 자세히 논의할 수 있다면 좋겠습니다. 197저는 목요일 오후와 금요일 오전에 시간이 됩니다. 언제가 더 좋으신가요?

올리버 코르테즈
197샬콘 교통부

어휘 inquiry 문의 handle 다루다, 담당하다 limitation 제약 general 일반적인 informational 안내하는, 안내의 latter 후자의

시에서 웹스터 로드 일부 구간을 커밍스로 명명

200(9월 29일)—콜먼 스트리트와 영 애비뉴의 사이에 있는 웹스터 로드의 일부 구간이 샬콘 최초의 여성 시장인 프랜시스 커밍스를 기리는 의미에서 공동 명명되었다.

200이번 추모안을 제안한 아를린 포스터 샬콘 시의원은 어제 웹스터 로드와 콜먼 스트리트 교차로 인근에서 고(故) 커밍스 시장의 가족 및 기타 일행과 함께 간소한 제막식을 가졌다.

199웹스터 로드를 가로지르며 해당 지점부터 이어지는 반 마일의 구간을 '프랜시스 커밍스 길'이라고 표시해 주는 새 다리형 표지판에서 방수포가 걷히자 군중은 환호했다. 이 도로 구간이 선정된 이유는 커밍스 시장이 재임 중 되살린 것으로 유명한 탤메이즈 공원과 가깝기 때문이었다.

200포스터 시의원과 커밍스 시장의 아들인 에드먼드 커밍스는 프랜시스 커밍스 시장이 샬콘에 행사한 긍정적인 영향을 강조하는 연설을 했다.

어휘 stretch (길게 뻗은) 구간, 지역 name A after B B를 따서 A의 이름을 짓다 in honor of ~를 기리며, ~에게 경의를 표하여 tribute (주로 고인을 향한) 추모, 헌사 gather 모이다 intersection 교차로 unveiling 제막 tarp 방수포 proclaim 표시하다, 선언하다 subsequent 뒤이은, 이어지는 proximity 근접, 가까움 revitalize 되살리다 tenure 재임 highlight 강조하다 impact 영향

---

196 사실 관계 확인

번역 웹페이지에서 포스터 씨에 관해 언급한 내용은?
(A) 샬콘 출신이 아니다.
(B) 여러 번 당선되었다.
(C) 영 애비뉴에 부동산을 소유하고 있다.
(D) 학위를 받은 분야에서 일하지 않는다.

해설 웹페이지의 첫 번째 단락에서 포스터 씨가 잰트리에서 자라 그곳에 있는 대학에 다녔다(She was raised and attended university in Zantry)고 했으므로, 현재 시의원을 맡고 있는 샬콘 지역 출신이 아님을 알 수 있다. 따라서 (A)가 정답이다.

---

197 연계   고난도

번역 코르테즈 씨와 포스터 씨는 언제 만나겠는가?
(A) 목요일 오전
(B) 목요일 오후
(C) 금요일 오전
(D) 금요일 오후

해설 이메일의 첫 번째 단락에서 샬콘 교통부(Shalkon Department of Transportation) 소속인 코르테즈 씨는 자신의 팀이 시내 도로 표지판을 담당하고 있어(as my team handles road signs in the city) 포스터 의원의 문의를 전달받았다고 한 후, 세 번째 단락에서 목요일 오후와 금요일 오전에 시간이 된다(I'm free on Thursday afternoon and Friday morning)며 가능한 회의 시간을 제시했다. 웹페이지의 두 번째 단락을 보면, 포스터 의원은 화요일 오전과 목요일 오후를 따로 비워 두고 오로지 대중과 만나는 일에 쓰고 있다(She ~ reserves Tuesday mornings and Thursday afternoons exclusively for meetings with the public)고 되어 있다. 코르테즈 씨는 일반 대중이 아닌 업무상 만나는 교통부 직원이므로, 목요일 오후가 아닌 금요일 오전에 만났을 거라 추론할 수 있다. 따라서 (C)가 정답이다.

---

198 동의어 찾기

번역 이메일에서 1번째 단락 1행의 "passed"와 의미상 가장 가까운 것은?
(A) 전달했다
(B) 제정했다
(C) 거절했다
(D) 능가했다

해설 'passed'를 포함한 부분은 '뷰캐넌 국장님이 의원님의 문의를 저에게 전달했습니다(Director Buchanan passed your inquiry on to me)'라는 의미로 해석되는데, 여기서 passed는 '전달했다, 넘겨주었다'라는 뜻으로 쓰였다. 따라서 '전달했다'라는 의미의 (A) relayed가 정답이다.

---

199 연계   고난도

번역 완성된 표지판에 관한 설명 중 가장 사실에 가까운 것은?
(A) 도시의 심벌 마크가 포함되어 있다.
(B) 공원 입구에서 보인다.
(C) 도시 경계 밖에 위치한다.
(D) 바탕은 녹색이다.

해설 기사의 세 번째 단락에서 완성된 표지판이 웹스터 로드를 가로지르고 있음(a new sign bridge that spans Webster Road)을 알 수 있는데, 이메일의 두 번째 단락을 보면 일반 교통 표지판(general traffic signs) 양식은 녹색 바탕에 흰색 문자(green with white lettering)이고, 샬콘 시 안내 표지판(Shalkon city informational signs) 양식은 연한 금색 바탕에 흰색 문자와 시 로고(light gold with white lettering and the city logo)가 들어가며 도로 한쪽에 서 있는 경우에만 가능하다(only available for signs that stand on one side of the road)고 되어 있다. 따라서 도로 양쪽에 걸친 새 표지판은 일반 교통 표지판 양식을 따라 바탕이 녹색임을 추론할 수 있으므로, (D)가 정답이다.

200 세부 사항

번역 포스터 씨는 9월 28일에 무엇에 관해 이야기했는가?

(A) 과학 프로젝트의 미래
(B) 지역 정치인의 업적
(C) 환경보존의 중요성
(D) 동네만의 특색

해설 기사의 두 번째 단락에서 포스터 씨가 어제 고(故) 커밍스 시장의 가족 및 기타 일행과 함께 간소한 제막식을 가졌다(Arlene Foster ~ gathered ~ yesterday for a small unveiling ceremony)고 했는데, 기사가 작성된 날짜(September 29)로 보아 제막식이 28일에 열렸음을 알 수 있다. 마지막 단락에서 포스터 씨가 커밍스 시장이 샬콘에 미친 긍정적인 영향을 강조하는 연설을 했다(Council member Foster ~ gave speeches highlighting the mayor's positive impact on Shalkon)고 했으므로, (B)가 정답이다.

어휘 endeavor 활동, 프로젝트, 시도 accomplishment 업적 conservation 보존 characteristics 특색

▶▶ **Paraphrasing** 지문의 **gave speeches** → 질문의 **speak**

지문의 **the mayor's positive impact on Shalkon** → 정답의 **The accomplishments of a local politician**

토익 주관사가 만든 고난도 적중실전

YBM
실전토익
RC 1000 3

___

토익의 페이스메이커 YBM이
이름을 걸고 만든 진짜 토익 실전서!

철저한 최신 경향 분석으로
실제 시험과 가장 유사한 문제 구성!

토익 주관사의 노하우가 집대성된
〈YBM 실전토익 3〉으로 만점에 도전하세요!